Sweden's War in Muscovy, 1609-1617

The Relief of Moscow and Conquest of Novgorod

Michael Fredholm von Essen

Helion & Company Limited
Unit 8 Amherst Business Centre
Budbrooke Road
Warwick
CV34 5WE
England
Tel. 01926 499 619
Email: info@helion.co.uk
Website: www.helion.co.uk
Twitter: @helionbooks
Visit our blog http://blog.helion.co.uk/

Published by Helion & Company 2024
Designed and typeset by Mary Woolley, Battlefield Design (www.battlefield-design.co.uk)
Cover designed by Paul Hewitt, Battlefield Design (www.battlefield-design.co.uk)

Text © Michael Fredholm von Essen 2024
Photographs and illustrations © as individually credited
Colour artwork drawn by Sergey Shamenkov © Helion & Company 2024
Maps by George Anderson © Helion & Company 2024

Illustrations attributed to Army Museum, Stockholm, are reproduced under the Creative Commons license and derive from the web site, <https://digitaltmuseum.se>. Illustrations attributed to Royal Armoury, Stockholm, or Skokloster Castle are reproduced under the Creative Commons license and derive from the web site, https://digitaltmuseum.se, with special thanks to Martin Markelius, curator at the Museum. Illustrations attributed to History Museum, Stockholm, or Economy Museum – Royal Coin Cabinet/SHM, Stockholm, are reproduced under the Creative Commons license and derive from the web site, <https://samlingar.shm.se>. Other illustrations are reproduced under GNU Free Documentation License (GNU FDL) coupled with the Creative Commons Attribution Share-Alike License, or derive from the author's personal collection. The art work by the late Tommy Hellman, an accomplished expert on the arms and equipment of early modern soldiers and a good friend, is reproduced with the permission of his family. Photographs attributed to Medström are reproduced with the permission of this publisher.

Every reasonable effort has been made to trace copyright holders and to obtain their permission for the use of copyright material. The author and publisher apologise for any errors or omissions in this work and would be grateful if notified of any corrections that should be incorporated in future reprints or editions of this book.

ISBN 978-1-804510-08-7

British Library Cataloguing-in-Publication Data.
A catalogue record for this book is available from the British Library.

All rights reserved. No part of this publication may be reproduced, stored in a retrieval system, or transmitted, in any form, or by any means, electronic, mechanical, photocopying, recording or otherwise, without the express written consent of Helion & Company Limited.

For details of other military history titles published by Helion & Company Limited contact the above address or visit our website: http://www.helion.co.uk.

We always welcome receiving book proposals from prospective authors.

Contents

Chronology		iv
Introduction		xxv
Dramatis Personae		xxvii
Prologue: A Bevy of Monarchs, a Chancellor, and Two Generals		xxxv
1	The Origins of Sweden's War in Muscovy	51
2	The Swedish Military Establishment	56
3	The Muscovite Military Establishment	112
4	The Commonwealth Expeditionary Armies	147
5	The Time of Troubles	171
6	De la Gardie's Intervention Army	186
7	Mutiny	200
8	The Polish Invasion	207
9	The Relief of Moscow	217
10	The Battle of Klushino	224
11	The Polish Tsar-Elect	240
12	The Struggle for Ingria and Kexholm County	243
13	The Death of False Dmitriy	260
14	The First National Militia	262
15	The Storm of Novgorod	268
16	The Siege of Pskov	282
17	The Siege of Ivangorod	289
18	Gustavus Adolphus, Tsar of Muscovy	295
19	The Rise of the House of Romanov	302
20	The Siege of Tikhvin Monastery	310
21	The Siege of Gdov	315
22	Gustavus Adolphus at Pskov	328
23	The Finnish-Muscovite Borderlands	336
24	The Treaty of Stolbovo and Truce of Deulino	342
25	The Legacy and Implications of the War	348
Colour Plate Commentaries		357
Further Reading		367
Bibliography		372

Chronology

All dates Old Style (O. S.). Events of particular relevance to the election of tsars are marked within borders.

1609

11 Jan	Polish-Lithuanian Commonwealth mercenary Jan Kiernożycki abandons the siege of Novgorod, which presently negotiates for Swedish military support
13 Feb	King Charles of Sweden orders Baltzar Bäck and Isaac Behm to march against and capture Kola Castle in the Arctic north (but the expedition is postponed because travel soon would become impracticable)
28 Feb	King Charles of Sweden and Tsar Vasiliy of Muscovy conclude a defensive alliance, the Treaty of Viborg, according to which Sweden will intervene in Muscovy to support the Tsar against internal and external enemies; immediately afterwards, the first units of the intervention army set out from Viborg under Christer Some
3 Mar	Rearguard of Swedish intervention army sets out from Viborg
5 Mar	Jacob De la Gardie arrives in Viborg to assume command of the Swedish intervention army; Grand Hetman of Lithuania Jan Karol Chodkiewicz conquers the Livonian port-town of Pernau; from which he soon goes on to lay siege to Dünamünde, Livonia
11 Mar	De la Gardie leaves Viborg en route to join the intervention army; soon after, the intervention army under Some crosses the border into Muscovy
16 Mar	De la Gardie reaches Systerbäck
29 Mar	De la Gardie reaches Kaporie
30 Mar	De la Gardie unsuccessfully attacks Kaporie

CHRONOLOGY

7 Apr	When faced with Muscovite reluctance to allow the intervention army quarters in Novgorod, De la Gardie threatens to return to Kaporie to secure Ingria against Chodkiewicz
7–8 Apr	Units loyal to Tsar Vasiliy defeat False Dmitriy's men at Yaroslavl', taking the town; soon after, they also take Kostroma
14–15 Apr	De la Gardie's intervention army marches into Novgorod, joins forces with Mikhail Skopin-Shuyskiy
2 May	Combined Swedish–Muscovite army under De la Gardie sets out from Novgorod
8 May	Swedish–Muscovite corps probably under Christer Some disperses a rebel corps that had laid siege to Porkhov between Novgorod and Pskov
10 May	Skopin-Shuyskiy sets out from Novgorod
12 May	De la Gardie enters Staraya Russa, until then held by Kiernożycki on behalf of Dmitriy
15 May	Evert Horn and Kornil Choglokov defeat Kiernożycki at Kamenka
16 May	Torzhok, on the road to Moscow, declares loyalty to Tsar Vasiliy; soon after, Skopin-Shuyskiy orders a loyalist unit under Kornil Choglokov to Torzhok; meanwhile, rebel commanders Prince Grigoriy Shakhovskoy and Aleksander Zborowski march north from Staritsa towards Torzhok to regain the town
18 May	Swedish–Muscovite corps probably under Christer Some attempts but fails to take Pskov; Toropets submits to Tsar Vasiliy
23 May	De la Gardie sets out from Staraya Russa
6 Jun	De la Gardie and Skopin-Shuyskiy, on the road to Moscow, again join forces
17 Jun	Horn and Semyon Golovin defeat Prince Shakhovskoy and Zborowski at Torzhok
27 Jun	De la Gardie and Skopin-Shuyskiy join forces with Horn and Golovin at Torzhok
30 Jun	King Charles instructs De la Gardie to take Novgorod as security in case Tsar Vasiliy fails to deliver Kexholm County as promised
4 Jul	Reinforcements from Smolensk under Prince Yakov Baryatinskiy and Semyon Ododurov join De la Gardie and Skopin-Shuyskiy
7 Jul	De la Gardie and Skopin-Shuyskiy set out from Torzhok towards Tver'

13 Jul		De la Gardie and Skopin-Shuyskiy defeat Zborowski outside Tver', but they fail to take Tver' itself (First battle of Tver')
15 Jul		De la Gardie and Skopin-Shuyskiy again defeat Zborowski outside Tver', this time with a more decisive result (Second battle of Tver'); Zborowski loses most men but again takes refuge in Tver'
16 Jul		De la Gardie attempts to storm Tver'; when the attempt fails, Skopin-Shuyskiy advices him to abandon Tver' and instead march towards Tushino, Dmitriy's headquarters; however, within days De la Gardie's Finnish units mutiny, refusing to continue the march into Muscovy – for which reason the Swedish army retreats to Tver'
3 Aug		Perceiving the growing threat from Skopin-Shuyskiy, Commonwealth mercenary Jan Piotr Sapieha hands over command of the siege of the Holy Trinity-St Sergius Monastery to subordinates, rides towards Skopin-Shuyskiy's headquarters at Kalyazin
9 Aug		Tsar Vasiliy writes to King Charles, requesting more men; around this time, the Swedish army again mutinies, and retreats to Torzhok
10 Aug		Christer Some, with a small Swedish detachment, joins Skopin-Shuyskiy at Kalyazin, begins to train Muscovite pikemen
18 Aug		At Kalyazin, Skopin-Shuyskiy defeats Sapieha's approaching Commonwealth mercenaries; at around this time at Torzhok, De la Gardie receives King Charles's orders of 30 June, after which he retreats in the direction of Novgorod with the soldiers who still follow orders
1 Sep		Semyon Golovin, Grigoriy Valuyev, and Christer Some march towards Pereyaslavl'
6 Sep		Golovin, Valuyev, and Some take Pereyaslavl' with local support; around this time, De la Gardie again sets out towards the east
7 Sep		King Charles replies to Tsar Vasiliy's request of 9 August, promising the requested support; King Charles orders the reserves in Stockholm to be sent to the eastern front under Henrik Wildeman
11 Sep		King Sigismund of the Polish-Lithuanian Commonwealth and Field Hetman of the Crown Stanisław Żółkiewski launch a full-scale invasion of Muscovy by leading the Crown Army across the border
19 Sep		King Sigismund and Żółkiewski's advance guard commence the siege of Smolensk

CHRONOLOGY

20 Sep	Having defeated and dispersed a Muscovite rebel corps from Ivangorod which attempts to prevent his passage, Horn reaches Narva with orders to collect the expected reinforcements
26 Sep	De la Gardie and Skopin-Shuyskiy again join forces at Kalyazin
29 Sep	In Livonia, Stiernskiöld surrenders Dünamünde to Grand Hetman of Lithuania Chodkiewicz
1 Oct	Skopin-Shuyskiy's cavalry raid Dmitrov
2 Oct	Skopin-Shuyskiy's cavalry begin operations in the vicinity of the Holy Trinity-St Sergius Monastery
3 Oct	In Sweden, King Charles orders Baltzar Bäck and Isaac Behm to begin preparations for a march against Kola Castle (the second attempt, to be carried out in February–March 1610)
6 Oct	Skopin-Shuyskiy and De la Gardie reach Pereyaslavl'; around this time, Wildeman arrives in Viborg with first batch of Swedish reinforcements for De la Gardie
9 Oct	Skopin-Shuyskiy and De la Gardie leave Pereyaslavl'; Golovin, Valuyev, and John Muir move into Aleksandrovskaya Sloboda without opposition; Davyd Zherebtsov successfully brings reinforcements into the Holy Trinity-St Sergius Monastery
18 Oct	Skopin-Shuyskiy and De la Gardie defeat Sapieha and Prince Roman Różyński at the village Karinskoye, near Aleksandrovskaya Sloboda; Christer Some seriously wounded in the battle
26 Oct	Tsar Vasiliy's representatives inform the Tsar that because of Bishop Silvester's agitation, Kexholm refuses to be annexed by Sweden
17 Dec	De la Gardie and Skopin-Shuyskiy, on behalf of their respective sovereigns, conclude an agreement on the practical details concerning the extension of the Swedish intervention, including the transfer of Kexholm; around this time, second batch of Swedish reinforcements to De la Gardie arrive in Viborg
27 Dec	False Dmitriy flees from his mutinous followers at Tushino to Kaluga
1610	
1 Jan	Valuyev brings additional reinforcements to the Holy Trinity-St Sergius Monastery
2 Jan	Wildeman with the Swedish reinforcements on the road to Aleksandrovskaya Sloboda, apparently along the northern route by way of Tikhvin and Ustyuzhna

12 Jan	Fearing the arriving Swedish–Muscovite army, Sapieha abandons the siege of the Holy Trinity-St Sergius Monastery, moves into a new camp at Dmitrov
17 Jan	Tsar Vasiliy ratifies the 17 December 1609 agreement with Sweden on the continued Swedish intervention; Swedish reinforcements under Wildeman reach De la Gardie at Aleksandrovskaya Sloboda, with others still on the way
28 Jan	De la Gardie and Skopin-Shuyskiy enter Sapieha's abandoned camp, greeted as saviours by the monks of the Holy Trinity-St Sergius Monastery
4 Feb	At Smolensk, King Sigismund makes public a manifest with the terms of an agreement between himself and envoys from Tushino headed by Mikhail Saltykov for the election of his son Władysław as new Tsar of Muscovy
9 Feb	Evert Horn, having set out from Viborg with the second batch of reinforcements to De la Gardie, enters Muscovy across the ice of the frozen Gulf of Finland near Kaporie
14 Feb	Bäck and his expedition to Kola Castle ready to set out (Bäck's second attempt to march to Kola); however, Behm has failed to send his men to the meeting place, so the expedition is again cancelled
16 Feb	De la Gardie sets out from Aleksandrovskaya Sloboda in an attempt to push Sapieha out of Dmitrov
18 Feb	De la Gardie offers Sapieha battle outside Dmitrov, but the outnumbered Sapieha refuses
19 Feb	De la Gardie storms Sapieha's camp; Sapieha takes refuge in the fortified administrative quarter of Dmitrov; afterwards, De la Gardie returns to Aleksandrovskaya Sloboda because of supply shortages
26 Feb	Sapieha burns the fortified administrative quarter of Dmitrov, retreats westwards by way of Klin to the Joseph-Volokolamsk Monastery
6 Mar	Prince Różyński abandons and burns the rebel camp in Tushino
7 Mar	Skopin-Shuyskiy and De la Gardie learn of the rebel departure from Tushino; at about this time, Horn reaches Novgorod
12 Mar	De la Gardie and Skopin-Shuyskiy enter Moscow; at around this time, Swedish cavalry under Pierre De la Ville successfully storm a Commonwealth camp at Rzhov
24 Mar	Prince Różyński critically injures himself, falling down the stairs while drunk; he dies shortly afterwards
23 Apr	Skopin-Shuyskiy dies from poison

CHRONOLOGY

2 May	De la Ville breaks through the outer defences of the Joseph-Volokolamsk Monastery, defended by Commonwealth mercenaries
23 May	Horn sets out from Zubtsov, aiming to retake Belaya from a Commonwealth army loyal to King Sigismund
28 May	Crown Field Hetman Stanisław Żółkiewski sets out from Smolensk with orders to relieve Belaya
29 May	Sheïn writes to Prince Dmitriy Shuyskiy, the Tsar's new chief commander, that Żółkiewski marches towards Belaya to attack Rzhov and Zubtsov
13 Jun	Learning of Żółkiewski's offensive, Tsar Vasiliy again orders the handover of Kexholm as part of an agreement with De la Gardie; at around this time, Horn's enlisted soldiers mutiny, but Horn puts down the mutiny with harsh measures
14 Jun	Żółkiewski lays siege to Tsaryovo Zaymishche, defended by Prince Fyodor Yeletskiy and his deputy, the experienced Valuyev
21 Jun	Horn's army join forces with De la Gardie's army at Myshkino, but the expected pay promised by Prince Shuyskiy is not at nearby Mozhaysk where the Tsar's army has assembled; De la Gardie reluctantly agrees to march towards Tsaryovo Zaymishche to relieve Prince Yeletskiy, Valuyev, and their garrison under siege by Żółkiewski
22 Jun	Part of the funds to pay De la Gardie's army arrives from Moscow; because of disputes relating to the number of men supplied, Prince Shuyskiy and De la Gardie cannot immediately pay the enlisted officers for their expenses
23 Jun	Prince Shuyskiy and De la Gardie reach Klushino
24 Jun	Żółkiewski defeats Prince Shuyskiy and De la Gardie at Klushino; most of De la Gardie's soldiers desert, so he accepts surrender under terms of free departure for himself and the remaining men
29 Jun	De la Gardie and his few loyal men reach Vydropuzhsk, from which he sends a report to Tsar Vasiliy that he is on the way to Viborg to raise a new army
1 Jul	De la Gardie reaches Khotilovo
2 Jul	Group of 300 assorted Spanish, English, Scottish, German, and French soldiers surrender to King Sigismund's representatives, being the last of the deserters from De la Gardie's remnant army
4 Jul	With Swedish troops moving into Kexholm County to annex the territory that Moscow had agreed to cede, skirmishes break out outside Kexholm; Arvid Wildeman and Lars Andersson lay siege to Kexholm

SWEDEN'S WAR IN MUSCOVY 1609-1617

6 Jul	De la Gardie reaches Viny
7–9 Jul	De la Gardie in Bronnitsa
17 Jul	Tsar Vasiliy IV deposed by the new boyar Council of Seven ('seven boyars') in Moscow, on 19 July tonsured as a monk to remove him from power
25 Jul	De la Gardie sets up camp at Novgorod
7 Aug	De la Gardie departs from Novgorod
13 Aug	Having despatched De la Ville to conquer Ladoga Town, De la Gardie reaches Nyen; soon after, De la Gardie exchanges fire with the Nöteborg garrison, after which he marches to Kexholm
15 Aug	De la Ville takes Ladoga Town in a surprise attack
17 Aug	In Moscow, Żółkiewski signs an agreement with the Council of Seven that gives the throne to Prince Władysław; the supporters of the Council of Seven swear loyalty to Tsar-elect Władysław
20 Aug	While Peder Jacobsköld lays siege to Ivangorod, neighbouring Narva accidentally catches fire; the Swedish army attempts to extinguish the fires, but Régis Du Vernet's French cavalry instead take the opportunity to plunder the burning town
24 Aug	De la Gardie writes to the Council of Seven in Moscow, warning them of the risks inherent in accepting a Polish candidate to the throne, and instead suggests one of the Swedish King's sons
6 Sep	Du Vernet's French cavalry mutinies, demanding more pay; around this time, De la Gardie reaches Kexholm
7 Sep	Ivan Saltykov and Grigoriy Valuyev set out from Moscow, leading a strong delegation to Novgorod in the name of Tsar-elect Władysław
21 Sep	Żółkiewski enters Moscow, occupies the Kremlin in the name of Tsar-elect Władysław
9 Oct	Du Vernet sent to Stockholm to answer for the mutiny, which by then had affected most Swedish units at Ivangorod
10 Oct	Patrick Rutherford's enlisted Scottish soldiers mutiny in Reval
12 Oct	Ivan Saltykov accepted as new governor in Novgorod, as representative of Tsar-elect Władysław
21 Oct	In the days leading up to this date, the mutinies within the Swedish army at Ivangorod cripple the siege operation, for which reason Philip von Scheiding soon accepts the Muscovite proposal of an Armistice of Ivangorod (ratified by King Charles on 16 November)

26 Oct	King Charles orders Bäck to make a third attempt to take Kola Castle
22 Nov	False Dmitriy murders Prince Oraz Muhammad Khan of the Kasimov Tatars
11 Dec	Prince Peter Urusov, a Tatar noble, kills False Dmitriy in revenge for the murder of the Kasimov Khan
28 Dec	King Charles orders De la Gardie and Evert Horn to resume the offensive into Muscovy, with the seizing of Novgorod a priority; Patriarch Hermogenes of Moscow, having learnt of the death of Dmitriy, is in the process of dispatching circular letters to Muscovite towns, asking them to unite against the Commonwealth army; in response, Commonwealth officers arrest Hermogenes

1611

15 Jan	De la Ville's brother Jacques captured by Muscovites when commanding a reconnaissance mission outside Ladoga Town
26 Jan	De la Gardie sets out from Viborg, bound for Muscovy
30 Jan	King Charles orders Colonel Andrew Stuart on a semi-diplomatic mission to seize Fort Suma on the River Suma and gain control of the Solovki Monastery, both on the White Sea
5 Feb	Convinced that De la Gardie would not relieve his garrison, and pressured by the Muscovites who used his brother as a hostage, De la Ville agrees to surrender Ladoga Town in exchange for the right of departure with all weapons, belongings, and full military honours
11–12 Feb	De la Gardie attempts a surprise night attack on Nöteborg, but fails
12 Feb	Bäck's expeditionary corps assembles in Rovaniemi, Finland, after which it finally sets out bound for Kola Castle
27 Feb	Not yet knowing that Dmitriy is dead, King Charles writes to him, offering Sweden's support in exchange for the territories already agreed with the previous regime and Ladoga Town
28 Feb	King Charles writes to Moscow and Novgorod, repeating his offer of support against the Commonwealth; King Charles also informs the governors of Ivangorod, Jama, Kaporie, Gdov, and Pskov about his offer to Dmitriy
2 Mar	Kexholm surrenders to Arvid Wildeman, Governor of Viborg; defenders depart
5 Mar	Hans von Rechenberger's Regiment and Robert Popler's company finally reach Nazya Yam, ready to join De la Gardie's army

SWEDEN'S WAR IN MUSCOVY 1609–1617

6 Mar	Acting upon orders of De la Gardie, Samuel Cobron attempts to take Ladoga Town in a surprise attack, but fails (and retreats on 13 March); soon after, a coup in Novgorod removes Governor Ivan Saltykov
18 Mar	De la Gardie writes to the notables of Novgorod, noting that since he had not received acceptable replies to his previous communications, he would send his army against the city
19 Mar	Moscow uprising against Commonwealth rule, Commonwealth garrison withdraws into Kitaygorod and the Kremlin, burning the outer city
21 Mar	Newly formed national militia, under Prokopiy Lyapunov, Prince Dmitriy Pozharskiy, and ultimately also Ataman Ivan Zarutskiy and Prince Dmitriy Trubetskoy, begins to take action against the Commonwealth garrison, with Prince Pozharskiy and his contingent first into the fray; Prince Pozharskiy badly wounded in combat, Prince Andrey Golitsyn killed
23 Mar	Yet another false Dmitriy announces himself, this time in Novgorod, but he is recognised as a cossack known as Sidorka and expelled
26 Mar	Colonel Stuart's expeditionary corps assembled at Kajaneborg, sets out but fails to reach Fort Suma because the snow is too deep (Stuart returns to Kajaneborg in late April)
27 Mar	King Sigismund offers Sapieha a contract to rescue the besieged Commonwealth garrison; at around this time, he also orders Grand Hetman of Lithuania Chodkiewicz to march with the army of Livonia to Moscow
28 Mar	False Dmitriy again announces himself, but in Ivangorod, held by former rebels and under threat from Swedes; claiming that he did not die in Kaluga after all, he gains support also in Jama, Kaporie, and Gdov – soon, Dmitriy attempts to negotiate an agreement of recognition with Sweden but the Swedes break off the talks
4 Apr	Denmark-Norway declares war on Sweden (the Kalmar War)
27 Apr	King Charles orders Baltzar Bäck, who failed to capture Kola Castle because he could not bring artillery across the Arctic wilderness, to make yet another attempt to conquer the Arctic coast
9 May	King Charles orders Bäck instead to invade the Norwegian province of Jämtland, because of the ongoing Kalmar War a more urgent task than the Muscovite Arctic coast
28 May	De la Gardie marches out of Sol'tsy, bound for Novgorod

CHRONOLOGY

2–3 Jun	King Sigismund's Commonwealth army storms Smolensk, after an almost two-year siege
2 Jun	De la Gardie's army at Luzhskiy in the vicinity of Novgorod
5 Jun	Horn leads cavalry reinforcements out of Viborg
6 Jun	Vasiliy Buturlin, the authorised representative of the national militia, requests that De la Gardie lead the Swedish army in support of the new regime; in private, Buturlin informs De la Gardie that the new regime would be happy to elect one of the Swedish King's sons as Tsar, as long as Muscovy is permitted to retain its Orthodox faith
7 Jun	Having been hired by King Sigismund against promises of future pay, Sapieha sets up a camp outside Moscow – but only to open negotiations with Commonwealth commander Aleksander Gosiewski in the Kremlin for the handover of the pay promised by King Sigismund
9 Jun	Buturlin and De la Gardie meet again; Buturlin requests negotiations to be postponed for two weeks; King Charles orders Colonel Stuart to make a second attempt against Fort Suma
16 Jun	Prince Trubetskoy, Zarutskiy, and Lyapunov, the commanders of the national militia, write to Governor Prince Ivan Odoyevskiy and Metropolitan Isidore in Novgorod, requesting them to persuade De la Gardie to hurry to their rescue; envoys of the national militia enter into negotiations with Sapieha in an attempt to hire him to their side
18 Jun	Envoys of the national militia leave Sapieha's camp, but maintain a channel for continued negotiations
23 Jun	The assembly of the national militia, represented by Prince Trubetskoy, Zarutskiy, and Lyapunov, formally elects Gustavus Adolphus Tsar of Muscovy, and sends this decree to Novgorod in order to hasten the arrival of De la Gardie's relief army
27 Jun	Sapieha demands his pay from King Sigismund, since Gosiewski is unable to pay what the King had promised
30 Jun	The assembly of the national militia agrees to make its grand council of war the highest judicial and administrative authority under the Tsar (a decree sometimes referred to as the constitution of the national militia), and elects Prince Trubetskoy, Zarutskiy, and Lyapunov as the chief officers of the council and state
2 Jul	The decree about the election of Gustavus Adolphus as Tsar of Muscovy, issued by Prince Trubetskoy, Zarutskiy, and Lyapunov, reaches Novgorod

SWEDEN'S WAR IN MUSCOVY 1609-1617

4 Jul	Sapieha leaves Moscow to plunder the vicinity for supplies to himself and Gosiewski
5 Jul	National militia units attempt to storm the Kremlin, but are pushed back with heavy losses
8 Jul	Meeting between De la Gardie and envoys from Novgorod at the Khutyn' Monastery at Kolmovo north of Novgorod degenerates into quarrel and fighting between the escorts of the two parties; in revenge, Swedish soldiers against orders plunder buildings belonging to the monastery; meanwhile, Dmitriy surrounds Pskov with his army, argues that he is Muscovy's only defender against perfidious foreigners, and demands Pskov's surrender
12 Jul	Novgorod army sallies out, but fails to make an impact on the Swedes
15–16 Jul	De la Gardie assaults and seizes Novgorod
17 Jul	Based on the decree about the election of Gustavus Adolphus as Tsar of Muscovy and acutely aware of his unfavourable situation, Governor Prince Odoyevskiy surrenders Novgorod Castle to De la Gardie
22 Jul	Members of the cossack faction of the national militia murder Lyapunov, whom they blame for the introduction of judicial safeguards to ban violence and robberies of the type they have grown accustomed to
25 Jul	Treaty of Novgorod; Novgorod formally appeals for Swedish protection, agrees to a union between Sweden and Novgorod against the Commonwealth, and pledges to give the throne of Muscovy to one of King Charles's sons
23 Aug	Learning that Swedes under Evert Horn march on Pskov, Dmitriy abandons the blockade of the city and withdraws to Gdov
28 Aug	Reporting the events in Novgorod to Stockholm, De la Gardie advises King Charles to send his son Charles Philip to Viborg as soon as possible for election as Tsar
31 Aug	Horn reaches Pskov but finds the city unwilling to yield to Sweden
5 Sep	Sapieha falls seriously ill
7–8 Sep	Horn attempts to storm Pskov, but fails
12 Sep	Ladoga Town surrenders to a Swedish army, and accepts the Novgorod Treaty; Tikhvin soon follows Ladoga Town's lead
26 Sep	Hetman Chodkiewicz reaches Moscow, temporarily relieves his countrymen there
30 Sep	Following an internal coup in Pskov, the city declares for Dmitriy

CHRONOLOGY

5 Oct	Sapieha dies from his illness
7 Oct	Horn abandons the siege of Pskov, marches towards Gdov to confront Dmitriy
28 Oct	Prince Pozharskiy arrives in Nizhniy Novgorod to assume command of the second national militia, raised by Kuz'ma Minin, a local merchant
30 Oct	King Charles dies from natural causes; Gustavus Adolphus inherits the Swedish throne at age 16
30 Nov	Having chased Dmitriy out of Gdov but having failed to take the town, Horn reaches Nöteborg, initiates negotiations with the defenders who are unwilling to surrender; Swedes blockade and lay siege to Nöteborg
4 Dec	Dmitriy arrives in Pskov, where he is acknowledged as Tsar of Muscovy

1612

Jan	Cossack faction of the national militia under Prince Trubetskoy and Zarutskiy sends a delegation to negotiate with the latest False Dmitriy in Pskov
10 Jan	Gustavus Adolphus accepts the offer of the Muscovite throne for himself, assumes the title Tsar of Muscovy, and orders free trade with Novgorod, which now is a Swedish dominion; letters to this extent are addressed to the Governor, Metropolitan, and Estates of Novgorod
Early Feb	Following a confused battle near Staraya Russa, Commonwealth Colonel Aleksey Mikhaylovich massacres the Swedish garrison under Oliver Popler
23 Feb	National militia, under Prince Pozharskiy, sets out from Nizhniy Novgorod, at first aiming for Moscow
25 Feb	Evert Horn defeats the Commonwealth Colonel Aleksandr Nalivayko at Borovichi
2 Mar	Cossack faction of the national militia under Prince Trubetskoy and Zarutskiy acknowledge False Dmitriy in Pskov as Tsar of Muscovy
9–10 Mar	Having failed to dislodge Horn from Borovichi, several units of Commonwealth freebooters retreat towards Ustyuzhna
14 Mar	Chodkiewicz writes to De la Gardie, suggesting that the Swedish commander switch sides to join King Sigismund; De la Gardie sends the letter on to Gustavus Adolphus as evidence of continued Commonwealth conspiracies against the Swedish Crown
18 Mar	Horn inflicts a severe defeat on Colonel Aleksey Mikhaylovich

SWEDEN'S WAR IN MUSCOVY 1609-1617

1 Apr	Prince Pozharskiy deploys the national militia at Yaroslavl' to safeguard a national assembly (*Zemskiy sobor*) of northern towns and hereditary servicemen to establish a provisional government; at around this time Nöteborg, finally starved of supplies, surrenders to Claes Slang
Early May	Prince Pozharskiy, Minin, and the national assembly send a delegation to Novgorod with letters to the Metropolitan Isidore, Prince Odoyevskiy, and De la Gardie, requesting further details of the Treaty of Novgorod and informing them that the national assembly would acknowledge and support the election of a Swedish prince as Tsar
16 May	De la Gardie forwards the documents of the national assembly to Stockholm
18 May	False Dmitriy flees Pskov
19 May	The emissaries of the national assembly return to Yaroslavl' to report about the successful meetings with the Metropolitan Isidore, Prince Odoyevskiy, and De la Gardie
20 May	Dmitriy captured and returned to Pskov; in June, he is handed over to representatives of Prince Trubetskoy's cossack faction, which ultimately executes him
26 May	Gustavus Adolphus asks Duke John of Östergötland to assume command in the war against Denmark and Norway, so that he can sail to Finland to assume the Tsardom and command in the war in Muscovy
3 Jun	Horn lays siege to Kaporie
5 Jun	Chodkiewicz advances towards Moscow
6 Jun	Mikołaj Struś brings reinforcements from Smolensk to Gosiewski in Moscow
7 Jun	Having learnt of the Danish successes on the western front, Gustavus Adolphus decides to postpone the voyage to Muscovy
14 Jun	Gosiewski hands over command in Moscow to Struś
16 Jun	Kaporie surrenders to Horn; Horn then turns to Jama, which surrenders a few days later
28 Jun	Horn reaches Ivangorod, where he builds a redoubt to cut the supply line between Ivangorod and Gdov; afterwards, Horn continues to Gdov which soon surrenders (in July)
26 Jul	Envoys from Novgorod advocate the election of a Swedish Tsar to Prince Pozharskiy and the national assembly's council of war; Prince Pozharskiy and the national militia set out from Yaroslavl' to counter Hetman Chodkiewicz

CHRONOLOGY

28 Jul	Prince Pozharskiy demands that the cossack faction abandon Zarutskiy and take him into custody; cossack faction suspects Zarutskiy of collusion with Chodkiewicz, so Zarutskiy and his remaining supporters withdraw to Kolomna, fetching Maryna and her baby boy Ivan
10 Aug	Having failed yet another attempt to take Pskov, Horn returns to Ivangorod
14 Aug	Prince Pozharskiy reaches the Holy Trinity-St Sergius Monastery
18 Aug	Prince Pozharskiy sets out from the Holy Trinity-St Sergius Monastery
20 Aug	Princes Pozharskiy and Trubetskoy arrive with their armies at Moscow; faced with an imminent attack by Chodkiewicz, the two princes agree to cooperate, urged on by the Holy Trinity-St Sergius Monastery
22–24 Aug	Prince Pozharskiy repulses Chodkiewicz outside Moscow (while Prince Trubetskoy holds back)
23 Aug	De la Gardie again writes to Stockholm, underlining the urgent need to send Charles Philip to Novgorod; on this date at the latest, Horn commences the siege of Ivangorod
25 Aug	Chodkiewicz retreats from Moscow
2 Sep	Death of ex-Tsar Vasiliy in Commonwealth captivity from murder or ill-treatment
15 Oct	Defenders of Ivangorod sally out in force, but fail to break the Swedish siege
22 Oct	Trubetskoy and his cossacks drive the besieged Moscow Commonwealth garrison, under Mikołaj Struś, out of Kitaygorod
24 Oct	De la Gardie again writes to Stockholm, underlining the urgent need to send Charles Philip to Novgorod
26 Oct	Commonwealth garrison under Struś in the Moscow Kremlin surrenders to Pozharskiy and Trubetskoy, and marches out on the following day (27 October)
Early Nov	National militia calls for towns and communities to send representatives for a national assembly in Moscow on 5 December for the election of a Tsar; King Sigismund marches to relieve the besieged Commonwealth garrison in Moscow, but abandons the effort (17 Nov) and retreats; due to the Commonwealth expedition, the Moscow national assembly is postponed
4 Dec	Ivangorod finally surrenders to Horn
11 Dec	Zarutskiy, Maryna, and baby Ivan reach Mikhaylov

	26 Dec	De la Gardie receives the communication that Charles Philip will be in Viborg before the end of February 1613; he sends a representative to Moscow with the news
1613		
	19 Jan	Kalmar War between Denmark and Sweden ends with Treaty of Knäred
	7 Feb	National assembly agrees in principle that a foreign tsar is the best choice, but postpones the election of Charles Philip until he arrives in Muscovy; King Sigismund back in Warsaw
	21 Feb	Armed cossacks move into the national assembly, threaten violence, and force the election of young Michael Romanov as Tsar of Muscovy
	2 Mar	Cossack faction sends a mission to Kostroma to persuade young Michael Romanov and his mother Marfa Ivanovna to accept the election
	14 Mar	Under strong cossack and clerical pressure, Marfa Ivanovna and young Michael accept the election, and set out towards Moscow on a circuitous route that first takes them to Yaroslavl' for meetings (from 21 March to 16 April) with Prince Pozharskiy's faction with the purpose of gaining guarantees for their personal safety
	18 Mar	De la Gardie advises Gustavus Adolphus to hasten Charles Philip's voyage to Muscovy but also reinforce the Swedish armies there, and in light of the election of Michael Romanov, hasten the consolidation of such territories in Muscovy that Sweden had gained
	29 Apr	Gustavus Adolphus admits to De la Gardie that the latter was correct in suggesting Charles Philip as Tsar, and that Gustavus Adolphus's decision to take the throne for himself had been hasty and resulted from ignorance of the situation
	2 May	Having negotiated mutual personal security guarantees with the leading nobles, Tsar Michael and his followers finally dare to enter the capital; soon after, Dmitriy Cherkasskiy sets out with an army loyal to Tsar Michael in a campaign to reconquer northwestern Muscovy from Swedes and roving Commonwealth mercenaries
	25 May	Tikhvin rises against and defeats its Swedish garrison, assisted by cossacks from Cherkasskiy's army
	4 Jun	Swedish corps under Robert Moore attempts but fails to retake Tikhvin
	9 Jun	Moore departs from Tikhvin
	Early Jun	Pskov Army takes Gdov (exact date unrecorded)
	18 Jun	Charles Philip sets out by sea from Stockholm, bound for Viborg but hampered by contrary winds

CHRONOLOGY

24 Jun	Prince Semyon Prozorovskiy's corps of Cherkasskiy's army reaches Tikhvin
29 Jun	Moore's vanguard returns to Tikhvin, which results in renewed skirmishes
29 Jun–3 Jul	Soldiers loyal to Tsar Michael defeat Zarutskiy at Voronezh; after which Zarutskiy, Maryna, and baby Ivan move on to Astrakhan' (where they arrive late in the year)
9 Jul	Charles Philip arrives in Viborg
10 Jul	Moore's significantly reinforced corps reaches Tikhvin
11 Jul	Michael Romanov crowned Tsar
17 Jul	With Moore engaging Muscovites at Tikhvin, De la Gardie orders Monickhouen's Regiment, by then newly arrived from Sweden to Viborg and under Paul Bettig, to march straight to Tikhvin
11 Aug	Moore's men begin to build redoubts and batteries at Tikhvin
17 Aug	After an extended bombardment, Bettig storms the Tikhvin nunnery but falls in the assault
18 Aug	Duke Julius Henry of Saxe-Lauenburg sets out from Ivangorod with a Swedish army to retake Gdov
21 Aug	Duke Julius Henry reaches Gdov (with the artillery arriving five days later)
28 Aug	Duke Julius Henry initiates an artillery bombardment of Gdov, ultimately breaching the town wall – but he fails to prepare an assault, and moreover is within days decisively defeated by a relief force from Pskov, after which the Swedes must abandon the siege; east of Tikhvin, Moore's men defeat and disrupt a strong Muscovite relief force
14 Sep	Reportedly inspired by the holy icon Our Lady of Tikhvin and religious fervour, defenders at Tikhvin sally out, taking prisoners and perhaps also spiking some cannons
14 Sep	Defenders at Tikhvin again sally out, taking prisoners
15 Sep	Defenders at Tikhvin sally out once more
14 or 17 Sep	De la Gardie orders Moore to abandon the siege of Tikhvin, and return to Novgorod
6 Oct	Horn sets out from Narva towards Gdov with the remnants of Duke Julius Henry's army and reinforcements from Sweden
18 Oct	Prince Trubetskoy advances with an army in the direction of Novgorod, demanding that De la Gardie abandon all Swedish conquests in Muscovy; the offensive soon loses momentum because of heavy snowfall, and results in little but the exchange of letters of complaint

SWEDEN'S WAR IN MUSCOVY 1609–1617

Late Oct–Nov	Horn lays siege to Gdov, but fails and ultimately abandons the endeavour
10 Nov	Gustavus Adolphus informs the Queen Dowager that he no longer has any hope that Charles Philip would become Tsar, but his brother must nonetheless remain in Viborg so that the Novgorodians would not renounce the treaty with Sweden
20 Nov	By this time, Muscovites from the direction of Tikhvin have initiated a siege of Ladoga Town
23 Dec	Gustavus Adolphus formally abandons his previous policy vis-à-vis Muscovy, henceforth desiring negotiations directly with the Estates in Moscow, or preferably, Tsar Michael; he insists on retaining Ivangorod, Jama, Kaporie, Nöteborg, Kexholm, Gdov, and Ladoga Town, which can be made to constitute a defensive ring of fortresses around Estonia and Finland
1614	
10 Jan	Truce concluded in Weltz between Sweden and the Commonwealth
12 Jan	Horn's army bound for Gdov and Pechory reaches Ivangorod; Charles Philip formally abandons his claims on Muscovy and Novgorod, instead leaving them to his brother the King
13 Jan	Gosiewski proposes a military alliance to De la Gardie, with joint operations against Tsar Michael's armies, since both he and De la Gardie currently lack necessary reinforcements; De la Gardie is tempted to accept Gosiewski's offer but knows that Gustavus Adolphus opposes cooperation with the Commonwealth
16 Jan	With Swedish hopes for Charles Philip becoming Tsar of Muscovy shattered, he leaves Viborg, and returns to Stockholm
22 Jan	Gustavus Adolphus modifies the Swedish policy vis-à-vis Muscovy further, henceforth insisting only on retaining Ivangorod, Jama, Kaporie, Nöteborg, and Kexholm as a defensive ring around Estonia and Finland
27 Jan	De la Gardie replies to Gosiewski that he can only agree to a truce, not an alliance against Muscovy
9 Feb	Before this date, Horn abandons the attempt to take Gdov, hampered by deep snow and lack of artillery
12, 14 and 16 Feb	Pierre De la Ville and Jacques Bourguignon de Corobel attempt to storm the fortified Pskov-Pechory Monastery; having failed, they abandon the attempt (before 19 February)

CHRONOLOGY

Late Feb–early Mar	Monickhouen lays siege to the recently built Muscovite redoubt at Staraya Russa, but ultimately abandons the siege because of the cold weather
5 Mar	Having pushed the Muscovite invaders out of Nöteborg and Kexholm Counties as well as relieved Ladoga Town, Herman Wrangel and Jesper Andersson Cruus reach Novgorod
Late Mar	Prince Trubetskoy sets out from Torzhok in the direction of Novgorod, but soon halts in the fortified camp at Kresttsy, where Cobron in vain attempts to invite him to battle
19 Mar	Gustavus Adolphus arrives in Tavastehus, Finland
20 Apr	Having moved out of his camp, Prince Trubetskoy's vanguard division reaches Bronnitsa
May	Zarutskiy, Maryna, and her three-year-old son Ivan escape from Astrakhan' to Yaik
19 May	Swedish naval victory on Lake Ladoga, in which 11 Swedish *lodja* vessels defeat a Muscovite squadron
8 Jun	Gustavus Adolphus sets out by sea from Viborg
16 Jun	Gustavus Adolphus arrives at Narva, delayed by unfavourable winds; he assumes personal command of the eastern front
25 Jun	Zarutskiy, Maryna, and child Ivan captured by government troops, brought to Moscow; subsequently, Zarutskiy and child Ivan executed
27 Jun	Cobron storms one of the Muscovite redoubts at Bronnitsa
8 Jul	Colonel Sidor again enters into De la Gardie's service in Novgorod, being the second Polish colonel to do so this summer
14–15 Jul	Cobron defeats Prince Trubetskoy at Bronnitsa
15 Jul	Andrey Palitsyn and his men abandon their position at Staraya Russa
27 Jul	Gustavus Adolphus gives Horn the task of assembling the army at Narva and then conquering Gdov; Hans Munck defeats Muscovites at Ristilahti in Uukuniemi in Karelia
15 Aug	Soon after this date, Cobron and Monickhouen join the siege of Gdov; eventually, the Muscovites repulse two attempts to storm the town, and Monickhouen falls in the siege
25 Aug	Gustavus Adolphus arrives at Gdov, assumes personal command of the siege
10 Sep	Gdov surrenders to Gustavus Adolphus
29 Sept	Two-year-truce between Sweden and the Commonwealth enters into force

SWEDEN'S WAR IN MUSCOVY 1609-1617

	4 Oct	Horn assumes command on the eastern front, while Gustavus Adolphus and De la Gardie temporarily return to Sweden
	15 Nov	Gustavus Adolphus back in Stockholm
	14 Dec	Horn demands that Novgorod accept a union with Sweden; but Novgorod continues to argue against the decision, saying that the city remains bound to its oath to Charles Philip
	22 Dec	John Merrick arrives in Moscow to mediate in the peace negotiations
1615		
	18 Jan	On this day, if not before, Horn sets out from Novgorod towards Pskov, attempts to blockade the city
	14 May	Gustavus Adolphus sends De la Gardie from Sweden to Finland to raise men and equip the army there
	Jun	Prince Nikita Volkonskiy goes on the offensive from Tikhvin towards Ladoga Town, but Cobron defeats and drives him and his men off, and then, at Tikhvin, inflicts a second defeat on the Muscovites, which effectively neutralises them as a threat
	10 Jun	De la Gardie in Åbo
	21 Jun	De la Gardie sets out from Åbo, bound for Novgorod by way of Narva
	28 Jun	Swedish main fleet with Gustavus Adolphus and the army bound for Pskov sets out from Stockholm
	3 Jul	Swedish main fleet leaves the outer Stockholm archipelago
	8 Jul	Gustavus Adolphus and the main fleet arrives in Narva; army disembarks
	20 Jul	Gustavus Adolphus sets out from Narva; De la Gardie remains in Narva to ensure that arriving reinforcements join the army
	25 Jul	Gustavus Adolphus reaches Gdov
	29 Jul	Gustavus Adolphus at Pskov with Swedish advance guard, lays siege to Pskov
	30 Jul	Field Marshal Evert Horn falls at Pskov
	31 Jul	Swedish main army arrives at Pskov
	14 Aug	Robert Moore, the senior Swedish siege expert, falls at Pskov
	18 Aug	De la Gardie and Merrick reach Novgorod
	20 Aug	Pskov cut off from Muscovite supply lines
	3 Sep	Swedish siege artillery arrives at Pskov
	12 Sep	Dutch mediators arrive in Narva, a few days later followed by Sweden's Chancellor Axel Oxenstierna
	17 Sep	Swedish siege artillery commences bombardment of Pskov

CHRONOLOGY

23 Sep	Swedish artillery opens a breach in Pskov's city wall, but the attempt to storm the city fails
30 Sept	Gustavus Adolphus orders preparations to be made for the retreat of the besieging army
8 Oct	Gustavus Adolphus renews bombardment of Pskov
9 Oct	Gustavus Adolphus attempts to storm Pskov, but fails to take the city
10–11 Oct	Gustavus Adolphus intensifies the bombardment of Pskov, until part of his gunpowder depot accidentally catches fire and explodes
13 Oct	First units of Gustavus Adolphus's army retreat from Pskov, bound for Novgorod
17 Oct	Gustavus Adolphus leaves Pskov with the main army, bound for Narva
27 Oct	Gustavus Adolphus reaches Narva
30 Nov	Truce agreed between Gustavus Adolphus, who spends the winter in Finland, and Tsar Michael

1616

3 Jan	First formal meeting for peace negotiations in Diderino between representatives of Gustavus Adolphus and Tsar Michael with Dutch and English mediators
22 Feb	Armistice in Diderino: a three-month truce between Gustavus Adolphus and Tsar Michael
27 Feb	Dutch delegation arrives in Novgorod, prepares to travel to Stockholm to meet Gustavus Adolphus for further negotiations between the parties (through the exchange of letters, not personal meetings)
13 Jun	Following the exchange of several letters, peace negotiations collapse (truce lapsed on 1 June)
18 Jun	Carl Gyllenhielm promoted to Field Marshal with orders to conquer Pskov
6 Jul	Gyllenhielm arrives in Narva
28 Jul	Gyllenhielm marches out of Narva, bound for Pskov
9 Aug	Gyllenhielm reaches Pskov, lays siege to the city
17 Sep	Muscovite surprise attack on Swedish riverine vessels with food supplies from Narva results in the loss of all supply vessels
23 Sep	Lacking food supplies, Gyllenhielm abandons the siege of Pskov, retreats to Narva while leaving a detachment in a fortified camp at Pskov
28 Sep	Gyllenhielm reaches Narva

SWEDEN'S WAR IN MUSCOVY 1609–1617

29 Sept	Two-year truce between Sweden and the Commonwealth allowed to lapse by King Sigismund's refusal to negotiate a mutually acceptable peace treaty; negotiations for a new truce continue
11 Oct	Pskov Army lays siege to the Swedish fortified camp at Pskov
3 Dec	Swedish relief expedition under Hans von Rechenberger sets out from Narva
11 Dec	Out of food, Swedes at Pskov surrender under terms of free departure
14 Dec	Rechenberger's relief expedition meets the retreating Swedish survivors; all return to Narva
31 Dec	Peace negotiations, never fully abandoned, resume in Stolbovo

1617

17 Feb	War between Sweden and Muscovy ends with Treaty of Stolbovo; Sweden returns Novgorod but gains Ingria and Kexholm County
26 Mar	Władysław and Chodkiewicz launch a new campaign against Moscow, which ultimately fails
6 June	Swedish–Commonwealth negotiations for a continued truce collapse
9 June	War resumes between Sweden and the Polish-Lithuanian Commonwealth; Swedes invade Livonia
12 Oct	Belated coronation of Gustavus Adolphus as King of Sweden

1618

13 May	Defenestration of Prague, outbreak of the Bohemian Revolt and the Thirty Years' War
15 Nov	Truce between Sweden and the Commonwealth
1 Dec	Truce of Deulino between Muscovy and the Commonwealth; King Sigismund gains Smolensk and the Chernigov region of Severia

Introduction

The present book aims to describe and analyse Jacob De la Gardie's Swedish intervention in Muscovy of 1609–1610 and the subsequent Ingrian War between Sweden and Muscovy of 1610–1617, both of which took place during Russia's Time of Troubles, a time of lawlessness and anarchy; and the Polish–Muscovite War of 1605–1618. Faced with a serious threat from the Polish-Lithuanian Commonwealth which supported a series of pretenders to the throne, Tsar Vasiliy IV of Muscovy entered into an alliance with King Charles IX of Sweden. Charles was already at war with his nephew, Polish King Sigismund III, since Sigismund claimed the Swedish crown that Charles had taken from him. As a result, a Swedish expeditionary army under Jacob De la Gardie marched to Moscow in order to save Muscovy from both pretenders and a Polish-Lithuanian invasion army, and relieve the Tsar. However, the Swedish–Muscovite coalition was defeated by a Commonwealth army in the battle of Klushino, and Sigismund proclaimed his son Tsar of Muscovy. Later, Sweden conquered Novgorod. Instead of accepting Sigismund's choice of Tsar, Moscow offered the throne to the young Gustavus Adolphus of Sweden, who later rose to pan-European prominence in the Thirty Years' War. While the representatives of Gustavus Adolphus ruled Muscovy from Novgorod, a coup in Moscow led to the assumption of power by the first Tsar of the Romanov dynasty. Sweden accordingly went to war against Muscovy: the Ingrian War, in which Gustavus Adolphus laid siege to Pskov. The war ended with the 1617 Treaty of Stolbovo, in which Muscovy ceded key territories to Sweden while Sweden recognised the House of Romanov as rulers of Muscovy. For Sweden, the Treaty of Stolbovo has been described as the most successful peace ever negotiated with Muscovy or its successor Russia. For Muscovy, the Treaty signified the ascension of the House of Romanov. For both countries, the war led to significant military reforms that, in time, would make both the Swedish and Muscovite military establishments forces to be reckoned with. For Gustavus Adolphus, who arrived in 1614 personally to take command of the Swedish war effort, the war in Muscovy proved a significant step on his path to become a successful commander in the subsequent Thirty Years' War.

While the focus of the present book is the Swedish intervention in the Time of Troubles, it also describes the military establishments of the countries involved in the conflicts, the context of and motivations of the various parties, and pertinent events that led up to and caused the wars.

At the time of the Time of Troubles, some of the belligerent powers followed different calendars. The Gregorian calendar, named after the sixteenth-century pope Gregory XIII who introduced it, had been developed as a correction to an observed error in the old Julian calendar. The visible result of the correction was that the date was advanced 10 days, that is, 4 October 1582 was followed by 15 October 1582. France and the Holy Roman Empire changed calendar on this date, as did most Catholic nations. However, many Protestant countries including Sweden initially objected to adopting a Catholic innovation. They retained the Julian calendar, which for this reason differed from the one used in Catholic nations and at present. Old Style (O. S.) and New Style (N. S.) are terms commonly used with dates to indicate that the calendar convention used at the time described is different from that in use at present. Unless noted otherwise, the dates given here will be O. S., since the events described primarily took place in Sweden and Muscovy which both used the Old Style.

The different calendars already caused confusion in seventeenth-century Europe, and at present the situation frequently causes problems for historians. Swedish and Muscovite/Russian archival documents and modern histories relating to the war commonly use the O. S. calendar. Meanwhile, Commonwealth documents and modern Polish-language histories naturally follow the N. S. calendar. I have yet to see a work on the Time of Troubles and Sweden's war in Muscovy without the occasional, wrongly calculated date, and no doubt there will be mistakes in the present volume, too.

An attempt has been made to include, in addition to English-language translations, the original names in Swedish, Polish, Lithuanian, Russian, Finnish, and German, where it seemed important to do so for reasons of clarity. However, since neither language had a codified system of spelling at the time, the forms used are not necessarily those used today. Still, anybody with a working knowledge of the language should be able to identify the word forms employed. The same goes for personal names, which were then spelled in a variety of ways. Moreover, names and titles were long and cumbersome, and often we do not know which of several given names an individual preferred.

Dramatis Personae

Sweden

Charles Philip (1601–1622), Duke of Södermanland, Närke and Värmland. Son of King Charles IX, younger brother of Gustavus Adolphus.
John (1589–1618), Duke of Östergötland. Youngest son of the late King John III and cousin of Gustavus Adolphus.
Julius Henry (1586–1665), Duke of Saxe-Lauenburg. German prince without prior military experience.
Andersson, Erik (Finnish: Eerikki Antinpoika; c. 1586–1634), interpreter, courier, and intelligence officer with long experience of Muscovy.
Andersson, Lars, of Botila (d. 1611), cavalry captain. Commander of a Karelian cavalry banner.
Banér, Svante Gustavsson (1584–1628), colonel. With his father executed by King Charles, he grew up destitute, going into Imperial service as a common cavalryman in Hungary, from which he rose through the ranks until Gustavus Adolphus gave him a regiment.
Bäck, Baltzar (d. 1618), Governor of Lapponia and sometime soldier.
Behm, Isaac (d. c. 1623), Governor of Österbotten and sometime soldier and admiral, known for acts of excessive violence.
Boije, Anders Nilsson (d. 1618), colonel. Commander of the Finnish cavalry, veteran of numerous wars, including on the side of King Sigismund in the civil war which brought Duke Charles to the kingship, and the brother-in-law of Colonel-General Axel Kurck. Governor of Kexholm in 1612.
Boije, Hans Mårtensson (1581–1617), cavalry captain. Governor of Kexholm in 1613. Nephew of Anders Boije.
Cobron, Samuel (earlier Cockburn; 1574–1621), captain, in 1610 promoted to colonel, in 1614 major general. Scotsman in Swedish service since either 1598 or 1606.
Colville, James (possibly Calvine; fl. 1609), lieutenant colonel. Head of the English contingent in De la Gardie's intervention army.
Clodt von Jürgensburg, Jost (d. 1621), captain, in 1615 promoted to major. German military professional in Swedish service.

Cruus, Jesper Andersson (1576–1647), colonel. Veteran of the wars on the eastern front against the Commonwealth.

Cruus, Jesper Matsson (1576 or 1577–1622), colonel, in 1615 field marshal. Veteran of the wars on the eastern front against the Commonwealth. Distant relative of Jesper Andersson Cruus.

De la Ville de Dombasle, Pierre (fl. 1609–1614), lieutenant colonel, in 1611 colonel. Commander of the French contingent in De la Gardie's intervention army and, since he could speak Dutch, other soldiers as well.

Du Vernet, Régis (fl. 1607–1610), colonel. French officer in Swedish service.

Frensham, Jacob (fl. 1609–1614), captain. English or Scottish officer in Swedish service.

Glasenap, Asmus von (d. 1629), cavalry captain, promoted to major in 1615. German officer in Swedish service.

Gyllenhielm, Carl Carlsson (1574–1650), colonel. An illegitimate son of King Charles, and half-brother of Gustavus Adolphus, Gyllenhielm went into French service under Henry IV, spent 13 years in chains in a Polish prison, served on the eastern front, and was in 1616 promoted to field marshal as a replacement for the late Evert Horn.

Gyllenhierta, Claes Christersson (d. 1617), cavalry captain. Veteran soldier who commanded a Finnish cavalry banner.

Gyllenmåne, Tönne Göransson (fl. 1592–1613), commissar. Diplomat and administrator. Governor of Kexholm in 1611.

Hammarskiöld, Per (Peder) Michaelsson (c. 1560–1646), cavalry captain, in 1611 promoted to colonel of cavalry in Småland.

Hästesko, Lindved Claesson (c. 1570–1615), cavalry captain, serving as colonel. Commander of a Karelian cavalry banner.

Hepburn, Daniel (fl. 1609–1611; in Sweden known as Hebron), captain. Poland-born Scottish officer in Swedish service.

Höök, Göran Hansson (d. 1611), cavalry captain. Noble of a family later known as Lilliehöök who commanded a Västergötland cavalry banner.

Horn af Kanckas, Evert Carlsson (1585–1615), cavalry captain, in 1613 promoted straight to field marshal because of his great responsibilities and military successes. In 1613 appointed governor of Narva, Ivangorod, Jama, and Kaporie. According to some accounts a veteran of the 1605 battle of Kircholm.

Jacobsköld, Peder Nilsson (1567–1611), secretary to the Governor of Reval. Official and diplomat dependent on and loyal to King Charles.

Kafle, Bengt Erlandsson (d. 1636), cavalry captain, promoted to lieutenant colonel in 1617. Commander of a Västergötland cavalry banner.

Kurck, Axel Jönsson (1555–1630), colonel-general. Veteran of numerous wars, including on the side of King Sigismund in the civil war which brought Duke Charles to the kingship.

Larsson, Anders, of Botila (d. 1613), Governor of Reval. Father of Lars Andersson.

Leslie, Alexander (1582–1661), lieutenant in Oliver Popler's company (1611). Scotsman in Swedish service since 1608.

DRAMATIS PERSONAE

Linck von Thurnburg, Johann Conrad (fl. 1609–1610), colonel. German officer in Swedish service.
Mansfeld zu Vorderort, Joachim Friedrich von (1581–1623), count and general. German veteran appointed commander of the army in Livonia.
Monickhouen, Johan (Jean) van (d. 1614), colonel. Dutchman from Brabant in Swedish service since at least 1608. A qualified military engineer and siege specialist who first served in Livonia, his name was often spelled Johan von Mönnichhofen.
Moore, Robert (d. 1615), captain. Accomplished military engineer in Swedish service who commanded an enlisted company and also functioned as senior quartermaster.
Muir or **Moore** or **Myr, Hans** or **John** (d. 1613), cavalry captain. Commander of an enlisted unit.
Munck, Hans Michaelsson (1588–1635), of Fulkila, cavalry captain. Promoted to commander in Kexholm County in 1614, and Governor of Kexholm in 1615.
Pedersson, Peder (also known as Petrus Petreius; 1570–1622). Swedish diplomat and expert on Muscovy.
Popler, Oliver (d. 1612), captain, in 1612 at the latest promoted to lieutenant colonel. Scotsman in Swedish service.
Popler, Robert (fl. 1609–1613), captain. Probably a relative of Oliver Popler.
Rechenberger, Hans von (d. c. 1650), colonel.
Rutherford, Patrick (1577–1618), colonel. Veteran of Swedish service on the eastern front and a good friend of Chancellor Oxenstierna.
Rutherford, Robert (fl. 1612–1617), major, in 1615 promoted to lieutenant colonel and acting commander of the King's Regiment.
Ruthven, Patrick (1572 or 1586–1651), captain. Scottish officer in Swedish service since 1608, who soon acquired a reputation as a bon viveur. Because of his frequent carousing he became known, in a pun on his real name, under the nickname Pater Rothwein ('Father Red Wine').
Rytter (Reuter), Johan Henriksson (1585–1644), major. Veteran of the 1605 battle of Kircholm, in 1615 ennobled as Rytter.
Scheiding, Philip von (1578–1646), Governor of Narva.
Scheiding, Otto von (1580–1651), cavalry captain. Younger brother of Philip von Scheiding.
Slang, Claes Eriksson (1558–1625 or 1626), captain, serving as acting colonel.
Some, Christer Abrahamsson (c. 1565–1618), field marshal. Veteran of the wars on the eastern front against the Commonwealth.
Stålhandske, Hans Jönsson (d. 1623 or 1624), cavalry captain. Commander of the Finnish retinue of nobles (1610–1612), deputy governor of Kexholm (1612), commander in Kexholm County (1614–1615), and governor of Kexholm (1616).
Stierna, Arvid Persson (1581–1641), colonel.
Stiernskiöld, Nils Göransson (1583–1627), colonel. Veteran of the wars on the eastern front against the Commonwealth, who in 1610 was so badly

wounded by an exploding cannon that for three years he could only walk with crutches.
Stuart, Andrew or **Anders**, of Starsäter (*c*. 1570–1640), colonel. Scottish soldier, diplomat, and veteran of the 1605 battle of Kircholm. Naturalised as a Swedish noble, in Swedish historiography known as 'Anders Stuart the Elder'.
Stuart, William (d. 1613), colonel.
Taube, Reinhold (d. 1613), lieutenant colonel, in 1613 promoted to colonel. Military professional who commanded first Jacob De la Gardie's Life Regiment of Foot, and then the King's Regiment of Foot which included the Drabant Company. His name was often spelled Tuffwe.
Wauchope, John (fl. 1608–1613), cavalry captain. Scottish officer in Swedish service.
Wildeman, Arvid Tönnesson (d. 1617), Governor of Viborg. Sometime admiral and soldier, veteran of the civil war and the war against the Commonwealth.
Wildeman, Henrik Tönnesson (d. 1612), vice-admiral. Brother of Arvid Tönnesson Wildeman.
Wrangel, Herman (1585–1643), cavalry captain.

Muscovy

Baryatinskiy, Yakov Petrovich (d. 1610), Prince. Loyalist veteran of the war with Sweden in the 1590s.
Bezzubtsev, Yuriy (fl. 1604–1617), captain (*sotnik*). Rebel noble. Although often described as a cossack leader and his patronymic appears to be lost in records, he was of noble lineage related to the important Houses of Sheremetyev and Romanov and commanded nobles from Putivl'.
Bolotnikov, Ivan Isayevich (1565–1608), freebooter.
Buturlin, Fyodor Leont'yevich (d. 1640), voivode. Deputy governor of Pskov (1614–1615).
Buturlin, Vasiliy Ivanovich (fl. 1605–1614), voivode. Loyalist. Holding the court rank of *chashnik* (cup-bearer), he served as commander of the Vanguard Division at Klushino (1610) and representative of the national militia (1611).
Cherkasskiy, Dmitriy Mamstryukovich (d. 1651), Circassian prince. In the service of False Dmitriy (1608–1610), the Commonwealth soldier of fortune Jan Piotr Sapieha (1611), Kuz'ma Minin (1612), and Tsar Michael Romanov (1613 onwards).
Choglokov, Kornil Nikitich (fl. 1609–1612), voivode. Loyalist commander who fought in the armies of Prince Skopin-Shuyskiy, the Council of Seven (on behalf of Tsar-elect Władysław), Prince Trubetskoy, and ultimately Prince Pozharskiy.
Chornyy-Obolenskiy, Fyodor Timofeyevich (1588–1650), prince.
Chulkov, Fyodor Danilovich (fl. 1588–1614), voivode. Loyalist veteran of wars against Sweden and the Khanate of the Crimea.

DRAMATIS PERSONAE

Filaret (*c.* 1553–1633), alternative Patriarch of Moscow. Born as Fyodor Nikitich of the House of Romanov, he served as soldier and diplomat before Tsar Boris forced him into monastic confinement as Filaret. Promoted as alternative Patriarch by False Dmitriy.

'Fyodor Fyodorovich' (real name unknown; d. 1608), Tsarevich ('Crown Prince'). Don cossack chief who claimed to be the nonexistent second son of Tsar Fyodor and accordingly the grandson of Tsar Ivan IV.

Gagarin, Afanasiy Fyodorovich (fl. 1573–1624), prince. Deputy governor of Pskov (1615).

Golitsyn, Andrey Vasil'yevich (d. 1611), prince. One of the Council of Seven.

Golovin, Semyon Vasil'yevich (d. 1634), voivode. Brother-in-law of Prince Mikhail Skopin-Shuyskiy.

Hermogenes (Russian: Germogen; before 1530–1612), Patriarch of Moscow. Uncompromising opponent of the False Dmitriys and everything foreign.

Isidore (d. 1619; Russian: Isidor), Metropolitan of Novgorod and Velikiye Luki.

'Ivan Augustus' (Russian: Ivan Avgust; real name unknown; d. 1608), Tsarevich ('Crown Prince'). Pretender who claimed to be the son of Tsar Ivan IV.

Izmaylov, Artemiy Vasil'yevich (d. 1634), voivode. Rebel noble and, from 1611, Prokopiy Lyapunov's successor as leader of the noble elite from Ryazan'.

Khovanskiy, Ivan Andreyevich (d. 1621), prince. Loyalist diplomat and commander who served Tsars Vasiliy and Michael.

Khovanskiy, Ivan Fyodorovich (d. 1625), prince. Loyalist governor of Pskov (1607), Ivangorod (1609–1610), and again Pskov (1612–1614). Distant relative of Ivan Andreyevich Khovanskiy.

Khvorostinin, Ivan Dmitriyevich (d. 1613), voivode. Rebel noble, diplomat, soldier, and veteran of the wars with the Khanate of the Crimea. Governor of Astrakhan'.

Kirill (Zavidov; d. 1619), Metropolitan of Rostov and Yaroslavl'.

Kropotkin, Pyotr Ivanovich (d. 1630), prince. Loyalist. Deputy governor of Ivangorod (1609–1610).

Kurakin, Ivan Semyonovich (d. 1632), prince. In the service of Tsar Vasiliy (1609–1610), Dmitriy (1611), and Tsar-elect Władysław (1612).

Lyapunov, Prokopiy Petrovich (1547?–1611), voivode. Veteran of various conflicts and leader of the noble elite from Ryazan'.

Lykov-Obolenskiy, Boris Mikhaylovich (1576–1646), prince. One of the Council of Seven.

Mezetskiy, Daniil Ivanovich (d. 1628), prince. Loyalist soldier and diplomat.

Minin, Kuz'ma (d. 1616). Wealthy merchant and close associate of Prince Dmitriy Pozharskiy. Although Minin made his fortune as a meat wholesaler in Nizhniy Novgorod, he was not necessarily low-born, commanded noble cavalry in battle, and it has been suggested that he was a recently baptised Tatar.

Molchanov, Mikhail Andreyevich (fl. 1589–1611), secretary and head of chancellery (*d'yak*). Rebel and opportunist who once claimed to be Dmitriy.

Morozov, Vasiliy Petrovich (d. 1630), Boyar. Loyalist governor of Pskov (1615).

Mstislavskiy, Fyodor Ivanovich (c. 1550–1622), prince. The most powerful of the Council of Seven, and Chairman of the national assembly (*Zemskiy sobor*) of 1613.

Myshetskiy, Yefim Fyodorovich (fl. 1609–1659), prince. Loyalist governor of Kexholm under Prince Skopin-Shuyskiy, followed by service at Nöteborg and elsewhere in northwestern Muscovy.

Ododurov, Ivan Grigor'yevich (fl. 1609–1617), voivode. Loyalist diplomat and commander.

Ododurov, Semyon Grigor'yevich (fl. 1609), voivode. Loyalist and brother of Ivan Ododurov

Odoyevskiy, Ivan Nikitich (d. 1616), prince. Loyalist veteran of previous wars with Sweden and the Khanate of the Crimea. Governor of Novgorod from 1610 onwards. Known as Ivan Odoyevskiy the Elder to distinguish him from his identically named younger brother (d. 1629) who served further east.

Odoyevskiy, Nikita Ivanovich (d. 1689), prince. Son of Ivan Odoyevskiy.

Oraz Muhammad Khan (1572?–1610; r. 1600–1610), Tatar prince and Khan of the Kasimov Khanate. Descendant of Chinggis Khan and veteran of the previous war against Sweden.

Palitsyn, Andrey Fyodorovich (d. 1640), voivode.

Pashkov, Filipp 'Istoma' Ivanovich (1583–1607), captain (*sotnik*). Formerly a hereditary serviceman, by this time a rebel leader of the noble elite from Tula.

'Petrushka (Peter)' (d. 1608), Tsarevich ('Crown Prince'). Also known as Ileyko (Il'ya) Muromets. Real name Il'ya Ivanovich Korovin, cossack pretender who claimed to be the nonexistent first son of Tsar Fyodor and accordingly the grandson of Tsar Ivan IV.

Pleshcheyev, Ivan Vasil'yevich (fl. 1607–1641), voivode. Governor of Kolomna, rebel noble in Tushino, and agent of Ivan Zarutskiy.

Pleshcheyev, Lev Afanas'yevich (d. 1645), voivode. Rebel noble in Tushino and, later, agent of Tsar-elect Władysław.

Pozharskiy, Dmitriy Mikhaylovich (1578–1642), prince. Loyalist commander, descendant of a line of minor sovereign princes.

Prozorovskiy, Semyon Vasil'yevich (c. 1586–1660), prince. Loyalist commander whose family was related to Tsar Vasiliy by marriage. Fought under Princes Cherkasskiy and Pozharskiy, including during the latter's 1612 eviction of the Commonwealth garrison in the Moscow Kremlin.

Putyatin, Ivan Semyonovich (d. 1624), prince. Governor of Nöteborg (1610) and supporter of Tsar-elect Władysław.

Romanov, Ivan Nikitich (d. 1640), Boyar. Younger brother of Filaret, and one of the Council of Seven.

DRAMATIS PERSONAE

Saltykov, Ivan Mikhaylovich (d. 1611), voivode. Rebel noble and Commonwealth supporter. Governor of Novgorod (1610–1611).
Saltykov, Mikhail Glebovich (fl. 1576–1620), Boyar. Father of Ivan Saltykov and himself a rebel noble. Governor of Ivangorod (1606–1609).
Shakhovskoy, Grigoriy Petrovich (fl. 1587–1612), prince. Veteran commander who had served as voivode since the reign of Tsar Ivan IV, but then transferred his allegiance to the False Dmitriys.
Shein, Mikhail Borisovich (1570s–1634), Boyar. Loyalist governor of Smolensk and head of spy network in the Grand Duchy of Lithuania. Veteran of wars against the Khanate of the Crimea and assorted rebels.
Sheremetyev, Fyodor Ivanovich (1570–1650), Boyar. One of the Council of Seven.
Silvester (Russian: Sil'vestr; fl. 1595–1615), Bishop of Korela (Kexholm), and subsequently, Archbishop of Vologda (1612) and Archbishop of Pskov (1613) until his death in 1615.
Skopin-Shuyskiy, Mikhail Vasil'yevich (1586–1610), prince. Loyalist general and younger distant cousin of Tsar Vasiliy IV.
Sunbulov, Grigoriy Fyodorovich (fl. 1606–1609), voivode. Together with Prokopiy Lyapunov, a leader of the noble elite from Ryazan'.
Sunbulov, Isay (Isaak) Nikitich (fl 1594–1630), voivode. Like his relative Grigoriy Sunbulov, at first in the service of Prokopiy Lyapunov, later followed by service on behalf of Tsar-elect Władysław.
Telepnyov, Yefim Grigor'yevich (d. 1636), secretary and head of chancellery (*d'yak*). In the service of Tsar Vasiliy, and after him, the Council of Seven.
Telyatevskiy, Andrey Andreyevich (d. 1612), prince. Rebel governor of Chernigov.
Trubetskoy, Andrey Vasil'yevich (d. 1611), prince. Veteran soldier who had fought every conceivable enemy ranging from the Commonwealth under Stephen Báthory (1533–1586) to Livonia, Sweden, the Crimean Khanate, and the Circassians of the Caucasus. One of the Council of Seven.
Trubetskoy, Dmitriy Timofeyevich (d. 1625), prince. Rebel noble and distant relative of Andrey Trubetskoy.
Urusov, Pyotr (Peter) Arslanovich (Tatar: Orak Yanarslan uly; d. 1639), Noghai Tatar prince.
Valuyev, Grigoriy Leont'yevich (d. 1626), voivode. Loyalist commander.
Vel'yaminov, Leontiy Andreyevich (fl. 1611–1613), Boyar. Loyalist.
Volkonskiy, Grigoriy Konstantinovich (*c.* 1560–1634), prince. Diplomat and soldier, veteran of the war against Sweden in the 1590s and the Khanate of the Crimea. Later in the service of Tsar-elect Władysław.
Volkonskiy, Nikita Andreyevich (d. 1620), prince. Loyalist.
Vorotynskiy, Ivan Mikhaylovich (d. 1627), prince. One of the Council of Seven.
Yeletskiy, Fyodor Andreyevich (d. 1638), prince. Loyalist.
Zarutskiy, Ivan Martynovich (d. 1614), ataman. Don cossack leader and serial rebel.
Zherebtsov, Davyd Vasil'yevich (d. 1610), voivode. Loyalist veteran and commander of men from Siberia and Arkhangel'sk.

Polish-Lithuanian Commonwealth

Chodkiewicz, Jan Karol (Lithuanian: Jonas Karolis Chodkevičius; c. 1570–1621), Grand Hetman of Lithuania. Veteran soldier who repeatedly defeated Swedish and other armies.
Gosiewski, Aleksander Korwin (d. 1639), voivode. Veteran of the 1605 battle of Kircholm and commandant of occupied Moscow (1610–1612).
Kiernożycki (Kiernozicki), Jan (fl. 1609), cavalry captain and sometimes colonel. Polish soldier of fortune serving False Dmitriy.
Lisowski, Aleksander Józef (c. 1580–1616), soldier of fortune, serial mutineer, and commander serving False Dmitriy but primarily himself. Veteran of wars against Moldavians and Swedes.
Mniszchówna or **Mniszech, Maryna** (c. 1588–1615). Daughter of a Polish nobleman and wife of two False Dmitriys.
Radziwiłł, Krzysztof (Lithuanian: Kristupas Radvila; 1585–1640), Field Hetman of Lithuania from 1615.
Różyński, Roman Kirykowicz (Ruthenian: Roman Kirillovich Rozhinskiy; 1575–1610), prince. Veteran officer of many wars who served as False Dmitriy's Hetman.
Sapieha, Jan Piotr (Lithuanian: Jonas Petras Sapiega; 1569–1611), soldier of fortune and hetman serving False Dmitriy. Veteran of the 1605 battle of Kircholm.
Sidor (full name unknown; d. 1614), colonel. Lithuanian volunteer and soldier of fortune.
Zborowski, Aleksander (1570–1637), mercenary commander.
Żółkiewski, Stanisław (1547–1620), Field Hetman of the Crown. Veteran soldier who had fought Swedish, Muscovite, and other armies for many years.

Prologue: A Bevy of Monarchs, a Chancellor, and Two Generals

Charles IX Vasa, King of Sweden

Charles IX (1550–1611; r. 1599–1611) of the House of Vasa was the youngest son of King Gustavus I. When King Gustavus died in 1560, Charles received a duchy that encompassed most of the provinces of Södermanland and Närke and parts of Västmanland and Västergötland. At age 15, he was put in command of the Swedish artillery for the conquest of Varberg Castle. Three years later, he joined his elder brother John in the rebellion that overthrew their half-brother, King Erik XIV.

Charles's elder brother then assumed the throne as King John III (1537–1592; r. 1569–1592). There was much rivalry within the House of Vasa. King John had a son, Sigismund, who in 1587 was elected King of Poland and accordingly ruler of the Polish–Lithuanian Commonwealth. With the death of King John in 1592 from natural causes, Sigismund inherited the Swedish throne. Duke Charles, Sigismund's uncle, was appointed regent in the King's absence. However, Sigismund was a Catholic whilst Sweden had become a Lutheran country. Moreover, Duke Charles regarded himself as better qualified than his nephew to rule Sweden and Finland.[1]

Duke Charles accordingly rose against King Sigismund. In 1598, Sigismund led a Polish–Swedish army to Sweden but was defeated at Stångebro. In 1599, Duke Charles called a parliament in Jönköping which duly declared Sigismund deposed from the Swedish throne and confirmed the Duke as regent. The Duke then explained his views on the succession order to the remaining members of the Swedish branch of the House of Vasa,

---

1   Sweden and Finland constituted the same country. Its provinces and peoples had the same rights and obligations. Hence, any reference to Swedish soldiers, nobles, and so on, can be assumed also to include those from Finland, unless stated otherwise. Estonia, too, was part of the Swedish kingdom. Soldiers from these territories were all national troops.

King Charles IX. (Gripsholm Castle)

after which a parliament in Norrköping in 1604 recognised Duke Charles as King of Sweden. From 1607 onwards, he styled himself, in the antiquarian style popular at the time, 'King of Swedes, Goths, Vandals, Finns, Karelians, Lapps in Northern lands, Cajanians, and Estonians in Livonia'.

The King was married twice, from 1579 with Mary of the Palatinate, with whom he had six children. After her death, he married Christina of Holstein-Gottorp, with whom he had three children, including the son Gustavus Adolphus.

Both as man and ruler, King Charles was unpredictable and ruthless. He was also suspicious, vindictive, unforgiving, and prone to violence. There was a streak of insanity in the House of Vasa, but King Charles seems not to have succumbed to it, even though he, like his father and brothers, displayed signs of psychopathy. He frequently regarded those who spoke out against him as traitors, for which he sentenced them to death. His reign was characterised, if not by terror, then at least by fear. Yet, King Charles was also an efficient and meticulous planner and skillful politician who successfully played out different groups within parliament against each other. In religion, King Charles leaned towards Calvinism, which did not prevent him from displaying the Lutheran façade required to become King of Sweden.

King Charles fell victim to a stroke in the summer of 1609. He never fully recovered, but died in Nyköping on 30 October 1611.

Sigismund III Vasa, King of Poland and Grand Duke of Lithuania

Sigismund III Vasa (Polish: Zygmunt III Waza; 1566–1632; r. 1587–1632), King of Poland and Grand Duke of Lithuania, was the son of the aforementioned King John III of Sweden (while he still was Grand Duke of Finland) and his first wife, Catherine Jagiellon, daughter of King Sigismund I of Poland. His parents raised young Sigismund as a Catholic so that he would be eligible for the Polish throne. Sigismund grew up speaking Polish

PROLOGUE: A BEVY OF MONARCHS, A CHANCELLOR, AND TWO GENERALS

and Swedish, and he also knew German, Italian, and Latin, which was the language of learning and diplomacy.

Sigismund was duly elected King of Poland in 1587. His competitors were significant men: Tsar Fyodor I of Muscovy, Andrew Báthory of Transylvania (brother of the late king of Poland), and four Habsburg Archdukes. Yet Sigismund, or rather his representative Erik Sparre, a Swedish Catholic, had one ace up his sleeve. Sparre ingeniously made the Polish parliament believe that if Sigismund was elected, then Sweden would relinquish its territories in Livonia to the Commonwealth. This, together with the hope of receiving Swedish help in creating a strong fleet and a desire not to intimidate the Ottoman Empire by electing a Muscovite or Habsburg candidate, clinched the deal. Crowned in the then capital of Cracow, Sigismund was also appointed Grand Duke of Lithuania and accordingly ruled the entire Polish-Lithuanian Commonwealth (the *Rzeczpospolita*). King Sigismund was eager to join Sweden, too, to this union.

When Sigismund in 1592 inherited the Swedish throne, we have seen that Duke Charles rose against him, in 1598 defeated the Polish–Swedish army at Stångebro, and in 1599 called a parliament in Jönköping which duly declared Sigismund deposed from the throne.

This did not prevent King Sigismund from still laying claim to the Swedish throne. Sigismund was King Charles's nephew and, moreover, represented the senior line of the Swedish royal House of Vasa. Sigismund could indeed be said to have a better claim to the throne than his uncle, King Charles, who ostensibly had deposed his nephew because of the younger man's Catholic beliefs. Formally, Charles referred to the provisions of the 1560 last will of King Gustavus I, his father, which stipulated that any of his children who left the Lutheran religion would lose his inheritance. Charles successfully fought for power over Sweden and took control of Finland, both of which he ruled sternly. Sigismund had to be satisfied with the wealthier but more loosely organised Commonwealth.

King Sigismund's life encompassed the Counter-Reformation, the period of Catholic resurgence that took place in response to the Protestant Reformation. This may have turned him into a religious zealot. Certainly, he favoured, and granted privileges to, the order of Jesuits, whom he employed as advisors. The Swedes suspected that he also employed Jesuits as spies. Indeed, the King's religious policies in 1606–1609 engendered a rebellion among Commonwealth nobles who opposed the King's expansion of the Catholic faith at the expense of the Protestant one and disliked the King's growing powers. The rebels ultimately surrendered in exchange for leniency. The rebellion failed to stem the expansion of state-supported Catholicism in the Commonwealth. Nonetheless, the rebels succeeded in affirming the elective nature of Polish kingship and the inviolability of noble rights and privileges in the Commonwealth political system. The rebellion simultaneously confirmed the continuous power and economic influence of the nobility. This made the Commonwealth a great power, yet planted the seeds of the state's decline due to the nobility's unwillingness to modernise and adopt such economic and military innovations that

Sigismund, King of Poland and Grand Duke of Lithuania, c. 1624. (Paul Soutman; photo: Medström)

took place in the rest of central and northern Europe, including Muscovy. Unlike the Commonwealth nobility, who preferred to look to the past, King Sigismund was in favour of modernisation. Yet, there was only so much that he could do in the face of a hostile aristocracy based on the magnates with their vast holdings and personal armies.

King Sigismund was married twice, first to Anne of Austria, and then to Anne's younger sister Constance. Family life seems to have been mostly happy, and King Sigismund had many children with each of his wives. Among them was a son, Władysław (1595–1648), who ultimately would succeed him. However, both his spouses were Habsburg princesses, which caused resentment primarily in Sweden but in the Commonwealth as well. It is fair to say that the brides, through no fault of their own, encountered more hostility than approval in their adopted country. Yet, the marriages cemented the King's alliance with the House of Habsburg. On their side, the Habsburgs were happy to employ King Sigismund as a buffer against hostile or potentially hostile powers elsewhere, including Protestant Sweden and the Ottoman Empire. Relations between the Commonwealth and the Habsburgs were mutually beneficial, but never quite as cordial as their shared interest in the promotion of Catholicism might suggest.

Like most members of the House of Vasa, King Sigismund was unpredictable, at times temperamental and impetuous, although generally not as vindictive as his uncle, King Charles of Sweden. Yet, two envoys from Pope Clement VIII, Cardinal Enrico Caetani and his secretary Giovanni Paolo Mucante, described King Sigismund's character as almost saintly. In the words of Mucante:

> Everyday he [Sigismund] says the prayers as if he were a priest, he daily attends mass, then hears choral music and sermons. He fasts piously, and abstains from the marriage bed every Wednesday and Friday, and two days before and after confession. He tries to propagate the Catholic faith as much as he can, and if it only

depended on him, there would not be a single schismatic, Calvinist, or Lutheran in this powerful kingdom. To the best of his ability, His Majesty has decided not to give any office except to a Catholic, denying it to all dissenters.[2]

When not attending to his religious needs, the King was interested in arts and crafts, and in apparent contradiction to the saintly character reported by the Pope's envoys, was a skilled dancer who enjoyed celebrations. This brings us back to the question of King Sigismund's character and motives. The descriptions of him as a zealot, when not based on hostile Protestant propaganda, derive from reports such as those of Mucante and Caetani, who had their own reasons for describing the King as a champion of the Counter-Reformation. Perhaps the answer to the question of the King's motives lie somewhere between those of his political opponents and most overly pious supporters. King Sigismund certainly wanted to regain the Swedish throne, and it is equally certain that he wished to safeguard Catholicism, but perhaps the rumours about his fervent desire to convert Sweden and Muscovy to the Catholic faith were no more than the pious desires of the clergy who stood behind and supported him against the powerful Commonwealth magnates.

King Sigismund extended his vast realm at the expense of those neighbouring states that his army could defeat. His reign marked Poland's greatest territorial expansion, before decline set in.

Vasiliy IV Ivanovich Shuyskiy, Tsar of Muscovy

Vasiliy IV (*c.* 1552–1612; r. 1606–1610), Tsar of Muscovy, belonged to the ancient aristocratic House of Shuyskiy. This made him a member of the Rurik Dynasty, the line that descended from the ninth-century Varangian chief Rurik who is generally credited with establishing the state of Kievan Rus' which laid the foundation for what ultimately would become Russia. Vasiliy was the last Rurikid who ruled as Tsar.

Although primarily remembered in history for his political activities, Vasiliy was an able army general who fought loyally under several consecutive tsars. As a young man, he served Tsar Ivan IV in a variety of military roles, ultimately as voivode (general) during the campaigns of 1581, 1582, and 1583. From 1585 to 1587, he served Tsar Fyodor I as voivode of Smolensk. In 1598 and 1605, he served Tsar Boris Godunov as voivode. In 1605, Vasiliy was one of the generals who inflicted a major defeat on the pretender known as the False Dmitriy (see below) at Dobrynichi.

---

2   X. Paweł Władysław Fabisz, *Wiadomość o legatach i nuncyuszach apostolskich w dawnej Polsce (1075.–1863.)* (Ostrów: J. Priebatsch, 1864), p.189.

SWEDEN'S WAR IN MUSCOVY 1609-1617

While loyal to Tsars Ivan, Fyodor, and Boris, Vasiliy for reasons not fully explained did not extend his loyalty to the latter's son, Fyodor. Soon after Fyodor in April 1605 was recognised as Tsar Fyodor II, Vasiliy suddenly recognised the pretender Dmitriy as genuine despite once having led the commission of inquiry that determined that the real Dmitriy died as a boy years ago. Although Vasiliy's action is generally regarded as opportunistic, the events during Dmitriy's ascension to the throne to some extent remain murky. A Swedish observer, Peder Pedersson, who was in Moscow at the time reported that Dmitriy's supporters seized Vasiliy, sentenced him to death, dragged him to the execution ground, and even forced his head down on the executioner's block as a means of extracting a recantation of his previous report that the real Dmitriy had died as a boy.[3] Under these circumstances, it was perhaps unsurprising that Vasiliy repudiated his report and changed allegiance. Meanwhile, young Tsar Fyodor was murdered, at least in part as the result of Vasiliy's repudiation. However, within less than a year Vasiliy again switched sides. Having gathered support from other senior nobles, Vasiliy turned against Dmitriy, and indeed led the conspiracy that brought about the pretender's murder in May 1606. The proximate cause was Vasiliy's sudden reconfirmation, in public, that the real Dmitriy indeed had died as a child and that the False Dmitriy who had assumed the throne was an impostor. Vasiliy then led the mob that broke into the Kremlin to lynch Dmitriy's Commonwealth supporters, bodyguards, and advisors. During the riot Dmitriy was murdered, too.

Vasiliy IV, Tsar of Muscovy

Two days after Dmitriy's murder, Vasiliy's followers on 19 May 1606 proclaimed him as the new Tsar. Vasiliy was then in his mid fifties, and apparently very nearsighted.[4] Henceforth,

---

3   Petrus Petreius [Peder Pedersson], *Een wiss och sanfärdigh Berättelse om några Förandringar som j thesse framledne åhr vthi Storfurstendömet Muskow skedde äre* (Stockholm: Andreas Gutterwitz, 1608). Original lacks page numbers. Facsimile edn: Margareta Attius Sohlman (ed.), *Stora oredans Ryssland: Petrus Petrejus ögonvittnesskildring från 1608*. (Stockholm: Carlssons, 1997), p.144. The French mercenary Jacques Margeret, who like Pedersson was in Moscow at the time, relates a similar although more muddled story. Jacques Margeret, *The Russian Empire and Grand Duchy of Muscovy: A 17th-Century French Account* (Pittsburgh: University of Pittsburgh Press, 1983), pp.68–9.

4   Chester S. L. Dunning, *Russia's First Civil War: The Time of Troubles and the Founding of the Romanov Dynasty* (University Park, Pennsylvania: Pennsylvania State University Press, 2001), p.206.

PROLOGUE: A BEVY OF MONARCHS, A CHANCELLOR, AND TWO GENERALS

his rule essentially hinged on the military success of his younger distant cousin, Prince Mikhail Skopin-Shuyskiy, who was a popular commander and campaigned with considerable success against the rebels and Commonwealth mercenaries who at this point plundered at will throughout major parts of the realm.

Vasiliy was married twice. His first marriage produced no children. Before he became tsar, Vasiliy married Princess Yekaterina Buynosova-Rostovskaya. Upon assumption of the throne, her name was changed to Maria, which was deemed more suitable. The couple had two daughters, Princesses Anna and Anastasia, but both died in infancy. Tsar Vasiliy had three brothers: Andrey (d. 1589), Dmitriy (c. 1560–1612), and Ivan (c. 1566–c. 1638). The brothers generally coordinated their activities to enhance the power of the House of Shuyskiy and its adherents.

False Dmitriy, Pretender to the Throne of Muscovy

False Dmitriy (d. 1610; 'Pseudo-Demetrius' in contemporary western and central European chronicles) was an impostor who in order to gain the throne passed himself off as the late Tsarevich Dmitriy Ivanovich of Muscovy, the youngest son of Tsar Ivan IV. Not only did he claim to have miraculously survived the real Dmitriy's death in 1591 at the age of eight, he also claimed to have escaped the 1606 murder in the Kremlin of the preceding pretender, the previous false Dmitriy.[5]

We hardly know anything of the real background of this particular false Dmitriy (or for that matter, of the earlier circumstances of most other false Dmitriys who presented themselves during the Time of Troubles). Like his predecessor, he only rose to power with Commonwealth support, and for reasons beyond his control, became an unwilling tool for King Sigismund and other Commonwealth notables in their aim to gain control of the Muscovite political landscape. This particular Dmitriy first appeared on the scene during the winter of 1606/1607 and then on the Commonwealth's border with Muscovy. He was apparently an educated man, since he could speak and write both Russian and Polish. He seems to have known Orthodox liturgy, which gave rise to a tradition that he might have been the son of a priest or at least a school teacher. Some claimed that he could also read the Talmud and other rabbinic literature, which possibly made him a converted Jew. One tradition identified him as the son of a noble or even a high-ranking boyar. Another claimed him as a Lithuanian secretary. Some claimed that he indeed had been a secretary, but a Muscovite in the service of the first false Dmitriy. Others believed that he was a retainer of the rebel leader Mikhail Molchanov, who himself once had claimed to be Dmitriy. The most fanciful tradition identified both false Dmitriys as a son of Prince

---

5 Although in modern historiography for this reason commonly designated False Dmitriy II, our Dmitriy in reality was the third who claimed the identity.

Andrey Kurbskiy, who in 1564 defected to Lithuania to escape the wrath of Tsar Ivan IV. Prince Kurbskiy remained in the Commonwealth until his death almost 20 years later, which would have allowed him to sire an unknown son of the appropriate age. The probably least credible tradition of Dmitriy's origin claimed that he was the son of a *strelets* (musketeer) from Starodub in Muscovy. Nobody can say whether any of these proposed backgrounds contained any kernel of truth. What the multitude of conflicting rumours do tell us is that hardly anybody, at least in his area of origin, believed that he really was Dmitriy.

When this enigmatic stranger first appeared, he had no known local ties. The Commonwealth authorities soon labelled him as either a vagrant or a Muscovite spy, and promptly threw him in prison. The shadowy vagrant apparently called himself Andrey Nagoy, which was a name that might link him to the House of Nagoy, the family of the late Tsarevich Dmitriy Ivanovich. Although there is nothing to suggest that the officials believed in the supposed claim of Nagoy kinship, it made the vagrant a useful tool for those Commonwealth notables who desired a military intervention in Muscovy. When interrogated, the mysterious 'Nagoy' ultimately 'confessed' that he in reality was Tsarevich Dmitriy. Or, as the story eventually was retold, perhaps this episode took place only later, when the Commonwealth plot was already in motion. In May 1607, the Commonwealth officials sent the new Dmitriy across the border into Muscovy, accompanied by two men to ease his way. The false Dmitriy and his entourage then rode to Starodub, where conveniently he was received also by a delegation from the rebel base at Putivl'. On 12 June 1607 this delegation found him to be the genuine article, their professed leader, and the rightful heir to the throne of Muscovy. The arrival a few days later of well-armed Commonwealth mercenaries ready to serve the new Tsar helped to convince any locals who doubted his identity.

The False Dmitriy of 1607, as he appeared in a seventeenth-century print later widely published in European countries. The somewhat rough look may or may not be genuine. There is no known reputable, contemporary depiction of this particular false Dmitriy.

The new Dmitriy was joined by numerous men who saw better opportunities under a false Dmitriy than under Tsar Vasiliy. Among them were several veteran rebel leaders, including Prince Grigoriy Shakhovskoy and the aforementioned Mikhail Molchanov, who had not given up the attempt to seize the throne. They raised a new rebel army of volunteer Commonwealth nobles, Ukrainian cossacks, Don cossacks, and their own personal retainers. In the spring of 1608, the rebels marched towards Moscow. Having defeated Tsar Vasiliy's brother Dmitriy Shuyskiy at Bolkhov, the false Dmitriy established a fortified camp at Tushino near Moscow, where he received additional Commonwealth reinforcements. Among them was the first False Dmitriy's widow, the Polish lady Maryna Mniszchówna or Mniszech (*c.* 1588–1615), who immediately 'recognised' her husband which in the eyes of some gave further legitimacy to his cause.

PROLOGUE: A BEVY OF MONARCHS, A CHANCELLOR, AND TWO GENERALS

Ladislaus or Władysław Vasa, Tsar-elect of Muscovy

Ladislaus or Władysław (1595–1648; claimant of the throne of Muscovy 1610–1634) was the eldest son of King Sigismund and his first wife, Anna of Austria.

Because of Władysław's young age, he played a limited personal role in the events in Muscovy. In 1610, the young man was elected Tsar of Muscovy by the group of Muscovite nobles (the 'seven boyars') who deposed Tsar Vasiliy. Young Władysław never assumed the throne, primarily due to his father's desire to take it for himself but also because of an uprising against the Commonwealth's influence. Władysław accordingly never reigned as Tsar of Muscovy, yet retained the claim to the throne.

Raised at court in Poland, young Władysław knew Polish, German, Italian, and Latin. Like his father, he was interested, and personally skilled, in arts and music. Based on Władysław's later life, he had a sense of humour, was friendly, outgoing, and generally popular with those he met. However, like most members of the House of Vasa he had a temper, and when angered might react rashly. Władysław appears to have been more tolerant in his religious views than his father, but for reasons already explained, the real level of personal piety of either man is hard to disentangle from contemporary propaganda and hence difficult to measure.

Władysław, 1613 or 1614.
(Uffizi Gallery)

Having come of age, Władysław continued to use the title of Elected Grand Duke of Moscow (*electus Magnus Dux Moscoviae*) until 1634, by which time he had succeeded his father as King of Poland and Grand Duke of Lithuania, and moreover repulsed a Muscovite attempt to retake Smolensk (the Smolensk War of 1632–1634). Władysław never dropped his formal claim to the throne of Sweden, even though he never set foot in that country.[6]

Gustavus Adolphus Vasa, Tsar of Muscovy and King of Sweden

Gustavus Adolphus (1594–1632; r. 1611–1632; claimant of the throne of Muscovy 1611–1617), Grand Duke of Finland, Duke of Estonia, and Duke of Västmanland, was still a very young man when the war in Muscovy broke out. He assumed the kingship after the death in 1611 of his father, King

---

6   The claim was retained also by his half-brother and successor, John Casimir, who only surrendered it after the Wars of the Swedish Deluge of 1655–1660.

Charles IX. Gustavus Adolphus was only one year older than his distant cousin Władysław, who enjoyed the luxury of maturing before he had to lead men in battle. Yet, and despite at this point being inexperienced and still untested in warfare, Gustavus Adolphus nonetheless soon grew into the truly charismatic commander who in later years would put his stamp on European affairs. Although the real character of Gustavus Adolphus is difficult to separate from the personality cult which because of later military successes was built around his person in his lifetime, and even more so after his death, many contemporary eyewitnesses have given evidence that he was well liked, even admired, by most of those who met him, whether nobles or commoners.

Gustavus Adolphus was generally friendly and in a good mood. He had a sense of humour, made jokes, and enjoyed social events such as banquets and dances. Like his father, he had a temper and sometimes reacted with anger. However, unlike his father, grandfather, and most uncles he was not cruel or vindictive, and did not physically violate those who displeased him. Although Gustavus Adolphus trusted his own counsel and would not allow himself to be ruled by others, he was cooperative and would listen to their opinions and advice.

Highly educated in both the sciences and humanities, Gustavus Adolphus was also well versed in languages. In addition to Swedish, German, and probably some Finnish (the three predominant languages of the Swedish kingdom), he spoke Latin, Italian, French, and Dutch. He understood Spanish, English and Scots, and knew some Polish and Russian.[7] He was trained in philosophy and jurisprudence, read and was influenced by the Dutch jurist Hugo Grotius (1583–1645), and (in striking contrast to many other rulers, then and later) grounded his arguments in these disciplines when speaking before the Council or Parliament. Yet, Gustavus Adolphus was also genuinely pious. God ruled over life and death, and the best that mankind, even a man born to kingship, could aim for was to do his duty in accordance with his Christian conscience, even if this conflicted with reasons of state.[8]

Gustavus Adolphus, 1610 or 1611. (Gold medal, possibly by Ruprecht Miller; photo: Gabriel Hildebrand, Economy Museum – Royal Coin Cabinet/SHM, Stockholm)

---

7   Nils Ahnlund, *Gustav Adolf den store* (Stockholm: Aldus/Bonniers, 1963), pp.22–3.
8   Sven Lundkvist, 'Verklighetsuppfattning och verklighet: En studie i Gustav II Adolfs handlingsramar', Robert Sandberg (ed.), *Studier i äldre historia tillägnade*

PROLOGUE: A BEVY OF MONARCHS, A CHANCELLOR, AND TWO GENERALS

In war, Gustavus Adolphus led from the front, sharing the labours and risks with his men. Already, as a child, he had encountered the Dutch model of warfare (more on which below). John of Nassau, one of the chief architects of the Dutch model, visited Sweden in 1601–1602. Given command of the Swedish army, he provided some ideas on how to reform organisation and tactics. Gustavus Adolphus, then eight years old, met John at least once, upon his departure from Sweden. Five years later, in 1607, Gustavus Adolphus first met his future major general, Dodo von Innhausen und zu Knyphausen, who previously had been in Dutch service and thoroughly knew the Dutch model. In 1608, at fourteen years old, Gustavus Adolphus spent two months of intensive training in the Dutch model under Jacob De la Gardie, who himself had been trained in its use in the Dutch Republic while he served as a colonel there. This ended Gustavus Adolphus's formal military training. However, he continued to read and observe, and moreover, in 1611 the outbreak of the Kalmar War obliged him henceforth to assume a leading role in warfare and gradually step in for his father.[9] When he inherited the Swedish throne in 1611, there was no more than a short-term truce between Sweden and the Commonwealth. By then, he had also been elected Tsar of Muscovy by a group of Muscovite nobles broadly representative of the country but under conditions (described below) which meant that in practical terms he only reigned through the city of Novgorod.

Axel Oxenstierna, Lord High Chancellor of Sweden

Axel Oxenstierna (1583–1654) was appointed Lord High Chancellor (Swedish: *Rikskansler*) of Sweden by the new King, Gustavus Adolphus, in 1612. Henceforth, the talented Oxenstierna was allowed to develop the state machinery as needed.

Axel Oxenstierna descended from one of Sweden's most powerful noble families. Following a conventional education, which naturally included Latin and major modern languages such as German and French, he in 1599–1602 studied at the universities in Rostock, Wittenberg, and Jena. Following his return, he went into the service of Gustavus Adolphus's father, the unpredictable and vindictive King Charles.

The 20-year-old Oxenstierna displayed great talent and rose rapidly in rank and position. He joined the Swedish Council of the Realm (Swedish: *Riksrådet*) in 1609, and in January 1612, aged 28, became Lord High Chancellor. This was in the middle of the Kalmar War, soon after Gustavus Adolphus had to assume sole military command after the death of his father Charles.

    Herman Schück 5/4 1985 (Stockholm: Festschrift, 1985), pp.227–41.
9 Michael Fredholm von Essen, *The Kalmar War 1611–1613: Gustavus Adolphus's First War* (Warwick: Helion, 2023).

Oxenstierna was only 11 years older than the young king, and the two rapidly developed a mutual respect. Although they did not always agree, they complemented and trusted each other.

The historian often attempts to understand a significant historical person through his or her writings, such as letters, treatises, and above all memoirs. Oxenstierna did not write memoirs, nor did he explain his actions to posterity. But he was a prodigious writer. During his long life of state service he drafted innumerable reports, memorandums, letters, and orders. He also maintained a substantial correspondence with friends and relatives.[10] If there is any key to Oxenstierna's character to be found in these thousands of documents, it is his devotion to affairs of state. His personal character remains in the shadow of the statesman and, to some extent, in the shadow of the King he served. Oxenstierna worked throughout the day. Over time, he got to know all important statesmen of his time, and such was his family background, power, and influence that he could soon speak freely to kings and first ministers everywhere.

Axel Oxenstierna, 1626. (Jacob Heinrich Elbfas; photo: Medström)

Oxenstierna in 1608 wedded Anna Åkesdotter Bååt (1579–1649). By all accounts, the marriage was a happy one. Yet, for Oxenstierna affairs of state always took precedence. Instead Anna managed, on her own and with considerable skill, the numerous manor houses and palaces that the couple acquired over the years, throughout the growing Swedish realm. Her husband had little or no time for such minor matters, since his task was the establishment and maintenance of the machinery of state. Indeed, Sweden at the time of Gustavus Adolphus's ascension to the throne can be said to not yet have had a machinery of state. Without Oxenstierna, it is unlikely that the country would have remained a functioning state after the Kalmar War, nor within a few years emerged as a great power.

One of few issues on which the King and his chancellor did not agree was the relationship with Muscovy. Gustavus Adolphus argued that an alliance with Muscovy, in one form

---

10 In 1888, the Royal Swedish Academy of Letters, History and Antiquities began to publish Oxenstierna's copious correspondence. The project only came to a conclusion of sorts in 2018, and resulted in multiple volumes and a database, maintained by the Swedish National Archives (*Riksarkivet*, RA).

or another, would benefit Sweden, certainly as long as the threat from the Commonwealth remained and possibly longer (and he was right; during the subsequent Thirty Years' War, Muscovy was Sweden's only unswerving ally among the neighbouring states). Oxenstierna, however, simply did not trust the Muscovites. In 1615, he went so far as to write to the Swedish overall commander in the east, Jacob De la Gardie, that 'there can be no doubt that, in the Muscovites, we have neighbours who are disloyal but also mighty, whom it is impossible to trust owing to their innate perfidy and falsity sucked in with their mothers' milk, but who, because of their strength, are feared not only by us but also by many others among their neighbours, as we well remember.'[11] Throughout his long career, Oxenstierna could never make himself trust Muscovy. It seems very likely that he based this judgement on the conflicting loyalties that the Swedes encountered on the eastern front in the years leading up to 1615, during the Time of Troubles when perfidy became a means of survival in Muscovite politics.

Michael Fyodorovich Romanov, Tsar of Muscovy

Michael Romanov (1596–1645; r. 1613–1645; Russian: Mikhail), Tsar of Muscovy, belonged to the House of Romanov, by lineage although not name one of the oldest aristocratic families. Young Michael's father harboured ambitions to gain the throne for himself, so Tsar Boris compelled him and his wife to take monastic vows.[12] When still a young child, the boy was accordingly sent together with his mother Marfa Ivanovna into a monastery. Tsar Boris had good reason for suppressing the House of Romanov, whose ambitions had grown both grand and aggressive. The Romanovs were closely linked to the previous tsars by marriage. Young Michael's great-aunt Anastasia Romanovna was the first wife of Tsar Ivan IV and the mother of Tsar Fyodor I, which made Michael a cousin once removed of Tsar Fyodor and a great-nephew-in-law of Tsar Ivan. Besides, Michael's grandfather had served as acting regent after the death of Tsar Ivan before Boris Godunov assumed this position.[13]

---

11   Translation based on B. F. Porshnev, *Muscovy and Sweden in the Thirty Years' War, 1630–1635* (Cambridge: Cambridge University Press, 1995), p.108.
12   On these events, see Dunning, *Russia's First Civil War*, pp.95–6. Monastic vows made a man ineligible for the throne. Michael's father Fyodor Nikitich Romanov (1553 or 1554–1633) assumed the name Filaret as a monk. Filaret remained in monastic confinement until he was released by a false Dmitriy, who in 1605 made him metropolitan of Rostov and Yaroslavl'. In 1609, another false Dmitriy promoted himto 'Patriarch of Moscow and over the whole of Russia' (*Patriarkh Moskovskiy i vseya Rusi*). Both false Dmitriys acknowledged the Romanovs as relatives and favoured them as part of playing the role of being Dmitriy. Filaret was then sent as an envoy to King Sigismund, who imprisoned him from 1610 to 1618.
13   After the death of Tsar Ivan IV, Michael's grandfather, Nikita Romanovich

Michael Romanov, Tsar of Muscovy

Michael became the first tsar of the House of Romanov on 21 February 1613, when the national assembly (*Zemskiy sobor*, 'assembly of the land'[14]), a parliament of the Estates which chiefly consisted of the aristocracy, hereditary servicemen, and Church officials, under highly irregular circumstances elected him Tsar of Muscovy.[15] There is nothing to suggest that the members of the national assembly regarded the 16-year-old boy as anything but a compromise candidate, elected so as to keep other, more powerful candidates out of power. In their eyes, his most favourable attributes were almost certainly his comparatively weak position in Moscow power politics (not least because his father was in Commonwealth captivity) coupled with the family link to the old dynasty. Young Michael was not even in Moscow at the time of his election. Sure enough, Tsar Michael did not become an assertive ruler. Nonetheless, his election resulted in the long-lasting and comparatively stable reign of the Romanov dynasty, under the rule of which Muscovy, and then Russia, would expand its borders to the Baltic and Black Seas as well as to the Pacific, gain lasting political and cultural influence, and ultimately surpass the Commonwealth and Sweden as the great power of northeastern Europe.

At the time of the wars described in this book, Michael Romanov remained unmarried.

Mikhail Vasil'yevich Skopin-Shuyskiy, the Tsar's Voivode (General)

Prince **Mikhail Skopin-Shuyskiy** (1586–1610) was a distant cousin of Tsar Vasiliy IV and accordingly a member of an ancient aristocratic House. Young Mikhail lost his father at an early age, so the future Tsar Vasiliy provided for

---

Zakhar'yin-Yur'yev (*c.* 1522–1586), served as acting regent for a few months until he was struck by the illness from which he later died. Boris Godunov only assumed the role of regent afterwards.

14 In seventeenth-century Russian, *zemskiy* ('territorial; of the land') carried essentially the same meaning as today's *narodnyy* ('national').

15 The office of Tsar was normally hereditary, not elective. The national assembly (*Zemskiy sobor*), an institution first called by Tsar Ivan IV in 1549, elected Boris Godunov as Tsar because of the succession crisis caused by the end of the Rurik Dynasty in 1598. The election of Michael Romanov was only the second occasion on which a national assembly elected a new tsar.

PROLOGUE: A BEVY OF MONARCHS, A CHANCELLOR, AND TWO GENERALS

him. The young man entered court service in 1604 under Tsar Boris Godunov. Like Vasiliy, he also served the pretender Dmitriy. Real military service began during the reign of Tsar Vasiliy, when Skopin-Shuyskiy rapidly emerged as the Tsar's primary voivode (general). He was an able commander who showed his ability and potential in many battles.

There is no information on Skopin-Shuyskiy's education, but because of his upbringing, it is unlikely that he was highly educated in either the sciences or the humanities, nor was fluent in any language except Russian. Even so, Skopin-Shuyskiy was not unwilling to learn new customs and is known to have adopted a number of western and central European practices, especially in military affairs. For instance, he carried a straight rapier in a red leather-covered scabbard instead of the more customary Muscovite sabre, and it will be shown that he encouraged his infantry to adopt Continental pike tactics.

Skopin-Shuyskiy married Aleksandra Vasil'yevna Golovina in *c.* 1607. The couple soon had a son, Vasiliy, but he died as a child. The spouse is best known under the name Anastasia, a name that she took upon entering a monastery after the death of her husband.

Mikhail Skopin-Shuyskiy, depicted in the style of a religious icon which in the early seventeenth century signified the artistic move from religious art into modern portrait painting.

Jacob Pontusson De la Gardie, the King's Lieutenant General

Jacob De la Gardie (1583–1652) was born in Reval (modern-day Tallinn) to Pontus De la Gardie, a French mercenary in Swedish service, and Sophia Gyllenhielm, an illegitimate daughter of King John. Because of the very early deaths of both parents, the boy grew up with his grandmother in Finland. His military career began early: at age 18, De la Gardie received a colonel's commission. However, in his first year of service (1601) he fell into Commonwealth captivity together with his friend and kinsman Carl Carlsson Gyllenhielm (1574–1650), an illegitimate son of King Charles. Against the advice of military professionals, the two young men enthusiastically volunteered to defend Wolmar in Livonia, which at the time was utterly exposed. Expectedly, the endeavour failed, and although the two commanders managed to negotiate the free departure of their men, this was at the price of giving themselves up to Commonwealth captivity. In a spiteful mood aimed at his rival King Charles, King Sigismund refused to ransom or exchange Gyllenhielm, who had to spend most of the next 13 years in chains under appalling conditions. Gyllenhielm was for the first four years imprisoned together with De la Gardie, who although offered release in exchange for a ransom after the first year, refused to abandon his comrade who was not offered the same terms. Ultimately, De la Gardie was released in a prisoner exchange. His friend Gyllenhielm was only released in 1614, after the death of King Charles and following an intervention by Gustavus Adolphus.

De la Gardie was released in 1606, against a promise not to fight the Commonwealth in the immediate future. To honour his pledge, De la Gardie went into Dutch service as a colonel under Maurice of Nassau, eventually Prince of Orange, where he remained for two years. Meanwhile, De la Gardie learnt the new Dutch model of warfare. Upon his return to Sweden in 1608, we have seen that De la Gardie for two months mentored Gustavus Adolphus in the Dutch model. Henceforth, De la Gardie was one of those officers who continued to promote the Dutch model of warfare in the Swedish army. As a result, King Charles in 1609 ordered the 25-year-old De la Gardie to assume command as the King's Commanding General on the eastern front, and as Lieutenant General of the intervention army sent to relieve Tsar Vasiliy and Muscovy. In effect, De la Gardie's task became to command the eastern wars in the King's absence. By coincidence or design, this meant that he was given the same task that his father, Pontus De la Gardie, had carried out in the years before his death.

Jacob De la Gardie, 1606. (National Museum, Stockholm)

Although De la Gardie seems not to have attended much formal education as a youth, he kept himself informed about a variety of subjects (even including astronomy albeit on an amateur level), spoke French, his father's language, as a native, and was able to communicate with adequate fluency in relevant languages such as Latin, German, Finnish, and of course Swedish, the language of his mother and grandmother. When the war in Muscovy began, De la Gardie quickly picked up some Russian, and by the end of the war he spoke the language with sufficient fluency to conduct diplomatic negotiations in it.

At the time of his appointment to overall command on the eastern front, De la Gardie remained unmarried.

1

The Origins of Sweden's War in Muscovy

Sweden's war in Muscovy broke out because of a complex set of interlinked events that originated in (1) Swedish–Commonwealth rivalry over the control of Estonia, (2) dynastic rivalries within the Swedish–Polish House of Vasa, (3) the conflicting territorial ambitions of Sweden and the Commonwealth in Muscovy, and (4) internal instability in Muscovy, which suffered from a severe succession crisis coupled with elite and regional rivalries unrelated to Sweden or the Commonwealth.

On 18 May 1595, the Treaty of Teusina (Finnish: Täysinä, Russian: Tyavzino; a village near Narva) concluded decades of war, begun in 1570, between Sweden and Muscovy.[1] Moscow acknowledged Sweden's acquisition of northern Livonia, brought under the Swedish Crown in 1561, which henceforth became known as Estonia. Sweden acknowledged Muscovy's acquisition of Kexholm County and Ingria, east of respectively Finland and Estonia. Sweden relinquished its claim on the Kola Peninsula, but Muscovy acknowledged the Swedish Crown's right to tax most of Lapponia (named after the indigenous Lapps, or Sami), the sparsely populated Arctic north. Muscovy agreed to rely on Viborg and Reval as ports for trade with western Europe, although in reality Moscow continued to trade through Arkhangel'sk in the Arctic as well as, when conditions allowed, the Commonwealth's Baltic Sea ports. On most issues, the treaty

---

1   The Treaty of Teusina was the first formal revision of the mutual border between Sweden and Muscovy since the 1323 Treaty of Nöteborg. Since then, growing migration into the sparsely populated border region of Finnish peasants from the west, and Muscovite peasants from the east, had caused problems. Both groups of settlers wanted to open up virgin farmlands, preferably out of reach of tax collectors. This resulted in confrontations not only between different groups of settlers, but also between Swedish and Muscovite tax collectors in search of their respective subjects. Both states claimed territorial control over the lands occupied by their tax subjects, which produced an untenable situation.

SWEDEN'S WAR IN MUSCOVY 1609-1617

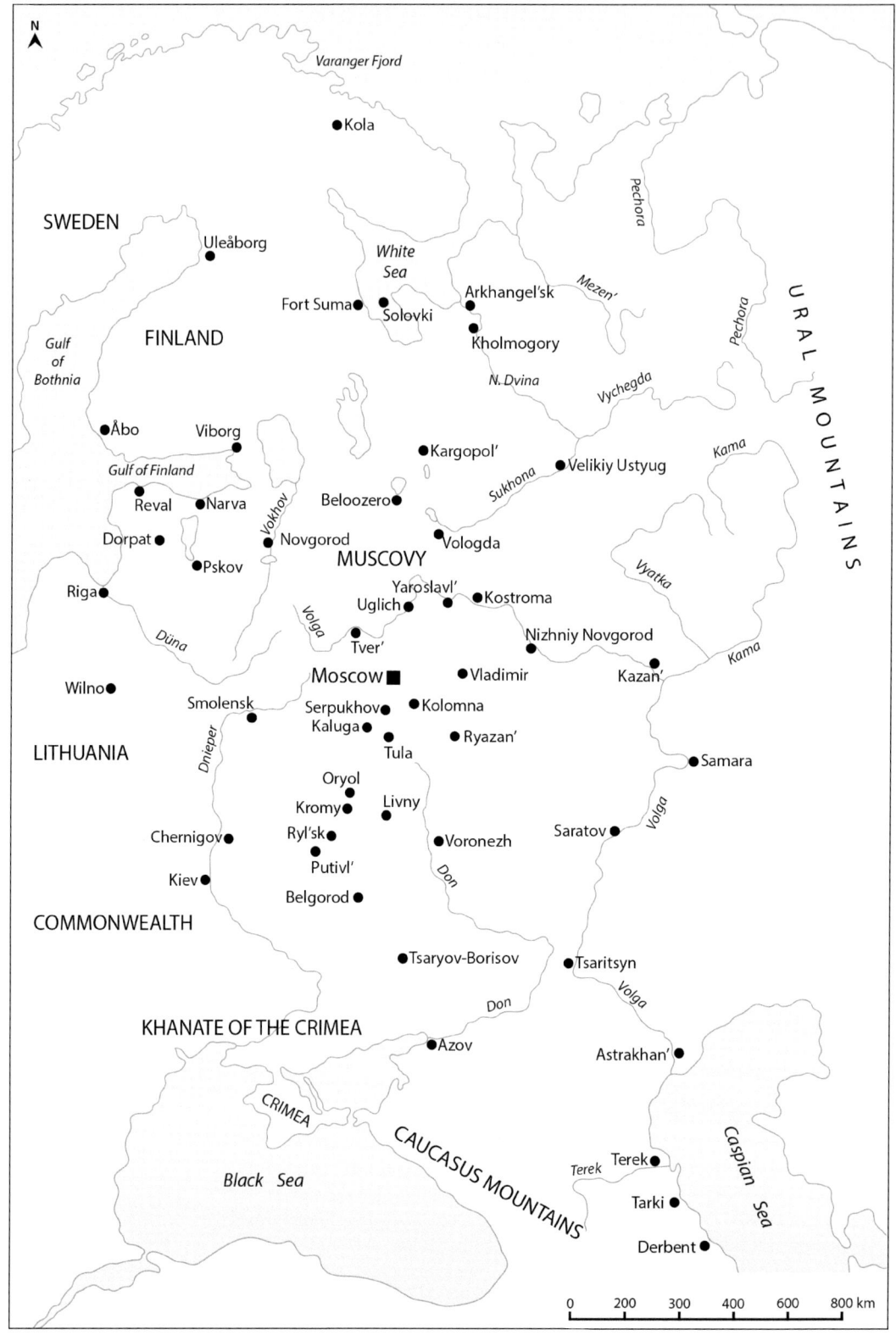

Map 1. Sweden, Muscovy, and the Polish-Lithuanian Commonwealth.

resolved the formal differences between Sweden and Muscovy, which then were the only remaining parties in the war. Neither party was happy with the agreement and both soon wished to revert parts of it.

The Commonwealth had joined the war on the Swedish side in 1578, but in 1582 concluded a 10-year ceasefire agreement with Muscovy, according to the terms of which Muscovy for the time being relinquished its claims on Estonia to the Commonwealth – even though Sweden already held this territory. Since the Commonwealth and Sweden by 1595 were ruled by the same king, this would not necessarily be an issue. However, the Commonwealth nobility could not abide Sweden's acquisition of Estonia, since in their view Muscovy had already given away the rights to this territory to them. They now argued their expectation that the joint King of Poland and Sweden, Sigismund, would transfer Estonia to its rightful owners, that is, the Commonwealth nobility.

Needless to say, this demand caused considerable anger in Sweden, whose nobles and soldiers had for years fought and died for Estonia. It also gave Sigismund's uncle, Duke Charles, yet another cause on which he could raise opposition to Sigismund's rule. Put in simple terms, the Swedish nobility did not wish to relinquish Estonia, while the Swedish Lutheran Church could not abide a Catholic king. Moreover, Sigismund was far away and his supporters in Sweden were few in number.

Duke Charles was the youngest son of King Gustavus I who had abolished the deep-rooted Germanic tradition of elective kingship and established his own family, the House of Vasa, on the Swedish throne. Although the establishment of the Vasa dynasty officially implied agnatic primogeniture, that is, the right of the firstborn legitimate son to inherit the throne, succession law remained malleable. King Gustavus's sons had already, for reasons of their own, interpreted succession as based on the principle of lateral agnatic seniority, that is, the election of the best qualified, mature male candidate among the dynasty's princes. Or, shorn of the legalese, the principle that might makes right – a conclusion eased by Swedish society's still recent memories of elective kingship.[2] In short, while still a Duke Charles concluded that he had a better right to the Swedish throne than his Catholic nephew, who in any case spent most of his time in Poland, far from his power base in Sweden.

Duke Charles accordingly rose against King Sigismund. He formally referred to the provisions of the 1560 last will of King Gustavus I, his

---

2   The malleability of the succession principle is evident from the reinterpretation taken up by Parliament in Norrköping in 1604, that King Charles's heir would be determined among his sons according to the principle of (reintroduced) agnatic primogeniture. This excluded Sigismund's heirs from the succession order. Nonetheless, Parliament also decided that in case no surviving male was available, a female heir of King Charles's line would inherit the throne (male-preference primogeniture). Following this principle, Christina, daughter of Gustavus Adolphus, in 1632 succeeded her father on the throne. In 1644, aged 18, she assumed full power as ruling queen.

father, which stipulated that a child who left the Lutheran religion would lose his inheritance. In 1597 Charles called a parliament in Arboga and mobilised an army, and in 1598 Sigismund led his army to Sweden. To gain Commonwealth support for the expedition, Sigismund before his departure had to promise the Polish parliament (*Sejm*) that Sweden would relinquish Estonia to the Commonwealth. Sigismund's army landed near Kalmar in southern Sweden, from which he marched and sailed north to confront Duke Charles. Other detachments landed and took the capital, Stockholm. Even so, Charles ultimately defeated Sigismund at Stångebro on 25 September 1598. Sigismund had to withdraw, losing most of his remaining Swedish supporters in the process, many of whom were captured and executed by the ruthless Duke. In 1599, Charles called a parliament which duly declared Sigismund deposed from the Swedish throne. Soon, as we have seen, he made himself King of Sweden.

This initiated a long conflict between the two countries that would not be resolved until 1660, after several devastating Swedish invasions of the Commonwealth and the involvement of numerous other powers as well.

Hoping to profit further from his victories, King Charles in 1600 sailed to Reval in Estonia with an army. He marched into the part of Livonia which still belonged to the Commonwealth, taking Pernau, Dorpat, and several smaller towns. The war continued in 1601 when the Swedes for a while laid siege to Riga but failed to take the city. Over the following years, Commonwealth forces won several victories over the Swedes, notably that at Kircholm (modern-day Salaspils) near Riga on 17 September 1605. The Commonwealth armoured cavalry, the famous hussars commanded by Field Hetman of Lithuania Jan Karol Chodkiewicz, cut down the Swedish infantry, and King Charles only escaped through the self-sacrifice of a Livonian noble, cavalry captain Heinrich Wrede, who gave up his horse to the King. Wrede then fell, together with most of the Swedish foot. A small consolation for the Swedish king was that King Sigismund because of unrest at home lacked men to follow up the victory.

Indeed, the parties in the theatre negotiated a ceasefire in 1608. It was terminated after a few months, primarily because King Charles had been unaware of the agreement. Meanwhile Charles worried about Sigismund's excellent relations with Spain, and persistent rumours that the King of Spain planned a naval expedition in support of Sigismund against Elfsborg Castle, the key to the Swedish west coast. Hostilities between Sweden and the Commonwealth continued until 1611, when a ceasefire was agreed, not least because both powers then were busy attempting to annex choice

Field Hetman of Lithuania Jan Karol Chodkiewicz. In recognition of his great victory over the Swedes at Kircholm, Chodkiewicz received letters of congratulation from Pope Paul V, Emperor Rudolph II of Habsburg, King James VI/I of Scotland and England, Sultan Ahmed I of the Ottoman Empire, and Shah Abbas I of Persia. Promoted to Grand Hetman soon after the victory, Chodkiewicz went on to play an important role in the subsequent wars in Muscovy.

Muscovite territories. The rivalry between Sweden and the Commonwealth did not subside, but the contestants moved to another chessboard. For the same reason, they subsequently extended the ceasefire in Livonia several times.[3]

In Muscovy, this was the nightmarish Time of Troubles (*Smutnoye vremya*, or *Smuta*), the period of lawlessness and chaos that followed the death in 1598 of Tsar Fyodor Ivanovich, the last of the Rurik Dynasty. During this time Muscovy suffered from uprisings, usurpers, anarchy, famine, and foreign interventions.

---

3   *Sverges Traktater med främmande magter* 5:1 (Stockholm: P. A. Norstedt, 1903), p.227.

2

The Swedish Military Establishment

By the early seventeenth century Sweden had a small population, an underdeveloped and poorly monetised economy, and an agricultural base that suffered from a short growing season.[1] The population constituted at most 1,350,000: some 850,000 in Sweden, 350,000 in Finland, and 150,000 in Estonia.[2] The military establishment was correspondingly small. While mobilisation potential was higher, the total Swedish military establishment rarely reached an actual strength exceeding 15,000 men, and expeditionary forces were usually no larger than 3,500 to 7,000 men.[3] The national army

---

1   For more information on the Swedish military establishment in the Swedish core territories of Sweden and Finland, see Fredholm von Essen, *The Kalmar War*, which also details Sweden's military architecture and the Swedish navy.

2   Although these high estimates are generally accepted by historians, they derive from research conducted by Hans Forssell around 1880 and Sigurd Sundquist in 1938. Hans Forssell, *Sverige 1571: Försök till en administrativ-statistisk beskrifning öfver det egentliga Sverige, utan Finland och Estland* (Stockholm: P. A. Norstedt, 2 vols, 1872–1883); Sigurd Sundquist, *Sveriges folkmängd på Gustaf II Adolfs tid: En demografisk studie* (Lund: Håkan Ohlsson, 1938). It has since been determined that central Sweden and Finland enjoyed rapid population growth in the period up to 1600. SvendGissel, Eino Jutikkala, Eva Österberg, Jørn Sandnes, and Björn Teitson, *Desertion and Land Colonization in the Nordic Countries c. 1300–1600: Comparative Report from The Scandinavian Research Project on Deserted Farms and Villages* (Stockholm: Almqvist & Wiksell International, 1981), p.234. Recent research finds that population growth continued throughout the seventeenth century as well. Moreover, based on the very detailed tax records of the Elfsborg Ransom 1613–1618, Sweden (as it then was) around 1620 appears to have had a population of only about 620,000 people. Lennart Andersson Palm, *Sweden's 17th Century: A Period of Expansion or Stagnation?* (Gothenburg: Gothenburg University, 2016), pp.10–11.

3   Michael Fredholm von Essen, *Lion from the North 1* (Warwick: Helion, 2020), p.96.

THE SWEDISH MILITARY ESTABLISHMENT

was thus no larger than it had been under King Gustavus I.[4] In 1600, King Charles asked the parliament to agree to a permanent military organisation based on horse and foot raised in provincial regiments and also funded by the provinces. Parliament turned down the proposal to fund a standing army, but agreed to the proposed permanent provincial regimental organisation in peacetime, since this corresponded to existing although less well-defined practices.[5]

By tradition, most Swedish troops were raised in the Swedish and Finnish heartland. In 1612, about 85 percent of the soldiers came from Sweden and Finland.[6] In comparison, Estonia provided only a few men, and they were primarily enlisted. Sweden and Finland constituted the same country, with equal rights and obligations, and records typically do not specify ethnic or linguistic background. When troops were identified as deriving specifically from Sweden or Finland, this only meant that they were raised there, not that they were Swedish- or Finnish-speakers. The coastal areas of Finland were primarily Swedish-speaking, and there were Finnish settlements in Sweden. From 1570 onwards, the number of Finnish troops in the army grew dramatically, until Finns were disproportionally represented. While in 1570 there had been only two Finnish infantry companies (Swedish: *fänika*) compared to 31 Swedish, in 1601 there were 25 Finnish, 68 Swedish, and two Estonian companies. By 1618 there were 23 Finnish and 36 Swedish companies. In 1601, there were 18 cavalry banners in Sweden (Swedish: *fana*; sometimes known as cornet), including the retinue of nobles and Court Banner, compared to eight in Finland including the retinue of nobles.[7] In 1604, it was decided to maintain 15 provincial cavalry banners in Sweden and 10 in Finland.[8]

Estonia was exempt from conscription. However, a locally enlisted infantry company garrisoned Reval. Another was raised to garrison Narva. The Estonian nobility provided a banner of the retinue of nobles.

There were two reasons for this significant growth in the share of Finnish troops. First, geography: the sixteenth-century wars against Muscovy had been fought on Finland's border, which naturally focused military attention to the eastern half of the country. Second, poverty: Finland was significantly poorer than the Swedish heartland, which meant that military service was regarded as no worse, and possibly better, than subsistence farming. The prospects of subsistence farming were uncertain, at best, where farmlands were scarce and the population growing. Over time, the poor farmlands

---

4   Generalstaben, *Sveriges krig 1611–1632* Vol. 1: *Danska och ryska krigen* (Stockholm: Generalstaben, 1936), p.67.
5   Generalstaben, *Sveriges krig* 1, p.85.
6   Lars Ericson and Fred Sandstedt, *Fanornas folk: Den svenska arméns soldater under 1600-talets första hälft* (Stockholm Armémuseum, 1982), pp.9–10.
7   Generalstaben, *Sveriges krig* 1, pp.86, 574–9. See also RainerFagerlund, 'De finska fänikorna under äldre Vasatid: Forskningsläge och problem', *Turun historiallinen arkisto* 38 (Turku, 1982), pp.94–116, on p.99.
8   Generalstaben, *Sveriges krig* 1, p.89.

probably constitute the chief explanation why Finland supplied troops at a level far above its relative share of the total population.

Enlisted units, whether cavalry or infantry, were by tradition primarily raised in Germany and Scotland. Dutchmen were enlisted from 1592 onwards. It was not unusual to appoint one particular military entrepreneur colonel of all enlisted soldiers from his nation in the Swedish army. This arrangement did not make the colonel exempt from Swedish military law or chain of command, but was helpful if his men did not speak Swedish or German. Military entrepreneurs of high rank might even insist of such an arrangement as part of their patent.[9]

Swedish commanders knew that enlisted units usually were good soldiers, but they often caused problems and mostly so when they did not receive their pay. After a particularly disruptive incident in 1609, King Charles remarked to a Muscovite envoy that 'there are men in the army of various nations, who would not live in peace even here without monthly and indisputable wages. If, therefore, they [the Muscovites] had received any damage from this, it was not so much to be imputed to His Royal Majesty as to themselves [for not paying the soldiers on time].'[10]

Tactical Doctrine

By the early seventeenth century Sweden's military organisation, armament, and tactics purported to follow the Dutch model of warfare.

The Dutch model, introduced between 1590 and 1610 by Maurice of Nassau (1567–1625), eventually Prince of Orange, and his cousins William Louis (1560–1620) and John of Nassau (1561–1623), relied on tactical units, battalions, each of which officially (but not in practice) consisted of 550 men in imitation of the ancient Roman cohort. On the field of battle, the battalions would form up in a linear formation, typically 10 but frequently only six ranks deep, each with pikes in the centre and musketeers on each side of them. Two or more battalions would form a regiment. The army as a whole would form up in two to three lines. The Dutch model was designed to exploit firepower to the fullest extent, since it allowed all musketeers to fire. This was accomplished by rotation of ranks, an evolution known as the countermarch, with each rank firing a simultaneous salvo. William Louis of

---

9   The complete contractual terms of this arrangement, together with all other details pertaining to the patent, survives in a 1607 agreement between King Charles and Henry Luxe de la Borde regarding the enlistment of 500 French cavalry. Lauri Juhani Eerikäinen and Bengt M. Holmqvist, 'En kondottiärs villkor på Karl IX:s tid', *Meddelande* 35 (Stockholm: Armémuseum, 1974–75), pp.45–57.

10 'Esse nempe in exercitu variarum nationum homines, qui absque menstruo eoque indubitato stipendio ne hic quidem pacate viverent. Itaque si exinde aliquid damni suscepissent, non tam Reg. M:ti quam sibi ipsis id imputandum.' King Charles to Muscovite envoy, 22 June 1609, Axel Oxenstierna, *Rikskansleren Axel Oxenstiernas skrifter och brefvexling* 1:1 (Stockholm: P. A. Norstedt, 1888), pp.495–6, on p.496.

Nassau in 1594 read an account of the drill practiced by the ancient Roman army and then suggested the countermarch in a letter to his cousin Maurice. Soon enough it became a key feature of the Dutch model, which primarily used the rotation of ranks of musketeers defensively. Having fired, each rank retired to reload while the next rank took its place.

The Dutch model focused on firepower and mobility, defined as rapidity of movement and ease of manoeuvre, rather than shock. Moreover, the linear formation was vulnerable to flank and rear attack. The Dutch model did not provide a significant role for artillery and cavalry. Artillery was typically dispersed along the front of the line of battle. Artillery could be moved only slowly, or not at all, so may change hands if overrun by the enemy, and if not spiked (made inoperable), be turned against its former owners. If the fortune of battle then turned again, the artillery might change hands several times in the same battle. Cavalry typically employed caracole tactics.[11] This meant that the cavalrymen would advance in deep formation, at less than a gallop. As each rank came into range, the men would discharge their carbines or pistols, then wheel to the left (most commonly, since the horseman was firing with the right hand), retire to the back of the formation to reload, and in due time repeat the manoeuvre. The whole unit might move slowly forward as each rank fired, or slowly retreat to keep its distance from an advancing enemy. It has been argued that the caracole was less significant for its practical use than for the drill itself, which integrated the horsemen in a tactical body governed by discipline, not by each man's individual fighting skill.[12] The cavalrymen were armed and sometimes armoured for melee, and the intention usually seems to have been to follow the caracole with a charge, in effect using the caracole to soften up the enemy. Nonetheless, infantry arquebusiers and musketeers enjoyed a much greater range and more reliable fire than the wheellock pistols of most cavalry, so the cavalry usually kept a respectful distance.

Both artillery and cavalry were accordingly relegated to what in effect was a support role. Cavalry held higher status due to its origin in noble service (the retinue of nobles, more on which below). Yet, in the Dutch model the infantry, the proverbial queen of battle (although the term had

---

11 A term meaning 'snail' (Spanish: *caracol*), translated into German as *Schnecke* and into French as *limaçon* (ultimately from Latin *limax*, 'snail'). Previously, before the introduction of the countermarch, the tactics was also used by infantry. Hans Delbrück, *History of the Art of War 4: The Dawn of Modern Warfare* (Lincoln: University of Nebraska Press, Bison Books, 1990), 123. On the caracole, see Wendelin Schildknecht, *Harmonia in fortalitiis construendis, defendendis & oppugnandis* 3 (Stettin: Johann Valentin Rheten, 1652), pp.168–9; Johann Jacobi von Wallhausen, *Kriegskunst zu Pferdt* 2 (Frankfurt am Main: Johann Theodor de Bry, 1616), p.65 (describes its execution without using the name); Theodor Jakobsson, *Lantmilitär beväpning och beklädnad under äldre Vasatiden och Gustav II Adolfs tid* (Stockholm: Generalstaben, 1938; published separately and as Suppl. Vol. 2 in Generalstaben, *Sveriges krig 1611–1632*), pp.149–51.
12 Delbrück, *Dawn of Modern Warfare*, p.124.

not yet come into common use), was regarded as the chief means of winning the field. Besides, warfare came to focus more on outmanoeuvring the enemy in an extended campaign than on defeating him in a major battle. Campaigns for this reason also tended to focus on fortified positions, since to deny the enemy an important stronghold was a means of wearing him down. Besides, during the siege there was finally an opportunity to fully utilise one's artillery.

The Swedish Crown had noted the advantages of the Dutch model of war and begun work to adapt to the new organisational and tactical doctrines. However, the Swedish military had not progressed very far. Besides, military units in Scandinavia were often understrength and not quite able to live up to the theoretical doctrines.

Raising Troops

The Nobility

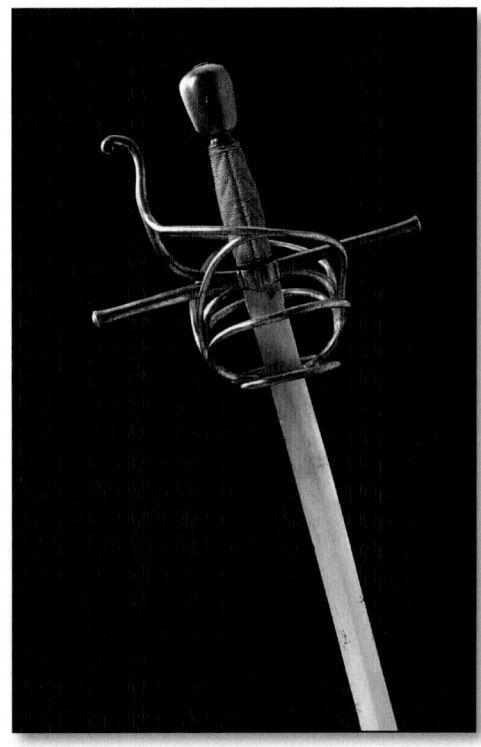

Rapier hilt dated to c. 1600, made either in the Swedish arms factory at Arboga or in Germany. Swept hilt of gilded steel with grip bound in gilded brass wire, attached to a later blade. Owned by King Charles, who employed it in tournaments. Total weight 1.59 kg. Blade length 93.6 cm, width 27.0 mm. Total length 112.4 cm. (Royal Armoury, Stockholm)

The Swedish and Finnish nobility was small but constituted the traditional core of the army and provided the bulk of the officer corps. By tradition, war was their primary purpose, and many, in particular among the Finnish nobility, benefited from military service. The early seventeenth century saw the transformation of the Finnish nobility from what could be referred to as a group of illiterate, medieval-style strongmen into members of a pan-European nobility, which sent its sons to study at the great universities on the Continent. The Swedish nobility had experienced the same change, although in the previous century. The nobility's collective wealth increased rapidly, too, in particular with regard to tax-free land grants.

However, many nobles remained individually poor, and from the second half of the sixteenth century, state service became an important path of both economic and social advancement for them. While military service no doubt provided opportunities to most, service as administrators and what might be called civil servants provided rewards, too. During the seventeenth century, salaries formed an important and increasing share of the income of most nobles, with only the highest-born as an exception to the rule.

Yet, the almost uninterrupted wars of the previous century had by the time of Sweden's war in Muscovy produced a situation in which a significant share of the officer corps was not of noble but common origin. In addition, it was understood that the mobilisation of real aptitude included the ennoblement of talented commoners, who then had to rely chiefly on state salaries

THE SWEDISH MILITARY ESTABLISHMENT

to support themselves. For them, military service was a career, not a social obligation. By 1610, commoners and newly created nobles constituted 14 percent of all cavalry captains and, yet more significantly, 68 percent of all infantry captains. The corresponding figure for colonels and generals was 11 percent.[13]

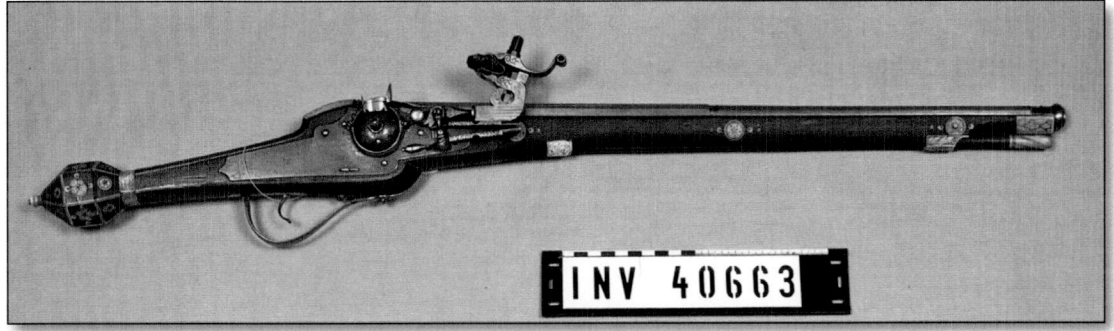

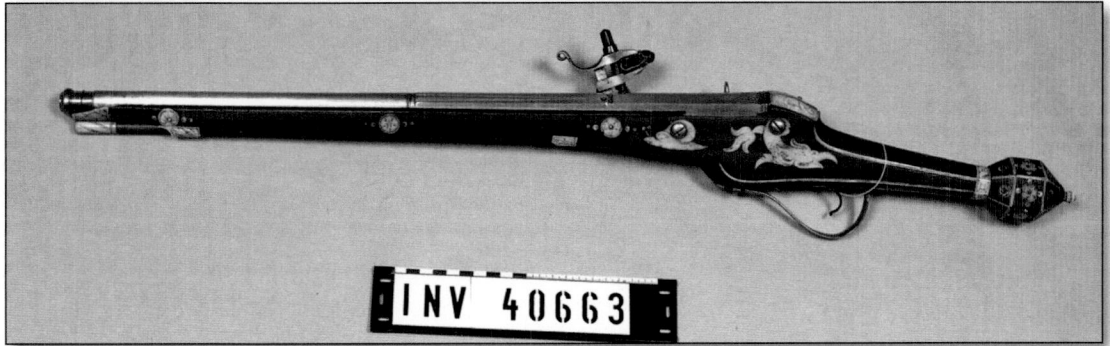

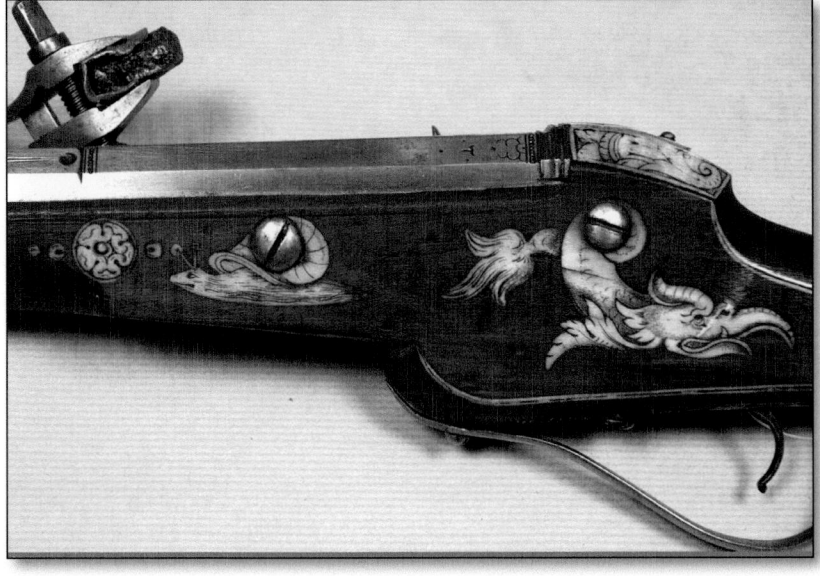

Wheellock pistol, one of a pair dated to 1608. Weight 1.88 kg. Barrel length 54.0 cm, total length 78.5 cm. Calibre 12.0 mm. (Army Museum, Stockholm; AM.040663; formerly of Gustav von Essen's collection, dispersed in 1898)

---

13   Gunnar Artéus, *Till militärstatens förhistoria: Krig, professionalisering och social förändring under Vasasönernas regering* (Stockholm: Probus, 1986), pp.47, 50.

Cavalrymen

Until the reign of Gustavus Adolphus, early modern Swedish kings (with the single exception of Erik XIV) regarded the cavalry as the primary combat arm. Unlike the infantry, which was conscripted or levied, the Swedish cavalry was raised on a voluntary basis, in exchange for noble status, land, and freedom from taxation. There was good reason for this; most campaigns were fought on the border with Muscovy or the Polish-Lithuanian Commonwealth in the east and Denmark in the south. While the Danish–Swedish borderlands were characterised by difficult terrain which brought its own particular tactical problems, the Scanian plains were excellent for cavalry operations. Meanwhile, cavalry retained a key role in warfare in the east. Cavalry in Scandinavia still operated in company-sized tactical units known as banners.

The nobility still provided some armed and equipped cavalrymen who fought as cuirassiers in the retinue of nobles. This duty was generally understood to have begun around the age of 17.[14] Although a noble was expected to serve in person, many hired a cavalryman to attend in their stead. The retinue of nobles was held to be the senior cavalry regiment in the army but usually only served at home, in defence of the country. The obligation to serve in foreign campaigns changed over time. Under King Erik XIV the retinue of nobles had been obliged to serve abroad at its own expense but for only three months per year, after which the Crown had to cover costs. Under King John III the retinue of nobles only had to serve abroad for up to two weeks per year. Under Gustavus Adolphus, the retinue of nobles was required to serve at its own expense for up to two months per year when away from home.[15] The retinue of nobles constituted three companies in Sweden, one in Finland, and one in Estonia.

In the eyes of Gustavus Adolphus, the retinue of nobles was a disappointment. Its members were also very few. When called up for war in 1612, no more than 30 men showed up for service out of the entire retinue, which technically should have consisted of at least 300 men in Sweden alone. Moreover, most were merely hired cavalrymen even though the nobles themselves were obliged to serve. Gustavus Adolphus reportedly described the resulting unit as a 'loose bunch of useless men'. Another eyewitness noted that no more than eight actual nobles served for the entire campaign.[16]

Due to the small size of the retinue of nobles, additional cavalry units had to be raised. Since it was difficult for the Crown to raise enough cash to pay for its troops, Swedish kings customarily employed land grants as a money-

---

14 Henning Hamilton, *Afhandling om krigsmaktens och krigskonstens tillstånd i Sverige, under Konung Gustaf II Adolfs regering* (Stockholm: Kongl. Vitterhets Historie och Antiquitets Academiens handlingar 17, 1846), p.175.
15 Hamilton, *Afhandling*, p.173; citing a decision dated 10 January 1612.
16 Hamilton, *Afhandling*, pp.179–80.

saving measure. Already in the 1540s, King Gustavus I had attempted to raise both horse and foot by hiring volunteers, each of whom would serve in exchange for a tax-exempt farmstead. For common soldiers, the farmstead typically consisted of a small cottage and some land to cultivate. Ultimately, the reform failed with regard to the infantry. However, for the cavalry the traditional concept of military service in exchange for tax-exempt farmsteads remained. King Charles in 1603 instructed that every cavalryman be provided a farmstead to provide for his upkeep and place of residence in times of peace. It also became possible for an individual to contract to provide a cavalryman with equipment in exchange for a farmstead exempt from taxation to defray the costs. Since the basis of the income was land revenues, this type of cavalry became known as territorial cavalry (Swedish: *landsryttare, landssåtare*). Some instead served as enlisted cavalry (*besoldningsryttare*). They received pay and board, usually in a royal castle but occasionally in a farmstead, which was then compensated through tax exemption. In reality, there was little difference between these two types of cavalry. They were also generally equipped and armed alike. Certain groups of specialists, too, who could afford to raise cavalrymen, went together to form cavalry units, in exchange for exemption from some types of taxation as well as conscription. These included the game wardens in 1611 and a group of mining professionals in 1612.[17]

The ongoing wars in the Polish-Lithuanian Commonwealth had shown that the Swedish cavalry as it then was armed, equipped, and trained – as unarmoured harquebusiers – could not withstand the fearsome Polish winged hussars. Most urgent was the reintroduction of armour, that is, cuirassiers of the Continental type. As a result of the disastrous defeat at Kircholm, King Charles in 1606 announced that anybody who could supply himself with helmet, breast- and backplate, vambraces, rerebraces, and cuisses of plate (that is, full armour), a warhorse, saddle, and the appropriate weapons

Nobles (but not necessarily their serving men) of the Swedish retinue of nobles were armed as cuirassiers. (Jacob de Gheyn, *Die Reitschule oder Übungen der Kavallerie*, 1599–1600)

---

17 Hamilton, *Afhandling*, pp.184, 187–8.

to serve as a cavalryman would, in effect, become a noble and enjoy a number of privileges including the right to carry a special coat of arms which depicted an armed hand in silver on a blue and yellow field. It was not hereditary nobility; the Crown could, if it wished, decline the services which effectively removed the exemption from taxation. This programme, which was called 'shield-knight service' (*skölderusttjänst*), resulted in some additional cuirassiers, but state poverty was too severe for the initiative to have a major impact. King Charles hoped to raise nine cavalry banners of such volunteers, but those who volunteered were too few to form banners of their own, so had to be incorporated into existing banners.[18] Besides, the announcement came several decades too late. Public attitude to what constituted noble rank was changing, and nobility was already being seen more as a matter of birth than a function within the army.

Infantrymen

In 1600 the Parliament in Linköping ruled that every province should raise a certain number of soldiers, and that the Crown should provide all soldiers, including infantrymen, with a farmstead. In 1604, Parliament in Norrköping again confirmed the principle that all soldiers, including infantrymen, be provided with a farmstead. Through these decisions, King Charles again extended the practice to the infantry. As a result, the officers of the national army were provided, as part of their salary, with tax-exempt Crown land to farm (farmsteads subsequently known as 'military homesteads', *militiehemman*), of a size appropriate to the rank held. Alternatively, the officer received the appropriate rent corresponding to the tax owed, while the farmstead remained in private hands. In 1611, King Charles ordered that officers and under-officers would continue to be paid according to this system. Moreover, he also ordered that those common soldiers of the national army who did not yet have any tax-exempt land should be provided with a small farm. Gustavus Adolphus issued the corresponding instruction in 1614.[19] The decision to establish a national army in part paid for with land grants was taken since such an army was cheaper to raise and maintain and because it enabled a degree of domestic control.

The principle of tax-exempt land grants as payment for military service laid the foundation for the organisation ultimately known as the *indelningsverk*, from a word perhaps best translated as the allotment authority. The *indelningsverk* provided for the existence of cavalry units (and in principle although not yet in practice, infantry units as well)

---

18 Hamilton, *Afhandling*, p.144 n.275, p.173 n.299; Josef Alm, *Blanka vapen och skyddsvapen från och med 1500-talet till våra dagar* (Stockholm: Rediviva, 1975), p.244; Generalstaben, *Sveriges krig* 1, p.93.

19 Hamilton, *Afhandling*, pp.143–5, 147–50.

through the permanent allotment (*indelning*, 'division') of sources of revenue for their needs.

However, the land grant system did not yet produce enough common soldiers for service on foot and as sailors. For this, the foundation had to be the old national army. Since already King Gustavus I had found that the once semi-voluntary character of the national army clearly was insufficient to produce enough men, the only answer remained conscription (*utskrivning*).

Conscription was the arbitrary raising of men from a population, in most cases from peasants on Crown land. Although resented, the concept still had a certain legitimacy since in Sweden the peasant Estate enjoyed parliamentary representation. Based on a decision by Parliament in Västerås in 1544, Parliament had to grant all acts of conscription. The conscripted soldiers had to be armed, trained, and provisioned by the Crown. On the other hand, they could be used anywhere, overseas or at home, as well as indefinitely. Many peasants regarded conscription as a death sentence, which ultimately it often was, and numerous conscripts attempted to desert, especially before they were shipped overseas.

Artillerymen

The Swedish artillery emerged as a service arm in the sixteenth century under German master artillerymen who previously had served under Emperor Charles V. For this reason, the Swedish artillery adopted Continental artillery traditions. One of them was the artillery's first right to the church bells in every captured town. This was a practice that went back to the need for bronze to cast cannons. Sweden had abundant copper deposits, yet the Swedish artillery retained this tradition at least until the 1660s.[20] Artillery personnel were enlisted among semi-civilian professionals. Most artillerymen were enlisted within the Swedish kingdom, so the artillery arm in many ways remained national in composition. Both Swedish and Finnish artillerymen were moved to Stockholm for training. In war, infantrymen were temporarily detached as labour to assist as needed.[21] Artillery personnel were generally detached to remote garrisons throughout the kingdom. Some were also included in the field army, when it mobilised.

Engineers and sappers, too, belonged to the artillery. The first professional engineers seem to have been enlisted in the Dutch Republic in 1610, and this source of manpower henceforth remained important for the development of a Swedish engineering arm. In the field, the supply train, too, fell under the command of the artillery, including replacement arms supplies that were brought along by the field army.[22]

---

20   Michael Fredholm von Essen, *Charles X's Wars* 1 (Warwick: Helion, 2021), p.80.
21   Jonas Hedberg (ed.), *Kungl. Artilleriet: Yngre vasatiden* (Stockholm: Militärhistoriska Förlaget, 1985), p.25.
22   Hedberg, *Kungl. Artilleriet: Yngre vasatiden*, pp.46, 304.

Levies and Burgher Militias

Neither conscription nor enlistment provided sufficient manpower for an extended war. If so, the Crown could still levy troops among the peasants. This was done through a quota that the peasants had to fill. Levied troops served on foot, received no training, and had to pay for their own weapons and supplies. On the other hand, they were only required to serve at home. Levied troops were usually used to man defensive redoubts along the external borders, in effect functioning as a border guard. The levied peasants would serve for a time, and then be replaced by other levies from the same area. The Crown directed that former soldiers should be selected as leaders of the levies.

In times of need, the Crown also had the right to raise a general levy. A general levy consisted of all men able to bear arms and was usually called out to defend an external border. The levied troops had to arm and supply themselves. Their use was accordingly restricted, for practical reasons, to certain geographical areas and short durations of time. Levies could also be called out in the form of burgher militias, which would have to take some responsibility for defending their towns when under siege.

Most towns were very small, and burghers might be counted in dozens, not hundreds. As a result, there was fundamentally little difference between most burgher militias and peasant levies. However, in the largest towns there was a degree of voluntary service in the burgher militias, and those burghers who served in them could usually be expected to afford the necessary military armament.

Levies were only rarely used for Sweden's war in Muscovy. There was little need for them, since the war was almost exclusively fought beyond Sweden's borders.

The Chain of Command

The King naturally stood at the apex of the chain of command. The military hierarchy remained underdeveloped. The Council of the Realm (Swedish: *Riksrådet*) carried out the functions of a national government. Its leading members were the five great officers of state. First among them was the Lord High Justiciar (*Riksdrots*), who took precedence. The second and third were respectively the Grand Marshal of the Realm (*Riksmarsk*), who was in command of home defence and the Army, and the Grand Admiral of the Realm (*Riksamiral*), who commanded the Navy.[23] These officers were

---

23 The position of Grand Admiral of the Realm was instituted in 1571 with the appointment of Claes Eriksson Fleming (*c.* 1535–1597), who supported King Sigismund against the future King Charles.

followed in precedence by the Lord High Chancellor (*Rikskansler*) and the Lord High Treasurer (*Riksskattmästare*).

The Grand Marshal and the Grand Admiral controlled the military establishment: the units of the Army and Navy. At the time of the wars covered in this volume, first Magnus Brahe (1564–1633) and then, from 1612, Axel Ryning (1552–1620) served as Marshal of the Realm. Until this advancement, Ryning instead served as Grand Admiral of the Realm, a position in which Göran Gyllenstierna (1575–1618) succeeded him. Their primary activities were administrative, not operational.[24]

The King could, and did, appoint provincial commanders as needed. By tradition, an army commander was called 'Field Colonel' (Swedish: *fältöverste*) or 'Colonel-General' (*generalöverste*), terms that essentially meant general. Such a man only commanded the provincial field army. Any garrisons within his area of operations remained under the command of their respective commandants. This at times caused difficulties in the chain of command, which only the King could override by issuing direct orders to the commandants. The reason for this anomaly was probably that in times of peace, the governors at Kalmar and Elfsborg Castles were in formal command of all soldiers in respectively Småland and Västergötland. Since these provinces were particularly exposed in times of war, it was natural then to appoint field colonels in command of provincial field units. Yet, the governors at these important castles remained in place and naturally retained an influential position vis-à-vis their respective garrisons. The situation was similar in Finland and Estonia, where governors often controlled even field units.

However, the situation could be quite different when a commander was appointed to exercise individual command in a theatre of war in which the King was not present, or likely to be present. Such a commander might be appointed Field Colonel-General (*generalfältöverste*). The only officer who received the full title and mandate was Pontus De la Gardie, who in 1581 received authority to command both land and naval units on the eastern front against Muscovy. An earlier title for this office was Commanding General (*fältherre*). Whilst the title remained in use and would reappear, the officer who served in this position was in the early 1600s instead known as a Lieutenant General (*generallöjtnant*), which meant that he served as the King's lieutenant or deputy. Soon, however, the title of Field Marshal (*fältmarskalk*) appeared for an officer in this position. Previously, this title had indicated a commander of cavalry, roughly equivalent to a colonel in status. Although the term field marshal sometimes appears in texts produced during the first two decades of the seventeenth century, the rank

---

24 After the Kalmar War of 1611–1613, Gustavus Adolphus and Lord High Chancellor Axel Oxenstierna began the process of establishing properly authorised government departments, including a department of war, to which the King in the late 1610s would delegate his authority.

was not really formalised until later, during the Thirty Years' War, when it gradually superseded the other two.

Military Organisation

Sweden was fortunate in having in the army a number of experienced soldiers who had fought in the long period of wars preceding the war in Muscovy. Already by the late sixteenth century, the majority of native officers in the Swedish army (captains, lieutenants, ensigns, and indeed sergeants) were already highly professionalised in everything but theoretical education. First, they were experienced in the military position they held. By 1590, 77 percent of native infantry captains and 62 percent of cavalry captains had served in their present rank for three years or more. In addition, most or all would have served in junior ranks for some time before being promoted to captain. Besides, 35 percent of all infantry captains and 31 percent of all cavalry captains had, in fact, served for 11 years or more, and most of this time had been spent at war. This fortunate situation endured. By 1610, 63 percent of native infantry captains and 71 percent of cavalry captains had served in their present rank for three years or more. By then, 29 percent of all infantry captains and eight percent of all cavalry captains had served for 11 years or more.[25] The latter figure can be explained that by this time, a far higher share of cavalry officers (48 percent of the total) were of foreign origin. The number of foreign infantry officers had risen too, but not as dramatically, to 27 percent. The foreign officers had, of course, not served for as long in the Swedish army, but they had often gained considerable experience elsewhere.[26] There was accordingly no need to build an army from scratch. A professional core already existed.

What was the origin of the foreign officers? Most were Germans, either from the Continent or the eastern side of the Baltic. Indeed, it is often difficult to distinguish in the records between Baltic Germans from Livonia or Estonia who were Swedish citizens and those who technically were foreign nationals. The second largest group consisted of the Scots, English, and Irish (who often are difficult to distinguish from the Scots in contemporary written sources). This group was followed in numbers by a mixed group of Frenchmen, Walloons, Swiss, Italians, and Spaniards, and a slightly smaller group consisting of men of Dutch, Frisian, or Flemish origin. Men of other background served too, including some Poles, Muscovites, Hungarians, and the occasional Dane or Norwegian.[27] It is obvious that Lutheran faith was not a prerequisite for service in the Swedish army, despite the latter's insistence on *attending* Lutheran sermons. It is also obvious that the Swedish army sought different types

---

25 Artéus, *Till militärstatens förhistoria*, p.36.
26 Artéus, *Till militärstatens förhistoria*, pp.47, 50.
27 Artéus, *Till militärstatens förhistoria*, p.87.

of military expertise in different foreign regions. By 1610, 67 percent of foreign cavalry captains were of German or Baltic German origin, 17 percent were Scots, English, or Irish, 16 percent had a French, Walloon, Swiss, Italian, or Spanish background, and only the occasional individual was of Commonwealth, Muscovite, or Hungarian origin. In comparison, by 1610, 56 percent of foreign infantry captains were of German or Baltic German origin, 32 percent were Scots, English, or Irish, six percent Dutch, Frisian, or Flemish, five percent had a French, Walloon, Swiss, Italian, or Spanish background, and, again, only the occasional individual was of Commonwealth, Muscovite, or Hungarian origin.

It is thus clear that officers of Scots, English, or Irish origin were more likely to serve in the infantry. Those of Dutch, Frisian, or Flemish origin almost invariably served in the infantry (or, coincidentally, in the navy, which hosted many officers of Dutch origin). In contrast, officers of French, Walloon, Swiss, Italian, or Spanish origin were far more likely to serve in the cavalry.[28] There was a reason for enlisting so many foreign officers for the cavalry. As noted, with Sweden's native cavalry force still based on the nobility, the available manpower was insufficient. A new source of cavalry officers was required, and for this foreign nationals were enlisted.

Unit Organisation

The existing Swedish army was obsolete and insufficient with regard to both organisation and armament. By the turn of the century, regiments in the Swedish army were temporary in nature, usually enlisted abroad, and had no standard establishment strength. The Swedish national military establishment was not organised in multiple-level formations, nor in higher formations. There was no military-administrative organisation. Each company or banner was independently raised, and in times of peace independent and directly subordinate to the king.[29] The only unit level that existed was that of the banner and company. It accordingly constituted the only administrative and tactical unit, with the two roles combined into one. There was no permanent regimental organisation, nor did the Dutch-style battalion yet exist in Sweden. An army was raised by combining a number of banners and companies. Although companies of foot would generally be deployed collectively in a line of battle, the line was no more than a practical solution for battlefield use. It did not signify any kind of permanent identity or higher formation.

---

28 Artéus, *Till militärstatens förhistoria*, p.89.
29 G. B. C:son Barkman, *Gustaf II Adolfs regementsorganisation vid det inhemska infanteriet: En studie över organisationens tillkomst och huvuddragen av dess utveckling mot bakgrunden av kontinental organisation* (Stockholm: Meddelanden från Generalstabens krigshistoriska avdelning, 1931), p.71.

The Crown had made some recent attempts to reform the cavalry. The old 300-strong cavalry banner was in 1603 reorganised as a company and reduced to a strength of 120 horse (cavalry units counted their strength in horses, not men).[30] However, in 1611 some cavalry companies were again increased to a strength of 200 or 300.[31] Whether this was the practical result of the outbreak of the Kalmar War (because war always necessitated the need for extra men) or because the new company was regarded as too weak, remains unclear. Some banners in any case never reached establishment strength.

There was no standard establishment strength for national companies of foot. Yet since the late sixteenth century there was an understanding that a company of foot should consist of some 300 men, even though many were significantly smaller. By the time of Sweden's war in Muscovy, a company of foot raised in Sweden generally speaking had a strength between 200 and 300 men.[32] In one perhaps ideal case, the company consisted of 191 common soldiers, 68 *doppelsöldner* (corporals or similar who presumably served as pikemen – common pikemen no longer received higher pay), four drummers, four pipers, 30 trainee officers (*adelsburst*, *adelsburs*; or *adelsbuss*; who presumably served as pikemen), and about three officers.[33] The trainees were often, but not invariably, young nobles who served as volunteers without pay. There is some uncertainty regarding their service conditions. According to the regulations of Kings John and Charles, young nobles not yet of age to serve on horseback must still serve, but as common soldiers.[34] However, the term seems to derive from the Dutch term *adelburst*, which signified a naval midshipman or cadet. If so, this group of soldiers may have served as volunteers (similar to the *adventurers* or *voluntaries* in England, *soldati di fortuna* in Italy, *soldats de fortune* in France, and *aventureros* in Spain, all of whom generally were youths of gentle or noble birth) who still were regarded as in training for later promotion to officer rank. From 1574 onwards, pikemen and arquebusiers received the same pay.[35]

Nor was there any standard establishment strength for enlisted foreign units. The foreign regiments in Swedish service at the time did not adhere to any particular type of organisation. The decisive factor seems to have been availability of men and opportunity to enlist them. These regiments generally included from five to eight companies of from 150 to 200 men

---

30 John of Nassau had in 1601 attempted to reduce the cavalry banner from the traditional 300 to 100, but the reform was never fully implemented; in 1602 establishment strength, such as it was, reverted to 300.
31 Hamilton, *Afhandling*, p.210.
32 Barkman, *Gustaf II Adolfs regementsorganisation*, pp.81, 207.
33 For another variant of this ideal, see G. Bertil C:son Barkman and Sven Lundkvist, *Kungl. Svea livgardes historia* 3:1: *1611–1632* (Stockholm: Stiftelsen för Svea livgardes historia, 1963), p.212.
34 Hamilton, *Afhandling*, p.128.
35 Bertil C:son Barkman, *Kungl. Svea livgardes historia* 2: *1560–1611* (Stockholm: Stiftelsen för Svea livgardes historia, 1939), pp.700–705.

each. Occasionally a regiment had more companies, which generally was the result of the amalgamation of two previous regiments.[36]

King Charles frequently experimented with different organisational forms and different types of armaments. However, over time he grew to favour the enlistment of professional soldiers abroad instead of training national units. In 1609, the Swedish army included no less than 10,000 soldiers enlisted abroad.[37] Most served on the eastern front.

A specialty that set the Swedish army apart from Continental armies was the employment of ski troops, which were used both for reconnaissance and surprise flank attacks. Every year, Finnish ski troops were sent to Livonia, and ski troops were frequently used in the campaigns against the Commonwealth and Muscovy.

In Livonia, the Crown introduced mobile defences such as swinefeathers, the use of wagon forts for protection and, upon the initiative of the Dutch expert John of Nassau, 100 carts with affixed pikes (Swedish: *spetskärror*) that might provide a modicum of protection against armoured cavalry such as those fielded by the Commonwealth.[38] Of these various measures, the most long-lasting was the swinefeather (elsewhere also known as Swedish feather). This was a short pike, with a total length of approximately 1.8 to 2 m including the 30 cm-long head. Under the right circumstances, the swinefeather formed an efficient protection against cavalry. A unit of arquebusiers or musketeers with swinefeathers firmly planted in the ground in front of them would give the appearance of a wall of spear points. Moreover, with the addition of logs to link them together, several swinefeathers could be arranged into a *cheval-de-frise*, an anti-cavalry obstacle that was positioned in front of the infantry ranks so as to provide protection against a cavalry charge.

Guard Units

King Gustavus I had founded the Court Banner (Swedish: *Hovfanan*) as an enlisted elite armoured cavalry unit. Its members received higher pay than the retinue of nobles (whose members, moreover, were only paid under certain conditions). King John in 1575 incorporated the retinue of nobles into the Court Banner, which in 1576 consisted of 156 men. The incorporation of the old retinue of nobles probably reduced the combat readiness of the Court Banner. Perhaps for this reason King John's son and successor, Sigismund, during his rule in Sweden in 1591, established yet

---

36 Barkman, *Gustaf II Adolfs regementsorganisation*, p.79.
37 Generalstaben, *Sveriges krig* 1, p.92.
38 Jakobsson, *Lantmilitär beväpning och beklädnad*, 14, 20. See also 'Egenhändiga anteckningar af Carl Carlsson Gyllenhjelm rörande tiden 1597–1601', *Historiska Handlingar* 20 (Stockholm: P. A. Norstedt, 1905), pp.258–395; 'Grefve Johans av Nassau relation angående kriget i Livland 1601–1602', *Historiska Handlingar* 20 (Stockholm: P. A. Norstedt, 1905), pp.396–438.

another guard cavalry unit: the Vanguard Banner (Swedish: *Kännefanan*; Finnish: *Päälippue*), under the command of Claes Hermansson Fleming (d. 1616) of the Finnish retinue of nobles. The Vanguard Banner was ranked higher than the Court Banner.[39] However, the unit was disbanded in 1593.

Having gained the throne, King Charles constituted a new permanent cavalry unit, henceforth known as the King's Life Banner (*Kungl. Majestäts Livfana* or *Konungens Livfana*) or, with the more modern terminology that came into use in the seventeenth century, the King's Life Company of Horse. This was an enlisted cavalry company which although technically a guard unit, in reality functioned as a permanent fighting unit.

There were two additional Life Banners in Sweden: the two ducal life banners or life companies of respectively Dukes Gustavus Adolphus and John. Yet another was being formed under Duke Charles Philip, who still was a minor.

When Gustavus Adolphus inherited the army from his late father, he immediately merged his Life Company of Horse into the King's Life Company of Horse. Since this was an enlisted cavalry company which functioned as a fighting unit, the company was no permanent structure and did not continuously follow the King. For instance, in 1613 the King's Life Company of Horse, under Herman Wrangel, deployed with the field army to Muscovy and in 1614 was present at Novgorod.[40]

The by tradition and for reasons of combat readiness most prestigious regiment of the Swedish army was the King's personal Life Guard of Foot. It was always enlisted. Being the military unit closest to the King, the Life Guard frequently changed designation, leadership, organisation, and to some extent armament. This was particularly the case at times of royal succession, when the new sovereign found it particularly important to retain a loyal guard unit.

The Life Guard, too, originated with King Gustavus I. In time, his small, personal infantry guard grew into a company-sized unit, known as the Drabant Guard (*Drabantkåren*). This unit continuously followed the King. In addition, there was a second, and generally larger, infantry unit at the King's disposal. This was the Household Company (*Gårdsfänikan*), which guarded the royal palace. King Charles in 1600 redesignated the Household Company as the Stockholm Company and turned his Drabant Guard into a regular infantry company, known as the Drabant Company (*Drabantfänikan*). He used both this and the Stockholm Company as regular combat units. However, he in 1608 reassigned the Stockholm Company in

---

39   Sebastian Jägerhorn, *Hårdast bland de hårda: En kavalleriofficer i fält* (Stockholm: Medström, 2018), pp.25, 233 n.67. The term *kännefana* (*kennefana*), with the apparent synonym *rännefana* (*rendefana*), was known since the Nordic Seven Years' War of 1563–1570, when both Danes and Swedes used it with the meaning of vanguard (Danish/Swedish: *Fortrav/Förtrav, Forvagt/Förvakt*).

40   Barkman, *Kungl. Svea livgardes historia* 3:1, pp.180, 215.

THE SWEDISH MILITARY ESTABLISHMENT

status to that of a provincial company in Uppland.[41] Between 1600 and 1605 King Charles also employed a third guard unit, the Arquebusier Company (Swedish: *Hakeskyttefänikan*).

When Gustavus Adolphus ascended to the throne in the middle of the Kalmar War, he inherited the Drabant Company from his late father. Gustavus Adolphus retained this unit as an independent Life Guard company (with a planned strength, in 1614, of 300 men, although less than 200 could be found before a cavalry company of Österbotten veterans was integrated into the unit[42]). In addition, he in 1613 ordered Colonel Reinhold Taube to enlist a whole infantry regiment for the King's personal use. Taube had commanded regiments in Swedish service since the campaign in Muscovy in 1609–1610, after which he fought in the Kalmar War. Primarily raised from Germans and Scots in Swedish service, the new regiment became known as the King's Regiment (formally, His Royal Majesty's Regiment, *Hans Kungliga Majestäts regemente*). It consisted of four companies, each with a planned strength of 300 men. In reality, the total strength reached only 915 men.[43] Taube and the King's Regiment fought in Muscovy in 1613, where Taube fell in battle. Because of the death of Taube, and the unit's considerable losses, Gustavus Adolphus in 1615 had the remnants of the King's Regiment reconstituted. In practical terms, this became a mostly new enlisted regiment but with the same name (apparently elongated into His Royal Majesty's Life Regiment) and again consisting of four companies.[44] Most of the soldiers were probably Germans. The regiment served with the King under Jost Clodt von Jürgensburg at the siege of Pskov in 1615, after which it was disbanded in 1616.[45]

---

41 Barkman, *Kungl. Svea livgardes historia* 2, pp.351–2, 417, 421–2, 425, 428, 429, 434, 437.
42 Barkman, *Kungl. Svea livgardes historia* 3:1, pp.217–18, 221.
43 Reinhold Taube's Company, of 245 men (primarily Germans); Patrick Learmonth's Company, of 215 men (Scots); John Handley's Company, of 168 men (Scots), and Anders Munck's Company, of 287 men (Germans). Figures from 20 September 1613; cited in Barkman, *Kungl. Svea livgardes historia* 3:1, p.213.
44 Jost Clodt von Jürgensburg's Company, of 150 men (including the remnants of Taube's Regiment); Paul de Courlas's Company, of 193 men (probably Germans); Wilhelm van Laer's Company, of 147 men (enlisted in the Dutch Republic); and Hans Ernst von Termo's Company, of 189 men (probably Germans). Courlas had previously served as lieutenant in Guillaume De la Barre's French harquebusiers who fought in Sweden during the Kalmar War and then joined Cobron's Regiment. Figures from 1615; cited in Barkman, *Kungl. Svea livgardes historia* 3:1, p.234.
45 Barkman, *Kungl. Svea livgardes historia* 3:1, pp.180–81, 211–15, 211–16, 230–2, 243–4.

Gustavus Adolphus's Organisational Reforms

Although Gustavus Adolphus early on realised that a comprehensive reform of the Swedish army was necessary, there was little opportunity to begin this work while Sweden fought the Kalmar War with Denmark and Norway at the same time as operations were ongoing on the eastern front. Yet, both the Kalmar War and the ongoing operations in Muscovy showed that some reform work simply could not wait. A particular glaring problem was the lack of regimental structures. Everybody still fought in independent infantry companies and cavalry banners, a custom inherited from the Middle Ages and rightfully regarded as obsolete.

The opportunity to reform the army came with the conclusion of the Kalmar War in 1613 and the simultaneous need to send reinforcements to the war in Muscovy. While Gustavus Adolphus wanted to form the reinforcements into regiments of the Dutch model, a problem was that the conscripted infantry companies were not necessarily mandated for service overseas. For this reason, Gustavus Adolphus began to set up new regiments based on enlistment among existing infantry companies. In short, the plan was to form enlisted provincial regiments of volunteers out of the existing structure of provincially conscripted men for homeland defence.

Although Gustavus Adolphus already favoured the Dutch organisational model, he realised that it was too early to implement the Dutch model throughout the entire army. One reason was to avoid the sudden imposition, in time of war, of a new organisational model. Perhaps even more important was that the old model also was cheaper, since an organisation into large companies needed fewer, highly-paid officers. Instead, Gustavus Adolphus retained the old infantry company style of 300 men, 10 of which would form a regiment of foot.[46]

It was a good plan, but conditions in war-ravaged Sweden did not allow for full implementation. In reality, he only managed to raise one infantry regiment of the intended type. This was Jesper Andersson Cruus's Regiment, which moreover only managed to raise nine companies, not all of which reached establishment strength. Nonetheless, the raising of the regiment proved to Gustavus Adolphus that provincially raised units could play a role in modern warfare as well (Table 1).

---

46   Barkman, *Gustaf II Adolfs regementsorganisation*, p.76; Generalstaben, *Sveriges krig* 1, p.102.

Table 1. Jesper Andersson Cruus's Regiment, 1613[47]

Colonel: Jesper Andersson Cruus

Province	Company	Strength
Västmanland and Mountain County (Bergslagen)	Jesper Andersson Cruus	288
Västerbotten	Erik Johansson Båge	300
Norrland except Västerbotten	Ernst Larsson Creutz	300
Uppland and Dalecarlia	Åke Oxenstierna	280
Dalecarlia	Nils Boije	246
Västergötland	Hans Campbell	240
Västergötland	Robert Douglas	238
Småland	Johan Henriksson Rytter (Reuter)	282
Småland	Erik Drake	245
In total		2,419

The regiment was retained until 1617, when it was dissolved at the time the first system of permanent territorial regiments of foot was formed.[48] At the time, desertion and losses had reduced the regiment to seven very weak companies.[49]

In 1614, yet another Swedish enlisted regiment was formed, under Svante Banér. Because of difficulties in retaining even Cruus's Regiment at some level of establishment strength, the new regiment only received six companies, mostly with a strength considerably lower than the purported establishment strength of 300 men. When the regiment departed for Muscovy in the summer of 1614, it remained significantly understrength (Table 2). The regiment returned to Narva in 1616, after which it was dissolved.[50]

---

47 Sources: Barkman, *Gustaf II Adolfs regementsorganisation*, p.77; Generalstaben, *Sveriges krig* 1, p.102.
48 Fredholm von Essen, *Lion from the North* 1, p.124. Gustavus Adolphus's continued reform of the Swedish army is described, pp.117–51.
49 Barkman, *Gustaf II Adolfs regementsorganisation*, p.77; Generalstaben, *Sveriges krig* 1, p.103.
50 Barkman, *Gustaf II Adolfs regementsorganisation*, p.77; Generalstaben, *Sveriges krig* 1, p.103.

Table 2. Svante Banér's Regiment, 1614[51]

Colonel: Svante Banér

Province	Company	Strength
Dalecarlia and Uppland	Svante Banér	167
Västerbotten	Jacob Frensham	310
Dalecarlia	Hans Nilsson	166
Småland	Evert Bamberg	202
Småland	Andreas Goossen van der Maan	206
Småland	Paul Wulf	269
In total		1, 320

When Gustavus Adolphus in 1615 decided to lay siege to Pskov, he needed additional reinforcements to the field army. For this purpose, he aimed to form two native infantry regiments, one in Sweden and one in Finland. However, it was believed that enlistment would not be successful, so the Crown returned to conscription. The two new regiments became dissimilar and also differed from the previous ones. The Swedish regiment consisted of eight companies, an organisational type that already was represented in Jacob De la Gardie's own Life Regiment. Gustavus Adolphus took personal command of the new regiment, which henceforth became known as His Royal Majesty's Own Regiment (*Hans Kungl. Majestäts eget regemente*). The name was indistinguishable from the aforementioned King's Regiment raised by Reinhold Taube in 1613. Below the King, command of the regiment was held by Lieutenant Colonel Robert Rutherford. This regiment, too, did not reach the planned establishment strength of 300 men per company (Table 3). The regiment participated in the siege of Pskov. Upon returning home, it was dissolved.[52]

---

51   Sources: Barkman, *Gustaf II Adolfs regementsorganisation*, p.77; Generalstaben, *Sveriges krig* 1, p.103.
52   Barkman, *Gustaf II Adolfs regementsorganisation*, p.78; Generalstaben, *Sveriges krig* 1, p.103.

THE SWEDISH MILITARY ESTABLISHMENT

Table 3. His Royal Majesty's Own (Swedish) Regiment, 1615[53] ()

Colonel: Gustavus Adolphus
Lieutenant Colonel: Robert Rutherford

Province	Company	Strength
Västerbotten	Robert Rutherford	197
Ångermanland and Medelpad	Matts Slumpare	167
Ångermanland and Medelpad	Jakob Velamsson	232
Hälsingland	Bengt Bagge	215
Dalecarlia	Olof Olofsson	240
Värmland	Eskil Hansson	278
Västergötland	Anders Munck	193
Västergötland	Sven Pjeske	136
In total		1, 658

It remains unclear from surviving documents what kind of organisation Gustavus Adolphus intended for the Finnish regiment. It seems that it became smaller than originally intended. The regiment was named after its colonel, Hans von Rechenberger. During the siege of Pskov, it consisted of five companies (Table 4). Only two companies reached establishment strength. The regiment was dissolved in 1618, when the new organisation of the Finnish infantry was established. However, before then some of the older companies had already been replaced.[54]

Table 4. Hans von Rechenberger's Regiment, 1615[55]

Colonel: Hans von Rechenberger

Province	Company	Strength
Österbotten	Hans von Rechenberger	299
Österbotten	Erik Tomasson	199
Tavastland	Reinhold Jacobsson	139
Tavastland	Matts Larsson	163
Nyland	Matts Olofsson	307
In total		1, 107

---

53 Sources: Barkman, *Gustaf II Adolfs regementsorganisation*, p.78; Generalstaben, *Sveriges krig* 1, pp.103–4.
54 Barkman, *Gustaf II Adolfs regementsorganisation*, p.79; Generalstaben, *Sveriges krig* 1, pp.103–4.
55 Sources: Barkman, *Gustaf II Adolfs regementsorganisation*, p.79; Generalstaben, *Sveriges krig* 1, pp.103–4.

SWEDEN'S WAR IN MUSCOVY 1609-1617

In similarity to these newly raised regiments, the foreign regiments in Swedish service at the time did not adhere to any particular type of organisation. The enlisted regiments generally consisted of from five to eight companies of from 150 to 200 men. Occasionally, a regiment counted more companies, but this was generally the result of the merger of two existing regiments.[56]

Weapons, Equipment, and Uniforms

Officers and Under-officers

As elsewhere in the region, officers provided their own arms and armour. In battle, each officer would be armed with two wheellock pistols and a rapier. A handful of officers may instead have carried a sabre, a sidearm that acquired a certain level of popularity during the years when the late King John maintained good relations with the Commonwealth. However, by the time of King Charles the use of sabres was mostly discontinued.

An under-officer, too, was armed with rapier and perhaps pistols. Unlike officers, under-officers in the Swedish army received their arms from the Crown. At the time of Sweden's war in Muscovy infantry under-officers typically carried halberds. In the sixteenth century, the Swedish halberd was essentially a short poleaxe fitted with a spearhead. The cutting edge was convex in the manner of an axe, and the weapon was primarily used as a cutting weapon. However, in the 1570s a more elaborate style of halberd with a concave cutting edge and a longer pole was introduced from Germany. This halberd was primarily used as a weapon for stabbing, in the Continental manner. The German halberd was used by Drabant Guards and likely under-officers in other infantry units as well. The Drabant-style halberd, as it was called, appears to have been larger and heavier as well as longer. Some halberds were apparently called 'double halberds' so are believed to have had two cutting edges.[57]

King Charles's rapier. German blade made by Clemens Horn, Solingen, c. 1595-1600. Swept hilt of silver made at the turn of the century by Johan Pedersson, Stockholm. Weight 1.50 kg. Blade length 92.7 cm, width 38.0 mm. Total length 114.4 cm. (Royal Armoury, Stockholm)

---

56 Barkman, *Gustaf II Adolfs regementsorganisation*, p.79; Generalstaben, *Sveriges krig* 1, p.104.
57 Barkman, *Kungl. Svea livgardes historia* 2, pp.606–17.

THE SWEDISH MILITARY ESTABLISHMENT

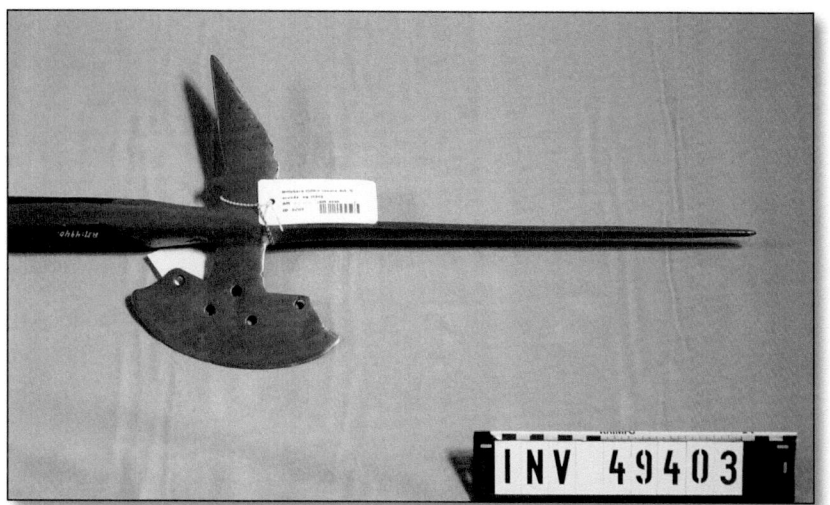

Swedish halberd of the traditional poleaxe style, sixteenth century. Found at Sorunda, Södermanland. (Army Museum, Stockholm; AM.049403)

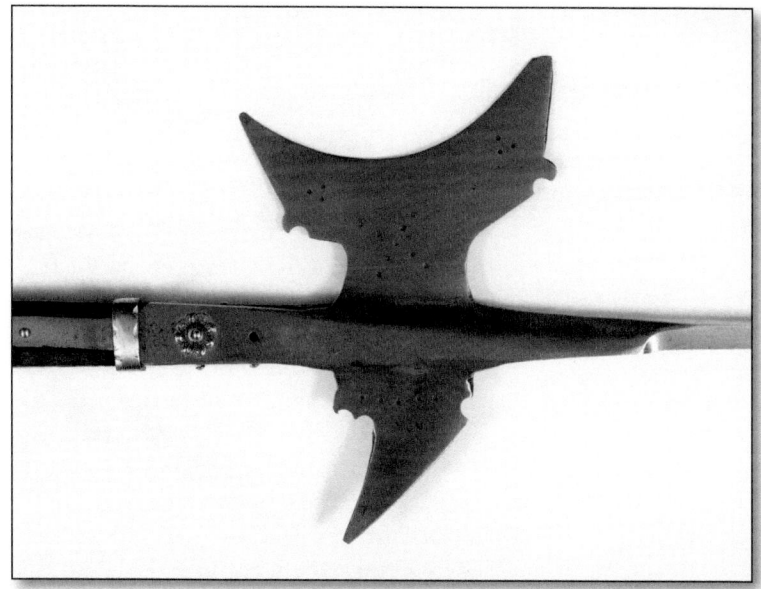

The Drabant-style halberd with concave cutting edge was introduced in the 1570s and known under this name from 1582 onwards. This more utilitarian Drabant-style halberd was probably manufactured in Germany. Halberds actually used by the Drabant Guard were often gilded, but by the time of Sweden's war in Muscovy, utilitarian Drabant-style halberds were likely delivered to many under-officers. (Army Museum, Stockholm; AM.056179)

SWEDEN'S WAR IN MUSCOVY 1609-1617

Partisan issued to King Charles's Drabant Guard, carrying the royal cypher C R S (*Carolus Rex Sueciae*, 'Charles, King of Sweden'). Manufactured in the period 1604-1611. (Royal Armoury, Stockholm)

Partisans were known in Sweden but were issued to under-officers instead of halberds only in 1590 and then again from some point between 1616 and 1622 (an exact year cannot be determined since records for these years seem to be missing).[58] In 1608, the Stockholm Armoury distributed 1,441 regular halberds, 207 Drabant-style halberds, and four partisans.[59]

From 1600 onwards, the captain and lieutenant of the Drabant Guard each carried a highly decorated gilded partisan with tassels. All other men of the Drabant Guard carried halberds, which from King Charles's coronation in 1607 onwards were gilded in the manner of the late King Erik's time.

Under-officers probably wore helmets as well as gorgets as a symbol of rank, at least judging from examples a decade later.[60] Some might also have worn a cuirass, with tassets to protect the upper thighs if serving in a pike unit.

In 1609, King Charles ordered the arms factory in Arboga to resume production of round shields (Swedish: *rudass*, *rundass*, or *rundel*; known on the Continent as *rondache*). His reasons for this decision are unclear. It is possible that some infantry officers, perhaps the company captains, each carried a round shield. While such shields were distributed in small numbers (apparently one per company), we do not know how they were used. Although originally intended for use on the battlefield by *rodeleros* or sword-and-buckler men in the Spanish and Dutch manner, in the Swedish army they were since the reign of King John far more frequently used in siege warfare.[61] The use of soldiers armed with round shields in the Life Guard of Maurice of Nassau may have influenced Swedish practices.[62] In 1610, Arboga delivered full sword-and-buckler gear for 162 men and 288 additional shields to the Crown.[63]

---

58   Barkman, *Kungl. Svea livgardes historia* 2, p.635; Jakobsson, *Lantmilitär beväpning och beklädnad*, p.90.
59   Jonas Hedberg (ed.), *Kungl. Artilleriet: Medeltid och äldre vasatid* (Stockholm: Militärhistoriska Förlaget, 1975), p.475 (Appendix 11).
60   Evident from the 1626 painting of the Norrland Territorial Regiment by Nicolas de la Fage, Karlberg Palace.
61   Hamilton, *Afhandling*, p.119; Jakobsson, *Lantmilitär beväpning och beklädnad*, p.115; Barkman, *Kungl. Svea livgardes historia* 2, p.212.
62   Eduard Wagner, *European Weapons & Warfare 1618–1648* (London: Octopus Books, 1979), p.104.
63   Barkman, *Kungl. Svea livgardes historia* 2, pp.622–3.

THE SWEDISH MILITARY ESTABLISHMENT

Soldier armed with round shield. A Swedish infantry captain was probably armed in this manner. (Adam van Breen, *De Nassausche Wapen-Handelinge*, 1618)

SWEDEN'S WAR IN MUSCOVY 1609-1617

Arquebusiers and Musketeers

In the early seventeenth century, most Swedish infantry were unarmoured arquebusiers. In Sweden, the infantry arquebus (Swedish: *hake* or *rör*) was, apparently, quite long, since they were known as 'long guns' (*långbössor*). The typical calibre tended to increase over time, from 30 bore (that is, drilled for a bore size equivalent to a ball weighing one thirtieth of a pound, or expressed differently, equivalent to 30 balls per pound of lead, which corresponded to a nominal calibre of 13.9 mm) in the early 1590s to mostly 16 bore (16 balls per pound of lead, with a nominal calibre of 16.8 mm) at the time of Sweden's war in Muscovy.[64] This weapon frequently came with a snaplock or snaphance lock which employed a fire-stone to strike fire. The fire-stone was often a flintstone, so the mechanism foreshadowed the later flintlock. The arquebus was not used with a fork rest.

The province of Småland was known for its production of fine-calibre, rifled hunting guns, which were sometimes used in war. We do not know if the men who carried them were dedicated snipers or simply had to rely on local stocks.[65]

The significantly heavier and more powerful Dutch 10-bore matchlock musket (10 balls per pound of lead, corresponding to a nominal calibre of 19.7 mm) was known in Sweden. It was possibly first introduced from the Dutch Republic in 1592, when 65 muskets were procured (even though the Dutch government pre-authorised the sale of 200).[66] These guns were used with a fork rest. In 1608, the Stockholm Armoury distributed 1,875 matchlock muskets, as compared to 1,108 snaplock ones. Yet, in the same year the Armoury also distributed 671 snaplock arquebuses, 536 arquebuses of other types, and 50 carbines.[67] Clearly, no uniformity with regard to firearms had yet developed in the army. Gustavus Adolphus soon learnt to prefer the heavy and sturdy 10-bore matchlock muskets, which were also cheaper to manufacture and maintain. When after the Kalmar War he modernised the armament of the Swedish army, he ordered the replacement of the arquebus with the matchlock musket.[68] Perhaps

Musketeer. (Jacob de Gheyn, *Wapenhandelinghe van Roers, Musquetten ende Spiessen*, 1607)

---

64 Josef Alm, *Eldhandvapen 1: Från deras tidigaste förekomst till slaglåsets allmänna införande*. (Stockholm: Rediviva, 1976), pp.151, 197.
65 Alm, *Eldhandvapen* 1, p.151.
66 Alm, *Eldhandvapen* 1, p.152; Generalstaben, *Sveriges krig* 1, p.76 n.2.
67 Hedberg, *Kungl. Artilleriet: Medeltid och äldre vasatid*, p.475 (Appendix 11).
68 Fredholm von Essen, *Lion from the North* 1, pp.155–65.

THE SWEDISH MILITARY ESTABLISHMENT

it was the inferior performance of the Swedish arquebus that convinced young Gustavus Adolphus of the need to re-arm.

At first, matchlock muskets were imported from the Continent where this weapon was already in common use. The matchlock was an old design and not the most advanced type of gun lock. However it was not the lock but the calibre of the old arquebus that was obsolete. Swedish gunsmiths were experienced in manufacturing both wheellock and snaplock (snaphance) guns, which relied on gun locks that were more advanced than the imported matchlocks.[69] It has been suggested that the snaplock was invented in Sweden, which is unknown but possible.[70] A wheellock works by spinning a spring-loaded steel wheel against a piece of pyrite to generate sparks, whilstin a snaplock, a spring-loaded cock strikes a flintstone onto hardened steel (known as the frizzen) to generate a shower of sparks. In either case, the sparks ignite the gunpowder in the priming pan. In comparison, a matchlock is a simple mechanism which merely lowers a burning slow-match, held in a clamp at the end of a small curved lever (known as a serpentine), into the priming pan to ignite the gunpowder.

In 1612, new muskets from the Continent arrived which were used to arm the infantry from Dalecarlia and Västmanland. The rest of the infantry was instructed to use snaphance weapons, which must have meant either their old 16-bore arquebuses or newly made 12-bore muskets, with a nominal calibre of 18.5 mm. In 1613, the Stockholm arsenal received 2,094 matchlock muskets but also 1,419 snaphance muskets. In some regiments, the old 16-bore arquebus remained in service into the 1620s.[71]

Even though Gustavus Adolphus after the war set out to re-arm his troops with muskets, re-armament took time. Snaphance weapons continued to be manufactured for many years, although when made for military use, they were henceforth more often 12-bore muskets.

During Sweden's war in Muscovy, arquebusiers and musketeers generally did not wear armour. As sidearm, they carried double-edged rapiers or

Musketeer. (Jacob de Gheyn, *Wapenhandelinghe van Roers, Musquetten ende Spiessen*, 1607)

---

69   The wheellock was in seventeenth-century German known as *Züntschloss*. Another common term was *Feuerschloss* (firelock), which, however, might be used for any gunlock. The corresponding Swedish terms were then *sintlås* and *fyrlås*. The modern German term for wheellock is *Radschloss*.
70   Josef Alm, *Arméns eldhandvapen förr och nu* (Stockholm: Kungl. Armémuseum, 1953), p.36
71   Alm, *Eldhandvapen* 1, pp.160, 163.

Late sixteenth-century tessak. (Royal Armoury, Stockholm; photo: Samuel Uhrdin, Livrustkammaren/SHM)

Early seventeenth-century tessak with clam shell hilt. War booty popularly known as 'Zisca's sword'. Blade length 78 cm, total length 90 cm, width 5 cm. (Skokloster Castle; photo: Göran Schmidt)

Musketeer, 1611. The jacket has several short tails and shoulder straps divided into tongues. Sleeves and breeches are fairly wide. The hat is decorated with tall plumes. The collar is flat and semi-wide. King Charles's funeral armour, made in Stockholm in 1611. (Strängnäs Cathedral)

possibly the occasional remaining sabre. In 1601, instructions for service sidearms described rapiers as broad at the hilt (for strength) and narrow at the point (for thrusting). Sabres should be straight and suitable for thrusting, that is, less curved than those employed in the Commonwealth from which the weapon type hailed. A sabre should have quillons and a bar to protect the hand, which made it look more like a rapier and less like a sabre. The 1601 instructions suggest that the two weapon types were converging in Sweden.[72] Some Swedes also carried the tessak (Swedish: *tasshake*), or the probably very similar cutlass (Swedish: *kortlass*, from French: *coutelas*, or Italian: *coltellaccio*; 'knife').[73] The tessak (from German: *Tisacke, Dusack,*

---

72 Alm, *Blanka vapen*, p.29.
73 Alm, *Blanka vapen*, p.30, Heribert Seitz, *Svärdet och värjan som armévapen* (Stockholm: Kungl. Armémuseum, 1955), pp.34–8, 92–4.

Dussägge, or Czech: *tesák* – the origin of the name is disputed[74]) was a cutting sword, occasionally curved but mostly straight and, unlike the Eastern sabre, always with a western hilt of the basket or clamshell type. Blade length varied from about 55 to 83 cm, with a total length of up to 96 cm. Blade width usually ranged from 3 to 5 cm. The tessak was already considered obsolete on the Continent. By the time of King Charles, all these terms seem to have been used more or less interchangeably.

Pikemen and Halberdiers

Most infantrymen who did not carry muskets were armed with pikes. The pike (early seventeenth-century Swedish: *spets*, 'point') was an important offensive and defensive weapon that also safeguarded the infantry from enemy cavalry. On the Continent and until recently also in Sweden, a pikeman was traditionally valued higher than an arquebusier. Yet, the task of carrying a pike and the associated armour had been unpopular with the men ever since their pay was reduced to that of an arquebusier.

First John of Nassau, and then King Charles himself at the disastrous defeat at Kircholm, realised that the Swedish army needed more armoured pikemen. As mentioned, Sweden also needed armoured cuirassiers, so the same means was taken to raise both. In 1606, the Crown announced the aforementioned programme known as 'shield-knight service' (*skölderusttjänst*), which essentially meant that anybody who could supply himself with the required armour and a warhorse would, in effect, become a noble and enjoy a number of privileges (but not, as we have seen, hereditary nobility). Although this programme was primarily introduced to raise cuirassiers, those who had the means to acquire a helmet, breast- and backplate, and pike and were willing to serve on foot as pikemen were eligible, too. King Charles hoped to raise 13 companies of such pikemen. However, the programme was a failure and produced few volunteers. Ultimately, two companies of pikemen were raised, one in Småland and one in Västergötland, and they remained in service when the war in Muscovy broke out. The programme was not extended to Finland, which lacked suitable men of means and moreover, needed immediate replacements for those men who had been lost at Kircholm.[75]

It seems that the failure of the shield-knight programme made King Charles rethink his options. From the defeat at Kircholm until the beginning of the Kalmar War (that is, from 1606 to 1611), the Crown issued

---

74 The weapon was commonplace in southern Germany, Austria, and the western Balkans in the late fifteenth and sixteenth centuries and remained in use among peasants and brawny Viennese journeymen into the eighteenth century. Many believe that the term derives from Old German *sax*, that is, a single-edged short sword.
75 Generalstaben, *Sveriges krig* 1, pp.93–5.

to the infantry so many halberds relative to the number of pikes that it seems possible that King Charles wanted to create units of halberdiers instead of pikemen. He possibly regarded the halberd with its increasingly long spearhead as a more versatile thrusting weapon than the longer pike.[76] If so, the plan failed. We hear nothing of units of halberdiers, even though individuals armed with this weapon may have fought in the war. Moreover, as soon as Gustavus Adolphus succeeded his father, he made a major effort to increase the number of pikemen. In 1612, he appointed a special pike manufacturer, who was ordered to make 'as many pikes as were needed or he could manage'.[77] In 1613 he ordered every peasant in Stockholm and Uppsala Counties to deliver two to three pike shafts. Similar instructions followed elsewhere, and in later years as well. Ash wood was recommended, but pine was acceptable, the instruction clarified. In 1613, the pikes were required to be 10 cubits (5.94 m) long. Because of the ongoing wars on the eastern front against the Commonwealth and Muscovy, Swedish officers generally held that pikes had to be longer than the long lances employed by Polish hussars for infantry to successfully withstand a Polish cavalry charge. However, in 1616 the regulation length was decreased to nine cubits (5.35 m), which corresponded to Continental practices and henceforth remained the standard Swedish pike length. Based on surviving seventeenth-century pikes in the Royal Armoury, Stockholm, and Skokloster Castle, the pike-head was made of hard steel, about 10 to 14 cm in length (longer if the socket was included), and four-sided in shape. The pike shaft had a non-uniform diameter that ranged from about 3 to 3.75 cm and was from the head downwards strengthened by two iron reinforcements, 50 to 70 cm in length.[78] The section used as a hand grip – sometimes designated with two rings, one at each side – was often square or grooved to facilitate a safe grip, or covered in cloth. Pike shafts were preferably ash or maple wood, although as noted, pine and eventually aspen were acceptable, too.[79] The

Pikeman. (Jacob de Gheyn, *Wapenhandelinghe van Roers, Musquetten ende Spiessen*, 1607)

---

76 Barkman, *Kungl. Svea livgardes historia* 2, pp.616–17.
77 Gustaf Petri, Kungl. *Första livgrenadjärregementets historia 1: Östgötafänikorna till och med år 1618* (Stockholm: P. A. Norstedt, 1926), pp.413–14.
78 Alm, *Blanka vapen*, pp.140–41.
79 Hamilton, *Afhandling*, p.122. The common practice among modern-day re-

THE SWEDISH MILITARY ESTABLISHMENT

pike shafts may have been painted black, especially later in the century since this seems to have been a common practice in Germany, and based on the surviving pikes, apparently in Sweden too. There is, unfortunately, no way of knowing whether surviving, black-painted pike shafts were painted when first issued or only later.

The pike was exclusively a battlefield weapon. Most garrison regiments only carried arquebuses. In fact, when a pike-armed unit was deployed to garrison a town or fortress, standard practice was to supply the pikemen with arquebuses instead of pikes. The commandant would be ordered to store the pikes until the unit again was ordered into the field.[80] Likewise, for obvious reasons pikes were not used when troops were sent out to forage,

Pikeman. (Jacob de Gheyn, *Wapenhandelinghe van Roers, Musquetten ende Spiessen*, 1607)

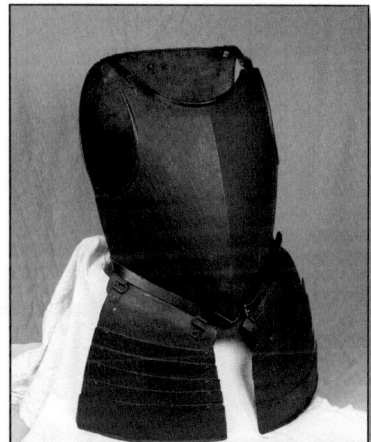

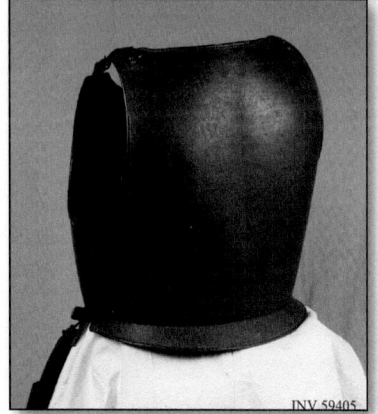

Pikeman armour, 1600–1630. (Army Museum, Stockholm, AM.059405)

---

    enactors to employ factory-made pike shafts of uniform diameter from point to butt does not correspond to early modern practices, and additionally makes the pike wobbly when in operation.

80 Alm, *Blanka vapen*, p.142; citing a letter dated 28 July 1630 to Lars Kagg, the commandant in Anklam. There is no reason to believe that the practice then was a new one.

SWEDEN'S WAR IN MUSCOVY 1609-1617

Infantry helmet, 1600–1630. (Army Museum, Stockholm, AM.061183)

or for small war. Pikemen deployed for shipboard duty were also re-armed, this time with guns with snaphance locks.[81]

Pikemen were expected to wear a full set of armour consisting of both breastplate and backplate, gorget, and tassets to protect the upper thighs. A pikeman would also wear a helmet, commonly of the cabasset type (in Scandinavia often referred as a pear helmet, because of its pear-, some say almond-shaped, top with a small point). Inside the helmet, the soldier wore padding made of flax or, for those officers who could afford it, cotton.[82] Some Swedish pikemen possibly wore helmets of the morion type. After the Kalmar War, the Danish Crown in 1615–1616 purchased 119 sets of captured Swedish infantry armour from a military entrepreneur, including helmets of a type in Danish referred to as a 'moulun'.[83]

Each pikeman carried a rapier as a sidearm. Pikemen in some regiments might be armed with an axe instead of rapier. For instance, in late 1611 an order was issued to supply some soldiers with axes instead of rapiers.[84] Whether this was the result of a shortage of rapiers, perhaps the most likely explanation, or an expected need for fortification tools remains unknown.

Harquebusiers

At the beginning of the seventeenth century, most Swedish cavalry, whether of provincial or enlisted origin, served as unarmoured harquebusiers. Unfortunately for the historian, the available narrative sources hardly ever distinguish between cuirassiers and harquebusiers, all of whom routinely are described only as cavalry. The armament was certainly similar. Each harquebusier carried a fine-calibre arquebus or carbine as primary armament, a rapier, and one or two wheellock pistols. Some may have worn a helmet, gorget, breastplate, and occasionally even a backplate and armour for the upper arms. The full set of harquebusier armour (Swedish: *skyttetyg*) was probably only worn by a minority.[85]

The cavalry arquebus usually came with a wheellock, although a few snaphances were used as well. The Continental manner of employing the cavalry arquebus at this time involved hanging it from a swivel attached to a bandolier across the left shoulder, so that it could be fired without unhooking from the bandolier. For this reason, the weapon was in Sweden referred to as a 'bandolier arquebus' (*bantlärhake*). Swedish harquebusiers

---

81 Alm, *Eldhandvapen* 1, p.161.
82 Alm, *Blanka vapen*, p.253; citing Wallhausen, *Kriegskunst zu Fuß*.
83 Otto Blom, *Kristian Den Fjerdes Artilleri, Hans Tøihuse og Vaabenforraad* (Copenhagen: C. C. Lose, 1877), p.336.
84 Hamilton, *Afhandling*, p.121.
85 Jakobsson, *Lantmilitär beväpning och beklädnad*, p.116.

THE SWEDISH MILITARY ESTABLISHMENT

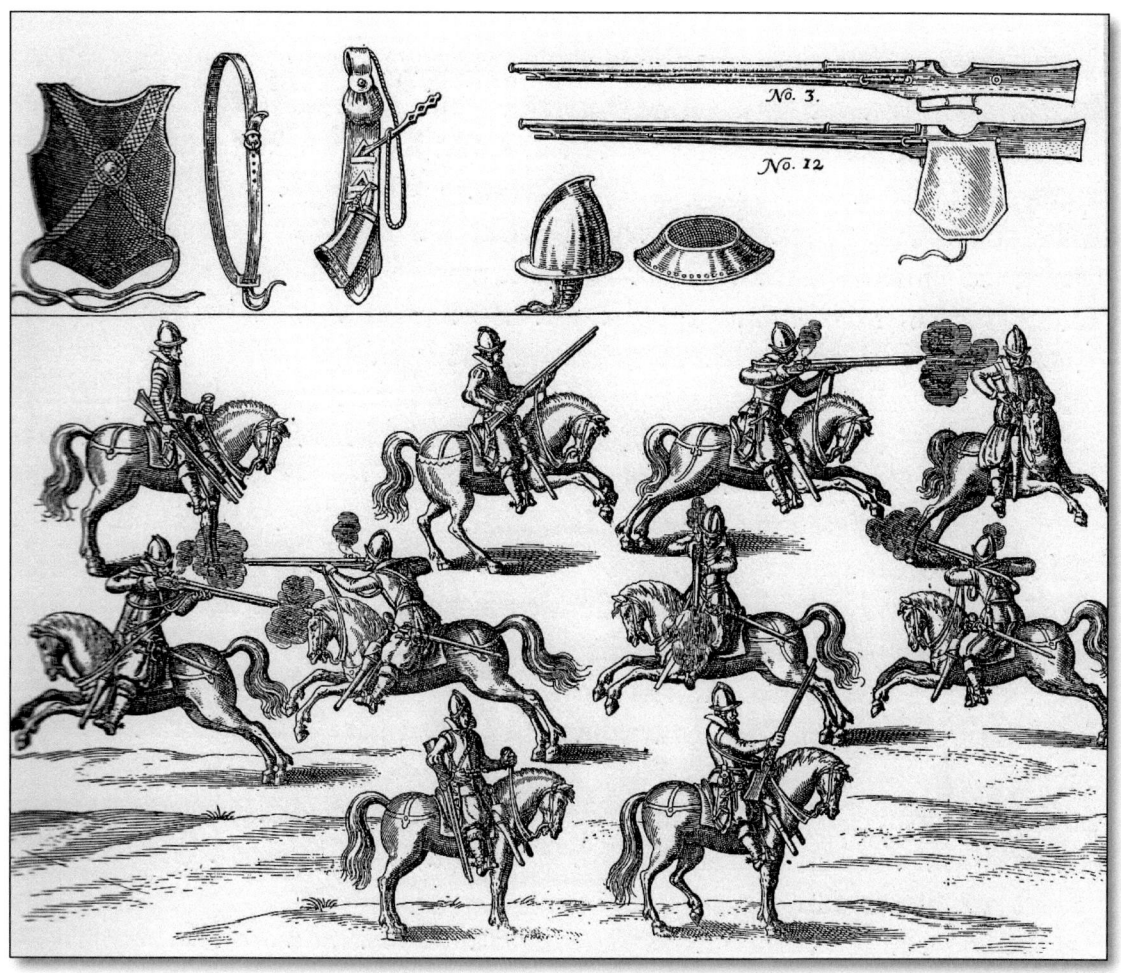

Harquebusier weapons and equipment. Breastplate, bandolier with arquebus hook, leather strap with ammunition pouch, wheellock spanner, gunpowder flasks; arquebuses, one with lock cover; helmet, gorget. (Wallhausen, *Kriegskunst zu Pferdt*, 1616)

were identical to those enlisted abroad. Following Continental style, the bandolier arquebus was commonly around 1.2 m long and had a calibre of 16 bore (16.8 mm). On the left side of the gunlock, a fairly large leather flap was screwed in place which could be folded over the gunlock to protect it. On his right side, the harquebusier carried a special leather strap from his belt with a powder-horn, priming flask, ammunition pouch, and wheellock spanner.[86]

The Swedish harquebusiers were already at this time in the process of replacing the arquebus with the carbine. As far as is known, carbines were first introduced to Sweden in 1600, when 100 such weapons were ordered from Copenhagen. They were to have a barrel length of about 0.7 m.[87] Based on later examples, total length was probably similar to the arquebus or possibly slightly shorter. A carbine, like the musket which was also

---

86 Alm, *Eldhandvapen* 1, pp.196–7.
87 Jakobsson, *Lantmilitär beväpning och beklädnad*, p.9.

introduced around this time, had a larger calibre than the obsolete arquebus. However, the wheellock remained in common use among horsemen.

The practice of firing the gun without unhooking it from the bandolier was discontinued with the introduction of carbines. Instead, the carbine was carried in a saddle holster. Likewise, the harquebusier's belt strap for equipment was in most cases discarded, too. Instead, the men would carry powder-horn, priming flask, ammunition pouch, and wheellock spanner on the outside of the saddle holster.[88]

Cuirassiers

Full set of shot-proof cuirassier armour, 1620-1630. Blackened and lined with soft leather. Those used during Sweden's war in Muscovy were in most cases identical. (Skokloster Castle)

First instituted in (probably) 1280, when members of the nobility agreed to raise a force of armoured cavalry from their retainers when called to arms, the oldest unit in the Swedish army was that of the noble cavalry. This traditional military duty was known by an old name that can be translated as military service but originally signified knight-service, that is, service on horseback (Swedish: *rosstjänst, russtjänst, rusttjänst*). From 1571 onwards, it was known as the retinue of nobles (*riddarskapets russtiänst*; later *adelsfanan*). The retinue of nobles served as cuirassiers but was numerically small, consisting only of a few hundred men. Swedish cuirassiers looked much the same as those on the Continent.[89]

Cuirassiers were few in the Swedish army, since the armour was costly and out of reach even for many nobles, and since the weight of the armour demanded the use of larger horses than Sweden easily could breed at home. According to regulations from 1621, which reflected older practices, each cuirassier should bring a good and strong horse of 14 hands (140 cm). He should also bring a second cavalryman on a horse of 13 hands, armed with helmet, breast- and backplate, rapier, and a pair of wheellock pistols. A third horse and baggage servant should be brought as well, but for the supply train.[90] Although these regulations were

---

88 Alm, *Eldhandvapen* 1, pp.121, 154, 196, 213; Alm, *Arméns eldhandvapen*, pp.121-2.
89 The retinue of nobles was last raised in 1743, and remained as an organisation until 1901.
90 Hamilton, *Afhandling*, pp.201-2; Jakobsson, *Lantmilitär beväpning och beklädnad*, p.118.

THE SWEDISH MILITARY ESTABLISHMENT

issued after the war in Muscovy, it is likely that the Crown held similar expectations beforehand.

A cuirassier was armed with a pair of wheellock pistols and a rapier. Pistols made in Sweden in the first years of the seventeenth century occasionally came with snaphance locks instead of wheellocks. However, wheellocks soon became standard equipment.[91] Early in the century, pistols were long, up to around 75 cm in length, with calibre varying widely around 57 or 58 bore (about 11 mm).[92] Later, the calibre increased to 18 bore (around 16.2 mm), which over time became the standard Swedish pistol calibre.[93]

Gorget, originally blackened, for cuirassier armour, first half of the seventeenth century. (Skokloster Castle)

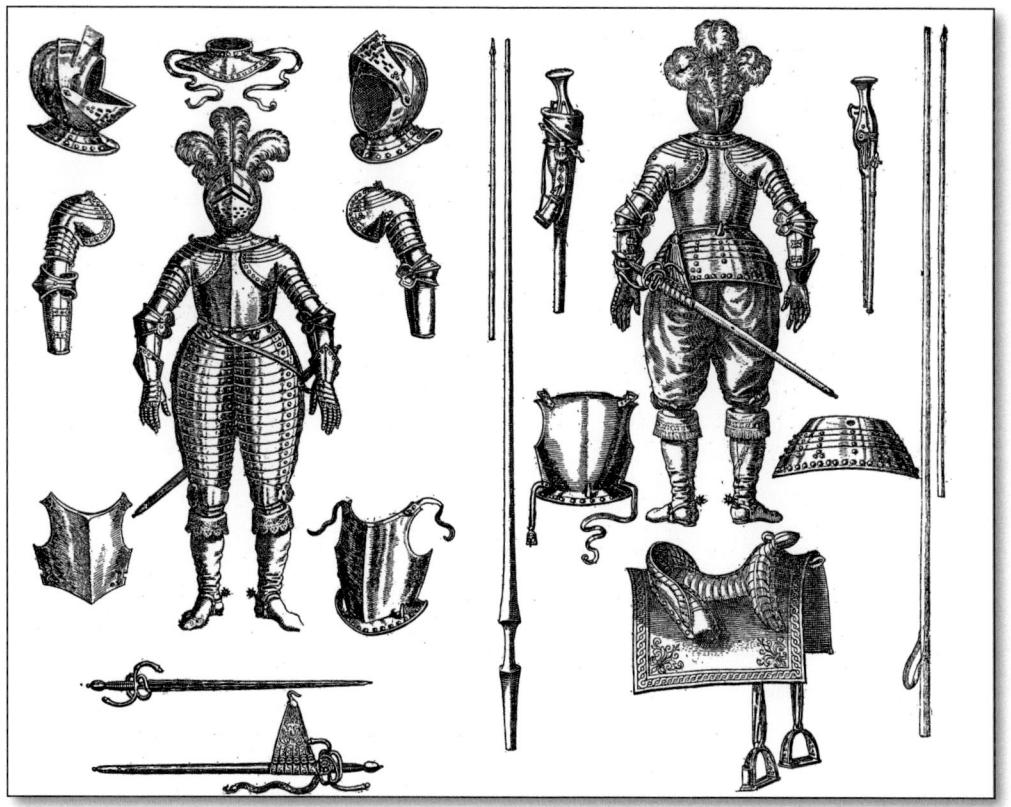

Cuirassier armour. (Wallhausen, *Kriegskunst zu Pferdt*)

---

91 Alm, *Eldhandvapen* 1, pp.154, 202, 213; Alm, *Arméns eldhandvapen*, pp.118, 121–2.
92 Alm, *Eldhandvapen* 1, p.200.
93 Jakobsson, *Lantmilitär beväpning och beklädnad*, p.116 n.3.

SWEDEN'S WAR IN MUSCOVY 1609-1617

Cuirassier on horseback. (Wallhausen, *Kriegskunst zu Pferdt*)

Full set of blackened Danish shot-proof cuirassier armour, 1620-1650. (Army Museum, Stockholm)

Blackened Danish cuirassier's visored helmet, 1620-1650. (Army Museum, Stockholm)

THE SWEDISH MILITARY ESTABLISHMENT

A cuirassier wore a visored close helmet or burgonet, a gorget for the neck, three-quarter armour that covered the entire upper body and both arms as well as the front half of the legs down to and including the knee, and high riding boots. A full set of Swedish cuirassier armour (Swedish: *drabbtyg*) weighed around 25 kg and was generally blackened. Until about 1620, the breastplate was commonly of the peascod belly or goose belly type, which then fell out of fashion. This had already happened in Germany, where Wallhausen in 1615, in *Kriegskunst zu Fuß*, had argued that the style was 'more suited to pregnant women than to soldiers'.[94]

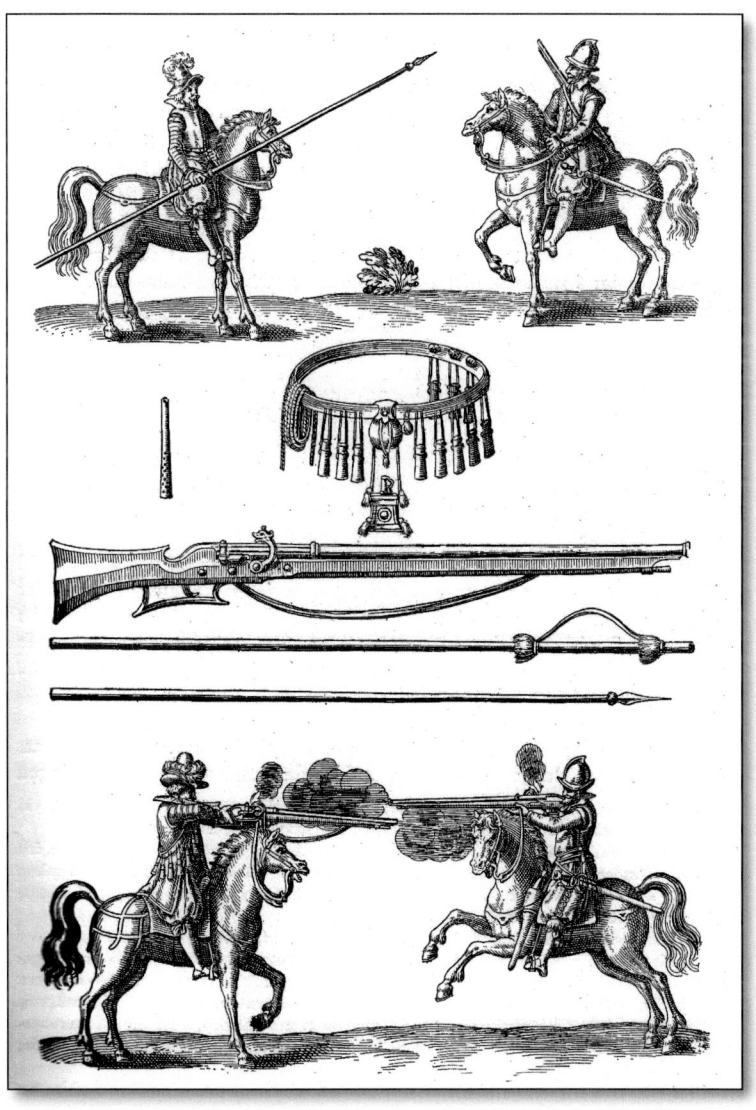

Dragoon with equipment. (Wallhausen, *Kriegskunst zu Pferdt*)

Dragoons

Dragoons were mounted musketeers who moved on horseback but fought on foot. Sweden began to use dragoons early: there were already dragoons in the Swedish army in 1580. There was also at least one French dragoon company, under Captain Adam Richard de La Chapelle (d. 1636), a French petardier and ultimately a dragoon officer who enlisted in 1611 for the Kalmar War, and from 1613 onwards served in Muscovy.

Dragoons used the same muskets as other infantry. Each also carried a rapier. Some may have been equipped with axes as well. Dragoons wore helmets but no breastplates. They wore shoes, not riding boots, and were not issued with spurs.

---

94   Alm, *Blanka vapen*, pp.242, 251.

Artillerymen

Sweden rapidly adopted the Spanish–Dutch artillery system, which was quickly becoming the common standard for central and north European artillery. The Spanish–Dutch system matured in 1609, when the General of Artillery in the Spanish Netherlands, Charles Bonaventure de Longueval (1571–1621), Count of Bucquoy, together with the artillery professionals Cristóbal Lechuga (d. 1621) and Diego Ufano (fl. 1609–1612) simplified and reduced the large number of previous artillery calibres into a comprehensive system of only four standard calibres. Ufano explained the need for reform because:

> the diversity and great confusion among the old cannons caused a lot of effort and labour in obtaining the appropriate cannon balls. Nowadays we have but a single range of artillery, all based on the full cannon and its fractions drawn to the eighth, so the appropriate munitions are easy to obtain and handle ...[95]

In the French edition, published within a year, the anonymous translator was so enthusiastic about the innovation that he expanded upon Ufano's declaration of intent with the following words:

> all the necessary munitions are very easy to find. It is truly remarkable to be content with these four calibres ...[96]

The Spanish–Dutch system used the same terminology as the obsolete sixteenth-century German system, from which it had emerged, but for different calibres. First, as in the past the new system divided the artillery into two basic classes: the short-barrelled, short-range siege artillery (German: *Mauerbrecher*, 'battering ram') and the long-barrelled, long-range field artillery (German: *Schlange*, 'snake'; in other languages better known as culverins, ultimately from Latin *coluber*, 'snake' and *colubrinus*, 'serpent-like'). The long-barrelled culverins were henceforth indeed regarded as the primary class of artillery, since they were more versatile, higher velocity weapons of longer range. While both classes of artillery also were used as shipboard cannons, the long-barrelled ones seem to have been preferred in this role.

---

95   Diego Ufano, *Tratado de la artilleria y uso della* (Brussels: Juan Momarte, 1613), p.38. Ufano's work is generally believed first to have appeared in 1612. Incidentally, Ufano seems to have been the first European artillery specialist to identify the origin of cannons and gunpowder in China.

96   Diego Ufano, *Artillerie, ou vraye instruction de l'arttillerie et de ses appartenances* (Rouen: Jean Berthelin, 1628), pp.14–15. The first French edition was published in 1614 by Johann Theodor de Bry, who simultaneously had the book translated into and published in German.

Then, each class of artillery was divided into four standard calibres. The system used the 48-pounder as baseline for siege artillery and the 24-pounder as baseline for field artillery (Table 5). In addition to the 48-pounder, the Spanish–Dutch artillery system made allowance for the continued use of the old *Doppelkartaune* or *cañon double*, a 96-pounder that was very difficult to move.[97] However, professionals soon noticed that even the 48-pounder was too heavy for easy operation. They also discovered that the 24-pounder was not only lighter, easier to move, and took up less space than the 48-pounder, but it also consumed less gunpowder and had a higher rate of fire, yet produced almost the same effect against a masonry wall. Henceforth, the 24-pounder became the standard siege cannon, a position it would retain until the end of the nineteenth century, when the 24-pounder was finally superseded by modern rifled artillery.

Although the Spanish–Dutch artillery system quickly became the common standard among professionals, master artillerymen occasionally used inconsistent terminology. A quarter culverin might, for instance, be called a pelican, and the falcon (more properly, eighth culverin) inspired the name falconet for yet smaller-calibre long-barrelled guns. Moreover, cannons for practical reasons often fired significantly lighter loads than their official rating would suggest.[98] Nonetheless, it is obvious from contemporary orders and reports that the north European armies fully embraced the Spanish–Dutch artillery system, and in fact had done so already by this time.

Table 5. The Spanish-Dutch artillery system, with the calibre determined according to the base weight in pounds of iron of the appropriate cannonball.

Siege Artillery

Name (in English / German / French / Spanish)	Munition (Calibre)
Full or whole cannon / *Volle* or *Ganze Kartaune* / *canon commun* / *cañon comun*	48
Demi-cannon / *Halbkartaune* / *demie canon* / *medio cañon*	24
Quarter cannon / *Quartierkartaune* or *Viertelkartaune* / *quart du canon* / *quarto de cañon*	12
Eighth cannon / *Achtelkartaune* / *huictiesme du canon* / *octavo de cañon*	6

---

97 Interestingly, the German term *Kartaune* derived from from Italian *quartana bombarda*, that is, a quarter cannon. Now it was the turn of the *Kartaune* to be subdivided into increasingly smaller fractions. Armies were rapidly exchanging the huge siege cannons of the past for more efficient lightweight models.

98 This, together with differences imposed by the quality of gunpowder, made some contemporary descriptions of artillery fire so unlike the manuals by Ufano and others that misunderstandings frequently arose among later scholars with regard to the respective calibre-weight ratios of the two classes of cannons.

Field Artillery (Culverins)

Name (in English / German / French / Spanish)	Munition (Calibre)
Full or whole culverin / *Volle* or *Ganze Feldschlange* / *couleurine commune* / *culebrina comun*	24
Demi-culverin / *Halbe Feldschlange* / *demie couleurine* / *media culebrina*	12
Quarter culverin / *Quartierschlange* or *Viertelschlange* / *quart de couleurine* / *quarto de culebrina*	6
Falcon / *Falkon, Falkaune*, or *Achtelschlange* / *faulcon* or *faulconneau* / *falcon*	3

The Swedish siege artillery included 96-pounders (Swedish: *dubbelkartoger*), 48-pounders (*helkartoger*), 36-pounders (*trekvartskartoger*), 24-pounders (*halvkartoger*), and 12-pounders (*kvartskartoger* or *kvarterstycken*).

In addition, the Swedish artillery included long-barrelled cannons of the culverin class: 24-pounders (*helslangor, notslangor*, or *fältslangor*; that is, 'field snakes'), 18-pounders (*trekvartsslangor*), 12-pounders (*halvslangor*), and 6-pounders (*kvartsslangor*). Smaller-calibre long-barrelled cannons were known as falcons (*falkoner*), and guns of even smaller calibre than these were known as falconets (*falkonetter*).[99]

The total number of cannons was large, but the cannons were distributed throughout the country's castles, in Sweden, Finland, and Estonia. In 1600 the Stockholm Armoury alone contained an artillery park consisting of two 96-pounders (more on which below), five 48-pounders, four 36-pounders, and ten 24-pounders. The number of culverins was far larger, including fifty-one 24-pounders, thirty-five 18-pounders (of which 18 were bronze), one hundred and four 12-pounders (of which 79 were bronze), and large numbers of cannons of smaller calibre.[100]

It was understood that common calibres were beneficial for logistics and generally made the army more efficient. However, this was not yet reflected in the existing artillery parks. When the Danes in 1611 and 1612 took the castles of Kalmar and Gullberg, they found cannons of several different calibres, including 12-pounders, 10-pounders, and 3-pounders.[101] In 1582, two remarkably large, long-barrelled 96-pounders (*fyrdubbla notslangor*) were cast in Stockholm. Having a weight of 10,200 kg each, the two cannons were named Makalös ('peerless').[102] The poor road conditions in Sweden meant that siege artillery could often not be moved at all, except by river boat or ship. Even the field artillery, established in 1541 and kept up to date since then, lacked mobility, which often precluded its efficient use. We will

---

99   Jakobsson, *Lantmilitär beväpning och beklädnad*, pp.165–8.
100 Hedberg, *Kungl. Artilleriet: Medeltid och äldre vasatid*, p.470 (Appendix 7).
101 Jakobsson, *Lantmilitär beväpning och beklädnad*, p.65 n.3.
102 Hedberg, *Kungl. Artilleriet: Medeltid och äldre vasatid*, p.196.

THE SWEDISH MILITARY ESTABLISHMENT

see that Swedish artillery was only seldom used in Muscovy, where road conditions were even worse.

Sweden had abundant copper deposits, so the production of bronze cannons was never a problem. Even so, quite a few iron cannons were in the inventory, too. The iron cannons were generally regarded as inferior. While iron cannons were much cheaper than bronze cannons, they were also heavier, since iron is weaker than bronze and an iron cannon accordingly needs a thicker barrel. Moreover, if suffering from manufacturing flaws, iron cannons might burst without warning. Bronze cannons might burst too, but if so, would usually show a revealing swell first.

Finally, there were mortars and petards, which were used for siege operations. Petards were first introduced in Sweden from France in 1592. Cast of bronze or iron, petard sizes varied from 20 to 70 kg.[103] From 1602 onwards, the Swedish army used petards in Livonia.[104] The Swedes found petards very useful during the first years of the war in Muscovy, but the Muscovites soon learnt to counter this tactics by erecting fences in front of important gates so as to deny hostile petardiers access. Copying the Muscovite countermeasure, King Charles ordered two or three fences to be erected in front of important gates of his own fortifications.[105] For the Swedish army in Muscovy, mortars henceforth became the weapon of choice when laying siege to Muscovite fortresses.

Swedish siege artillery played only a minor role in the war in Muscovy. Considering the number of sieges, they should have been a prominent part of every siege. However, logistical difficulties and the poor quality of the road network prevented their use except in exceptional circumstances. Although possibly fired from Narva against neighbouring Ivangorod in 1610, we can only say with certainty that siege cannons proper were finally employed when Gustavus Adolphus laid siege to Pskov in 1615. The Swedish army had by then already deployed 24-pounder siege cannons in the castles of Viborg, Reval, Narva, and after its conquest, Ivangorod. It is believed that 48-pounder siege cannons were shipped from Sweden for the siege of Pskov.

Mines were manufactured to destroy the walls of enemy fortresses. The Stockholm Armoury contained huge mines, of gunpowder weights corresponding to 270, 1,303, and 1,480 lb (that is, 112, 541, and 614 kg).[106]

Hand grenades were in common use, especially during sieges. These were handled by artillerymen.

Although nowadays little known, Sweden employed pyrochemical munitions of various types. Rockets for battlefield illumination and incendiary uses were already in common use. This was a field in constant development, and the numbers and types of pyrotechnics in Sweden grew

---

103 Hedberg, *Kungl. Artilleriet: Medeltid och äldre vasatid*, pp.196, 203.
104 Barkman, *Kungl. Svea livgardes historia 2*, p.406.
105 Hedberg, *Kungl. Artilleriet: Medeltid och äldre vasatid*, p.203.
106 Hedberg, *Kungl. Artilleriet: Medeltid och äldre vasatid*, p.227.

Petard attached to a gate, with its constituent parts on the floor below. (Christoph Dambach, *Büchsenmeisterey*, 1605)

rapidly from 1540 onwards. A firework corps, separate from the Ordnance Corps, was established in 1570.[107] Pyrotechnical munitions remained in use in the seventeenth century, when mortars of various types capable of launching pyrotechnics were added to the weapons package. The artillery on occasion also fired toxic fuming balls (Swedish: *dunstkulor*), smoke-filled cannon balls which emitted toxic fumes – an early form of chemical warfare.

Since artillerymen also served as sappers, they carried a variety of tools such as pickaxes, spades, shovels, and axes. Attempts were made to introduce combination tools that also served as weapons. In 1600, the Crown ordered 6,000 military forks (German: *Sturmgabel*; Swedish: *stormgaffel*), a weapon type commonly employed for the destruction of gabions and fascines when storming enemy field fortifications.[108] Being essentially a civilian tool with some added offensive capability, the shape of military forks varied considerably. Most seem to have had hooks on the back so as to enable the pulling down of fascines and, possibly, enemies. However, the military fork is often confused with the *roncone* (also known as *runca*), which existed in great numbers on the Continent and by this time seems to have been more

---

107 Hedberg, *Kungl. Artilleriet: Medeltid och äldre vasatid*, p.241.
108 Barkman, *Kungl. Svea livgardes historia 2*, pp.617–18.

THE SWEDISH MILITARY ESTABLISHMENT

common than the outwardly somewhat similar partisan.[109] The *roncone* was characterised by its tines which were widened out to form cutting blades, while the central prong often was extended into a spike or spearhead. Since the Swedish Crown ordered such a large number of military forks at a time when soon-to-be King Charles experimented with halberds as surrogate pikes, there is some doubt about which weapon type he had in mind and exactly what the Swedish military fork looked like.

Artillerymen also handled most aspects of field engineering. The Swedish artillery train for this reason also carried 12 or 13 pontoons or boats, each about 4.5×2 m in size, for the construction of temporary bridges, together with all other necessary materials.[110]

Swedish artillerymen were armed with muskets and rapiers for personal protection and as a means to protect their cannons.[111] They generally dressed similarly to the infantry.

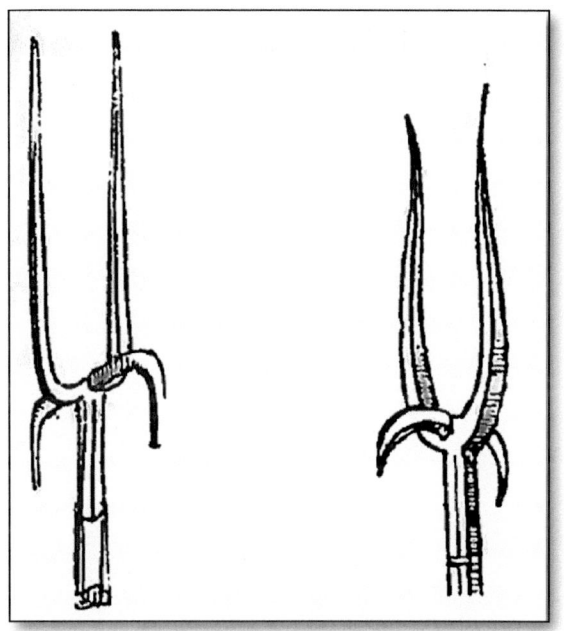

Right: Italian military fork employed at Geneva, 1612. Left: Italian or Swiss military fork from roughly the same period. Swedish military forks are generally believed to have been of similar type. (August Demmin, 1893)

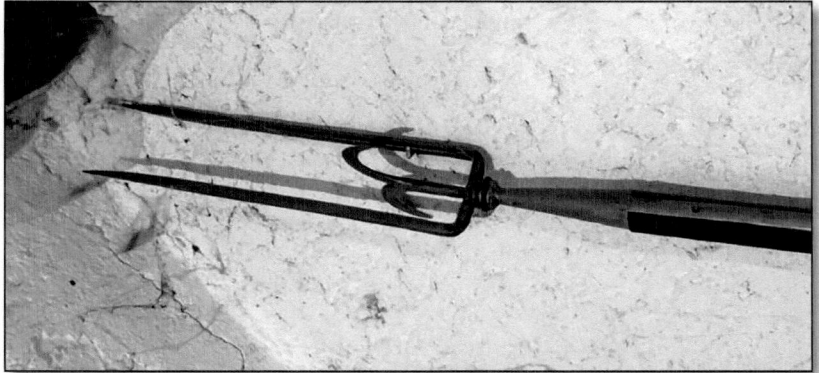

Military fork of Continental type.

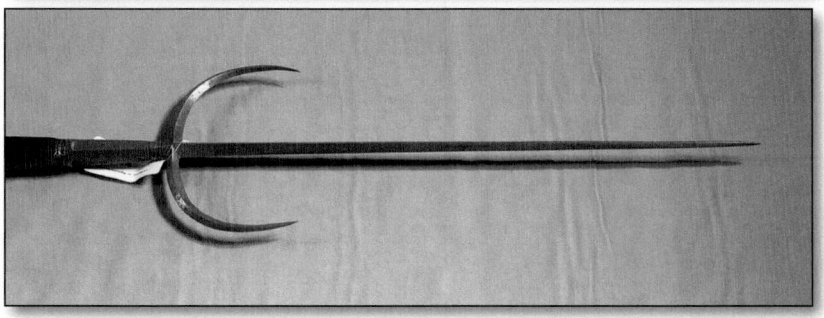

Roncone of uncertain date and provenience, from a Swedish collection. Essentially a civilian hay fork with an extended prong functioning as spike or spearhead, the *roncone* just as easily functioned as a partisan or half-pike. (Army Museum, Stockholm; AM.049495)

---

109 To confuse matters further, there was also a presumably Corsican variant, known as *korseke*.
110 Hedberg, *Kungl. Artilleriet: Medeltid och äldre vasatid*, p.231.
111 Hedberg, *Kungl. Artilleriet: Yngre vasatiden*, p.80.

Uniforms

Although national uniforms were not worn at the time of the war in Muscovy, units often presented a uniform appearance, since most Swedish soldiers received cloth for uniforms. Since cloth of the same type and colour (plain woollens were rarely issued except to the navy) were distributed at the same time, this meant that the men of a given unit commonly shared the same style and colour – at least until clothes wore out and individuals had to replace them wherever garments were found. However, details usually remain elusive. Some information gleaned from archival records show units and colour combinations which still may have been current at the time of the war in Muscovy (Table 6). Even so, we know from later records that cloth sometimes was issued every year or every second year, and the colour of the new cloth was typically different from the previous distribution. In short, the units would indeed often present a uniform appearance, but there were no fixed or even customary colours for particular units (with, occasionally, the only exception being guard units dressed up for festive occasions in the colours of the ruler's house). It is clear that Swedish and Finnish infantry often wore blue garments, but this was presumably because of common availability rather than choice.

Table 6. Known Swedish unit uniform colours (with their geographical origin in parenthesis), 1609–1617[112]

Drabant Guard	
King Charles's Drabant Guard of Foot (1610)	Yellow and blue, with grey woollen casack and hat
Gustavus Adolphus's Drabant Guard of Foot (1616)	Yellow-brown or red jackets with blue bands
- Officers and pikemen	Elk-skin buff coat with yellow silk threads
- Musketeers	Yellow jackets with black trimming
Cavalry	
Newly raised Swedish cavalry banners (1609)	
- Officers	Red, purple, sky blue, liver brown, or black
- Cavalrymen	Red, blue, or black of inferior quality
Hans Boije's Cavalry Banner (Finland, 1609)	Red, blue, black, or brown

---

112   Sources: primarily Höglund, *Från Karl Knutsson till Kristina*, pp.43–4, 95–9.

THE SWEDISH MILITARY ESTABLISHMENT

Lorentz Wagner's Cavalry Banner (Västergötland, 1609)	Brown, orange, red, liver brown, green, or fiole brown
Erik Bertilsson's Cavalry Banner (Finland, 1609)	Liver brown, blue, green
Daniel Golowitz's (Golovachev's?) Cavalry Banner (1609)	Red, blue, or green
Tomas Olofsson's Cavalry Banner (Finland, 1609)	Red or blue
Hans von Lünden's Cavalry Banner (Germany, 1609)	Green, blue, or red
Lindved Claesson Hästesko's Cavalry Banner (Finland, 1609)	Green, red, or liver brown
Lars Andersson's Cavalry Banner (Karelia, 1609)	Green, brown, or red
Carl Lake's Cavalry Banner (Västergötland, 1609)	Blue
Herman Dücker's Cavalry Banner (Germany, 1609)	Brown, red, orange, or green
Sten Carlsson's Cavalry Banner (Uppland, 1609)	Blue
Unidentified cavalry banner (1609)	Green or blue
Jacob De la Gardie's Life Cornet (1610)	
- Ensign	Red English cloth
- Corporals and cavalrymen	Blue or red
Life Banner (*Livfanan*, under Herman Wrangel, enlisted in Sweden, 1616)	Red and grey
Duke Julius Henry of Saxe-Lauenburg's Company of Horse (1613)	
- Officers	Pale blue velvet
- Cavalrymen	Blue, red, and grey cloth
Knut Håkansson Hand's Cavalry Banner (Småland, 1613)	Pale blue cloth
Samuel Cobron's Regiment (Scotland/England, three companies of horse, five of foot)	
- One company of horse (1613)	Fiole brown
- The others (1613)	blue
- All (1614)	Blue and grey cloth
- All (1615)	Black, green, red, and grey cloth
Jacques Bourguignon de Corobel's Cavalry Banner (1613)	Blue and grey
Carl Carlsson Gyllenhielm's Cavalry Company	
- Officers (1615)	Black velvet
- Cavalrymen (1615)	Black or blue cloth

SWEDEN'S WAR IN MUSCOVY 1609-1617

- Cavalrymen (1616)	Blue English cloth, grey and black cloth
Commanding General's Life Cornet of Horse (*Fältherrens livkornett*; that is, Jacob De la Gardie's guard cavalry, of two companies, 1615)	Red and black cloth
Livonian Retinue of Nobles' Banner (1615)	Red, black, and green cloth
Axel Mårtensson's Cavalry Banner (Finland, 1615)	Red and black
Henrik Månsson Spåre's Cavalry Banner (Finland, 1615)	Black, red, brown, and fiole brown cloth
Anders Paul's Cavalry Banner (Finland, 1615)	Brown, green, and black
Claes Wachtmeister's Enlisted Banner (1615)	Red, black, and green cloth
Polish Enlisted Banner (1615)	Red, black, and green cloth
Erik Jönsson's Cavalry Banner (Finland, 1617)	Blue English and grey cloth
Lars Andersson's Cavalry Banner (Karelia, 1617)	Blue cloth and grey cloth from Lübeck
Hans Ekholt's Cavalry Banner (Finland, 1617)	Grey cloth and grey woollens
Dragoons	
Adam Richard de La Chapelle's Dragoon Company	
- Dragoons (1613)	Blue and grey cloth
- Dragoons (1615)	Red
Infantry	
Jacob (James) Balfour's Company (Scotland, 1609)	Red, blue, or liver brown
Thomas Kennedy's Company (Scotland, 1609)	Blue
Gustav Hansson's Company (unknown origin, 1609)	Brown
Josef Jönsson's Company (Finland, 1609)	Blue
Mats Larsson's Company (Finland, 1609)	Blue
Nils Jönsson's Company (Dalecarlia, 1609)	Blue
Grels Jönsson's Company (Finland, 1609)	Blue
Peter Ogilvie's Company (Scotland, 1609)	Blue
Carl Hansson's Company (Dalecarlia, 1609)	Blue
Jesper Andersson Cruus's Regiment (Sweden, 1613)	
- Officers	Blue English cloth
- Infantrymen	Grey cloth and red stockings
Patrick Rutherford's Regiment (1613)	Blue and grey cloth, grey stockings
Samuel Cobron's Regiment	

- Infantrymen (1613)	blue
- Infantrymen (1614)	Blue and grey cloth
- Infantrymen (1615)	Black, green, red, and grey cloth
Johan van Monickhouen's (reconstituted) Regiment (1614)	Blue and grey cloth
Svante Banér's Regiment (Sweden, 1614)	White (pale grey), black, and red cloth
Hans von Rechenberger's Regiment (Finland)	
- Infantrymen (1615)	Grey
- Officers (1617)	Black cloth and velvet
- Infantrymen (1617)	Black or grey cloth
Erik Johansson Båga's Norrland Company (Hälsingland and Ångermanland, 1613)	Blue and grey
Eskil Hansson's Company (Värmland, 1615)	Grey
Olof Bryngelsson's Company (Karelia, 1615)	Grey woollens
Lars Nilsson's Company (Österbotten, 1617)	Blue and grey
Sigfrid Larsson's Company (Österbotten, 1617)	Blue English cloth, grey cloth
Christopher Assersson's Norrland foot (1617)	
- Officers	Black velvet
Commanding General's Life Regiment (*Fältherrens livregemente*; that is, Jacob De la Gardie's)	
- Grey (1614)	
- Red and black (1615)	
- Grey and black (1616)	
Franz Dücker's Company (1614)	Blue and red cloth (issued while on garrison duty in Staraya Russa)
Issued to 'the soldiers in Narva', that is:	
- Svante Banér's and Samuel Cobron's Regiments	
- Carl Carlsson Gyllenhielm's and Finnish cavalry banners	
- Finnish infantry companies	
-- Cavalrymen and infantrymen (1615)	Grey or blue Scottish cloth
-- Officers? (1616)	Blue English cloth

SWEDEN'S WAR IN MUSCOVY 1609-1617

-- Cavalrymen and infantrymen (1616)	Blue and grey cloth
Issued to 'the soldiers in Estonia and Livonia':	
- Officers (1617)	'Fine-quality' cloth
- Infantrymen (1617)	Lübeck grey cloth
Artillery	
Artillerymen in Ivangorod (1614)	Blue cloth

Banners

By the turn of the seventeenth century, Swedish infantry colours and cavalry standards are believed mostly to have retained the characteristics of the previous century in that they consisted of only two colours and were geometrically divided into squares, rhombi, lines, and similar patterns. Such banners may have remained in use at the time of Sweden's war in Muscovy. Yet, by then the Swedish army had adopted similar styles in military banners and colours to those already predominant on the Continent. Colours and banners were painted with royal cyphers and devices in the form of texts or emblems in the Continental tradition. King Charles used the device C R S (*Carolus Rex Sueciae*; Charles, King of Sweden), while his son Gustavus Adolphus upon succession adopted the cypher G A R S. (*Gustavus Adolphus Rex Sueciae*).

Until about 1620, colours were three to four m in breadth and length. Hand grips were still short, less than about 30 cm in length. The hand grip might be covered with green wax, with the grip itself covered in cloth. Cavalry units carried standards of a type known as cornet. The cornet was usually about 50 to 55 cm in breadth and 50 to 70 cm in length and edged with a fringe of thread. Based on surviving specimen in the Trophy Collection, Stockholm, a cornet pole was shaped like a fluted lance and usually painted. Since all dragoon units were enlisted, we can assume that dragoon guidons had swallowtails

Cavalry cornet in cuirassier armour. Cornets in Swedish service, especially those in the retinue of nobles or any of the life banners, would have dressed in a similar manner. (Jacob de Gheyn, *Die Reitschule oder Übungen der Kavallerie*, 1599-1600)

THE SWEDISH MILITARY ESTABLISHMENT

in the Continental style. As far as is known, they commonly were about 1 m in breadth and from 1.4 to 1.8 m in length.[113]

Almost the only reasonably comprehensive early seventeenth-century information we have on Swedish colours and banners derive from the epic poem *Carolomachia*, which was written by Laurentius Bojerus, a Swedish Jesuit, to celebrate the Commonwealth victory at Kircholm in 1605.[114] The poem's descriptions are sufficiently detailed to allow the identification of each banner with a particular provincial unit – as long as we accept the premise that Swedish cavalry units already flew banners with the coat of arms of their respective province. This conclusion indeed seems likely, since the provincial coats of arms already played an important heraldic role and they certainly appeared on banners later in the century. Yet, we should bear in mind that Bojerus's descriptions do not constitute conclusive evidence. In the absence of actual surviving banners, the possibility remains that the poet intended his banner descriptions as allegoric, not literal, descriptions.

In no case does Bojerus mention the colour of the field of the provincial banners. If more than one unit was raised in a province, we can assume that each carried a banner with the same provincial coat of arms but on fields of different colour.

Based on Bojerus, King Charles's Life Banner of Horse flew a snow-white cornet with the three golden crowns of Sweden. Apparently, the colour white already signified the status of a life company.[115]

The Uppland cavalry flew a cornet with the royal orb and cross (Latin: *globus cruciger*, 'cross-bearing orb'; in the Empire and Sweden somewhat

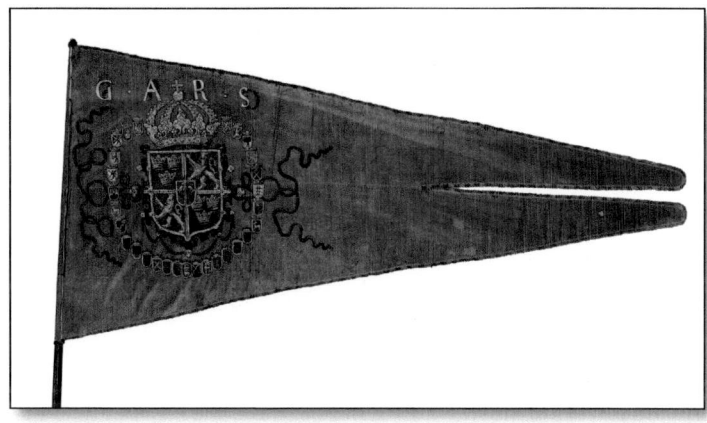

The Swedish national banner was not carried in the field but used for ceremonies. Painted by the craftsman Holger Hansson on blue silk, the national banner was employed at the coronations of both King Charles (in 1607), for whom it was made, and Gustavus Adolphus (in 1617), for whom the cypher G A R S (*Gustavus Adolphus Rex Sueciae*) was added. Breadth 1.75 m, length 3.82 m

---

113 Richard Brzezinski, *The Army of Gustavus Adolphus 2: Cavalry* (London: Osprey, Men-at-Arms 262, 1993), pp.39, 41.
114 Laurentius Bojerus, *Carolomachiae liber 3* (Vilnius: Jesuit Academy, 1606). Bojerus (1563–1619) was a Swedish Jesuit who mostly wrote poems on religious topics. The *Carolomachia* is his best-known work. Bojerus published his poems under various pseudonyms.
115 The custom of white standards may have derived from the practice on the Continent to display, in the immediate vicinity of the commanding general, a small white flag. Berthold von der Becke, *Soldaten-Spiegel: Historische Anweisung welcher Gestalt ein Guarison oder Vestung nicht allein mit aller jhrer Notturfft vnnd Zugehörung wohl zu versorgen hohen vnd nidern Aemptern recht anzuordnen* (Frankfurt am Main: Johann Spieß und Johann Jacob Porschen, 1605), p.85. Possibly, the standard was known (in Dutch or German) as *Kendefahne* ('recognition banner'), a term that disseminated to Sweden (as *Kännefana*), where the expression was known since at least 1565, and which became the name of the aforementioned Vanguard Banner.

irreverently known as apple of the state (German: *Reichsapfel*; Swedish: *riksäpple*).

The Småland cavalry flew a cornet with a standing lion carrying a crossbow.

The Östergötland cavalry flew a cornet with a fierce griffon.

The Västergötland cavalry's cornet displayed a proud lion on a bi-colour field, which based on later banners can be assumed to have been black and yellow.

The Södermanland cavalry flew a cornet with a black griffon, which the poet described as terrible in countenance.

The Finland cavalry (later to be known as the Åbo and Björneborg regiment) cornet was decorated with a standing bear wielding a sword. According to Bojerus, the cornet also displayed a star, although two stars is more likely since this was included in the contemporary coat of arms.

The Nyland cavalry from Finland (later to be known as Nyland and Tavastehus regiment) flew a cornet with a helmet crowned with two flags (presumably blue with a cross of yellow or white – that is, heraldic gold or silver).

Other information on colours and standards is limited. In 1607, the Drabant Guard of Foot fought under a yellow colour. In 1609, newly raised cavalry banners, including Lars Andersson's Cavalry Banner in Karelia,

The cornet of the Finland cavalry, as described in the poem *Carolomachia*. (Author's illustration)

The cornet of the Nyland cavalry, as described in the poem *Carolomachia*. (Author's illustration)

THE SWEDISH MILITARY ESTABLISHMENT

The cornet of the Småland cavalry, as described in the poem *Carolomachia*. (Author's illustration)

The cornet of the Östergötland cavalry, as described in the poem *Carolomachia*. (Author's illustration)

received cornets of red damask. In 1610, Jacob De la Gardie's Life Cornet of Horse (of two companies) received cornets of unknown but likely white damask with silver embroideries including four flames each, presumably one in each corner.[116]

In early 1612, the cavalry (the Life Banner?) under Gustavus Adolphus flew a black cornet.[117] A hand-drawn copy of one of Karel van Mander II's tapestries for Frederiksborg Castle which depicted a Danish naval landing later in the same year shows two Swedish infantry colours of the early type. One features the cross of St Andrew, while the other looks like a modern Swedish blue and yellow flag. Although the original colours of the tapestry are no

The cornet of the Västergötland cavalry, as described in the poem *Carolomachia*. (Author's illustration)

---

116 Lars-Eric Höglund, *Från Karl Knutsson till Kristina: Svenska fälttecken och beklädnad från senmedeltid till trettioåriga kriget* (Karlstad: Acedia press, 2012), p.44.
117 Anonymous [Ernst Werckman], 'Journal über alles des Jenige, so sich in dem so genannten Calmarschen Krieg zugetragen', Holger Rørdam (ed.), *Monumenta Historiæ Danicæ 2: 2: Historiske kildeskrifter og bearbejdelser af dansk historie, især fra det 16. aarhundrede* (Copenhagen: G. E. C. GAD, 1887), pp.671–762, on p.728.

SWEDEN'S WAR IN MUSCOVY 1609-1617

longer known, the blue and yellow flag is known from the 1550s and is believed to have been older still.

Kettledrums and trumpets were accompanied by flags, too, of unknown colour but with silver embroideries.[118] As noted, colours and standards, as well as musical instruments, were regarded as important trophies, so they were eagerly captured in battle. It was deemed a disgrace to lose a standard, since a captured standard was a sure sign of defeat. The loss of standards and musical instruments also made it difficult to gather and reorganise the survivors of a unit, since standards and music were important means of leading a military unit. In the Swedish army, each company standard was carried in battle by the ensign who in turn was protected by two men armed with long, straight two-handed swords of the Continental *Zweihänder* style.[119] The custom reached Sweden with the Landsknechts in the early sixteenth century.[120] By the time of Sweden's war in Muscovy, the sword-armed guard primarily played a ceremonial role, and Gustavus Adolphus abolished the custom early in his reign.

Soldier with ceremonial two-handed sword, 1611. The jacket is buttoned all the way down and has protruding shoulder straps. Sleeves are slit, and breeches are fairly narrow. The linen collar has elongated tips. King Charles's funeral armour, made in Stockholm in 1611. (Strängnäs Cathedral)

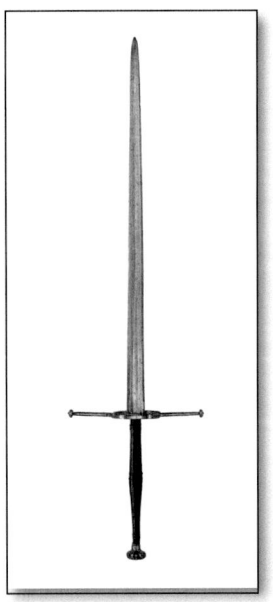

Two-handed command sword of the type used by some officers, dated to the end of the sixteenth century. Made in Germany, with the running wolf mark of Passau and Solingen swordsmiths inlaid in brass. Blade length 102.9 cm, width 51 mm. Total length 142.2 cm. Weight 2.7 kg. Owned by Axel Oxenstierna. (Royal Armoury, Stockholm)

The command sword owned by Axel Oxenstierna next to two ceremonial double-handed *Zweihänder* swords, dated to c. 1600, with parts of a suit of armour. Under Gustavus Adolphus, command swords were only used in the navy, while the use of ceremonial double-handed swords was discontinued altogether. (Royal Armoury, Stockholm)

---

118 Höglund, *Från Karl Knutsson till Kristina*, p.44.
119 Barkman, *Kungl. Svea livgardes historia 2*, p.633.
120 Seitz, *Svärdet och värjan*, p.46.

THE SWEDISH MILITARY ESTABLISHMENT

Regimental Music

A Swedish infantry unit contained drummers and pipers, while cavalry units included trumpeters and kettledrummers (one kettledrum on each side of the horse). When possible, a cavalry trumpeter rode a piebald. Back in 1594, when the Drabant Guard participated in a parade on foot, they employed kettledrums hung on the back of a soldier and played by the man behind him.[121] This practice may have continued later as well. As noted, the music played an important role in maintaining order, since it could be used for signalling on the field of battle and elsewhere. The music, no doubt, was also intended to reinforce the men's morale both in battle and on the march.

Drummer. (Jacob de Gheyn)

---

121   Göte Göransson, *Gustav II Adolf och hans folk* (np: Bra Böcker, 1994), p.217.

Skis

No description of the Swedish army would be complete without mentioning the use of skis when snow conditions permitted. When John of Nassau in 1601–1602 commanded the Swedish army, the exotic skis made such an impression on him that he documented them in a drawing with accompanying text.[122] He described the skis as eight feet long. Both the point and rear were turned up, and the left ski was lined with reindeer skin underneath so as not to slip backwards when moving uphill. Although Nassau did not mention them, other types of skis were used, too, each designed for a certain activity or type of snow cover. Skis had been used in previous wars, and most men from northern Sweden and Finland were experienced in their use. In the Arctic North, entire units regularly travelled on skis, accompanied by Lapp auxiliaries with reindeer for the carrying of provisions. In the previous century, Finnish ski troops had been armed with arquebuses, and in the reigns of King Charles and Gustavus Adolphus, they likely carried either arquebus or musket.[123]

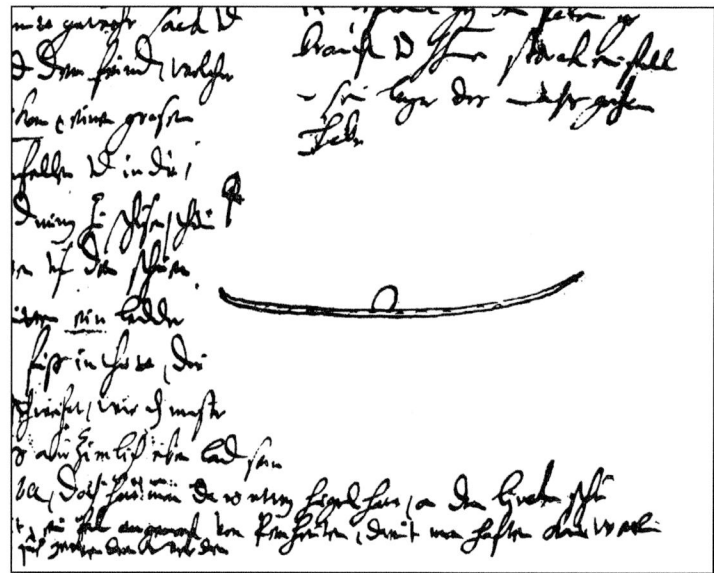

John of Nassau's description and drawing a Swedish ski. (Staatsarchiv Wiesbaden, Abt. 174 K 924, Altes Dillenburger Archiv fol. 123)

Armament industry

At the beginning of the seventeenth century, Sweden had only rudimentary arms production facilities. There was only one arms factory, in the town of Arboga, and it belonged to the Crown. Some manufacture took place in the province of Hälsingland as well. Despite efforts to increase production there and elsewhere, Sweden still had to import handheld weapons.

It need not import artillery, however. Although tin had to be imported, primarily from England, Sweden had large copper reserves, so had the capability to cast large numbers of bronze cannons. Foundries existed in several locations in Sweden including Stockholm, Kalmar, and Nyköping

---

122 For details, see 'Grefve Johans av Nassau relation', pp.396–438; Barkman, *Kungl. Svea livgardes historia* 2, pp.403–5.
123 Michael Fredholm von Essen, *Muscovy's Soldiers: The Emergence of the Russian Army 1462–1689* (Warwick: Helion, 2018), p.59.

and as well as in Reval in Estonia and Viborg in Finland. Gunpowder production facilities were available in the same locations or nearby. Sweden was self-sufficient in cannon and gunpowder production.

A persistent problem, however, was slow-match, which was needed for artillery but also for matchlock muskets. Sweden never became self-sufficient in slow-match production.

3

The Muscovite Military Establishment

Swedish and Commonwealth sources tend to exaggerate the number of Muscovite soldiers, sometimes considerably so. However, Muscovy was able to raise a significant number of men, and moreover, was growing increasingly proficient at it. This had little to do with the available male population, which in reality was lower than that of the Commonwealth. Muscovy had for some time worked to establish better procedures for raising soldiers and at the outset of the seventeenth century compared favourably to both Sweden and the Commonwealth in this respect. Yet, the system was still far from flawless. Besides, Muscovy controlled a vast territory, and to secure distant borders, it was impossible to raise all available men for every campaign. Moreover, we will see that Muscovy presently suffered from all sorts of internal problems, ranging from famine to succession issues and what can be termed a constitutional crisis, in which the periphery revolted against the centre.

The total population of Muscovy is estimated at around 11 to 12 million people.[1] Both contemporary and modern observers have assessed the potential maximum size of the Muscovite armed forces at the end of the sixteenth century as being probably around 110,000, of which somewhat more than 40,000 might be called out for campaign service ('division service,' *polkovaya sluzhba*) in any given campaign season.[2] The rest would be available for garrison service ('town service,' *gorodovaya sluzhba*). This means that less than one percent of the population was available for mobilisation, and of them, only about a third was actually called up at any

---

1 John L. H. Keep, *Soldiers of the Tsar: Army and Society in Russia, 1462–1874* (Oxford: Clarendon, 1985), p.88.
2 Richard Hellie, *Enserfment and Military Change in Muscovy* (Chicago: University of Chicago Press, 1971), pp.267–73, attempts to summarise what is known about the numbers of the Muscovite military forces in the sixteenth and seventeenth centuries. See also Fredholm von Essen, *Muscovy's Soldiers*, pp.121, 170.

THE MUSCOVITE MILITARY ESTABLISHMENT

one time. However, it also means that significantly higher numbers were available, including for rebellions against the centralising tendencies of the tsars. Centralisation had culminated in the second half of sixteenth century under the ambitious Tsar Ivan IV (1530–1584, r. 1533–1584), the first great reformer of the Muscovite army and state. Young Ivan grew up in a brutal environment, which goes some way in explaining why he became known (in English) as 'the Terrible'.[3] His Russian nickname, *Groznyy*, in reality meant the Dreaded or Threatening, which in sixteenth-century Russian did not have a negative connotation per se but rather suggested awe-inspiring authority, a person who was respected and worthy of respect.[4] In English, Ivan the Terrifying would perhaps have been a better translation of the cognomen. A brilliant reformer and an intellectual of sorts, Tsar Ivan nonetheless was a ruthless ruler who carried out brutal and probably excessive purges among the Muscovite nobility and within his own court. Some of the turmoil in early seventeenth-century Muscovy can be explained by the attempts of noble lineages purged by Tsar Ivan to reassert their former power.

The Muscovite military system was very different from the Swedish one. The close association with the Mongol Golden Horde during the Middle Ages had transformed the Muscovite military establishment. The Muscovite army consisted primarily of cavalry, organised along Mongol lines.[5] During the more than two centuries of Mongol rule, Moscow copied, and made its own, numerous political, military, and social institutions borrowed from the Mongols. These included, in addition to the organisation and armament of the army, the Mongol system of taxation and civilian administration, the diplomatic forms and customs of Inner Asia, the postal service, and some aspects of criminal law. Moscow became part of an Inner Asian community of shared customs and institutions. Muscovites thereby gained an excellent understanding of Inner Asian culture, diplomatic conventions, protocol, and steppe politics and dynamics.[6] Muscovite foreign policy towards the steppe powers generally was considerably more adroit than its policy towards the other European powers, which were less well understood in Moscow due to the physical distance and comparable isolation of Muscovy. The isolation was augmented by Muscovy's attachment to its own form of Orthodox Christianity that stayed aloof from both the Catholic and Lutheran creeds. Furthermore, the most prominent noble families in Muscovy, such as the Mstislavskiys, Shuyskiys, and Bel'skiys, all regularly

---

3 See for example, Ivan's own account of his early life, in J. L. I. Fennell (ed.), *The Correspondence between Prince A. M. Kurbsky and Tsar Ivan IV of Russia 1564–1579* (Cambridge: Cambridge University Press, 1955), pp.69–101.

4 Carolyn Johnston Pouncy (ed.), *The Domostroi: Rules For Russian Households in the Time of Ivan the Terrible* (Ithaca: Cornell University Press, 1994), p.63 n.5.

5 For further information on the Muscovite military system see Fredholm von Essen, *Muscovy's Soldiers*.

6 Charles J. Halperin, *Russia and the Golden Horde: The Mongol Impact on Medieval Russian History* (Bloomington: Indiana University Press, 1987), p.90.

intermarried with the Tatar nobility. Indeed, by 1600, at least 60 princes of Mongol ancestry, together with their families and retainers, had gone into Muscovite service. Estimates of the Mongol component of Muscovite nobility varies, but based on surnames, as many as 17 percent might then have been of Mongol, Tatar, Caucasian, or Siberian ancestry. In fact, the real number may have been higher, since many adopted Russian names when they converted to the Orthodox faith.[7]

Another Mongol legacy was the postal service. This was a means for the ruler to receive and send messages, but it was also a means to keep outlying regions under control and observation. The system relied on post stations (*yam*, pl. *yama*) and couriers and stage coaches for transportation of messages and goods. In times of peace, communications speed was accordingly quite high. A courier could bring a message from Moscow to Novgorod in six or seven days. However, the disruptions caused by the Time of Troubles made travel difficult and very slow. By 1612–1613, it might take three to five weeks for a message to reach Novgorod from Moscow, if it arrived at all. These problems remained for a long time. Even after the end of the war between Sweden and Muscovy in 1617, travel between Moscow and Novgorod took about two weeks.[8]

An army, if not led by the Tsar himself, was commanded by the most senior ranking prince or noble. The Tsar's own troops were also, in particular if the Tsar was absent, commanded by military officers known as voivodes (*voyevoda,* pl. *voyevody*). *Voyevoda* merely means 'military commander', and the title, originally signifying the leader of a traditional princely retinue (*druzhina*) or a general levy of commoners (*opolcheniye*), was used for the commander or deputy commander of a division (*polk*) within a Muscovite army.[9]

On the tactical level, an early Muscovite army fundamentally operated as a Mongol one. The Muscovite military system relied on the Mongol division of armies into five tactical units: an advance guard, a main force, left and right wings, and a rearguard. The army generally formed up in either a small array, consisting of three divisions, or a large array, of five. The small array consisted of the centre or great division (*bol'shoy polk*), the right wing or arm (*pravaya ruka*), and the left wing or arm (*levaya ruka*).

---

7 Donald Ostrowski, *Muscovy and the Mongols: Cross-Cultural Influences on the Steppe Frontier, 1304–1589* (Cambridge: Cambridge University Press, 1998), pp.55–8.

8 Adrian A. Selin, 'Communications in the Novgorod Region during the Crisis Period of the Time of Troubles', *Vestnik SPbGU Istoriya* 63:3 (2018), pp.748–762, on p.759.

9 The term *polk* is often incorrectly translated as regiment since this is the modern meaning of the term. Of non-Slavic origin, this military term had a very long history and ultimately derived from ancient Gothic *fulk* ('battle formation'), which in the Eastern Roman Empire became *fulcum*. At the same time, the term disseminated into the Slavic languages, in time becoming Russian *polk* and Polish *pułk*.

THE MUSCOVITE MILITARY ESTABLISHMENT

To this were added, in the large array, the vanguard (*peredovoy polk*) and the rearguard (*storozhevoy polk*). Each was commanded by a voivode, selected from among the princes and boyars. The size of the divisions varied greatly, from 300 to more than 15,000 men.[10] Most common were probably divisions consisting of some 2,000 to 5,000 men, but the great division in particular might be considerably stronger. The great division was commanded by the 'great voivode' (*bol'shoy voyevoda*), who in the absence of the Tsar simultaneously served as army commander. Each voivode had a subordinate deputy voivode within his division.

The order of seniority was the great division which held primacy, followed by the right arm division, the vanguard division, the rearguard division, and the left arm division, in this order, which is confirmed by the surviving elite service registers. It follows that this was also the order of seniority of the divisional voivodes.

The Muscovite army organisation was based on the old Inner Asian division into units of nominally 10, 100, and 1,000 men. Organisationally, the great division was divided into 'thousands' (*tysyachi*), 'hundreds' (*sotni*, sing. *sotnya*), 'half-hundreds' (*polusotni*), and 'tens' (*desyatki*), respectively commanded by 'leaders of thousand' (*tysyatskiye*, or *voyevody*), 'leaders of hundred' (*sotniki*) or, in the infantry, 'headmen' (*golovy*), 'leaders of fifty' (*pyatidesyatniki*), and 'leaders of ten' (*desyatniki*).

Muscovite cavalryman in *tegilyay* padded hemp armour, sketched from a serviceman in the retinue of the Muscovite embassy to Georgia, 1641. (Teramo Cristoforo Castelli)

The great division was the main force of the army while on the march and in battle formed its centre in the line. Every army could have its own great division. Along with the five main divisions, there might also be a light cavalry reconnaissance division (*yertaul'nyy polk*; from Turco-Mongol *yortaghul*, 'raiding party') commanded by another voivode (*voyevoda yertaul'nyy*), and possibly a force of artillery (*naryad*), commanded by an artillery voivode (*voyevoda ot naryada*). Other voivodes commanded any units of non-Russian troops, such as Tatars. If a *gulyaygorod* or fortified wagon

---

10   A. V. Chernov, *Vooruzhennyye sily Russkogo gosudarstva v XV–XVII vv.: S obrazovaniya tsentralizovannogo gosudarstva do reform pri Petre I* (Moscow: Voyennoye Izdatel'stvo Ministerstva Oborony Soyuza SSR, 1954), ch. 1. Available from Biblioteka Khronosa website, <www.hrono.ru/libris/lib_ch/chrnv00.html>, accessed on 25 January 2018.

SWEDEN'S WAR IN MUSCOVY 1609-1617

Muscovite mounted archer in *tegilyay*, with his sabre fastened to a strap so that he can drop it when shooting the bow. Although this illustration is a century older than the previous one, the cavalry had changed little. (Sigismund von Herberstein, 1549)

Muscovite mounted archers in *tegilyay*, one with his sabre fastened to a strap, another with whip in hand. (Sigismund von Herberstein, 1549)

fort (more on which below) was used, it was commanded by an officer known as the *voyevoda gulyavyy*.

On the battlefield, the Muscovite army had fully embraced Mongol tactical doctrine. Highly mobile horse archers were used for harassing slow-moving enemy forces. When confronted with enemy cavalry, the Muscovite cavalry aimed first to engage with archery, then withdraw in feigned flight until the pursuing enemy could be attacked in the flank by other Muscovite cavalry or rashly followed all the way into the range of fire of the Muscovite artillery or arquebusiers, or into an ambush by the infantry. Raiding and looting were frequently used as a weapon of terror, to reduce the enemy population's will to fight. In this context, raiding was not merely random looting but a deliberate strategy to gain specific military objectives, in this case the subjugation of the enemy population, parts of which might even be relocated to areas within one own's territory that suffered from a shortage of labour. Many of the enemies of Muscovy concluded, wrongly,

THE MUSCOVITE MILITARY ESTABLISHMENT

that the raiding served no other purpose than destruction. This was not quite true, although a number of campaigns admittedly consisted of little but the raiding, looting, and burning of border villages. Raiding and looting also formed a means to feed and thus retain the army when logistics broke down, which commonly happened.

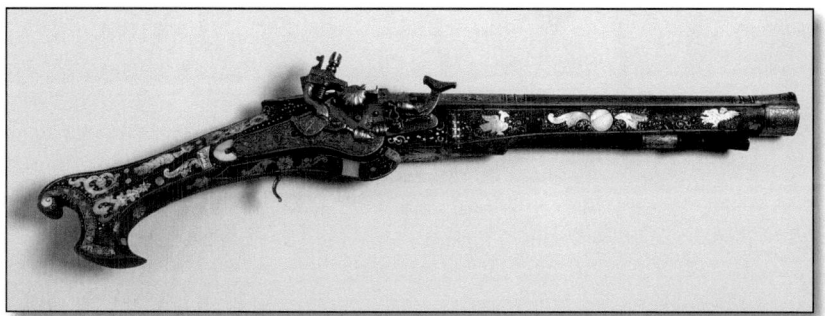

Muscovite gunsmiths already produced beautiful and advanced guns, such as this rifled snaplock pistol, made by Pervusha Isayev in the first quarter of the seventeenth century. Total length: 58.0 cm; barrel length: 35.9 cm; calibre: 16 mm. (Moscow Kremlin Armoury)

Muscovite snaplock pistol with revolver magazine, made by Pervusha Isayev about 1625. Total length: 57.7 cm; barrel length: 29.2 cm; calibre: 11 mm. (Moscow Kremlin Armoury)

Pair of Muscovite snaplock pistols, dated to the first quarter of the seventeenth century. (Moscow Kremlin Armoury)

Raising Troops

The Muscovite population traditionally fell into two categories: those who performed military service (*sluzhilyye lyudi*) and those who paid taxes (*tyaglyye lyudi*). The latter included the church, except in the frequent cases when church representatives made themselves exempt from taxation for spiritual reasons. The upper level of those who performed military service consisted of the boyars (*boyarin*, pl. *boyare*) or nobility, originally a warrior elite akin to the princely retinues of the Middle Ages. The lower level consisted of a socially inferior group of fighting men who had been recruited into service or had contracted to serve in exchange for payment ('contract servicemen', *sluzhilyye lyudi po priboru*). Between these two groups stood the 'hereditary servicemen' (*sluzhilyye lyudi po otechestvu*), who provided the bulk of fighting men in Muscovy.

All hereditary servicemen served on the basis of land ownership, either an inherited patrimonial freehold (*votchina*, pl. *votchiny*; 'in the family') or a service land grant (*pomest'ye*, pl. *pomest'ya*) which was conditional on lifelong and unlimited military service. Service landholders of the later category were known as *pomeshchiki*. The land grant privilege, too, was heritable; however, although a son was entitled to a land grant, it would not necessarily be the same land that his father had held. The service landholding system was the result of the Muscovite government's persistent problem in how to mobilise and use resources that were both limited and scattered over a vast territory, without at the same time allowing centrifugal forces to break up the quite recently unified Muscovite state. The land grant system may have been adopted from the similar system employed within the Golden Horde.[11] There was a common understanding that in times of war, 'should anyone show himself to be courageous in battle and stain his hands with the blood of the enemy, he would be honoured with gifts, both movable and immovable.'[12] The immovable gift would be a land grant.

Over time, many freehold estates were withdrawn, and the Muscovite government instead parcelled out land grants in exchange for service. By this process, the traditional nobility was transformed into a service nobility. They became the servitors of the state, whose rank and prestige no longer depended on lineage alone but also on what office they held. Yet, the hereditary servicemen were divided into a number of subdivisions, including the Moscow-ranked men who served in the capital, with extensive lands and numerous peasants at their disposal, and those who served in the provinces, with limited lands and few or no peasants, and accordingly were deemed to be of lower social standing. Although often referred to as 'nobles' by outsiders, the term hereditary serviceman better conveys the importance

---

11 Ostrowski, *Muscovy and the Mongols*, pp.48–9, 54.
12 J. L. I. Fennell (ed.), *Prince A. M. Kurbsky's History of Ivan IV* (Cambridge: Cambridge University Press, 1965), p.23.

THE MUSCOVITE MILITARY ESTABLISHMENT

of the individual's rank of military service and lineage, yet does not imply an exalted aristocrat and accordingly gives a better understanding of the man's position in society.[13]

By tradition, the son of a hereditary serviceman would be enrolled for service at the age of about 15 by undergoing the military initiation (*verstan'ye*, pl. *verstan'ya*). For some, entry into service might be delayed until an age as late as 18, while others might begin service at 14. The name of the young serviceman would be recorded in one of the elite service registers or deployment books (*razryadnyye knigi*) that were sent to the Military Deployments Chancellery (*Razryadnyy prikaz*) in Moscow, which best can be described as a ministry of defence. The young servicemen, now initiated (*verstannyy*, pl. *verstannyye*), were divided into different ranks (*stat'i*) according to their family background which also determined what kind of military position they could receive. The elite who were Moscow-ranked (*sluzhilyye lyudi po moskovskomu spisku*) were divided into ranks with elaborate titles, in descending order *stol'niki*, *stryapchiye*, *dvoryane moskovskiye*, and *zhil'tsy*. Yet, most servicemen were provincials. The three provincial grades were, in descending order, *vybornyy* ('selected'), *dvorovoy* ('court-ranked'), and *gorodovoy* ('town-ranked').[14]

The initiated hereditary servicemen in Moscow were generally no more than some 2,600 to 3,300. However, they were comparatively rich, which allowed them to muster many fighting men. It is likely that the sovereign's division (*gosudarev polk*), under the direct control of the Tsar, often reached a strength of some 20,000 men.[15] This was because each land grant-holder was obligated not only to appear in person but for each allotment of 100 populated *chetverti* of land (one *chetvert'*, or quarter, being 1.35 acres) bring one serving man, with a horse and full armour, and with two horses for a distant campaign.[16] Service was always with 'with horses, men, and weapons'. The number of serving cavalrymen to be raised depended on the size of his land grant, with the nobility providing many while poorer hereditary servicemen only being obliged to provide one or two. Since the elite service registers only noted the servicemen, not their armed serving men, the number of serving men can only be estimated. Yet, given the significant and growing number of sons of poor hereditary servicemen, the total number of serving men was likely not lower than the number of servicemen on the register and might have been considerably higher. The mustered troops were assigned to either campaign service or garrison service. They were not paid or supplied by the state, since the land grant

---

13 Carol Belkin Stevens, *Soldiers on the Steppe: Army Reform and Social Change in Early Modern Russia* (DeKalb: Northern Illinois University Press, 1995), p.xi.
14 Chernov, *Vooruzhennyye sily*, ch. 3; Keep, *Soldiers of the Tsar*, pp.22, 32.
15 Hellie, *Enserfment and Military Change*, pp.268–72; Alexander Filjushkin, *Ivan the Terrible: A Military History* (London: Frontline Books, 2008), p.29.
16 hernov, *Vooruzhennyye sily*, ch. 2; Hellie, *Enserfment and Military Change*, p.38; Keep, *Soldiers of the Tsar*, p.30.

was expected to provide for all their necessary supplies while on campaign. Giles Fletcher (1546–1611), an English diplomat in Muscovy, noted: 'Every man is to bring sufficient for himself to serve his turn for four months, and, if need require, to give order for more to be brought unto him to the camp from his tenant that tilleth his land or some other place.'[17]

Individuals were appointed to military command according to an elaborate order of precedence (*mestnichestvo*). Originally a system to reconcile and integrate the often-conflicting status claims of the original Muscovite servicemen and those Tatars and others who had joined and taken service with Muscovy later, the basic assumption was that a serviceman could only be appointed to positions that were commensurate with those occupied by his ancestors. For instance, somebody whose ancestor had held higher rank than the ancestor of another could not be appointed to a position subordinate to the other. This frequently caused difficulties, since appointments thereby were subordinated genealogy, and often led to considerable disunity of command. On the other hand, the system also promoted greater loyalty to the new identity as members of Muscovy's hereditary service class. It was not only Tatars and others of an Eastern origin who had joined the Muscovite service class in large numbers. According to some estimates, as many as 49 percent of the Muscovite nobility had surnames that indicated a Polish, Lithuanian, or western and central European origin.[18] The order of precedence system was probably originally derived from Mongol traditions.[19]

The elite service registers listed appointments to military command, together with the size of the division commanded, for both campaign and garrison duty. In the 1560s, the earliest period for which reasonably complete records exist, such sources indicate that the maximum strength of the hereditary serviceman cavalry was some 30,000 to 35,000. By the end of the century, this number had fallen to some 25,000.[20] However, the deployment books, although generally very detailed, do not give the full story, since they did not record the sometimes-considerable number of serving men brought by each hereditary serviceman. Nor did they necessarily record other types of troops such as streltsy, cossacks, or Tatars (more on which below). They also did not include any muster rolls for provincial troops available for mobilisation. Moreover, because their primary purpose was to support the order of precedence system, they focused on the past, not the present, and included no data on the number and disposition of current

---

17   Giles Fletcher, *Of the Russian Commonwealth* (1591), in Lloyd E. Berry and Robert O. Crummey (eds), *Rude & Barbarous Kingdom: Russia in the Accounts of Sixteenth-Century English Voyagers* (Madison: University of Wisconsin Press, 1968), p.184.
18   Ostrowski, *Muscovy and the Mongols*, p.58.
19   Ostrowski, *Muscovy and the Mongols*, pp.47–8.
20   Hellie, *Enserfment and Military Change*, p.267.

THE MUSCOVITE MILITARY ESTABLISHMENT

military forces.[21] This means that only estimates are available for Muscovy's total military strength.

A nobleman commonly spent far more time on campaign than on his estate. This was a problem, since his absence often resulted in the estate being ruined by lack of competent management, corruption, or the loss of labour caused by peasants moving elsewhere. Reasons for peasants abandoning an estate were manifold, including the ravages of wars, better opportunities elsewhere, or indeed at times forced removal by more powerful estate holders. In most cases, peasant departures were not clandestine operations but well planned, with entire peasant families departing with livestock, belongings, agricultural tools, and seeds at a time when the nobleman was absent on service. They also did not usually move very far, in most cases no longer than from one province to the next. Entrepreneurial peasants, however, would move on to the southern frontier, where there were virgin lands and plenty of opportunities, including finding official employment. Those who moved greater distances, such as to the frontier, were usually well-to-do who could afford both the journey and taking advantage of any opportunity that materialised upon arrival. Those who were guilty of crimes, or simply were more adventurous, could push on further, beyond the border, and join the free cossack communities.

When peasants took employment elsewhere, moved south, or were even forcibly removed to the estate of a more powerful neighbour, this wreaked havoc on the serviceman's ability to support himself. Eventually, the loss of labour became such a problem that Tsar Ivan IV introduced a system of temporary prohibition on the transfer or voluntary removal of peasants from their estate. In 1580, Ivan issued a code (*Ulozheniye*) which restricted the conveyance of peasants from one estate to another to St George's Day. Moreover, the following year was declared interdicted, that is, peasants were not allowed to leave the land to which they were attached at all. The interdiction remained in force until 1586. In addition, Ivan in 1581 ordered a census to be carried out, during which the names of all peasants should be listed with the estate on which they served. The census was completed in 1592. The interdiction and the census, when taken together, represented the introduction of enserfment in Muscovy, and this was the direct result of the need to guarantee the availability of labour on the land grants so that servicemen could support themselves while on military duty. Subsequent Muscovite governments followed the practice initiated by Tsar Ivan and had interdicted years alternated with free years. This practice, which also favoured wealthy and powerful monasteries, continued until the day of transfer on St George's Day was abolished in 1607.[22] Nonetheless, peasants continued to leave for a variety of reasons. Serfdom, with its unintended

---

21 Marshall Poe, 'Muscovite Personnel Records, 1475–1550: New Light on the Early Evolution of Russian Bureaucracy', *Jahrbücher für Geschichte Osteuropas* 45:3 (1997), pp.361–78.
22 Hellie, *Enserfment and Military Change*, pp.237, 240.

negative consequences for the development of Muscovy's and, later, Russia's political and social organisation, was accordingly the solution to urgent labour shortages that hampered the hereditary servicemen's ability to carry out their military duties.

The hereditary servicemen were not only intended to be self-supported financially and logistically, they were also fundamentally self-trained. This meant that their personal martial capacity varied considerably, with those of a military bent being far more proficient than those who merely served to uphold family tradition and safeguard their land grant. Moreover, they were generally not proficient in operating as a unit, since they hardly ever trained in formation. Although it can be assumed that those hereditary servicemen who spent their life on campaign would develop a certain proficiency, regardless of personal circumstances, there was no military training in times of peace, beyond the occasional roll call for muster purposes. There were also no tactical exercises and manoeuvres.

The Tsar relied primarily on his own retinue, the household or 'court' (*dvor*). His retainers (*dvoryanin*, pl. *dvoryane*, 'household retainers'), based in Moscow and by origin often bondsmen, in time received service land grants to support themselves. The Tsar's retinue was, in effect, a standing army, albeit one that depended on individual prowess, not unit training. It was commanded by a quartermaster-general (*okol'nichiy*), a title perhaps of Mongol origin that by then had become one of the highest ranks within the *dvor*.

On campaign, the Tsar's *dvor* was augmented by provincial retainers, generally from, and as groups named after, the towns ruled by Moscow. Such a man was known as a 'son of a boyar' (*syn boyarskiy*, pl. *deti boyarskiye*). The relationship was not necessarily one of kinship, since the term also could refer to a dependent of a noble household. Registered in the towns and dependent on service land grants for their upkeep, they served in town contingents. Each was obliged to bring his own armed serving men, provided for and armed at his expense. Such men, too, might be bondsmen in status, but others were relatives who lacked the means to serve independently. Either way, the majority were probably professional warriors. They were also usually well-armed. Since it was only a wealthy hereditary serviceman who could afford to bring his own armed men, he could also afford to arm them properly. The result would be a large cavalry army, consisting of men of different categories: members of the Tsar's personal retinue (*dvoryane*), nobles (*boyare*), hereditary servicemen (*deti boyarskiye*), and serving men (*sluga*, pl. *slugi*) in the attending retinues.

There was little difference between the court retainers and the sons of boyars. They were often referred to, collectively, as *dvoryane i deti boyarskiye*.

The Tsar could also count on the assistance of his relatives and numerous vassal princes and boyars, each of whom would bring his own, frequently considerable *dvor*. Unlike the boyars, the vassal princes were often the descendants of comparatively recent arrivals at the Muscovite court, men from other principalities who had taken service with Muscovy as it emerged as the leading regional power.

THE MUSCOVITE MILITARY ESTABLISHMENT

Weapons and Equipment

The chief Muscovite weapon was the Inner Asian composite bow, which like the accompanying bowcase and quiver was of Mongol type. A complete set of cavalryman's armament, including a bow in its bowcase and a quiver full of arrows, was known as *saadak*. Those who could afford it wore mail or scale armour of traditional Turco-Mongol type, with metal plates, joined by straps, to protect the chest, back, arms, and legs, such a suit of armour being known as *zertsalo* ('mirror'). If this was beyond their means, Muscovite cavalry instead often wore a short-sleeved, high-collared, densely padded hemp coat (*tegilyay*, from the corresponding Mongol term), a type of armour which indeed grew more common in this period until metal armour fell out of use among all except the highest and most wealthy nobility. Sometimes the *tegilyay* included iron bands or even armour plate fastened inside. A related type of armour was the brigandine (*kuyak*, again from the corresponding Mongol term), a garment of cloth or leather reinforced with metal plates from both sides, of the type commonly used by Mongols. Like Tatars and Mongols, those Muscovites who could afford it wore silk garments under their armour.[23] The conic, spiked iron helmet, too, was of Mongol, or to be more specific, Turco-Persian type. It was known as *misyurka* (from *Misr*, Arabic for 'Egypt'). Originally quite tall, helmets over time gradually grew more flattened. Others wore the *shishak* helmet, which also was of Inner Asian origin and which by way of Poland (where it was known as *szyszak*) was disseminating into Germany under the name *zischägge*. Some who could not afford an iron helmet instead wore a padded cloth or brigandine (*kuyak*) helmet with a metal nasal sewn on.

Muscovite steel helmet restored for Tsar Michael Romanov by Nikita Davydov in 1621. Made of wootz steel with gold, precious stones, and silk fabric. (Believed to have belonged first to Prince Aleksandr Nevskiy, Moscow Kremlin Armoury)

---

23 Richard Chancellor, *Voyages* (1589), in Berry and Crummey, *Rude & Barbarous Kingdom*, p.28.

SWEDEN'S WAR IN MUSCOVY 1609-1617

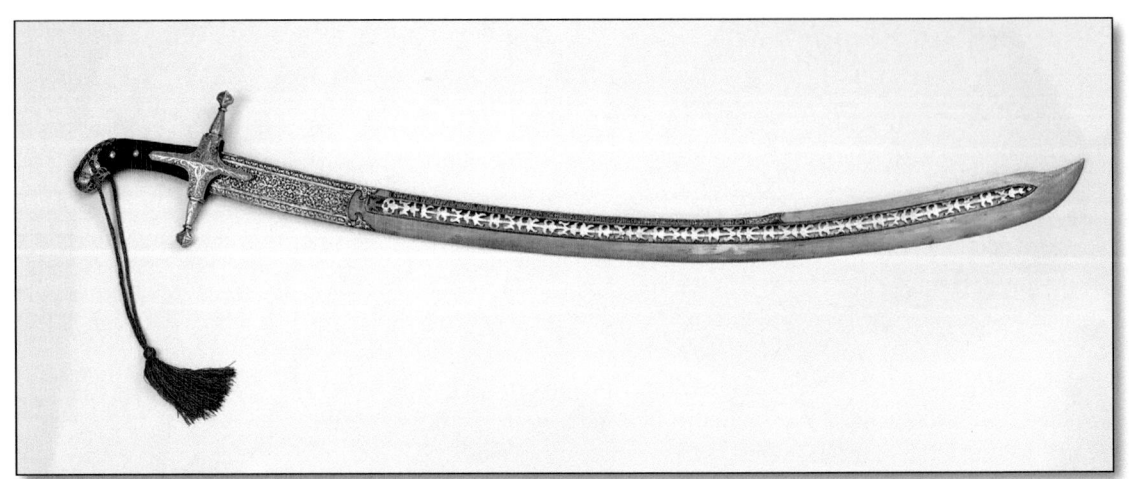

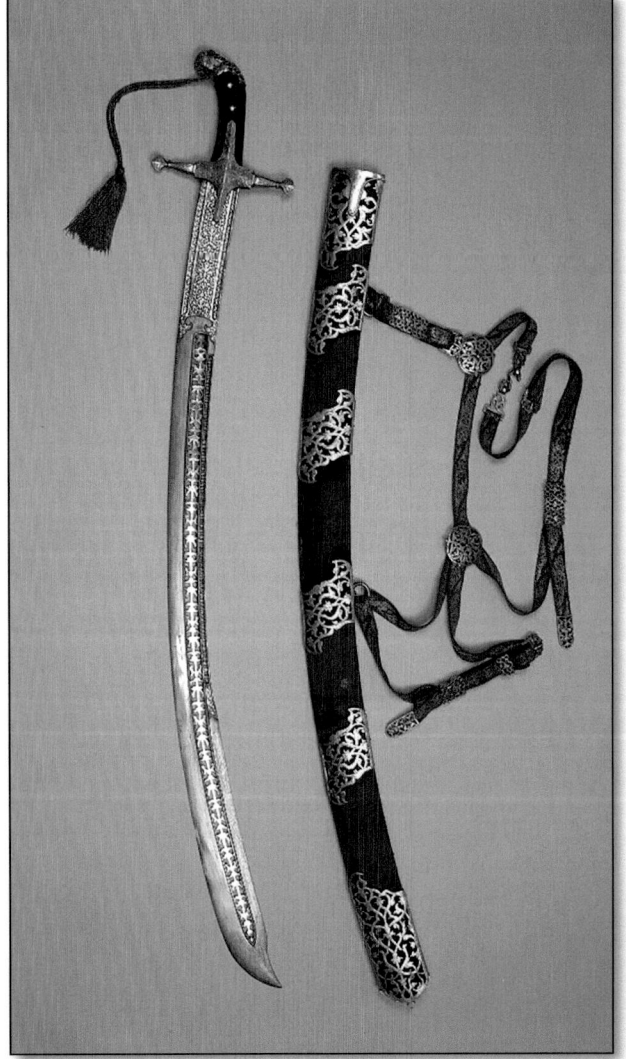

Muscovite sabre made for Tsar Michael Romanov by Iliya Prosvit in 1618. The blade is decorated with openwork ornament that reduces the weapon's weight. Made of wootz steel with gilded silver inlays. Total length: 106.2 cm; blade length: 93.2 cm; scabbard length: 95.0 cm. (Moscow Kremlin Armoury)

THE MUSCOVITE MILITARY ESTABLISHMENT

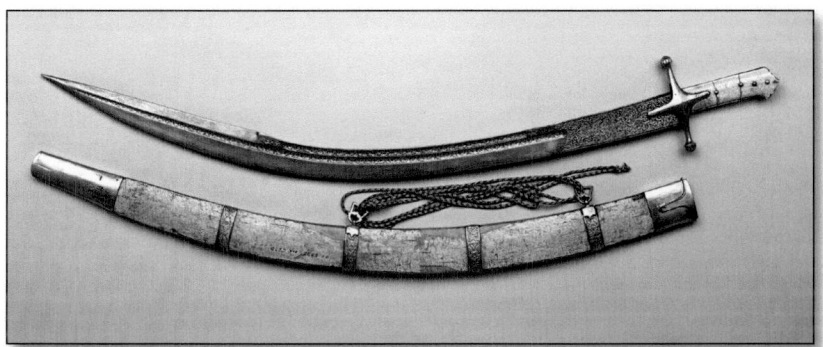

Muscovite sabre, early seventeenth century. Belonged to Prince Aleksandr Lobanov-Rostovskiy. Made of wootz steel with gilded silver inlays. Total length: 95.5 cm; blade length: 84.5 cm; scabbard length: 86.3 cm; blade width at the ricasso: 4.3 cm. (Moscow Kremlin Armoury)

Muscovite suit of armour of the *zertsalo* ('mirror') type, made by Dmitriy Konovalov and Andrey Tarman, 1616. (Moscow Kremlin Armoury)

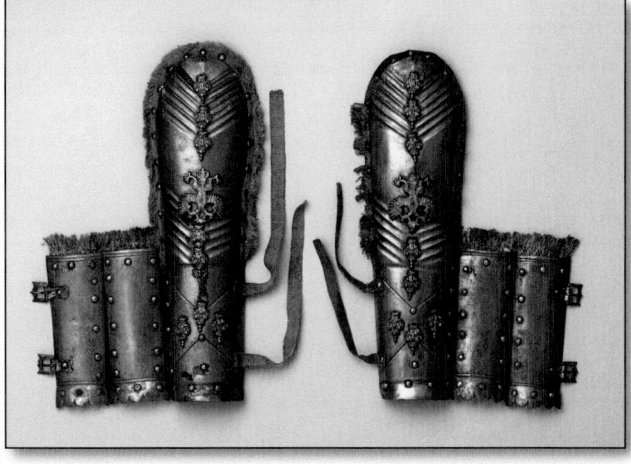

Pair of Muscovite vambraces, seventeenth century. Armguard length: 32.3; interior plate length: 14.0 cm. (Moscow Kremlin Armoury)

SWEDEN'S WAR IN MUSCOVY 1609-1617

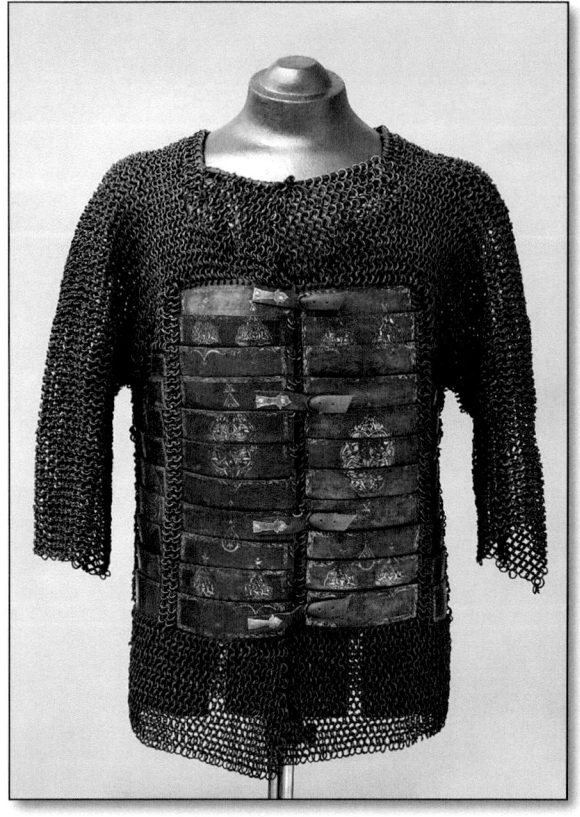

Muscovite chainmail and plate armour, late sixteenth or early seventeenth century. Belonged to Boyar Nikita Romanov. Total length: 70.0 cm. (Moscov Kremlin Armoury)

Muscovite *saadak* set, consisting of bow case and quiver, seventeenth century. Bowcase height 68.0 cm; bowcase width 33.0 cm; quiver height 37.0 cm; quiver width 17.0 cm. Made by Prokofiy Andreyev. (Moscow Kremlin Armoury)

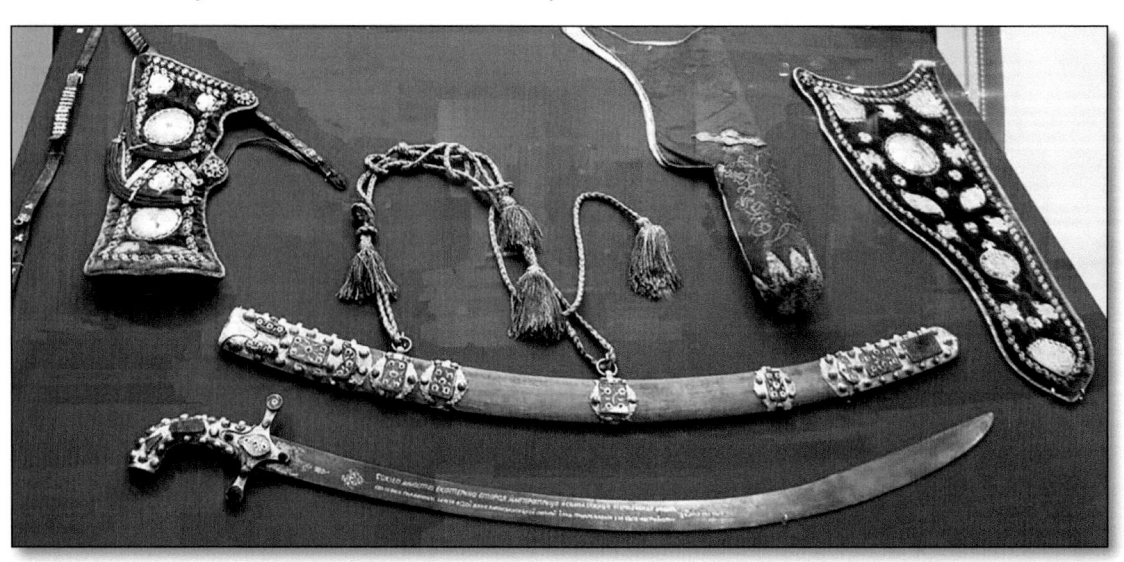

Parts of a Muscovite *saadak* set, including bow case and quiver, together with a highly embellished sabre. (Moscow Kremlin Armoury)

THE MUSCOVITE MILITARY ESTABLISHMENT

Over time the use of not only metal armour, but also lance and shield disappeared, and the cavalryman became a mounted archer with only a sabre, a dagger, and perhaps an axe hanging at the saddle-bow as sidearm. Only a few Muscovite cavalrymen carried handguns or muskets. A horseman carried both his whip and sabre fastened to his hands with lanyards, so that he could drop them both when shooting the bow.

Fletcher described the Muscovite mounted archer: 'The common horseman hath nothing else but his bow in his case under his right arm and his quiver and sword hanging on the left side, except some few that bear a case of dags or a javelin or short staff [bear spear; *rogatina*] along their horse side.'[24] But the nobles presented a different and considerably more splendid view. Fletcher continued:

> The under captains will have commonly some piece of armour besides, as a shirt of mail or such like. The general with the other chief captains and men of nobility will have their horse very richly furnished, their saddles of cloth of gold, their bridles fair bossed and tasselled with gold and silk fringe, bestudded with pearl and precious stones, themselves in very fair armour, which they call *bulatnyy* [of Damascus steel], made of fair shining steel, yet covered commonly with cloth of gold and edged round with ermine fur, his steel helmet on his head of a very great price, his sword, bow, and arrows at this side, his spear in his hand, with another fair helmet and his *shestopyor* or horseman's scepter [six-flanged mace] carried before him.[25]

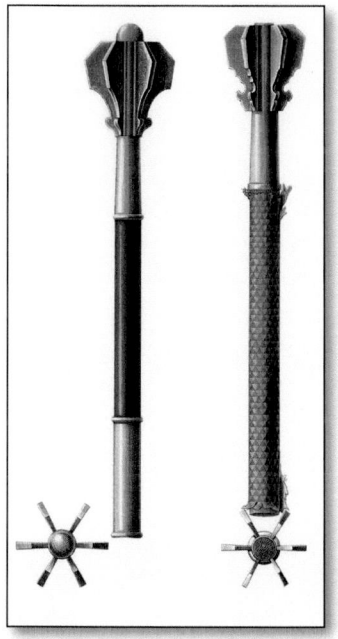

Muscovite officer's six-flanged maces of the *shestopyor* ('six feathers') type. A mace with a different number of flanges was called a *pernach* or *pernat*, from the same Slavic root for 'feather' (*pero*). (Drawing by Fyodor Grigor'yevich Solntsev, 1846–1853)

Ceremonial *pernach* or *pernat* flanged mace made of silver and wood, late seventeenth century. Length: 55.3 cm. (Moscow Kremlin Armoury)

---

24 Giles Fletcher, *Of the Russian Commonwealth* (1591), in Berry and Crummey, *Rude & Barbarous Kingdom*, p.183.
25 Giles Fletcher, *Of the Russian Commonwealth* (1591), in Berry and Crummey, *Rude*

SWEDEN'S WAR IN MUSCOVY 1609-1617

Right: Muscovite *djid* set of javelins, mid seventeenth century. Length: 82.0 cm; length of quiver: 76.0 cm. (Belonged to Prince Vasiliy Golitsyn, Moscow Kremlin Armoury)

Furthest Right: Bear spear (*rogatina*), seventeenth century. Spearhead length: 27.8 cm; width: 5.5 cm. (Moscow Kremlin Armoury)

Fletcher noted that both weapons and tactics were of Eastern origin: 'Their swords, bows, and arrows are of the Turkish fashion. They practice like the Tatar to shoot forwards and backwards as they fly and retire.'[26] In other words, the Muscovite, an excellent mounted archer, commonly employed the Parthian shot as a tactical device.

The contemporary English merchant George Turberville (1540?–1610?) noted the same. In a letter in verse, written in 1568 or 1569, he described the Muscovite bow further:

& *Barbarous Kingdom*, pp.183–4. Spelling or Russian terms have been normalised.
26 Giles Fletcher, *Of the Russian Commonwealth* (1591), in Berry and Crummey, *Rude & Barbarous Kingdom*, p.184.

THE MUSCOVITE MILITARY ESTABLISHMENT

Their bows are very short, like Turkish bows outright,
Of sinews made with birchen bark in cunning manner dight.
Small arrows, cruel heads, that fell and forked be,
Which being shot from out those bows, a cruel way will flee.[27]

Muscovite cavalrymen rode horses in the Mongol style, with Mongol saddles and short stirrups that allowed them to stand clear of the saddle. They relied on a Mongol-style short whip instead of spurs. Horses were unshod. Many rode mid-size Noghai horses acquired from the Tatars of this name who controlled vast territories north of the Caucasus. This was indeed the most common horse breed in Muscovy.[28] The Noghai was a small but sturdy steppe breed, of up to 14½ hands (145 cm). It was not suitable for heavy shock cavalry but could endure extended journeys, foraging on the way. Turberville reckoned that they easily rode 80 km per day, which corresponds with known travel times.[29] In fact, the Noghai influenced Muscovite horsemanship to the extent that even the whip became known as a *nagayka*, from the Russian pronunciation of Noghai.

In similarity to so many other aspects of Muscovite culture, even the clothes customarily worn in Muscovy were of Inner Asian origin, ranging from the *caftan*, a long narrow gown, to the high, soft boots associated with equestrian nomads.

The Muscovite state awarded valuable objects (furs, cloth, precious metals, and so on) in recognition of achievement, in particular to commanders. But Moscow also awarded medals. Fletcher describes them as 'a piece of gold stamped with the image of St George on horseback, which they hang on their sleeves and set in their caps.'[30] In reality, this was a golden kopek coin, which the recipient commonly would display fastened to his hat.

Streltsy

The streltsy (*strelets*, pl. *strel'tsy*; 'shooters') was a standing corps of infantry matchlockmen. Probably based on the Ottoman janissaries, the Muscovite streltsy soon acquired a role similar to the Ottoman corps. The streltsy were selected men, and full-time soldiers. Unlike the hereditary serviceman cavalry, they were not disbanded at the end of a campaign.

---

27 George Turberville, *Letter* (1589), in Berry and Crummey, *Rude & Barbarous Kingdom*, p.82.
28 Ostrowski, *Muscovy and the Mongols*, p.124.
29 George Turberville, *Letter* (1589), in Berry and Crummey, *Rude & Barbarous Kingdom*, p.82.
30 Giles Fletcher, *Of the Russian Commonwealth* (1591), in Berry and Crummey, *Rude & Barbarous Kingdom*, p.186.

Each streltsy regiment (*prikaz*) was divided into companies of about 100 men each, a company accordingly being known as a *sotnya* (hundred) like the corresponding unit in the traditional cavalry. The regiment was commanded by a headman (*golova*), under whom served a deputy (*podgolova*), below whom were commanders of respectively 100 men (*sotniki*), 50 men (*pyatidesyatniki*), and 10 men (*desyatniki*).[31] Some streltsy regiments were larger, so that a regiment could consist of from 500 to 1,000 streltsy. The streltsy corps trained regularly, and each Moscow-ranked regiment had its integral artillery, consisting of from six to eight cannons.

As heads of the regiments were appointed hereditary servicemen. A regiment was named after its town, or if more than one, its commander. The troops were recruited from free townsmen and peasants. Recruits were to be 'young and quick', and vouched for by somebody in authority, a group of elders, or the whole male population of an existing streltsy cantonment.[32] The streltsy lived in cantonments, separated from the rest of the town by law, fortifications, and/or natural obstacles. They were paid with food supplies and money, and service was for life. It was also hereditary. Despite being regarded as standing forces and maintained by the state, Muscovy could not afford to pay continuous wages. As a result, the streltsy were to be maintained in part by wages, and in part by trade privileges and land grants. Each strelets received a plot of land on which he built a house for himself and his family, at his own expense but for which he received a government subsidy. Since service was hereditary, his family could remain after the soldier's death but it was expected that a male relative would take his place in the regiment. In addition, service came with a number of privileges, for instance the right to bring goods into town without paying a toll. Such privileges in time caused the streltsy increasingly to identify and ally with their town's other small traders. In contrast to the hereditary servicemen who generally came from a rural background, the streltsy were closely associated with the towns in which they were based. Regardless of the ambition to build a standing force, individual streltsy had to engage in trades to support themselves and their families, just like poor hereditary servicemen who had to engage in agriculture, with or without serfs as labour, for the same reason.

Streltsy were divided according to their garrison town into 'selected' (*vybornoye*) or Moscow-ranked streltsy and town streltsy (*gorodovoye*), stationed elsewhere. In times of peace, the streltsy served in garrisons or as part of the border defensive lines. At war, both Moscow and town streltsy participated in campaigns and battles. The streltsy were under

---

31 Grigori Carpofsson Cotossichin [Kotoshikhin], *Beskrifning om muschofsche rijkets staat* (Stockholm: Ljus, 1908; first published in 1669), p.73; Chernov, *Vooruzhennyye sily*, ch. 2.
32 Chernov, *Vooruzhennyye sily*, ch. 3.

THE MUSCOVITE MILITARY ESTABLISHMENT

the administration of a special government office (*Streletskiy prikaz*) commanded by a voivode.[33]

What really characterised the streltsy, beyond their new form of organisation and the fact that they at regular intervals engaged in unit training of sorts (usually shooting contests), was that they received arms, equipment, and cloth for garments from the state. They were accordingly uniformly armed and clothed. Moscow streltsy received cloth for their uniform every year, while provincial streltsy only received this stipend every third or fourth year.[34] As a result, a streltsy regiment would present a uniformed appearance. As daily dress, the Moscow streltsy wore heel-length caftans made of grey, black, or brown cloth with wide sleeves that narrowed at the wrist. They also wore hats trimmed with fur, and the customary Muscovite boots. Some Moscow streltsy also had a full-dress uniform consisting of a similar but better-quality caftan of red cloth with gilded braiding on the chest, together with a whitish belt and heeled boots with turned-up toes. Uniforms may have changed in colour but not in style. By the end of the sixteenth century, certain regiments wore yellow or blue caftans. Some regiments wore silver braiding instead of gilded. The streltsy who marched out of Moscow in June 1610 as part of Prince Dmitriy Shuyskiy's army were dressed in green caftans.

A selected group of streltsy, the 'streltsy at the stirrup' (*stremyannyye strel'tsy*), served mounted, or more likely, as an early form of dragoons who were supposed to follow the tsar on horseback but stay at his side, fighting dismounted. They were reportedly armed with bows as well as matchlock muskets. This unit, up to 2,000 strong and dressed in red, formed the Tsar's primary bodyguard.[35]

Local streltsy units were also raised, in particular by wealthy monasteries. So for instance, in the early seventeenth century the strategically important Novodevichiy Monastery had an independent garrison of 300 to 350 streltsy.

By the end of the sixteenth century there were possibly as many as 20,000 to 25,000 streltsy, of whom about 7,500 to 10,000 garrisoned Moscow.[36]

The main armament of the streltsy was the matchlock arquebus or musket, in the words of Fletcher 'with a plain and straight stock, somewhat like a fowling piece; the barrel is rudely and unartifically made, very heavy, yet shootheth but a very small bullet.' The calibre was indeed often small, the muskets varying in calibre from 14 to 18 mm. In addition to his musket, the strelets carried a sabre, and the *berdysh* (a term perhaps derived from Polish *berdysz*), a pole-axe with a 40 to 100 cm-long head mounted on a pole (in exceptional cases up to two metres long). It was used as a musket rest as well as for hand-to-hand combat, in particular against horsemen. When

---

33   Filjushkin, *Ivan the Terrible*, p.34.
34   Cotossichin, *Beskrifning*, pp.80, 95, 96.
35   Giles Fletcher, *Of the Russian Commonwealth* (1591), in Berry and Crummey, *Rude & Barbarous Kingdom*, p.180; Cotossichin, *Beskrifning*, p.95.
36   Chernov, *Vooruzhennyye sily*, ch. 3.

SWEDEN'S WAR IN MUSCOVY 1609-1617

Strelets, surrounded by two Muscovites in caftans, c. 1610. (Excerpt from *Tabula Russiae ex autographo, quod delineandum curavit Foedor filius Tzaris Boris desumta*, a map of Moscow by Hessel Gerritszoon, second edition 1614)

not in use, the weapon was carried slung in a shoulder-loop, or, according to Fletcher who saw them, fixed on each soldier 'at his back' which some have interpreted as thrust through the belt on the man's back.[37]

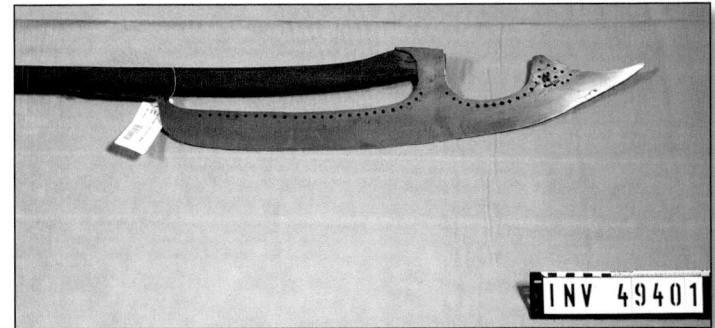

Muscovite berdysh poleaxe, seventeenth century. Total length 211.0 cm. (Army Museum, Stockholm; AM.049401)

---

37   Giles Fletcher, *Of the Russian Commonwealth* (1591), in Berry and Crummey, *Rude & Barbarous Kingdom*, p.184.

Although the streltsy were occasionally called up in units for military training, this fundamentally consisted of training in marksmanship only. There were no tactical exercises, nor manoeuvres. Moreover, and this was a feature of the streltsy as much as of other troop types, the Muscovite army fundamentally failed to address the need for continuous training. The key reason for this was that the Muscovite economy simply was unable to sustain a large, standing army. The persistent lack of funding meant that the men had to be effectively demobilised when no longer needed, and then switched to individual trades to support themselves. With few exceptions, such as some of the Moscow streltsy, the streltsy units were standing forces on paper only. They could be mobilised, but to prepare them for campaign duties, training often would have to start all over from scratch, at least if they were expected to operate at full capacity.

Artillery

Cannons known variously as *pushki* and *tyufyaki* were omnipresent in Muscovy. Artillery was perhaps introduced from the east and the west at the same time, as these two words appear to be of respectively Czech and Turkic origin.

Fortress artillery used for firing clusters of multiple small shot or stones early on consisted of small-calibre, forged and welded iron guns (*tyufyaki*), which were from about 40 to 120 cm long, with a calibre of 50 to 75 mm. Although never much used in the field, they still remained in the arsenals of towns and fortresses. Yet, true cannons (*pushki*), designed for high-trajectory firing, soon became a speciality of Muscovy. They fired stone or iron balls, iron case shot, and eventually also explosive grenades. Calibres ranged from about 30 mm (for fortress types) to about 250 mm (for siege guns). Lengths varied from 0.8 to more than 6 metres; weight of the gun from 20 to 7,500 kg. Large cannons fired balls up to 30 kg in weight or occasionally more. The cannon with probably the largest bore of its day was cast in Moscow in 1586. This was the Tsar Cannon (*Tsar'-pushka*) of bronze, cast by Andrey Chokhov (*c.* 1545–1629). It is preserved in the Kremlin to this day but since 1835 is mounted on an ornamental carriage. The cannon barrel alone weighs nearly 40 tons and is 5.34 m long. Its calibre is 890 mm. The Tsar Cannon was positioned to defend one of the main gates of the Kremlin when the Tatars threatened Moscow in 1591, but in the end the great cannon did not get the opportunity to fire a single shot.

With the new technology also arrived the concept of light field artillery (*pishchal'*, pl. *pishchali*, from Czech).[38] By the 1520s horse-drawn, wheeled gun carriages became available, which made field artillery a more successful proposition than in the past. Yet, most *pishchali*, too, were used from fortress

---

38   George Vernadsky, *The Mongols and Russia* (New Haven: Yale University Press, 1953), pp.365–6.

walls. The use of such pieces as wall guns (*zatinnyye pishchali*) continued into the seventeenth century, when they typically ranged in calibre from 20 to 30 mm. Wall guns were fixed to the walls they were meant to defend.

Artillerymen (known as *pushkar'*, pl. *pushkari*, and *zatinshchik*, pl. *zatinshchiki*, respectively, depending on whether they manned cannons or wall guns) formed a prominent part of Muscovy's armies. Artillerymen were recruited contract servicemen (*po priboru*) who served in exchange for wages. Like other groups of Muscovite soldiers, artillerymen lived in separate neighbourhoods. They were paid in cash and provisions and also received land so that they could support their families. However, they were not numerous. A small fortress might only have from five to 50 artillerymen. The artillerymen were regarded as specialists. In times of war, existing soldiers were detached or fresh ones conscripted to assist with the cannons.

Tsar Ivan IV created the first Muscovite 'regimental' artillery, by detaching part of the old artillery division and forming units (*naryad*, pl. *naryady*; 'patrols') of artillery that, in times of war, were attached to the individual divisions of the army. Each division accordingly received its own artillery support.

The period also saw other innovations in artillery, including multi-barrelled ones such as the organ gun (*soroka*). Its barrels, up to 100 or more in number, were fixed side by side, and/or in several tiers. Guns with the barrels fixed in a revolving drum appeared, too.[39]

Because of the popularity of the artillery, most fortresses and towns soon had far more cannon than could be manned by the specialist artillerymen alone. When the Muscovites in the sixteenth century left Livonia, the Polish monk Abbé John Piotrowski noted about the fortresses that they abandoned: 'We were all amazed to find in all the fortresses numerous cannon and an abundance of powder and cannon balls, more than we ourselves could collect in our own country.'[40] Fletcher was impressed, too, based on what he heard and saw: 'It is thought that no prince of Christendom hath better store of munition than the Russe emperor.'[41]

Fortresses and Fortifications

The cities and towns of Muscovy were habitually fortified, since raids were commonplace and nomad horsemen often lacked the inclination and capability to carry out a siege. Medieval forts were generally built of

---

39 V. M. Krylov, et al., *The Military-Historical Museum of Artillery, Engineer and Signal Corps: The Guide* (St Petersburg: The Military-Historical Museum of Artillery, Engineer and Signal Corps, 2008), p.52.

40 Cited in Wipper, *Ivan Grozny* (Moscow: Foreign Languages Publishing House, 1947), p.224.

41 Giles Fletcher, *Of the Russian Commonwealth* (1591), in Berry and Crummey, *Rude & Barbarous Kingdom*, p.186.

THE MUSCOVITE MILITARY ESTABLISHMENT

wood, commonly a stockade or palisade (*tyn*), from two to five metres high, consisting of timber driven directly into the ground or on top of an earthen rampart. To make the rampart even more difficult for an intruder, tree branches, too, were often driven into the ground. Additional protection was provided by an outer moat or natural obstacle such as a river or gully. A vertical palisade was referred to as a standing barrier (*stoyachiy ostrog*). Often built on a rampart, with the timber driven into the ground to provide a vertical wall, in elaborate forts it had log scaffolding on the inside so as to provide a fighting platform. But the palisade could also be driven into the ground in a slanting manner, inclined inwards, which made the palisade more difficult to scale. This was known as a slanting barrier (*kosoy ostrog*). Such a barrier, too, was built on a rampart, often with scaffolding on the inside.[42]

Wooden town walls were generally secure in the face of Tatar marauders. Tatars seldom employed artillery, particularly not during raiding. Over time, the wooden palisades developed into elaborate structures, with towers and fighting platforms built in the style of timber block houses.

More important fortifications were built of stone. Commonly built in major cities such as Moscow, Novgorod, and Pskov, they primarily consisted

Ivangorod, 1615. (Anthonis Goeteeris, who in 1619 mistakenly labelled the drawing as Narva)

---

42   Konstantin Nossov, *Russian Fortresses 1480–1682* (Oxford: Osprey Fortress Series 39, 2006), p.14.

of a combination of brickwork and stone, with walls from 10 to 20 metres high and from two to 12 metres thick. The walls were additionally fortified with battlements and towers. Traditional fortifications were polygonal, depending on the terrain for its choice of shape.

Italian military architects began to apply their skills in Muscovy in the late fifteenth century. Among the first modern castles was the powerful Ivangorod on the border with Estonia, built in 1492. Ivangorod was a particularly appropriate choice for a modern castle, since Livonians and Swedes customarily employed siege artillery. Swedish invaders for reasons of logistics seldom brought siege cannons much deeper into Muscovy. Fortresses developed further along European lines in the sixteenth century. As far as is known, the first bastions were added to a fortress in 1585–1586 at Ladoga Town, which was then within Swedish reach.[43]

From the sixteenth century onwards, all new towns were built by orders of the Tsar and according to decrees that established standards for fortifications. This meant that from this period onwards, European designs became standard for newly erected fortresses throughout the territories under the Tsar's control.

A Muscovite town typically consisted of two parts, a walled 'administrative quarter' (*gorod*), which housed soldiers, administrators, and clergy, and a 'trading quarter' (*posad*), which often was located outside the wall and which housed the town market, merchants, and artisans. For this reason, a town was principally a military and administrative centre, not a place of commerce. A town was under the control of a governor or rather commandant who answered to the Tsar and whose primary responsibility was tax collection and defence. The governor was, among other duties, responsible for the recruited contract servicemen (*sluzhilyye lyudi po priboru*) who served as town garrison. Most also worked in shops or farms outside the fortified section of the town to make ends meet.

Cossacks

Beyond streltsy and levies, infantry existed in the form of town cossacks (*gorodovyye kazaki*). Town cossacks were voluntary recruits who served as infantry in exchange for monetary wages in garrisons in towns and along the borders in the south and east.

The town cossacks emerged much earlier than the better-known free cossacks on the southern Russian and Ukrainian steppes. Originally, most were of Tatar origin. The term cossack derived from a Turkic word, *qazaq*, meaning 'seceder' or 'wanderer', by which was meant a man who for one reason or another had left the service of his ruler and accordingly lived as a freebooter outside the control of the Khan. The first cossacks were almost certainly men who had lost their position and affiliations during

---

43   Nossov, *Russian Fortresses*, p.12.

the disintegration of the Golden Horde, and then turned to mercenary employment instead. A cossack owed allegiance to neither khan nor sultan, prince nor tsar. The earliest reference to town cossacks pertains to those in the service of the Principality of Ryazan', who in 1443/1444 fought in alliance with Grand Prince Vasiliy II of Muscovy against the Tatars of the Great Horde, one of the Mongol successor states, at the River Listan' (modern-day Listvyanka). This contingent of town cossacks almost certainly consisted of mercenary Tatars displaced by the disintegration of the Golden Horde.[44] The recruitment of town cossacks increased significantly a century later, under Tsar Ivan IV. He contracted numerous men, regardless of ethnic background, for service as town cossacks, especially but not exclusively in the towns that constituted the primary defensive lines in the south. Southern Muscovy, and sometimes Moscow itself, remained vulnerable to the regularly recurring grand raids of the Crimean Tatars. The Tatars came to acquire slaves, on which the Crimean economy depended, so the raids caused much human suffering and were highly disruptive.[45]

Contracted for service among free commoners, town cossack contingents were generally named after the town in which they served. In the army, they were regarded as holding a position below that of streltsy and artillerymen. They were paid in a similar way, receiving some cash and provisions but also a little land so that they could sustain their families, and were exempt from paying taxes. Like streltsy and artillerymen, they were settled in towns in their own distinct neighbourhoods. A town cossack unit was headed by a headman (*golova*). His unit was subdivided into hundreds, and further on, into tens. Town cossacks could be mustered for both garrison and campaign duty. Their term of service was not fixed. Town cossacks served on foot or occasionally as cavalry and brought their own weapons. But there were also wealthy cossacks who instead served as cavalrymen and, as a result, might receive a personal land grant, in effect becoming provincial hereditary servicemen (*sluzhilyye lyudi po gorodovomu spisku*). They were not many, by the turn of the seventeenth century constituting no more than about 12 to 15 percent of all service cossacks.[46] Although important especially along the borders, the number of town or service cossacks was never great. Their total numbers reached no more than an estimated 5,000 to 10,000 men.

Moscow also regularly solicited the services of the free cossacks who from the sixteenth century onwards lived along the rivers Don, Volga, and Dniepr. Since these technically were not subjects of the Tsar, and accordingly neither servicemen nor taxpayers, relations with them were increasingly often handled by the Ambassadors' Chancellery (*Posol'skiy*

---

44 Nikolay Sergeyevich Borisov, *Ivan III: Otets russkogo samoderzhaviya* (Moscow: Akademicheskiy proyekt, 2nd edn 2017), pp.70–71.
45 On the Crimean Khanate, its military establishment, and the grand raids, see Fredholm von Essen, *Charles X's Wars* 1, pp.242–61.
46 Chernov, *Vooruzhennyye sily*, ch. 4.

prikaz), which functioned as Muscovy's foreign ministry.[47] Free cossack units were frequently hired to serve in the southern Russian steppes, in particular as a defence against Tatar raids. The cossacks were paid in cash and also received weapons and food supplies.

The origin of the free cossacks was as obscure and opaque as many of the individual cossacks themselves. The Don had for long been the home of a variety of peoples who did not recognise the rule of any Russian prince. Following the Mongol conquest, Tatars became a prominent population group of the steppe and forest steppe. However, the population also came to include large numbers of resettled inhabitants as the result of Mongol and Tatar raiding. As Slavic and Turkic ethnic elements merged, a new distinct cossack culture emerged. Cossacks served as either infantry or cavalry under their own leaders, their chief being known as hetman (*ataman*). He organised his band into a retinue (*druzhina*).

Yet, the early inhabitants were not destined to form more than a minor share of the cossack population. The first cossack settlements (*stanitsa*, pl. *stanitsy*) on the Don emerged only in the 1530s or 1540s. The settlements were fortified and attracted many Muscovite deserters and outcasts. Many were criminals escaping from the law, while others were fugitive peasants from central Muscovy (and Poland or Lithuania, although most of the latter ended up at the lower Dnieper where other cossack settlements appeared) in search of better opportunities. Numbers grew rapidly from the 1550s onwards, as an increasing number of migrants from the north trickled south, abandoning their own ruined estates or those of others on which they had served, hoping to find better opportunities as cossacks. As political and social dislocation in the heartland increased, so did the number of migrants. They made a living from horse-rearing, hunting, and fishing, but also from robbery and piracy, sailing their river boats down the Volga to the Caspian Sea or from the Dnieper to the Black Sea. Although less romantic occupations, eventually some took up farming and salt production as well.

The cossacks used riverine crafts such as the *chayka* ('seagull'), which was commonly used by Ukrainian cossacks in the sixteenth and seventeenth centuries. Such a vessel could be 20 metres long, with a width of from three to four metres, and carry a fighting crew of some 50 to 70 men, in addition to from two to six small cannons (falconets).[48] Although primarily designed for riverine transport, such craft carried sails and were sufficiently seaworthy to carry out raids along the shores of the Black Sea and the Caspian Sea. Similar craft, but for obvious reasons without falconets, had been used in

---

47 I. D. Belyayev, *O russkom voyske v tsarstvovaniye Mikhaila Feodorovicha i posle ego, do preobrazovaniy, sdelannykh Petrom Velikim: Istoricheskoye izsledovaniye* (Moscow: Universitetskaya tipografiya, 1846), p.17.

48 Based on a reconstruction in the Odessa Maritime Museum, in turn based on a contemporary depiction. Michael Fredholm von Essen, 'The Cossack Chaika', *Arquebusier* 25:2 (1999), p.19.

the region for raiding purpose since the third century AD, by groups such as Goths, Heruls, Slavs, and Vikings.

The Don cossacks became the origin of many other groups of cossacks, including the first Volga cossacks, from whom in turn emerged the Yaik (Ural) cossacks, the Terek cossacks, and the Siberian cossacks. Cossack boatmen sailed the Volga already before Muscovy annexed Astrakhan' and its surrounding territory. Their piratical activities caused problems for trade, so in 1577 Muscovy sent troops to pacify the Volga and remove all cossacks. While some of the Volga cossacks returned to the Don, others joined the recently emerged Yaik cossacks on the River Yaik (now Ural). Others instead set out across the Caspian Sea and sailed up the River Terek, where there was already a Muscovite outpost. They settled below the Caucasus mountains as the Terek cossacks in about 1578. The Terek cossacks were soon engaged in frontier fighting with the various peoples of the Caucasus – Kabardians, Circassians, Chechens, and Noghai, from whom they took up many customs including what much later would become known as the 'traditional' cossack dress of *cherkesska* (a long, narrow-waisted caftanwith wide sleeves) and *burka* (a goat-hair felt cloak with wide square shoulders), as well as new recruits and wives. Indeed, it was little but their Christian Orthodox faith that set them apart from the neighbouring Caucasian tribes. Yet others instead sailed up the Volga and its tributary the Kama to the Urals, where in the service of the Stroganov merchant family they began to push into Siberia.

Moscow began military cooperation with the Don cossacks in 1549 to apply pressure, by raiding, on the Tatar Khanate of the Crimea, as a means to hamper their regular expeditions to catch slaves in southern Muscovy. Henceforth, whole cossack groups (*stanitsy*) from the Don, Volga, and Terek Rivers entered Muscovite service. They usually served in the role of a frontier force.

In 1586, Muscovite regular troops returned to the mouth of the Terek. The Terek cossacks continued their activities but henceforth did so in the service of Moscow. The Terek cossacks were soon joined by the Greben' cossacks (cossacks of the 'mountain ridge'), a smaller group of cossacks.

The nature of the cossacks changed during the Time of Troubles. We will see that large numbers of men of any origin then went cossack out of necessity, that is, joined any cossack warlord willing to take them in. Moreover, when Michael Romanov became the first Tsar of his dynasty in 1613, his court's power and finances were so diminished that the Tsar and his advisors had no choice but to hire roving cossack bands for service in the army. No less than 15 such bands (again referred to as *stanitsy*), altogether more than 1,500 men, joined the Tsar's army. Many were former rebels, others were Tatars, and some were Commonwealth deserters or mercenaries. Arms, equipment, and even dress varied widely, since many by then had adopted Polish dress styles. In an attempt to mould them into an army, the cossack bands received new standards issued by the Treasury Chancellery (*Kazennyy Prikaz*) through the Military Deployments Chancellery (*Razryadnyy prikaz*). The number of cossack units so hired, most of them of company size, grew rapidly until their number in 1619 had reached at least 245. The majority of the men had never been free cossacks. Moreover, most of these cossack units were established not in the traditional cossack manner but by the state, which is evidenced by the manner of issuing standards. Many cossack atamans and some of their men also received land grant and salaries from the new government. Not all cossack units served at the same time, because many were lost or disbanded during operations. Others, dissatisfied, rebelled, especially from 1614 onwards. Nonetheless, the cossacks units established by Moscow under these circumstances provided the core of Tsar Michael's early armies.[49]

Tatar and Tribal Troops

Tatar allies formed important contingents within the Muscovite army. There were several Tatar enclaves in Muscovy, including, most importantly, those in Kasimov and Temnikov. These were integral parts of the Muscovite state and their soldiers fought as part of the Muscovite army. Most were nominally Muslims. The Tatars served under their own chiefs, generally a prince or *murza* (noble), and were organised into units based on the traditional steppe decimal system. Each group was generally allotted a town and its surroundings for subsistence. A typical example was the Tatar Khanate of Kasimov, which emerged in 1445 as a client state of Muscovy. The Kasimov Tatars regularly contributed strong contingents of Tatar cavalry to the Muscovite army and played a significant role in the Muscovite military system. Muscovite armies also might include groups of Noghai Tatars from the steppes north of the Caucasus. From a military point of view, Kasimov and Noghai Tatars probably differed little from other, originally Inner Asian Tatars.

There were non-Tatar tribal forces too. Among them were the Meshchory, a Finno-Ugrian population linked to the Kasimov Tatars who fought as irregular tribal cavalry. So did large numbers of Bashkirs, Chuvash, and Mordvins, who entered Muscovite military service in tribal groups.

It seems likely that up to 10,000 Tatars may have served in the armies of Muscovy at any given time, together with up to some 8,000 Chuvash, Mordvins, and others.[50] When mentioned in the sources, Tatars and other tribal troops appear under the leader's name, typically recognisable by his choice of title, most commonly that of *murza*.[51] They often operated

---

49 Alexander Malov, 'Standards of Russian Cossacks in 1613–1619', Karin Tetteris (ed), *In Hoc Signo Vinces: The Vexillological Seminar, Stockholm 2011 & 2013* (Stockholm: Armémuseum, 2016), pp.79–88.
50 Chernov, *Vooruzhennyye sily*, ch. 4, based on the estimate for 1630.
51 For an example from 1614, see Oleg A. Kurbatov, *Tikhvinskoye osadnoye sideniye 1613* (Moscow: Zeughaus, 2006), pp.35–6.

THE MUSCOVITE MILITARY ESTABLISHMENT

in conjunction with cossack cavalry, since their style of fighting was very similar.

The main difference between the tribal troops and other Muscovite forces was that the tribals less frequently carried firearms and accordingly were limited to the light cavalry role. Fletcher described the Tatar way of war:

> Their manner of fight or ordering of their forces is much after the Russe manner (spoken of before), save that they are all horsemen and carry nothing else but a bow, a sheaf of arrows, and a falcon sword [sabre] after the Turkish fashion. They are very expert horsemen and use to shoot as readily backward as forward. Some will have a horseman's staff like to a boar spear besides their other weapons. The common soldier hath no other armour than his ordinary apparel, viz., a black sheepskin with the wool side outward in the day time and inward in the night time, with a cap of the same. But their *mirza* or noblemen imitate the Turk both in apparel and armour.[52]

The sheepskin garments of the Tatar rank and file were quite different from that of the often splendidly dressed Tatar nobility.

Prominent Muslim Tatars, such as the Khan of the Kasimov Tatars, did not form part of the *mestnichestvo* system of order of precedence and served as commanders as the tsar saw fit. However, most Tatars in Muscovite service converted to Christianity, married into the Muscovite nobility, and in time were assimilated. As noted, a considerable number of Muscovite noble families claimed Tatar descent. However, this pattern began to change in the early seventeenth century.[53] The explanation may be as simple as most Tatars by then already having been assimilated into Muscovite society. But it is equally possible that the xenophobia encouraged by the Church, which labelled all foreigners as heathens and, moreover, wanted to forget Muscovy's old links to the Mongol Khans, had produced an environment in which Tatar descent was no longer regarded as desirable. Certainly, the Church by then had formulated an ideology according to which Mongols were evil, had contributed nothing to Orthodox Muscovy, and had to be resisted at all costs. By the late sixteenth century, the Church had already begun to spread the myth of the 'Tatar yoke' which supposedly had held the Christians back.[54]

---

52 Giles Fletcher, *Of the Russian Commonwealth* (1591), in Berry and Crummey, *Rude & Barbarous Kingdom*, 193. Spelling slightly amended.
53 Halperin, *Russia and the Golden Horde*, p.113.
54 Ostrowski, *Muscovy and the Mongols*, pp.244–5.

Foreign Mercenaries

The attitude of the Church towards foreigners clashed with the state's need for foreign expertise. Foreign mercenaries had been employed already in the fifteenth century, in particular as military engineers, artillerymen, and gunsmiths, and in the sixteenth century the number of foreign soldiers increased further. Some Italians still served with the Muscovite army, and the number of Germans and Lithuanians rose. Scots, English, Dutch, French, Danes, and Swedes also appeared in Muscovite service. In most Russian-language sources, all western and central Europeans were labelled Germans (*nemtsy*), since this term, which originally meant 'mute', implied anybody who could not speak the Russian language.

According to the (almost certainly incomplete) service registers, there were in 1578 a total of 400 'Germans' in Muscovite service in Moscow.[55] About a decade later, an English merchant and diplomatic agent, Jerome Horsey (d. 1626), noted about 1,200 foreign mercenaries in the Muscovite army. Horsey, who was in Muscovy from 1572 to 1591, presumably thought primarily of the western and central Europeans in Muscovite service, mentioning French, Scots, Dutch, Poles, and a few English.[56] There were others as well. In addition to Tatars who for one reason or another had been incorporated into the Muscovite army, the other contemporary Englishman, Fletcher, added: 'Of mercenary soldiers that are strangers (of whom they call *nemtsy*) they have at this time 4,300 of Poles; of Circassian that are under the Poles about 4,000 whereof 3,500 are abroad in his garrisons; of Dutch and Scots about 150; of Greeks, Turks, Danes and Swedes, all in one band, an 100 or thereabouts.'[57] At the time of Fletcher's writing, his description 'Circassian that are under the Poles' most likely referred to the Petyhortsy Circassians who began to migrate to Poland in 1562 (more on which below) but then, nonetheless, often took service with Muscovy.

Levies and Logistics

In wartime, the Tsar could still raise a general levy of commoners (*opolcheniye*; a term often translated as militia). However, the Mongol style of fighting had diminished the value of infantry, mostly reducing it to town garrison duty and support functions. Both townsmen and free peasants of taxpaying background were levied for military service, which was regarded as a hereditary obligation. Known as as *ratniki*, *pososhnyye lyudi*, or from

---

55 Viktor Ivanovich Buganov (ed.), *Razryadnaya kniga 1475-1598 gg.* (Moscow: Nauka, 1966), p.301.
56 Jerome Horsey, *Travels* (concluded in 1621), in Berry and Crummey, *Rude & Barbarous Kingdom*, pp.287, 288–9.
57 Giles Fletcher, *Of the Russian Commonwealth* (1591), in Berry and Crummey, *Rude & Barbarous Kingdom*, p.180.

THE MUSCOVITE MILITARY ESTABLISHMENT

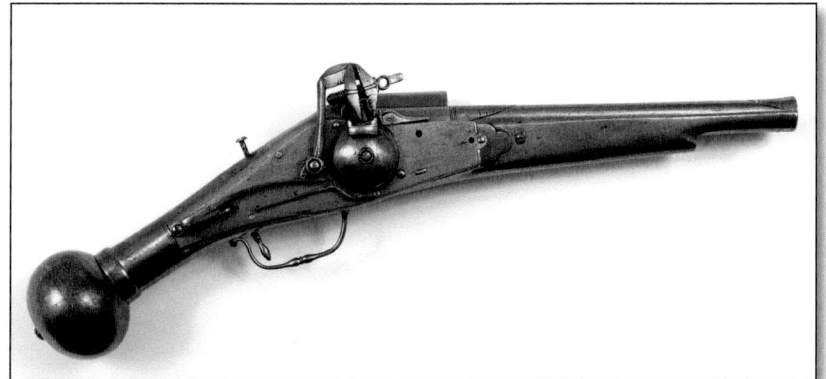

Wheellock pistol made in Germany, late sixteenth to early seventeenth century. Total length: 53.2 cm; barrel length: 23.4 cm; calibre: 13 mm. (Moscow Kremlin Armoury)

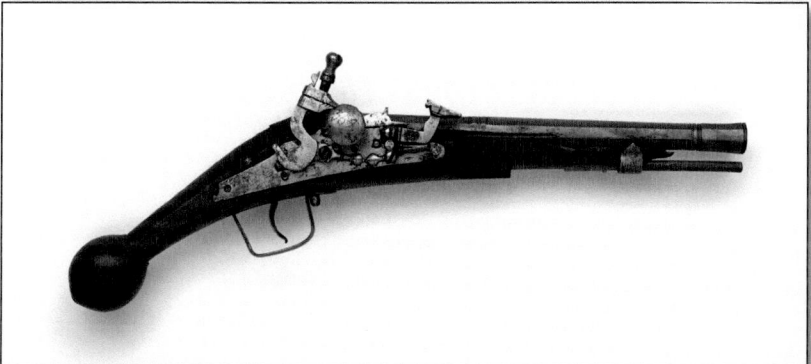

Snaplock pistol made in England, 1600–1610s. Total length: 36.5 cm; barrel length: 23.0 cm; calibre: 10.5 mm. (Moscow Kremlin Armoury)

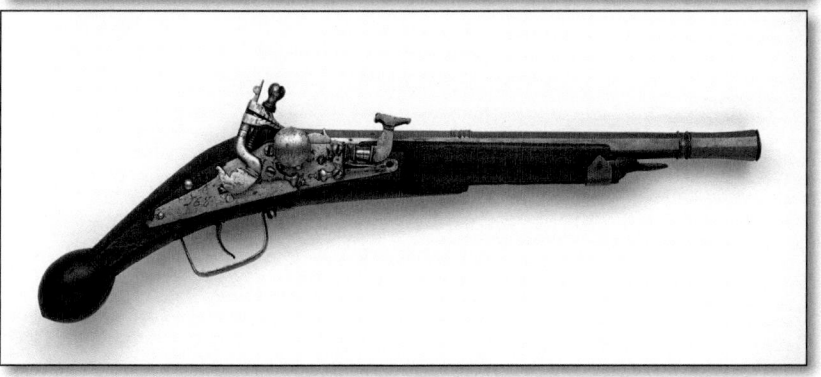

Snaplock pistol made in England, 1600–1610s. Total length: 39.0 cm; barrel length: 26.3 cm; calibre: 10 mm. (Moscow Kremlin Armoury)

the seventeenth century, *datochnyye lyudi*, meaning 'donated men', these men served in the host (*pososhnaya rat'*, named after the tax assessment units – *sokha*, pl. *sokhi* – according to which they were levied) and did so as foot as well as 'horse'.

Those on foot mostly served as conscripted labourers, tasked with the construction of field fortifications, bridges, and roads, repair of fortresses, disposal of the dead, and so on. The 'horse' (*konevoy*) consisted of men who served as coachmen in transportation units that provided the many horse-drawn carts and sledges necessary for the transportation of men, supplies, and the artillery train. Some were based on the postal service, consisting of men for this reason known as *yamshchiki*. Neither category was expected to take part in combat, except in self-defence. Although some of the foot occasionally served as infantry, the majority were only involved in physical labour.

The host was assembled upon order from the Tsar and fell under the authority of the *okol'nichiy*. It was commanded by voivodes and headmen (*golovy*). Numbers could be substantial, typically counted in the thousands in each Muscovite army. When called up, these men were paid by the state so that they could support themselves. At times, every third or fourth adult male of a certain region might be called up.[58]

Muscovy was slow to establish a logistical arm. Carts and wagons were not always sufficient. For transportation purposes, river boats played a major role because of Russia's network of large rivers. In particular heavy artillery was almost invariably moved by river.

Having said this, one legacy of the Mongol military system was that a Muscovite cavalry army often preferred not to encumber itself with a baggage train. As an additional bonus when operating in hostile territory, this put severe psychological pressure on the defenders, as they saw their property being systematically lost.[59]

Another device taken from the Mongol military system was the concept of the wagon fort, the use of one's wagons as a mobile defensive line. The wagon fort was particularly often used on the steppes, where there was no natural defensive cover. The horses were unharnessed and the wagons formed up into a square or a circle, with each wagon-pole pushed above the wagon ahead, or taken off. The wagons were chained together and whenever there was time, a ditch was dug in front of the carts. However, exits were always left at front and rear to allow for sallies in force. These exits were temporarily blocked with woodwork and chains until they were needed. The horses were kept inside the formation, available for cavalry sorties.

With the introduction of firearms, the Muscovites developed the wagon fort concept into the *gulyaygorod* ('walking town'), made up of a circle of wagons, fortified with about two-metre high mantlets and similar devices constructed of planks or logs and mounted on wheels or sledges, with holes bored for the musket-barrels. The timber was framed to clasp together one piece within another, as when building a log cabin.[60] The *gulyaygorod* was essentially a fortified camp. The wagon fort was an old steppe tradition, and the practice survived even after the new innovation, the *gulyaygorod*, had ultimately grown obsolete. In fact, the wagon train tactics were of considerable antiquity and common throughout Eurasia. On the other side of the continent, Chinese and Manchus used similar tactics. Because of the cavalry-oriented nature of the Muscovite army, the use of a wagon fort or *gulyaygorod* was defensive, not offensive.

---

58   Filjushkin, *Ivan the Terrible*, p.20.
59   Carol B. Stevens, *Russia's Wars of Emergence 1460–1730* (London: Routledge, 2013), p.45.
60   Giles Fletcher, *Of the Russian Commonwealth* (1591), in Berry and Crummey, *Rude & Barbarous Kingdom*, p.186.

THE MUSCOVITE MILITARY ESTABLISHMENT

Banners and Music

Each cavalry division had its own banner, made of silk damask, unpatterned silk, or cloth of taffeta, with sewn-on or painted ornaments. The most common ornaments were the six-armed Orthodox cross and biblical scenes, the image of Christ, the Virgin and the Holy Child, a saint such as the Archangel Michael, or even a multitude of saints with their hands extended in prayer. These images often appeared in combination. The sun, moon, stars, and other ornaments were common, too.[61]

In comparison, streltsy regiments and – from 1613 onwards – cossacks in the Tsar's service were issued standards of cheap cotton or, cheaper, dyed linen. The standards of these cossack units were regarded as purely utilitarian, so did not employ religious motifs. The most popular and easiest to produce motif seems to have been the six- or eight-pointed Orthodox cross. The colour of the fabric varied but included red, dark blue and purple, light green, and yellow. It was also common for cossacks to use captured enemy standards as their own.[62]

Following steppe fashion, Muscovites used copper kettledrums attached to the drummer's saddle for signalling. Moreover, Fletcher noted, they had kettledrums so big that they were:

> [carried] upon a board laid on four horses that are sparred together with chains, every drum having eight strikers or drummers, besides trumpets and shawms [a wind instrument of the oboe class] which they sound after a wild manner much different from ours. When they give any charge or make any invasion, they make a great halloo or shout altogether as loud as they can, which, with the sound of their trumpets, shawms, and drums, maketh a confused and horrible noise. So they set on first discharging their arrows, then dealing with their swords, which they use in a bravery to shake and brandish over their heads before they come to strokes.[63]

In addition to the customary music, Prince Dmitriy Shuyskiy's army that marched out of Moscow in June 1610 reportedly brought about 10 large bells, mounted on horse-drawn wagons.

---

61 Several have been preserved in the Army Museum, Stockholm.
62 Malov, 'Standards of Russian Cossacks', pp.79–88.
63 Giles Fletcher, *Of the Russian Commonwealth* (1591), in Berry and Crummey, *Rude & Barbarous Kingdom*, p.185.

Artist's drawing of two Muscovite standard-bearers. (Drevnosti Rossiyskogo gosudarstva, 1849–1853)

4

The Commonwealth Expeditionary Armies

The manpower potentially available to the Polish-Lithuanian Commonwealth in the early seventeenth century is difficult to estimate. The Commonwealth's total population has been estimated at about 11 to 12 million, of whom some 7.5 to 8.5 million lived in Poland and only some 3.5 million inhabited Lithuania and Ruthenia (modern-day Belarus and Ukraine).[1] Poland was more populous and wealthier than Lithuania and much more so than Ruthenia. When united, the Commonwealth compared favourably to Muscovy in population and wealth, which is unsurprising based on geography and agricultural potential. In comparison, Sweden was significantly smaller and had fewer resources, even when compared to Lithuania alone.

However, unlike Sweden and Muscovy the Commonwealth did not have a system for general mobilisation. Moreover, the military might of the Commonwealth was fragmented between the Crown of Poland, the Grand Duchy of Lithuania, numerous wealthy magnates, and a variety of other officeholders and local strongmen.[2] Poland had a king, but he was elected, kingship was not hereditary, and royal powers were limited. The Commonwealth perceived itself to be not a kingdom but a republic of nobles. The key interest of the nobility (*szlachta*, a term likely derived from German *Geschlecht*, 'family' or 'clan' although other hypothetical explanations have been suggested) was to preserve traditional noble liberties, that is, the right

---

1   Iwo Cyprian Pogonowski, *Poland: A Historical Atlas* (New York: Hippocrene Books, 1987), p.115; Andrej Kotljarchuk, *In the Shadows of Poland and Russia: The Grand Duchy of Lithuania and Sweden in the European Crisis of the mid-17th Century* (Södertörn University College, dissertation, 2006), p.28.
2   For an overview, see Richard Brzezinski, *Polish Armies 1569–1696* (London: Osprey Men-at-Arms Series 184 and 188, 2 vols, 1987); and in additional detail, Michal Paradowski, *Despite Destruction, Misery and Privations… The Polish Army in Prussia during the War against Sweden 1626–1629* (Warwick: Helion, 2020).

of every nobleman, however poor, to abstain from following the orders of autocratic kings. Incidentally, this also meant that there was widespread opposition to the formation of a regular army, in particular one based on the lowly infantry. A standing army was regarded as the tool of the Crown and accordingly, through its very existence, an existential threat to noble liberties.

Within the Commonwealth, the key fighting force was accordingly the one supposedly provided by the nobility. In theory, all nobles were available for military service. The nobility in the Commonwealth has been estimated as having constituted between six and eight percent of the total population. The nobility's share of the total population was far higher in the Commonwealth than elsewhere in Europe, except in Spain and Hungary. There were regional differences. The percentage of nobles as compared to the rest of the population was much higher in Royal Prussia and Poland than in Lithuania and Ruthenia, that is, even higher than the six to eight percent proposed as an average share.[3] In theory, the nobility should have been able to raise a fighting force of several hundred thousand well-armed and trained men. However, the Commonwealth never managed to raise more than a small share of all who supposedly should have served. There is no information on the share of the nobility, or of the general population, which the Commonwealth actually managed to raise for purposes of mobilisation.

Yet, the large share of nobles within the total population meant that there were always men willing to serve in wars, whether abroad or at home. Many were nobles in name only, since they lacked lands to sustain the lifestyle expected of them. For them, war was always the best option to make a living. Others might better be called rural gentry, although they certainly considered themselves nobles. Since their lands were too small to support numerous sons, some would instead search out opportunities as soldiers of fortune. Moreover, in the Commonwealth, rebellions were so commonplace that many were regarded as entirely lawful according to customary law and tradition. Participants in failed revolts often sought better opportunities elsewhere. Others went into foreign service for monetary gain. The men who in the early seventeenth century went to fight in Muscovy, on behalf of the various False Dmitriys or as part of King Sigismund's expeditionary armies, belonged to all these social groups.

The Commonwealth was the product of a meeting of Eastern and Western cultural, military, political, and religious ideas. Since the Middle Ages, the Polish nobility had grown increasingly close to their western, primarily German neighbours and adopted many of their customs. At the

---

3   Robert I. Frost, *After the Deluge: Poland-Lithuania and the Second Northern War, 1655–1660* (Cambridge: Cambridge University Press, 2003), p.10. There is no academic consensus on the share of the nobility of the total population, and some argue for higher figures. Kotljarchuk, *In the Shadows*, p.1, proposes a figure of 10 to 11 percent for Lithuania and Ruthenia.

THE COMMONWEALTH EXPEDITIONARY ARMIES

same time, major parts of the Commonwealth, in particular Lithuania and Ruthenia, remained part of an Eastern cultural, military, and religious tradition. This was obvious in the case of the predominant religion, which was Orthodox Christianity that looked to the east, not the west. Less obvious to the casual observer, but of no less importance, were the strong military influences inherited from the Mongol Empire and its successor states. The Mongol Empire had impacted upon the constituent parts of the Commonwealth no less than on Muscovy. Even so, Lithuanian and to some extent Ruthenian nobles, too, followed in the footsteps of their Polish peers, accepted polonisation, often converted to Catholicism, and over time grew closer to the German West than the Tatar East.

The complex mixture of Eastern and Western traditions was obvious in the Commonwealth's military affairs. With the exception of some enlisted units which fought in the Continental manner adopted from Germany, the Commonwealth's military forces employed forms of organisation and types of tactics which differed radically from those in Germany and Sweden. The Commonwealth's traditional military remained greatly influenced by the Inner Asian cavalry tactics habitually employed by Eurasian steppe nomads. Its core was formed by heavy cavalry, supported by highly mobile horse archers, or the traditional equivalents thereof in the form of Tatar or 'cossack' light cavalry. Incidentally, we will see that 'cossack' (Polish: *kozak*) was the customary term for any cavalry not labelled hussar, nor identified by an ethnic label, for which reason most Commonwealth light cavalry were called cossack-style.

The Commonwealth's military forces were divided into two distinct organisations: the Army of Poland, also known as the Crown Army, and the Army of Lithuania, also known as the Grand Ducal Army. Although both were under the authority of King Sigismund, since he was simultaneously King of Poland and Grand Duke of Lithuania, the two armies had separate chains of command so often experienced coordination problems.

The foundation of the Commonwealth army consisted of the *Kwarciani* or 'Quarter' army, so called after the quarter share (Polish: *kwarta*) of the royal revenues technically set aside for its maintenance.[4] Yet, the Commonwealth military establishment also included a panoply of other units. Of most interest to the King was the Royal Guard, which was the King's small personal army. However, there were also the standing garrisons of certain fortresses, the independent armies of cities and major towns, and the private armies of the magnates (the wealthier nobles). Units of unpaid noble volunteers often played a major role, too, serving not for pay

---

4 Introduced in 1562–1563 as a means to finance the army, the quarter was already in 1567 reduced to a fifth. Subsequently, it continued to be levied at the same fixed rate, regardless of ongoing inflation which over time greatly reduced the monetary value of what once had been intended as a quarter of real total revenues. It was only the Polish Crown which had a quarter army; Lithuania never had one, nor any other standing force under Commonwealth control.

(since they did not receive any) but for the right to plunder the supposedly enemy territories through which they passed. As might be expected, these freebooters were poorly disciplined and often caused major disruptions. On occasion, 'district soldiers' were raised locally as needed, as the availability of funding allowed and the district parliament (*sejmik*; 'small parliament') permitted.

Peasant and townsman levies could be raised, too. Levies were known under names such as *wybraniecka* ('chosen' which in this case meant 'conscripted') or *łanowa* ('acreage-based'), depending on the basis for the levy, which fundamentally was a form of taxation. Those raised from the towns served as infantry, while those raised in the country generally served as mounted soldiers. Peasant and townsman levies were not used for the expeditions into Muscovy, so will not be further described here.

In similarity to the situation in Muscovy, the clergy habitually preached hatred between Protestant, Catholic, and Orthodox Christians and between these and non-Christians such as Jews. In this regard, there was little difference between the Commonwealth and Muscovite clergy (or for that matter, the clergy in Sweden). For this reason, religious strife customarily hampered cooperation further, both within the Commonwealth and between the Commonwealth and its neighbours.

Tactical Doctrines

The Commonwealth army was primarily a cavalry army. By tradition, the cavalry was divided into 'hussars' (*husaria*; armoured cavalry) and 'cossacks' (*jazda kozacka*; in effect everything else, since in this context the term only signified a non-hussar horseman, not necessarily a Ukrainian cossack).

The traditional troop types of the Commonwealth military employed no formal tactical doctrine. Instead, the different troop types fought in their respective customary manner. The hussars fought as shock cavalry, while the cossack-style cavalry employed traditional steppe tactics, including feigned flights and other types of disruptive attacks to soften up the enemy and the provision of flank cover to the shock cavalry. They also played an important role in reconnaissance and foraging.

A Commonwealth cavalry army customarily drew up in half-moon array, with cossack-style cavalry on the flanks where it was deployed in a forward position, heavy cavalry in the centre where it was held back until the decisive charge, and any infantry and artillery deployed between the units of horse. The Lithuanian cavalry, with its higher share of Tatar and Circassian cavalry, may have fought in even looser formations than the Polish cavalry. However, this should not be interpreted as a lack of an order of battle. By tradition, a Commonwealth army deployed in what was known as the 'Old Polish Order'. In reality, this was a remnant of the Mongol division of armies into five tactical units: vanguard, main force, left and right wings, and rearguard. The same order of battle was used by Muscovites, Tatars, and others who had emerged from the same tradition.

THE COMMONWEALTH EXPEDITIONARY ARMIES

The Commonwealth cavalry regarded itself as the key arm of any army. Commonwealth commanders were confident that a shock by the hussars would defeat any enemy, in particular after he had been softened up by cossack-style cavalry. Within a few decades, developments in Swedish and Continental tactics and armament would expose the fallacy of this notion, but so far, Commonwealth hussars faced no enemy that they could not beat. They had proved it against the Swedes in the 1605 battle of Kircholm and they would soon prove it again, against Swedish and Muscovite armies. The confidence of the hussars remained unshaken, and for good reason.

Infantry, regardless of type, was by tradition strictly used for holding or attacking fortifications or for the provision of fire support to the cavalry. Infantrymen were not expected to fight on an open field, and they were certainly not expected to gain honour at the expense of the cavalry.

Well-to-do Polish hussar, early seventeenth century. Armed with lance, two wheellock pistols, palash, and sabre, for protection he wears the customary half-armour, a *kapalin* helmet (inspired by the Eastern *szyszak*) which later would also form the pattern for Swedish cavalry helmets (Fredholm von Essen, *Lion from the North* 1, p.179), and a leopard fur. Not all hussars wore wings. The armoured hussar was a formidable opponent. (Tommy Hellman)

As a result, infantry played a very limited role in the Commonwealth expeditionary armies, or did not participate at all.

Organisation and Training

We have already seen that the Commonwealth fielded two military establishments: the Crown army of Poland and the Ducal army of the Grand Duchy of Lithuania. The King and Grand Duke appointed four individuals as commanders of his two armies. The Grand Hetman of the Crown and the Field Hetman of the Crown commanded the Polish army. Likewise, the Grand Hetman of the Grand Duchy of Lithuania and the Field Hetman of the Grand Duchy of Lithuania commanded the Lithuanian army. In theory, it was the Field Hetman (*hetman polny*) who commanded the army's operations in the field, for which reason he was marginally inferior in rank to his Grand Hetman (*hetman wielki*). In reality, both hetmans maintained independent commands and often preferred not to cooperate in operations. Hetman was a title which betrayed both German and Turkic linguistic influences. Its ultimate origin was the German word *hauptmann* ('captain') which was borrowed into Polish as *hetman*.

A hetman carried a spherical mace (*buława*) as the symbol of command. This tradition was found throughout eastern Europe and ultimately derived from the Mongols. As with all royal appointments, the tenure of these offices was for life. The King had the right to appoint, but he could not dismiss.

Immediately before the events under consideration here, from 1581 to 1605, the statesman and soldier Jan Sariusz Zamoyski (1542–1605) served as Crown Grand Hetman in addition to his already-existing position as Grand Crown Chancellor. Politically, Zamoyski aimed to follow an independent course for the Commonwealth which also included constitutional reforms. This made him clash, for different reasons, with the policies and desires of both King Sigismund and the nobility, so the position of Crown Grand Hetman remained vacant from his death until 1618 when the veteran soldier Stanisław Żółkiewski (1547–1620) was appointed. Żółkiewski had then already served as Crown Field Hetman from 1588 to 1618. When he was promoted, the position of Crown Field Hetman fell vacant instead. In the Lithuanian army, Jan Karol Chodkiewicz (*c.*1570–1621), another veteran soldier, served as Lithuanian Grand Hetman from 1605 onwards. Meanwhile, the position of Lithuanian Field Hetman remained vacant until 1615, when Krzysztof Radziwiłł (1585–1640) was appointed.

Both the Crown army and the Grand Ducal army were in turn divided into two distinct administrative units, each known as an *autorament* (perhaps best translated as 'contingent' or 'enlistment'). The 'national autorament' (*narodowy autorament*) consisted of those troops raised according to the traditional, Eastern, and ultimately medieval system, while the 'foreign autorament' (*cudzoziemski autorament*) consisted of those raised along the modern Continental model adopted from Germany. The two types of units, national and foreign, were organised in fundamentally different ways and employed very different tactics. They were also characterised by different standards of training. While the men of the national autorament might be good fighters, they only seldom trained in units. On the other hand, the men of the foreign autorament might well have received training in modern tactics and methods, especially if they had served in Germany.

The National Autorament

The national autorament consisted primarily of cavalry. Its smallest administrative unit was the 'retinue' (*poczet*), which consisted of a gentleman cavalier known as a 'companion' (*towarzysz*) and his retainers (*pocztowy*, pl. *pocztowi*), each also sometimes referred to as a 'lad' or 'servant' (*pachołek*), who might number between one and 24 depending on the gentleman's rank and wealth. In addition to retainers, each 'retinue' included a number of non-combatants: camp followers such as wives or other dependents and civilian servants whose duties included the handling of wagons and supplies.

A number of 'retinues' constituted a 'company' (*rota*, alternatively 'banner', *chorągiew*), which was the smallest administrative and tactical unit within the national autorament. The same Polish term was used for both horse and foot. For practical purposes, the unit will here be referred to either as a banner of horse or a company of foot. It was commanded by a 'rotamaster' (*rotmistrz*), who had received a patent or contract to raise a unit of a certain number of horses (or portions, if infantry; Polish: *porcje*). He would then gather a suitable number of companions, each of whom would bring his own retinue of retainers and civilians. The rotamaster would appoint one of them his 'lieutenant' (*porucznik*) as second in command. The position of rotamaster was often nominal only, and the lieutenant would then lead the banner or company. Another retainer would be appointed ensign to carry the unit's banner. The rotamaster, too, would bring his own 'retinue', but this was significantly larger than the others. In part, because of his rank, but also because he needed to appoint several drummers or pipers for his banner or company.

The size of a newly raised banner or company varied according to the patent issued. Hussar companies ranged from 100 to 200 in strength. Companies belonging to senior nobles or generals tended to be significantly larger.

While most units of the national autorament were cavalry, it included some arquebusier or musketeer infantry companies, mostly of a type inspired by the Hungarian haiduk system. Such infantry had played a significant role in sixteenth-century Commonwealth armies, but in comparison to Continental companies, this type of unit was already becoming obsolete. Nonetheless, such companies were formed, in the same manner as the banners of horse, with a company strength usually between 100 and 300 portions.

SWEDEN'S WAR IN MUSCOVY 1609-1617

A number of banners or companies were temporarily assembled into a formation known as a *pułk*. As noted, this was a term of ancient origin which previously best was described as a division but henceforth was acquiring the meaning of regiment.[5] This constituted the main tactical unit intended to operate independently. This formation was commanded by the senior rotamaster who accordingly was known as 'colonel' (*pułkownik*). A

Polish hussar in half-armour, helmet, and leopard fur. Armed with a war hammer and sabre, he would also carry a lance, a palash or armour-piercing sword, and probably wheellock pistols as well. (*Tablica Gołuchowska*. Oil panel painting by unknown artist, 1600-1625. Originally in Gołuchów Castle, presently in the National Museum, Poznań.)

Wealthy noble in Polish dress. He wears a *żupan* garment, cloak, soft leather shoes, and feathered cap, all of Eastern origin. (*Tablica Gołuchowska*. Oil panel painting by unknown artist, 1600-1625. Originally in Gołuchów Castle, presently in the National Museum, Poznań.)

---

5   We have seen that this military term disseminated into the Slavic languages, in time becoming Polish *pułk* and Russian *polk*.

regiment might consist of no more than two or as many as 40 companies, but from five to 12 seem to have been most common. The *pułk* was not a permanent formation, nor did it have a staff unit.

The Foreign Autorament

Things worked differently in the foreign autorament. It was so named because it to a significant degree consisted of enlisted soldiers raised in the customary Continental manner in western and central Europe. There was little fundamental difference between soldiers enlisted in this manner, whether they were in Commonwealth, Swedish, or Muscovite service, with regard to skills and training, and prisoners of war could usually be inserted into existing units without difficulties.

However, not all men within the foreign units were foreigners. Numerous Germans lived within the Commonwealth, in Prussia, Courland, and Livonia, and yet more importantly, in the great merchant cities such as Danzig. Significant numbers of them served in foreign units of the state armies.

The foreign units included both cavalry and infantry, organised and trained in the Continental manner. They were often referred to as German units, since most of the soldiers enlisted in these units were Germans and German was used as the language of command. Besides, we have seen that it was common for speakers of Slavic languages customarily to label all western and central Europeans as Germans, since this term, which originally meant 'mute', implied anybody who could not speak the language. Many Commonwealth nobles regarded the foreign autorament with suspicion.

The Royal Guard

The Royal Guard (*Gwardia królewska*) existed independently of the state army, and was paid from the King's household treasury. The Royal Guard included the Court Hussar Banner and the Trabant Guard; the latter was a traditional princely guard formation in Germany, the name of which seems to derive from the fifteenth century. From an organisational and linguistic perspective, it was the equivalent of the Swedish Drabant Guard. King Sigismund also had about 400 haiduk infantry in the Royal Guard.

Private Armies

The great Polish and Lithuanian magnates commonly maintained private armies for the protection of their vast estates. In times of peace, it was not unusual for a wealthy magnate to control an army which outnumbered the combined strength of the state army and Royal Guard. Bishops, abbots, and many other senior churchmen likewise controlled huge estates, and like the magnates, they too maintained substantial private military forces, sometimes entire regiments and complete artillery trains. In exceptional cases, a private army might number up to 10,000 men.

The private armies were used for private family feuds and for the protection of the estates. They were generally not employed in support of the state army, since they were privately funded and the best the King could offer the magnates was in most cases no more than additional land and civil titles, both of which they already had aplenty. As a result, a magnate might provide a few hundred men as a token force to support the Commonwealth army in times of need but he would generally not deploy the bulk of his forces, unless he found his own lands at risk.

Large towns and cities raised private armies, too. Each would have a professional town guard which also functioned as a police force, and a burgher militia, which in times of war was raised for defensive purposes. Large towns and cities also had the means to hire enlisted units of soldiers. Richest and most powerful was the city of Danzig, which had the means and will to invest in an arsenal with a vast stock of modern arms and armaments, a comprehensive system of fortifications of the most up-to-date type, the enlistment of entire regiments of foreign professional soldiers, a well-armed burgher militia strong enough to field yet more well-organised regiments, and a private fleet for maritime protection and for securing the city's access to the Baltic Sea. Danzig was, except in name, an independent state.[6]

The Levy of the Nobility

The Levy of the Nobility (*Pospolite ruszenie*) was a mobilisation of nobles performed according to a custom which (like its Swedish counterpart, the Retinue of Nobles) derived from the Middle Ages. The Levy could be raised as a 'small' one, if the problem was only regional in nature, or as a 'grand' one, with the King in command. The Grand Levy of the Nobility would in theory include all nobles within the realm, although that many were never successfully raised.

When raised, the Levy was organised into units based on province (Polish: *województwo*, a term in English variously translated as a voivodeship or palatinate; each was governed by a voivode or palatine, *wojewoda*), land (*ziemia*), and district (*powiat*). Each noble was responsible for bringing his own arms, armament, and provisions. He also had to provide the same for his men.

A regional Levy was usually commanded by a castellan (*kasztelan*; a position which originally signified the keeper of a royal castle and hence ranked below the voivode). In times of war, the castellan served as the

---

6   Werner Hahlweg, *Das Kriegswesen der Stadt Danzig 1: Die Grundzüge der Danziger Wehrverfassung 1454–1793* (Berlin: Junker und Dünnhaupt, 1937), p.16.

pułkownik of the men of his district. The nobles formed up in banners each under a rotamaster. Most were cossack-style cavalry, since this troop type was cheaper to raise and thus more accessible to the average noble.

In theory, the nobles of the Levy had to participate in annual musters in each district so that it could be ascertained that each had acceptable arms, armour, and equipment. As we have seen, the total number of adult male nobles who should have shown up for these musters was considerable, especially in Royal Prussia and western Poland, and probably more so than available logistics would have allowed. It is accordingly hard to escape the conclusion that the idea of a Commonwealth army based on the Grand Levy of the Nobility always was a fiction, primarily entertained by the nobles themselves. Moreover, in Royal Prussia and western Poland, the Levy seldom had to face actual combat. The situation was very different in the south and east, where the Lithuanian Levy often had to mobilise to confront raids by Crimean Tatars. This gave the individual members of the Levy in these regions significantly more combat experience than their counterparts in western Poland.

The Levy, particularly within the Crown army, had a well-established reputation for poor discipline. Every Commonwealth noble, even a minor one, claimed the right to question and veto orders, including those from the King. For this reason, it was always difficult and time-consuming to gather the Levy in one location, and when eventually mobilised, it was equally or yet more difficult to keep it together, and persuade it to actually to attack the enemy. This was not necessarily because of lack of bravery, but because some of its constituent nobles might feel that they had a better grasp of tactics and strategy than their commanding officer. Since each noble had to provide his own provisions, many returned home as soon as their initial supplies ran out. It was a common belief that as long as the Levy had participated in at least one action, whether a victory or defeat, it had fulfilled its obligations with honour, and so could dissolve, regardless of the strategic circumstances. Besides, every noble claimed the right to depart for personal business, whenever needed, so when confronted by an able enemy, panic easily broke out, with each man departing in a hurry. A Commonwealth army based on the Levy might disintegrate overnight.

Hussars

The foremost Commonwealth troop type was the hussar. Famous as the winged hussars, they were levied from the nobility in both Poland and Lithuania and served as armoured lancers. Each man brought armour and dress as splendid as he could afford, so while a hussar unit presented a spectacular appearance, there was little or no uniformity. Many Commonwealth hussars wore 'wings', a wing being made of a line of feathers inserted into a wooden frame which was affixed to the hussar's saddle.[7] The feathers might be eagle, vulture, or falcon, although poorer nobles at times used painted goose feathers instead. The hussar troop type first seems to have emerged in Serbia and was common also in Hungary. In sixteenth-century Poland, this type of soldier had replaced the western and central European-style knight in full plate armour who had dominated warfare there since the late Middle Ages.

Most hussars wore a lobster-tailed pot helmet of the originally Inner Asian *szyszak* type, which also was used by Muscovites and from the late sixteenth century was becoming common in Germany under the name *zischägge*. They also wore half-armour, that is, plate armour covering the upper body and arms (vambraces), or a combination of chainmail and plate. A set of hussar armour commonly weighed from 18 to 20 kg. Yet the breastplate was only around 3 to 3.5 mm thick, which made it vulnerable to the fire of heavy muskets such as the Dutch 10 bore weapon. The armour was often ornate, especially among those who had the means, which would have been the majority of those nobles who served as hussars.

The hussar carried a light lance, about five metres long. It was beautifully painted, and made from two separate pieces which were hollowed out for lightness. Above the polygonal handgrip was a flattened ball which provided some balance and to a certain extent served as a hand-guard. Since the hollow lance broke easily when it made contact, it was necessary to bring large numbers of spare lances in the supply train.

Because of the Polish hussar's origin in the medieval knighthood of western Poland, some hussars by this time still carried a two-handed knightly sword akin to the Swedish command sword as their weapon of choice for use when the lance had shattered. However, in the sixteenth century Ottoman Turkish influences strongly affected hussar armament.

Hussars of Aleksander Zborowski's White Hussar Banner at the 1610 battle of Klushino, with sidearms hanging from the wrist, attached to lanyards, to keep up the momentum during the charge. (Szymon Boguszowicz, c. 1620; L'viv National Gallery of Arts at Oles'ko)

---

7 Later in the century, the feathered wooden frame was more commonly affixed to the hussar's armour backplate.

Henceforth, it became common to carry, as sidearms, not one but at least two weapons: a curved sabre, suspended from a waist belt in the customary manner, and a long, straight sword, either the type with a sabre hilt known as a backsword or palash or an armour-piercing sword, hung on the horse under the left side of the saddle. When the horseman needed his sidearm quickly he would hang it from his wrist, attached to a lanyard in the same manner as Muscovite horsemen.

The sabre was a variation of the Turco-Mongolian wide-bladed and slightly curved cavalry sword. It reached the Commonwealth from Hungary, which also gave the weapon its name: Hungarian *szablya*, Polish: *szabla*. Ultimately, however, the weapon derived from the Ottoman Empire, where the name was known, in Turkish, as *kılıç*; 'sword'. The Hungarians adopted the sabre widely after the Ottoman victory over them in the battle of Mohács in 1526. The sabre had a moderately curved, single cutting edge, except for the end of the blade around the point which was flared and double-edged (and known in Turkish as the *yalman*). In the Commonwealth, a variant of the sabre known as a *karabela* (a term possibly derived from Turkish *karabela*, 'black curse') soon evolved. This was a regular sabre but with the grip stylised as the head of a bird. Both this variant and the more common one, styled on the Hungarian sabre, became widespread.

The backsword or palash (Polish: *pałasz*; German: *Pallasch*; Hungarian: *pallos*, 'sword'), a long, straight broadsword with a sabre grip, was introduced to the Commonwealth soon after the introduction of the Ottoman sabre. The palash is traditionally believed to have been an East European invention, aimed to be more efficient against plate armour than the slashing sabre and also better suited for thrusting. However, the weapon type was used already by the Ottomans who in turn may have been inspired by blades in existence during the pre-Ottoman Abbasid Empire. In the Commonwealth, the palash was commonly single-edged, except that it had

Hussar, in customary half-armour, *szyszak* helmet and leopard fur, 1620. (woodcut by Wojciech Rakowski, in *Pobudka zacnym synom Korony Polskiey do służby Woienne* ('Call to arms of worthy sons of the Polish Crown to military service'))

SWEDEN'S WAR IN MUSCOVY 1609–1617

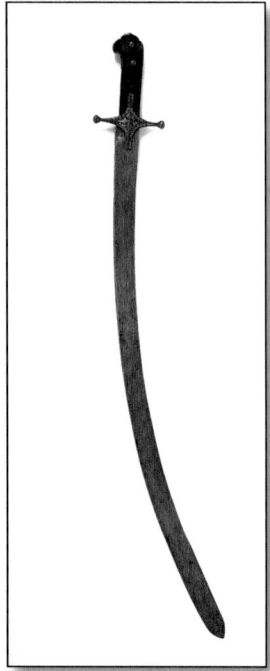

Karabela, dated and attributed to seventeenth-century Poland. Total length 88.0 cm, blade length 76.6 cm. (Royal Armoury, Stockholm; photo: Samuel Uhrdin)

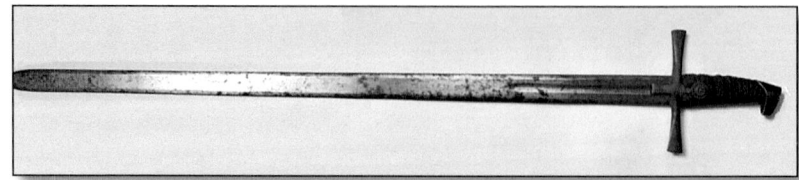

Above: Backsword or palash (*pałasz*), seventeenth century. (Private collection)

Right & Below: Armour-piercing sword (*koncerz*), seventeenth century. (Private collection)

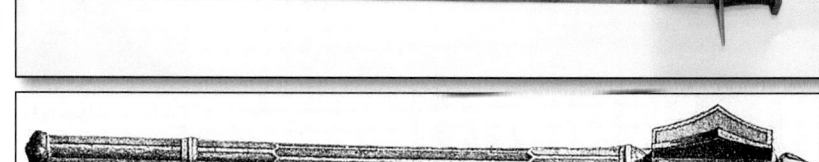

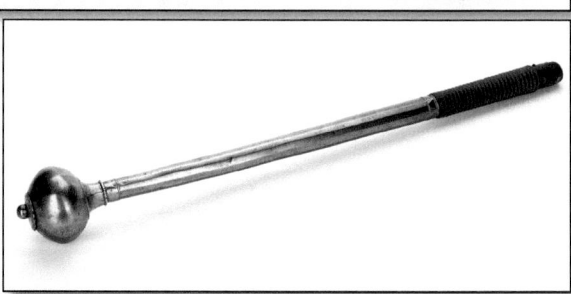

Above: Flanged mace of the *buzdygan* type, carried as the symbol of rank of a rotamaster. (Zygmunt Gloger)

Spherical mace of the *buława* type in Ottoman style, carried as the symbol of rank of a hetman. Steel, with a hollow wooden grip covered in black leather. Total length 285 mm, head length 87 mm, grip length 135 mm with end-piece damaged. Dated to about 1600. (Skokloster Castle; photo: Erik Lernestål)

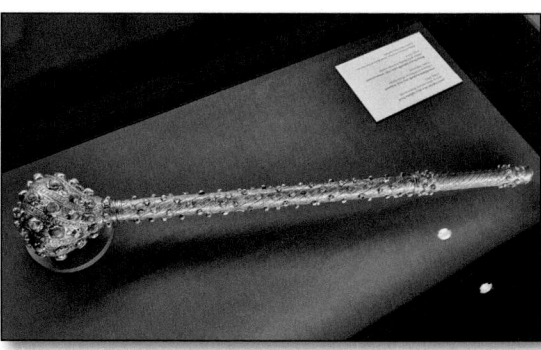

Another, yet more decorated mace of the *buława* type in Ottoman style. Belonged to Janusz Radziwiłł, Field Hetman of Lithuania in 1646. (Private collection of Maciej Radziwiłł; photo: Pofka)

THE COMMONWEALTH EXPEDITIONARY ARMIES

a Turkish-style *yalman*. This suggests an Ottoman origin for this weapon as well. The weapon's blade length reached up to about 94 cm.[8] The palash was longer than the sabre and primarily intended to be used from horseback.

Even longer was the armour-piercing sword (Polish: *koncerz*; German: *Panzerstecher*). Suitable for piercing chainmail armour and solely intended to be used from horseback, it was very long, with the blade alone from 1.25 up to 1.39 m long.[9] Total length might exceed 1.5 m. The weapon was of pre-Ottoman origin and probably developed in central Europe during the late Middle Ages.

As if this was not enough, officers and many nobles added a war hammer to their set of sidearms. This weapon was also the sign of somebody in command. The rotamaster might instead carry a flanged mace (Polish: *buzdygan*) as a symbol of his rank. A hetman, as noted, carried a spherical mace (Polish: *buława*) as the symbol of supreme command.

By this time, most hussars also carried firearms, likely a pair of wheellock pistols and/or a wheellock carbine.

Since each Commonwealth noble supplied his own arms and equipment, they wore fundamentally civilian dress. Noble dress was expensive, with plenty of silks, satins, and velvets. Those who had the means added gold and silver. Customary Commonwealth male dress consisted of a long undergarment (Polish: *żupan*), of Inner Asian origin and known by a name of Turkic or Tatar origin. It was closed from right to left and had sleeves terminated with a characteristic elongated cuff (known as a 'dog's ear') that could be used to cover part of the hand.

Noble in Polish dress, from a stucco relief with the popular motif 'Death and the noble' in Tarłów dated to the 1640s. Although of a slightly later date, this noble is typical of those who served in the Commonwealth cavalry, whether as hussar, cossack-style cavalryman, or officer in other units. He wears a *żupan* undergarment, caftan, soft leather boots, and high, fur-lined cap, all of Eastern origin. Armed with a sabre and a long-shafted war hammer which also served as a walking-stick, he in addition carries a short whip (instead of spurs), a wheellock spanner for his pistol or carbine, and a flat sabretache container on his side. The sabretache, in the early 1630s often made of red leather, was intended for carrying ammunition, but contemporary observers noted that they were equally often employed for carrying letters, documents, a comb, and money. Although less frequently depicted in illustrations from the Time of Troubles, the sabretache had a long history in the region and certainly existed by then.

---

8   Wojciech Zablocki, *Szable świata* (Warsaw: Bellona, 2011), p.83.
9   Zablocki, *Szable*, p.84.

SWEDEN'S WAR IN MUSCOVY 1609-1617

Noble on horseback, unarmoured but with a hussar wing fastened to his saddle in the customary manner to give a festive air to the occasion. His two haiduk infantrymen carry pole-axes of the *berdysz* type and wear particularly distinctive headgear, again to fit the occasion. (Commonwealth envoys to Paris, 1645)

Among nobles, the dog-ears were usually worn upturned to show the different-coloured lining. Over this garment was worn a caftan (Polish: *kontusz*), to this was added high but soft leather boots, and typically a high, fur-lined cap (Polish: *kuczma*; Ukrainian: *kuchma*) of Tatar origin, frequently decorated with a feather or two. Many men shaved their foreheads and necks but for a long lock on the top, combed onto the forehead, and wore long moustaches, a custom derived from the Tatars and common also in the Ottoman Empire. Others did not go to this extreme, but still shaved more of their heads and necks than was common in western and central Europe. Poles who left the Commonwealth for travels within Germany or further afield customarily adopted European hairstyles.

Many wealthy hussars wore the fur of a wild animal, preferably a leopard or bear, over his armour. Those who could not acquire a leopard fur might have another suitable fur dyed with spots so that it looked like leopard. Less wealthy nobles might have to make do with a wolf fur as a cloak.

Since Commonwealth hussars were the lineal descendants of the western and central European-style, Polish knight in full plate armour, unlike most other Eastern Commonwealth cavalry they used spurs in the

Noble on horseback, unarmoured but with a hussar wing fastened to his saddle in the customary manner. The use of hussar wings for festive purposes was common. (Stefano della Bella)

THE COMMONWEALTH EXPEDITIONARY ARMIES

European manner and their horse-riding manner was more European than Inner Asian in style. Hussars were expected to build up the charge from a walk (for 100 paces, or 75 m), to a trot (for the next 200 paces, or 150 m), followed by a gallop (for another 120 paces, or 90 m), until the charge itself began at a distance of 80 paces (60 m) from the enemy line.[10]

Being the socially most prestigious of Commonwealth military men, hussars formed the smallest share of the cavalry. Many small battles were fought wholly without hussars, since they tended to attach themselves to commanders of a certain social stature, which meant that they primarily served in the larger armies. Senior commanders had almost invariably

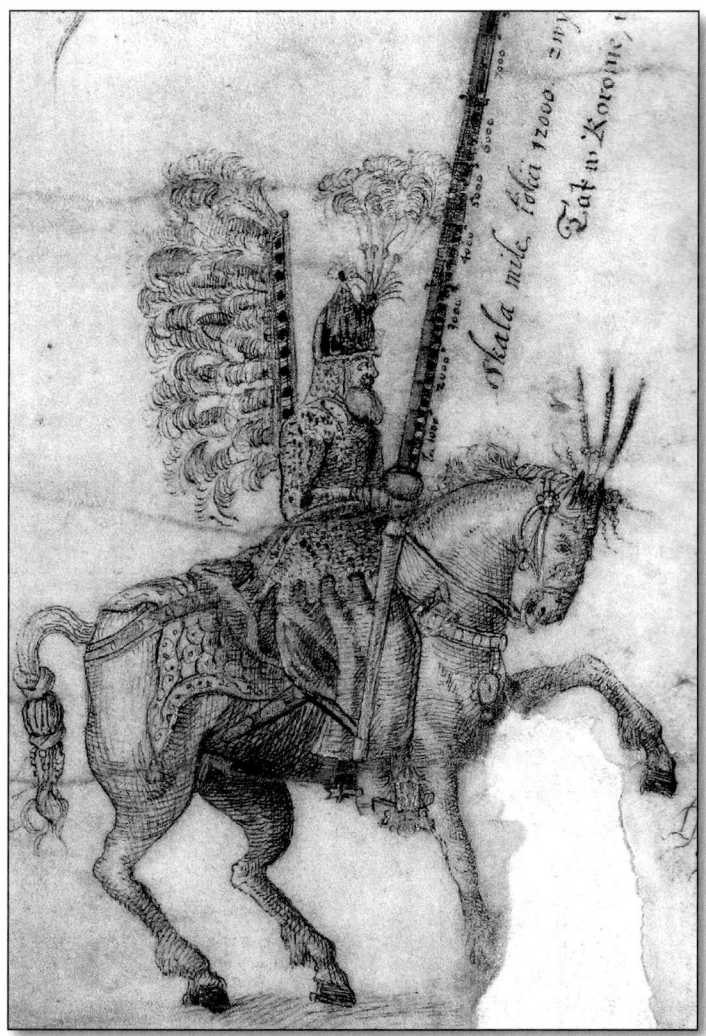

Lithuanian hussar, 1645. The depiction was used for a map, which explains why the lance is drawn as a scale indicator – certainly not the normal manner in which a lance was painted. Otherwise, the depiction shows some of the differences in appearance between Lithuanian and Polish hussars. This hussar, for instance, wears a *pancerni*-style chainmail cuirass, not half-armour like the wealthier Polish hussars. Yet more conspicuously, he wears a full beard in the manner of northern Ruthenians and Muscovites. (Biržai Region Museum Sėla, Biržai, Lithuania)

---

10 *Regulamen exercerunku dla regimentow Konnych Gwardyi J. K. Mci Koronney y WX. Lit.* (Warsaw: Drukarnia nadworny J. K. Mciy PP. Kom. Eduk. Narod., 1786), p.577. The Crown Horse Guard regulations from 1786, which seemingly all modern-day Polish historians hold as representative also for previous centuries.

served as hussars. However, and again for reasons of social prestige, the average hussar served only for a short period of time, so as to fulfil family expectations, and most were in no way professional soldiers.

Cossack-style Cavalry and Pancerni

As noted, in the Commonwealth cavalry the term 'cossack' had little if anything to do with the Ukrainian cossacks of the Lower Dnieper. In a similar manner to the first Muscovite cossacks, the Commonwealth 'cossacks' originated among Tatars in Polish and Lithuanian service. By the early seventeenth century, soldiers referred to as cossacks were raised throughout the Commonwealth. Indeed, we have seen that cossack was the customary term for any cavalry not labelled as hussars, for which reason we will refer to them as cossack-style cavalry.

Cossack-style cavalrymen were primarily armed with composite bows, carried in a bowcase on the left side and a quiver on the right. Some, but by no means all, also carried a wheellock carbine and/or several wheellock pistols. Others might bring a musketoon, a musket with a short barrel for use on horseback. Even so, they would still carry a composite bow in the customary manner. Many still wore a round shield (Polish: *kalkan*) for protection, of the type prevalent among the Crimean Tatars, in the Caucasus, and incidentally within the Ottoman Empire. As a sidearm, they would carry a sabre.

Like Muscovites and other easterners, cossack-style cavalrymen rode horses in the Mongol style, with short stirrups that allowed them to stand clear of the saddle. They used Mongol-style saddles and stirrups, and relied on a Mongol-style short whip instead of spurs.

Over time, many cossack-style cavalrymen acquired chainmail or splint-mail armour with vambraces and so became 'armoured' (*pancerni*). They would also acquire helmets. Some well-to-do cossack-style companies might be better armoured and equipped than hussars from poor families.

The *pancerni* cossacks are best known for their use of chainmail cuirasses and the *misiurka* helmet (from *Misr*, Arabic for 'Egypt', a term derived by way of Russian *misyurka*, of the same origin). Despite its name, this type of helmet was of Inner Asian origin and also very common in Persia and on the Indian subcontinent. The sub-type of this helmet most common in the Commonwealth was a low variant characterised by the small, round metal plate which only covered the crown of the skull (a style known in Persian as *kulah-zirah*). This type of helmet came with a long chainmail coif or neck guard, which was fastened under the chin when preparing for battle. Many mem no doubt wore the chainmail coif unfastened when no danger was expected. The helmet included a significant layer of flat padding underneath the round metal plate, which made it look taller.

Although the *misiurka* was closely associated with the *pancerni*, a *pancerni* cossack-style cavalryman might instead wear the *szyszak* helmet of hussar fame, just as some hussars instead wore the *misiurka* helmet.

THE COMMONWEALTH EXPEDITIONARY ARMIES

Polish cossack-style cavalry officer, armed with bow and sabre. Note the costly brocade dress and the single vambrace to protect the left arm. (*Tablica Gołuchowska*. Oil panel painting by unknown artist, 1600–1625. Originally in Gołuchów Castle, presently in the National Museum, Poznań.)

Lithuanian *pancerni*, 1645, although illustrated without lance. (Biržai Region Museum Sėla, Biržai, Lithuania)

The Lithuanian *pancerni* differed slightly from those raised elsewhere in the Commonwealth. The Lithuanian *pancerni* seem more commonly to have been of Tatar or Circassian origin (and were hence often known as Petyhortsy; see below) than their counterparts in the Crown Army. They were also differently armed: in similarity to some Muscovite and Caucasian troops most carried, instead of firearms, a 2.5 m long bear spear (a heavy spear with a leaf-shaped head, known as *rogatina* or, in Ruthenian, *rohatyna*) and a short lance (*dzida*), about 1.8 to 2.0 m long. The lance derived from a type of javelin known as *djid* (a term from the Caucasus), which was previously in widespread use and remained common in Muscovy.

Tatar Cavalry

In previous centuries, a number of Tatar and Circassian groups because of the fortunes of war ended up on the territory that would become the Commonwealth. Most found themselves settled in the Grand Duchy of Lithuania, where some of their descendants in modern-day Lithuania and Belarus still recognise their origin. Known as Lipka Tatars or Lithuanian Tatars (the term Lipka derived from the Tatar name of Lithuania), many married Christian women, although they and their offspring remained Muslims, and over time most adopted the Ruthenian language. Their nobles commonly learnt Polish.[11]

Most notable among the Tatar cavalry (*jazda tatarska*), however, were the Petyhortsy Circassians, who derived from the Caucasus (and strictly speaking were no Tatars, although their chiefs were related to the Tatar nobility). In 1561 a number of Kabardian princes opposed to Muscovy and, more importantly, their local rivals who had allied with Muscovy, left the territory in the Caucasus known as the Five Mountains and brought their Circassian followers to Poland to petition for help. The Polish king granted them refuge, so in 1562, five Kabardian princes (known in Poland as Onyszko/Aleksander Kudadek, Kassim and Gawrila Kambulatowicz, and Kudadek's relatives Solgien and Temruk Szymkowicz) moved permanently to Poland with their families and 300 men. Most were, or became, Christians but a number remained believers in the old animist religion. Since they came from the Five Mountains, they became known in Poland as Petyhortsy (Polish: *Petyhorcy*), which was the Polish pronunciation of the Russian name of their ancestral home. These men formed the backbone of a number of special Petyhortsy cavalry regiments in Polish service, which for decades regularly came to receive fresh volunteers from the Five Mountains Circassians.[12]

Not all Petyhortsy Circassians who went to Poland ended up in Polish service. Some served in Crimean Tatar armies. Others forgot their earlier animosity and went into Muscovite service. In either case, the Petyhortsy retained their traditional dress (red and grey caftans with shaggy fur cloaks) and weapons, primarily lance, composite bow, and chainmail.

Whenever the Levy of the Nobility was raised, or upon the King's request, the Tatars in the Commonwealth were expected to provide men, too. Other Tatars served for pay in the various armies within the Commonwealth. Tatar cavalry served in Commonwealth-style banners of 60 to 200 men, and chainmail-armoured cavalry of this kind formed a major part of the better-armed cossack-style cavalry.

---

11 On the Lipka Tatars, see Stanisław Kryczyński, 'Tatarzy litewscy: Próba monografii historyczno-etnograficznej', *Rocznik Tatarski* 3 (1938).

12 See for example, Amjad Jaimoukha, *The Circassians: A Handbook* (New York: Palgrave, 2001), pp.117–18.

Wealthy Tatars wore a hussar-style wing on the saddle behind the back, in the hussar manner. Composite bow and sabre were the most common armament, except for nobles and Petyhortsy, who as noted wore armour and carried spears (*rogatina*).

German Cavalry

In the Commonwealth, a cavalryman armed and equipped in the Continental style was known as a *reiter* (Polish: *rajtar*), from the German term *Reiter* ('horseman'). Reiter units (Polish: *rajtaria*) generally rode heavier horses than those used by native Commonwealth cavalry. Some were heavily armoured, in the style of cuirassiers, while others were equipped as harquebusiers. There was little difference in organisation, equipment, dress, and training between those cavalry units which enlisted for Commonwealth service and those which served in the Swedish army.

Haiduk Infantry

As noted, haiduk infantry were musketeers. Each man carried an arquebus or musket as his primary weapon, with a sabre and an axe as sidearms. They wore Eastern dress but lacked armour and helmets. When a unit was raised, the men would receive cloth of a uniform colour, so that each unit presented a uniform appearance. Blue in various shades was most common, but pictorial evidence shows that other colours were used, too. An under-officer (Polish: *dzięsiętnik*; 'commander of ten') typically wore a uniform different in colour from his men, and was armed with a polearm (*darda*), commonly a halberd, half-pike, or partisan. Haiduk infantry had played a significant role in sixteenth-century Commonwealth armies, but in comparison to Continental companies, this type of unit was already becoming obsolete.

Haiduk infantryman with full armament, that is, an arquebus, sabre, and axe. He carries wound on his left arm a burning slow-match, with the rest of his implements in the gunpowder flask and pouch for shot at his belt. He has slung an empty canvas bag for his arquebus over his left shoulder. His dress consists of a black *magierka* felt cap in Hungarian style with peak and side flaps that could be folded down in cold weather, with several small pipes stuck into the brim, a white *żupan* undergarment, and a short-sleeved, white *delia* overcoat, folded up and fastened to the waist, with red lining and passementerie loops and buttons. The uniform is kept together by a belt tied around the waist. He wears tight red trousers and black *trzewiki* short boots. (*Tablica Gołuchowska*. Oil panel painting by unknown artist, 1600–1625. Originally in Gołuchów Castle, presently in the National Museum, Poznań.)

German Infantry

The Commonwealth also employed what was known as German infantry, that is, enlisted infantry units in the Continental style. Organisation, equipment, dress, and training did not differ from enlisted units in Continental Europe, so it was easy for enlisted soldiers to switch to the victorious army after a battle. Commonly, about a third of the men were pikemen, at least some of whom would be armoured, whilst the remaining two-thirds were unarmoured musketeers.

Artillery

Commonwealth artillery had not developed as much as its counterparts in Sweden and Muscovy. Equipment was often obsolete, and the vast range of calibres employed posed significant logistical problems. Most artillery was based in towns and fortifications. There was no field artillery, and the cavalry-based Commonwealth armies were seldom able to bring along their heavier cannons, even when such were needed.

Artillerymen were professionals, often of German origin. They dressed in a variety of garments, unsurprisingly usually following German fashion.

The Commonwealth expeditionary armies sent into Muscovy brought few, if any, cannons. Artillery did not play a prominent role in these expeditions.

Banners and Music

Polish cavalry banner often associated with the *topacz* coat of arms, a winged eagle's talon, which was a military symbol that originated in Hungary and the south. Like many Commonwealth banners, the motif includes an attached heart symbol. The heart and field are red, while the wing and border are white. The banner has been variously dated to the late sixteenth, early seventeenth century, or the first half of the seventeenth century. The banner, made of patterned European silk damask, has a breadth of 148 cm and a length of 240 cm. (Army Museum, Stockholm, ST 29:123)

ST 29:123

Banner motifs followed different traditions in the Crown and Ducal Lithuanian armies. A common symbol of Crown banners was the silver or white eagle on a red field, or alternatively, a white cross on a red field. Meanwhile, a common symbol of Lithuanian banners was what in later history became known as the 'chase' or 'pursuit' (Lithuanian: *Vytis*; Polish: *Pogoń*) motif, which consisted of a mounted knight – the 'pursuer' or 'warrior-hero' (Lithuanian: *Vytis*; Russian: *Vityaz*') who gave rise to the term. The knight, often depicted on a red field, was invariably depicted with sword raised

THE COMMONWEALTH EXPEDITIONARY ARMIES

against his enemies and with a double cross (a variant of the patriarchal cross) emblazoned on his shield. The symbol was based on the seal of the Grand Duke of Lithuania Algirdas (r. 1345–1377), who expanded his borders to the Black Sea, and there is some evidence that the symbol was already in fairly common use in his time. In addition, banners with religious motifs were very common, including but not limited to the Virgin Mary and the Holy Child, perhaps standing on a crescent moon with a sunburst as background.

Standards of the national autorament were often straightforward in style, commonly only displaying a suitable device on a plain field. Cossack-style units generally carried square, unfringed standards roughly 1.25 m in breadth and 1.15 m in length. Hussar units sometimes carried larger standards, from around 1.5 to 2.5 m in breadth and from around 2.5 to 3.5 m in length, which in addition often had two to three, or even four, tails. Infantry colours in the national autorament followed Continental practices with regard to size and patterns. They were usually square in shape with a breadth and length of from 3 to 4 m.

Standards of the foreign autorament differed little from those fielded by other Continental-style units.

Colours and standards, but also musical instruments, were regarded as important trophies, so they were eagerly captured in battle. It was deemed a disgrace to lose a standard, since this was a sure sign of defeat. However, the loss of standards and musical instruments also made it difficult to gather and reorganise the survivors of a unit, since standards and music were important means of leading a military unit. As for music, Commonwealth armies primarily employed a variety of trumpets and kettledrums.

Polish cavalry banner with a white eagle as the main motif, on a red field. Made of silk, with a breadth of 160 cm and a length of 176 to 313 cm. The yellow wheat-sheaf on the eagle's breast dates the banner to the reign of the Polish Vasa dynasty. The banner is of an early type and may date to the late sixteenth century. (Army Museum, Stockholm, ST 28:58)

Logistics

The Commonwealth had no centralised supply system. Nor was it possible to establish one, since the Crown Army and the Grand Ducal Army constituted separate military establishments each with its own sources of funding. As noted, nobles and other cavalry were supposed to provide their own supplies, so each man brought individual baggage, while the units of the foreign autorament maintained separate supply trains, provided for by the state. Most units included an excessive number of servants, camp followers, and wagons. Because of the lingering Eastern traditions of steppe warriors, traditional cavalry (primarily Tatars but sometimes also Poles and Lithuanians) might still choose to operate in what was called *komunik* (without infantry support and wagons) when speed was of the essence. If so, they supplied themselves by plunder and contributions from the territories which they passed through. In the period under consideration here, the mercenary cavalry army of Aleksander Józef Lisowski (c. 1580–1616), a soldier of fortune, serial mutineer, and commander who at times served False Dmitriy but mostly himself, was notorious for operating in this manner. The appearance of such a cavalry army was generally no more welcome than a foreign invasion, since either would live off the land.

However, it was far more common to use a wagon train (*tabor*, a designation in common use at the time which probably originated during the fifteenth-century Hussite uprising, since the Hussites invoked the image of the Biblical Mount Tabor). The wagons of the supply train were occasionally positioned as a defensive line to shield the army from raiding enemy horsemen. Unlike in Muscovy, the wagons were usually not specially modified for this purpose, except that they might be manned by armed men and even small ordnance such as wall guns. However, a wagon train of this type could advance slowly together with the units it shielded. We have seen how Muscovites and cossacks habitually used wagon trains on the steppe against Crimean Tatar incursions, and Commonwealth units were no strangers to such tactics. Swedes employed them, too.

While logistics may have been somewhat less developed than desired, the Commonwealth had excellent engineers. Along the borders, especially in but not limited to Prussia, cities, towns, and fortresses were protected by modern fortifications. Even monasteries often had up-to-date fortifications. While many old cities in the interior, including Warsaw, Cracow, Posen (modern-day Poznań), and Wilno (modern-day Vilnius), still retained their medieval walls, engineers were available to improve their fortifications, if funding was allocated. Prussian cities and major towns such as Danzig were very well protected and fortified, with defences of a quality that had few equals elsewhere in Europe.

5

The Time of Troubles

Although Sweden in 1609 was in firm control of Estonia and held important strongholds in southern Livonia, the already precarious Swedish position on the frontier with the Commonwealth went from bad to worse. This should have been no surprise, since Commonwealth forces for the last five years had repeatedly inflicted serious defeats on Swedish armies. In March, the Grand Hetman of Lithuania Jan Karol Chodkiewicz conquered the important port-town of Pernau. An enraged and characteristically vindictive King Charles had the defeated Swedish commandant, Daniel von Wochen, sentenced to death for treason and executed in the possibly most cruel and gruesome manner ever employed in early modern Sweden: his body was torn apart by two horses with the remnants then displayed on racks and wheels. Predictably, the execution did nothing to ameliorate the Swedish position in Livonia. Chodkiewicz next laid siege to the strategically important Dünamünde, which controlled the exit to the sea of Livonia's chief mercantile city, Riga. After a long siege, and following a failed Swedish attempt to the relieve the stronghold, Dünamünde's commandant, Nils Stiernskiöld, in September had no choice but to surrender.[1]

---

1 Stiernskiöld found himself in an exceedingly tough situation. His few artillerymen died from disease at an early stage in the siege, so Stiernskiöld personally had to take over some of their responsibilities. When he in spring 1609 fired a cannon, it exploded and wounded him so badly that he could not walk again until August. Moreover, Stiernskiöld had left his young wife, infant son, and sister-in-law in the apparent safety of Pernau. When Pernau fell, Chodkiewicz brought the family to Riga, where they were treated harshly. Stiernskiöld knew this, because Chodkiewicz attempted to use the captives as leverage to make Stiernskiöld surrender without further ado. Stiernskiöld responded that he hoped Chodkiewicz would treat his family honourably, in the manner that the Poles wanted the Swedes to treat their women and children, if they fell into captivity. Chodkiewicz then released the captives. Yet, Dünamünde could ultimately not be defended. Perhaps because of the numerous difficulties, Stiernskiöld evaded the wrath of King Charles. We will see that Stiernskiöld fought in Muscovy already in 1610, and in the Kalmar War against Denmark from 1611 onwards. In 1617, King Charles's son and successor Gustavus Adolphus put Stiernskiöld in command of the next, more successful

SWEDEN'S WAR IN MUSCOVY 1609–1617

King Sigismund accordingly had every reason to be satisfied with his victories in Livonia. This enabled him to deal with other urgent problems elsewhere, which meant that in the following years Sweden faced less pressure from Commonwealth armies than before. This was fortunate for King Charles, since by then the Swedish focus had shifted towards the east.

Much had happened in Muscovy while Swedish and Commonwealth armies fought over Livonia. Upon the death in early 1598 of the deeply religious Tsar Fyodor I Ivanovich (1557–1598; r. 1584–1598), the son and heir of the ambitious Tsar Ivan IV who greatly expanded Muscovy's borders, there was no heir to the throne of Muscovy. Tsar Fyodor had only ever had one child, a daughter named Feodosia, but she had died aged two. Besides, in his lifetime Tsar Fyodor had displayed little interest in politics. Instead, he had handed over effective rule to his brother-in-law and subsequent successor, Boris Godunov (1552–1605; r. 1598–1605). Boris continued Tsar Ivan's policies, including the expansion of trade with England and western Europe through the White Sea and Arkhangel'sk in the Arctic. Boris also presided over considerable territorial expansion in Siberia and the northern Caucasus. After Tsar Fyodor's death, Boris after some hesitation had himself elected Tsar. For several years, business continued as usual, and Tsar Boris appeared to have made himself master of Muscovy.

However, in the autumn of 1601 severe frosts caused disastrous crop failures. Northern Europe had already suffered weather-related crop failures since the 1590s, with a particularly negative impact in Sweden and Finland, and now the severe frosts extended in a southeasterly direction. As usual in the premodern and early modern world, this brought famine, which in turn engendered rampant diseases. Tsar Boris ordered the provision of such relief there was, in fact made huge efforts to alleviate the famine, but the government's supplies were limited. Soon, rumours emerged about grain hoarding by nobles and merchants. For the next three years, starvation and disease caused widespread suffering. The growing tax burden and the acute labour shortage that, among other problems, critically displayed the state's inability to provide for its hereditary servicemen, contributed further to the general sense of dissatisfaction with government policies.

Nils Stiernskiöld. (Epitaph, Gillberga Church, Södermanland)

Swedish invasion of Livonia.

Even so, the key problem was elite rivalry. Quite a few powerful boyars hoped eventually to displace Tsar Boris. Yet, none dared to challenge the Tsar unless they could rally around an external force.

Then, in autumn 1604, a young and well-educated man who claimed to be Dmitriy Ivanovich, the youngest son of Tsar Ivan IV, suddenly appeared to claim the throne. The previous years of famine had been bad, but the real Time of Troubles began with the sudden appearance of the pretender to the throne who became known to history as False Dmitriy. As far as is known, the real Dmitriy (1582–1591) had died at age eight, apparently in an accident sustained during an epileptic seizure, even though some subsequently believed that Boris Godunov's henchmen had murdered the boy. The claim to the throne was in any case dubious, since the real Dmitriy had been illegitimate according to Orthodox Canon law and thus ineligible for succession even had he been alive. However, this was a technicality, because the succession order in Muscovy was just as malleable as that in Sweden, a situation which we saw that King Charles used to his benefit only a few years before. Besides, the pretender who now called himself Dmitriy may really have believed in his royal blood.[2] The story that his supporters, primarily the nobles who opposed Tsar Boris, now circulated far and wide was that the true Dmitriy had been hidden by his relatives, who then indicated another boy to the assassins who carried out the murder.[3] Hence, they argued, the pretender was the real Dmitriy and a lawful claimant to the throne.

The validity of the pretender's claim accordingly became a question of military might, and it was no coincidence that Dmitriy in October 1604 arrived by way of Kiev on the wings of a Commonwealth army. The Commonwealth connection was no coincidence either: in March 1604 young Dmitriy visited the court of King Sigismund in Cracow, and in the following month, he in a semi-public act converted, probably insincerely, to the Catholic faith.

Nonetheless, the pretender was accepted by those who for one reason or another opposed Tsar Boris. Among them were high-ranking nobles effectively displaced from their ancestral lands by the policies introduced by Tsar Ivan (and upheld by his successors Fyodor and Boris) as a means to increase central power at the expense of the old nobility. Appointed to military posts on the southern border, they included notables such as Prince Andrey Telyatevskiy, the governor of Chernigov; Prince Grigoriy Shakhovskoy, the governor of nearby Putivl'; Prokopiy Lyapunov, a voivode who assumed the leadership of the nobles from Ryazan'; and Filipp 'Istoma' Pashkov, a mere *sotnik* (commander of 100) who in a similar manner became the leader of the nobles from Tula. Among others who eagerly

---

2 Dunning, *Russia's First Civil War*, p.132.
3 Many European observers liked Dmitriy because he could communicate in foreign languages and wore Continental dress, so they propagated the story. Among them was the French mercenary Margeret. *Russian Empire*, pp.17, 80–81.

accepted the pretender were the Don cossacks, who strongly resisted the Tsar's attempts to make them conform to the legislation and taxation that governed other Muscovites and would much rather support somebody who promised them additional freedoms.

Dmitriy also seems to have acquired a certain level of popular support, not least because he promised his supporters exemption from all taxes for 10 years. In comparison, Tsar Boris had lost significant popular support because of the previous years of famine and suffering. A sober analysis of the situation shows that none of the rebel leaders had any desire to change the basic characteristics of the Muscovite state. Rather, each considered himself more suited to rule than the Tsar, or for that matter, any other rebel commander.

Dmitriy's army rapidly moved into Chernigov, Putivl', Ryl'sk, Kursk, Sevsk, and Kromy. Advancing from the south against the River Oka defensive line, which traditionally protected the Muscovite heartlands from Crimean Tatar raids, all went well until a mutiny broke out among Dmitriy's Commonwealth mercenaries due to the fact that he had not paid them. Having lost their primary military force, the rebels suffered a major defeat on 21 January 1605 at Dobrynichi. Dmitriy had little artillery, and his attempts to gain the support of either the Tatar Khanate of the Crimea or the Noghai Tatars failed. For a while, it seemed that his cause was lost.

Tsar Fyodor II

However, on 13 April Tsar Boris suddenly died. He was succeeded by his young son, Fyodor II (1589–1605). Young Fyodor was talented but had no time to assert his power, because on 1 June a group of nobles who saw better prospects under Dmitriy staged a coup in the Kremlin, imprisoned Fyodor and his mother and murdered them both on 10 June 1605. Young Fyodor was both intelligent and physically strong for his age. When his corpse was put on display, the Swedish observer Peder Pedersson concluded that based on the wounds, young Fyodor had resisted the assailants, but to no avail.[4]

Ten days later, on 20 June 1605, Dmitriy entered Moscow as Tsar Dmitriy of Muscovy (r. 1605–1606). He faced no resistance. By then the late Tsar Boris's family was dead, with the sole exception of his daughter Xenia (Russian: Kseniya; 1582–1622) who had witnessed the murders of her mother and brother. Dmitriy forced himself upon the young woman. He retained her for several months as a concubine until his Polish bride, Maryna Mniszchówna or Mniszech

---

4 Petreius, *Een wiss och sanfärdigh Berättelse*.Facsimile edn: Sohlman, *Stora oredans Ryssland*, p.130.

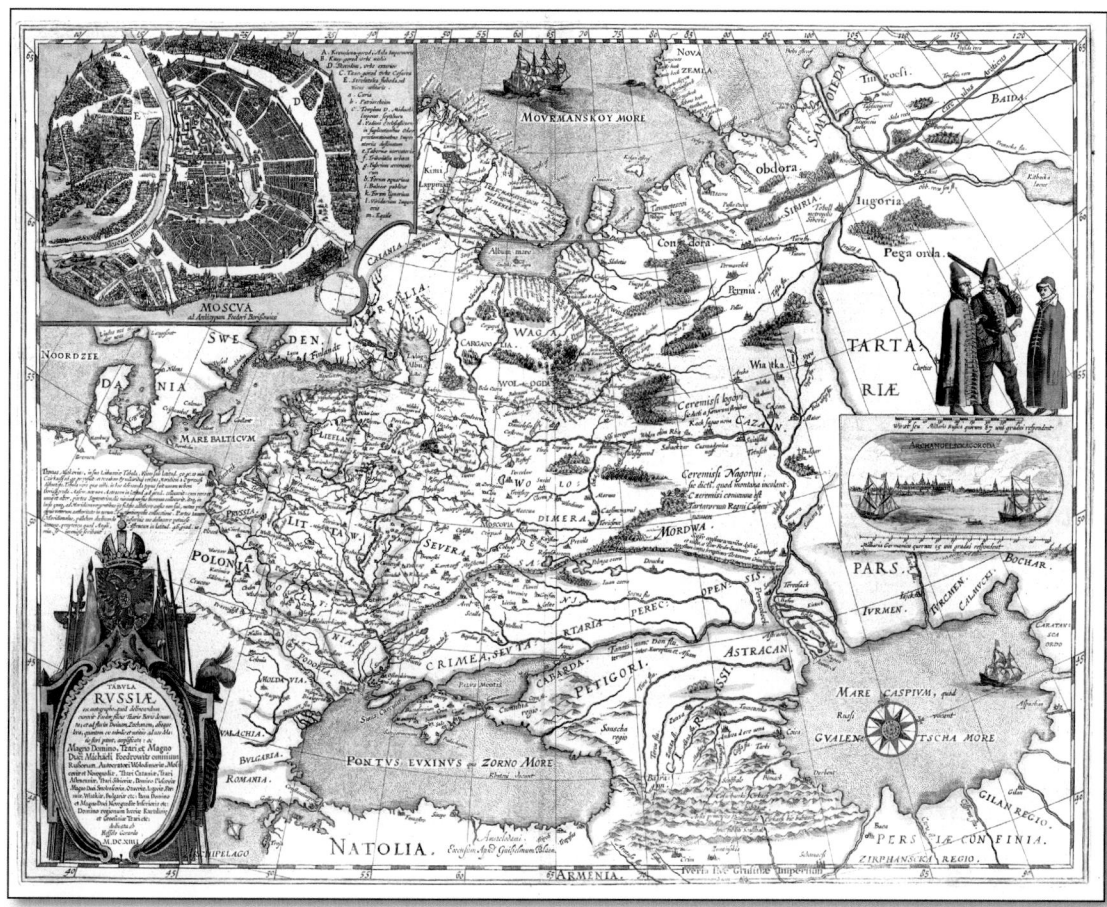

Map of Muscovy by Hessel Gerritszoon, originally designed by the talented Tsar Fyodor II. With two insets: a plan of Moscow and a view of Archangel'sk. The map was compiled from manuscript maps and notes brought back to Amsterdam by Isaac Massa. (*Tabula Russiae ex autographo, quod delineandum curavit Foedor filius Tzaris Boris desumta*, second edition 1614)

(*c.* 1588–1615), arrived in Moscow to become his wife.[5] The reasons for Dmitriy's treatment of Xenia can now only be guessed at. Perhaps, he intended to retain her as a potential future bride with a convenient link to the old House of Rurik in case the Catholic faith of Maryna caused public discontent. The Orthodox Church exercised a deep cultural and spiritual influence, so many Muscovites resented foreign faiths. Indeed, Maryna's father, concerned that his daughter ultimately might be rejected and his own influence correspondingly reduced, asked Dmitriy to distance himself from Xenia. In the end, Dmitriy married Maryna, who certainly came with the option of continued Commonwealth support. He confined Xenia in a convent. Some said that she gave birth to a son of Dmitriy's there, but if so the boy probably did not survive childhood, since he was not heard of again.[6]

---

5   Petreius, *Een wiss och sanfärdigh Berättelse*. Facsimile edn: Sohlman, *Stora oredans Ryssland*, p.132. Dunning, *Russia's First Civil War*, p.201, downplays Dmitriy's treatment of Xenia, likely because it was inconsistent with his assessment of Dmitriy as a great Tsar beloved by his subjects.

6   Pierre De la Ville, *Discours sommaire; De ce qui est arrivé en Moscovie depuis le*

SWEDEN'S WAR IN MUSCOVY 1609-1617

False Dmitriy in coronation dress. (Szymon Boguszowicz, 1606)

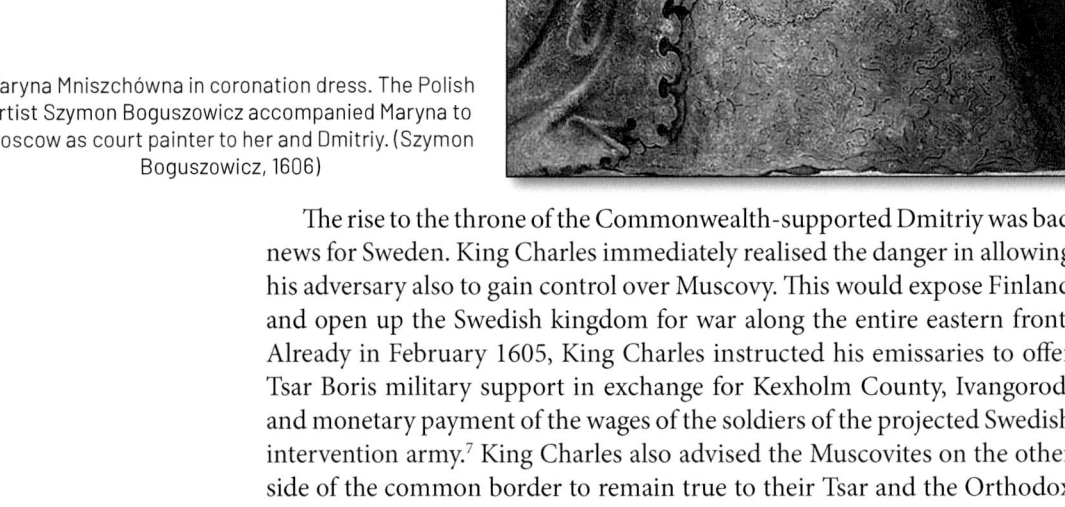

Maryna Mniszchówna in coronation dress. The Polish artist Szymon Boguszowicz accompanied Maryna to Moscow as court painter to her and Dmitriy. (Szymon Boguszowicz, 1606)

The rise to the throne of the Commonwealth-supported Dmitriy was bad news for Sweden. King Charles immediately realised the danger in allowing his adversary also to gain control over Muscovy. This would expose Finland and open up the Swedish kingdom for war along the entire eastern front. Already in February 1605, King Charles instructed his emissaries to offer Tsar Boris military support in exchange for Kexholm County, Ivangorod, and monetary payment of the wages of the soldiers of the projected Swedish intervention army.[7] King Charles also advised the Muscovites on the other side of the common border to remain true to their Tsar and the Orthodox religion.[8] It was commonly assumed that King Sigismund, together with the Pope, wished to convert the Muscovites to the Catholic faith.

règne de Ivan Wassiliwich, empereur, jusques à Wassili Ivanovitz Sousky (1611), Louis Paris (ed.), *La Chronique de Nestor*, Vol. 1 (Paris: Heideloff et Campé, 1834), pp.404–28, on p.407.

7   Helge Almquist, *Sverge och Ryssland 1595–1611: Tvisten om Estland, Förbundet mot Polen, de ryska gränslandens eröfring och den stora dynastiska planen* (Uppsala: Uppsala University, dissertation, 1907), p.91.

8   Almquist, *Sverge och Ryssland*, p.94

Learning about Dmitriy's subsequent progress towards Moscow, King Charles in autumn 1605 moved enlisted German units to Finland. He also increased the Viborg garrison by raising additional national troops. Sure enough, Dmitriy soon demanded that Sweden return Narva, gained through the Treaty of Teusina in 1595. Surely King Sigismund's hand was behind this, or so the Swedes may have argued. In reality Tsar Boris had already, in times of apparent Swedish weakness, demanded the return of Narva and indeed all of Estonia.[9] But it was also true that Dmitriy, upon gaining the throne, offered military support to King Sigismund against Sweden and, for a while, made preparations for this contingency.[10]

King Charles did not need to worry, as the false Dmitriy soon lost whatever popular support he had gained. His pro-Commonwealth policies angered many nobles, while the Church detested his acceptance of the Catholic faith.

In May 1606, unrest broke out in Moscow. Muscovites under Vasiliy Shuyskiy and other senior nobles broke into the Kremlin, where they on 17 May murdered the false Dmitriy and many of his Polish supporters. Although King Charles was uninvolved in the coup, a large share of the nobles who joined the Shuyskiys came from Novgorod and Pskov, that is, those regions that, for geographical reasons, were somewhat receptive to Swedish influences.[11] Dmitriy's corpse was first put on display and then cremated, after which the ashes were reportedly shot from a cannon in the direction of the Commonwealth, whence he had come. On 19 May, Vasiliy Shuyskiy had himself elected as the new Tsar, Vasiliy IV. King Charles immediately sent a congratulatory message to Tsar Vasiliy, noting that the latter's ascension to the throne had saved Muscovy and the Orthodox religion from the evil schemes of King Sigismund and the Pope. In the message, King Charles also expressed his hope that an alliance between Sweden and Muscovy against the Polish King now would be possible. Finally Charles offered Vasiliy military support, and to add spice to the offer informed Muscovy that he had intelligence that the Habsburg Emperor and the King of Spain intended to support King Sigismund by sending a Spanish fleet to conquer Arkhangel'sk. But there was no cause for alarm, Charles assured

---

9   When in January 1599 Charles's position in Sweden had remained as uncertain as the Tsar's position now was in Muscovy, Tsar Boris had offered then Duke Charles his support against King Sigismund, in either money or soldiers, in exchange for the Estonian lands of Narva and Wask-Narva (Russian: Syrensk; modern-day Vasknarva), the former an important port-town and the latter a stronghold then better known as Neuschloss.
10 Dunning, *Russia's First Civil War*, p.220.
11 Isaac Massa, *Een cort verhael van begin en oorspronck desser tegenwoordighe oorlogen en troeblen in Moscouia totten jare 1610* (Brussels: J. Olivier, 1866), p.164; Isaac Massa, *Histoire des guerres de la Moscovie (1601–1610)* (Brussels: J. Olivier, 1866), pp.176–7.

Vasiliy, because the Swedish army and navy would safeguard Muscovy from any such designs.[12]

However, King Charles's hopes for an alliance led nowhere. Because of difficulties in diplomatic relations (caused by epidemics as much as Muscovy's continuous instability, and not everybody recognised Tsar Vasiliy), Charles soon began to make plans to go to war in order to recover Kexholm (Russian: Korela; modern-day Priozersk) and Nöteborg (Russian: *Orekhov*, alternatively *Oreshek*; meaning Fortress Hazelnut), which Sweden had lost to Muscovy in the 1595 Treaty of Teusina. He even devised plans to persuade Novgorod to voluntarily secede from Muscovy and turn itself into a Swedish protectorate, and began to make designs on Ivangorod.[13]

Only months after the ascension of Tsar Vasiliy, yet another false Dmitriy appeared, travelling from Moscow to the Ukrainian part of the Commonwealth where he established a base. This time it was a minor noble named Mikhail Molchanov, one of those who had participated in the murder of Tsar Fyodor II, who began to play out the role of Dmitriy.[14] He claimed that he had survived the events in Muscovy and that a substitute had been murdered in his stead. Molchanov was too cautious himself to join the army that other nobles now formed in the name of Dmitriy to march on Moscow. Instead, he found a freebooter named Ivan Bolotnikov. As a young man of military background, Bolotnikov had run away to join the cossacks and then, captured by Crimean Tatars, spent several years as a slave on an Ottoman galley. Now he was on his way home through the Commonwealth, and what better way to travel than with a rebel army? Molchanov accordingly sent Bolotnikov to Putivl' where his superior, the aforementioned Prince Grigoriy Shakhovskoy, in July 1606 put Bolotnikov in charge of the mostly cossack army that was set to march on Moscow. On the way to the capital, yet more rebels joined Bolotnikov, including the aforementioned Pashkov, Lyapunov, and several others. The rebel army again advanced towards the River Oka defensive line. It was divided into two columns, one from the south-west under Bolotnikov by way of Kromy and Kaluga, and the other from the south-east under Pashkov and Lyapunov by way of Tula, Ryazan', and Kolomna. The Tsar's army confronted the rebels at the River Ugra near Kaluga, where on 23 September 1606, an army under Tsar Vasiliy's brother Ivan Shuyskiy inflicted a defeat on Bolotnikov.[15]

Yet, the loyalist victory over Bolotnikov produced no significant strategic gains. Pashkov's column took Kolomna in early October. The two rebel armies then converged on Moscow and established positions on the southern outskirts of the city, from which they blockaded traffic to the south. In October 1606, the rebels laid siege to Moscow and also sent letters into the city, urging the inhabitants to rise. The Tsar responded by

---

12   Almquist, *Sverge och Ryssland*, pp.105–6.
13   Almquist, *Sverge och Ryssland*, p.108.
14   Dunning, *Russia's First Civil War*, pp.250–52.
15   Dunning, *Russia's First Civil War*, pp.281–2.

sending his younger distant cousin, Prince Mikhail Skopin-Shuyskiy, to conduct hit-and-run raids on the rebel camps. Moreover, Bolotnikov's army was soon torn by dissension. The rebellious nobles wanted political power, which meant that their priorities were different from those of most cossacks, who wanted freedom from taxation, central government, and in the more extreme cases, unrestricted license to plunder. Ultimately the loose confederation of rebels fell apart, and on 15 November Lyapunov and his associate Grigoriy Sunbulov defected to Tsar Vasiliy. A streltsy unit soon followed them. Pashkov defected on 2 December, within days followed by Yuriy Bezzubtsev's unit, although Bezzubtsev himself remained loyal to the pretender's cause.[16] Meanwhile the Tsar received reinforcements from Smolensk in the west and the towns of the north, which remained loyal. The country had in effect been divided, with the south and the lands along the middle and lower Volga from Nizhniy Novgorod to Astrakhan' opting for the rebels, while core lands and the north remained on the side of the Tsar.

There was a reason for this particular geographical divide, but it lay two generations back in time. In 1565, Tsar Ivan IV had set aside about half of the realm as his private domain (*oprichnina*), from which he distributed conditional land grants in return for military service to such men who were willing to serve him loyally as an absolute ruler. Many had not previously owned freeholds, so found themselves bound to the Tsar as their main source of income. The rest of Muscovy remained the 'land' (*zemshchina*), which constituted everything that the Tsar did not bring into the *oprichnina*. Now, 40 years later, the geographical divide roughly corresponded to that of the *oprichnina*: the lands in the north where the Tsar had settled the service nobility which depended on him for revenues – and which now remained loyal – and the outlying *zemshchina*, mostly southern lands where Tsar Ivan IV sent those who in most cases had patrimonial freeholds of their own and whom he for this reason did not fully trust – and which now rebelled.[17] Meanwhile, the lands around Smolensk remained loyal because of the recurring conflicts with the Commonwealth, which Smolensk rightly saw as the sponsor of the false Dmitriys.

As a result of Prince Skopin-Shuyskiy's successful raids against rebel bases, the arrival of loyalist reinforcements from the west and north, the rebel defeat in conjunction with Pashkov's defection on 2 December, and the continuous defections by other rebels, Bolotnikov's army abandoned the siege of Moscow and retreated.

Those rebels who remained in the field withdrew to Tula, where they were joined also by Terek and Volga cossacks under a leader named Il'ya Korovin but who called himself Tsarevich ('Crown Prince') Petrushka (Peter). The leader of a band on the River Terek in the Caucasus who made a living out of robbing merchants, Peter claimed to be the (nonexistent) son of Tsar Fyodor and accordingly the grandson of Tsar Ivan IV. Wanting a share of

---

16 Dunning, *Russia's First Civil War*, pp.307–9, 314–17.
17 Fredholm von Essen, *Muscovy's Soldiers*, pp.47–50.

the spoils, he made contact with Prince Grigoriy Shakhovskoy in Putivl'. Shakhovskoy announced that Fyodor's long-dead daughter Feodosia in fact had been a boy named Peter, who now would join the rebels. Preparing for a new offensive against Moscow, Prince Andrey Telyatevskiy, who once had been the original master of Bolotnikov, and Prince Grigoriy Shakhovskoy, who had produced the pretenders, now joined forces with Bolotnikov.

Meanwhile, yet another pretender arose, this time in Astrakhan' in the south-east. Astrakhan' had joined the rebellion under its governor, Ivan Khvorostinin. He soon found somebody, possibly a former bondsman, who had been to Moscow and who now claimed to be Tsarevich Ivan Augustus (Ivan Avgust), the son of Tsar Ivan IV and his fourth wife Anna Koltovskaya, whom Ivan had divorced and with whom he had no offspring. This claim was very useful, since it made 'Crown Prince' Ivan Augustus the elder brother of Dmitriy and the uncle of 'Crown Prince' Peter. Ultimately, 'Crown Prince' Ivan Augustus made no real impact on national events. However, for some time he ruled by terror in the south-east, torturing and executing any loyalists he could find.[18]

This time, Tsar Vasiliy wanted to pre-empt the rebel onslaught. In May 1607 the Tsar's army moved against Bolotnikov's and 'Crown Prince' Peter's camp at Tula. In June, the Tsar laid siege. After a long struggle, which included the flooding of Tula through the construction of a dam, the surviving rebels surrendered on 10 October, including Bolotnikov and 'Crown Prince' Peter. Tsar Vasiliy had both men executed. Prince Telyatevskiy seems not to have been punished, so had presumably made some kind of deal with the Tsar. Prince Shakhovskoy, who because of his production of one pretender after the other was generally regarded as the instigator of the insurgency, was banished to the north.

Presumably feeling secure at last, Tsar Vasiliy informed King Charles that he certainly intended to keep the peace between the two countries but did not need the military support which the Swedish King had offered.

Tsar Vasiliy's assessment was premature. Muscovy had already seen two false Dmitriys, both emerging from the Commonwealth and with Commonwealth military support, one false Peter, and a false Ivan Augustus. The story of the false Dmitriys is notable, because although some of the general public were swayed by their claims, the pretenders were fundamentally pawns introduced by Commonwealth notables in attempts to gain control over Muscovy. Not even the Commonwealth nobles who fought for the false Dmitriys believed in their claims. Even so, in July 1607 yet another false Dmitriy appeared, and again with Commonwealth support. It was not Mikhail Molchanov, who had dropped this show. The new Dmitriy, too, claimed to have survived the first Dmitriy's murder in the Kremlin[19] and was joined by numerous men who saw better opportunities

---

18 Dunning, *Russia's First Civil War*, pp.356, 362.
19 In traditional historiography the new Dmitriy is designated False Dmitriy II, although as we have seen, in reality he was the third who claimed this identity.

under a false Dmitriy than under Tsar Vasiliy. Among them were several previous rebel leaders, including Prince Shakhovskoy, who returned from his banishment in the north, and Molchanov. Others who early gravitated towards Dmitriy were a number of small-time Commonwealth mercenaries, among them Jan Kiernożycki, Jan Mikuliński, and the infamous marauder Aleksander Lisowski. They were soon followed by Prince Roman Różyński, a professional Ruthenian mercenary and veteran of many wars who had a well-deserved reputation for violence and heavy drinking and rapidly became Dmitriy's chief hetman.[20] As before, the rebel armies consisted of Commonwealth nobles, Ukrainian cossacks, Don cossacks, and the retainers of rebellious Muscovite nobles.

In November 1607 another pretender also emerged in the south. A Don cossack chief who claimed to be Tsarevich Fyodor Fyodorovich, the younger brother of Tsarevich Peter, joined forces with Dmitriy in Starodub. Pledging support to his 'uncle Dmitriy', Tsarevich Fyodor reportedly brought as many as 3,000 Don cossacks.[21]

In the spring of 1608, the rebels loyal to the new Dmitriy marched towards Moscow. On 30 April–1 May 1608, Dmitriy's mercenary general Prince Różyński defeated Tsar Vasiliy's brother Dmitriy Shuyskiy at Bolkhov.

Dmitriy then, in June, established a fortified camp at Tushino, a village strategically located 12 km north-west of Moscow, which controlled some of the roads that linked the capital to the west. Over time, the camp at Tushino grew into an enormous wooden town. On top of a hill, Dmitriy had a 'palace', in reality a wooden house, erected for his personal use. Commonwealth commanders and noble rebels had smaller wooden cottages built around the 'palace'. Further away, the rest of the army lived in temporary cabins or tents.

Meanwhile, the Tushino army sustained itself by living off the land in the manner of an occupation army. The various commanders and units savagely plundered any villages, and indeed any towns, they could lay their hands on. Dmitriy had neither revenues nor supply mechanisms, so his men had little choice. Hence, Dmitriy became known as the 'robber at Tushino' (*tushinskiy vor*). He also did not tolerate rival pretenders, and had both the alleged Tsareviches, Fyodor Fyodorovich and Ivan Augustus, put to death, after they unwisely joined him at Tushino to gain their share of the wealth.[22]

Contemplating the tumultuous events in Muscovy, King Charles understood that at this point, anything might happen over there. Not wishing to miss a good opportunity, he again began to plan for a military intervention, and in February 1608, he again offered the Tsar military

---

20   Almquist, *Sverge och Ryssland*, p.116.
21   Dunning, *Russia's First Civil War*, p.389.
22   Altogether, up to 10 pretenders ultimately announced themselves among various cossack groups, but Dmitriy accepted none of them, instead offering substantial rewards for their capture and execution. Dunning, *Russia's First Civil War*, p.395.

support – but he also pointed out that if he did not receive a positive response before midsummer, he would instead enter into an alliance with the Commonwealth against Muscovy (an impossibility under current circumstances but Tsar Vasiliy could not know this).

In August and September, Dmitriy received additional Commonwealth reinforcements, most of whom had reasons of their own to keep some geographical distance to King Sigismund and were more than willing to ride to Tushino. Among them was the first False Dmitriy's widow, Maryna Mniszchówna, who for reasons we can only guess at – possibly her own desire to be an empress or perhaps under pressure from her father – immediately 'recognised' Dmitriy as her tsar husband to provide further legitimacy to his cause. The Commonwealth nobles who now joined Dmitriy's banners should not at this point be regarded as under the command of King Sigismund. However, most enjoyed good relations with the Polish Crown, so it was perhaps only a question of time before the question of divided loyalties would arise. Yet, numerous Muscovites joined Dmitriy, too. Among them was the former boyar of the House of Romanov who had been forced into monastic confinement as Filaret by Tsar Boris but later was released by the first false Dmitriy – who had in 1606 made him metropolitan of Rostov and Yaroslavl'.

Jan Piotr Sapieha at the Holy Trinity-St Sergius Monastery. (Willem Hondius, 1630)

In August 1608 the experienced Lithuanian mercenary Jan Piotr Sapieha arrived in Tushino with some 7,000 Commonwealth cavalry. On 2 September 1608, men loyal to Dmitriy gained control over the important northwestern mercantile centre of Pskov and the nearby towns of Gdov, Ivangorod, Jama (Russian: Yama), and Kaporie (Russian: Kopor'ye).[23] Nöteborg and Kexholm acknowledged Dmitriy in late November 1608, although apparently with less enthusiasm.[24]

Sapieha and his fellow mercenary Aleksander Lisowski on 23 September 1608 laid siege to the strongly fortified Holy Trinity-St Sergius Monastery, in Sergiyev Posad (then commonly known as Troitsa, 'Trinity') 66 km north-east of Moscow. This was, and remains, the country's most important monastery and the spiritual centre of the Russian Orthodox Church. The wealthy monastery was protected by a 1.25

---

23 Almquist, *Sverge och Ryssland*, pp.123–4. Sapieha had already offered Dmitriy his support in August 1607, Almquist, p.116. A true soldier of fortune at heart, Sapieha offered his services to anybody who might be willing to pay.
24 Almquist, *Sverge och Ryssland*, p.131.

km stone wall with 12 towers and an integral garrison. Under normal conditions, a total of 2,780 people lived within the monastery, which even maintained direct trade links to several foreign countries. In short, the monastery had more of the characteristics of a fortified town than of a mere place of worship. The Tsar had sent reinforcements into the monastery, which was now defended by an estimated 2,300 soldiers and about 1,000 monks, servants, and peasant levies, under the experienced Prince Grigoriy Borisovich 'Roshcha' Dolgorukov and his deputy Aleksey Ivanovich Golokhvastov, together with Abbot Ioasaf. Other leading monks included Avraamiy Palitsyn, who presumably was the author of the monastery's answer to Sapieha's and Lisowski's order to surrender:

> To the proud commanders Sapieha and Lisowski! Your dark majesties and your warriors are the opposers of God, the abomination of dissolution, and know that you attempt in vain to lead us, a flock of Orthodox Christians, into temptation. You should know that even a ten-year-old Christian youth from the Holy Trinity-St Sergius Monastery would laugh at your request. And as far as your letter is concerned, we spit on it upon receiving it. What man would, at the expense of his soul, prefer darkness to light, a lie to the truth, dishonour to honour, and bitter slave labour to freedom? How could we forsake our eternal, holy, and true Orthodox Christian Faith of the Greek Confession and submit ourselves to the new heretical law which betrays the Christian Faith and which was cursed by the four ecumenical patriarchs [of the cities of Constantinople, Antioch, Jerusalem, and Alexandria, who broke with the Pope of Rome owing to the latter's claim for primacy]? What would be our gain and honour in betraying our Orthodox Sovereign and Tsar and submitting ourselves to our enemy, the impostor and rebel? And you, people of the Latin faith, have become like Jews, and even worse, for the Jews did not recognise the Lord and consequently crucified him. Yet how can we, who know our Orthodox Sovereign, concede to your request to forsake our Christian Tsar despite the fact that our grandfathers were born in the vineyard of our true pastor Christ and under the rule of a Christian Tsar? And how can you attempt to tempt us with false kindness, vain flattery, and ill-gained wealth? We shall remain faithful to the pledge we gave on the cross, for we do not care for all the wealth in the entire world.[25]

Sapieha and Lisowski brought a significant army, possibly as many as 10,000 men with no less than 63 cannons, towards the Holy Trinity-St Sergius

---

25 Based on the translation in Serge A. Zenkovsky (ed.), *Medieval Russia's Epics, Chronicles, and Tales* (New York: E. P. Dutton, 1963), pp.308–9.

Monastery. The mercenaries constituted less than half of this army, with the rest being rebels.

While Sapieha laid siege to the monastery, Lisowski set out to ravage and overthrow the territories to the north. For a while, the towns of Kostroma, Yaroslavl', and Vologda fell into his hands (until northern Muscovy rose against Lisowski in spring 1609). From late November to early January 1609, Dmitriy's men, under the command of the Polish cavalry captain Jan Kiernożycki, also laid siege to Novgorod, defended by Prince Skopin-Shuyskiy.[26]

Militarily weak, Tsar Vasiliy now had to request support from abroad. It was only Sweden that had the means and inclination to step in. On 10 August 1608, Tsar Vasiliy wrote to his distant cousin and commander, Prince Skopin-Shuyskiy in Novgorod, asking him to enter into negotiations with the Swedes for military support.[27]

Tsar Vasiliy had little choice but to rely on Swedish support: militarily, his supporters by then only controlled Moscow, Smolensk, and the Holy Trinity-St Sergius Monastery. A Swedish representative, Måns Mårtensson Palm, travelled to Novgorod, where he and Prince Skopin-Shuyskiy entered into a preliminary agreement. King Charles instructed his agents that he wanted Kexholm, Nöteborg, and the stronghold of Kola Castle (the strongest fortress on the Kola Peninsula, known in Sweden as Kolahus) in the Arctic. Furthermore, he wanted to make the Muscovite representatives agree to a plan in which the combined Swedish–Muscovite army first would take Kaporie, Ivangorod, Gdov, and Pskov, which had already given their allegiance to the false Dmitriy, and then take Dorpat (modern-day Tartu), which was held by a Commonwealth garrison. This, Charles argued, would also distract the Commonwealth commander in Livonia, Hetman Chodkiewicz, from continuing his offensive against the Swedes at Dünamünde, Kokenhusen, and Salis.

Soon, it was obvious that this plan was unrealistic. Sweden no longer had the men to go on the offensive in Livonia. Moreover, Skopin-Shuyskiy needed help in Novgorod, where by then he was under siege.[28] King Charles on 28 December 1608 accordingly instructed the newly appointed Commanding General, Jacob De la Gardie, only to move into Muscovy if Tsar Vasiliy remained in power, and when doing so, advancing by way of

---

26 Dunning, *Russia's First Civil War*, p.400.
27 Generalstaben, *Sveriges krig* 1, p.325.
28 Jan Kiernożycki, with possibly 4,000 men, laid siege to Novgorod in November 1608. Skopin-Shuyskiy defended the city with 150–200 of his own men and Novgorod's integral army. Novgorod remained under threat until January 1609, when Skopin-Shuyskiy received reinforcements (1,000 men from Tikhvin under Stepan Gorikhvostov and a somewhat smaller contingent from the Onega lands in the north under Yevsey Ryazanov). This brought Skopin-Shuyskiy's contingent to almost 2,000 men, in addition to the Novgorod Army. As a result, Kiernożycki abandoned the siege. Vadim Viktorovich Kargalov, *Moskovskiye voyevody XVI-XVII vv.* (Moscow: Russkoye slovo, 2002), pp.95, 100.

THE TIME OF TROUBLES

Kexholm and Nöteborg. If he could take these towns, he should garrison them with Swedish soldiers, even though ostensibly it was in the name of the Tsar. Any rebels should be punished with murder and fire, and in Charles's characteristically harsh words, children in the cradle should not be spared. After taking Kexholm and Nöteborg, De la Gardie should attempt to assist Skopin-Shuyskiy in Novgorod. If the latter wanted him to march to Moscow, De la Gardie should first confirm this decision with the King.

In 1609, the new Dmitriy promoted Filaret Patriarch of Moscow, despite or more likely because of the fact that there was already a Patriarch of Moscow, the old, uncompromising Patriarch Hermogenes (d. 1612) who hated the Catholic faith of Dmitriy's Commonwealth supporters. To maintain their claims, the Dmitriys had to acknowledge the Romanovs as relatives, for which reason they also favoured them. As a result, by 1609 Muscovy had two Tsars, two Patriarchs, and two governments ruling the country – one in Moscow and the other in nearby Tushino. The city of Moscow itself, Smolensk, and much of the northern lands supported Tsar Vasiliy, while much of the south recognised the authority of Dmitriy. Kolomna, under Prince Dmitriy Pozharskiy (1578–1642), remained loyal to Tsar Vasiliy, which was fortunate for Moscow since Kolomna controlled the road to the Ryazan' region in the south-east, which supplied the capital with grain.

6

De la Gardie's Intervention Army

Throughout the winter of 1608–1609, the representatives of King Charles and Prince Skopin-Shuyskiy negotiated terms. On 28 February 1609 they concluded the Treaty of Viborg, which established a defensive alliance between Sweden and Muscovy.[1]

King Charles did not offer support out of the goodness of his heart but as a means to extend Swedish power. Tsar Vasiliy negotiated from a position of weakness, and realising that he needed a strong ally to retain power, he was prepared to offer concessions. The Treaty of Viborg was a diplomatic success for King Charles, and the Tsar confirmed the Treaty of Teusina. Both parties agreed not to conclude a separate peace treaty with the Commonwealth, and Charles agreed to send an intervention army of 5,000 men (2,000 horse and 3,000 foot, fully armed) to Muscovy in support of Tsar Vasiliy. In return, Sweden would acquire Kexholm Country for all eternity. Muscovy must also pay the Swedish army at a price of 32,000 roubles per month, which as calculated corresponded to 104,000 Reichsthalers.[2] The Swedish army would operate in conjunction with a Muscovite army of some 3,000 men.

Moreover, while King Charles for the time being abandoned his designs on Ivangorod and any neighbouring Muscovite towns, he had not yet given up hope for the Arctic north. On 13 February 1609, while treaty negotiations were still ongoing, he ordered his governors in Lapponia ('Norrland', that is, Northern lands) and Österbotten, Baltzar Bäck and Isaac Behm, to march against and capture Kola Castle in the name of Tsar Vasiliy with a corps

---

1   Almquist, *Sverge och Ryssland*, pp.132–3.
2   Actually, 96,000 Reichsthalers. Merchants then valued one rouble as three Reichsthalers. Payment was agreed as follows: 25 Reichsthalers to each cavalryman, 12 Reichsthalers to each infantryman, 5,000 Reichsthalers to De la Gardie in his role as supreme commander, the cavalry and infantry colonels each 4,000 Reichsthalers, and a total of 5,000 Reichsthalers for the other officers. Almquist, *Sverge och Ryssland*, p.128 n.1. De la Gardie never appointed officers to the largely administrative posts of cavalry and infantry colonels, so there is no discrepancy in the exchange rate.

DE LA GARDIE'S INTERVENTION ARMY

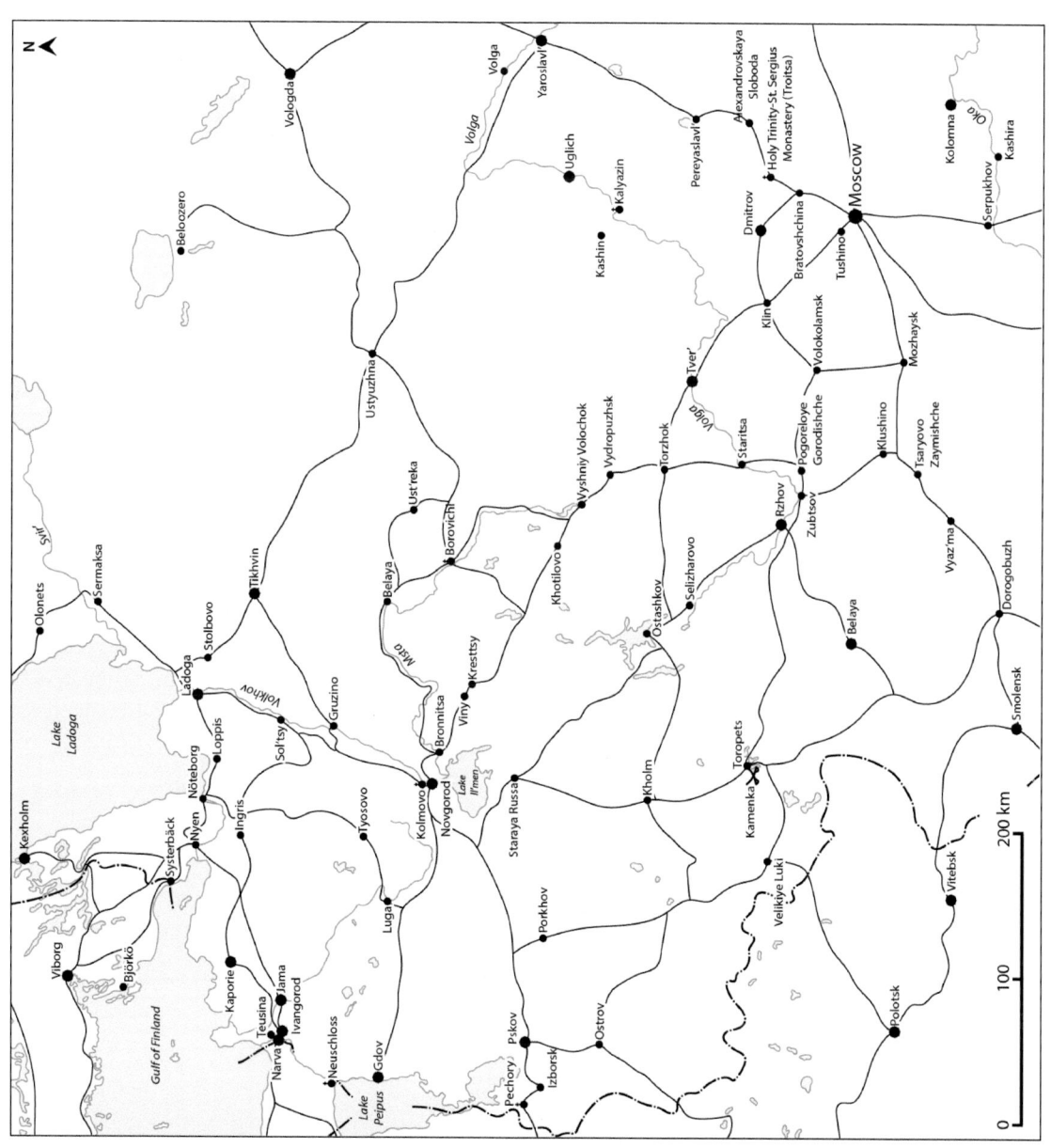

Map 2. Northwestern Muscovy.

of 200 to 300 men with skis, and to make contact with Muscovite officials at Fort Suma (Swedish: Soma) on Sumskiy Island on the River Suma, and the fortified Solovki (Solovetsk) Monastery, both at the White Sea. A few enlisted soldiers were sent north to take part in the expedition. Charles ordered Bäck and Behm to stick to the story that they only acted in the best interest of Tsar Vasiliy. However, the King's order could not then be carried out in time, because only March was a suitable month for a venture of this kind.[3]

The main Swedish intervention army set out from Viborg bound for Muscovy as soon as the Treaty of Viborg was concluded. The army was accompanied by the Muscovite representatives and for the time being commanded by Christer Some, a veteran of the wars on the eastern front against the Commonwealth who had occasionally held the rank of field marshal and would function as the deputy commander of the expedition. King Charles had already on 28 December 1608 ordered the 25-year-old Jacob De la Gardie to assemble the soldiers in Finland and also authorised his use of the taxes raised in Finland to provide for their wages. Technically, De la Gardie was appointed Lieutenant General under Gustavus Adolphus, Grand Duke of Finland, and accordingly was commander of all military forces in Finland. He was also put in command of several cavalry banners.[4] Since neither King nor Grand Duke was present on the eastern front, in reality this meant that De la Gardie became Commanding General in the east, that is, supreme commander of the intervention army sent to relieve Tsar Vasiliy and Muscovy. In effect, De la Gardie's task became that of commanding the eastern wars in the absence of the royals.

Because of unstable winter weather, De la Gardie had to travel overland, north of the Baltic Sea, to reach his command. For this reason, he arrived in Viborg only on 5 March 1609, within days of the conclusion of the Treaty. At this point, the Swedish intervention army had already commenced the march towards the east. The rearguard had set out two days before his arrival.

This was a dangerous moment on the eastern front. On the same day that De la Gardie arrived in Viborg, we have seen that Grand Hetman of Lithuania Chodkiewicz conquered the Livonian port-town of Pernau in a surprise attack.

The Swedish plan was to deploy primarily foreign enlisted soldiers on Muscovite soil. However, Sweden's total number of available enlisted soldiers in 1609 was only 3,334 horse and 4,602 foot, not all of whom were available for the expedition. In early 1609, De la Gardie's army consisted of no more than 912 horse and some 450 foot; another approximately 1,200 men remained in Estonia.[5] This meant that national units from Finland (both horse and foot) must be sent, too. The enlisted foreign companies included

---

3   Almquist, *Sverge och Ryssland*, pp.167–8; Generalstaben, *Sveriges krig* 1, pp.327–8.
4   Almquist, *Sverge och Ryssland*, p.136.
5   Generalstaben, *Sveriges krig* 1, p.329 n.2.

French and German cavalry and German infantry. Since not all units had been ready to march, reinforcements would have to be sent eastwards when they had concluded their preparations. De la Gardie's deputy commander was the aforementioned Christer Some. His other senior officers included Colonel-General Axel Kurck, a Finnish veteran of numerous wars, including fighting on behalf of King Sigismund in the civil war which brought then Duke Charles to power and for which the vindictive Charles imprisoned him. Other officers were colonel Anders Boije, another Finnish veteran and Kurck's brother-in-law, and Evert Horn, born in Estonia as the son of a field colonel who had commanded in both Finland and Livonia. Kurck was now an elderly man, in poor health because of many years spent on campaign and in prison. Boije, too, was elderly. In contrast, Horn was an educated man in his prime, spoke German, Latin, and French in addition to his native Swedish and presumably Finnish, and would soon prove himself a very brave, able, and even chivalric officer.

Then there was the need for military intelligence, including men with good knowledge of the Russian language. For operations in Muscovy, the Viborg local government had instituted two separate functions, both based on the recruitment of Russian-speakers in eastern Finland and Karelia. One was the 'Russian interpreters' (Swedish: *ryssetolkar*) who handled diplomatic tasks, interpretation, and translation. They were employed by the Crown, listed as government interpreters, and paid a salary, after which they served both in their formal capacity and as couriers and intelligence agents. The other consisted of the 'peasant intelligencers' (*kunskapsbönder*, from the corresponding word *kunskapare*; German: *kundschafter*), individuals who were familiar with Muscovy and often went there, after which they reported back to Viborg any intelligence found. One of the government interpreters was Erik Andersson (Finnish: Eerikki Antinpoika; *c*. 1586–1634). The son of a previous Russian interpreter, Andersson frequently travelled to Muscovy and was accordingly the perfect choice to accompany De la Gardie's intervention army.[6] Another Swede with experience of Muscovy who travelled with the intervention army was the Swedish diplomat Peder Pedersson (also known as Petrus Petreius; 1570–1622). He had spent 1601–1605 in Muscovy, witnessed the dramatic events in Moscow, and in December 1605 returned by way of the Commonwealth, where he had the dubious pleasure of being interrogated by King Sigismund and several notables in Cracow.

The King had ordered De la Gardie to march to Novgorod by way of Kexholm and Nöteborg on Lake Ladoga further to the north and east, respectively, to claim these towns before he moved further into Muscovy. However, because of the existing road network (of which Stockholm may have been poorly informed) De la Gardie had to march directly to Novgorod, where Skopin-Shuyskiy already awaited him with the Tsar's army. There

---

6   Fredholm von Essen, *Lion from the North* 1, pp.224–5; Kari Tarkiainen, 'Rysstolkarna som yrkeskår 1595–1661', *Historisk Tidskrift* 92 (1972), pp.490–522.

SWEDEN'S WAR IN MUSCOVY 1609-1617

During the Muscovite wars, terrain was difficult, roads poor or nonexistent, and guerrilla warfare and raiding common. This road consists of a causeway of round logs pushed into the ground perpendicular to the direction of travel so as to provide footing when inclement weather resulted in muddy roads, which was common. As individual logs were frequently broken or rotten to the core, loose adjacent logs rolled and shifted back and forth, and the roads were difficult and dangerous to get across, in particular for horses. Known in English as corduroy roads, they were common in the borderlands between Muscovy, Finland, and Livonia. Roads further to the north were far worse, or nonexistent. (The Ivangorod Road, somewhere between Vruda and Tyosovo post stations. Anthonis Goeteeris, 1619)

was no time first to move against Kexholm and Nöteburg.[7] King Charles had hoped that De la Gardie's and Skopin-Shuyskiy's combined army also could be employed to recover part of Livonia, but this hope turned out to be impossible, too, for the same reason.

The Swedish army entered Muscovy along the road from Viborg in the middle of March 1609. They were met by a Muscovite corps under Ivan Ododurov, who was sent to accompany the Swedes. The Swedish soldiers, mostly professionals, looked down on Ododurov's men, regarding them better suited as peasants than soldiers.[8]

Having entered Muscovy, what was the legal status of De la Gardie's army? In contemporary Muscovite correspondence and chronicles, they seemingly play a role out of all proportion to their limited numbers. In contrast, later Polish and Russian historiography tend to regard the Swedish units as mere mercenaries enlisted into Muscovite service in a personal capacity and De la Gardie essentially as the military entrepreneur who had hired and brought them to Muscovy – which makes the Swedish units essentially invisible in later histories. On the surface, it might seem to be a certain logic in this interpretation, because De la Gardie and his men entered Muscovy to fight on behalf of Tsar Vasiliy and they were, to some extent, paid by the Tsar. However, the abundant correspondence with Stockholm makes it clear that De la Gardie and the Swedish intervention army the

---

7 Generalstaben, *Sveriges krig* 1, p.328.
8 Almquist, *Sverge och Ryssland*, p.138.

Plate A
1. Swedish Cuirassier, Finnish Retinue of Nobles, 1610
2. Swedish Harquebusier, Hans Ekholt's Finnish Cavalry Banner, 1617

(Illustrations by Sergey Shamenkov, © Helion & Company)
See Colour Plate Commentaries for further information.

Plate B
1. Swedish Guardsman, Drabant Guard, 1617
2. Swedish Pikeman, Olof Bryngelsson's Karelian Company of Foot, 1615

(Illustrations by Sergey Shamenkov, © Helion & Company)
See Colour Plate Commentaries for further information.

Plate C
1. Swedish Arquebusier, the Commanding General's Regiment of Foot, 1614
2. Swedish Ensign, the Commanding General's Regiment of Foot, 1611
(Illustrations by Sergey Shamenkov, © Helion & Company)
See Colour Plate Commentaries for further information.

Plate D
1. Polish Hussar, Aleksander Zborowski's White Hussar Banner, 1610
2. Polish or Lithuanian Cossack-style Cavalryman, Jan Piotr Sapieha's Banner, 1610
(Illustrations by Sergey Shamenkov, © Helion & Company)
See Colour Plate Commentaries for further information.

Plate E
1. Polish Reiter Cavalryman, Jacques Margeret's Banner, 1610
2. Polish *Lisowczyk* Cossack-style Cavalryman, 1610
(Illustrations by Sergey Shamenkov, © Helion & Company)
See Colour Plate Commentaries for further information.

Plate F
1. Polish Haiduk Infantry Arquebusier, 1610
2. Muscovite Voivode, 1609
(Illustrations by Sergey Shamenkov, © Helion & Company)
See Colour Plate Commentaries for further information

Plate G
1. Muscovite Cavalryman, 1609
2. Muscovite Strelets Infantry Musketeer, 1609
(Illustrations by Sergey Shamenkov, © Helion & Company)
See Colour Plate Commentaries for further information.

vii

Plate H
1. Muscovite Don Cossack Cavalryman, 1609
2. Muscovite Service Tatar Cavalry Officer, 1613
(Illustrations by Sergey Shamenkov, © Helion & Company)
See Colour Plate Commentaries for further information.

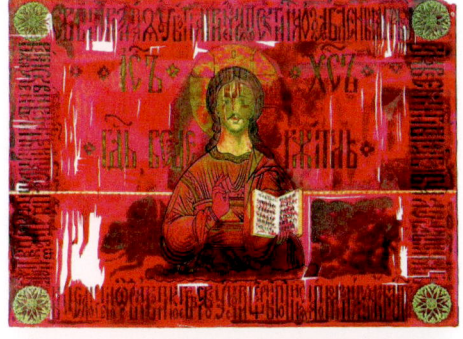

Plate I
1. Sweden: Nyland Cavalry Cornet
2. Sweden: Finland Infantry Colour
3. Muscovy: Prince Dmitriy Pozharskiy's Personal Banner

(Illustrations 1 and 2 by Lesley Prince, © Helion & Company, Illustration 3 by Fyodor Grigor'yevich Solntsev)
See Colour Plate Commentaries for further information.

Plate J
The Polish-Lithuanian Commonwealth: King Sigismund's Grand Royal Banner
(Illustration J1 by Olek Remesz, © Wikipedia)
See Colour Plate Commentaries for further information.

Plate K
The Polish-Lithuanian Commonwealth: Hussar Officers and Hussar Banner, 1605
Details from the Stockholm Roll, attributed to Balthasar Gebhardt, 1605
See Colour Plate Commentaries for further information.

Plate L
The Polish-Lithuanian Commonwealth: Colour of Gostomski's Haiduk Company and King Sigismund's Trabant Guard, 1605
Details from the Stockholm Roll, attributed to Balthasar Gebhardt, 1605)
See Colour Plate Commentaries for further information.

entire time remained within the Swedish chain of command and ultimately took orders only from King Charles. We will see that De la Gardie and his men were also expected to bring pressure on Tsar Vasiliy, or whoever ruled Muscovy, to make sure that he handed over those territories that Charles desired. The conclusion must accordingly be that De la Gardie's intervention army remained under Swedish control, and although temporarily detached to prop up the Tsar in Muscovy, at all times served as a Swedish instrument of force projection. To the senior Swedish and Muscovite commanders involved in De la Gardie's venture, there was no doubt whatsoever that De la Gardie only took orders from King Charles, not Tsar Vasiliy, and that he primarily operated to further Swedish, not Muscovite objectives, if these diverged. The intervention army fought to sustain the rule of the Tsar, but only to the extent that the Tsar's interests corresponded with those of King Charles.

Ododurov and the Muscovite emissaries who now accompanied the army recommended a detour to the west for an immediate attack on Kaporie. The Swedes duly attempted to storm the town with the help of a petard, but the assault failed. De la Gardie had requested additional petardiers from Narva, but ultimately one had to be sent all the way from Reval, and he arrived late. Since De la Gardie also lacked adequate artillery support, he then ignored the town and continued towards Tyosovo on the road to Novgorod. There, the army built a temporary camp. Meanwhile, De la Gardie himself rode on the Novgorod to discuss the practical details of the campaign with Skopin-Shuyskiy. The latter again confirmed the Treaty of Viborg, but he could only offer 5,000 roubles in cash and 3,000 sable furs as payment, since this was all he had.⁹ Moreover, Skopin-Shuyskiy preferred not to accommodate the Swedes in Novgorod itself (a sensible precaution, since the provision of quarters to foreign soldiers in a city tended to ruin it). Instead, he suggested that De la Gardie should conquer the town of Staraya Russa further south, which was held by men loyal to the false Dmitriy, and quarter his men there.¹⁰

De la Gardie wanted to allow his men to rest in Novgorod, so he suggested that if they were not paid, then he would instead return to Kaporie, Jama, and Ivangorod, to make sure that these Ingrian towns

---

9   Sable furs were small but could be sold for very high prices. When used in lieu of currency, they came in bundles of 40 furs in a packet. When in autumn 1610 a representative of De la Gardie disposed of the latter's share of the sable furs acquired and successfully brought to Stockholm during the campaign, the total turned out to be 1,000. They were evaluated as corresponding to 3,660 roubles or 10,980 Reichsthalers. De la Gardie had gone to war burdened with debts from his time as prisoner in the Commonwealth and from his stay in the Dutch Republic, with hardly a Reichsthaler to his name. With the help of the 1,000 sable furs, he could repay his debts and emerge as a moderately wealthy man. Erik Grill, *Jacob De la Gardie: Affärsmannen och politikern, 1608–1636* (Gothenburg: Gothenburg University, PhD Dissertation/Wettergren & Kerber, 1949), p.18.
10 Almquist, *Sverge och Ryssland*, p.138.

renounced their previous declaration of loyalty to Dmitriy and remained secure from attack by Chodkiewicz's Commonwealth army. This would, of course, have set the Swedish intervention army on a course that would have greatly delayed its employment further inland and ultimately might result in the loss of Moscow to rebels. Skopin-Shuyskiy accordingly located and offered another 6,000 roubles and agreed to let the Swedish army march into Novgorod for a period of rest. De la Gardie accepted, and on 14–15 April 1609, the Swedes entered Novgorod. There, De la Gardie discovered that Skopin-Shuyskiy only had between 1,000 and 1,500 men at his disposal for campaign service, not even half of what had been promised.[11] These were the survivors of Skopin-Shuyskiy's own men and the reinforcements from Tikhvin and the Onega lands in the north. The Novgorod Army would not participate in the campaign. But there were other units elsewhere that also remained loyal to the Tsar. While Skopin-Shuyskiy was in Novgorod with De la Gardie, other loyalist units retook Yaroslavl' and Kostroma much further to the east. Vologda became a centre for loyalist forces, and Uglich and Kashin declared for the Tsar, too. All sent some men, but these still remained far away.[12]

Evert Horn. (Epitaph, Åbo Cathedral, Finland)

De la Gardie set out from Novgorod on 2 May. Skopin-Shuyskiy and De la Gardie seem to have planned that the Swedes first would drive off the rebels west and south of Lake Il'men', between Novgorod and Pskov, and then join forces with loyalist Muscovites at Torzhok or elsewhere on the highway from Novgorod to Moscow. The advantage of this plan, in Swedish eyes, was that De la Gardie was able to still keep an eye on Livonia, in case Chodkiewicz planned yet another offensive there. He accordingly divided his army into three, dispatching one corps probably under Christer Some in the direction of Pskov to the west and another under Evert Horn towards Staraya Russa in the south. Some of Skopin-Shuyskiy's men accompanied each corps.

On 8 May the first Swedish–Muscovite corps, probably under Christer Some, dispersed a rebel corps that had laid siege to Porkhov between Novgorod and Pskov. The same Swedish–Muscovite corps attempted to take Pskov itself on 18 May. Pskov was a major city, with a population of at least 25,000 and probably 30,000 people. Together with Novgorod, of a similar size, Pskov was an old merchant city with a long and proud history that rivalled Moscow in size and mercantile importance. While many nobles of Pskov remained loyalists, they were greatly outnumbered by those who supported Dmitriy, and the latter apparently included hardcore rebel demagogues who preached hatred

---

11   Almquist, *Sverge och Ryssland*, p.139.
12   Kargalov, *Moskovskiye voyevody XVI–XVII vv.*, pp.102, 109, suggests that Skopin-Shuyskiy had 5,000 men in Novgorod, of whom he immediately sent 2,000 to Vologda, Staraya Russa, and other towns. Since all loyalist contingents came from the north-east, not the Novgorod Lands, Kargalov's estimate appears incorrect.

DE LA GARDIE'S INTERVENTION ARMY

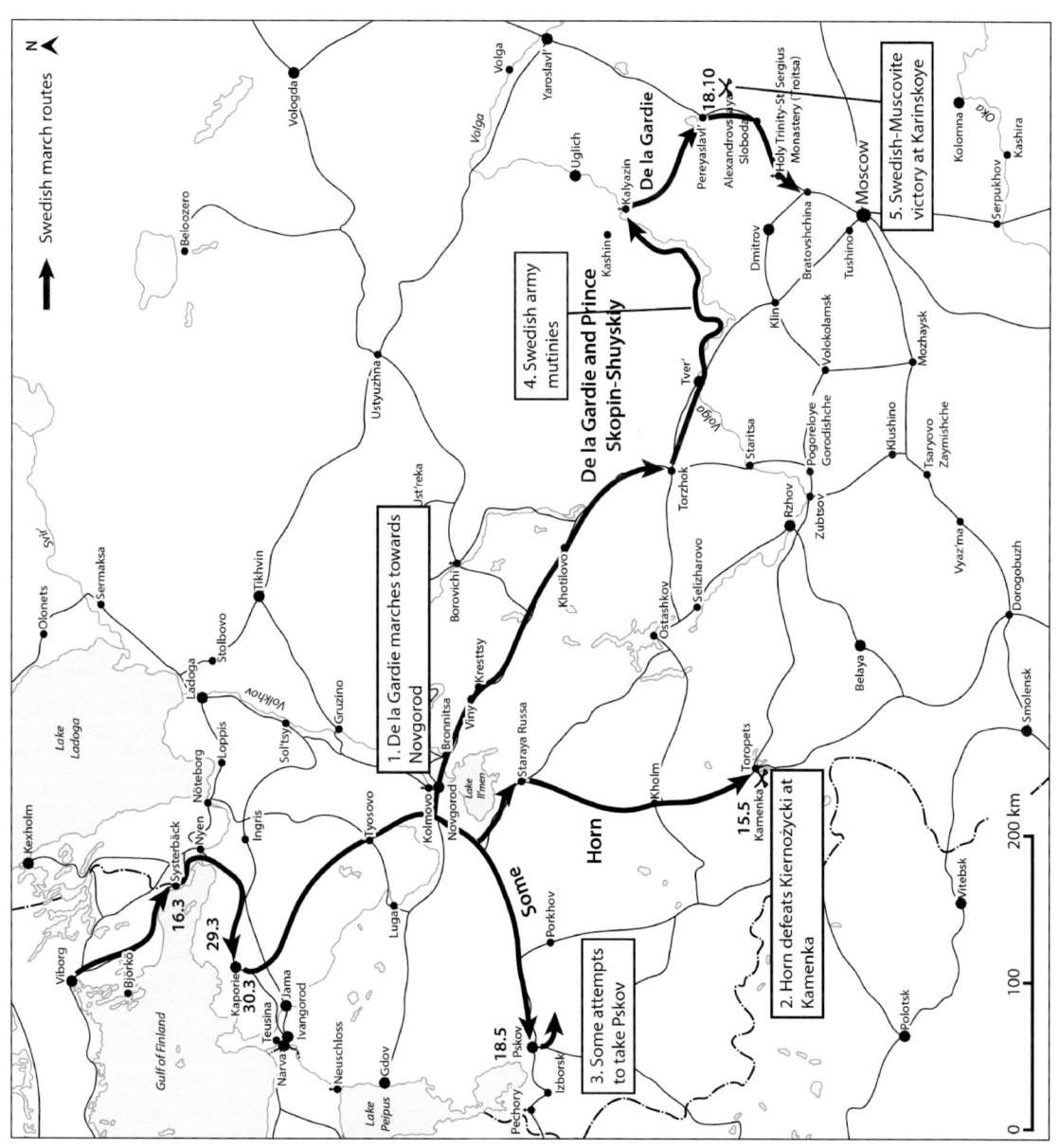

Map 3. De la Gardie's Intervention in Muscovy, 1609.

towards the old regime and anybody who supported it. As a result, Pskov defended itself vigorously, and the attempted surprise attack failed.[13]

Meanwhile the second Swedish–Muscovite corps, some 500 men under Evert Horn and the elderly but experienced Anders Boije, moved against Staraya Russa, in which Kiernożycki and his Commonwealth mercenaries had taken refuge after their failure at Novgorod. As soon as Horn approached, Kiernożycki burned the town and retreated further south, reportedly with some 2,000 men, all described as cossacks or cossack-style Commonwealth cavalry. Whatever remained of Staraya Russa then surrendered, and on 12 May De la Gardie and the main army, accompanied by 500 Muscovite cavalry under Semyon Golovin, Fyodor Chulkov, and Kornil Choglokov, marched into the town.[14] In particular Chulkov was an experienced commander who also knew something about the Swedes, having participated in the previous war against Sweden from 1588 onwards. Golovin and Choglokov were talented commanders. Golovin was also Skopin-Shuyskiy's brother-in-law.

The Battle of Kamenka

Pursuing the retreating rebels towards the south by way of Kholm, Horn on 15 May finally overtook Kiernożycki and his men at the village of Kamenka, 10 km south-west of the town of Toropets. The rebels immediately fled 'as hares'. In the ensuing battle, the Swedes and Muscovite loyalists dispersed Kiernożycki's men, of whom only about 500 out of some 2,000 managed to extricate themselves. Kornil Choglokov played a particularly important role in the battle. Based on the interrogation of two captured rebel captains, Horn reported that Kiernożycki's corps had consisted primarily of mercenaries: 700 Polish nobles, 700 Zaporozhian (Ukrainian) cossacks, 350 cossacks from southern Muscovy, 200 streltsy, and several retainers of rebel boyars. Horn claimed to have lost only four men (of his Swedish soldiers, that is; there is no information on loyalist Muscovite losses), in exchange for the capture of seven cannons, horses, supplies, valuables, and money. The rebels also abandoned many women in their camp. Horn took them under his protection and ultimately had them released.[15]

A number of northwestern Muscovites towns including nearby Kholm, Ostashkov, Rzhov, Zubtsov, Staritsa, and Torzhok abandoned Dmitriy's cause and submitted to Tsar Vasiliy as soon as they heard of the victory at Kamenka. Naturally so did nearby Toropets, the leading notables of which sent a delegation with this message to Horn, and in addition requested a Swedish relief army to overpower the rebels in the town's vicinity. They

---

13 Almquist, *Sverge och Ryssland*, p.142.
14 Almquist, *Sverge och Ryssland*, p.141.
15 Almquist, *Sverge och Ryssland*, pp.141–2; citing Horn's report. The battle of Kamenka is often referred to as the battle of Toropets.

tried to convince Horn by pointing out that their town was a key node in the road network of the region between Novgorod, Pskov, and Smolensk – the key cities in the region. Whilst true, an extended expedition to Toropets would have taken the Swedes dangerously far to the south at a time when Horn lacked supplies, so he deferred the decision to De la Gardie. Horn's corps already suffered shortages of bread and beer, and some desertions had taken place, both among the enlisted soldiers and those from Finland. It would soon become clear that the Finnish soldiers in particular much disliked marching deep into Muscovy. Meanwhile, Toropets also sent emissaries directly to De la Gardie. Nonetheless, he decided not to divide his intervention army. Toropets would have to rely on the important loyalist city of Smolensk for support.

No longer worried by rumours of imminent Commonwealth operations in Livonia, De la Gardie on 23 May marched out from Staraya Russa, this time bound for Moscow. On 6 June, and on the road to Moscow, he again joined forces with Skopin-Shuyskiy, who had set out from Novgorod a few days later than the Swedes.

By then the false Dmitriy had already decided to go on the offensive against the Swedish–Muscovite army. His first objective became retaking Torzhok, on the road to Moscow, which because of De la Gardie's and Skopin-Shuyskiy's victories had declared loyalty to Tsar Vasiliy. Skopin-Shuyskiy had already ordered a loyalist unit (of possibly 4,000 horse) under Kornil Choglokov to garrison Torzhok. Now, Dmitriy sent Prince Grigoriy Shakhovskoy and Aleksander Zborowski north by way of Staritsa towards Torzhok with 3,000 men (2,000 mercenary hussars and 1,000 Tushino rebels) to regain the town. Remnants of Kiernożycki's men and other Commonwealth mercenaries may have joined as well, possibly producing a total of up to 6,000 men.[16] In response, De la Gardie and Skopin-Shuyskiy sent 2,000 men, half of them Swedes and half Muscovites, under Horn and Golovin, to confront the rebels which then stood outside the town. On 17 June the combined Swedish–Muscovite corps attacked the rebels. It was a sharp engagement, and the two sides seem to have been roughly equal in numbers. Zborowski's hussars failed to break through the Swedish pike and shot, but pushed back the French and Muscovite cavalry. The rest of the Swedish–Muscovite corps pushed on, until at the critical moment Choglokov led a sally out of Torzhok which hit the rebels in the rear. Zborowski's men disengaged in disorder, and the remaining rebels retreated, having suffered significant but otherwise unknown casualties. Horn claimed negligible losses, only some 15 men out of the Swedish force. We do not know the number of Muscovite casualties. In fact Zborowski claimed a victory, despite his ignominious retreat, and to cover up his failure spread the greatly exaggerated story that his men had killed 2,000 Muscovites and 500 foreigners.[17] Horn then moved into Torzhok to join

---

16 Kargalov, *Moskovskiye voyevody XVI–XVII vv.*, pp.110–111.
17 Almquist, *Sverge och Ryssland*, p143. Zborowski's story is retold in Sapieha's diary.

forces with Choglokov. Because of Torzhok's important strategic location on the main highway to Moscow, the victory of Horn and Golovin was decisive for further operations.

It was obvious to the loyalists in northwestern Muscovy that the Swedish–Muscovite army made an impact on the rebels. Soon, reinforcements began to arrive. Mikhail Sheïn sent a significant contingent from Smolensk, between 3,000 and 4,000 men under Prince Yakov Baryatinskiy and his deputy Semyon Ododurov.[18] The Smolensk men marched east by way of Dorogobuzh, Vyaz'ma, and Belaya, all of which they cleared of rebels.

Fighting over Tver'

From Torzhok, the combined Swedish–Muscovite army continued along the main road towards Tver', strategically located on the River Volga, and arrived on 13 July. There, De la Gardie and Skopin-Shuyskiy confronted a rebel army of at least 5,000, possibly 6,000 men commanded by Zborowski and Kiernożycki. Prince Shakhovskoy may have been in the army, too, but this seems uncertain. Most or all of Zborowski's men were cavalry. The numbers had risen because Sapieha had sent 1,000 men from the ongoing siege of the Holy Trinity-St Sergius Monastery as reinforcements. Sapieha had also advised Zborowski to send a letter to De la Gardie, arguing that because of their shared religion, the Swedish general should join the Poles in supporting Dmitriy instead of fighting for Tsar Vasiliy. Possibly Sapieha and Zborowski thought that De la Gardie was a French Catholic. While De la Gardie immediately rejected this request, we will see that similar letters reached in particular the enlisted French soldiers in Swedish employ.[19]

We do not know the strength of the combined Swedish–Muscovite army, but it is unlikely at this point to have consisted of fewer than 8,000

Aleksander Zborowski. (Unknown eighteenth-century artist; photo: Volodymyr Dk)

Aleksander Hirschberg (ed.), *Polska a Moskwa w pierwszej połowie wieku XVII: Zbiór materyałów do historyi stosunków polsko-rossyjskich za Zygmunta III* (Lviv: Ossoliński, 1901), pp.167–332, on p.230.
18   Kargalov, *Moskovskiye voyevody XVI–XVII vv.*, p.112.
19   Almquist, *Sverge och Ryssland*, p.148.

DE LA GARDIE'S INTERVENTION ARMY

men. It may well have been significantly stronger. De la Gardie, assuredly in agreement with Skopin-Shuyskiy, deployed the Muscovite units behind the Swedish line. The Muscovites were commanded by Skopin-Shuyskiy, Baryatinskiy, and Golovin. De la Gardie personally commanded the Swedish right wing, which consisted of Finnish cavalry, possibly cuirassiers or at least more heavily armoured men than most harquebusiers.[20] The left wing consisted of French and German harquebusiers. The centre was infantry. De la Gardie personally led the right wing's cavalry attack against Zborowski's cavalry, which soon dispersed and ultimately took refuge in the town. A sudden shower of rain made the infantry muskets and the arquebuses of the French cavalry temporarily inoperable due to a shortage of dry gunpowder, which enabled the rebel right wing, presumably under Kiernożycki, to carry out a counter-attack. The infantry in the centre held firm, but the French harquebusiers fled into the Muscovite lines behind them, which caused panic. The German harquebusiers appear to have fled too, and some of the fleeing Muscovites began to loot the supply train. However, when shooting again became feasible, Kiernożycki's right wing also retreated.

Neither De la Gardie nor Skopin-Shuyskiy had the means to lay siege to the strongly fortified Tver', so they withdrew into camp. Heavy rain prevented further hostilities until 15 July, when the rebel army again accepted battle outside the town. De la Gardie deployed the combined Swedish–Muscovite army in a half-moon formation, with the cavalry on the wings and the infantry in the centre. The Muscovites again deployed in a second line behind the Swedes. This time, the Swedish musket fire made a strong impact on the rebel line, which wavered, and when charged, the entire rebel army dispersed. Zborowski and some 500 men managed to take refuge in the fortified administrative quarter of Tver', but most rebels fled or fell as the Swedes pursued them. The next day the Swedes attempted to storm Tver' with the help of a petard. However, this attempt failed.[21]

After the July battles of Tver', De la Gardie reported his total strength to Stockholm. Soon after, other hands added the planned reinforcements to De la Gardie's summary, which shows that by this time he commanded about 3,500 men – although many were wounded or sick – and expected to receive another 1,000 soon, in a first batch of reinforcements. And yet more were to follow. King Charles clearly had great expectations for De la Gardie's intervention in Muscovy (Table 7).

---

20 Although few records remain, one of the Finnish banners was commanded by Hans Munck. Although wounded in the battle and ordered back to Finland, he would soon rise to prominence.

21 Almquist, *Sverge och Ryssland*, pp.148–9. While the two battles of Tver' are often dated wrongly, these dates are confirmed by official Muscovite reports.

Table 7. De la Gardie's expeditionary army, 18 August 1609, with expected reinforcements [22]

De la Gardie's Expeditionary Army		
Units	Fit	Wounded or sick
Seven banners of Swedish, French, and German cavalry	586	78
Eight banners of Finnish cavalry	1, 035	118
Nine companies of Finnish foot	917	315
Four companies of enlisted foreign foot	341	97
Total	2, 879	608
Grand total (fit and sick combined): 3, 487		
Reinforcements to be sent		
Cavalry		
Johan De Witt's (Flemish?) Banner	170	
Johann Jost von Quarnheim's (German) Harquebusier Banner	140	
Thomas Chamberlain's (English?) Harquebusier Banner	120	
Thomas Crichton's (Scottish) Harquebusier Banner	120	
Samuel Cobron's (Scottish?) Harquebusier Banner	110	
Total	660	
Infantry		
Johann Conrad Linck von Thurnburg's (German) Regiment	1, 021	
Sir James (Jacob) Spens's (English) Regiment, under Lieutenant Colonel James Colville	1, 000	
John Craul's (English) Company	140	
Total	2, 821	

---

22 De la Gardie's report, cited in Almquist, *Sverge och Ryssland*, pp.270–71.

DE LA GARDIE'S INTERVENTION ARMY

Units presently with the army in Livonia, under Count Joachim Friedrich von Mansfeld zu Vorderort		
Cavalry		
Régis Du Vernet (Frenchmen)	637	
Pierre De la Ville (Frenchmen)	730	
Livonians	500	
Christopher von Schee	112	
Per Hammarskiöld	200	
Otto von Scheiding	200	
Måns Pedersson (Stierna?)	170	
Total	2, 549	
Infantry		
Georg Köpken's Regiment	540	
(Oliver?) Popler's Company	300 (together)	
John Sutherland's Company		
Patrick Rutherford (Scots and possibly Irish)	460	
Five companies of Swedes	1, 000	
Total	2, 300	
Grand total	4, 849	
On the road to De la Gardie		
Cavalry		
Nicholas Andreas's Banner	607	
The first to be sent		
Infantry		
Daniel Hepburn's Company	257	
Robert Sim's Company (Scots)	76	
Sebastian de Pechels's Company	110	
Total within De la Gardie's expeditionary army and the first batch of reinforcements	6, 941	

7

Mutiny

Mikhail Skopin-Shuyskiy was in a hurry to relieve Moscow, so he insisted that they should not waste time on a siege, but instead continue the march as soon as possible. In fact, he regarded it as pointless to spend time taking any towns along the way, if they closed their gates. He must also have advised De la Gardie to leave the highway to Tushino, the headquarters of the false Dmitriy, and Moscow, and instead march along the River Volga towards Kalyazin, north of Moscow. De la Gardie accepted Skopin-Shuyskiy's counsel.

The news of the successful Swedish intervention in support of Tsar Vasiliy spread widely through Muscovy, and an increasing number of towns reasserted their loyalty to the Tsar. However, not all news was positive. Neither Tsar Vasiliy nor Skopin-Shuyskiy had the necessary funds to pay the Swedish army, which they had promised to do. Skopin-Shuyskiy could only provide 2,000 roubles and some fresh horses. As a result, some Swedish soldiers plundered the country along the route of march. The exact details remain caught up in accusations, counter-accusations, and propagandistic statements, but there is little doubt that incidents took place. Shortages in supplies also affected morale in the Swedish army. In particular the units from Finland complained over what they regarded as deplorable conditions in lands far away from home. Moreover, Tsar Vasiliy had promised King Charles the handover of Kexholm, but the Muscovite notables there procrastinated, constantly inventing new reasons to delay the execution of this part of the agreement. While De la Gardie and Skopin-Shuyskiy got along well together, and as far as is known even became good friends, policy differences certainly remained between King Charles and Tsar Vasiliy, neither of whom was particularly willing to trust the other.

Skopin-Shuyskiy sent about 2,000 Muscovites ahead to prevent Jan Mikuliński from gaining control of the Holy Trinity-St Macarius Monastery at Kalyazin before the combined Swedish–Muscovite army arrived.[1] Yet

---

1   Almquist, *Sverge och Ryssland*, p.149.

trouble was brewing in the Swedish army. On the way to Kalyazi the Finnish units mutinied, both cavalry and infantry, since they did not wish to march further into Muscovy, and despite De la Gardie's attempts to persuade them to stay with the army, the Finns simply turned around and marched entire back towards home in good order. Soon after their departure, the German and French enlisted units also mutinied. They wanted to receive their outstanding pay, else they would leave the army and join the enemy. Soon they departed as well.

De la Gardie tried to take resolute action, apparently even riding up to a Finnish standard-bearer to pull the colour from his hand in an attempt to stop the retreat. Yet, he could not risk initiating combat with the mutinous soldiers, since the entire army then would disintegrate. Ultimately, there was little De la Gardie could do. The men were set on returning to familiar lands.

While De la Gardie attempted to negotiate with his men, he counselled Skopin-Shuyskiy to continue the march towards Kalyazin. The Muscovite commander, who was fortunate to command men who operated in familiar surroundings, soon reached and moved into Kalyazin. Meanwhile De la Gardie accepted the reality on the ground and followed his retreating army. He then led his men into Tver', which Zborowski by then had abandoned. There, De la Gardie hoped to await the reinforcements from Sweden that he had been promised. For a while, the men were content with their surroundings.

However, the discontent within the Swedish army continued. A few weeks later, unrest again broke out in the Swedish camp. Ultimately a major part of the army set out from Tver', again following the highway back towards Novgorod and ultimately Finland. De la Gardie had little choice but to follow the army to Torzhok.

By then, Skopin-Shuyskiy was under attack from Commonwealth mercenaries determined to take Kalyazin. Although there was little that De la Gardie could do to help as long as his men did not follow orders, he nonetheless managed to send Christer Some in the direction of Kalyazin with 300 men who remained loyal, with orders to support Skopin-Shuyskiy.[2] It seems that the men consisted of both foot and horse, perhaps because De la Gardie and Some had to make do with those who had not yet mutinied.

We have seen that De la Gardie expected to receive reinforcements from Sweden, and emissaries from Sweden actually caught up with him in Torzhok. Unfortunately for De la Gardie they did not bring the promised reinforcements, but among them was a courier from King Charles. In a letter dated 30 June he asked De la Gardie to inform the Muscovites that if Tsar Vasiliy could not pay the Swedish soldiers, the Swedish Crown would

---

2   Almquist, *Sverge och Ryssland*, p.151. The number ('no more than 300') is confirmed by Sapieha's diary. Hirschberg, *Polska a Moskwa*, p.238. *Contra*: Kargalov, *Moskovskiye voyevody XVI–XVII vv.*, p.121, suggests 250 horse and 720 foot.

cover this cost, but only in exchange for Nöteborg, Ladoga, and Kola Castle, which Sweden would hold as security for the fulfilment of Tsar Vasiliy's promises. Deep inside Muscovy and without funds, the letter must have sounded like a bad joke to De la Gardie. Moreover, King Charles ordered him to take Novgorod instead, if Kexholm was not handed over as the Tsar had promised.[3] Essentially, Charles wanted De la Gardie to take Novgorod as security in case the Muscovites failed to honour their promises, or if Tsar Vasiliy's cause could not be upheld.[4] The King had also devised a plan to send a fleet into the River Neva, ostensibly to bring supplies to De la Gardie but in reality to take Nöteborg in any way possible. In addition, he coveted Ivangorod, the conquest of which he had contemplated in 1608 and again in January 1609, although neither option then had turned out to be feasible in light of Commonwealth operations in Livonia.[5] In fact, the Swedes in Estonia had continued to make designs on Ivangorod for most of the year, and in February 1609 one of Dmitriy's supporters there, Fyodor Aminov, had fallen into Swedish captivity. During the summer King Charles ordered his representatives to turn Aminov, and with his help take the town. Aminov was persuaded to write to Ivan F. Khovanskiy, Ivangorod's governor, however, Khovanskiy rebuffed Aminov's proposal.[6] Although negotiations continued, they led to nothing.[7]

However, these various plans had not produced any tangible gains, and certainly nothing that De la Gardie could make use of under present circumstances. Neither were the instructions from King Charles very helpful when it came to stemming the mutiny in his rebellious army. Despite De la Gardie's continued attempts to cajole his surly soldiers, a major part of the army decided to continue the retreat back to Finland, and the return march continued towards Novgorod. By then, at most 2,000 men continued to take occasional orders from De la Gardie.[8] He certainly did not have the resources to take Novgorod, as King Charles had ordered him, nonetheless he decided to remain in Muscovy in the hope that the expected reinforcements would arrive. If none arrived, he would anyway attempt to move against Ivangorod, Jama, and Kaporie. De la Gardie accordingly sent Horn with a few hundred Swedish and enlisted cavalry ahead to Narva to meet and accompany the expected reinforcements. Horn reached Narva on 20 September, after first defeating and dispersing a Muscovite corps from Ivangorod which attempted to prevent his passage. He found no waiting

---

3 Almquist, *Sverge och Ryssland*, p.146.
4 King Charles was assembling a reserve corps of 920 horse and 2,000 foot in Stockholm for insertion on the eastern front in case of need. Generalstaben, *Sveriges krig* 1, p.330.
5 Almquist, *Sverge och Ryssland*, p.147.
6 Fyodor Grigor'yevich Aminov (c. 1560–1628) ultimately went into Swedish service, but only in 1615. He naturalised as a noble, and founded the Swedish noble family of Aminoff.
7 Almquist, *Sverge och Ryssland*, pp.164–5.
8 Almquist, *Sverge och Ryssland*, p.152.

reinforcements. Moreover, in Narva his remaining men against orders commandeered ships with which they left Estonia.[9]

Victory at Kalyazin

While these events took place, Skopin-Shuyskiy had to deal with the rebels at Kalyazin as best he could on his own. While he received reinforcements in the form of loyalists from several towns, most men were untrained and apparently quite a few were no more than peasant levies. This did not deter Skopin-Shuyskiy. He urged any loyalists to rise against the rebels, denied the rumours that the Swedish intervention army had self-destructed, and promised the support of 40,000 Tatars who were on their way to help the Tsar. On one account, at least, he had tangible evidence for his claims: the small Swedish detachment under Christer Some marched into Skopin-Shuyskiy's camp at Kalyazin on 10 August. Some assured Skopin-Shuyskiy of De la Gardie's continued support, on condition that Skopin-Shuyskiy immediately sent him 1,000 roubles and made sure that Novgorod raised another 7,000 roubles so that he finally could pay, and hopefully regain control over, his men.

Some then set out to train a unit of Muscovite soldiers in how to use pikes in the Continental manner – the first record of Muscovite infantry trained as pikemen.[10] He divided his men into small units which deployed dispersed among the Muscovite infantry, and helped to stiffen the line of battle.

Skopin-Shuyskiy constituted a sufficient threat to Sapieha for him to hand over the siege of the Holy Trinity-St Sergius Monastery to subordinates, and then ride towards Kalyazin. However, Skopin-Shuyskiy had built strong fortifications at Kalyazin, a task for which his levies were eminently suitable. Moreover, he had received trained reinforcements. The loyalist governor Davyd Zherebtsov brought a northern army of hereditary servicemen and streltsy from Siberia and Arkhangel'sk into

---

9   When King Charles received the first news of the mutinies, on 8 September he exhorted the soldiers to serve Sweden loyally wherever they were deployed. Then on 4 October, he issued orders that any soldiers who returned to Finland should be apprehended and told to return to De la Gardie, or be punished as deserters.

10 Some described in a letter how he exercised the Muscovites 'with long pikes [Swedish: *spetzer*] in our manner'. Almquist, *Sverge och Ryssland*, p.153 n.3. Although a few sixteenth-century streltsy were armed with spears, there is no information that Muscovite infantry then functioned as pikemen in the Continental manner, nor that foreign officers trained them as such. Fredholm von Essen, *Muscovy's Soldiers*, p.47. *Contra*: Kargalov, *Moskovskiye voyevody XVI–XVII vv.*, p.122, argues that Yaroslavl' infantry were already armed with pikes (Russian: *kop'yo*). This may be so, but since the Russian term *kop'yo* may mean either spear, pike, or cavalry lance, its use alone without further context does not confirm the deployment of pikemen in the Continental manner.

Skopin-Shuyskiy's camp (reportedly as many as 1,200 from Siberia and 600 from Arkhangel'sk), and on 18 August, Sapieha assaulted Kalyazin. Skopin-Shuyskiy's cavalry first lured the rebel vanguard into an ambush through a feigned flight. The fortifications prevented Sapieha's cavalry from taking full advantage of their mobility, yet it was a hard-fought full-day battle. Ultimately, Skopin-Shuyskiy's men successfully pushed back Sapieha's mercenaries and rebels. The freshly trained pikemen displayed their worth: after only a week of training, they successfully held the line against the mercenary Commonwealth cavalry. Meanwhile, Christer Some fought on horseback, since he described in a letter that he and his cavalry rode with the Muscovites.[11]

Minor as the victory was, it caused Sapieha to abandon his offensive. Ordering Lisowski and his cavalry to stay behind to follow and harass Skopin-Shuyskiy's army, Sapieha returned to the siege of the Holy Trinity-St Sergius Monastery by way of Pereyaslavl', where he inserted a garrison.

Sapieha's failure at Kalyazin was not the only defeat suffered by Dmitriy's armies. Further to the east, the loyalist boyar Fyodor Sheremetyev advanced with some 3,500 Kazan' men from Nizhniy Novgorod to Vladimir, from which he harassed Dmitriy's poorly coordinated units. Meanwhile the Crimean Tatar army, under Qalgha Sultan Janibeg Geray, approached from the south – a peril to loyalists and rebels alike, as the Crimean Khanate sustained its economy by raiding for slaves. This time the Crimeans struck Serpukhov, Borovsk, Kolomna, and several other towns before riding home with their living plunder.[12]

Skopin-Shuyskiy now went on the offensive. He sent Semyon Golovin, Grigoriy Valuyev, and Christer Some towards Pereyaslavl', which they, together with locals inside the town, took on 6 September. The Commonwealth garrison was thoroughly disrupted, and many perished. This neutralised the opposition on the road from Rostov to Aleksandrovskaya Sloboda, and forced Lisowski to return to Suzdal'.

Meanwhile, De la Gardie again managed to gain control over his army, not least because Skopin-Shuyskiy had succeeded in raising 3,000 roubles in cash and yet more sable furs (which together apparently reached a combined value of 11,000 roubles) with which to pay the men. Those who were most mutinous continued the march towards the Swedish border, but others finally agreed again to follow De la Gardie's orders. They were not many; De la Gardie could only muster 830 horse and 130 foot.[13] The Swedish army then resumed the march towards the east. He reached Kalyazin on 26 September, where he again joined forces with Skopin-Shuyskiy.

---

11   Almquist, *Sverge och Ryssland*, p.154; citing Some's letter.
12   Janibeg Geray (1568–1636) became Khan of the Crimean Khanate in 1610. As Qalgha Sultan, the Khan's deputy, he commanded grand raids in Muscovy in both 1609 and 1610.
13   Generalstaben, *Sveriges krig* 1, p.333.

It was a happy meeting. Yet the difficulties that they needed to overcome were profound. Skopin-Shuyskiy urgently wanted to push on towards Moscow to defeat the rebels. De la Gardie, however, wanted to await the expected reinforcements from Sweden, the handover of Kexholm, and the agreed-upon outstanding pay to his men. In particular the long-promised handover of Kexholm was important to the Swedish Crown, and King Charles had expressed this demand in no uncertain terms. Tsar Vasiliy had indeed done what he could to effect the handover. Having sent repeated written orders to complete the transfer, he had finally even dispatched his trusted emissaries Fyodor Chulkov and Yefim Telepnyov to make sure that it happened. However, in late October the two emissaries had to inform the Tsar that they had only managed to reach Ladoga Town, and that in any case the fanatical Bishop Silvester in Kexholm had inflamed the population as well as the town's young governor, Prince Yefim Myshetskiy, against the Tsar's order. They refused to give up their town to heathen Lutherans.[14]

Not wishing to wait longer than necessary, Skopin-Shuyskiy began to raise peasant levies for the construction of bridges on the road to Pereyaslavl' which would take them to the besieged Holy Trinity-St Sergius Monastery. Together, Skopin-Shuyskiy and De la Gardie then set out on the road. On 6 October, they reached Pereyaslavl'. Soon afterwards, a combined contingent under Golovin, Valuyev, and John Muir moved into Aleksandrovskaya Sloboda, about 120 km north-east of Moscow, without facing any opposition.[15] Meanwhile, Skopin-Shuyskiy sent a relief force of 300 selected cavalrymen from Kostroma, Yaroslavl', and the northern towns under Zherebtsov towards the monastery. Zherebtsov managed to breach the rebel blockade and enter the monastery, whose garrison still fought on.[16] By then, Skopin-Shuyskiy's cavalry was already carrying out raids in the vicinity, which greatly disturbed the Commonwealth mercenaries. While he had received reinforcements from various towns in northwestern Muscovy, the strength of the combined Swedish–Muscovite army is not known. According to a deserter, it consisted of 15,000 Muscovites and seven banners of foreigners.[17] The deserter may have exaggerated the number of Muscovites, but at least De la Gardie's corps was, if anything, slightly stronger than he reported.

Sapieha felt the threat from the combined Swedish–Muscovite army, which had already defeated him once. Yet, there were other Commonwealth mercenaries in the area. Having received reinforcements of some 2,000 cavalry under Prince Roman Różyński from Tushino and another contingent under Colonel Jarosz Strawiński from Suzdal', Sapieha decided to attack. The ensuing battle took place on 28 October at the village of Karinskoye,

---

14 Almquist, *Sverge och Ryssland*, p.159.
15 The term *sloboda* indicated a settlement whose inhabitants were exempt from taxes and other duties. The town's name was Aleksandrov.
16 Kargalov, *Moskovskiye voyevody XVI–XVII vv.*, p.122, suggests 600 men.
17 Almquist, *Sverge och Ryssland*, p.158 n. 2.

near Aleksandrovskaya Sloboda. As at Kalyazin, Skopin-Shuyskiy made sure that his men built field fortifications. The Commonwealth cavalry was met with fire from Skopin-Shuyskiy's streltsy and De la Gardie's handful of musketeers. This repulsed the rebels. The number of casualties remain as uncertain as the total number of men in the respective armies. Swedish losses included Christer Some, who was badly wounded in the battle and ultimately had to be sent home.[18]

---

18   Almquist, *Sverge och Ryssland*, p.158. Christer Some did not get much time to recuperate. On his subsequent activities, see Fredholm von Essen, *Kalmar War*, pp.163, 205, 207–8.

8

The Polish Invasion

We have seen that King Sigismund provided either passive or active support to the false Dmitriys. In similarity to other proponents of regime change, then and later, he no doubt hoped that the pretender, if successful, would become a docile tool. However, King Sigismund never enjoyed the support of the entire Commonwealth nobility in these schemes. The Commonwealth nobles and cossacks who volunteered to fight for a false Dmitriy largely did so for reasons of their own. In some cases, they joined him not to ingratiate themselves with King Sigismund but because they had rebelled against him. In 1606, resentment within the Commonwealth nobility towards Sigismund's second Habsburg marriage and his plans to have his son, Władysław, elected as his successor already *vivente rege* (in the King's lifetime) caused a sufficiently strong reaction that some nobles, many of them Protestants, rebelled against what they perceived to be autocratic kingship.[1] The rebellion escalated into civil war. Although King Sigismund defeated his opponents the following year, the outcome of the rebellion was the abandonment of the King's plan to modernise the country's obsolete political system.

On 25 July 1608, King Sigismund and Tsar Vasiliy negotiated a ceasefire agreement that supposedly guaranteed Commonwealth neutrality in the Muscovite civil war for the duration of the agreement, which was set at three years and 11 months.[2] However, already by the end of the year King Sigismund made up his mind nonetheless to intervene in Muscovite affairs. This was not a suddenly discovered ambition: Sigismund had already at the

---

[1] The discontented nobles assembled at Sandomierz in 1606. Arguing that the rebellion was in defence of the constitution and that sovereignty rested in the assembly of the entire nobility *en masse*, not merely their parliamentary representatives, the rebels called it *rokosz* after the town of Rakosz near Budapest, where the Hungarian nobility had claimed their rights in 1526.

[2] Almquist, *Sverge och Ryssland*, p.118

SWEDEN'S WAR IN MUSCOVY 1609-1617

death of Tsar Fyodor in 1598 intended to suggest himself as successor to the Muscovite throne.[3]

For King Sigismund, an invasion of Muscovy was a golden opportunity and well worth breaking the 1608 ceasefire. It was a means to accomplish his goals of adding new lands to the Commonwealth under his own dynastic rule. Possibly he had grandiose hopes of bringing the entire Muscovite state under the Commonwealth, in similarity to his earlier ambition to include Sweden into a union with the Commonwealth. For the Commonwealth magnates, this meant an opportunity to extend their territories further into Ruthenia. The Polish king also hoped to gain the support of the Pope, for whom the invasion was a means to extend the Catholic faith also to Muscovy, and with a little luck to supplant the Orthodox church.

The three objectives could, in theory, be accomplished by conquering Muscovy and making it into a union partner within the Commonwealth. In reality, this objective conflicted with the more proximate goals of the campaign: the conquest of Smolensk and its lands. Commonwealth opinions were clearly divided on what goals should be aimed for. Veteran soldiers such as Grand Hetman of Lithuania Jan Karol Chodkiewicz and Field Hetman of the Crown Stanisław Żółkiewski argued for a cautious strategy and seem to have favoured the extension of union membership to Muscovy, while others were more eager for immediate territorial expansion.

Papal backing resulted in no more than verbal support, and funding for the expedition took longer than expected to raise. Ultimately, the unintended delays worked in King Sigismund's favour, since they brought the unexpected boon that he could use Tsar Vasiliy's treaty with King Charles as a pretext for the long-planned intervention. Sigismund portrayed the Swedish–Muscovite defensive alliance as a cause for war. Ostensibly, the Polish king would intervene to protect the Catholic Church from Swedes, Turks, and Tatars.

King Sigismund at Smolensk (As depicted by King Sigismund's court painter, Tommaso Dolabella, 1611)

---

3   Almquist, *Sverge och Ryssland*, p.41.

THE POLISH INVASION

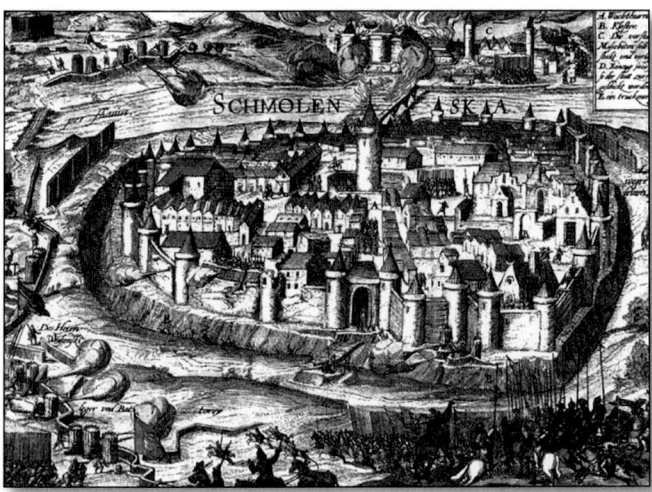

The siege of Smolensk, 1609–1611.

Preparations were completed in August 2009. The Crown army, an estimated 10,000 to 12,000 men under the command of King Sigismund and Crown Field Hetman Żółkiewski, crossed the border and in September 1609 laid siege to the important border city of Smolensk, defended by the resolute Mikhail Sheïn.[4] It was a full-scale invasion. Receiving intelligence on the approach of King Sigismund's army, Shein gathered some 5,400 men to defend the city. The strongly fortified Smolensk had a population of about 20,000.[5] Whilst some defences were obsolete, the Commonwealth soldiers had limited experience with modern siege warfare.

King Sigismund had ordered Lithuanian Hetman Chodkiewicz to invade Muscovy with the Livonian army through an attack on Pskov at the same time that he laid siege to Smolensk. However, the men of the Livonian army complained that they had not been paid, and instead of marching against Pskov, they retreated south into Lithuania to claim compensation. When none was forthcoming, they instead seized royal lands as security for the missing pay. They would not fight for King Sigismund until money was forthcoming. Clearly it was

Field Hetman of the Crown Stanisław Żółkiewski.

---

4 Almquist, *Sverge och Ryssland*, p.161.
5 Kargalov, *Moskovskiye voyevody XVI–XVII vv.*, p.196; Dunning, *Russia's First Civil War*, p.310.

SWEDEN'S WAR IN MUSCOVY 1609-1617

Field Hetman of the Crown Stanisław Żółkiewski at the battle of Klushino, 1610. (Szymon Boguszowicz, c. 1620; L'viv National Gallery of Arts at Oles'ko)

not only De la Gardie who experienced disciplinary problems caused by monetary difficulties.

King Sigismund's full-scale invasion of Muscovy changed the strategic landscape overnight. Tsar Vasiliy, for obvious reasons, and King Charles in distant Sweden, noted Sigismund's invasion with concern. False Dmitriy and his supporters worried, too, since the invasion seemed to confirm that the Polish king wanted the throne for himself, or possibly his son. Even Dmitriy's Commonwealth supporters grew apprehensive. The Commonwealth mercenaries among Dmitriy's men much preferred the opportunities offered by civil war with no king in the vicinity to claim his due. A full-scale Commonwealth takeover would deprive them of the rewards that Dmitriy already had promised. Besides, many of Dmitriy's Commonwealth followers enjoyed the extensive freedoms under the pretender. The bands in Tushino under the Polish freebooter Aleksander Lisowski, from his name known as *lisowczyki*, particularly opposed direct Commonwealth rule since many of them had previously rebelled against King Sigismund.

In October, Prince Różyński persuaded the volunteers to enter into a confederation against Sigismund. A confederation (Polish: *konfederacja*) was an association formed through constitutional means for the attainment of particular, stated aims, which often took the form of armed rebellion. A basic tenet in Polish constitutional law was that if the monarch did not respect the rights and privileges of the nobility, the nobles were no longer bound to obey him and had the legal right to rebel. If Sigismund gained the throne of Muscovy he might deprive the Commonwealth volunteers of their rightful rewards, which would make the invasion unconstitutional. Prince Różyński accordingly argued for a confederation, with the stated objective to remain loyal to Dmitriy until Moscow recognised him as Tsar, so that the Commonwealth mercenaries would receive their reward from state revenues.

Sapieha, however, informed King Sigismund that he was open to any opportunity, including service on behalf of the King, as long as the monarch agreed to guarantee the wages that Dmitriy had promised him and his men. Soon, negotiations between the Commonwealth mercenaries and Sigismund were underway, of which Dmitriy was not informed. By December, the Commonwealth mercenaries had accepted the transfer to King Sigismund of Smolensk (although the city had not yet fallen). In return, the Polish king guaranteed to provide the wages and other wealth that Dmitriy had promised.

Harassing the Rebels

Following the victory over Sapieha at Karinskoye in October, an increasing number of Muscovite towns declared for Tsar Vasiliy. Those which could sent soldiers to Skopin-Shuyskiy's army. Yaroslavl' reportedly sent 1,500 well-armed horse and foot. Meanwhile, Skopin-Shuyskiy continued the march towards the Holy Trinity-St Sergius Monastery. At the same time, Fyodor Sheremetyev attacked Lisowski at Suzdal', attempting to break through to join forces with Skopin-Shuyskiy. Although some of his units were repulsed towards Vladimir, he managed to bring a small force to Aleksandrovskaya Sloboda. Moscow sent an army, reportedly 3,000 men with artillery, under Princes Ivan Kurakin and Boris Lykov-Obolenskiy to join forces with Skopin-Shuyskiy.[6]

Meanwhile, Skopin-Shuyskiy took a number of measures to limit the freedom of manoeuvre of the rebels, and established fortifications and block houses in strategic locations. A siege war of little manoeuvring was a new and unfamiliar experience for the rebels, and some Poles, including Żółkiewski, argued that it was De la Gardie, Christer Some, and other Swedish officers who taught this strategy to the Muscovites.[7] De la Gardie and Skopin-Shuyskiy also sent out ski patrols to disrupt the enemy's supply lines and harass rebel units tied down in the snow by their horses. While northern Muscovites certainly knew how to ski, some of the patrols may have consisted of Finnish soldiers, since they tended to be particularly experienced in this manner of warfare and were present in the army. In hindsight it is difficult to say how much of Skopin-Shuyskiy's strategy and tactics derived from Swedish initiatives. Certainly, contemporary Muscovites and Poles regarded the Swedish participation as decisive. Yet, we have seen that De la Gardie's intervention army was never very large, and most of what Swedes and Finns could do, Muscovites could do equally well. The Swedish infantry employed more up-to-date tactics and weapons than the Muscovites, and probably had more experience in modern siege

---

6 Hirschberg, *Polska a Moskwa*, p.247; Almquist, *Sverge och Ryssland*, p.158.
7 Almquist, *Sverge och Ryssland*, p.159 n.2.

warfare, but other differences were less decisive.⁸ Perhaps it was the mere presence of the Swedes that was crucial. Despite the disciplinary problems, the Swedish presence proved to the Muscovite soldiers that Tsar Vasiliy had strong allies. Commonwealth mercenaries and cossacks no longer appeared quite as powerful as before. Most Muscovite servicemen found no particular difficulties in cooperating with their Swedish counterparts.

The one group that consistently disapproved of the Swedish presence was the Orthodox churchmen. Many of them repeatedly engaged in venomous diatribes against the presence of, in their words, the hated heathen foreigners, be they Swedes, Poles, Tatars, or Turks. While this caused resentment among some rural groups who never, or only seldom, met foreigners, the real impact of the church propaganda would come only later.

Arctic Operations

On 17 December 1609, De la Gardie and Skopin-Shuyskiy, on behalf of their respective sovereigns, concluded an agreement in Aleksandrovskaya Sloboda concerning the remuneration and practical details of the continued Swedish intervention. The Muscovite side promised full compensation, in addition to Kexholm County which would be ceded immediately. Yet the Tsar had to promise more than this: the agreement also granted King Charles any other town, district, or county that he might reasonably want in fair compensation for his expenses. In return, Sweden promised 4,000 well-equipped and fully armed soldiers, to be paid by Muscovy in the same manner as the previous units. Tsar Vasiliy ratified the agreement in a letter to King Charles, dated 17 January 1610.⁹ Indeed, King Charles had plenty of other demands, in particular Nöteborg, Ivangorod, and Kola Castle. We have seen that Charles had long entertained hopes for new territories in the Arctic north. He wanted the entire Kola County, but also Fort Suma, the wealthy, fortified Solovki Monastery, located on an island in the White Sea, and even Arkhangel'sk.¹⁰ As noted, already in early 1609 Charles had ordered Baltzar Bäck and Isaac Behm to command a ski march into the Arctic to take Kola Castle – in the name of Tsar Vasiliy. However, nothing

---

8   Since foreign officers had served in the Muscovite army since the sixteenth century, it must have had some contact with Continental tactics. One of them was the aforementioned Margeret, a veteran French mercenary who in consecutive order had served Tsars Boris, Dmitriy, and for a brief time, Vasiliy. Some credit him with the introduction of Continental tactics in Muscovy, including Chester Dunning in Margeret, *Russian Empire*, p.98 n.36.
9   *Sverges Traktater med främmande magter* 5: 1 (Stockholm: P. A. Norstedt, 1903), pp.189–97.
10 Generalstaben, *Sveriges krig* 1, p.324.

THE POLISH INVASION

had come of these plans because it was too late in winter and travel would soon have become impracticable.[11]

Impatient to gain these territories, King Charles now ordered Bäck again to assemble units in the Arctic north for a second attempt to conquer Kola Castle, which, he argued, belonged to Sweden. We have seen that Kola was the strongest fortress on the Kola Peninsula, with a garrison of about 200 to 300 men.[12] This time, King Charles had ordered preparations to begin early enough to set out during winter. In October 1609 he had instructed Bäck to bring some soldiers (Tidemann von Schrowe's company and a Polish company in Swedish service) and also raise 500 men in northern Sweden and another 500 men (to be raised by Isaac Behm in addition to Jacob Frensham's company) in northern Finland for the expedition to conquer Kola Castle. All of them must be good skiers.[13] These units were normally deployed in the coastal towns on the shore of the Gulf of Bothnia, the northernmost arm of the Baltic Sea.

In February 1610, Bäck's expeditionary corps stood at Torneå, ready to march at the appointed time. The corps then consisted of Colonel Hans von Rechenberger as military commander, the three Norrland companies of foot under respectively Per Clemetsson, Gulik Larsson, and Anders Olsson, and Matthias Houwald's Polish company of foot.[14] However, Behm was slow to send his men to the expedition, which in March resulted in a furious letter from King Charles, who threatened him with '7,000 devils' and the loss of his head if he did not immediately set out. For good measure, Charles sent the same threat to Bäck, Rechenberger, and Frensham.[15] Unfortunately, it was then again too late in the season. As a result, the expedition to Kola was again cancelled. During the summer of 1610, Bäck instead set out on the second scheme for the year planned by King Charles, namely, an expedition to the Varanger Fjord between Norway and Muscovy (presently in modern-day Norway) with six arquebusiers, 100 levies, and various other men including shipbuilders to establish an embryo naval base on the Atlantic side of the Arctic coast, supported by a supply train of Sami with

---

11   Sweden was not the only neighbouring state that desired Muscovy's Arctic north. King Christian IV of Denmark and Norway also hoped to capitalise on Muscovy's weakness during the Time of Troubles, and called on Moscow to renounce the Arctic territories and evacuate the Muscovite population from the Kola Peninsula.
12   In the mid seventeenth century, Muscovy maintained no less than 500 streltsy and nine artillerymen in Kola.
13   Johan E. Waaranen (ed.), *Samling af urkunder rörande Finlands historia 3 (1609–1611)* (Helsinki: Finska Litteratur-Sällskapet, 1866), pp.47–9. Incidentally, Tidemann von Schrowe, a veteran of the 1605 battle of Kircholm, is generally known in Swedish sources as Tideman Schrou.
14   King Charles's order dated 14 February 1610. Waaranen, *Samling*, pp.66–7. Matthias Houwald was probably a Baltic German and accordingly not the same as the Hungarian Michael Horvath (Erwat) who together with Tidemann von Schrowe fought for Sweden at Kircholm.
15   King Charles to Behm, 24 March 1610. Waaranen, *Samling*, pp.68–9.

Kola Castle. Although populations were small in the Arctic north, military operations still took place there in times of war and conflict. (Gerrit de Veer, 1598)

200 reindeer. They reached the Varanger Fjord, but the plan to establish a naval base ultimately failed.[16]

The Relief of the Holy Trinity-St Sergius Monastery

Yet, northwestern Muscovy remained the key theatre of operations for Swedish armies. In October 1609, Henrik Wildeman brought the expected Swedish reinforcements to Viborg.[17] These were Johann Conrad Linck von Thurnburg's regiment of foot and Posse's and Johann Jost von Quarnheim's cavalry companies. The following month, Wildeman marched into Muscovy with his corps. King Charles, as usual, wanted him first to take Ivangorod, but this fortress remained too strong for an attempt to be contemplated. Alternative plans were instead made to take the weaker Jama and Kaporie, but it is unclear what happened with this scheme. The winter cold and the habitual supply problems caused desertions, and when Wildeman in January 1610 arrived at Aleksandrovskaya Sloboda with the expected reinforcements, his corps had shrunk to only some 850 men fit for service.[18] Soon, additional reinforcements arrived, raising the number to 503 horse and 707 foot. Altogether, De la Gardie now commanded 1,330 horse and 900 foot.[19]

---

16 King Charles's order dated 19 December 1609. Generalstaben, *Sveriges krig* 1, pp.331–2; Waaranen, *Samling*, pp.60–66.
17 Many Swedish nobles still preferred to use first name and patronymic instead of family name. Henrik Tönnesson Wildeman personally seems not to have used the family name Wildeman, but it was his by right and is here used for simplicity.
18 Linck von Thurnburg's Regiment consisted of 549 fit men and 104 who were too sick to fight. The two cavalry companies together counted 302 fit and nine sick men. Almquist, *Sverge och Ryssland*, p.170.
19 Generalstaben, *Sveriges krig* 1, p.333.

THE POLISH INVASION

Meanwhile, Grigoriy Valuyev in early January succeeded, under the cover of darkness, in bringing possibly 500 additional reinforcements into the Holy Trinity-St Sergius Monastery, which further raised the ability of the defenders to hold out.

Sapieha had laid siege to the monastery since September 1608, nearly 16 months. Hitherto holding all the cards, the mercenaries and rebels had grown complacent. Now, the strategy employed by Skopin-Shuyskiy and De la Gardie of limiting the freedom of manoeuvre of the rebels and harassing and cutting their supply lines changed everything. When the mercenaries and rebels at the monastery understood that Skopin-Shuyskiy and De la Gardie were approaching, the latter with fresh Swedish reinforcements, they panicked, and many rebels simply fled. On 12 January Sapieha abandoned his camp without even attempting to destroy any remaining war booty or supplies. He established a new camp at Dmitrov for his remaining 1,000 or so men. Most were Commonwealth cavalry but he also retained a significant contingent of Don cossacks. On 28 January, Skopin-Shuyskiy and De la Gardie moved into the abandoned camp.

This was fortunate for the monastery's defenders, of whom more than 2,000 had died during the long siege, primarily of scurvy and epidemics. When De la Gardie and Skopin-Shuyskiy arrived, fewer than 1,000 men remained alive, of whom merely 200 had formed part of the original garrison. Relieving them was a great success for the Tsar.

De la Gardie's enlisted soldiers were less impressed, however. Hearing rumours about the wealthy monastery, they had expected to be paid in full immediately upon saving it. Where was the money? Surely the monks had a treasury? Yes, but considering the ruined state of the monastery, Skopin-Shuyskiy did not wish to coerce the monks into paying up as soon as he had rescued them. An enforced loan would ultimately be necessary, but perhaps not quite yet. Perhaps there still was some money left in Moscow?

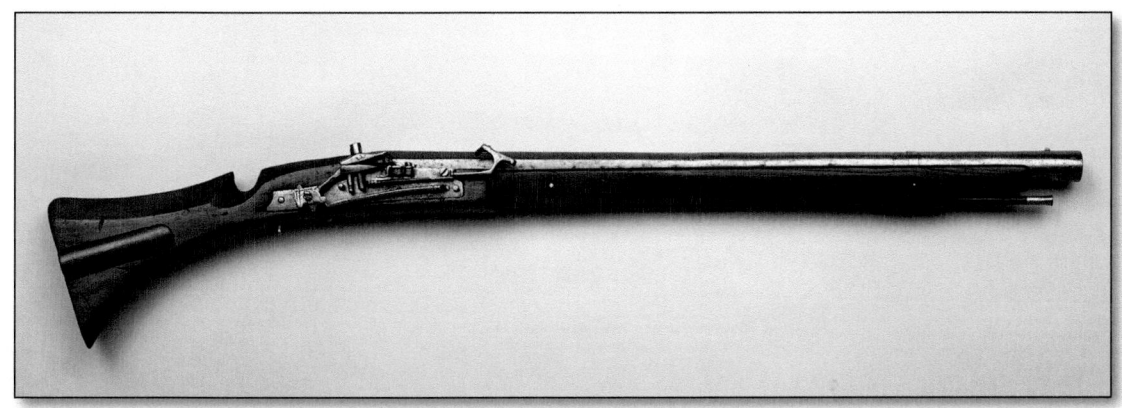

Muscovite snaplock arquebus, late sixteenth century or early seventeenth century. From the armoury of the of the Holy Trinity-St Sergius Monastery. Total length: 103.0 cm; barrel length: 70.5 cm; calibre: 14 mm. (Moscow Kremlin Armoury)

SWEDEN'S WAR IN MUSCOVY 1609-1617

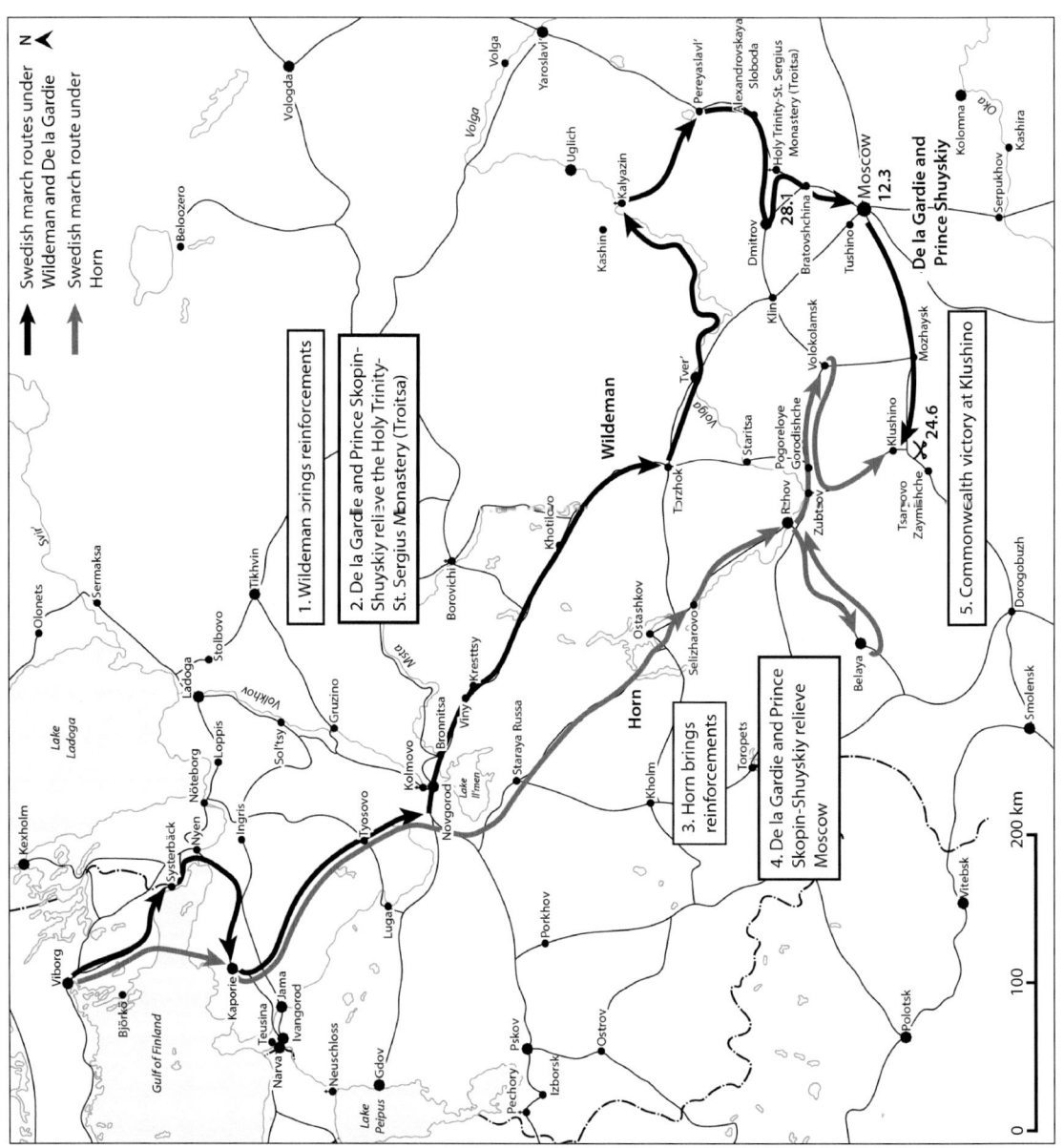

Map 4. De la Gardie's March to Moscow and Klushino, 1610.

9

The Relief of Moscow

Indeed, funds to pay the enlisted soldiers soon arrived. Skopin-Shuyskiy and De la Gardie could continue the march towards Moscow, but first they would have to deal with Sapieha and Lisowski. De la Gardie sent Wildeman with a corps against Lisowski, who was at Suzdal', while he personally led most of the Swedish intervention army against Sapieha at Dmitrov. Muscovite ski patrols already harassed Sapieha's supply lines. De la Gardie hoped that this would disturb Lisowski and Sapieha sufficiently to push them into the main rebel camp at Tushino. If so, all rebels could be handled at once through a pincer attack, with Skopin-Shuyskiy and De la Gardie approaching from the north and part of the Moscow garrison approaching from the south-east.

By then, the rebel camp at Tushino was already in a state of utter confusion. Everybody had understood that Dmitriy's most efficient soldiers, the Commonwealth mercenaries, were already negotiating terms with King Sigismund – and that Dmitriy was excluded from these negotiations. The news of the approaching Swedish–Muscovite army produced yet more fear. For these reasons Dmitriy had already left the camp in late December, with a few loyal retainers. He took refuge in Kaluga, which was strongly fortified and retained links with the cossack south.

Dmitriy's departure shattered what little then remained of rebel confidence. The Commonwealth mercenaries immediately ransacked his abandoned 'palace' and pilfered his remaining belongings. Some accused Prince Różyński of having scared away Dmitriy, his avowed master. Maryna vacillated between asking King Sigismund for mercy and persuading the Commonwealth mercenaries to stay loyal to a daughter of Poland. The latter would have been a futile task. Prince Różyński soon convinced the Muscovite rebel nobles – Patriarch Filaret and the House of Romanov, Mikhail Saltykov, and Mikhail Mochanov – that their best hope now was to promise King Sigismund they would not recognise any other candidate as tsar except one proposed by the Polish king. Most rebel nobles immediately dropped their professed loyalty to Dmitriy, and instead sent envoys to Sigismund, who was still laying siege to Smolensk. The envoys were headed by Mikhail Saltykov and also included his son Ivan Saltykov. Henceforth, father and son would attach their standards to the Polish cause. The Tushino envoys suggested the election of King Sigismund's son Władysław as the new Tsar but demanded safeguards for their own interests and those of the Orthodox faith. King Sigismund agreed with the proposal, and on 4 February made public a manifest in which he announced the agreed-upon terms.[1] Moreover, he promised vast estates in Muscovy to those Tushino rebels and mercenaries who supported him. He demanded an oath from the Tushino envoys that until the proper coronation of Władysław, they must remain loyal to King Sigismund himself. He also attempted to persuade Sheïn to surrender Smolensk to his new suzerain, but the loyal Sheïn refused to recognise the authority given to King Sigismund by a bunch of rebels without a cause.

Meanwhile Dmitriy attempted, from his refuge in Kaluga, to rally the rebels against King Sigismund. With the help of his wife Maryna, he also attempted to fan the anger of the rebels against Prince Różyński. The result was internal fighting in Tushino between the Commonwealth mercenaries and some of the Muscovite rebel nobles on the one side, and the cossacks and Tatars who remained loyal to Dmitriy on the other. In the ensuing chaos, Maryna felt her life at risk from Prince Różyński, so she fled the camp. Trying to join Dmitriy in Kaluga, she lost her way and had to ask for sanctuary in Dmitrov with Sapieha, who took her in.

On 16 February, De la Gardie set out from Aleksandrovskaya Sloboda towards Dmitrov. He brought most Swedish units, including Linck von Thurnburg's Regiment, and yet more Muscovite units under Zherebtsov and Prince Lykov-Obolenskiy. Skopin-Shuyskiy, meanwhile, established a camp at the village of Shepilovka. In this manner, the two commanders controlled more territory and ensured better access to supplies. Two days later, De la Gardie offered Sapieha battle outside Dmitrov. Sapieha, outnumbered, failed to take the bait. By then, the fit men under his command had been reduced further, to 400 Commonwealth cavalry and 300 Don cossacks. On 19 February De la Gardie stormed Sapieha's camp, which his men then plundered. Sapieha took refuge in the fortified administrative quarter of Dmitrov. He feared that the Swedes would storm the town as well. The risk was real: Colonel Linck von Thurnburg wrote in a letter a few days later that he could have stormed Dmitrov, had the Muscovites only followed his advice, and then they would have captured Sapieha. However, De la Gardie was now out of supplies. He accordingly returned to Aleksandrovskaya Sloboda, having left a garrison at a block house at Dmitrov.[2] Realising his position was vulnerable, Sapieha on 26 February burned Dmitrov, and then retreated westwards by way of Klin to the Joseph-Volokolamsk Monastery, as the name suggests located near Volokolamsk (then often called Volok

---

1 Almquist, *Sverge och Ryssland*, 171–2, with sources.
2 Almquist, *Sverge och Ryssland*, 174–5; citing a letter from Linck von Thurnburg, 4 March 1610; Sapieha's diary, Hirschberg, *Polska a Moskwa*, 253–4.

Lamskiy). Meanwhile, ski patrols from the block house at Dmitrov pursued the retreating mercenaries and cossacks, causing them considerable harm.

Having dealt with Sapieha, the only remaining threat on this side of Moscow was Lisowski's fast-moving cavalry. Apparently, Wildeman had not succeeded in pinning him down in Suzdal'. However, Lisowski's marauders posed only a minor threat to the combined Swedish–Muscovite army, so Skopin-Shuyskiy and De la Gardie decided not to postpone the march to Moscow any further.

Ultimately the anarchy, infighting, plotting, and fears among the rebels and mercenaries at Tushino caused their destruction as a fighting force. On 6 March, Prince Różyński had the Tushino camp burned. He then withdrew with most Commonwealth mercenaries, by way of Volokolamsk towards Staritsa further to the west, and later to Osipovo. There he soon died, fatally injuring himself falling down the stairs while drunk. Other Commonwealth men instead rode to King Sigismund's camp at Smolensk. Most cossacks and Tatars rode to Kaluga, where Dmitriy waited. The rebel evacuation of Tushino took place at the last moment. The combined Swedish–Muscovite army received the news of the rebel departure on the following day, having then reached the village of Bratovshchina, less than 50 km from Tushino and almost halfway to Moscow. On 12 March, Skopin-Shuyskiy and De la Gardie entered Moscow; thus ended the almost two-year blockade of the capital.

In Moscow, Tsar Vasiliy's supporters greeted Skopin-Shuyskiy and De la Gardie as heroes. The Tsar lavished gifts on De la Gardie, and nobody complained about the Swedish general's refusal to relinquish his rapier as he approached the Tsar, a custom normally mandated by Muscovite court protocol. Vasiliy also found money to pay De la Gardie's soldiers.

The Swedish intervention army stayed in Moscow for two months. There is evidence that Swedish representatives in Moscow intended to purchase additional cuirasses and rapiers there for the army but unfortunately we do not know whether they succeeded, or whether the armaments were of Continental or Muscovite design.[3]

By this time the Swedish emissary to the Tsar, Peder Pedersson, had voiced a new proposition. He informed Tsar Vasiliy that King Charles suggested that the Tsar send 2,000 or 3,000 men to Finland. There, Swedish officers would train them in modern warfare (the Dutch model), after which they would be enlisted for Swedish service against the Commonwealth. They would serve under native Russian-speaking officers who were already in the Swedish army. Afterwards, the soldiers would return to Muscovy, where they could contribute their skills and experience in modern warfare to the Tsar's army.

---

3   Almquist, *Sverge och Ryssland*, p.164 n.3; citing De la Gardie to Tsar Vasiliy, 14 January 1610.

Pedersson also had instructions to attempt to enlist several thousand Tatars, either men already in Muscovite service or Tatars from the Khanate of the Crimea. King Charles requested the Tsar's support in this matter.

Charles hoped that the proposed Muscovite and Tatar soldiers would join a Swedish army in Estonia that already consisted of Finnish soldiers and enlisted men from elsewhere. The army would then move into Commonwealth-held Livonia, conquer Dorpat, and then move into Muscovy by way of Pskov so that the units could join De la Gardie there. Charles pointed out that in this manner, the new army would serve both Swedish and Muscovite interests. Both King Charles and Tsar Vasiliy wanted King Sigismund out of Muscovy, he argued.[4]

However, the ambitious plan to bring Muscovite and Tatar soldiers for training in Finland led to nothing. Muscovy remained under immediate threat, and King Sigismund still stood at Smolensk. Since February 1610, Novgorod was directly threatened too, this time by the rebel Lev Pleshcheyev, and possibly some 6,000 cossacks based around Staraya Russa. Skopin-Shuyskiy asked De la Gardie to help in rescuing Novgorod, and the Swedish general seems to have promised to deal with Pleshcheyev.

Horn Brings Reinforcements

De la Gardie's promise was not empty, because the means for this were suddenly available to him: King Charles had dispatched another batch of enlisted reinforcements to Viborg in December. There, Horn assumed command of the reinforcements, who were paid in furs from the supplies brought from Muscovy. Since Wildeman had been unable to seize Nöteborg, Ivangorod, Jama, and Kaporie on the way to join forces with De la Gardie, King Charles ordered Horn to get it done. However, Charles greatly underestimated the logistical difficulties in laying siege to a major fortress in Ingria. Horn remained in Viborg, until in early February 1610 he was ready to set out. Because of the favourable winter conditions he marched straight across the frozen Gulf of Finland to Kaporie with 2,250 enlisted foreign soldiers. Among them were Scots and English under respectively Samuel Cobron and James Colville and French horse under Pierre De la Ville.[5] The Finnish units remained behind, since they were needed to defend the Swedish border.

From the outset, Horn found it difficult to get supplies. The local peasants immediately fled into the forests, taking their food with them or hiding it. The plan was that the governor of Kaporie, on behalf of Tsar Vasiliy, should provide supplies, but whilst the governor acknowledged this instruction,

---

4   Almquist, *Sverge och Ryssland*, pp.176–7.
5   Generalstaben, *Sveriges krig* 1, p.334. Although detailed evidence is lacking, it seems likely that the celebrated future Scottish field marshal Alexander Leslie (1582–1661) served in one of these units.

and Horn's need for supplies, he caused difficulties in other ways. Soon, violence broke out between Horn's quartermasters and the governor's men.

Nonetheless, Horn's arrival soon changed the strategic balance in the region. His enlisted captains were eager to attack Dmitriy's men, or for that matter, any rebels, since this offered the opportunity to carry out some plundering of their own. Pierre De la Ville led his cavalry to Staraya Russa, from which they chased off Pleshcheyev's cossacks (which raises questions as to whether the cossacks were as many as reported). Colonel De la Ville then rode to Novgorod, requesting quarters for his men. Although there was an agreement that the Swedish reinforcements would detach 200 soldiers to safeguard Novgorod, none had expected De la Ville to bring his cavalry there at this time, and on his own initiative. The Novgorod nobles accordingly tried to direct him against Pskov instead, where men loyal to Dmitriy still held sway.

Horn followed in the tracks of De la Ville with the rest of his army. In Novgorod he received instructions from De la Gardie, who had devised a campaign plan together with the Tsar. The objective was to clear out the remnants of the Tushino army, whether Commonwealth marauders or Muscovite rebels, from the region south and south-west of Tver'. Horn's orders were accordingly to march by way of Staraya Russa and Ostashkov to Staritsa, where he would join forces with De la Gardie and the Tsar's army. Then, the combined Swedish–Muscovite army would attack the Commonwealth camps in Zubtsov and Rzhov. Horn followed the plan. His first contact with the enemy was between Ostashkov and Selizharovo. However, the rebel cavalry again dispersed when he approached, just as at Staraya Russa.

In mid April, Horn sent De la Ville with 400 horse towards the Commonwealth camp at Rzhov, the base of reportedly 4,000 soldiers. In a daring attack, De la Ville charged into and disrupted the mercenaries, who fled. This decisive victory was followed up three days later when Horn arrived with the main army. He bypassed the Commonwealth position at Zubtsov and instead attacked and dispersed a smaller unit in Pogoreloye Gorodishche. Horn then continued towards the fortified Joseph-Volokolamsk Monastery, where reportedly 2,000 (but based on later events hardly more than 1,500) Commonwealth mercenaries under Paweł Rucki and Mikołaj Marchocki had moved in following the exodus from Tushino. The mercenaries now found themselves trapped between Horn's men from the west and Grigoriy Valuyev's Muscovite cavalry from the east. The Muscovites lacked the capacity to assault the fortified monastery, but by the end of April Horn sent an advance guard of six banners of cavalry and 100 foot under De la Ville with orders to take it, together with Valuyev's men. The Swedish petardiers broke through the outer defences, and the Commonwealth mercenaries had to seek cover behind the inner stone walls.[6]

---

6   Almquist, *Sverge och Ryssland*, p.182.

De la Ville moved into the settlement near the monastery, while Valuyev and his men took cover in and around a nearby block house. De la Ville offered the Commonwealth men the opportunity to exchange prisoners. During the exchange, Rucki and Marchocki suggested that the Frenchmen abandon the Swedes and Muscovites and instead join the Commonwealth mercenaries, who shared their religion. Besides, they argued, King Sigismund was a very generous employer, while the Muscovites would not even allow them to leave the country when their term of service was concluded. According to Marchocki, the French officers replied that their honour as soldiers ruled out a switch in allegiance, yet they did not interrupt negotiations but continued to meet their Commonwealth counterparts.[7]

The Swedish corps may have been short of supplies; in any case, De la Ville did not make another attempt to storm the monastery. However, the Commonwealth mercenaries suffered even more from the lack of supplies, so ultimately attempted to break out to flee elsewhere. This turned out to be a bad decision, because Valuyev's cavalry pursued them efficiently and mercilessly, killing many of the mercenaries. Of 1,500 men only 300 survived.[8]

Meanwhile, Horn moved into Zubtsov, which the Commonwealth mercenaries by then had abandoned.

The Swedish operations in Muscovy had begun in the north-west, but the relief of Moscow and the hunting down of assorted rebels and Commonwealth mercenaries elsewhere in the region meant that Swedish units henceforth had to operate in close vicinity to King Sigismund's Commonwealth armies which now approached from the south-west. The Polish King was tied up at Smolensk, but he had other armies at his disposal. Demoralised Commonwealth mercenaries and rebels had not been very difficult to deal with, but King Sigismund's armies were motivated and led by experienced commanders.

In April 1610, a Commonwealth army of reportedly 3,000 men loyal to King Sigismund under Aleksander Gosiewski took the strategically important town of Belaya. He then held it in the name of Władysław, the Polish Tsar-elect of Muscovy. On 23 May, Horn set out from his quarters in Zubtsov together with a Muscovite army, and marched to Belaya with the intention to storm the town. He had already contacted the Muscovite inhabitants, who had promised to set fire to the town and open the gates at the given moment. Somebody betrayed the plan to Gosiewski, but nonetheless Horn engaged in battle with him outside Belaya. Although Gosiewski's men ultimately had to take refuge within the town, Horn lacked petards and artillery, so the attempt to storm Belaya failed. There was nothing to be done except march back to Zubtsov.

---

7   Mikołaj Ścibor z Marchocic Marchocki, *Historya wojny moskiewskiej* (Posen: Orędownik, 1841), pp.79–80; Almquist, *Sverge och Ryssland*, p.182.
8   Marchocki, *Historya wojny moskiewskiej*, p.70.

During the retreat to Zubtsov discontent again grew in the Swedish army. This time it was particularly among the foreign units that problems occurred. Horn could not fail to notice that the French were attracted by the rewards offered at the Joseph-Volokolamsk Monastery, since they spoke openly about switching sides as soon as they had received the money that they were due. The English had been complaining ever since they arrived in Viborg and now grumbled that Swedish pay was so low that they wanted neither to stay in Muscovy nor return to Sweden. As usual, there was not enough money to pay the enlisted soldiers what they regarded as their due. In mid June, Colville and his associate Captain Nicholas Pinnart inveigled the English to desert, and in one night alone, as many as 60 English soldiers absconded. Then several entire units mutinied, threatening to kill Horn, unless they were paid. Horn put down the mutiny harshly. He hanged the ringleaders – a few English and Scottish soldiers – and also replaced Colville and Pinnart with loyal officers. Samuel Cobron was appointed colonel in Colville's stead.[9] Then Horn resolved to join De la Gardie, who remained in Moscow.

---

9   Almquist, *Sverge och Ryssland*, pp.183–4.

10

The Battle of Klushino

The combined Swedish–Muscovite army's stay in Moscow was pleasant but possibly ill-advised. The soldiers were growing complacent during their time in the capital. Then, on 23 April, somebody poisoned Mikhail Skopin-Shuyskiy, who died soon after. It seems that De la Gardie heard rumours of the plot and attempted to warn his comrade, but to no avail. The identity of the mastermind of the plot has been debated ever since. Perhaps it was Tsar Vasiliy's younger brother Dmitriy, who may have feared that his childless brother would appoint the young general as his successor. Or, perhaps one of the numerous enemies of the House of Shuyskiy ordered the deed so as to deprive the Shuyskiys of their best general. Or, perhaps Skopin-Shuyskiy's popularity and apparent easy cooperation with the Swedes alienated this or that Muscovite noble or clergyman who felt an urge to take action. Or yet again, perhaps it was somebody else. The Time of Troubles was not a forgiving period. Whoever ordered the deed, Skopin-Shuyskiy's death was a real blow to De la Gardie. First, the two had become good friends. Second, Skopin-Shuyskiy was one of those comparatively few Muscovite officers who were sincere about cooperation with the Swedes. Later Russian folk songs interpreted Skopin-Shuyskiy's friendship with De la Gardie as real kinship, claiming that they were brothers-in-law.[1]

With Skopin-Shuyskiy dead, the Tsar's brother Dmitriy assumed overall command of the Muscovite army. Meanwhile, the Swedish envoys continued negotiations with Tsar Vasiliy. Although the army had still not been fully paid, the real problem was Kexholm. The fortress-town, securely located on an island and thus almost unconquerable, had never displayed any particular enthusiasm for Dmitriy (although reluctantly acknowledged the Dmitriy at Tushino in late 1608), but its fiery bishop, Silvester, also refused to submit to the Tsar's repeated orders to surrender the town to the Swedish Crown. In May, the Tsar again wrote an instruction that formally ceded Kexholm to Sweden, but again Silvester and his devotees refused to

---

1   The songs russified De la Gardie's name into Mitrofan Puntusov, from his patronymic Pontusson, 'son of Pontus'.

budge. Following instructions from King Charles, De la Gardie declined to go on another offensive before Kexholm had been handed over and his soldiers paid.

Then, in early June 1610, Tsar Vasiliy and De la Gardie received intelligence that King Sigismund had detached Field Hetman of the Crown Stanisław Żółkiewski with a part of the Commonwealth army at Smolensk. King Sigismund wanted Żółkiewski to relieve Belaya. Since Belaya now was safe, King Sigismund may have intended the operation primarily as a show of force. After all, his main army remained tied up by Mikhail Sheïn, the stubborn defender of Smolensk. Be that as it may, Żółkiewski instead marched deeper into Muscovy. Augmented by the arrival of several additional Commonwealth cavalry banners, Żółkiewski advanced to Tsaryovo Zaymishche, where the able Valuyev, serving as the deputy of Prince Fyodor Yeletskiy, commanded a forward Muscovite garrison. By then, Żółkiewski probably commanded some 3,000 men. Ultimately, yet more men joined his command, including about 1,400 experienced Commonwealth mercenaries under Aleksander Zborowski who had given up all hope of retrieving the pay he felt he was due from False Dmitriy and for this reason instead wanted to extort the equivalent funds from King Sigismund. Żółkiewski's army also included an unknown number of enlisted Continental soldiers under Jacques Margeret, a veteran French mercenary who since 1600 had served several Muscovite rulers. Having left Muscovy in autumn 1606, he returned in 1609 to take service with a new Dmitriy in Tushino. Shortly afterwards, Margeret and his men went into Commonwealth service together with his long-time associate Mikhail Saltykov and, soon afterwards, Ivan Zarutskiy and his contingent of Don cossacks, who temporarily lacked means or allies elsewhere and for this reason joined forces with Żółkiewski. It was by no means certain that Prince Yeletskiy, Valuyev, and their probably 5,000 men would be able to withstand the Polish hetman's onslaught.[2]

While Żółkiewski's army threatened Tsaryovo Zaymishche, and in extension all Muscovite outposts between Smolensk and Moscow, it also constituted a threat to Horn who operated in the same area. And as if this was not enough, rumours reached Moscow that a murderous army of Crimean Tatars was riding into southern Muscovy.[3] Żółkiewski's offensive

---

2   Przemysław Gawron, 'The Battle of Klushino', Grzegorz Jasiński and Wojciech Włodarkiewicz (eds), *Polish Battles and Campaigns in 13th–19th Centuries* (Poznań: Wojskowe Centrum Edukacji Obywatelskiej im. płk. dypl. Mariana Porwita/Stowarzyszenie Historyków Wojskowości, 2016), pp.67–86, on pp.74–5; Dunning, *Russia's First Civil War*, p.409. Johannes Widekindi, *Thet Swenska i Ryßland Tijo åhrs Krijgz-Historie* (Stockholm: Niclas Wankijff, 1671), p.197, notes Prince Yeletskiy's and Valuyev's strength as 6,000 men, apparently based on De la Gardie's reports.

3   In reality, it was Dmitriy and Sapieha who suffered the brunt of the Crimean Tatar operation – but since Crimeans primarily fought for slaves they were so unpredictable that nobody in Moscow could yet know whom they would target.

focused attention on the necessity of reviving the Swedish–Muscovite alliance. On 13 June, the Tsar again promised that Kexholm would be handed over, before Midsummer, and that the Swedish army would be paid in full for six months. If these promises were not kept, the Tsar assured De la Gardie, he would release the Swedes from their duty to assist Muscovy. Mindful of both the Tsar's promises and the greater strategic picture, De la Gardie agreed to march out, in return promising to clear the lands between Moscow and Smolensk from Commonwealth invaders. De la Gardie immediately led his army out of Moscow together with the Muscovite army, which was now commanded by the Tsar's brother, Prince Dmitriy Shuyskiy. The plan was to gather other Muscovite units along the way and also allow time for Horn and his men to join the combined army at Mozhaysk. There, Prince Shuyskiy would meet them with pay and supplies.

Horn joined De la Gardie on 21 June. The arrival of Horn's men (who probably met De la Gardie at Myshkino north-west of Mozhaysk) brought De la Gardie's army up to some 1,800 horse and 1,400 foot.[4] Following a pattern already established in Livonia which in the coming years would become yet more conspicuous in Swedish overseas armies, most Swedish soldiers were enlisted professionals from the Continent or the British Isles. Most units had been raised by military entrepreneurs at their own expense.

On the evening of the following day, some of the money to pay the army finally came through from Moscow. However, Prince Shuyskiy, De la Gardie, and the enlisted officer-entrepreneurs could not agree on the number of men for which they would be paid. The officers demanded pay according to the original muster rolls, to cover their expenses for raising men, while De la Gardie wanted to pay them only for those men who were actually present, not those who had deserted or died. Perhaps the available money was simply insufficient to cover all claims. Perhaps Prince Shuyskiy and De la Gardie could not agree on what the Tsar owed the Swedes. Ultimately, De la Gardie could not immediately pay what the enlisted officers demanded,

---

4   Swedish numbers are tentative only, since updated muster rolls, if they ever existed, seem not to have survived. Widekindi, *Thet Swenska i Ryßland*, p.196, says that De la Gardie ordered a roll call, since his only records were those from the muster in Stockholm, but implicitly seems to suggest that no roll call was carried out. Generalstaben, *Sveriges krig* 1, p.334, suggests three cavalry and four infantry regiments, that is, at most some 1,500 horse and 2,500 foot. However, the only known figure for De la Gardie's army is the number of units which deserted him: 19 banners of cavalry and 12 companies of foot. Widekindi, *Thet Swenska i Ryßland*, p.204; Johannes Widekindi, *Historia belli sveco-moscovitici Decennalis* (Stockholm: Niclas Wankijff, 1672), p.170. To this number (the accuracy of which is hard to assess) can be added the approximately four banners of cavalry and two companies of foot who remained after the desertion. Widekindi is believed to have relied on De la Gardie's battle report, which was later lost. For his descriptions in Widekindi, see *Thet Swenska i Ryßland*, pp.196–208 (until the list of Muscovite names). The same goes for Widekindi, *Historia*, pp.160–2 and occasional later paragraphs, although this text is intermixed with information from Polish histories which makes it less useful as a near-primary source.

and he accordingly decided to postpone paying the soldiers until after the Commonwealth army had been vanquished. When the enlisted officers grumbled, he ordered the enforcement of strict disciplinary measures, including the shooting of the most rebellious soldiers, so as to prevent any new outbreaks of mutiny.

Meanwhile, Prince Shuyskiy insisted that De la Gardie immediately continue the march to relieve Tsaryovo Zaymishche, where Żółkiewski laid siege to Prince Yeletskiy and Valuyev.

On 23 June 1610, De la Gardie and Prince Shuyskiy passed through the village Klushino. By then De la Gardie's army, as noted, consisted of at most, 3,200 men (Table 8). The Muscovite contingent was larger, consisting of likely 15,000 soldiers accompanied by possibly thousands of non-combatant levies (Table 9). It was commanded by Princes Dmitriy Shuyskiy, Andrey Golitsyn, Daniil Mezetskiy, and Ivan A. Khovanskiy. Vasiliy Buturlin led the important vanguard division. Although some Muscovites were experienced soldiers, and the army also included units enlisted abroad including harquebusiers, an estimated half of the Muscovite army consisted of peasant levies or recently raised men. The Muscovites brought an estimated 11 cannons.[5]

Żółkiewski was too experienced to remain at Tsaryovo Zaymishche, where he ran the risk of being attacked by the combined Swedish–Muscovite army from one side and the Muscovite garrison from the other. He left a few units at Tsaryovo Zaymishche to prevent Prince Yeletskiy and Valuyev from sallying out, and then set out in the evening for a night march in the hope to take the Swedish–Muscovite army by surprise. The army that he brought towards Klushino was smaller than his combined Swedish–Muscovite adversary. Żółkiewski commanded an estimated 4,000 Commonwealth cavalry and 200 haiduk infantry, in addition to one or more enlisted companies of Continental, mainly German, cavalrymen under Margeret and Zarutskiy's mostly Don cossack contingent, all of whom went unreported in the Polish sources and whose numbers accordingly remain unknown to later historians (Table 10). De la Gardie reported Żółkiewski's strength as 5,000 armoured cavalry, 4,000 cossacks, and 1,000 haiduk infantrymen.[6] Although presumably an exaggeration, his report nonetheless suggests that Margeret's and Zarutskiy's contingents were not negligible in numbers. There is no way to determine exact numbers. While Zarutskiy's contingent, or most of it, possibly remained behind at Tsaryovo Zaymishche, Margeret certainly was at Klushino, and we will see that he was not the only French officer in Commonwealth service there. Besides, Zarutskiy's contingent was not the only Muscovite unit in Żółkiewski's army: the aforementioned Ivan Saltykov was there, too. He may not have brought as many fighting men, but

---

5   Very few credible sources mentioning the numbers and composition of the Muscovite army have survived, so the numbers presented here are estimates only.
6   Widekindi, *Thet Swenska i Ryßland*, p.199; Widekindi, *Historia*, p.163; believed to be based on De la Gardie's lost battle report.

he employed spies and agents who were busy encouraging defections and betrayals within Prince Shuyskiy's command. We have seen that Margeret and Saltykov's father were old associates. Żółkiewski's army brought two or possibly four falconets.

At dawn on 24 June, Żółkiewski's army deployed for battle outside the Swedish and Muscovite camps.[7] He had hoped to carry out a surprise attack on unsuspecting enemies, but this plan failed because the Commonwealth units did not stay together during the night march. They almost bypassed the enemy camps in the darkness, only realising their location when they overheard the early morning trumpet reveille as the Swedes and Muscovites called their soldiers to the standards. Moreover, the Swedes and Muscovites had settled in separate camps, which they also had protected by surrounding them with the supply wagons in the customary wagon fort formation. In addition, the Muscovite commanders had ordered the levies to build barricades around the camps.[8] The Muscovite camp occupied the left wing, shielded by the River Gzhat', while the Swedish camp took up the right wing, which was shielded by the village of Pyrnevo and beyond this, a forest. In addition, a number of fences and farm buildings blocked the open fields between the Commonwealth men and the Swedish and Muscovite camps.

Żółkiewski was clearly outnumbered. However, he had two major advantages. First, his army consisted of quality soldiers, most high-spirited Polish hussars who expected to win because of their noble qualities. Almost as many were experienced Polish and Lithuanian mercenary cavalry, many of whom also were hussars. Second, unlike De la Gardie's enlisted soldiers, who were in a mutinous mood because of the missing pay, most of Żółkiewski's men were highly motivated. Finally, in comparison with both Żółkiewski's and De la Gardie's men, the Muscovite army under Prince Shuyskiy was mostly newly raised, at times poorly armed, and most importantly, lacked the motivation to fight. Let the Swedes do the fighting, most officers and men argued, and Prince Shuyskiy agreed with them.

---

7   Both contemporary sources and modern historians disagree on many aspects of the battle, including the numbers involved. While Polish historians have made extensive studies of the battle, most habitually estimate the Swedish army as twice as strong as existing records suggest. It seems very likely that Muscovite numbers are yet more inflated. Commonwealth numbers may be exaggerated, too. Przemysław Gawron, 'The Battle of Klushino', Grzegorz Jasiński and Wojciech Włodarkiewicz (eds), *Polish Battles and Campaigns in 13th–19th Centuries* (Poznań: Wojskowe Centrum Edukacji Obywatelskiej im. płk. dypl. Mariana Porwita/Stowarzyszenie Historyków Wojskowości, 2016), pp.67–86, gives an excellent overview of the numerous Polish sources and the so far few known Russian sources, but neglects most Swedish ones. Later testimonies by those enlisted officers who switched to the Commonwealth side during the battle cannot always be taken at face value, since they were written to exonerate them from their actions.

8   Widekindi, *Thet Swenska i Ryßland*, p.197; believed to be based on De la Gardie's lost battle report.

THE BATTLE OF KLUSHINO

Table 8. Tentative Swedish order of battle at Klushino, 24 June 1610[9]

Commander: Commanding General Jacob De la Gardie	
Cavalry	
Jacob De la Gardie's Swedish-Finnish Life Cornet, under Posse:	200
- 2 companies	
Samuel Cobron's English-Scottish Harquebusier Regiment:	500?
- Samuel Cobron's Harquebusier Banner	
- John Craul's Harquebusier Banner	
- Hugh Kendrick's Harquebusier Banner	
- Benson's Harquebusier Banner	
- Thomas Crichton's Harquebusier Banner	
- Thomas (?) Kerr's Harquebusier Banner	
Pierre de la Ville's French Harquebusier Regiment:	300?
- 4 banners, commanded by his lieutenant	
Evert Horn's Finnish Banner	100
Claes Christersson Gyllenhierta's Finnish Banner	91
Johann Jost von Quarnheim's German Harquebusiers	150?
Asmus von Glasenap's Flemish/Dutch Harquebusiers	180?
Rinckholm's Cavalry Banner	100?
Total	23 banners (not all of which are identified), corresponding to an estimated 1,800 horses
Infantry	
Jacob De la Gardie's German Life Regiment of Foot, under Lieutenant Colonel Reinhold Taube	
- 5 companies	500?
Samuel Cobron's English-Dutch Regiment of Foot, commanded by his lieutenant	
- 4 companies	300?
Johann Conrad Linck von Thurnburg's German Regiment of Foot	
- 5 companies	600?
Total	14 companies, corresponding to an estimated 1,400
Artillery	
- 4 cannons	
Grand Total	3,200

---

9   Sources: various, primarily Generalstaben, *Sveriges krig* 1, pp.334, 337 n.1; Sikora, *Battle of Kłuszyn*, p.28.

229

Unit strengths should be treated as estimates only. The enlisted units also contained men of other nationalities than those mentioned. There are no surviving muster rolls. Note that Pierre De la Ville with two of his French banners were away from the army at the time and did not participate in the battle.

Table 9. Muscovite order of battle at Klushino, 24 June 1610 [10]

Commander: Prince Dmitriy Shuyskiy

Vanguard Division, under Vasiliy Buturlin and probably Prince Yakov Baryatinskiy	
Great Division	
- Moscow units, under Prince Daniil Mezetskiy	
- Moscow units, under Prince Andrey Golitsyn	
Unknown Division(s)	
Rzhov units, under Ivan A. Khovanskiy	
Volokolamsk units	
Osipovo units	
Zubtsov units	
Total	Likely 15, 000 soldiers accompanied by possibly thousands of non-combatant levies used as labour, drivers, and so on

Ultimately, very few Muscovite units actually fought in the battle.

Table 10. Commonwealth order of battle at Klushino, 24 June 1610 [11]

Commander: Field Hetman of the Crown Stanisław Żółkiewski	
All cavalry, exceptthe two haiduk infantry companies	
Stanisław Żółkiewski's Division (*pułk*), commanded by Janusz Porycki	
- Stanisław Żółkiewski's Hussar Banner, commanded by Lieutenant Mikołaj Górski	250
- Janusz Porycki's Hussar Banner, commanded by his lieutenant	130
- Krzysztof Zbaraski's Hussar Banner, commanded by his lieutenant	100
- Aleksander Bałaban's Hussar Banner, commanded by himself as rotamaster	100

---

10   Various but sadly very limited sources.
11   Primarily Sikora, *Battle of Kłuszyn*, p.27.

- Jan Daniłowicz's Hussar Banner	100
- Stanisław Chwalibog's Petyhorcy Banner, commanded by himself as rotamaster	100
- Krzystof Zbaraski's four cossack-style cavalry banners ('Pohrebiszczanie'), commanded by Piaskowski	400
- Stanisław Żółkiewski's Haiduk Infantry Company, commanded by his lieutenant	100
Total	Nominally 1,180 horses and 100 infantry
Mikołaj Struś's Division (*pułk*), commanded by himself	
- Mikołaj Struś's Hussar Banner, commanded by his lieutenant	200
- Mikołaj Herburt's Hussar Banner, commanded by himself as rotamaster	100
- Adam Olizar Wołczkowicz's Hussar Banner	100
- Niewiadomski's cossack-style banner, commanded by himself as rotamaster	100
- Mikołaj Struś's Haiduk Infantry Company, commanded by his lieutenant	100
Total	Nominally 500 horses and 100 infantry
Marcin Kazanowski's Division (*pułk*), commanded by himself	
- Marcin Kazanowski's Hussar Banner, commanded by his lieutenant	100
- Andrzej Firlej's Hussar Banner, commanded by himself as rotamaster	100
- Janusz Skumin Tyszkiewicz's Hussar Banner	100
- Spodwiłowski's cossack-style banner, commanded by his lieutenant	100
- Abraham Zylicki's cossack-style banner, commanded by himself as rotamaster	150
Total	Nominally 550 horses
Ludwig Weiher's Division (*pułk*), commanded by Samuel Dunikowski	
- Ludwig Weiher's Hussar Banner, commanded by Lieutenant Grzegorz Trajan	100
- Samuel Dunikowski's Hussar Banner, commanded by his lieutenant	100
- Krzysztof Wasiczyński's Hussar Banner, commanded by himself as rotamaster	100
Total	Nominally 300 horses
Aleksander Zborowski's Mercenary Division (*pułk*), commanded by himself	
- Aleksand erZborowski's Hussar Banner (White Banner), commanded by Lieutenant Stanisław Gruszewski	

- Aleksander Zborowski's Hussar Banner (Black Banner), commanded by his lieutenant	
- Aleksander Zborowski's Hussar Banner, commanded by his lieutenant	500 (in total)
- Stanisław Bąk Lanckoroński's Hussar Banner, commanded by himself as rotamaster	200
- Mikołaj Marchocki's Hussar Banner, commanded by himself as rotamaster	100
- Szymon Kopyczyński's Hussar Banner, commanded by himself as rotamaster	200
- Marek Wilamowski's Hussar Banner, commanded by himself as rotamaster	100
- Wilkowski's Hussar Banner, commanded by Lieutenant Józef Chłuski	100
- Andrzej Młocki's Hussar Banner, commanded by himself as rotamaster	200
Total	Nominally 1,400 horses
Unknown Divisional Affiliation	
- Wysokiński's cossack-style banner, commanded by himself as rotamaster	100
- Jacques Margeret's Reiter Company, and possibly other units from western Europe	Unknown number
- Ivan Zarutskiy's mainly Don cossack contingent	Unknown number
- Ivan Saltykov's contingent	Unknown number
Total	Nominally 100 horses, in addition to enlisted companies and Don cossacks
Artillery	
- 2 or possibly 4 falconets	
Grand Total	Nominally 4,030 horses and 200 infantry, in addition to an unknown number of soldiers in enlisted companies and the Don cossack contingent

Unit strengths should be treated as nominal only. While this estimate of manpower seems to be the best one currently available, Commonwealth military strength can only be estimated with some difficulty. Existing figures derive from accounts relating to Commonwealth military funding procedures, and real numbers were customarily at least 10 percent lower. Moreover, enlisted foreign companies, Muscovites, and Don cossacks were not recorded in Polish sources.

THE BATTLE OF KLUSHINO

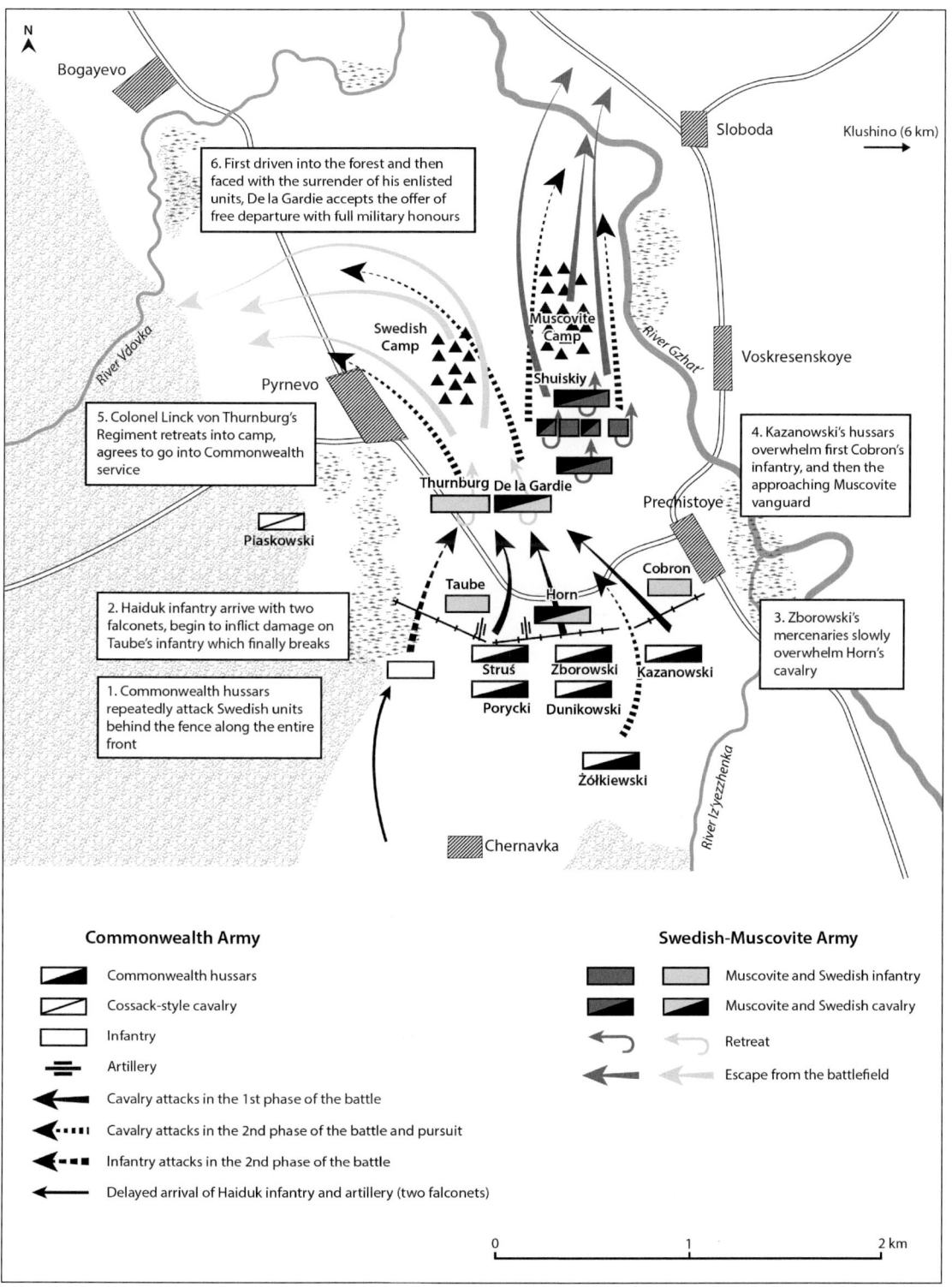

Map 5. The Battle of Klushino, 24 June 1610.

SWEDEN'S WAR IN MUSCOVY 1609–1617

When Żółkiewski's men approached, De la Gardie responded by deploying Taube's and Cobron's pike and shot in the first line, just behind the palisades and fences. Horn's, Posse's and Quarnheim's cavalry took up a position between the two infantry regiments. De la Gardie deployed the English–Scottish and French harquebusier cavalry in reserve in a second line. Meanwhile the Muscovite Vanguard Division, under Vasiliy Buturlin and probably Prince Yakov Baryatinskiy, began to move out of camp, forming a third line somewhat to the left of the Swedish units. We have no information on Prince Shuyskiy's plans for the battle. So much seems clear, however, that he wanted the Swedes to take the brunt of the Commonwealth attack. There is no need to look for malice in such a plan:

Aleksander Zborowski's White Hussar Banner attacks Evert Horn's Finnish Banner, flying a red cornet, at the battle of Klushino. If correctly depicted, the Finnish cavalry consisted of cuirassiers. (Szymon Boguszowicz, c. 1620; L'viv National Gallery of Arts at Oles'ko)

Mikołaj Struś's hussars attack De la Gardie's German Life Regiment of Foot under Reinhold Taube, at the battle of Klushino, displaying the difficulties faced by hussars in defeating pikemen in good order. (Szymon Boguszowicz, c. 1620; L'viv National Gallery of Arts at Oles'ko)

Prince Shuyskiy's commanders knew that the Swedish pike and shot under these circumstances had a greater chance of halting a hussar attack than the Muscovite units. Besides, most commanders everywhere, including Swedish King Charles, preferred to expose enlisted foreign soldiers to enemy action before risking their own.

Although the deployment for these reasons was customary, for De la Gardie the situation was grave. His enlisted units were mutinous. The fences that separated Swedes and Commonwealth hussars included a few gaps, and Commonwealth soldiers had already begun to open up passages by tearing down fences and burning farm buildings.

Muscovite cavalry of the Vanguard Division, under Vasiliy Buturlin and probably Prince Yakov Baryatinskiy, at the battle of Klushino. The men are correctly depicted as armed with firearms but no lances. (Szymon Boguszowicz, c. 1620; L'viv National Gallery of Arts at Oles'ko)

The battle of Klushino, 24 June 1610. This painting was commissioned by Field Hetman of the Crown Stanisław Żółkiewski to commemorate his victory, so is assumed to be reasonably accurate in its depiction of the events and units. (Szymon Boguszowicz, the Hetman's court painter, c. 1620; L'viv National Gallery of Arts at Oles'ko)

SWEDEN'S WAR IN MUSCOVY 1609-1617

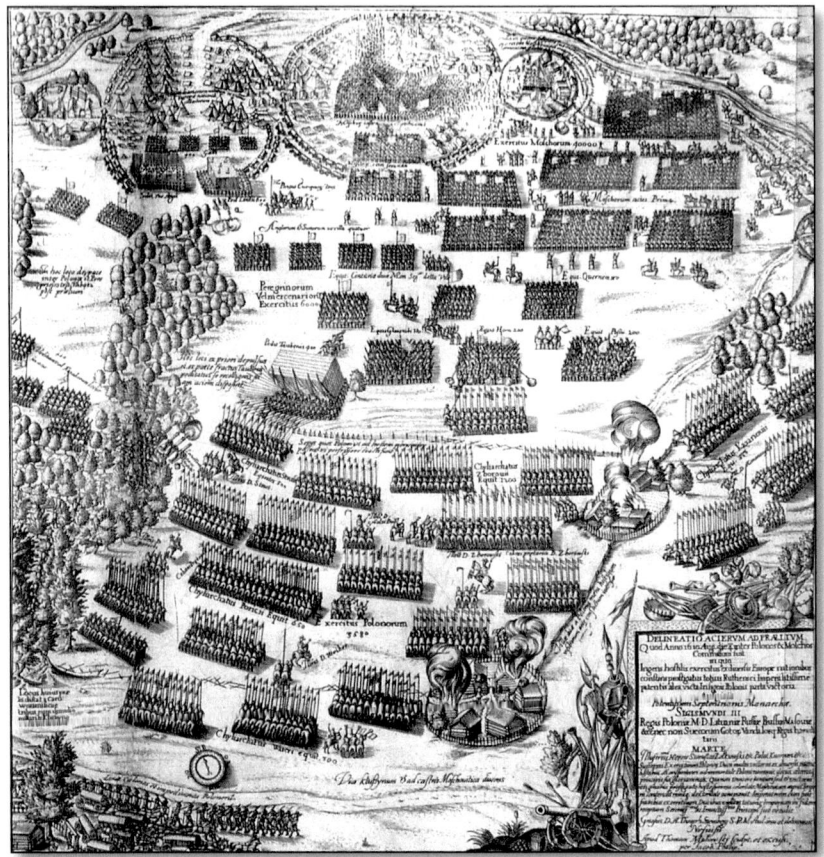

The battle of Klushino, 24 June 1610. Engraving by Jakub Filip, based on a drawing by military engineer Teofil Szemberg, who participated in the campaign but not the battle, during which he was deployed near Smolensk.

The first Commonwealth charge was carried out by hussars, who charged through gaps in the fences. Among them was Samuel Maskiewicz, who later described how his unit charged from eight to 10 times without being able to penetrate the Swedish defences. It was in particular the well-trained Swedish pike and shot which repulsed the hussars. They inflicted significant losses, at least in horses, each time the hussars charged. The Commonwealth cavalry attacks continued for several hours, during which the Swedish infantry remained in cover behind their palisades.

After about three hours, the haiduk infantry finally arrived with two falconets. They managed to open up additional breaches in the palisades, while the falconets began to inflict damage on Taube's infantry, which already had withstood numerous attacks from Mikołaj Struś's hussars. The Swedes had no artillery with which to respond: their four cannons were still in the camp.

In the middle of the field, Zborowski's experienced mercenaries were slowly overwhelming Horn's Finnish cavalry. Zborowski had achieved local superiority in numbers, and his hussars were also better armed for hand-to-hand combat than Horn's Finns. It is likely that some or all of Horn's cavalry employed the caracole, but this tactic only worked if the hussars failed to close with them.

Near the River Gzhat', Marcin Kazanowski's hussars, too, ultimately broke through the fences. Engaging Cobron's infantry, commanded by his lieutenant, Kazanowski's hussars seem to have driven some of the English and Scots into the approaching Muscovite vanguard. This may well have disordered Buturlin's cavalry, which enabled the hussars to follow up with a charge against them as well.

With the Swedish line breaking up, men began to retreat towards the nearest cover. On the Swedish right flank the surviving cavalry, and likely some infantry, too, took cover in the forest next to their camp. Both De la Gardie and Horn took cover there together with their cavalry, which of course also meant that they no longer could affect the developing situation. Żółkiewski and his hussars, who had pursued the fleeing cavalry until the forest, then returned, threatening the camp from the rear.

At this point, the main Swedish infantry reserve, Johann Conrad Linck von Thurnburg's German regiment of foot and three French banners which had not yet taken part in the combat, simply retreated towards the camp. Annoyed by De la Gardie's inability to pay his men, Colonel Linck von Thurnburg at this point decided to negotiate a better deal with the Commonwealth instead of joining the fight. Meanwhile, on the Swedish left flank, the uncommitted Muscovite units abandoned their camp and fled the field. With the exception of the vanguard they, too, never entered into combat.

Seeing that everything was falling apart, De la Gardie managed to make his way into the camp, which by then was thoroughly disordered. Despite his best efforts, the enlisted soldiers there refused to fight. Then the men began to loot the camp, including the tents of the Swedish officer, and took all De la Gardie's personal possessions. For good measure, they then moved into and looted the abandoned Muscovite camp, too. Meanwhile, Colonel Linck von Thurnburg concluded his negotiations with Żółkiewski, formally surrendered, and immediately entered into Commonwealth service with his men. De la Gardie handed out the 12,450 roubles (5,450 in gold and silver and the equivalent of 7,000 in furs[12]) which he had in an attempt to retain those enlisted soldiers who had not already gone over to the Commonwealth. They took the money but then still left, threatening to kill Horn and De la Gardie if they tried to stop them. Discord also broke out between the Germans and English, on the one side, and the French, on the other, which resulted in some bloodshed.

At this point, Żółkiewski offered De la Gardie, too, the chance to surrender. He sent a Polish officer, Piotr Borkowski, together with a French captain, Jacques Du Pont (Jacob Pontius), to negotiate with De la Gardie.[13] By then, the Swedish commander had hardly any loyal men left. Following a brief negotiation, De la Gardie accepted the offer of free departure with full

---

12   Widekindi, *Thet Swenska i Ryßland*, p.205.
13   Widekindi, *Thet Swenska i Ryßland*, p.202; Widekindi, *Historia*, p.168.

military honours including weapons and colours in return for a promise not to fight on behalf of Tsar Vasiliy.

Having agreed to these terms, De la Gardie marched out with those of his men who still followed him: some 400 mostly Swedes and Finns and remnants of the enlisted units, being 60 horse and 75 foot of Samuel Cobron's men and 108 foot of De la Gardie's Life Regiment, under Reinhold Taube.[14] They marched to Pogoreloye Gorodishche, where a Swedish cavalry corps of two French banners under Pierre De la Ville remained as garrison. De la Ville was ill in bed at the time. However, when the French cavalry heard of the defeat they (excluding De la Ville) mutinied too, as evidently did quite a few others of the enlisted soldiers who still remained, because on 2 July a group of 300 assorted Spanish, English, Scots, German, and French soldiers surrendered to King Sigismund's representatives.[15]

Meanwhile, Prince Shuyskiy fled to Moscow by way of Mozhaysk.

Total losses for the armies that fought at Klushino are generally unknown. The Swedish army certainly lost most of its men, but the majority simply went into Commonwealth service. Captain Thomas Crichton fell in the battle. Captain John Craul was shot in the knee and died from his wound soon afterwards. Craul's wound, incidentally, shows that the hussars who fought in the first line carried not only lances but firearms as well. Captain Kendrick suffered several head wounds from which he soon died. Commonwealth losses are very uncertain and, in any case, the sources only mention hussars. Żółkiewski estimated hussar losses as approximately 100. Other sources give different figures, ranging from 180 to 300 men killed and wounded.[16] The Commonwealth army captured numerous banners and colours as well as the 11 Muscovite cannons known to have been in the camp. Muscovite losses are otherwise unknown. Prince Yakov Baryatinskiy fell in the battle, while Vasiliy Buturlin was wounded and captured. The loss of these men can be explained by them both fighting in the vanguard, which seems to have been the only Muscovite formation that actually went into combat at Klushino.

After the battle, Żółkiewski returned to Tsaryovo Zaymishche, where he intimidated the besieged Muscovites into surrendering by displaying the captured banners, colours, and other evidence of his victory. Valuyev, not a timid commander, must have understood that Tsar Vasiliy's army was lost and no relief could be expected. Soon afterwards, the towns of Zubtsov, Rzhov, and the Joseph-Volokolamsk Monastery surrendered, too.

---

14 The Swedish and Finnish units were De la Gardie's Life Cornet (200 horse on 10 June), Claes Christersson Gyllenhierta's Banner (91 horse on 10 June), and Evert Horn's Finnish Banner (100 horse when they reached Narva in August). Generalstaben, *Sveriges krig* 1, p.337 n.1; Widekindi, *Thet Swenska i Ryßland*, p.209.

15 Gawron, 'Battle of Klushino', p.84.

16 Gawron, 'Battle of Klushino', p.83.

The mutinous enlisted units joined the Commonwealth army with all their booty from Klushino: weapons, furs, garments, and cash. They brought so many sable furs that the Poles at Smolensk could acquire whatever furs they wanted for prices far below customary market prices. Ultimately, the enlisted units went their separate ways. Most companies of English foot remained with Żółkiewski. Some of the French joined King Sigismund's army at Smolensk. Among the commanders, Colonel Linck von Thurnburg and Captains Asmus von Glasenap, Johann Jost von Quarnheim, James Colville, Paul Bettig, Edmund Kolb, and Cornelius Post went on to Germany. Quite a few later eventually returned to Swedish service, including Bettig, Glasenap, and Kolb, as well as Post's scribe Marcus Höijer.[17]

De la Gardie's retreating army, or rather the stump that was left of it, set out on the way to Novgorod by way of Torzhok.[18] On 29 June they reached Vydropuzhsk. De la Gardie sent a despatch to Tsar Vasiliy, explaining what had happened. He blamed Prince Shuyskiy's unwillingness to hand over the enlisted men's pay before the battle as the chief cause of the disaster. De la Gardie promised that he would gather the remaining Swedish units in Jama, Kaporie, Kexholm County, Viborg, and elsewhere in Finland with which the Swedish Crown would continue to support the Tsar. However, Tsar Vasiliy needed first to hand over Kexholm, as agreed and promised many times. De la Gardie then resumed the retreat towards the north-west. The Swedish intervention on behalf of Tsar Vasiliy was over.

This became particularly evident when in early July De la Gardie and his remaining men July approached Novgorod. He wrote to the governor there, informing him of the defeat and requesting quarters for his men while he called for reinforcements from Finland. However, the governor forbade De la Gardie from approaching the city, instead urging him to immediately return to Finland. In mid July, a Swedish convoy with chancellery documents and personal belongings of the officers on the way from De la Gardie to Viborg was apprehended at Nöteborg. Seemingly the Swedes were no longer welcome in northwestern Muscovy. De la Gardie ignored the instruction and set up camp at Novgorod.

---

17 Almquist, *Sverge och Ryssland*, p.191 n.1; with references.
18 Generalstaben, *Sveriges krig* 1, p.337, suggests some 600 horse and 200 foot, which appears too high.

11

The Polish Tsar-Elect

Without the military and moral support of the Swedish intervention army, Tsar Vasiliy's position became untenable. Żółkiewski's Commonwealth army continued towards Moscow, without facing any opposition. Meanwhile, the false Dmitriy's army approached from Kaluga to the south. Żółkiewski laid plans to go on a joint offensive with Sapieha against Moscow, however, in early July Sapieha was July halted by a Crimean Tatar army under the two brothers Batyr Begh Geray and Khan Temir Murza of the Noghai Horde. The Crimeans also dispersed Dmitriy's units, after which they set up a base at Serpukhov. Whilst technically they had come to assist Tsar Vasiliy, everybody knew that in reality they had come for slaves.

Tsar Vasiliy was trapped in his capital without an army to defend it, and on 17 July a group of nobles deposed him. Vasiliy was forcibly tonsured a monk, to make him henceforth ineligible for the throne. With the removal of the Tsar, seven leading boyars assumed collective power in Moscow. These were Princes Fyodor Mstislavskiy (the most powerful of the group), Ivan Vorotynskiy, Andrey Trubetskoy, Andrey Golitsyn, and Boris Lykov-Obolenskiy, as well as Boyars Ivan Romanov and Fyodor Sheremetyev. Thus commenced the 'Rule of the Seven Boyars' (Russian: *Semiboyarshchina*), a 'Council of Seven' which took it upon itself to govern Muscovy.

The Council of Seven was not per se a problem for Sweden, but the Swedish commanders were uneasy about what King Sigismund might do after the removal of the Tsar. On 24 August, De la Gardie wrote to the Council of Seven in Moscow, informing them that he had heard that they had deposed Tsar Vasiliy and instead wanted to elect a ruler from a foreign country. He warned them of the risks inherent in accepting a Polish candidate to the throne. The primary threat, De la Gardie argued, was to the Orthodox religion, which the Poles were keen to replace with their own faith. However, there was also a risk that the Swedish Crown would have to make territorial demands on Muscovy as a means to safeguard Sweden's own security. For these reasons, De la Gardie pointed out in what can only be described as a veiled threat, a Swedish candidate – one of the Swedish

THE POLISH TSAR-ELECT

King's sons – would be preferable and also safer for Muscovy.[1] De la Gardie wrote the letter as if in response to intelligence that some in Moscow had voted for King Sigismund's son Władysław, while others instead had voted for one of the sons of King Charles. Whether this was true, or whether such rumours by then were in circulation, or whether De la Gardie invented the story, remains unclear. If De la Gardie invented the rumour, he by chance or design through his letter originated the suggestion of a Swedish candidate to the throne of Muscovy which at a later stage would gain much traction. At this point, De la Gardie was unable to do much else to back up the Swedish position. Because of the loss of the army at Klushino, Sweden was temporarily unable to act forcefully in central Muscovy. It was a different matter with the border towns, and neither De la Gardie nor King Charles now harboured any hesitation to take the necessary towns by force, if they did not submit voluntarily.

On 17 August 1610, Żółkiewski and the Council of Seven concluded an agreement that would pave the way for a union between Poland, Lithuania, and Muscovy. The Council of Seven formally elected King Sigismund's son Władysław Tsar of Muscovy, in return for which King Sigismund would end the siege of Smolensk. The boyars also sent Filaret and other notables as envoys to King Sigismund at Smolensk.

The Swedish eastern strategy appeared to lie in ruins. De la Gardie's expedition to Muscovy, which had seemed an excellent opportunity to prevent a war on two fronts, had failed. Now there was a ruler of the Vasa dynasty on the throne of Muscovy, but from the Polish, not the Swedish branch. King Sigismund was in the process of wresting control over Muscovy in addition to the Commonwealth.

On 21 September, Żółkiewski and his Commonwealth army marched into Moscow and occupied the Kremlin in support of the new regime. Żółkiewski had Vasiliy carried off in a caged cart to Warsaw, where King Sigismund in October 1611 displayed him as living proof of his triumph. Vasiliy died in a Polish prison in September 1612, of either poison or maltreatment.[2] However, in Moscow problems arose almost immediately. The Commonwealth army in Moscow immediately established itself as an occupation army. At first, Żółkiewski made great attempts to maintain order. He was well aware of the dangers in quartering his soldiers in any city, let alone one such as Moscow where there were already tensions between the locals and his men. He instituted special courts with instructions to deal with the inevitable acts of looting and violence that took place. Yet, he also needed money to pay his men. Since King Sigismund did not have any to spare, Żółkiewski had to plunder the Muscovite government

---

1   Almquist, *Sverge och Ryssland*, p.198.
2   Żółkiewski also had Vasiliy's brothers Dmitriy and Ivan brought to Poland as captives. Dmitriy died at the same time as Vasiliy and under similar circumstances. Their younger brother Ivan lived on, but was not released from his Polish prison until 1620.

treasury to get funds. Moreover, the Muscovite envoys to King Sigismund brought demands that the Polish king had no intention of accepting. Chief among them was that young Władysław must convert to the Orthodox faith, preferably should marry a Muscovite lady, and not bring an excessive number of Poles to Moscow as his entourage. Displeased with such demands, King Sigismund had Filaret and the other Muscovite envoys detained, and ordered the siege of Smolensk to continue.

Soon, King Sigismund began to assume the powers that he claimed in the name of his son. He handed out Muscovite titles, and also distributed the lands of the followers of ex-Tsar Vasiliy to any Muscovite fortune-seeker who was willing to swear him loyalty. Although Żółkiewski had agreed with the Muscovites that Władysław would become Tsar, it seemed increasingly obvious that he desired this title for himself, perhaps as part of a union project. We do not really know if Sigismund had a future union in mind. We do know, however, that the proposal of a union was anathema to the Commonwealth nobility. Such an agreement would have surrendered the freshly-captured territory back to Muscovy. This was politically unacceptable, and would have been comparable to the aforementioned feelings of having lost Estonia to Sweden. Feeling betrayed by his sovereign, and probably by many of his peers as well, Żółkiewski relinquished his command.

Besides, there was already another candidate for the throne of Muscovy (and even more would follow[3]): the Khan of Crimea wanted to win the throne for himself or a son. According to rumours then in circulation he even offered, in the case that a Crimean was elected as Tsar, to abolish the traditional tribute to which the Khanate was entitled in its role as a successor of the Mongol Empire.[4] The traditional tribute was no anachronism but derived from the very real power of the Crimean Khanate to inflict punishment on its northern neighbours, should the Khan wish to do so. Both the Commonwealth and Muscovy paid the tribute, and both polities continued paying for decades after the events covered in this book.

---

3   King James VI/I of Scotland and England wanted his son Charles, the future King Charles I, to be sent to Muscovy as a candidate to the throne, and the Habsburgs had similar ideas for a candidate of their own. Dunning, *Russia's First Civil War*, pp.423, 582 n.30; with references. See also Chester Dunning, 'James I, the Russia Company, and the Plan to Establish a Protectorate over North Russia', *Albion* 21: 2 (1989), pp.206–26; Chester Dunning, 'A "Singular Affection" for Russia: Why King James Offered to Intervene in the Time of Troubles', *Russian History* 34: 1–4 (207), pp.277–302.

4   Almquist, *Sverge och Ryssland*, pp.202–3.

12

The Struggle for Ingria and Kexholm County

Meanwhile, De la Gardie returned to northwestern Muscovy. The threat of an impending union between the Commonwealth and Muscovy, as well as the never-implemented promise to cede Kexholm County, convinced both him and King Charles that the war in Muscovy could not be abandoned.

The result was the conflict which in Swedish historiography is known as the Ingrian War of 1610–1617.[1] The term is somewhat of a misnomer, since operations also took place in Novgorod, Pskov, and Kexholm County well beyond Ingria. We will see that an alternative and possibly better designation might be the War of the Muscovite Succession. Swedish attention now shifted from Moscow back to the borderlands that wrapped around the southeastern shores of the Gulf of Finland. Nor was the Arctic north forgotten.

The Swedish objectives reverted to safeguarding the eastern border and gaining control over the trade routes between Muscovy and western Europe. Novgorod presented a key opportunity. The city had formerly been independent of Moscow and might be made into a Swedish subsidiary or even, perhaps, annexed as a Swedish territory in the same manner as Estonia. It would also be preferable if the Swedish border could be extended to include the Muscovite town of Gdov, and yet more importantly the city of Pskov to the west of Novgorod. It was essential to deny these strongholds to the Commonwealth armies that presently operated in Muscovy on behalf of Tsar-elect Władysław. Then there was the Kexholm issue, which was the most urgent task. Sweden wanted Kexholm County, as had been agreed with Tsar Vasiliy. Preferably, the northeastern border would be extended

---

1   The term Ingrian War was introduced by Ulf Sundberg for reasons of clarity, and because the war's outcome was Sweden's acquisition of Ingria – see Sundberg, *Svenska krig 1521–1814* (Stockholm: Hjalmarson & Högberg, 1998), with the revised and extended edition Ulf Sundberg, *Sveriges krig* Vol. 2: *1448–1630* (np: SMB, 3 vols, 2010).

all the way to the White Sea, since this would enable Sweden to control the profitable Arctic trade route.

Swedish attention remained focused on the north all the way up to the Kola Peninsula. On 26 October 1610, King Charles again ordered Governor Baltzar Bäck to set out against Kola Castle, making a third attempt. Having already failed twice to march to the castle, Bäck's expeditionary corps assembled in Rovaniemi, Finland, on 12 February 1611. This year, the seasonal timing was right.

Bäck's expeditionary corps consisted of the Västerbotten company of foot under Per Clemetsson (309 men), Per Springfelt's levied company of foot, also from Västerbotten, and the aforementioned Polish company of foot. The corps also included 40 levied ski soldiers from Österbotten, under a commander known as Claes Tårfinnen. The supply train consisted of 30 Sami and 400 reindeer. At first, Jacob Frensham's Irish or possibly Scottish company of foot was earmarked to join the corps, but ultimately Frensham's men received other orders.[2] This time, Bäck's corps did set out in time and reached Kola Castle, their objective, but since they could not bring artillery across the Arctic wilderness, the endeavour to take the castle failed. Bäck returned with his men in early April 1611.[3]

King Charles also retained his plans to gain Fort Suma and the fortified Solovki Monastery. In early 1611 he ordered Colonel Andrew Stuart (c. 1570–1640) to carry out the semi-diplomatic mission. The King probably hoped that diplomatic persuasion backed up by military might would do the job. Stuart was allocated Knut Håkansson Hand's harquebusier banner, a company of foot from Hälsingland under Hans von Akern, an Irish or possibly Scottish company of foot under Robert Sim (Syme?), and 1,000 levies from Österbotten. He was ordered to set out from Uleåborg, assemble his men at Kajaneborg (the castle of Kajana, modern-day Kajaani), and then march into Muscovy. Altogether, Stuart's corps consisted of 80 horse and 1,300 foot. The corps set out in late March. However, the snow turned out to be too deep to reach their destination, so Stuart returned home in late April.[4] Perhaps this was just as well. Solovki Monastery was a heavily fortified island fortress located across a wide bay; the monastery's garrison was in 1611 based on 100 to 200 streltsy, but the monastery also had many able-bodied construction workers and servants that could be armed.[5] Ten years later the monastery maintained a total of 1,040 soldiers.[6]

---

2   Generalstaben, *Sveriges krig* 1, p.349.
3   Waaranen, *Samling*, 150–1; Generalstaben, *Sveriges krig* 1, p.349.
4   Generalstaben, *Sveriges krig* 1, pp.349–50; Waaranen, *Samling*, pp.132–4. Hans von Akern was originally known as Hans von Eckeren.
5   Chester S. L. Dunning, 'The Richest Place in the World: An Early 17th-Century English Description and Military Assessment of Solovetskii Monastery', Chester S. L. Dunning, Russell E. Martin, and Daniel Rowland (eds), *Rude & Barbarous Kingdom Revisited: Essays in Russian History and Culture in Honor of Robert O. Crummey* (Bloomington, Indiana: Slavica, 2008), pp.309–25, on p.315.
6   Yury F. Lukin, 'Solovki as an Object of Cultural Heritage of the Arctic', *Arctic and*

THE STRUGGLE FOR INGRIA AND KEXHOLM COUNTY

Whilst the forested borderlands between Livonia, Lithuania, and Muscovy – and between the major cities of Novgorod, Smolensk, and Moscow – were somewhat rough and characterised by poor roads, they were highly developed in comparison to those further to the north, in Ingria, Kexholm County, Karelia, and the wild borderlands along Finland's eastern and northern borders. The northern borderlands, whether on the Finnish or Muscovite side of the poorly delimited common border, collectively constituted a sparsely settled frontier region. Towns were small and mostly built of wood. Most peasants practiced slash-and-burn agriculture which resulted in temporary swidden fields. Others lived by fishing in the rivers and lakes. The settlements of the first were temporary, while those of the latter were seasonal. Neither group cared much about on which side of the border they operated. Agriculture was barely sustainable, and even if the peasant settlements could be located, they did not have the surplus food supplies to sustain any major military operation. From a logistical viewpoint, supplies always had to be brought in from elsewhere. Winters were long and harsh, but the cold season at least enabled movement along the frozen rivers or across frozen marshes. In comparison, spring caused severe flooding which might prevent military operations and logistics altogether. The forest cover was extensive, which usually prohibited the deployment of military units in the Continental manner. The dense forest made cavalry charges difficult, and at times impossible. Infantry was useful, but there are no indications that pikemen were ever used in Kexholm County during this war or previously, and probably not in eastern Ingria or Finland either.

Settlement in Ingria, 1615. Most buildings and many forts in northern Europe were log houses. (Anthonis Goeteeris)

North 26, 2017, pp.148–65, on p.153.

The forests also impeded cavalry movement. It was easy to close the few rough roads, in particular against cavalry incursions, with timber obstacles (abatis, *zasyeka* in Russian), which consisted of barricades of felled trees and constituted a traditional feature of northern warfare. Although there were usually paths between settlements, these were commonly known only to local guides and smugglers. Except for a limited number of small, medieval stone castles once built at traditional market places, most strongholds consisted of wooden blockhouses. Despite attempts by both the Swedish and Muscovite governments to bring law and order into the region through the introduction of officials and military garrisons to monitor the cross-border trade, the borderlands were essentially lawless.

Muscovite church in the village of Romanovo in the vicinity of Pskov, 1615. (Anthonis Goeteeris)

The Siege of Ivangorod

Preparations for a Swedish land grab in Muscovy began in early 1610, while De la Gardie's campaign was still ongoing. King Charles insisted upon the conquest of Ivangorod and Ingria as a preliminary to the annexation of Kexholm County.[7] Possibly the King felt that Ivangorod and Ingria were his due reward for helping Tsar Vasiliy, who after all, as we have seen, in December 1609 had promised Charles other territories beside Kexholm

---

7   Ivangorod lay just across the river from Narva in Estonia. Russian-language chronicles sometimes referred to both as Rugodiv, which may have been the original name of Ivangorod.

in compensation for Sweden's expenses. Or possibly, Charles was merely greedy for more lands.

The timing for an expansionist policy was perhaps not the best, because Sweden by this time faced threats on all its borders. It was becoming increasingly obvious to most Swedish commanders, except King Charles who was obsessed with his eastern designs, that Denmark was again becoming a serious threat. Meanwhile, the ongoing war with the Commonwealth in Livonia had never been properly concluded, only temporarily halted. This increased the risk that in the near future Sweden might have to simultaneously fight wars with Denmark in the south, Norway (also under the Danish King) in the west, Muscovy on the eastern front in Ingria, Karelia, and the Arctic, and the Commonwealth in Livonia.

Ignoring the threat of war from Denmark, the King in early 1610 ordered essentially all available Swedish army units to the eastern front. The reinforcements were sent in July. King Charles dispatched five of the seven provincial cavalry banners and one of the three Swedish banners of the retinue of nobles. However, he sent only five provincial companies of foot, since these usually were unwilling to serve abroad and moreover tended to lose a significantly higher share of men to diseases when shipped overseas. He also ordered fundamentally all enlisted foreign units in Sweden to the eastern front: seven cavalry banners and 11 companies of foot. To this could be added the garrison of Narva (four companies of foot) and already available, mostly Finnish, units on the eastern border. This produced an army of 19 cavalry banners and 20 infantry companies, altogether approximately 7,000 men. The army was led by the Governor of Reval, Anders Larsson of Botila, an elderly man weakened by an old wound which prevented him from wearing armour and made horseriding difficult. Colonel Per Hammarskiöld commanded the Swedish cavalry, Colonel Arvid Stierna the Swedish infantry, and Colonel Lindved Hästesko the Finnish units. Colonel Régis Du Vernet commanded a French cavalry regiment, while Colonel William Stuart a mostly Irish regiment of foot.[8] Cavalry Captain Herman Wrangel joined the army, too, in which he seems to

Colonel Per Hammarskiöld.

---

8   In 1609, perhaps 1,300 Irish soldiers were deported from Ulster for enlistment in the Swedish army, to allow Scottish and English settlement (the 'Plantation of Ulster'). Unhappy about their fate, the Irish soldiers were even more mutinous than other enlisted units.

Reval, 1615. (Anthonis Goeteeris)

have functioned as Larsson's chief of staff.[9] The experienced Colonel Nils Stiernskiöld, too, left Stockholm in July to travel to rejoin the army on the eastern front.

Larsson had orders to take Ivangorod, Jama, and if necessary Kexholm, and to persuade Pskov to submit either to Swedish rule or Tsar Vasiliy.

The internal political situation in Ivangorod, Jama, and Pskov was complicated. While the governor of Ivangorod, Prince Ivan F. Khovanskiy, and his deputy Prince Pyotr Kropotkin knew that the Swedes then were in Muscovy as the Tsar's allies and had received instructions to support them, the town streltsy and many townsmen by far preferred to accept the distant rule of a false Dmitriy than either the Tsar or the Swedish King, since a distant, weak, or preferably nonexistent ruler surely was better than a nearby, authoritarian one.

The campaign began in May, when Hästesko moved into Ingria from Finland to blockade Jama.

In June, intelligence reached King Charles from Narva, informing him that the garrison of Ivangorod faced shortages in food supplies and had sent some soldiers elsewhere. The King accordingly ordered his men to take advantage of this opportunity to capture the fortress. Hästesko with his men (five banners of cavalry and four companies of foot) was already blockading Jama, so he could easily continue to nearby Ivangorod. The King ordered Governor Larsson and his secretary, Peder Jacobsköld, to lead the

---

9   Generalstaben, *Sveriges krig* 1, pp.145, 338.

THE STRUGGLE FOR INGRIA AND KEXHOLM COUNTY

Jama, 1630s. (Adam Olearius)

operation. Jacobsköld was essentially an official and diplomat, ennobled for his loyalty to the King, and not a soldier. Yet, because of Larsson's advanced age he became the real commander of the operation.

Hästesko reached Ivangorod in early July, where he soon learnt of De la Gardie's defeat at Klushino. The Swedes estimated Ivangorod's garrison as some 1,000 men.[10] When negotiations got underway the governor of Ivangorod, Prince Khovanskiy, and his deputy Prince Kropotkin, not yet knowing that Tsar Vasiliy was deposed, expressed willingness to hand over the town to the Tsar's Swedish allies. However, as in Pskov and Jama, the town streltsy and many townsmen thought that Dmitriy's distant and lax rule offered more benefits than a significantly stricter Swedish regime, and refused to hand over the town.

When negotiations led nowhere, Larsson and Jacobsköld in August laid siege to Ivangorod. The Ivangorod garrison hoped for support from both Pskov and Lisowski's marauders, believed still to be operating on behalf of Dmitriy but by this time, if not before, surely more interested in the opportunities for plunder than whoever sat on the throne. Sure enough, Lisowski's marauders, reportedly some 2,000 horse, turned up in the area – which disturbed the siege operation. Lisowski had no interest in actually attacking the Swedes, but he and his men were eager to plunder food supply deliveries and remote outposts. By the end of the month, Evert Horn (who recently had arrived from De la Gardie with instructions to ascertain the availability of reserves for an action against Novgorod) led 1,000 horse against Lisowski, which temporarily dispersed the marauders.[11] Meanwhile, the Ivangorod garrison defended itself valiantly, with frequent

---

10 Generalstaben, *Sveriges krig* 1, p.338.
11 Generalstaben, *Sveriges krig* 1, pp.339–40.

sallies. Colonel Stiernskiöld participated in the siege, but in August he was again seriously wounded and had to leave the army. His wounds took half a year to heal.

Whilst the garrison of Ivangorod soon ran out of supplies, just as the Swedes had expected, the logistical situation was no better among the Swedes, who ran out of supplies too, and a supply ship sank in the Narva roadstead which made the situation worse. The enlisted soldiers grumbled and misbehaved. Nearby Narva accidentally caught fire on 20 August. Whilst the Swedish soldiers attempted to extinguish the fires, Régis Du Vernet's French cavalry instead took the opportunity to plunder the town savagely, stealing anything from livestock to cutlery. Confined to the camp, Du Vernet's men then set about agitating among Stuart's Irish foot. As a result, the Irish refused to follow orders and began talking about joining the enemy, so had to be guarded at all times by more reliable units. News of the mutiny at Klushino probably affected the mood in the army at Ivangorod. On 31 August, Jacobsköld wrote in a letter that he 'had never been on an unluckier campaign',[12] but when he wrote this line, he had not yet seen the worst. On 6 September, Régis Du Vernet led the French soldiers in a mutinous protest rally, demanding their pay that they believed Jacobsköld had hidden away. The Swedish commanders ordered the mutinous French cavalry to Dorpat, but in early October the latter instead marched away in an attempt to seize the stronghold Neuschloss (Swedish: Nyslott[13]) as security for their monetary claims. On 9 October Du Vernet, possibly upon his own request, was sent to Stockholm to answer for his mutiny. By some reports, he was shot during an attempted escape en route. Swedish and Finnish cavalry were sent out to deal with the mutinous Frenchmen, who dispersed in all directions. Meanwhile, 200 of Stuart's Irishmen defected to the Muscovites in Ivangorod or joined forces with Lisowski, whose operation was more to their taste. The mutiny also spread to the national units. Soldiers from Östergötland and Västergötland said that they wanted to follow the French, and threatened to kill any officer who tried to impose order. The third major mutiny in two years, it illustrated the risks in relying on enlisted foreign soldiers if readily available funds in large quantities were not available at all times. The mutinous mood even reached Reval: in October 1610 the Scottish soldiers there mutinied, too. They served under Colonel Patrick Rutherford, a veteran of Swedish service on the eastern front and a good friend of Chancellor Oxenstierna, so we can assume that he did his best to restore order. Fortunately, fresh funds had by then arrived from Stockholm, so he and his officers managed temporarily to appease the mutineers.[14]

---

12 Peder Nilsson Jacobsköld to Erik Elfsson and Bo Wernersson, 31 August 1610; cited in Almquist, *Sverge och Ryssland*, p.208 n.4.
13 Not to be confused with its Finnish namesake Nyslott, Finnish: Savonlinna.
14 Almquist, *Sverge och Ryssland*, p.209; Generalstaben, *Sveriges krig* 1, p.340; Waaranen, *Samling*, pp.109–10.

The mutinies notwithstanding, the defenders at Ivangorod were in no better shape than Jacobsköld's few remaining men. Ivangorod's garrison, too, had now realised that Lisowski was as great a threat to them as to the Swedes. Lisowski and the Irishmen who had joined him had already plundered the countryside around Gdov during which they also attacked the Muscovite garrison at Gdov. Most Muscovites in Lisowski's army then deserted. Henceforth, Lisowski did not even pretend to serve any master but himself.

As a result, Ivangorod in October sent envoys to Philip von Scheiding, the governor of nearby Narva. Ivangorod now wanted a ceasefire agreement that would allow a return to the customary cross-border trade relationship which had existed between Swedish Estonia and Muscovite Ivangorod before hostilities began. At this point, Dmitriy's supporters in Ivangorod clearly feared Lisowski and King Sigismund's Commonwealth armies more than they feared the Swedes. The Swedish commanders at this point had no more than 600 cavalry and hardly any infantry at Ivangorod who still followed orders.[15] Without infantry and supplies, they could not hope to continue the siege. The negotiations resulted in the Armistice of Ivangorod of October 1610.

King Charles ratified the armistice agreement on 16 November, but he also sent reinforcements. On 28 December, he ordered De la Gardie again to go on the offensive into Muscovy, from the Swedish base at Viborg where the reinforcements then assembled.

The Conquest of Kexholm

At the beginning of July 1610, only days after the defeat at Klushino and before De la Gardie returned to the region, Swedish units from Finland marched into Kexholm County to annex the territory that Moscow had repeatedly agreed to cede. Kexholm was the oldest town in the northern borderlands. The town had first been established by the local Karelians before 1143, on what then was the main waterway and trade route between the Novgorod Republic and Finnish markets. The first castle was built in 1294. Kexholm was built on an island, had a town wall, and occupied a strategic location. De la Gardie estimated the number of fighting men in Kexholm as about 2,000, of whom some were streltsy but most consisted of levied townsmen.[16]

Skirmishes broke out outside Kexholm itself on 4 July. What the Swedes estimated as some 1,000 Muscovite cavalry together with 200 foot from Kexholm attacked the approaching Swedes, but were repulsed and disrupted. It turned out that regardless of Tsar Vasiliy's repeated orders to

---

15 Generalstaben, *Sveriges krig* 1, p.340.
16 Generalstaben, *Sveriges krig* 1, p.355. We will see that his assessment was reasonably correct, with 1,600 apparently being the correct number.

SWEDEN'S WAR IN MUSCOVY 1609-1617

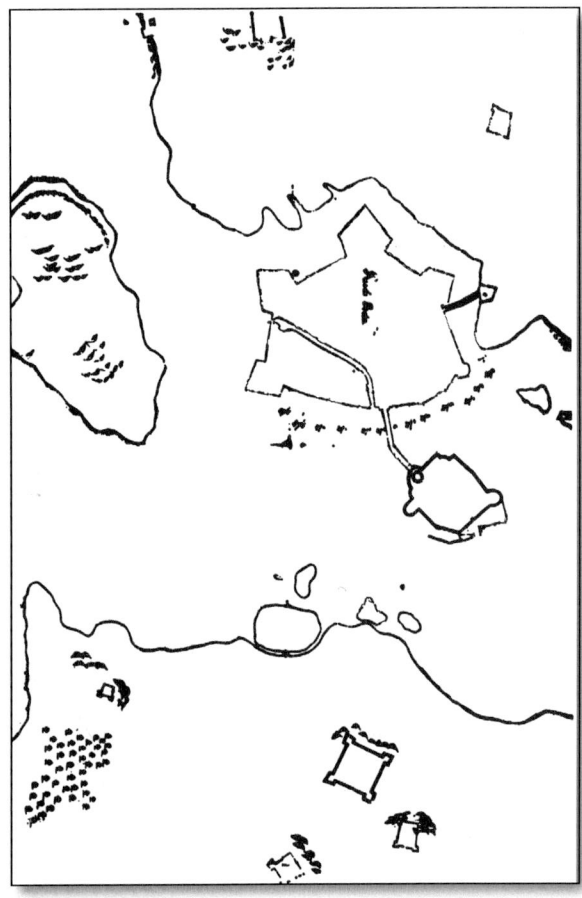

Hand-drawn sketch of Kexholm in 1656. Kexholm's location on an island made the fortress almost invulnerable. (Swedish Military Archive (KrA), Finska handritade kartor, Kexholm nr 17)

surrender Kexholm to Swedish representatives, the inhabitants still had no intention of giving up their town. We have seen that it was the Orthodox bishop, Silvester, who inveigled the inhabitants into resisting the Swedish takeover. In response, a Swedish army under Governor Arvid Wildeman of Viborg and cavalry captain Lars Andersson laid siege to Kexholm. The Swedish besiegers soon grew into two banners of horse, two or three companies of foot, and units of levies from Karelia and Savolax.[17] Unimpressed and trusting in God and their secure location, Bishop Silvester and his supporters refused to surrender.

King Charles also wanted Novgorod. To create conditions for an eventual operation against it, inearly August De la Gardie sent Pierre De la Ville towards Ladoga Town with orders to take this important stronghold on Lake Ladoga. Meanwhile, De la Gardie himself marched towards Nyen, which he reached on 13 August. The occupation of Ladoga Town would enable the Swedes to sever Novgorod's riverine link along the River Volkhov with Lake Ladoga and in extension Nöteborg and Kexholm as well. On 15 August, De la Ville managed to take Ladoga Town and its integral fortress in a surprise attack. This was a particularly impressive feat, since the fortress was very strong, with modern bastions added in 1585–1586, which probably made it the first of its kind in Muscovy. Having no petards, De la Ville and his men took bells from nearby monasteries, and using them as makeshift petards took Ladoga 'with

---

17   Generalstaben, *Sveriges krig* 1, p.355. The cavalry consisted primarily of Karelian cavalry under Lars Andersson, and from August Lindved Hästesko. The infantry consisted of the companies of Hans Prytz, Hans Root, and Hans Persson, the latter from Österbotten. By the end of October, Per Nilsson's company from Björneborg County (Satakunta) joined the besiegers, but the Karelian cavalry had by then redeployed elsewhere. The Karelian levies were commanded by Samuel Jacobsson, Lars Persson, and Anders Tolk, while those from Savolax were commanded by Henrik Christersson. Incidentally, Anders Tolk ('Anders the Interpreter') was presumably Anders Pettersson (Finnish: Antti Pekanpoika), the father of De la Gardie's intelligence officer Erik Andersson. Anders Pettersson had been captured by the Muscovites in 1572 and sent to Kazan'. In 1585 he managed to return to Karelia, where he married. Having learnt both Russian and Tatar, he joined the Swedish administration in Viborg, which handled most contacts with Muscovy including intelligence work. Eventually, Anders's son Erik succeeded his father as Sweden's leading intelligence officer in the region.

THE STRUGGLE FOR INGRIA AND KEXHOLM COUNTY

Ladoga Town. (Christian Lorenzen Rothgiesser, 1659)

bells [*avec des cloches*]'.[18] As a result, the Swedes gained control over the River Volkhov. Swedish rule was, however, contested, and soon Muscovite units, including the very streltsy whom De la Ville had evicted from Ladoga Town, showed up to lay siege to the isolated garrison.

Although the Swedish commanders at Ivangorod and Viborg wanted De la Gardie to remain at Nyen to protect this region from Lisowski's marauders, De la Gardie instead marched to Kexholm, which he reached in early September.

With De la Gardie arrived additional units, both from his own army and that at Ivangorod. This increased the numbers of the besiegers. About eight *lodja*-type vessels and other boats, crewed by 86 sailors, were brought from Savolax and probably also Viborg to assist in the siege and to blockade it from access across Lake Ladoga.[19] This flotilla was necessary, because until then the defenders were able to bring in food supplies by boat, something which Reinhold Taube, put in charge of the flotilla, henceforth could prevent. However, the Swedish artillery at Kexholm remained limited, consisting of only one 12-pounder culverin, a double falconet (possibly a 2-pounder), and a cluster of wall guns. De la Gardie had no siege artillery.[20]

---

18 De la Ville, *Discours sommaire*, p.415.
19 A *lodja* was an open rowing boat which also might carry a mast or two. It was sufficiently large to take soldiers and the occasional 5- or 3-pounder cannon.
20 The units brought by De la Gardie included Jacques Bourguignon de Corobel's French cavalry banner, Claes Christersson Gyllenhierta's Finnish cavalry banner, Göran Hansson Höök's Västergötland cavalry banner, John Wauchope's Scottish cavalry banner, the infantry companies of Reinhold Taube (who led the remnant of De la Gardie's Life Company), Robert Moore, Hemming Grass, and two French petardiers (La Plante and La Rose) from Viborg. A troop of 25 French cavalry, under a lieutenant, joined the army from De la Ville's garrison in Ladoga Town. Generalstaben, *Sveriges krig* 1, p.356.

SWEDEN'S WAR IN MUSCOVY 1609-1617

Muscovite *lodja* rowing vessels, 1590s.

After a failed attempt to storm Kexholm with the use of petards, De la Gardie reduced the besieging units to two banners of horse, four companies of foot, and some levies. He then ordered cavalry captain Lars Andersson to resume command, and to blockade and starve Kexholm until the town surrendered. On 20 October Andersson commanded 1,166 horse and foot at Kexholm.[21] De la Gardie also took measures to gain control over the rural population, and by late November 1610 the inhabitants of the southern parts of Kexholm County had sworn fealty to the Swedish Crown.[22] De la Gardie then travelled to Viborg to receive the expected reinforcements from Sweden.

Not knowing that Tsar Vasiliy had already been deposed, King Charles wrote to De la Gardie, accepting his plan to return to Muscovy to support the Tsar's weakening rule. He also repeated, and emphasised, the urgent need to gain control over Novgorod. This would be particularly important if Tsar Vasiliy lost power. Another desired objective, the King wrote, was Pskov, so as to secure the flank against Commonwealth forces in Livonia. As soon as Ivangorod had been conquered, the army would be available for this endeavour. Moreover, enlisted foreign units would be sent from Sweden as reinforcements.[23] Because of the distance to Stockholm, the King's orders could be regarded as no more than guidelines; De la Gardie would have to make his own decisions. With the mutiny at Ivangorod, the army with which De la Gardie had hoped to march to Novgorod no longer existed.

The poor relations between Novgorod and Sweden deteriorated further when the city acknowledged the Polish Tsar-elect. On 12 October, Novgorod accepted Ivan Saltykov as its new governor. Saltykov represented Tsar-elect Władysław, and in effect saw himself as the representative of King Sigismund. For this reason, Saltykov sent reinforcements under Prince Grigoriy Volkonskiy to assist the men who laid siege to De la Ville in Ladoga Town. He also wrote to De la Gardie, demanding that the Swedes

---

21   Lindved Hästesko's and Lars Andersson's banners of horse (together 380 horse), Reinhold Taube's, Per Nilsson's, Matts Sigfridsson's, and Robert Moore's companies of foot (together 356 men), and 430 levies. Sigfridsson's company derived from Österbotten. Almquist, *Sverge och Ryssland*, p.201; Generalstaben, *Sveriges krig* 1, p.356 n.7.

22   De la Gardie to King Charles, 9 December 1610. Generalstaben, *Sveriges krig* 1, p.357.

23   Generalstaben, *Sveriges krig* 1, p.346.

immediately leave Muscovy and return any territories which they already had taken.[24]

Nöteborg (then under Prince Ivan Putyatin) and Kexholm seemed to share Novgorod's preferences for Tsar-elect Władysław.[25] Neither was ready to submit to Swedish rule. Yet, De la Gardie's sources told him that the Muscovites in Novgorod and Nöteborg doubted that Władysław would actually arrive. Meanwhile, Dmitriy and men loyal to him still controlled Kaluga and Severia, as well as the great city of Pskov and the neighbouring towns including Ivangorod, Jama, Kaporie, and Gdov. In 1608 Pskov and the other towns had been seized by followers of the false Dmitriy and housed many who still opposed orders from Moscow. They refused to acknowledge Novgorod Governor Saltykov's, and in extension Władysław's, authority. Meanwhile, eastern Muscovy, Kazan', Astrakhan', and Siberia had adopted a wait-and-see policy.[26]

King Charles had ratified the armistice with Ivangorod, so another assault on this town was not permitted. However, in mid December De la Gardie received the order from King Charles (sent in early November) that he must conquer Kexholm and Nöteborg and relieve Ladoga Town. Since Kexholm was out of supplies and soon had to surrender anyway, and since it was equally difficult to supply a large Swedish army there, De la Gardie chose to focus on Nöteborg and Ladoga Town.

He decided first to take Nöteborg, and then relieve Ladoga Town. On 20 October, De la Gardie had 383 men at Nöteborg, including cavalry captains Lorentz Wagner with 97 horse, Jacques Bourguignon de Corobel with 150 French horse, and John Wauchope with 60 Scots.[27] He had sent Wagner with 150 men, and 25 of De la Ville's men, to Ladoga Town. However, Wagner failed to reach the town due to an encounter with a numerically stronger force of enemy cavalry under Governor Saltykov who marched against the town. Even so, De la Ville had succeeded in sending messengers to the Swedish army, and they informed De la Gardie that the town contained supplies for a year.[28]

Meanwhile, King Charles issued orders to assemble a new army in Viborg. Although he had promised foreign enlisted units, few were available, in particular with regard to cavalry. In early November, Charles ordered available units to assemble in Viborg by Christmas or at the latest in early January.[29] As before, De la Gardie would function as the commanding general in the east.

---

24 Almquist, *Sverge och Ryssland*, p.206.
25 Prince Putyatin may have been influenced by Luka Ivanovich Miloslavskiy, secretary (*d'yak*) and head of chancellery at Ivangorod (1609–1611), who also opposed Swedish rule.
26 Generalstaben, *Sveriges krig* 1, pp.348, 351.
27 Almquist, *Sverge och Ryssland*, p.201. Wagner arrived to Viborg during the autumn of 1610 and ultimately became head of De la Gardie's Life Cornet.
28 Generalstaben, *Sveriges krig* 1, p.351.
29 Generalstaben, *Sveriges krig* 1, p.348.

On 28 December, King Charles ordered De la Gardie and Horn to resume the offensive into Muscovy, with the seizing of Novgorod a priority.³⁰ De la Gardie marched out of Viborg on 26 January 1611. Because of the dispatching of units from several locations, their arrival at different times, and the ad hoc nature of regimental formations, the strength of De la Gardie's army as it marched out remains uncertain.³¹ Many units were still on their way to the theatre of operations.³² The army possibly consisted of 11 banners, 14 companies, and some field artillery, altogether an estimated 4,500 men. The field artillery remained limited, consisting of a 12-pounder culverin, a double falconet, and a cluster of wall guns.³³

No pay had arrived, so De la Gardie, his commissar Tönne Gyllenmåne, and Governor Wildeman of Viborg had to contribute their personal funds and whatever loans they could take.³⁴ De la Gardie's immediate objectives seem to have been, first, to prevent any Commonwealth army from advancing in relief of Kexholm (rumours, which ultimately turned out to be false, claimed that Chodkiewicz planned such a campaign), and second, to finally relieve De la Ville in Ladoga Town, which remained under siege by Governor Saltykov and his men.

De la Gardie first marched to Kexholm to inspect the ongoing siege operation. Everything looked fine. The army then continued to Nöteborg, to which De la Gardie brought about 1,700 men.³⁵ The men had been

---

30 By then, both the Swedish and Commonwealth commanders were more preoccupied with events in Muscovy than their ongoing, mutual war in Livonia. Little of consequence took place in Livonia in the campaign season of 1610. In spring 1611, Commonwealth and Swedish commanders agreed to a local truce which held until June 1612, when it was extended to October 1613. *Sverges Traktater med främmande magter* 5:1 (Stockholm: P. A. Norstedt, 1903), pp.225–9.

31 The army was based on those units that already were mobilised in Finland, the remnants of De la Gardie's previous army, and what remained of the army that had laid siege to Ivangorod: 11 national and two foreign banners, and three national and seven foreign companies of foot. In addition, Sweden sent one banner and seven companies of foot of enlisted soldiers and one Swedish banner and Hans von Rechenberger's four companies of foot from Norrland and Österbotten (but Rechenberger joined the army only in early March, together with Robert Popler's company of foot). If so, this meant that De la Gardie's army was planned as altogether 15 banners and 21 companies. Generalstaben, *Sveriges krig* 1, p.348. See also King Charles to De la Gardie, 6 November 1610. Waaranen, *Samling*, pp.114–7.

32 When De la Gardie marched out, only one of the expected four companies from Finland had arrived, under Captain Carl Heusser. He had seven cavalry banners: De la Gardie's Life Cornet under Wagner, Gyllenhierta's Finnish banner, Höök's Västergötland banner, Kafle's Västergötland banner, Corobel's French banner; Ruthven's Scottish banner, and Wauchope's Scottish banner. The enlisted infantry included Cobron's Regiment of foot and the companies of Captain Andreas Goossen van der Maan and Daniel Hepburn. Almquist, *Sverge och Ryssland*, p.213.

33 Hedberg: *Kungl. Artilleriet: Medeltid*, p.408.

34 Almquist, *Sverge och Ryssland*, p.213.

35 Cavalry: De la Gardie's Life Cornet under Wagner (120 men), Höök's Västergötland

THE STRUGGLE FOR INGRIA AND KEXHOLM COUNTY

given fur coats and woollen stockings, and many had received Sami shoes to protect them against the winter cold.[36] On the night of 12 February he attempted a surprise attack on Nöteborg. However, the attack failed. The strongly fortified Nöteborg was a medieval castle built on an island at the exit of the River Neva into Lake Ladoga, commanded a strategic location which dominated shipping along the Neva, and was almost invulnerable to assault. It was a fortress, not a town, and there were few civilians inside. Although the Swedes managed to break both the outer and inner gate with petards, the defenders barred the passage with a strong iron fence (or possibly a portcullis), and the assault failed. De la Gardie lost 20 men including Captain Heusser, which suggests that the Finnish units carried out the assault.[37] Since De la Gardie then lacked artillery, he did not attempt

Nöteborg, seventeenth-century print. Nöteborg was built on an island and almost invulnerable to assault.

Nöteborg, as seen from the north, 1650s. Nöteborg was built on an island and almost invulnerable to assault. (Swedish Military Archives, KrA)

---

    banner (180 men), Kafle's Västergötland banner (127 men), Gyllenhierta's Finnish banner (85 men), Ruthven's Scottish banner (120 men), Wauchope's Scottish banner (108 men), and Corobel's French banner (155 men), altogether 895 horse. Infantry: Cobron's Regiment of three (or possibly four) companies of altogether 460 foot, and three independent infantry companies, together 356 men. Generalstaben, *Sveriges krig* 1, p.352.
36 Generalstaben, *Sveriges krig* 1, p.351 n.3.
37 Generalstaben, *Sveriges krig* 1, p.352; Almquist, *Sverge och Ryssland*, p.214. A century later, Tsar Peter the Great would rename the fortress Schlüsselburg (modern-day Shlissel'burg), German for Key Castle, since he regarded it as the key to Ingria.

to lay siege, and the Swedes merely burned the exposed outer buildings on the shore.

Another blow was that De la Gardie learnt that De la Ville, having defended Ladoga Town against Muscovite units for several months, had surrendered to the besiegers. On 15 January, De la Ville's younger brother Jacques De la Ville and a few others were captured by Muscovites under Prince Grigoriy Volkonskiy when he commanded a reconnaissance mission outside Ladoga Town. To intimidate De la Ville, the commanding Muscovite officer had two prisoners killed in sight of the walls and informed him that his brother would be killed as well, unless he surrendered.[38] Believing that De la Gardie would not relieve his garrison, De la Ville on 5 February agreed to surrender Ladoga Town to Governor Saltykov of Novgorod in exchange for the return of the prisoners, and the right of free departure with all weapons, belongings, and full military honours. Saltykov had Prince Ivan Afanas'yevich Meshcherskiy, who seems to have been in immediate command for most of the siege, escort De la Ville and his men to Swedish territory. Based on his own account, De la Ville could not believe that King Charles and De la Gardie had sent a relief force under Lorentz Wagner in an attempt to assist. Perhaps he learnt of the relief attempt later, because he continued his service in Sweden during the Kalmar War later in the year, and again in Muscovy in 1613.[39]

In besieged Kexholm, the supply situation grew unbearable during the winter. Numerous Kexholm inhabitants died from starvation, cold, and diseases, including scurvy. The well-fortified fortress town could no longer sustain a long period under siege. In February 1611, the defenders finally agreed to negotiate. Yet, they also made preparations to blow up themselves and the fortress, unless the Swedes accepted honourable terms of surrender. Initially the Swedish commanders offered harsh terms, in effect allowing the Muscovites to depart only with the clothes they wore and their 'wooden gods' (by which the Swedes presumably meant icons and crucifixes). Moreover, Bishop Silvester would have to go into Swedish captivity. The Kexholm defenders refused to accept these terms, and instead threatened to blow up both the town and themselves.

Following long and complicated negotiations, during which the defenders of Kexholm managed to hide their desperate circumstances, it was agreed that the town would surrender in return for free departure with all personal belongings and all ecclesiastic paraphernalia, except church bells. They must also leave behind all Muscovite chancellery files, and primarily the tax records. These records were necessary for the Swedes to identify the county's peasants, who after the annexation of the territory otherwise might escape taxation. The artillery must stay behind too, but the value of such cannons that had been brought in since 1597 would be deducted from Muscovy's debt to King Charles. This time, the defenders

---

38 De la Ville, *Discours sommaire*, p.420.
39 De la Ville, *Discours sommaire*, p.418.

agreed. The terms were generous, probably overly so since the Swedes did not know that only about 100 fighting men remained alive. On 2 March 1611, Kexholm surrendered to Arvid Wildeman, Governor of Viborg,[40] and the surviving Muscovites departed. As many as 1,500 corpses were found in the town, primarily victims of disease, and they now had to be buried. King Charles appointed Tönne Gyllenmåne governor of Kexholm.[41]

The surrender of Kexholm, the chief town in the area and an important trading post, effectively brought the whole of Kexholm County under Swedish control.

De la Gardie's units then moved into Ingria to protect the coast of the Gulf of Finland and bring the towns of Kaporie and Jama under Swedish control.

---

40 Cavalry captain Lars Andersson died at around this time.
41 Almquist, *Sverge och Ryssland*, p.228. Gyllenmåne was in 1612 followed in this post by Anders Boije.

13

The Death of False Dmitriy

Meanwhile, the false Dmitriy remained at Kaluga, still claiming the throne. Much of southeastern Muscovy remained in rebellion, and many cossacks still supported Dmitriy, since he did not impose taxes on them, did not interfere with their private plundering, and remained unable to form any form of central government. Dmitriy had also, since 1608, enjoyed the support of Prince Oraz Muhammad Khan, the Kasimov Khan. However, in 1610 Commonwealth agents forged documents that appeared to compromise the Kasimov Tatars, and placed them in the hands of Dmitriy.[1] As a result, Dmitriy had the Kasimov Khan murdered and threw the Khan's associate and friend, Prince Peter Urusov, a Noghai Tatar noble, into prison. Possibly influenced by sentiments then prevalent in the Commonwealth and among both Catholic and Orthodox churchmen, Dmitriy carelessly assumed that his personal prestige was such that he still could retain the Khan's friends and followers in his service, so he soon released Prince Urusov from prison. He may have looked down on the Tatars; on 11 December 1610 the Tatar noble killed Dmitriy in revenge for the murder of the Kasimov Khan.

Based on what he later heard from others, Field Hetman of the Crown Stanisław Żółkiewski gave a vivid, yet credible description in his memoirs of the false Dmitriy's death:

> Having drunk plenty at dinner, … he ordered a sleigh to be harnessed, bringing a flask of mead into the sleigh; driving out into the open country, he drank with some boyars. Prince Peter Urusov, together with those several dozen horsemen with whom he was in league, was following him, apparently escorting him; and when the imposter and the boyars had drunk their fill, Urusov drew a pistol from his holster which he had ready, and galloping up to the sleigh shot him first with the pistol, then cutting off his head and hand with his sabre, he set off on his way, never returning to Kaluga.[2]

---

1   Dunning, *Russia's First Civil War*, p.414.
2   Stanisław Żółkiewski, *Początek i progres wojny moskiewskiej* (Paris: Rouge, Dunon

Yet Another False Dmitriy

The false Dmitriy in Kaluga was barely dead before in early 1611 yet another false Dmitriy declared his arrival, this time in Ingria.[3] Amazingly, at around the same time, one more false Dmitriy appeared in the south-east, based in Astrakhan'.[4] Suddenly there were two of them. The Astrakhan' Dmitriy was raised by the aforementioned Prince Peter Urusov, apparently as his own candidate to the throne. However, this Dmitriy never played a significant role, and soon faded into oblivion. Nothing is known of his fate.

Not so with regard to the new, northwestern Dmitriy. His story began on 23 March 1611, when he announced himself in Novgorod. Unfortunately for the pretender, he was soon recognised as a cossack known as Sidorka (nickname for Isidor; but perhaps not his original name) and expelled from the city. This did not prevent the pretender from again announcing himself on 28 March, but then in Ivangorod, controlled by former rebels, and as we have seen, under threat from Swedish units. False Dmitriy claimed that he did not die in Kaluga after all. He soon gained support in those towns, in particular Ivangorod, Jama, Kaporie, and Gdov, that already had been reluctant to acknowledge strong tsars. Dmitriy attempted to negotiate an agreement of recognition with the Swedes but the Swedish envoy Peder Pedersson who had met the man who first claimed to be Dmitriy could soon confirm that this pretender was not the same, hence a fraud, so the Swedes broke off the talks.

Whilst King Charles would have been ready to negotiate support in exchange for the new ruler of Muscovy ceding the strongholds in Ingria and Kola to Sweden, De la Gardie upon learning that the new Dmitriy definitely was a fraud, instead aimed for renewed cooperation with Novgorod, where sentiments despite much animosity remained reasonably strong in favour of continued Swedish–Muscovite cooperation, at least against the Commonwealth.

---

   et Fresné, 1866), p.66.
3 In traditional historiography, the new Dmitriy is designated False Dmitriy III, although he in reality was at least the fourth who claimed the identity.
4 The Dmitriy in the south-east is traditionally designated False Dmitriy IV.

14

The First National Militia

Meanwhile, Muscovite discontent with King Sigismund and his absent son Władysław was growing. Having learnt of the death of Dmitriy in Kaluga, Patriarch Hermogenes of Moscow in December 1610 dispatched a series of circular letters to Muscovite towns, asking them to unite against the Commonwealth invaders since their presence threatened the independence of the Orthodox Church; in response, Commonwealth officers arrested Hermogenes. The circular letters brought some resonance among those governors who did not have to worry about the presence of any Commonwealth garrison, yet were obliged to answer when Commonwealth commanders demanded contributions.

As a result, several notables rose against the Commonwealth presence. They were led by the former rebel Prokopiy Lyapunov, now the commandant in Ryazan', the town which provided the bulk of food supplies to Moscow. Lyapunov wrote and distributed a manifest against the Commonwealth presence, after which he led a contingent of fighting men to Moscow. Like-minded contingents arrived also from Yaroslavl', Vologda, Vladimir, Galich, Kostroma, and Nizhniy Novgorod. The core consisted of men who formerly had fought for Tsar Vasiliy under Skopin-Shuyskiy and Sheremetyev against the Tushino rebels. However, Lyapunov also recruited rebel boyars and soldiers whom Dmitriy had left in Kaluga, including the old Dmitriy loyalist Prince Dmitriy Trubetskoy (d. 1625). Lured by promises and supplies and in the hope of renewed plunder, a major part of the rebel cossacks joined, too, under Ataman Ivan Zarutskiy, who it will be remembered had fought on the Commonwealth side in the battle of Klushino, and Ataman Andrey Zakhar'yevich Prosovetskiy. By this time, a significant share of the cossacks were recent arrivals, not from the cossack south but from ruined villages and towns in central Muscovy. Having lost everything, they found that their only remaining option was going cossack, that is, joining any cossack warlord willing to take them in. These men, in social background ranging from serfs to free townsmen but including destitute hereditary servicemen as well, were less lured by renewed plunder than the hope of finding food supplies, and ultimately, some semblance of stability. Even Sapieha volunteered his services to Lyapunov's uprising, in the hope that a new tsar

THE FIRST NATIONAL MILITIA

would give him the outstanding pay that he considered his due. Lyapunov rightly regarded Sapieha's offer with some suspicion. Sapieha continued negotiations also with King Sigismund, whose generous promises ultimately made the mercenary rejoin his compatriots.

By the end of March 1611, the diverse contingents of what henceforth became known as the national militia (Russian: *zemskoye opolcheniye*, 'levy of the land'[1]) gathered around Moscow, where tensions were rising between Muscovites and Commonwealth soldiers. On 19 March 1611, a brawl developed into full-scale combat in Moscow. The Moscow streltsy joined the townsmen, overwhelming the Commonwealth soldiers, but three enlisted companies of foot (about 400 men) under the veteran French mercenary Jacques Margeret successfully extricated them. Two days later, the first units of the national militia under Prince Dmitriy Pozharskiy entered Moscow, renewing the assault on the Commonwealth garrison. However, when the Prince was badly wounded in the struggle, his men retreated, bringing him to safety. Meanwhile, members of the Council of Seven including Prince Fyodor Mstislavskiy, Fyodor Sheremetyev, and Ivan Romanov threw in their lot with the Commonwealth commandant, Aleksander Gosiewski, since they expected little mercy from the former rebels. So did Mikhail Saltykov, for similar reasons. Unable to hold the entire city, Gosiewski

Map of Moscow by Georg Braun and Frans Hogenberg. The map shows Moscow before the destruction of 1612 and the subsequent changes to the street network. The top of the map indicates the geographical west. Centre: The Kremlin. Lower centre: The fortified Kitaygorod. The origins of the map trace back to a survey reportedly ordered by Tsar Boris Godunov. Whilst the original plan has not survived, it is believed that Braun and Hogenberg based their work on a copy made for King Sigismund in 1610. The map includes the coats of arms both of King Sigismund (top left) and Muscovy (top right). (*Moscovia urbs metropolis totius Russiae Albae*, 1617)

---

1   In modern literature, the Russian name of the formation is often given as *narodnoye opolcheniye*, 'national levy'. It will be remembered that in seventeenth-century Russian, *zemskoye* ('territorial, of the land') carried essentially the same meaning as today's *narodnoye* ('national'). Incidentally, because of later events this particular formation is nowadays commonly called the first national militia.

and his 2,300 soldiers withdraw into the Kremlin and Kitaygorod, starting fires in the outlying parts of the city to cover the retreat. In due time, more national militia units moved into the city to occupy major parts of it and lay siege to the Commonwealth garrison.[2]

Encouraged by the letters of Hermogenes and Lyapunov's manifest, Metropolitan Isidore of Novgorod also began to champion the new cause. In early March the Novgorod government imprisoned, tortured, and ultimately beheaded Ivan Saltykov, the Polish Tsar-elect's governor, displayed his head on a pole, and offered the city's support to the national militia. Following Saltykov's downfall, the previous governor, Prince Ivan Odoyevskiy, resumed power in Novgorod. Nöteborg switched side, too, while Pskov and the neighbouring towns retained their loyalty to the false Dmitriy.

The new developments also persuaded the governments of Novgorod and Nöteborg to resume negotiations with De la Gardie. They had good reason for this, since the leaders of the national militia hoped that the Swedes would again intervene, driving the Commonwealth units away from Moscow.

Confrontation with Novgorod

To the disappointment of the Novgorod notables, De la Gardie again demanded the annexation of Kexholm County as well as Nöteborg and Ladoga Town in compensation for Swedish support. He also demanded the Muscovites elect a tsar who was independent of the Commonwealth.

Meanwhile, acting upon orders from De la Gardie, Cobron on 6 March attempted to retake Ladoga Town from the men loyal to King Sigismund's representative Saltykov. It was a surprise attack with 600 men. Cobron successfully opened up the outer gate with a petard, but the defenders managed to block the inner gate so that the Swedes could not break through. In addition, the Muscovites defended themselves vigorously, and a sudden spell of poor weather prevented the attackers from using muskets or siege ladders, so the attempt failed.

Allegiances remained complex in the border region. Soon after, the aforementioned coup took place in Novgorod, which resulted in Saltykov's downfall. Yet, De la Gardie had no way of knowing how the new Novgorod leadership would side. Besides, when De la Gardie demanded food supplies from Kaporie, the leading notables there – Governor Ivan Grigor'yevich Trusov and his deputy Andrey Timofeyevich Nagoy – procrastinated, saying that they expected imminent instructions from Tsar Dmitriy and could do nothing before these arrived.

De la Gardie sent Cobron with his detachment towards Novgorod as a show of strength versus Prince Odoyevskiy, the city's new governor. On 18

---

2 Dunning, *Russia's First Civil War*, p.418.

March, De la Gardie sent a letter to the notables of Novgorod. Noting that he had not received acceptable replies to his previous communications, he informed them that he would send his army against the city.[3] De la Gardie had established his headquarters at Sol'tsy, on the River Volkhov between Novgorod and Ladoga Town. This enabled him to block all river traffic between the two. The position also secured his communication line to Finland. He wrote to Viborg, requesting suitable river vessels to blockade the outlet of River Volkhov into Lake Ladoga, and also requested river vessels and men to build a redoubt at Nyen to block the River Neva's exit into the Gulf of Finland.[4] By spring the Swedes had built a redoubt at Nyen, 12 km from the mouth of the River Neva, as a means to control river traffic.

De la Gardie also received reinforcements. In early March, Hans von Rechenberger arrived at Nazya Yam (Swedish: Loppis) between Nöteborg and Ladoga Town with a regiment of four companies of foot from Norrland and Österbotten in northern Finland and Robert Popler with a company of enlisted English/Scots infantry. By the end of the month, the major part of the expected Finnish units arrived as well.[5]

Meanwhile, events took place in the Arctic north. On 27 April, King Charles ordered Bäck to make yet another attempt with Clemetsson's Västerbotten company and the Polish company, with 200 to 300 levies, to conquer Kola Castle and the Arctic coast, and to bring hand grenades this time.[6] He also ordered them not to plunder, since he intended to keep these territories. However, this time the outbreak of the Kalmar War prevented the expedition. A month later, King Charles received news of Colonel Andrew Stuart's failure to reach Fort Suma, and beyond the sea, the Solovki Monastery. On 9 June he then ordered Colonel Stuart to make a second attempt against Fort Suma.[7] Again, the outbreak of the Kalmar War and the subsequent death of King Charles put an end to the plan. Yet this did not prevent the monks at Solovki from panicking when during the summer they received reports of unknown ships observed approaching Solovki and staying in its vicinity for several days. Surely, these must be Swedish warships, and no doubt Swedish soldiers were on the way overland, too! When the mystery ships turned away and disappeared, the monks attributed this to divine intervention and wrote up the story as a Swedish invasion miraculously defeated by Saints Savvatiy and Zosima.[8]

---

3   Almquist, *Sverge och Ryssland*, p.224.
4   Nyen, a Swedish name derived from the River Neva, was a small settlement previously known as Landskrona. The redoubt built at Nyen ultimately became the origin of modern-day St Petersburg.
5   Almquist, *Sverge och Ryssland*, p.225.
6   King Charles to Bäck, 27 April 1611. Waaranen, *Samling*, pp.150–51.
7   Generalstaben, *Sveriges krig* 1, p.350; Waaranen, *Samling*, pp.152–3.
8   The pious story was accepted at face value by most modern historians. Dunning, 'The Richest Place in the World', p.316.

The Commonwealth Garrison in Moscow

The uprising in Moscow and the emergence of the national militia caught King Sigismund at a bad time. There is no doubt that the Polish king wanted to relieve his besieged garrison. However, he was still tied up with the siege of Smolensk. Sigismund first attempted to hire Sapieha for the job, but negotiations did not seem to lead anywhere. In late March 1611, he ordered Grand Hetman of Lithuania Chodkiewicz to march with the army of Livonia to Moscow. Chodkiewicz first attempted to negotiate a ceasefire agreement in Livonia with the Swedes. However, King Charles was unwilling to accept any ceasefire agreement with a duration of less than five years. Moreover, the eagerness displayed by Chodkiewicz made the King suspect that in reality he attempted to take Ivangorod or attack De la Gardie. Chodkiewicz did take time to assault the fortified Pskov-Pechory Monastery, but his army refused to march deeper into Muscovy without first receiving their pay. Chodkiewicz laid siege to the monastery for six weeks, without success – despite the insistent demands from King Sigismund that he instead march to Moscow as soon as possible. It would take six months before Chodkiewicz and his army reached Moscow.

Having finally been promised sufficient pay from the Muscovite state budget, Sapieha in early May 1611 set out towards Moscow. On 7 June, he set up a camp at Poklonnaya Mountain, a flat hill west of the city. Then, he initiated a new series of negotiations, but this time with Gosiewski who was besieged in the Kremlin. Lacking money, Gosiewski offered Sapieha choice pieces from the Kremlin treasury as partial payment for a rescue.

Concerned about the threat from Sapieha, Prince Dmitriy Trubetskoy, Ataman Ivan Zarutskiy, and Prokopiy Lyapunov, the commanders of the national militia, sent Vasiliy Buturlin, whom De la Gardie had met already in Moscow, to Novgorod as the authorised representative of the national militia to arrange a deal with the Swedes. On 16 June, Prince Trubetskoy, Zarutskiy, and Lyapunov also wrote to Governor Odoyevskiy and Metropolitan Isidore in Novgorod, requesting them to persuade De la Gardie to hurry to their rescue. They instructed Odoyevskiy and Isidore to accept the handover of Nöteborg and Ladoga Town, and also to promise the payment of the Swedish soldiers, although not at a rate as high as Skopin-Shuyskiy earlier had promised since money now was scarce. On the same day they also sent envoys to Sapieha, with the intention of, if at all possible, hiring him for their own purposes, or if this did not work out, at least play for time until the arrival of the much-hoped for Swedish relief army under De la Gardie. Sapieha was not that easily persuaded; he advised the envoys to stay loyal to the Polish Tsar-elect Władysław. Nonetheless, negotiations continued, and Sapieha made no attempt to save Gosiewski.

On 23 June 1611, the assembly of the national militia (the 'council of the whole land', *Sovyet vsey zemli*), represented by Prince Trubetskoy, Zarutskiy, and Lyapunov, formally elected Gustavus Adolphus, the eldest son of King Charles, Tsar of Muscovy. The decision, signed and sealed by the leading notables, was unanimous. This was significant, because the assembly was the most representative body of the Muscovite Estates that had gathered ever since the death of Tsar Boris. To emphasise the urgent need for a Swedish army, Prince Trubetskoy, Zarutskiy, and Lyapunov sent the decree about the election of Gustavus Adolphus to Novgorod, together with renewed instructions to Odoyevskiy and Isidore to hasten the arrival of De la Gardie's relief army. As soon as the expected treaty with De la Gardie was concluded, the assembly would send envoys to the Swedish King, whom they hoped would travel to Viborg together with his son so that they were within easier reach of Muscovy. The assembly also promised to hand over both Nöteborg and Ladoga Town, although not Kola Castle which was the only fortification that safeguarded the Arctic trade. In fact, while Prince Trubetskoy, Zarutskiy, and Lyapunov instructed Novgorod to make every effort to secure a Swedish relief army, they also wanted Odoyevskiy and Isidore to complain about the ongoing Swedish designs in the Arctic against Kola and their suspected designs against Fort Suma and the Solovki Monastery.[9] The urgent message and the decree about the election of Gustavus Adolphus as Tsar of Muscovy seem to have reached Novgorod on 2 July.

Sapieha probably learnt nothing of this. On 27 June he sent messengers to King Sigismund, but merely to demand from him the pay that Gosiewski obviously was unable to give. Sapieha continued to negotiate with all parties until 4 July, when he left Moscow to plunder the vicinity for supplies to himself and Gosiewski.

Meanwhile, King Sigismund had finally conquered Smolensk. The siege of Smolensk, begun on 19 September 1609, had lasted almost two years, until the effective garrison was reduced to 200 men. On the night of 2–3 June 1611, the Commonwealth soldiers stormed the city and killed most of the remaining defenders. The governor, Sheïn, fell into Commonwealth captivity, where he was harshly treated.[10] King Sigismund had finally gained the territory that most interested him and for which he had come. He probably regarded the precarious position of his garrison in Moscow as being of less importance. Deeming himself the master of Muscovy, King Sigismund returned to Warsaw.

---

9 Almquist, *Sverge och Ryssland*, p.242, with references.
10 Kargalov, *Moskovskiye voyevody XVI–XVII vv.*, p.205.

15

The Storm of Novgorod

De la Gardie expected reinforcements to arrive in the summer, when the dry weather improved road conditions, and accordingly sent Horn to the border with Finland to receive the expected units. De la Gardie also instructed Horn to set up a riverine communications route along the River Volkhov with Novgorod, by way of Nöteborg and Ladoga Town, both of which must be bypassed because of the hostile garrisons there; the Nöteborg authorities in particular had caused difficulties. Without riverine transportation, it would be impossible to supply the army. For the same reason, he also ordered Horn to see to that the work on the redoubt at Nyen proceeded as planned (it did). De la Gardie then, on 28 May, set out from Sol'tsy towards Novgorod with an army perhaps 4,000 strong. Finally it was time to assume control of the city on behalf of Sweden.[1]

By 4 June, De la Gardie's army had reached the vicinity of Novgorod, which was a major city with a population of at least 25,000, probably 30,000 people. The number of soldiers there is unknown, but unlikely to have been more than 3,000 men.[2] Novgorod had a city militia, but its combat value was likely limited. Most soldiers were streltsy or cossacks, and there must have been a small number of hereditary servicemen. The city had a comparatively strong artillery, consisting of one 96-pounder siege cannon, four 24-pounder culverins, 21 other cannons, and more than 50 small-calibre cannons and mortars.[3] However, considering the size of the city, the cannons were dangerously spread out.

Upon arrival, De la Gardie was met by a delegation of representatives from those city notables who opposed the Commonwealth-imposed Tsar. Among them was the national militia's Vasiliy Buturlin, whom De la Gardie knew from Moscow, who had fought and bled with the Swedes at Klushino, and who because of his antipathy towards the Commonwealth intervention

---

1 Almquist, *Sverge och Ryssland*, p.233; Generalstaben, *Sveriges krig* 1, p.363.
2 Generalstaben, *Sveriges krig* 1, p.368.
3 Hedlund, *Kungl. Artilleriet: Medeltid*, p.408.

THE STORM OF NOVGOROD

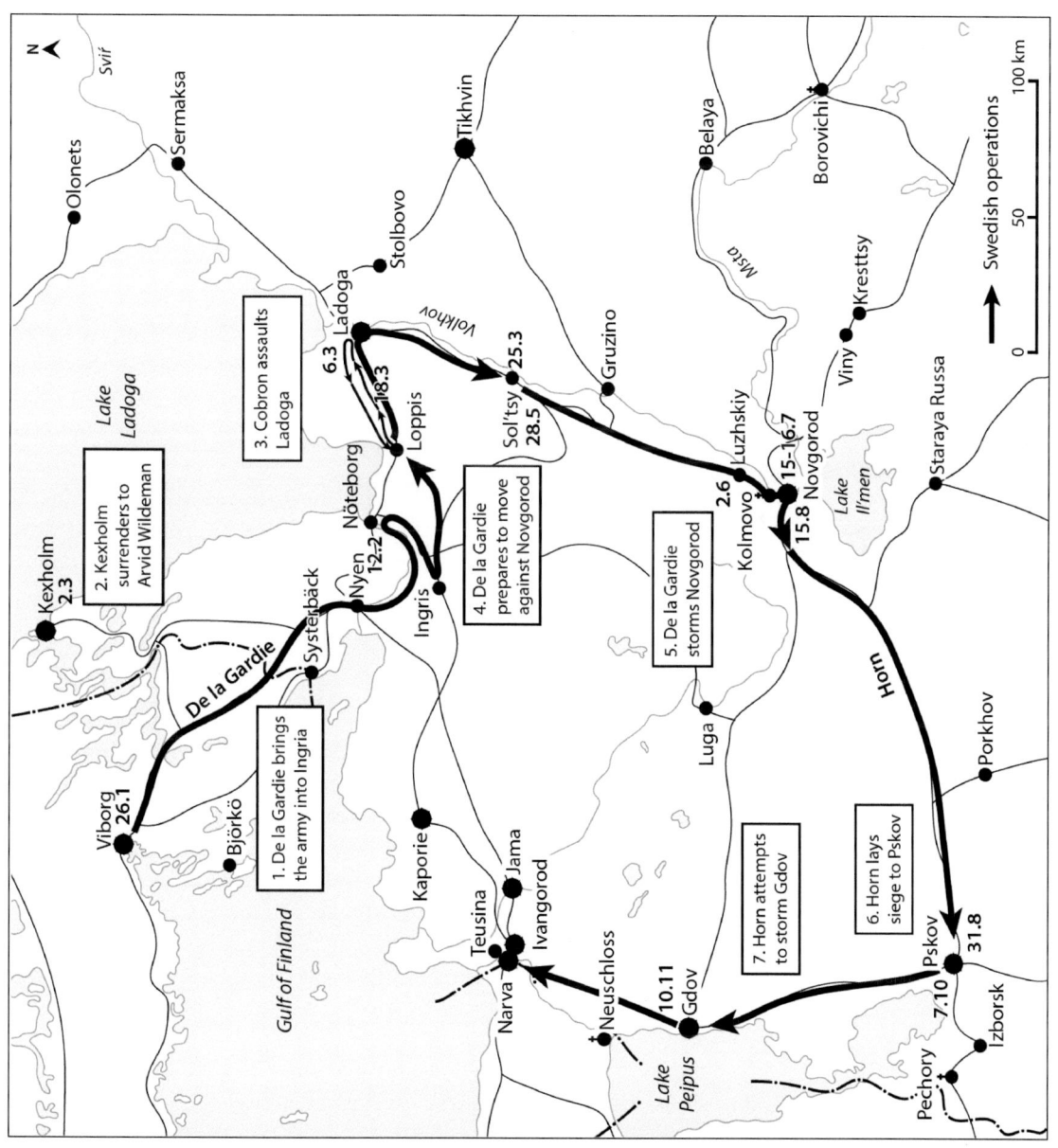

Map 6. De la Gardie's and Horn's Operations in 1611.

seemed to favour a Swedish alternative more than many others. The Governor, Prince Odoyevskiy, was there too.

De la Gardie initiated negotiations about cooperation against the Commonwealth intruders as well as Novgorod's promises to pay the Swedish soldiers. The first issue was of key interest to the Novgorod officials (as noted, a Commonwealth army had just stormed Smolensk). At first, negotiations went very well. We have seen that the assembly of the national militia was already willing to elect one of the Swedish King's sons as tsar. The delegates were also willing to cede Nöteborg and Ladoga Town in return for Swedish military support against the Commonwealth invaders.

On 6 June, Buturlin requested that De la Gardie lead the Swedish army in support of the new assembly of the national militia. In private, Buturlin informed De la Gardie that the assembly would be happy to elect one of the Swedish King's sons as tsar, as long as Muscovy could retain its Orthodox faith.

Then, as instructed, De la Gardie informed the Novgorod representatives of King Charles's demand for Kexholm, Gdov, Ivangorod, Jama, Kaporie, Nöteborg, and Ladoga Town, that is, Ingria entire. The notables in Novgorod thought this price too high; they had been prepared to offer Nöteborg and Ladoga Town, but not all the rest. Negotiations were accordingly postponed for about two weeks.

De la Gardie did not yet know that the national militia was in the process of formally electing Gustavus Adolphus as Tsar of Muscovy (this decree reached Novgorod only on 2 July but was not made public), and that Novgorod, too, formally had bound itself to the decision. So far, relations with Novgorod had been far from smooth. The Novgorodians clearly pursued a policy of their own in the negotiations with De la Gardie, which differed from that proposed by Moscow.

With the arrival in mid June of Horn's corps (two banners and two companies), the Swedish army at Novgorod consisted of 13 banners of cavalry and 16 companies of foot, altogether some 4,000 men (Table 11). At the same time, Sweden maintained garrisons in Kexholm, Nyen, Viborg, and levies on guard duty at the border with Savolax, Finland (Table 12), so the eastern borderlands were well defended.

On 8 July, De la Gardie met envoys from Novgorod at the Khutyn' Monastery at Kolmovo north of the city. During the meeting, mutual suspicions led to a quarrel, which in turn caused the drawing of weapons and the exchange of gunfire between the escorts of the two parties. In revenge, Swedish soldiers against orders then began to plunder buildings belonging to the monastery at Okol'nyy Gorod next to Novgorod itself. Afterwards, De la Gardie and Buturlin attempted to smooth over the incident. However, the tensions between the Swedes and some segments of the population of Novgorod remained. In particular the secretary (*d'yak*) and head of chancellery Afinogen Golenishchev was hostile towards any Swedish involvement in the city's affairs, and he seems to have been the one who provoked the incident.⁴ There was discord within Novgorod, too: Governor Odoyevskiy and Buturlin did not get along, and the servicemen and townsmen did not share the same goals.⁵

On 12 July the Novgorod army sallied out, but failed to make an impact on the Swedes. Upon their return, they burned the outskirts of Novgorod so as to prevent Swedish units from using buildings there as cover.

De la Gardie knew that his army could wait no longer. Supplies were low, and the men wanted their pay. However, De la Gardie had no siege artillery at his disposal, and hardly any field artillery. He faced other problems, too. Many of his soldiers were ill and could not be moved, and it was becoming increasingly difficult to find food supplies. A retreat under such conditions might easily end in disaster. Negotiation seemed to have played out its role; the only remaining options were military action or an ignominious retreat.

De la Gardie and his commanders had already laid plans for an assault upon Novgorod. Russian-language sources, but no Swedish ones, mention a Muscovite prisoner named Ivan 'Ivashko' Schwall (Shval') or Prokof'yev who supposedly told De la Gardie about the weakest point of Novgorod's fortifications. Whether there ever was such a prisoner (a chancellery scribe of this name later served the Swedish administration in Novgorod as under secretary), or whether De la Gardie learnt of this weakness from his envoys or intelligence officers, is both unknowable and matters little. What matters is that on the night between 15 and 16 July, De la Gardie set the operation in motion.

Table 11. Jacob De la Gardie's army at Novgorod, 15 July 1611[6]

Unit	Origin	Coy	Men
Cavalry			
Jacob De la Gardie's Life Cornet, under Lorentz Wagner	Sweden/Finland	1	120
Evert Horn's Cornet, under Otto Grothusen	Finland	1	100
Finnish Retinue of Nobles, under Hans Jönsson Stålhandske	Finland	1	150
Göran Hansson Höök's Banner	Västergötland	1	175
Bengt Erlandsson Kafle's Banner	Västergötland	1	127
Erik Bertilsson Ljuster's Banner	Finland	1	77
Lindved Claesson Hästesko's Banner	Karelia	1	100
Claes Christersson Gyllenhierta's Banner	Finland	1	77
Richard Isaacsson Rosencrantz's Banner	Finland	1	108

---

4   *D'yak* was a court rank derived from the word for deacon.
5   Almquist, *Sverge och Ryssland*, pp.245–6.
6   Generalstaben, *Sveriges krig* 1, pp.586–7.

SWEDEN'S WAR IN MUSCOVY 1609-1617

Franz Strych's Banner	Finland	1	241
Patrick Ruthven's Banner (enlisted)	Scotland	1	128
John Wauchope's Banner (enlisted)	Scotland	1	108
Jacques Bourguignon de Corobel's Banner (enlisted)	France	1	167
In total		13	1,678
Infantry			
Jacob de la Gardie's Life Company (enlisted)			
- Daniel Hepburn	Germany	1	325
Hans von Rechenberger's Regiment			
- Olof Helsing	Norrland	1	230
- Jacob Velamsson	Norrland	1	270
- Evert Bamberg	Österbotten	1	230
- Christopher von Damb	Österbotten	1	213
Samuel Cobron's Regiment (enlisted)	British Isles		
- Samuel Cobron		1	122
- Richard Band		1	84
- Harry Elphinstone		1	86
- Jacob Frensham		1	83
- Nicholas Gent		1	98
- Robert Kinnaird		1	120
- Robert Moore		1	75
- Oliver Popler		1	149
- Robert Popler		1	133
Jost Clodt von Jürgensburg's Company (enlisted)	Germany	1	75
Casper Möller's Company (enlisted)	Switzerland	1	92
In total		16	2,385
Grand total		29	4,063

Table 12. Swedish border garrisons at the time of the assault on Novgorod, 1611. Afterwards, De la Gardie redeployed some of these units to active duty[7]

Unit	Origin	Coy	Men
Kexholm			
Matts Sigfridsson's Company of Foot	Österbotten	1	117
Lars Larsson's Company of Foot	Björneborg (Satakunta)	1	90
Nyen			
Lars Andersson's Banner of Horse (most of the unit)	Karelia	1	254
Sigfrid Larsson's Company of Foot	Österbotten	1	216
Viborg			
Reinhold Jacobsson's Company of Foot	Tavastland	1	150
Mårten Simonsson's Company of Foot	Karelia	1	236
Hans Prytz's Company of Foot	Karelia	1	133
Hans Root's Company of Foot	Karelia	1	339
Levies on guard duty at the border with Savolax, Finland			
Lars Göransson Posse's Company of Foot	Savolax	1	
Mårten Eriksson's Company of Foot	Savolax	1	
Per Larsson's Company of Foot	Savolax	1	
Erik Nilsson's Company of Foot	Savolax	1	
- All levies			690

Novgorod consisted of two districts, the weakly fortified 'merchant side' or trading quarter, on the eastern side of River Volkhov, and the heavily fortified 'Sophia side' or administrative quarter on the western, which included the venerable Cathedral of St Sophia, the Holy Wisdom of God, and the city's castle. The merchant side was the commercial centre, while the Sophia side constituted the centre of government.

De la Gardie sent some units across the River Volkhov, which made the city notables conclude that the main threat faced the weakly fortified merchant side. When hostilities got underway on 15 July, Hans von Rechenberger launched an attack along the River Volkhov, with the help of river boats, on the northern sector of the wall of the Sophia side. However, both Rechenberger's operation and the apparent preparations on the merchant side were feints. The real objective of the attack was the southwestern sector of the Sophia side. In fact, De la Gardie realised that

---

7   Generalstaben, *Sveriges krig* 1, p.587.

SWEDEN'S WAR IN MUSCOVY 1609-1617

Reconstruction of Novgorod's merchant side. (Russian postcard, 1908-1909)

the Sophia side was the only real option, since even if his men took the merchant side, this would mean they would then have to find means to cross the river and carry out a landing on the other side, which was fortified. The Sophia side was far safer to attack overland.

At night, the Swedes attempted to blow the Chudintsev and Prussian gates to the Sophia side with petards, reportedly under the command of a French (or possibly Swiss) petardier known as Major Artzian Kurtz. Although the results were less than satisfactory, the Swedes nonetheless stormed the city wall. Evert Horn commanded the Swedish units in the centre, supported

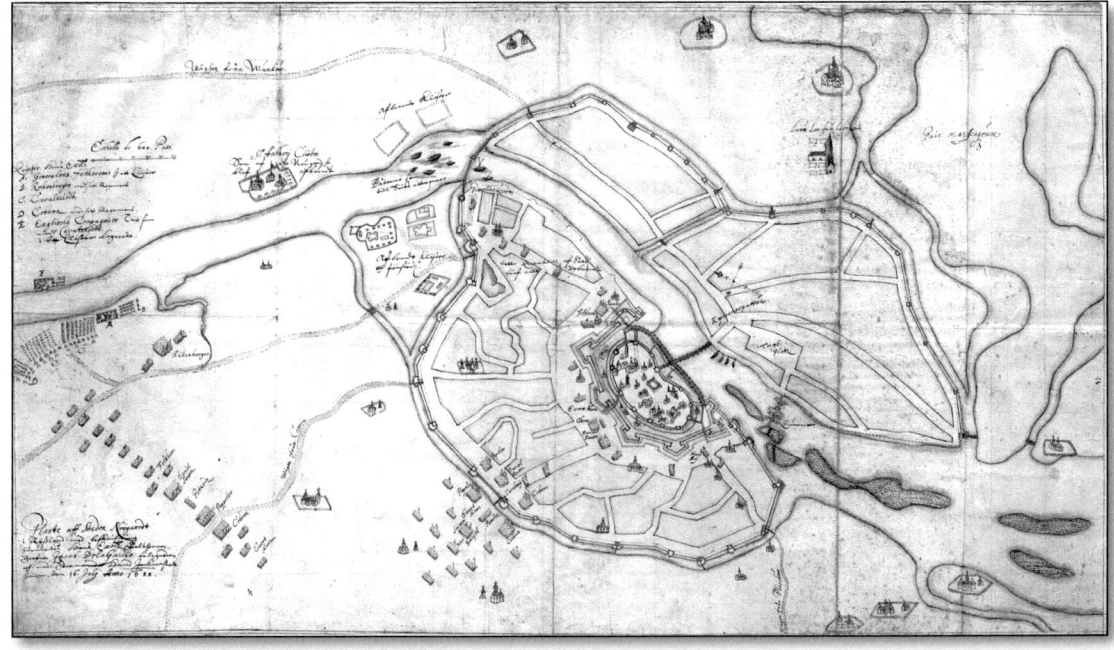

The storm of Novgorod, 15–16 July 1611. The map shows the original Swedish deployment in order of battle, the feint river boat assault in the northern sector, the assault on the outer wall, and the army's deployment in front of the castle. (Map possibly by Olof Hansson Örnehufvud)

THE STORM OF NOVGOROD

by Cobron and one of the Poplers who commanded the enlisted soldiers on the wings. Möller's Swiss foot followed immediately behind them. With Swedish infantry gaining control of the gates, Evert Horn then led the cavalry into Novgorod. The defenders, apparently surprised by the sudden assault, seemed completely unprepared. The Swedes gradually gained control over the entire Sophia side except the castle. The most hard-fought struggle took place around the tower where, on the city's northern side, the city wall stopped at the River Volkhov. Panicking, some Muscovite soldiers and nobles attempted to flee by boat across the river to the merchant side. Many drowned in the attempt. Buturlin, who was in command of the city's defences, brought other soldiers across on the river's only bridge, in this way saving them and himself. He did not wish to risk his men only because the Novgorodians out of mere stubbornness had sabotaged the national militia's agreement with Sweden. The soldiers hurriedly plundered the houses and stores on the merchant side, justifying the action by claiming that nothing must be left to the Swedes, and then departed the city, retreating eastwards towards nearby Bronnitsa (then often called Bronnitsy).

The aforementioned Afinogen Golenishchev fought until he fell in battle, together with the head of the streltsy, Vasiliy Golyutin, and the cossack officer Timofey Sharov. Another casualty was the fanatic Amos, the archpriest (*protopop*) of the Cathedral of St Sophia, who took an active part in the fighting and chose to perish in a burning building rather than surrender to heathens.[8]

By dawn, Novgorod was in Swedish hands. The soldiers had received strict

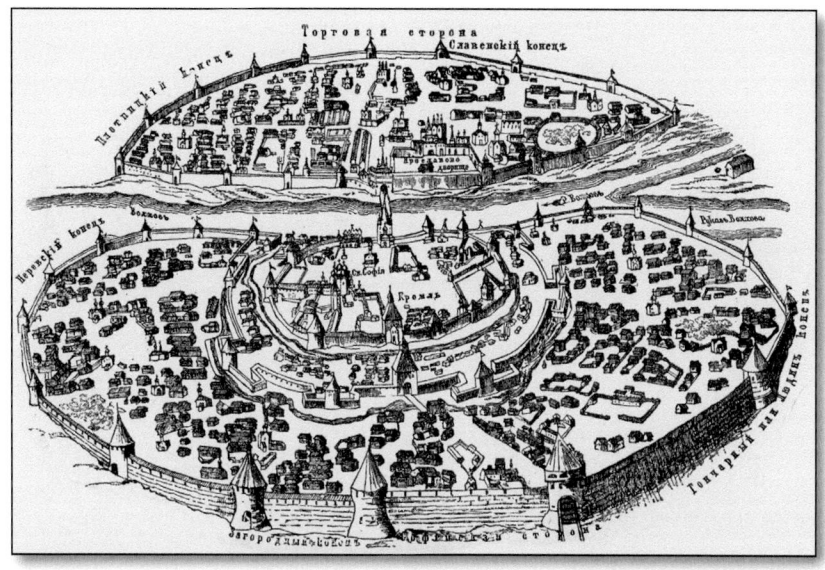

Depiction of Novgorod. (Anonymous reconstruction, 1675)

Cathedral of St Sophia, the Holy Wisdom of God, 1900. (Photo: Swedish National Heritage Board)

---

8   Harald Hjärne, 'Utdrag ur ryska krönikor, hufvudsakligen angående Jakob De la Gardies fälttåg', *Historiskt bibliotek* 6 (1879), pp.605–18, on pp.617–18.

SWEDEN'S WAR IN MUSCOVY 1609-1617

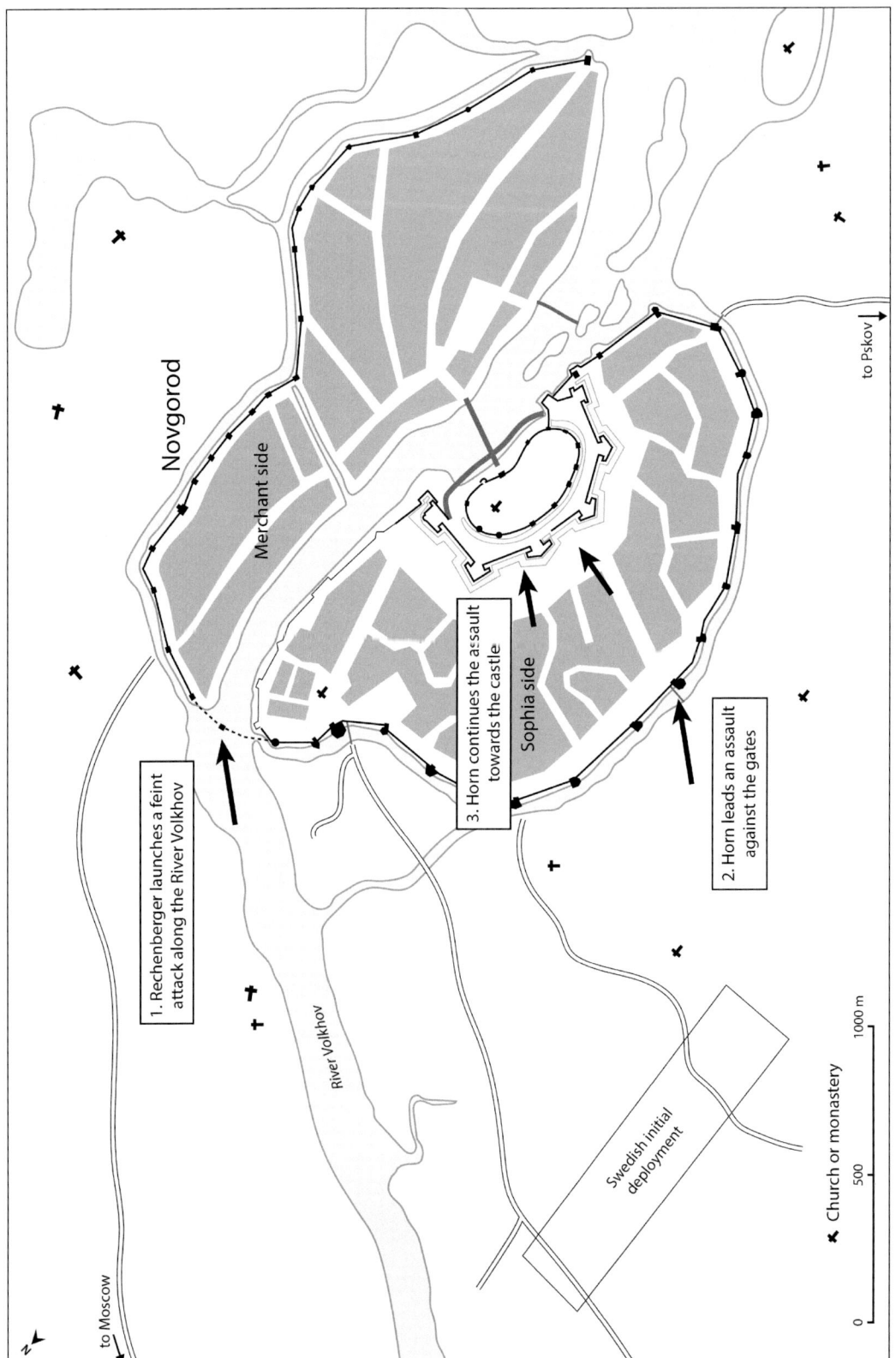

Map 7. The Storm of Novgorod, 1611.

orders not to loot the city or kill civilians, but incidents had probably taken place. To prevent further looting, De la Gardie closed the bridge to the merchant side and instead laid siege to the castle in the centre, where the city's governor, Prince Odoyevskiy, and Metropolitan Isidore, had taken refuge. On 17 July, when the Swedes prepared to storm the castle with a petard, both men hurriedly agreed to negotiate and immediately offered to surrender the castle to De la Gardie. They based their position on the decree that Moscow had already elected a Swedish prince as Tsar of Muscovy. Enticed by the news about the decree, and aware that the Muscovites had demolished the bridges across the moat and filled the gates with earth and gravel to prevent their opening by petards, De la Gardie accepted their offer and the same day entered the castle with his life company.[9]

We know little of public opinion in Novgorod. While pious Orthodox believers such as the late Amos resented foreigners, others probably still remembered how Tsar Ivan IV sacked and looted the city in 1570, massacring thousands of townsmen in the process. Besides, until its 1471 incorporation as the Novgorod State in Muscovy, by Ivan III, the old Novgorod Republic had been an independent polity. Novgorod remained a merchant city with numerous and prosperous links to the heathen west. It is possible that feelings in the city were ambiguous with regard to both Stockholm and Moscow.

The Treaty of Novgorod

The immediate result of Prince Odoyevskiy's and Isidore's surrender was the Treaty of Novgorod on 25 July 1611. Most of the treaty was based on the decree from Moscow, but taking full advantage of his position of strength, De la Gardie removed such clauses that he regarded as disadvantageous for the Swedish Crown. The treaty was written in two copies: one was sealed and signed by the Estates of Novgorod, led by the Metropolitan and the Governor, the other was signed by De la Gardie on behalf of King Charles. The treaty contained an appeal from Novgorod for Swedish protection, an agreement for a union between Sweden and Novgorod against the Commonwealth, and a pledge to give the throne of Muscovy to a son of King Charles, either Gustavus Adolphus or his younger brother Charles Philip (1601–1622), Duke of Södermanland, Närke and Värmland. Presumably understanding the need for Gustavus Adolphus to remain available for the Swedish kingship, De la Gardie probably already at this time (and certainly when he reported to Stockholm a month later) suggested Charles Philip as the more realistic choice. The treaty also confirmed the 1595 Treaty of Teusina, all treaties that were subsequently agreed between Tsar Vasiliy and King Charles, and Muscovy's ceding of Kexholm County to Sweden. In return, the Swedish Crown guaranteed to respect the Orthodox faith,

---

9   Almquist, *Sverge och Ryssland*, pp.247–8, with references.

promised not to interfere with the lives, lands, and property of Muscovy's inhabitants, and to grant the right to free trade. Peasants would remain linked to the soil, while present cossack liberties would not be circumscribed. The treaty included provisions to continue negotiations about the details of the dynastic union between the two countries, additional remuneration to Sweden for its military involvement, and fulfilment of the already outstanding pay owed to Sweden for De la Gardie's intervention army.[10] The provision about peasants remaining linked to the soil was almost certainly inserted to appeal to aristocratic and serviceman elements of the national militia, while the one about cossack liberties surely was intended to appease its cossack elements.

These provisions were necessary, because as we have seen, the national militia consisted of separate elements, commanded respectively by Prince Dmitriy Trubetskoy, cossack Ataman Ivan Zarutskiy, and Prokopiy Lyapunov. All three had formerly been rebels, but for quite separate reasons. Lyapunov saw himself as representing the interests of the nobility and the hereditary servicemen. Their chief interest was the restoration of domestic security and safeguards for their lands. Prince Trubetskoy and in an even higher regard, Ataman Zarutskiy, represented those of the cossacks. They were aware that law and order were necessary, but they also knew that their positions of leadership depended on their ability to give the cossacks regular payments and significantly more liberties than were granted to other Muscovite nationals. The leaders of the various interest groups must cooperate to reach their goals, and they did so in a grand council of war of the national militia which in many ways was akin to a national assembly (*Zemskiy sobor*). On 30 June Trubetskoy, Zarutskiy, and Lyapunov had pushed through and made public an agreement on how to rule and administer the country (a decree sometimes referred to as the constitution of the national militia). The grand council of war became the highest judicial and administrative authority under the tsar. It alone could sentence culprits to death or exile. Trubetskoy, Zarutskiy, and Lyapunov became the three chief officers of state. Laws for the safeguarding of property were introduced, and decrees to this effect were made public. The cossacks would, in a similar manner to other soldiers, receive support in the form of land grants or monetary payments. However, runaway serfs would be returned to their owners, and robbery and plundering were henceforth strictly prohibited.

Charles Philip, Duke of Södermanland, Närke and Värmland, 1610 or 1611. (Gold medal, possibly by Ruprecht Miller; photo: Gabriel Hildebrand, Economy Museum – Royal Coin Cabinet/SHM, Stockholm)

---

10 *Sverges Traktater med främmande magter* 5: 1, pp.200–211. On extant and lost copies of the treaty, see Almquist, *Sverge och Ryssland*, p.250 n.1.

Most rank-and-file cossacks realised that regardless of the high principles referred to, the agreement effectively constrained their accustomed liberties, which although never formally acknowledged in practice were tolerated while the revolt was underway. The cossacks had, over the years of rebellion, grown used to plundering any lands they passed through and seizing anything they wanted. Being denied these liberties after growing accustomed to them during years of plundering was an unpalatable proposal – and especially so because the cossacks in reality were not paid for their services and by this time must resort to plunder merely to supply themselves with food and other necessities.

Most cossacks particularly blamed Lyapunov for the miseries that the new regime of law and order surely would inflict upon them. They regarded him as the chief architect of the new legal and administrative regime, and they hated him for it. In addition, some veteran rebels remembered how Lyapunov had once betrayed their hero Bolotnikov and switched to the government side. The cossacks also disliked the Swedes, who had frequently fought them and chased them away from their gains, but Lyapunov became their scapegoat for everything that had gone wrong, and Trubetskoy and Zarutskiy did nothing to prevent their men from directing their anger at him. There is reason to believe that in particular Zarutskiy was happy to deflect all blame for the new decrees on Lyapunov, in order to safeguard his own position and favour with the cossacks. But there was also a conspiracy underway. The Polish commandant Gosiewski had cleverly had a letter forged in Lyapunov's name, which called for the death of all cossacks.[11]

The hatred towards the new regime culminated on 22 July, when Lyapunov met with an assembly of cossacks to discuss the new legislation. Ahead of the meeting, a Commonwealth agent put the aforementioned forged letter into the hands of those whom Lyapunov would meet. When Lyapunov came to the meeting, the enraged cossacks confronted him with the letter, and then murdered him.

The murder of Lyapunov shattered the noble and hereditary serviceman faction of the grand council of war. While Artemiy Izmaylov, another former rebel noble, assumed the late Lyapunov's role as a leader of the noble faction, he lacked his predecessor's prestige and influence. Henceforth, Prince Trubetskoy and Zarutskiy controlled the national militia, and did so to further their own power and that of the cossack faction. Prince Trubetskoy and Zarutskiy did not seem to mind the elimination of their colleague and rival, and henceforth claimed to rule the country in their own manner, which essentially meant that they punished anybody they disliked and ravaged such territories where they could find supplies and loot.

The nearby monasteries, including those which previously had resisted the cossack rebels, suddenly found themselves without military protection. At the same time, they had already sent letters calling the believers near and far to support the national militia against all foreigners and heretics.

---

11   Dunning, *Russia's First Civil War*, p.429.

The letters had been aimed at the Commonwealth invaders and the Polish tsar-elect, but they had also resulted in the beginning of a religious national awakening which, the cossack commanders immediately understood, equally well served as a tool against a Swedish, or for that matter, a Tatar candidate to the throne. In the view of pious clergymen, all non-Orthodox foreigners were equally evil, an interpretation which suited Prince Trubetskoy and Zarutskiy eminently since it enhanced their own position as leaders of the cossack faction and undermined that of other factions.

When Göran Brynno (Brunow), the Swedish envoy to Moscow, arrived to negotiate with the three leaders of the national militia, Prince Trubetskoy and Zarutskiy simply threw him in prison (where Brynno remained until March 1613). While Gosiewski and the other Commonwealth representatives in the Kremlin applauded the breakdown in negotiations with Sweden, they soon found a new problem. On 5 September Sapieha fell seriously ill, and died a month later. This removed the one military commander who, if he had wanted, might have rescued them. Moreover, the cossack army soon received additional reinforcements from Kazan'.

De la Gardie may not yet have known of these developments, but he had made a contingency plan in case a Commonwealth-backed pretender seized the throne in Moscow: he would then have Novgorod declare independence from Muscovy and turn itself into a Swedish county. Following the Treaty of Novgorod, an increasing number of towns joined Novgorod in its acceptance of a Swedish tsar. When in August Hans Muir led a Swedish corps to Porkhov and Torzhok, these towns readily joined Novgorod in accepting the treaty, and Ladoga Town and Nöteborg also expressed some willingness to join. When in September a Swedish army under Claes Slang arrived at its gate, probably on the 12th, Ladoga Town surrendered and fully accepted the treaty. So did nearby Tikhvin. Lars Anfestsson moved into Ladoga Town's administrative quarter with a garrison of Finnish soldiers (Sigfrid Larsson's company) but allowed a company of 50 streltsy to remain in the town's trading quarter, outside the town walls.[12]

Among the northern towns and strongholds, open anti-Swedish sentiments remained only in Nöteborg. This was perhaps not a coincidence. Among its defenders was Prince Yefim Myshetskiy who as governor of Kexholm had fallen under the spell of Bishop Silvester and accordingly hated the idea of handing over lands to the heathen Swedes. When Slang led the rest of the Swedish army to Nöteborg, he found the fortress divided between those – primarily the leading notables – who wanted to join the rest of the region in accepting the Novgorod Treaty, and those – primarily the streltsy and Prince Myshetskiy – who did not, at least not until the new Swedish tsar had actually arrived.[13] As a result, Nöteborg remained defiant.

Nonetheless, Swedish units already had or were gaining control over most of the Novgorod Lands, or the Principality of Novgorod for those

---

12 Almquist, *Sverge och Ryssland*, p.257; Generalstaben, *Sveriges krig* 1, pp.380, 381.
13 Almquist, *Sverge och Ryssland*, p.257.

who preferred this term. Even so, De la Gardie continued to face difficulties in supporting and paying his soldiers. Ultimately, supplies had to be brought in from Sweden and Finland. The national units were no more willing to obey orders, unless they were paid, than those enlisted abroad. The Västergötland units were particularly upset, and for them at least a contributing factor was certainly the news of the outbreak of the Kalmar War. They knew that their homes were at risk, and saw little purpose in staying in distant Novgorod when their own families and farmsteads suffered from Danes and Norwegians. Bengt Kafle's banner mutinied, but the insubordination was stifled through the rapid action of the unit ensign. Not so the mutiny in Göran Höök's Västergötland banner. The whole banner of cavalry abandoned their officers, deserted, and rode back to Viborg – where they were taken into custody. In November, they were shipped to Sweden, together with Kafle's banner.[14] With the possible exception of a few ringleaders, Höök's cavalrymen seem not to have been punished; Sweden needed soldiers at the time.[15]

---

14 Almquist, *Sverge och Ryssland*, p.258; Generalstaben, *Sveriges krig* 1, pp.380, 386.
15 A *Furier* (Swedish: *furerare*; a sergeant with added duties) known as Lood served in the banner. He was probably the later well-known soldier Olof Lood, in 1638 ennobled as Silfverlood and ultimately an army legend. The event did not stain Lood's career.

16

The Siege of Pskov

The situation was different in Ingria and around the Lake Peipus where loyalty to the new false Dmitriy instead remained strong, following his arrival in Ivangorod in late March 1611. Taking a cue from Ivangorod, neighbouring Jama, Kaporie, and Gdov declared for Dmitriy.

On 8 July 1611, Dmitriy surrounded Pskov with an army that Swedish intelligence estimated as 1,500 men and some artillery. Arguing that he was Muscovy's only defender against the perfidious foreigners, Dmitriy demanded Pskov's surrender.[1]

In response, De la Gardie in August sent Evert Horn against Pskov in command of a corps consisting of six banners – the major part – of the Finnish cavalry in a regiment under Hans Boije, Patrick Ruthven's banner of Scottish cavalry, John Wauchope's banner of Scottish cavalry, and Samuel Cobron's entire regiment of nine companies of foot. Horn's corps also included Muscovite units from Novgorod and even Pskov (described as 300 'good men' in the Pskov Chronicle). Horn had no artillery.[2]

Learning that Swedes under the well-known Horn marched on Pskov, Dmitriy immediately abandoned negotiations with the city and on 23 August instead withdrew to Gdov.

Horn reached Pskov on 31 August. He offered the city the opportunity to join the Swedish–Muscovite alliance under the terms of the Treaty of Novgorod. However, like Novgorod, Pskov (in western and central Europe known, in Latin, as Plescovia) had a history of independence as the Principality of Pskov or the Pskov Republic. The inhabitants of Pskov

---

1 Generalstaben, *Sveriges krig* 1, p.381.
2 Boije's cavalry consisted of the banners under Erik Bertilsson Ljuster, Lindved Hästesko, Claes Gyllenhierta, Franz Strych, the Finnish retinue of nobles under Hans Jönsson Stålhandske, and Evert Horn's cornet under Otto Grothusen. Cobron's Regiment consisted of the companies of Samuel Cobron, Richard Band, Harry Elphinstone, Jacob Frensham, Nicholas Gent, Robert Kinnaird, Robert Moore, Oliver Popler, and Robert Popler. Generalstaben, *Sveriges krig* 1, p.382; Yakov Nikolayevich Rabinovich, 'Gdov v smutnoye vremya, 1610–1621 gg.', *Voyenno-istoricheskiye issledovaniya v Povolzh'ye* 8 (2008), pp.17–32, on p.18.

were no less conscious of their proud history and importance than those of Novgorod. Pskov only became part of Muscovy in 1510. As a result, the defenders in Pskov whipped the messenger who brought the offer, and declared themselves ready to fight to the last man against the hated Swedes. Horn accordingly sent for a petardier and two petards from Novgorod. On the night between 7 and 8 September, he attempted to storm Pskov. The petardier succeeded in breaching a gate, taking the Muscovites by surprise, so the Swedes encountered no serious opposition. With three companies from Cobron's Regiment under Harry Elphinstone poised to move into the city, victory seemed to be at hand. Yet, to Horn's surprise, the men of the leading company suddenly panicked and retreated. The other two companies withdrew, too. This enabled the defenders to resume control over the open gate. Horn blamed Elphinstone, whom he accused of cowardice, but added that the entire unit was unreliable since they had not received their pay. Afterwards, the soldiers expressed shame at their behaviour and asked to make another attempt, but this time during the day and with siege ladders. Horn granted their request, but they were again repulsed.

Horn lacked adequate artillery support, and none could be sent because of the poor road conditions, so his one remaining chance was to employ a mine. However, most soldiers refused to carry out the digging associated with mining. Only Reinhold Jacobsson's Finnish company of foot, until recently part of the garrison of Porkhov, did not refuse. Horn ordered day labourers from Porkhov, but apparently they never came. The defenders carried out several sallies, and Horn's men spent most of their shot and gunpowder. As if this was not enough, the autumn weather brought rain, which caused difficulties in moving across the soaked ground.[3]

Meanwhile, Pskov suffered from internal tensions. On 30 September an internal coup took place in Pskov, in which locals with 300 cossacks from Izborsk gained control over the city, imprisoned its leading citizens, and declared for Dmitriy.[4] This brought increased attention to Sweden's unresolved problems with Dmitriy and Lisowski. De la Gardie had wanted Horn to neutralise them first, while Horn argued that the two caused as much, or more, problems for the defenders of Pskov. At the outset of the campaign, De la Gardie had thought that Pskov would fall quickly, and advised Horn to take Gdov, Izborsk, and Pechory as well. This would have brought the entire Lake Peipus under Swedish control. Horn had sent Hans Muir with a corps to take Izborsk and reconnoitre Pechory. However, Izborsk was successfully defended by 300 cossacks, and Muir gained nothing from the expedition. As for Gdov, rumours held that the Lithuanian Hetman Chodkiewicz might go on the offensive from Livonia (in reality, he was on the way to Moscow). For this reason, Horn did not wish to advance further in this direction. In the end, the campaign was a failure. Horn left Pskov on

---

3   Almquist, *Sverge och Ryssland*, pp.259–60; citing Horn's report.
4   Generalstaben, *Sveriges krig* 1, p.384.

7 October, instead marching towards Gdov, where Dmitriy was said to have only 300 men with him.[5]

Horn sent a letter to Dmitriy, offering him the chance to submit to the Swedish tsar in exchange for remaining as governor in Gdov. Dmitriy had no such intention, but he also feared staying in Gdov. After skirmishes with the approaching Swedes, he fled north to Ivangorod.

Horn then prepared to lay siege to Gdov. By this time, he sorely lacked gunpowder. He requested reinforcements with artillery and supplies for the siege from Philip von Scheiding, the governor of Narva, however, Scheiding refused to send artillery and the requested supplies since he claimed to need them for the defence of his own town. In early November the exchange of letters rapidly deteriorated into a heated argument between Governor von Scheiding and Horn and his officers at Gdov, in which Horn accused Scheiding of profiting from the trade with hostile Ivangorod, yet refusing to aid the army. Scheiding, in his turn, accused Horn of having set out with too little gunpowder to begin with. Although De la Gardie expressed his support and approval for Horn's request, the winter was already upon them and the campaign had to be interrupted.[6] Horn sent some of the Finnish cavalry back to Finland, and the rest to Novgorod.

However, things did not go much better for Dmitriy. Many of his men deserted him, instead joining the Swedes, and Dmitriy suffered additional losses when he pulled out of Gdov and retreated to Ivangorod; moreover he was wounded in the fighting that took place during the withdrawal. He found that he was little welcome in Ivangorod, and realising that he had better leave, rode back to Pskov, where he arrived in early December. This time, the population welcomed him. With the city under new management, propped up by the streltsy, Dmitriy felt comparatively safe.

Meanwhile, De la Gardie had given up hope of convincing Nöteborg to surrender through arguments and intimidation. He ordered Horn to Nöteborg, where Claes Slang was in charge of the siege. It is unclear how many men Horn then had at his disposal; only some 370 infantry from Rechenberger's Regiment and Casper Möller's Swiss company of foot are known to have been present, soon joined by Lars Andersson's and Lindved Hästesko's Karelian cavalry banners and probably some infantry from Nyen.[7] Horn arrived at Nöteborg on 30 November and immediately advised the fortress to accept a Swedish garrison. If they persisted in refusing, the rest of Muscovy would curse and extinguish them and their family lines, he said, since this refusal delayed the arrival of the Swedish tsar, and also put the entire country at risk of again falling under 'a bunch of Dmitriys, Poles, Turks, and [Crimean] Tatars'.[8]

---

5   Almquist, *Sverge och Ryssland*, p.261.
6   Almquist, *Sverge och Ryssland*, p.262.
7   Generalstaben, *Sveriges krig* 1, p.386.
8   Horn to De la Gardie, 30 November 1611, cited in Almquist, *Sverge och Ryssland*, p.263.

In reality, Horn believed that it was impossible to gain the almost impregnable Nöteborg by siege. It was defended by many men and could still easily bring in supplies by ship across Lake Ladoga. Any besieging army, in contrast, had to transport supplies from distant depots across a wild country. He needed clandestine action. Horn selected three or four men who could be counted on to enter Nöteborg, each unknown to the others. Then, at the appointed hour, they would set the fortress on fire. Unfortunately, there is no surviving information on whether Horn's plan ever was set in motion, and if so, how the clandestine action developed. Nöteborg remained defiant.

Despite the setbacks at Pskov, Gdov, Ivangorod, and Nöteborg, De la Gardie had by the end of the year managed to rally major parts of northwestern Muscovy around the elected Swedish tsar, King Charles's son. The problem was, he had no idea what Stockholm would think of the plan to install one of the King's sons in Moscow. Naturally De la Gardie had sent full reports about his negotiations to Stockholm, but unfortunately King Charles had been preoccupied with the ongoing Kalmar War against Denmark and Norway, and on 30 October he died from natural causes. The tsar-elect, Gustavus Adolphus, had suddenly become King of Sweden. De la Gardie had, of course, anticipated that the elderly King would pass away in due course, so he had from the outset suggested that Charles Philip should ascend the throne of Muscovy instead of his elder brother. De la Gardie explained the advantages of sending Charles Philip and expressed his sincere hope that the Prince accompanied by a few hundred men would travel to Viborg and the border with Muscovy during the winter. Meanwhile, a senior delegation from Novgorod would travel to Stockholm to offer the throne to one of the late King Charles's sons. The delegation came with a warranty of the highest authority, with guarantees from both the Orthodox Church in the name of the Metropolitan and the secular authorities in the name of Prince Odoyevskiy in Novgorod and the Estates of Muscovy. Not only did Novgorod's warranty explain the election of the Swedish tsar in Moscow on 23 June, it also linked the event to the historic Varangian, that is, Viking-Age Swedish, origin of the ancient House of Rurik which had produced so many distinguished tsars.[9]

It was an excellent plan. Unfortunately, nobody in Stockholm responded. For obvious reasons, Stockholm's attention was on the more proximate Kalmar War and the recent death of King Charles. Gustavus Adolphus

---

9   The twelfth-century Russian *Primary Chronicle*, also known as *The Tale of Bygone Years*, describes how the tribes of northwestern Russia in 862 invited the Varangian chieftain Rurik to rule over their lands. In Novgorod, he founded the Rurik dynasty, which went on to rule Kievan Rus', its principalities, and ultimately Muscovy. Linguistics, archaeology, geography, and popular tradition alike suggest that Rurik came from the coastal region of the Swedish core territories. It was thus natural for the scholarly churchmen of Novgorod, now that fanatics such as Amos no longer were with them, to remind their adherents that the Russian-speaking peoples already had a long-established tradition of inviting Swedish rulers.

inherited the Swedish throne at age 16, but because of the Kalmar War, he had no resources and little time to invest in Muscovy. By the end of the year, De la Gardie had no idea of what Sweden's new King, Gustavus Adolphus, thought about his scheme.

Confrontation with Commonwealth Freebooters

Although Hetman Chodkiewicz finally reached Moscow in late September 1611, and temporarily relieved his countrymen there, supply difficulties meant that he was unable to remain in the Moscow area. Chodkiewicz accordingly sent many units further afield to gain quarters wherever they could. Some moved into the region east of Novgorod. As we have seen, quite a few units in the Commonwealth army consisted of unpaid noble volunteers who served not for pay (since they did not receive any) but for the right to plunder the supposedly enemy territories through which they passed. In late January or early February 1612, one colonel from Chodkiewicz's Lithuanian army, known as Aleksey Mikhaylovich and judging from his name probably a Ruthenian, moved to Staraya Russa with reportedly some 1,500 cossack-style cavalry freebooters. Staraya Russa was guarded by a Swedish garrison of a few cavalrymen and 200 foot under Lieutenant Colonel Oliver Popler. The garrison was probably a combined force of men from Popler's, Elphinstone's, and Richard Band's companies. Believing that Mikhaylovich only controlled 300 or 400 men, Popler carried out a surprise attack on the Commonwealth camp. Apparently succeeding in destroying or at least disrupting a unit of 300 men, Popler was then in turn surprised by the arrival of Mikhaylovich with the main force. Having failed to fight his way out, Popler surrendered under terms of free departure; Mikhaylovich did not honour the agreement, but massacred him and his men, killing about 100 and taking 30 captives. Popler and probably also Elphinstone were killed, while Band fell into captivity.[10]

The depredations of Chodkiewicz's freebooters threatened to disintegrate the recently introduced Swedish administration of the Novgorod Lands. De la Gardie accordingly sent Horn (who had already begun to prepare an operation against Kaporie) to clear the territory of Commonwealth cavalry. Horn received a significant army: at least five cavalry banners, including De la Gardie's life cornet under Erik Börjesson and a Finnish banner under Franz Strych (Strijck), a contingent of Muscovite cavalry, and most of Cobron's regiment of foot and the Commanding General's Life Company under Daniel Hepburn. Learning from prisoners that the Commonwealth freebooters were planning a joint action aimed at Novgorod, Horn first marched to Borovichi, where on 25 February he disrupted the Lithuanian colonel Aleksandr Nalivayko's contingent of reportedly 2,000 Commonwealth noble cavalry. Nalivayko and half of his men fled towards

---

10 Generalstaben, *Sveriges krig* 1, pp.388–9.

the east, while the rest surrendered and went into Swedish service. Four days earlier, Nalivayko had sent a letter to De la Gardie, informing him that Chodkiewicz had ordered him back to Lithuania. Nalivayko expressed his sincere hope that the Swedes would not mind if he and his men took contributions from the Muscovites during the retreat, and also stopped for rest and recuperation from time to time, at the expense of the locals. The letter did not reach Novgorod in time to prevent the ensuing battle and is unlikely to have received a positive response, even if it had.

Learning that other Commonwealth freebooters were approaching, and that they planned to move on Novgorod, Horn abandoned the pursuit of Nalivayko and instead entered into a fortified position at Borovichi. Horn's men repulsed a night attack by Commonwealth freebooters – but could not prevent those freebooters who had gone into Swedish service from escaping to join their compatriots. Nonetheless, the engagement was a victory of sorts, and on the night of 9 and 10 March the Commonwealth freebooters abandoned their plans, instead riding north-east towards Ustyuzhna. Horn learnt of their retreat from scouts and ski patrols. Incidentally, Nalivayko took his defeat with good grace, in April writing a new letter to De la Gardie, thanking him for the provisions but complaining that De la Gardie had taken his emissary into custody and not yet released him.

Cobron was wounded in the night attack, so Horn sent him and his infantry together with the Commanding General's Life Company under Hepburn back to Novgorod. He then sent the Muscovite cavalry to Ust'reka to raise money and supplies. Meanwhile, he led the Swedish on a patrol, possibly to Vyshniy Volochok, from which he returned to Novgorod – but not before on 18 March inflicting a severe defeat on the Commonwealth commander Aleksey Mikhaylovich, who reportedly lost some 800 dead. The defeat was sufficiently decisive that it persuaded yet another Commonwealth colonel of freebooters, Matvey Shiryy, to abandon the area.[11]

Some Commonwealth freebooters remained, however, and lacking other means to sustain themselves, many went into Swedish service. In June 1612, three banners of Commonwealth noble freebooters, altogether about 350 men, served the Swedish cause.[12] In a twist of fate, De la Gardie put them under the command of Richard Band, whom, it will be remembered, the very same Commonwealth freebooters had recently captured and then released. De la Gardie promoted Band from captain to lieutenant colonel, and told him to assume command of his former captors. The Commonwealth banners were ultimately paid off and sent home in autumn 1612, with written assurances that they had served De la Gardie and the Swedish Crown loyally.

---

11 Generalstaben, *Sveriges krig* 1, pp.390–92.
12 Generalstaben, *Sveriges krig* 1, p.396.

SWEDEN'S WAR IN MUSCOVY 1609–1617

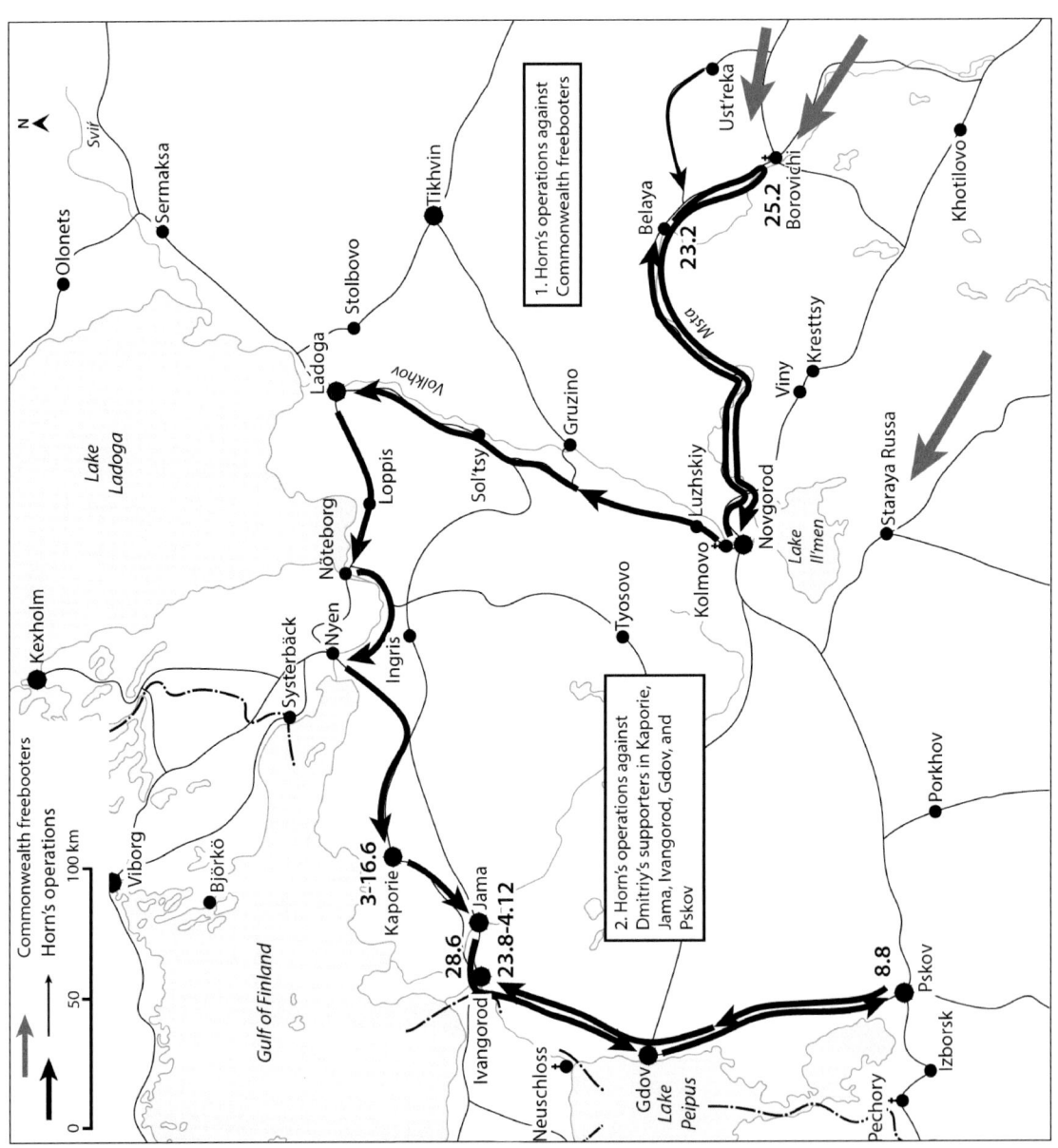

Map 8. Horn's Operations in 1612.

17

The Siege of Ivangorod

De la Gardie had hoped to use the late winter and spring of 1612 for Horn to conquer the remaining northwestern Muscovite strongholds, with Kaporie his first objective. However, the conflict with the Commonwealth freebooters approaching from the east had prevented these plans. As soon as the roads became passable again in late spring, preparations resumed.

By then, the Swedish blockade and siege of Nöteborg had finally borne fruit: Nöteborg surrendered to Claes Slang in April. Nöteborg was out of supplies, and of the garrison of between 1,300 and 1,500 men, only 100 remained.[1] Among the survivors was the aforementioned Prince Myshetskiy.

In Novgorod, De la Gardie retained only two or three Swedish banners, the aforementioned three Commonwealth banners, Rechenberger's Regiment, Lars Göransson Posse's company of Finnish foot from Savolax, and a composite company of foot from Cobron's Regiment under Lieutenant Colonel Robert Popler. The remaining five companies (at least the most displeased 366 men) from Cobron's Regiment were sent to Finland under Cobron because they refused to serve without first being paid.[2]

Two weak companies from Cobron's Regiment, under respectively Robert Moore and Jacob (James) Balfour, were detached, together with Ruthven's and Wauchope's banners of cavalry, for Horn's army. Horn also received 100 men under Daniel Hepburn from the Commanding General's Life Company of foot. Horn joined these units with those that, after the fall of Nöteborg, were deployed at Nyen and in Kaporie County (*uyezd*). This resulted in an army consisting of 10 banners of cavalry (eight from Finland and two from Scotland), about eight enlisted companies of foot, and at least two Finnish companies of foot. Altogether, the army consisted of, at most, 2,750 men. Horn also brought artillery, apparently six mortars, from the arsenal of Novgorod.[3]

---

1 Generalstaben, *Sveriges krig* 1, p.388.
2 Generalstaben, *Sveriges krig* 1, p.394.
3 Generalstaben, *Sveriges krig* 1, p.395.

Horn's first target was Kaporie, a stronghold defended by thick walls and a garrison of 100 streltsy, about 150 cossacks, and some town militia. While Horn marched towards Kaporie, a cossack unit under Mark Kozlov attempted to attack the Swedish units, under Hästesko, already near the stronghold. However, Horn's cavalry quickly rode to the rescue, dispersed the cossacks, and captured Kozlov. Horn's army initiated the siege on 3 June, if not before. He informed the garrison about the recent downfall of Dmitriy (see below), and demanded the town's surrender. Kaporie refused. The siege artillery then began to bombard the fortress artillery, while Horn's men dug trenches and prepared to storm the stronghold. Kaporie surrendered on 16 June. Horn deployed a garrison of 100 Finnish foot in Kaporie, under a Muscovite commandant.[4]

Having taken Kaporie, Horn turned to Jama, which surrendered to his siege artillery a few days later. Horn inserted a garrison of 130 enlisted German soldiers under their captain Hemming Grass. He later reinforced Jama's garrison with 40 streltsy from Kaporie and the Karelian cavalry banner formerly commanded by the late Lars Andersson but now led by Matts Jacobsson Braxen.[5]

Horn then turned against Gdov. He marched by way of Ivangorod, which he reached no later than 28 June and where he had a redoubt built so as to cut the supply line between Ivangorod and Gdov. By then, Horn had received reinforcements in the form of the three Commonwealth banners under Band. Horn deployed Braxen's banner, Reinhold Jacobsson's company of foot, and 80 town cossacks from Kaporie in the redoubt.[6]

In early July, Horn continued to Gdov which soon surrendered, certainly before the end of the month since Viborg, six to 12 days' ride away, saluted the victory on 26 July.

Having proceeded that far, Horn decided to make another attempt against Pskov, in the hope that his successes against Kaporie, Jama, and Gdov would make the people of Pskov more accommodating. The defence at Pskov was then led by the city's governor, Prince Ivan F. Khovanskiy. Although Horn's men easily repulsed the Pskov Army in the field outside the city, it was obvious that Pskov remained hostile, and Horn lacked both the men and equipment to lay siege to such a significant city. His men suffered from disease, and the enlisted soldiers complained about the missing pay. Horn took a personal loan to pay the Commonwealth cavalry, but neither money nor promises could prevent Ruthven's and Wauchope's Scottish banners from returning to Finland on their own initiative, against given orders.

Horn accordingly gave up the endeavour, and instead marched back towards Ivangorod. He left two contingents behind to secure the region and to make sure that supplies were gathered in the neighbouring Somero

---

4 Generalstaben, *Sveriges krig* 1, p.395.
5 Braxen fell at the storm of Tikhvin on 17 August 1613.
6 Generalstaben, *Sveriges krig* 1, p.396.

Region.⁷ The first contingent, under Robert Moore, had orders to secure the territories east of Pskov. It consisted of Franz Strych's and Claes Gyllenhierta's banners of cavalry and a Muscovite unit under Nikita Zinov'yev, who until recently had been Dmitriy's chief henchman but after his fall went into Swedish service. The other, consisting of Horn's cornet of cavalry and the Finnish retinue of nobles under Christer Hansson, was assigned Gdov County. Hemming Grass and his enlisted German foot was transferred to Gdov, which they garrisoned. For the stubborn defenders of Pskov, the Swedish presence further complicated a difficult situation. Lisowski's marauders also operated in the region, more intent on looting supplies intended for Pskov than on fighting any particular side in the war.

Horn commenced the siege of Ivangorod before 23 August. By then, his army consisted of four Finnish banners of cavalry, three enlisted foreign companies of foot, and probably three Finnish companies of foot. The Commonwealth banners were there, too, although their value in a siege operation was minimal.⁸

Horn knew that Ivangorod would take time to defeat, and that his only real option was to blockade the town until it ran out of supplies. This would take additional time, since the townsmen had horses and cattle inside the walls, and could even fish in the River Narova which separated Ivangorod from Narva. He accordingly had a second (and possibly even a third) redoubt built, so as to complete the encirclement of Ivangorod. Recurring cavalry patrols made sure that nobody from Ivangorod could slip through the line. Sure enough, townsmen soon attempted to escape the town. Horn ordered them pushed back into Ivangorod, in his own words 'to help the others consume' the town's supplies.⁹ Three years of warfare had hardened Horn's feelings towards non-combatants, whom he had hitherto been inclined to take under his protection.

Horn could also take advantage of the fortress artillery in Narva, which easily fired across the river against targets in Ivangorod. Horn's own artillery was presumably in operation, too, but its effect must have been correspondingly lower than that of the heavy artillery in Narva. Besides, Horn's men suffered greatly from disease.

Ivangorod's garrison defended itself vigorously, through repeated sallies. Ivangorod also responded to the bombardment from Narva by firing incendiaries into the Swedish town.¹⁰ They managed to set fire to a

---

7   Somero Region (*Somerskiy volost'*; modern-day *Slantsevskiy Rayon*) was a fertile agricultural area in southern Ingria which was vital for food production.
8   Generalstaben, *Sveriges krig* 1, pp.397–8.
9   Horn to De la Gardie, 16 September 1612; cited in Generalstaben, *Sveriges krig* 1, p.398.
10 The towns in northwestern Muscovy had the capacity to manufacture excellent incendiaries. In 1615, Gustavus Adolphus ordered incendiaries for the entire Swedish army in the east to be manufactured in Novgorod, under Horn's supervision. Novgorod also supplied the Swedish army with slow-match, for which production facilities in Sweden were insufficient. Generalstaben, *Sveriges*

SWEDEN'S WAR IN MUSCOVY 1609-1617

few buildings, but wise from earlier conflagrations, Narva was prepared to deal with them.

On 15 October, the defenders of Ivangorod sallied out in force. Horn wrote in his report that both men and women fought in the action. The experienced Swedish soldiers managed to disrupt and push back the desperate attack, but Captain Möller, the commander of the Swiss company of foot, was shot through the shoulder, a wound from which he later died.[11]

It turned out that the people of Ivangorod by then suffered from diseases of the same type as in Nöteborg. Nonetheless, resistance continued until 4 December, when Ivangorod finally surrendered. Following the example of De la Gardie, Horn let the town capitulate on the same terms as Novgorod. He made sure that the defenders knew that Sweden only aimed to replace Moscow's rule, and in no way wanted to destroy them. He moved in a

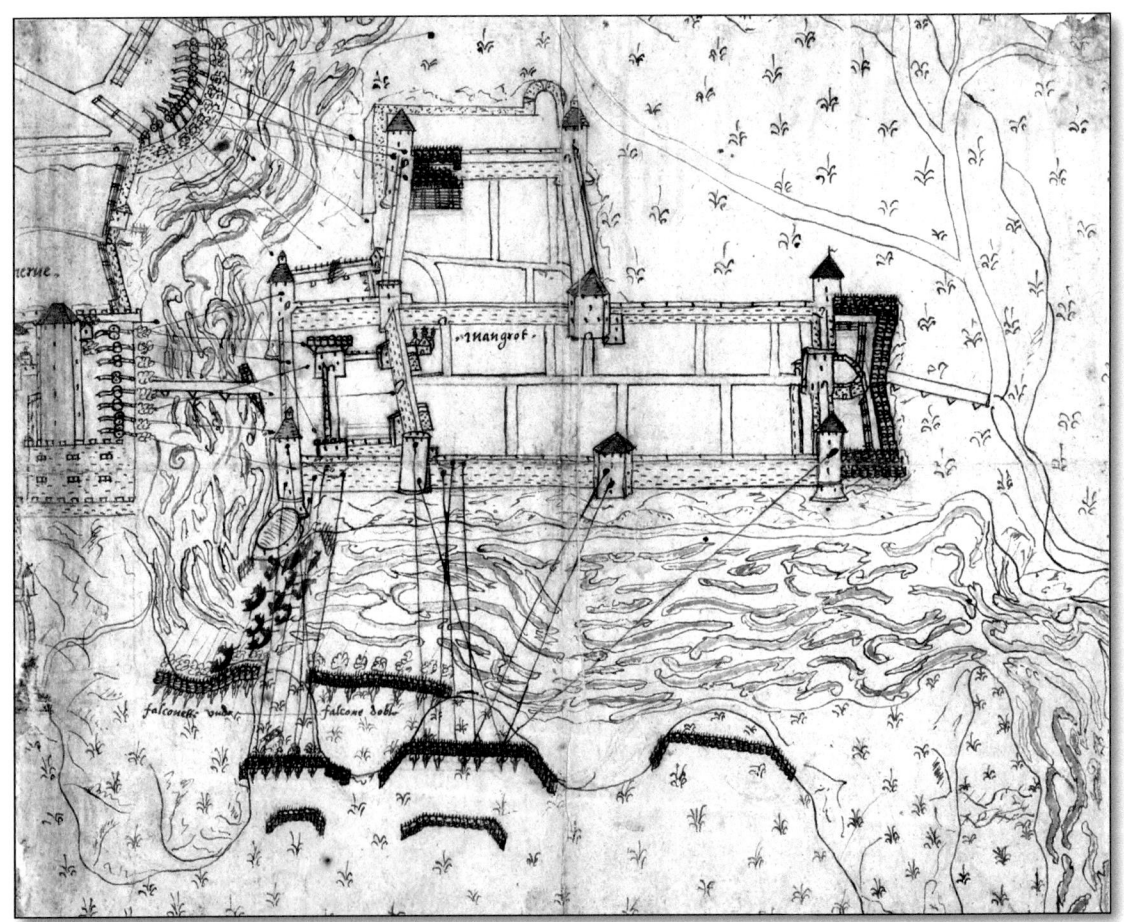

The siege of Ivangorod, 1612. Ivangorod (centre) is under artillery bombardment from Narva (on the left) across the river, and from falcons and falconets in Horn's redoubts to the south. Meanwhile, a Swedish storming party is in the process of crossing the river in assault boats (bottom left). (Royal Library, Stockholm)

---

krig 1, pp.503, 526.

11   Horn to De la Gardie, 18 October 1612; cited in Generalstaben, *Sveriges krig* 1, p.399.

garrison of three companies of Finnish and two companies of German infantry, together with a company of 100 Muscovite soldiers.[12]

By the conquest of Ivangorod, De la Gardie and Horn successfully carried out the strategy of securing the entire coastline around the Gulf of Finland. Further south, only Pskov remained, still defiant as much against Moscow as against Stockholm and Warsaw.

Yet De la Gardie and Horn had achieved all that could be accomplished. The Swedish armies were exhausted and had been stretched to the limit. The only real source of remaining worry was the never-ending presence of bands of Commonwealth marauders, but they were the shared enemy of Swedes and Muscovites alike.

The Swedish successes of 1612 can probably be best explained by the fact that those Muscovite units that resisted the Swedes were really only those that were loyal to false Dmitriy. When the last Dmitriy died during the summer, many of these units dissolved. We have seen that some went into Swedish service. Others rode east to join Muscovite armies. Likewise, when in August the Commonwealth Grand Hetman of Lithuania Chodkiewicz was halted outside Moscow, King Sigismund and his son lost their remaining power base in Muscovy, even though countless Commonwealth marauders continued their depredations in the country. These developments meant that in autumn 1612, the Swedish presence was the only remaining force of stability in northwestern Muscovy.

The Fate of the False Dmitriy in Pskov

In January 1612 the cossack faction that remained the only viable contingent of the first national militia sent a delegation to the latest false Dmitriy, who in Pskov in early December 1611 had been acknowledged as Tsar of Muscovy. On 2 March 1612, the cossack host at Moscow under Prince Trubetskoy and Zarutskiy also acknowledged the new Dmitriy as tsar. They also requested Dmitriy join them at Moscow, so that they could resume the lenient rule of the former Dmitriy from Tushino.

Dmitriy did not come, and it was soon obvious that he feared leaving Pskov. Dmitriy had no intention of going to Moscow; possibly he feared meeting those who had seen the original false Dmitriy. Yet more likely he feared Zarutskiy, who was already known to harbour plans for installing Maryna's baby son (born in early 1611 and named Ivan) on the throne as a means of elevating his own position. Dmitriy had good reason to fear for his safety.

Nonetheless, Dmitriy was now acknowledged as Tsar of Muscovy – in Moscow and Pskov, at least. However, his days of glory did not last long. Discontent grew in Pskov, and Dmitriy soon found that he had overstayed his welcome. Meanwhile, Zarutskiy had sent an agent, Ivan Pleshcheyev,

---

12 Generalstaben, *Sveriges krig* 1, p.399.

into Dmitriy's inner circle. Soon, Pleshcheyev made a deal with the city's governor, Prince Khovanskiy, to seize and hand over Dmitriy to the national militia at Moscow. Feeling that Pskov was no longer safe for him, Dmitriy fled the city on 18 May. However, two days later Khovanskiy's men managed to capture him. Dmitriy was returned to Pskov, and ultimately sent on to Moscow where he was executed.[13]

This concluded the saga of the recurring false Dmitriys. Although rumours of fresh Dmitriys still emerged from time to time, and having succeeded his father, the Polish King Władysław subsidised a certain 'Ivan Dmitriyevich' until 1634, no more false Dmitriy would wield power in Muscovy.[14]

13　Dunning, *Russia's First Civil War*, p.433.
14　Dunning, *Russia's First Civil War*, p.453.

18

Gustavus Adolphus, Tsar of Muscovy

In Sweden, the Muscovite offer of the throne and the Treaty of Novgorod became subject to careful deliberation between Gustavus Adolphus, Axel Oxenstierna, and the Council of the Realm. Oxenstierna argued that whichever decision they took on the offer, it must first and foremost favour Swedish interests. A union with Muscovy would enhance Sweden's position vis-à-vis the Commonwealth. Moreover, the offer from Muscovy could not really be refused, since this would constitute an insult and might upset the delicate balance of power between Sweden, the Commonwealth, and Muscovy. Yet, Charles Philip was already Duke of Södermanland, Närke and Värmland, and history had shown that it was not always advantageous for Sweden to send a ruler with large, personal lands in the country to gain a kingdom abroad. After all, this was how all the trouble with King Sigismund had started. If Charles Philip founded a new dynasty in Moscow, nobody knew, in the case of a future war between Muscovy and Sweden, whether his heirs and their possessions in Sweden then might jeopardise the internal security of the homeland.

Ultimately, there was only one solution to the matter. On 10 January 1612, Gustavus Adolphus accepted the offer of the Muscovite throne for himself, assumed the title Tsar, and ordered free trade with Novgorod, since the territory now was a Swedish dominion. He signed letters to this extent, addressed to the Governor, Metropolitan, and Estates of Novgorod. He also signed a number of land grants in Novgorod, in his new role as Tsar of Muscovy. Indeed, surviving Novgorod land grants from this year show that Gustavus Adolphus then used the title of Tsar.[1]

---

1   Gustavus Adolphus to Novgorod, 10 January 1612; cited in Generalstaben, *Sveriges krig* 1, pp.377, 407; Elisabeth Löfstrand and Laila Nordquist, *Accounts of an Occupied City: Catalogue of the Novgorod Occupation Archives 1611–1617*, Vol. 2 (Stockholm: Riksarkivet, 2 vols, 2005 and 2009), p.41.

SWEDEN'S WAR IN MUSCOVY 1609-1617

Gustavus Adolphus, 1616.

The decision to accept the offer and assume the eastern throne was genuine. Despite the ongoing Kalmar War, Gustavus Adolphus on 26 May went so far as to ask his cousin, Duke John of Östergötland (1589–1618), to assume command in the war against Denmark and Norway, so that he could sail to Finland and then cross the border into Muscovy to lead the war there, as Tsar of Muscovy or at least sovereign of Novgorod.[2] However, within days Gustavus Adolphus learned that both Elfsborg and Gullberg Castles had fallen to the Danes. These were Sweden's most important strongholds on the west coast. Meanwhile, the Danish fleet dominated the southern Baltic Sea, and two Danish armies stood on Swedish soil, one in the west and the other in the east. Gustavus Adolphus decided that he must postpone the voyage to the eastern front. He would not gamble the homeland for the chance to gain Muscovy.

From the viewpoint of Stockholm, the Swedish King's decision to accept the Tsardom for himself was logical and eminently rational. However, from an eastern perspective, his decision sounded ominous. Was not this exactly what King Sigismund had done two years ago, when envoys from Tushino offered the then still-occupied throne of Muscovy to his son? King Sigismund had accepted the offer, appointed his son Tsar of Muscovy, but then retained all power in his own hands, clearly intending to unite Muscovy with his own lands. When learning of the Swedish King's decision, De la Gardie found himself in the uncomfortable position of sharing the viewpoint of his Muscovite subordinates. Surely, it would be better to send Charles Philip instead? De la Gardie wrote back to Gustavus Adolphus, explaining his and the Novgorodians' concerns. So did the Novgorodians. They asked that the King must not abandon them 'as orphans' but soon send Charles Philip as Tsar.[3]

Then a letter from Gustavus Adolphus dated 19 February 1612 reached De la Gardie in Novgorod: it hinted that the King actually might send Charles Philip to rule Muscovy, after all.[4] In Novgorod, the notables grasped at this promise, an interpretation which would affect events both there, and yet more importantly further afield – in Moscow.

Gustavus Adolphus, c. 1616. (Gold medal, dated to 1614–1618, Gustavianum, Uppsala)

---

2   Henrik Horn to Duke John, 26 May 1612; Gustavus Adolphus to Duke John, 30 May 1612; both cited in Petri, *Kungl. Första livgrenadjärregementets historia* 1, pp.397–8.

3   De la Gardie to Gustavus Adolphus, 22 April 1612; De la Gardie to Axel Oxenstierna, 22 April 1612; Novgorod to Gustavus Adolphus, 24 April 1612; all cited in Generalstaben, *Sveriges krig* 1, p.379.

4   Gustavus Adolphus to De la Gardie and Evert Horn, 19 February 1612; cited in Generalstaben, *Sveriges krig* 1, p.378.

The Second National Militia

Southern Muscovy was in complete disorder. Northern Muscovy was overrun by marauders, some from the Commonwealth, others from the cossack hosts. Because of the continuous turmoil caused by cossacks and other former rebels, many merchants saw the need to form a new national militia. The calls from Patriarch Hermogenes legitimated the plans. The prime mover of the undertaking was a wealthy merchant known as Kuz'ma Minin, who in autumn 1611 had already begun to gather funds for the endeavour. Although Minin made his fortune as a meat wholesaler in Nizhniy Novgorod, he was a close associate of Prince Dmitriy Pozharskiy. Minin was not necessarily low-born, ultimately commanded noble cavalry in battle, and it has been suggested that he was a recently baptised Tatar.[5]

The result was a new national militia. Headed by Prince Pozharskiy with Minin as treasurer and financial guarantor, the army at first consisted of volunteers from Nizhniy Novgorod. The town had about 8,000 inhabitants, a garrison of 500 streltsy, and maintained profitable mercantile links with most other towns on the Volga, in central and northern Muscovy, and in Siberia.[6] As a result, Nizhniy Novgorod wielded considerable influence. Soon, funds and contingents arrived also from Kazan', Kolomna, Ryazan', and other towns. The new army set out from Nizhniy Novgorod in February 1612, bound for Moscow. For merchants, nobles, and hereditary servicemen, the second national militia offered hope. Some even saw it as their last and best hope of gaining security from the cossack faction, which following the murder of Lyapunov had profited greatly from the anarchy and whose commanders did not hesitate to take full advantage of the situation. There was every reason to believe that unless some level

---

5   Vladimir Leonidovich Makhnach, 'Igo lzheumstvovaniya', *Zolotoy Lev* 61–62, 2001 (<www.zlev.ru>); interview with Vladimir Makhnach, 'Nichego ne bylo', *Ogonyok* 30 (July 2002). The hypothesis of Minin's Tatar background is disputed. Aleksey Vladimirovich Morokhin and Andrey Aleksandrovich Kuznetsov, 'Kuz'ma Minin: Fakty i legendy', *Smutnoye vremya v Rossii: Konflikt i dialog kul'tur* (St Petersburg: Trudy Istoricheskogo fakul'teta Sankt-Peterburgskogo universiteta, 2012; <http://cyberleninka.ru/article/n/kuzma-minin-fakty-i-legendy>), pp.207–11. Whilst the Tatar background hypothesis upset the later, but now traditional, image of the second territorial army as a national Slavic movement, no seventeenth-century observer would have been surprised to find large contingents of Tatars and other non-Slavs in a Muscovite army. In modern-day Russia, the hypothesis of Minin's Tatar background upset Slavic nationalists and soccer hooligans to the extent that President Vladimir Putin in 2010 personally stepped in to rebuke a group of soccer club supporters. He told them that nationalism had no place in a soccer stadium, that throughout history non-Slavs contributed significantly to Russia, and that Minin's Tatar background was not an issue. He also cautioned them that relations in a multi-ethnic state such as Russia must be based on mutual respect. 'Vladimir Putin vstretilsya s futbol'nymi bolel'shchikami', *Sportcom*, 21 December 2010 (<www.sportcom.ru/portal/2010/12/21/74572.html>).

6   Dunning, *Russia's First Civil War*, p.416.

of unity could be achieved against the cossacks, the chaos would merely continue indefinitely. In comparison with the anarchic cossack leadership, the council of war of the second national militia increasingly began to play the role of a national assembly.

The army was diverted on its way to Moscow, when Prince Pozharskiy and Minin heard of a cossack detachment on the way to threaten Yaroslavl', which held an important strategic position, controlling the routes of communication between central and northern Muscovy. The northern lands supplied the new national militia with funding, clothing, and weapons, so the town was of key importance. In early April 1612, the army deployed at Yaroslavl', which for the following four months functioned as its headquarters.

Pozharskiy and Minin strongly denounced the cossack faction for acknowledging the false Dmitriy. They also denounced the Polish tsar-elect Władysław and Maryna's baby son Ivan, whom some, in particular Zarutskiy, already regarded as a potential candidate to the throne. Instead, they called for representatives of the nobility, hereditary servicemen, and northern towns to meet in Yaroslavl' for a formal national assembly (*Zemskiy sobor*) and to establish a provisional government. Pozharskiy and Minin promised to continue the struggle against both Commonwealth invasion armies and bandits, which everybody knew meant the marauding cossacks. Significantly, Pozharskiy and Minin did not mention the Swedes among the national militia's – and in extension the country's – enemies.

In mid May Prince Pozharskiy, Minin, and the representatives of the national assembly sent a delegation to Novgorod with letters to the Metropolitan Isidore, Prince Odoyevskiy, and De la Gardie. They requested further information on the Treaty of Novgorod and informed them that the national assembly would acknowledge and support the election of a Swedish prince as tsar. The letter to De la Gardie included a request from the national assembly for permission to send emissaries to negotiate with him, and with Stockholm if required, about the election of a Swedish prince as tsar.[7]

Metropolitan Isidore and Prince Odoyevskiy informed the emissaries about the treaty, and also pointed out that De la Gardie had followed the agreement to the letter. Because Gustavus Adolphus now was King of Sweden and could not abandon his kingdom, they instead asked for his younger brother Charles Philip. They explained that Charles Philip did not need to convert to the Orthodox faith, as long as he promised to respect the faith and privileges of his new subjects. De la Gardie, in turn, informed the emissaries that Gustavus Adolphus certainly was willing to take Muscovy under his protection, that he would not infringe upon the faith and customs of the Muscovites, and that he surely would send his brother to Muscovy, as

---

7   Helge Almquist, 'Tsarvalet år 1613: Karl Filip och Mikael Romanov', *Historiska studier tillägnade Prof. Harald Hjärne på hans sextioårsdag den 2 maj 1908* (Uppsala: Almqvist & Wiksell, 1908), pp.197–224, on 204.

soon as the Muscovite emissaries requested this to himself, Duke Charles Philip, and their mother the Queen Dowager, Christina of Holstein-Gottorp. De la Gardie also forwarded the documents of the national assembly to Stockholm.[8]

It is thus clear that the national assembly in May and June seriously considered a Swedish candidate to the throne, as agreed in the Treaty of Novgorod, and also engaged in negotiations to further this cause. Presumably, they thought the Swedish option the best to safeguard their interests, restore order, and protect the country from yet more Commonwealth designs.

On 26 July, envoys from Novgorod advocated the election of a Swedish tsar to Prince Pozharskiy and the national assembly's council of war. They pointed out that the late King Charles of Sweden had given his blessing to Duke Charles Philip as future tsar, and Gustavus Adolphus was now king. Both Gustavus Adolphus and the Queen Dowager had approved the election. Charles Philip was surely already on the way to Novgorod, or was already there, if he had not stayed in Viborg. The envoys also reminded them that the first national militia already a year ago had elected a Swedish prince as tsar and drawn up the fundamental plans for his rule.

Based on the protocol of the meeting in Yaroslavl', Prince Pozharskiy was at first cautious about the Swedish project. He worried that Stockholm would act as treacherously as Warsaw, that is, only going forth with the project as a pretext and means to annex more Muscovite territory. He also wondered why Charles Philip had not gone to Novgorod earlier. After all, a year had passed since the Treaty of Novgorod. The envoys from Novgorod explained that Charles Philip had already been on the way to Muscovy when he heard of his father's death. Naturally, he must return home for the royal funeral. And then, he had to participate in the war with Denmark, which logically had taken priority. But lately both the King and the Queen Dowager had approved the voyage to Muscovy, and he was expected in Viborg in late June.

Again based on the preserved protocol, Pozharskiy declared himself satisfied with these explanations, and would send emissaries to Novgorod as soon as Charles Philip had arrived and converted to the Orthodox faith. He would not risk sending a delegation to Stockholm, since the previous Muscovite delegation sent abroad, to King Sigismund of Poland, had been imprisoned there upon arrival. Moreover, the national assembly responded to Novgorod that they stood behind the decision (of 23 June 1611) of the first national militia about the election of a son of the Swedish king as tsar. They pointed out, however, that Muscovy needed a tsar, and if Charles Philip had not showed up before the end of the summer, this might cause problems. Until then, they agreed to unite against the Commonwealth invaders and promote trade between Novgorod, Yaroslavl', and the rest of Muscovy.[9]

---

8   Almquist, 'Tsarvalet', p.205; with references.
9   Almquist, 'Tsarvalet', pp.207–8; with references.

The envoys from Novgorod had exaggerated on certain aspects of the agreement with Sweden, most importantly with regard to the whereabouts of Charles Philip. The young duke was barely 11 years old, and his mother Christina was reluctant to send him unprotected into the rough politics of Muscovy. Charles Philip had not yet set out from home.

The cossack faction of the original national militia under Prince Trubetskoy and Zarutskiy found the emergence of the second national militia greatly disturbing. They could hardly welcome the decision taken in Yaroslavl' and Novgorod to respect the election of a Swedish tsar. Prince Trubetskoy and Zarutskiy realised that Prince Pozharskiy and Minin, in alliance with Novgorod and its Swedish principal, posed a threat to cossack liberties just as great as the threat they posed against Commonwealth interests in Muscovy.

However, a Commonwealth army of about 2,000 men under Hetman Chodkiewicz was marching on Moscow, and Prince Trubetskoy and Zarutskiy needed the support of the second national militia. In early August, Prince Pozharskiy advanced on Moscow with his national militia to counter Chodkiewicz. The Prince refused to join forces with the cossack faction, unless it first deposed Zarutskiy from his leadership position and, moreover, took him into custody. In late June, two cossacks had attempted to murder Prince Pozharskiy, and when interrogated, they had claimed to act upon orders from Zarutskiy. Prince Pozharskiy also made sure to explain to De la Gardie that while the national assembly of nobles, hereditary servicemen, and merchants stood behind Charles Philip, the cossack faction remained hostile to the idea, since they preferred a weak central government. On 23 August, De la Gardie again wrote to Stockholm, underlining the urgent need to send Charles Philip to Novgorod. He emphasised that the arrival of Charles Philip would by itself give the Swedish prince northwestern Muscovy, and moreover, prevent the formation of a pro-Commonwealth faction in Moscow.[10] The letter arrived at a time when skirmishes between Danish and Swedish warships had just taken place in the Stockholm archipelago, so perhaps unsurprisingly, the government in Stockholm did not immediately prioritise De la Gardie's suggestion.

Prince Pozharskiy's demand to take Zarutskiy into custody came at a bad time for the cossack ataman; simultaneously, many cossacks had begun to suspect him of collusion with Chodkiewicz. To save himself, Zarutskiy and his 2,000 supporters withdrew to Kolomna, where Maryna and her baby boy Ivan waited.

On around 20 August, Princes Pozharskiy and Trubetskoy arrived with their respective armies at Moscow. Faced with an imminent attack by Chodkiewicz, the two princes agreed to cooperate, urged to this decision by the monks of the Holy Trinity-St Sergius Monastery.

Prince Pozharskiy on 22–24 August repulsed Chodkiewicz's army. He attributed the victory to a famous icon, Our Lady of Kazan', which he

---

10   Almquist, 'Tsarvalet', pp.211–12; with references.

carried with his personal baggage. Perhaps the Lady really assisted Prince Pozharskiy, because Prince Trubetskoy chose to hold back in the battle, even though some of his men participated on their own initiative. The failure of Chodkiewicz's relief expedition doomed the besieged Commonwealth garrison in the Moscow Kremlin.

When Sigismund learnt of the failure of Chodkiewicz at Moscow, he personally marched towards Moscow with his son and a relief army, but was unable to get there in time. His men were in no hurry, since they were poorly paid. The King's army reached Vyaz'ma and Volokolamsk, but with winter approaching, Sigismund ordered a retreat back towards Smolensk. This time, the Muscovites refused to negotiate with him.

By October, the besieged Commonwealth garrison in the Moscow Kremlin no longer had either the means or the will to continue the struggle. In June 1612, Gosiewski had handed over command to Mikołaj Struś (1577–1627). On 26 October 1612, Struś surrendered to Princes Pozharskiy and Trubetskoy.[11]

In early November, the national militia called for towns and communities to send representatives for a continued national assembly meeting in Moscow on 5 December for the formal election of a tsar. However, King Sigismund's offensive delayed the arrival of many representatives, so the meeting had to be postponed.

By the end of November, the adherents of Prince Pozharskiy still expressed their continued support for Charles Philip as Tsar. Meanwhile, De la Gardie eagerly waited for confirmation from Stockholm that Charles Philip was on the way. On 26 December 1612, he finally received the communication that the boy would be in Viborg before the end of February 1613. De la Gardie immediately sent a representative to Moscow with the good news. However, he found it prudent not to tell Moscow about the instruction from Stockholm to make sure that Muscovy also ceded the long-promised lands that Sweden wanted.[12]

---

11 Having left Moscow, Gosiewski assumed command of Commonwealth units in the region between Smolensk, Toropets, Belaya, and Vyaz'ma. Even after the surrender of the Commonwealth garrison in the Kremlin, a significant number of Commonwealth units remained all over western Muscovy, where they lived off the land. In 1613, Gosiewski accordingly remained a latent threat to the Swedish presence in Novgorod.
12 Almquist, 'Tsarvalet', pp.215–16; with references.

19

The Rise of the House of Romanov

The postponement of the national assembly meeting enabled some notables to begin the promotion of a 16-year-old noble named Michael Romanov for the election of a tsar of Muscovy. Young Michael probably appeared a pliable choice, for reasons of his youth, his family link to the old dynasty, and most importantly, lack of a personal power base, not least because his father Filaret was in Commonwealth captivity. The family link made young Michael particularly attractive to the clergy, who regarded him as a guarantor for the supreme role of the Church. Other candidates emerged as well, not least Prince Trubetskoy, the powerful leader of the cossack faction, but the other notables distrusted him for this very reason.

Most representatives reached Moscow in January 1613. Prince Pozharskiy argued for the election of Charles Philip. He pointed out what everybody already knew, namely, that the raising to the throne of all recent native tsars had resulted in civil strife and, moreover, they had patently been unable to prevent the country's numerous calamities. However, a Swedish tsar would bring stability and enable a unified response to Commonwealth aggression, not least since Sweden, too, was at war with the Commonwealth. But there were other concerns, he noted. If the Swedish candidate was rejected, then Sweden would join Muscovy's enemies and the result would likely be war with both the Commonwealth and Sweden. Moreover, a rejection of Charles Philip would also jeopardise the reunification of Novgorod with the rest of Muscovy. Based on such arguments, the national assembly agreed that it would be inadvisable to elect a native tsar.[1]

On 7 February 1613, the national assembly agreed in principle that a foreign tsar was the best choice. However, the actual election was postponed until the end of the month.[2] In short, the national assembly desired that Charles Philip actually arrived in Muscovy before he was formally elected. This cautious attitude was hardly surprising, in particular in light of the

---

1   Almquist, 'Tsarvalet', pp.216–17; with references.
2   Almquist, 'Tsarvalet', p.218; with references.

promise from Stockholm that Charles Philip would be in Viborg before the end of February – from which he easily could enter Muscovite soil.

However, this display of caution also inadvertently offered the cossack faction more time to act. Both sides sent emissaries to the various towns to broadcast their particular choice of candidate and the reasons therefore. The cossack party enjoyed the support of most of the clergy, including the influential monks at the Holy Trinity-St Sergius Monastery, who loathed anybody who did not follow the Orthodox faith which in extension meant all foreigners, regardless of background.

Yet, the cossack faction soon realised that agitation was not enough. Charles Philip might show up at the border any day, and then the national assembly could be expected to elect the Swedish candidate as the country's new tsar. Surely, the hated foreigner would put an end to traditional cossack liberties, and he might very well bring an army of foreign soldiers to enforce the peace. Now was the time for resolute action.

Soon, bands of cossacks began to engage in violent protests. They threatened members of the national assembly, attacked the residences of not only Prince Pozharskiy but also, for good measure, their own leader of sorts, Prince Trubetskoy, whom the cossacks now increasingly suspected of fraternisation with other nobles in support of the Swedish tsar.[3] Finally, armed cossacks even fought their way into the meeting hall of the national assembly in the Kremlin, vowing that they would not leave until young Michael Romanov was elected. In the middle of this tumult, the national assembly on 21 February 1613 fearfully agreed to elect Michael Romanov their new tsar. To ensure that nobody contested the will of the cossack faction, the decision was hurriedly copied in numerous communications that were dispatched to the various towns. It was a coup, not an election. Significantly, neither Prince Pozharskiy, the now increasingly sidelined Prince Trubetskoy, or the generally respected Prince Mstislavskiy – who was the actual chairman of the national assembly – spoke out in support of the decision, nor did they sign the decree. Instead, the decision was announced by Metropolitan Kirill of Rostov and Yaroslavl', who presented it as a unanimous decision under the eyes of God which finally would liberate the true believers from the accursed plague of heathens. For the first time during the war, the kings of Sweden and Poland were both described as enemies of the Orthodox faith.[4]

The cossacks and clergy had successfully pushed through the election of Michael Romanov, but they had not yet persuaded the young man and his family to accept the honour. On 2 March, they sent a mission to Kostroma to persuade young Michael and his mother, Marfa Ivanovna. Neither Prince Pozharskiy, Minin, Prince Trubetskoy nor any other leader of their factions joined, or were permitted to join, the mission. Instead, they were for a while

---

3   De la Gardie to Gustavus Adolphus, 13 April 1613; cited in Almquist, 'Tsarvalet', p.219.
4   Almquist, 'Tsarvalet', pp.219–20; with references.

put under house arrest in Moscow. Moreover, neither young Michael nor his mother wanted to accept the election. Marfa Ivanovna had presumably heard of the coup in the national assembly and must have feared to allow her son to be pushed into the murderous strife that for the last few years had characterised political life in the capital. There was also the risk that King Sigismund would take revenge on Filaret, Michael's father, if Filaret's son assumed the throne that the Polish king had wanted for himself or his son. Yet, the envoys did not take no for an answer, or tolerate any delay. According to intelligence that De la Gardie later reported to Gustavus Adolphus, the cossacks went so far as to use force in an attempt to abduct the elected tsar and bring him to Moscow.[5]

As a result, the armed might of the cossack delegates and the God-fearing exhortations of the clergy ultimately persuaded Marfa Ivanovna and her son to accept the election. On 14 March, they were ready to set out towards Moscow. Obviously still cautious, they chose a circuitous route that first took them to Yaroslavl'. Prince Pozharskiy and his faction had been outmanoeuvred, but they retained considerable influence. It seems very likely that the detour to Yaroslavl' included meetings during which Princes Pozharskiy, Mstislavskiy, and others agreed to give guarantees for the personal safety of the Romanovs – and also receive guarantees that Michael, as tsar, would not allow the cossack faction to take vengeance against their noble opponents.[6]

By early April, the boyars had indeed recovered some of their traditional power, and Prince Mstislavskiy entered into negotiations with young Michael and the Romanov family. Soon afterwards, Princes Pozharskiy and Trubetskoy formally submitted to Tsar Michael. By then, the parties had negotiated mutual security assurances, and the senior nobles knew that a formal submission would not bring any negative repercussions on themselves. The relief was presumably mutual, because only then, on 2 May, did Tsar Michael finally dare to enter his capital. Formal documents on the election were drawn up so as to legitimise the new tsar. His election was now made to appear as the inevitable outcome of the national assembly's deep desire to elect a member of the old nobility of the Orthodox faith. To add yet more legitimacy to the decision, and as a means to counter the anticipated Swedish protests, those who drew up the documents included references to the advice of the late Swedish King Charles, who once had written to the nobility that they should not elect a Polish prince but instead find a native ruler.[7]

However, the formal announcement of Tsar Michael's election was postponed for some time, in the futile hope that his father Filaret first would be released from Commonwealth captivity. When this outcome no

---

5   De la Gardie to Gustavus Adolphus, 13 April 1613; cited in Almquist, 'Tsarvalet', p.220.
6   Almquist, 'Tsarvalet', p.221; with references.
7   Almquist, 'Tsarvalet', p.222; with references.

THE RISE OF THE HOUSE OF ROMANOV

longer seemed likely, the coronation took place in an elaborate ceremony on 11 July. Princes Pozharskiy, Mstislavskiy, and Trubetskoy attended the ceremony, but received no tangible rewards for their efforts in gathering the national assembly that ultimately had elected Tsar Michael.[8] It must have been obvious to the participants that even though all parties upheld the peace, there was little trust between the various factions and their representatives. As a deliberate and probably necessary policy to ensure national stability, Muscovite historians gradually set out to produce a sanitised version of recent events around which all parties could unite. The story of the events that led to election of the first tsar of the House of Romanov thus transformed into a romanticised fiction, which greatly affected subsequent Russian historiography and in extension, much of traditional Western historiography. The new story focused on national unity and downplayed existing divisions and rivalries, including Muscovite support to alternative candidates to the throne. As the real events show, the election of Tsar Michael was the result of a coup, not well-intentioned deliberations among patriots who only had in mind the best interests of the country.[9]

Prince Dmitriy Pozharskiy in his later years, as depicted in an engraving based on a near-contemporary painting of the coronation of Tsar Michael Romanov.

Even so, the ascension of Michael to the throne ultimately brought stability to Muscovy. Peace did not come overnight, nor without further atrocities. A number of former rebels and potential political opponents never reconciled themselves with the new regime, and they were hunted down without mercy. Among them was Maryna Mniszchówna, the wife of two false Dmitriys. Having delivered the baby boy Ivan, we have seen that Maryna took refuge with cossack leader Ivan Zarutskiy, who seems to have entertained ambitions to gain the throne for himself. He accordingly took baby Ivan under his protection. Zarutskiy's primary motive was probably to employ Maryna and the baby as tools to increase his own power. Yet, Zarutskiy may ultimately have grown fond of Maryna and the boy (whom some claimed was his son). Be that as it may, Zarutskiy's ambition was enough of a threat for the uncompromising Patriarch Hermogenes to denounce both the cossack ataman and baby Ivan as traitors and demand their death. In June 1614 the entire family was captured by government soldiers (under Ivan Odoyevskiy the Younger, brother of Novgorod's able governor Ivan Odoyevskiy the Elder) and brought to Moscow. The time of the False Dmitriys was over, and the new regime, supported by the Church, wanted to make an example to the public.

---

8   Almquist, 'Tsarvalet', p.223; with references.
9   On how this affected traditional interpretation of the Swedish candidacy, see Almquist, 'Tsarvalet', p.223. See also Alexej Smirnov, *Den svenske tsaren* (Stockholm: Karneval, 2017), pp.176–81, 209–10.

First, the executioners killed Zarutskiy by impaling him on a stake. Then, in possibly the most heinous act of cruelty during the entire Time of Troubles, the government hanged the three-year-old baby Ivan in public. Officials of the new regime argued, from their perspective possibly correctly, that baby Ivan had to die a public death to pre-empt future pretenders. Maryna died in prison a few months later, from grief or poison or a combination thereof.

Gustavus Adolphus and Charles Philip

Denmark and Sweden finally concluded a peace treaty in January 1613. Taking the advice of his chancellor, Axel Oxenstierna, Gustavus Adolphus accepted harsh terms to gain time to reform his country and resolve the campaigns in the east. There, the most urgent problem was the ongoing campaign in Muscovy.

On 18 March 1613, De la Gardie in a letter advised Gustavus Adolphus to hasten Charles Philip's voyage to Muscovy but also reinforce the Swedish armies there with units from the concluded Kalmar War. In light of the recent election of Michael Romanov, De la Gardie also advised the King to hasten the consolidation of such territories in Muscovy that Sweden had already gained, and by conquest increase them all the way to the Arctic coast. Moreover, he advised Gustavus Adolphus that it would be beneficial to enter into an alliance with the Commonwealth and divide western Muscovy between himself and King Sigismund.[10] With regard to the Arctic plan, so beloved by the late King Charles, De la Gardie had no way of knowing that Gustavus Adolphus, in light of the Treaty of Knäred which just had concluded the Kalmar War with Denmark, had abandoned it as unrealistic.

Having sent this well-intentioned advice to Gustavus Adolphus, De la Gardie's personal position was suddenly complicated by a Polish plot. Unexpectedly, he received a letter from King Sigismund, in which the Polish king wrote that Hetman Chodkiewicz had informed him that De la Gardie was willing to switch sides, and that Sigismund not only would allow De la Gardie to retain his present position but also give him generous rewards.[11] The letter was delivered by an emissary of the aforementioned Gosiewski, who on 11 March 1613 forwarded it to De la Gardie. Gosiewski argued that he and De la Gardie were in the same position, alone and vulnerable in a hostile foreign country, so they really should help each other.

Regardless of whether Chodkiewicz had lied to King Sigismund about De la Gardie's response to a failed attempt to turn him, or whether a devious Sigismund wrote a letter with this content in a deliberate attempt

---

10   De la Gardie to Gustavus Adolphus, 18 March 1613; cited in Generalstaben, *Sveriges krig* 1, p.415.
11   Sigismund to De la Gardie, 18 December 1612 (O.S.); cited in Generalstaben, *Sveriges krig* 1, pp.415–16.

THE RISE OF THE HOUSE OF ROMANOV

to undermine De la Gardie's position, the Swedish commander had little choice but to send the entire correspondence to Gustavus Adolphus and Chancellor Oxenstierna together with a message that he was innocent of the Polish king's insinuations.[12]

Yet, De la Gardie also had to safeguard the Swedish position in Novgorod. He contacted Gosiewski, explained that he could not without his King's decision enter into an alliance, but he suggested a local truce, which was beneficial for both parties.

Fortunately for De la Gardie, Gustavus Adolphus was not his father King Charles. Having received the various letters and reports, Gustavus Adolphus replied to De la Gardie that he did not doubt his loyalty. However, he was against any plans for 'an uncertain and false armistice' with the Commonwealth, since this only would make the Muscovites yet more suspicious.[13]

The correspondence did not change the fact that Gustavus Adolphus still intended to send his brother Charles Philip to Viborg and then Novgorod. As late as November 1612, the King had again suggested his own name for the tsardom of Muscovy, but this idea was not well received in Sweden. On 29 April 1613, Gustavus Adolphus admitted to De la Gardie that the latter was correct in suggesting Charles Philip as Tsar, and that Gustavus

The pinnace was a small full-rigged ship of a type that later would develop into the frigate, and accordingly could fulfil a number of roles for which larger warships were unsuitable. Although this pinnace, in the port of Wismar, is the Commonwealth ship *King David*, Swedish pinnaces were identical. The crew has taken down the main yard and are bending (tying) on the mainsail.

---

12 De la Gardie to Gustavus Adolphus, 21 March 1613; cited in Generalstaben, *Sveriges krig* 1, p.416. De la Gardie's correspondence was dispatched with the aforementioned Göran Brynno, who had by then been released from custody in Moscow and was now on the way back to Sweden.
13 Gustavus Adolphus to De la Gardie, 28 April 1613, 29 April 1613; cited in Generalstaben, *Sveriges krig* 1, p.417.

Adolphus's decision to take the throne for himself had been hasty and resulted from ignorance of the situation.¹⁴

On 18 June 1613, Charles Philip finally set out by sea from Stockholm, bound for Viborg. He sailed protected by a fleet of four warships and a pinnace under Admiral Hans Claesson Bielkenstierna. Hampered by contrary winds, it took until 9 July before Charles Philip reached Viborg.

Prince Cherkasskiy Strikes Back

By then, relations between the Muscovites and Swedes were deteriorating rapidly.

In May 1613, Prince Dmitriy Cherkasskiy led some of Tsar Michael's men in an offensive aimed as much against the Swedes in northwestern Muscovy as the Commonwealth army at Smolensk. Since the Swedes were geographically closer, most fighting took place with them. An initial Muscovite army, by the Swedes estimated as 6,000 men, moved into a fortified camp at Ust'reka. The major part of Prince Cherkasskiy's army consisted of Moscow's recently formed cossack units, since few other soldiers were available. A small corps of an estimated 500 cossacks appeared somewhat later around Staraya Russa.¹⁵

Most of the Swedish army still remained in Sweden itself, because of the recently concluded Kalmar War. It accordingly took time before reinforcements reached De la Gardie, who had few men at his disposal,¹⁶ and having to retain strong units to defend Novgorod, he could only raise a field army of 1,000 men. He also lacked funds to continue the war, and had to take personal loans and even pawn some of his cannons to raise cash for the most essential expenses.

De la Gardie in late May accordingly enlisted a Commonwealth colonel, Sidor, who commanded eight banners of cavalry, altogether from 1,500 to 2,000 men as the Swedes estimated his strength. De la Gardie ordered Robert Moore, with a detached corps of 1,000 soldiers, and Sidor to advance against the Muscovites at Ust'reka. However, they failed to disrupt the Muscovite army and withdrew to Belaya.¹⁷

As a result, both Tikhvin and Gdov rose against Swedish rule. At Tikhvin, a combined force of townsmen under Abbot Onufriy, cavalrymen and at least two companies of streltsy originally from Ivangorod, Nöteborg, and Ladoga Town under Andrey Grigor'yevich Trusov, and from 400 to 700 cossacks from Ust'reka under Dmitriy Bayimovich Voyeykov in May surprised the local commandant, Jean De la Combe (known to the Muscovites as Ivan Lakumbov) and the Swedish garrison of 120 men. In

---

14   Gustavus Adolphus to De la Gardie, 29 April 1613.
15   Generalstaben, *Sveriges krig* 1, pp.431, 435.
16   The details are presented in Generalstaben, *Sveriges krig* 1, pp.432–5.
17   Generalstaben, *Sveriges krig* 1, p.434.

light of the difference in numbers, the outcome was inevitable. The attackers killed 60 Swedish soldiers, and captured the survivors. De la Combe, his wife, and a few Swedes barricaded themselves in the commandant's house. They repelled several attacks, but when the attackers brought cannons to destroy the building, were forced to evacuate it. De la Combe and his wife were soon captured as they attempted to escape across the roof. Voyeykov sent them to Moscow as prisoners.

Gdov, too, fell to a combination of rising townsmen and external force, this time from nearby Pskov. The Swedish commandant, Wolmar von Ungern, suppressed a first rising in May. Ungern had no more than a Swedish company of foot from Jämtland at his disposal, so De la Gardie detached a Finnish company of 150 soldiers as well. Nonetheless, in early June the Pskov Army made a second attempt, and this time they conquered Gdov, reportedly because the Jämtland company abandoned the town. Cornered, Ungern surrendered. He, too, ended up in Muscovite captivity.[18]

Porkhov, too, rose against Swedish rule. However, Swedish units quickly suppressed the rebellion and regained the town.

In comparison, the cossacks at Staraya Russa proved no problem. A composite Swedish–Novgorodian corps from Staraya Russa, under Horn and Prince Fyodor Chornyy-Obolenskiy, which included 300 Novgorodian cavalry including many newly baptised Tatars, drove them away in late July.

---

18   Generalstaben, *Sveriges krig* 1, p.434; Smirnov, *Den svenske tsaren*, p.193.

20

The Siege of Tikhvin Monastery

Tikhvin consisted of a town and monastery on the south bank of the River Tikhvinka, and a nunnery on the north bank. Both settlements were fortified. An outer defensive line surrounded both the southern and northern settlements.[1]

Learning about the fall of Tikhvin, De la Gardie immediately sent Robert Moore with a detached corps to retake the town. Moore managed to take the outer areas, but failed to regain the town, monastery, or nunnery. Moore then retreated to Gruzino on the way to Novgorod.

Following Moore's retreat, a large Muscovite contingent from Ust'reka under Prince Semyon Prozorovskiy and his deputy Leontiy Vel'yaminov marched to Tikhvin. The Swedes at first estimated its strength, townsmen levies included, as about 3,000 men. Later, the estimate was reassessed as 1,200 in addition to civilians.[2] Prince Prozorovskiy established a command post in the nunnery, while Vel'yaminov did likewise in the monastery.

De la Gardie made another attempt in early July, when the first reinforcements had finally arrived. He sent Robert Moore, Daniel Hepburn, and Colonel Sidor by way of Gruzino to Tikhvin with possibly 4,000 men (about 2,000 Swedish regulars, Sidor's 1,500 cavalry, perhaps 300 Polish cavalry under Maciej Chalaim, and 300 Novgorodian hereditary servicemen under Prince Nikita Odoyevskiy, the son of Governor Odoyevskiy).[3] Moore's army included artillery. The Muscovites attempted to meet Moore's force as it approached, but were pushed back into Tikhvin.

Not having enough men to surround both the southern and northern settlements at Tikhvin at the same time, the Swedes built two camps, the

---

1   On the siege of Tikhvin Monastery, see Harald Hjärne, 'Utdrag ur ryska krönikor, hufvudsakligen angående Jakob De la Gardies fälttåg', *Historiskt bibliotek* 7 (1879), 208–42; Kurbatov, *Tikhvinskoye osadnoye sideniye*; Generalstaben, *Sveriges krig* 1, 434–8.

2   Generalstaben, *Sveriges krig* 1, 435. Kurbatov, *Tikhvinskoye osadnoye sideniye*, 31, suggests a total of 2, 500 men.

3   Kurbatov, *Tikhvinskoye osadnoye sideniye*, 32.

THE SIEGE OF TIKHVIN MONASTERY

larger one facing the town and the smaller one the nunnery. The Swedish artillery opened up with incendiary bombs fired from gun barrel artillery, possibly mortars.

On 17 July De la Gardie ordered Monickhouen's Regiment, by then newly arrived from Sweden to Björkö (modern-day Primorsk), about 45 km south of Viborg, to march straight to Tikhvin. Samuel Cobron's three possibly understrength cavalry banners joined the reinforcements on the way, probably at Nyen. Monickhouen's Regiment was then under the command of Lieutenant Colonel Paul Bettig, whom we last saw going into Commonwealth service during the battle of Klushino three years earlier. He was now back in Swedish employ. When the regiment arrived at Tikhvin, it only consisted of 900 men (down from 1,148 since the departure from Stockholm). Having arrived at Tikhvin, Bettig assumed command over the siege operation. Altogether, he then reportedly commanded some 1,500 men. It is unclear if Moore's and Sidor's men were included in this total.[4]

Bettig first concentrated his efforts on the nunnery, and after an extended bombardment, he stormed it on 17 August. One of the defenders, a certain Gavrilka Smol'yanin, took the opportunity to switch side with his men; the rest panicked and fled out into the open field, where Bettig's men cut down most of the defenders, reportedly some 700 cossacks. As the nunnery fell, Prince Prozorovskiy and his surviving cossacks fled into the nearby monastery. Prince Matvey, the general's younger brother, fell into Swedish captivity. However, the Swedes lost several experienced and difficult to replace officers. Among them was Bettig, who fell in the struggle, but also the experienced Major Artzian Kurtz (then of the Commanding General's Life Regiment), the skillful petardier who had blown the gate of Novgorod and also handled petards during the assaults on Pskov and other towns. Christer Hansson, captain of the Finnish retinue of nobles fell too, whilst Prince Odoyevskiy was wounded.

Tikhvin had a strong connection with the House of Romanov, so the defenders naturally hoped for assistance from the Muscovite army that slowly assembled at Ustyuzhna further to the east. The original leaders of the uprising, Abbot Onufriy, Trusov, and Voyeykov,

The Tikhvin Entry (Vvedenskiy)of the Mother of God nunnery, as depicted in 1678. The main buildings and outline then remained unchanged since 1613.

---

4   Generalstaben, *Sveriges krig* 1, 437.

accordingly rode east to plead for reinforcements. Prince Prozorovskiy and Vel'yaminov remained behind to lead the defence. A relief force of reportedly some 1,500 cossacks and Tatars under Isay Sunbulov set out for Tikhvin. However, the Swedes learnt from a snatched Muscovite courier that the relief force was approaching, and decisively defeated it east of Tikhvin on 28 August, capturing in the process 22 standards and several notables including Abbot Onufriy. On the same day they also beat back a sally from Tikhvin, which apparently was coordinated with the relief army. Even so, it seems that Prince Prozorovskiy's men managed to take or spike three cannons, including one which they had lost together with the nunnery on 17 August.[5]

The Swedes then focused their activities on the monastery, which was defended by some 800 cossacks. Their modern methods of siege warfare greatly impressed some of the less experienced Muscovites, in fact so much that when, after the siege, the survivors returned home to tell about the experience, nobody believed them. Henceforth, the expression 'towers on wheels' came to signify a brazen lie. The inspiration for the expression is believed to have been one or other of the siege implements employed at Tikhvin. Yet, the monastery was too strongly fortified, and the resident priests were energetic in encouraging the men to fight to the end against the heathen Swedes, not least because the monastery was the home of a holy icon, Our Lady of Tikhvin Mother of God (*Theotokos*). If the church historians can be believed, visions of Our Lady repeatedly appeared before the faithful defenders. On the other hand, the church historians also described an ongoing flow of faithless defectors from the monastery who found it more convenient to switch side than to trust in the holy icon. Nonetheless, neither bombardment with incendiary bombs nor assaults managed to convince the defenders to surrender. The Swedes then tried mining, but without the professional technical expertise of men such as Kurtz, the attempts failed.[6] Moore and Hepburn seemed to be at a loss as to how to continue the operation. Meanwhile, the Swedes suffered shortages of everything from experienced officers to money to pay the men, garments, munitions, and food supplies. Because of the lack of cash, the bulk of Colonel Sidor's cavalry was dismissed, and only the Colonel and 100 men were retained. The rest set out towards the north, aiming for what they hoped would be easier pastures in Olonets, Kholmogory, and perhaps even distant Arkhangel'sk. The now leaderless Monickhouen's Regiment soon began to lose whatever discipline they had once possessed – and when out of Colonel Monickhouen's sight, they had misbehaved already in Sweden – and they lost 200 men in a Muscovite sally, primarily because of their unwillingness to post sentries. In the first half of September, the regiment mutinied. All but 50 men departed to find their fortune – and supplies – elsewhere.

---

5   Generalstaben, *Sveriges krig* 1, 437; Kurbatov, *Tikhvinskoye osadnoye sideniye*, 38.
6   Generalstaben, *Sveriges krig* 1, 438.

THE SIEGE OF TIKHVIN MONASTERY

Seeing little hope in taking Tikhvin under present conditions, in mid September De la Gardie ordered the remaining units there back to Novgorod.

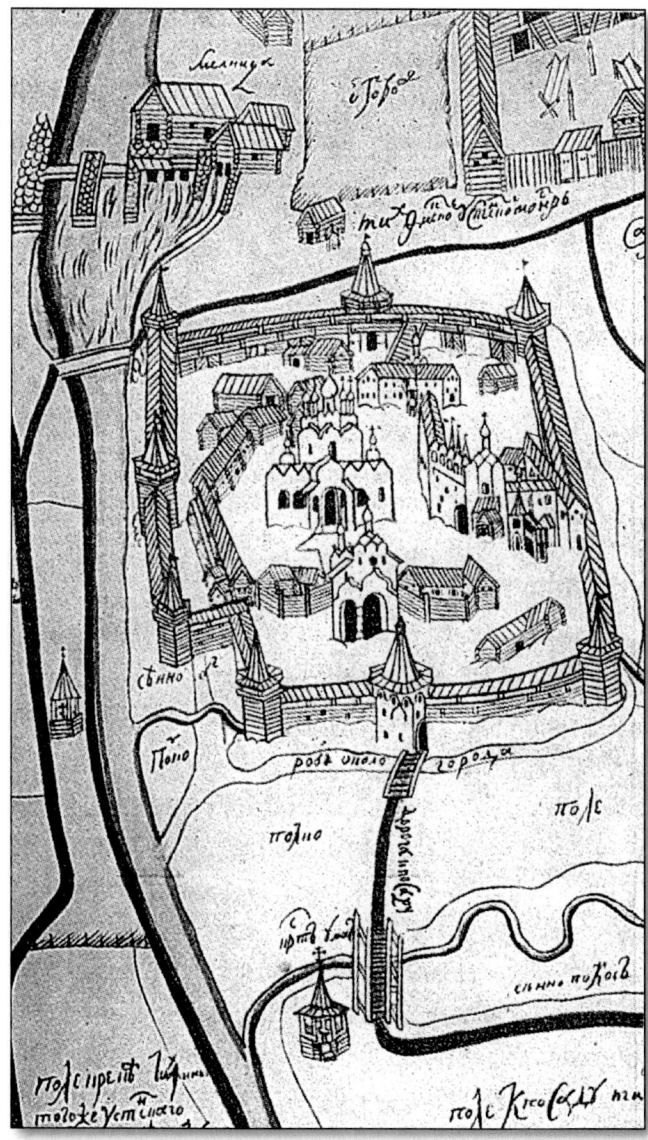

The Tikhvin Assumption (Uspenskiy) of the Mother of God Monastery, as depicted in 1678. The main buildings and outline seen then had remained unchanged since 1613.

SWEDEN'S WAR IN MUSCOVY 1609-1617

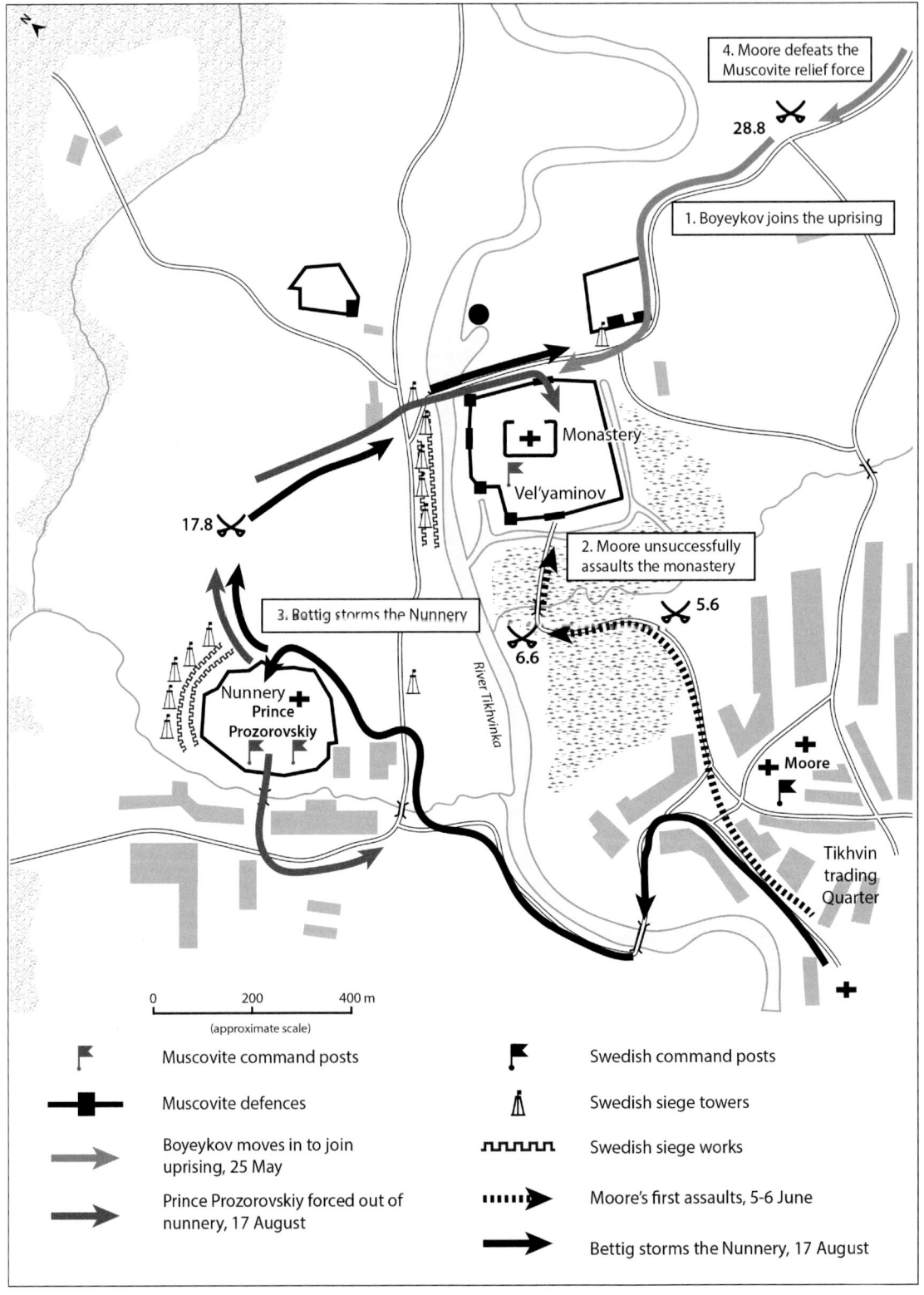

Map 9. The Siege of Tikhvin, 1613.

21

The Siege of Gdov

Then there was Gdov. De la Gardie gave the task of retaking it to Julius Henry, Duke of Saxe-Lauenburg. The Duke had gone into Swedish service with a cavalry banner (presumably harquebusiers), and Gustavus Adolphus had directed him to march to Novgorod with his own banner as well as the Livonian cavalry banners. However, the Duke was a Prince of the Empire and accordingly refused to accept a position subordinate to De la Gardie. A compromise solution had to be found. To appease the Duke's feelings, De la Gardie accordingly sent him to Gdov with an independent command. Ultimately, this was a mistake: the Duke was, in the words of the able Evert Horn, 'young and inexperienced'.[1] Horn was only one year older than Duke Julius Henry, but as we have seen already a veteran soldier with years of active duty behind him.

De la Gardie assigned Cobron's Regiment of Foot of 540 men, a Finnish infantry company of 140 men, and a Novgorodian unit of unknown type and strength to Duke Julius Henry for the siege operation. The Duke also received command of Knut Håkansson Hand's harquebusier banner from Småland, apparently again at full strength of 230 or possibly even 380 horse, Hans Boije's 300 Finnish cavalry, the five Livonian banners of horse, each of which had fewer than 100 men, and six cannons. We can assume that the Duke's own cavalry banner was there as well.

Duke Julius Henry and his army reached Gdov on 21 August. However, the Swedish and Finnish cavalry units were then sent onwards to Novgorod, because De la Gardie needed them to retake a monastery at Staraya Russa, which had been occupied by a force of some 1,000 cossacks. This left the Duke only the Livonian cavalry banners, altogether an estimated 400 horse. He accordingly laid siege with about 680 foot, 400 Livonian horse, an unknown number of Novgorodians, and very likely the Duke's own cavalry banner.[2]

---

1   Horn to De la Gardie, 21 September 1613; 29 September 1613; cited in Generalstaben, *Sveriges krig* 1, pp.432, 439.
2   Generalstaben, *Sveriges krig* 1, pp.432, 439, 440.

The Duke built a single redoubt for his infantry, and then an artillery battery for the bombardment of Gdov, which soon opened up a breach in the town wall. However, he was slow to carry out an assault, so the defenders repaired the wall before one could be organised. Moreover, the Duke put all his cavalry in a separate camp, at some distance to Gdov, and also neglected to maintain cavalry patrols – despite receiving reports that a relief force from Pskov might be on its way. This was a fatal mistake. Soon, 600 Muscovites from the Pskov Army arrived in the Swedish rear, and assaulted the Duke's redoubt at the same time that the defenders of Gdov sallied out. Cobron's Regiment lost some 200 men, abandoned the redoubt, and fled. They abandoned the cannons, too, which were seized by the Pskov Army. The Novgorodian contingent also suffered heavy casualties. The cavalry was too far away to intervene, and the Duke followed the infantry in its flight; the remnants of his Swedish army eventually assembled at Narva and Ivangorod. Contemporaries laid the entire blame for the debacle on Duke Julius Henry, and there is nothing to suggest it should be otherwise.[3]

The only consolation was that Knut Hand's harquebusier banner from Småland and Hans Boije's Finnish cavalry successfully drove the cossacks out of the monastery at Staraya Russa.

Since so far only a few reinforcements from Sweden had arrived, De la Gardie was concerned about whether he would be able to defend Novgorod itself against a determined offensive. Horn was in Narva to receive the promised reinforcements, which meant that De la Gardie also lacked experienced field commanders.

Nonetheless, it was necessary to retake, or at least contain, Gdov. Otherwise, Kaporie, Jama, and Ivangorod were at risk, too, and tax collection in Ingria would become difficult or impossible. De la Gardie could not abandon this source of revenue and supplies since it was necessary to feed his men – and the civilian population in Novgorod under his rule.

He accordingly ordered a new attempt against Gdov. This time, Duke Julius Henry remained in formal command of the operation, but the real commander was Horn, whom De la Gardie recalled from Narva. This laid the ground for a format that henceforth became standard when Imperial princes went into Swedish service: the Imperial prince was put in command, but the Swedish Crown invariably appointed a trusted Swedish deputy commander to assist the prince and, equally important, keep an eye on him.

The siege of Gdov was accordingly resumed in late October by Horn, in effective control, and Duke Julius Henry. The available units were probably those which had taken part in the first siege, together with such reinforcements that had arrived, including a composite regiment under Reinhold Taube and a strong cavalry contingent under De la Ville, both of whom had previously been in Sweden to fight in the Kalmar War. Altogether, Horn and the Duke seem to have led between 800 and 1,000 cavalry and some 1,600 foot, in addition to seven cannons. Yet, soon disaster struck:

---

3   Generalstaben, *Sveriges krig* 1, p.439.

Colonel Taube fell, hit by artillery fire as he leaned over the bulwark to aim a cannon, and so did Lieutenant Colonel Patrick Learmonth, one of Taube's company commanders, during a failed attempt to storm Gdov. De la Ville, a cavalry officer, led two operations to mine the wall, but both failed because of problems with the mines, which failed to explode as expected. In early November, Colonel Johan van Monickhouen arrived with a group of siege specialists, and orders to prepare the setting of mines under the walls. The Dutchman Monickhouen was an experienced siege expert. However, he fared no better. The early winter caused difficulties, too, with logistics but also with growing disciplinary problems. Horn abandoned the venture in late November, ordering the army to Novgorod.[4] Duke Julius Henry went to Sweden.[5]

With the Kalmar War against Denmark over, Gustavus Adolphus was finally able to send substantial reinforcements to De la Gardie. By the end of the year, some 5,000 to 6,000 men arrived on the eastern front. This was also a good opportunity to remove foreign enlisted soldiers from the Swedish heartlands, where it was feared that they might cause problems. The foreign soldiers were also more tolerant of service in Muscovy than Swedish and Finnish soldiers, who generally disliked being there.

On 20 December, De la Gardie had at his disposal 3,708 horse, divided into 19 banners, and 6,708 foot, divided into six field regiments and nine Finnish garrison companies in Ivangorod, Jama, Kaporie, Nyen, Nöteborg, and Ladoga Town. Altogether, he had 10,416 men.[6] Even so, the King's Life Banner of Horse under Herman Wrangel and Jesper Andersson Cruus's Regiment of Foot, were by then still on the march from Viborg and had not yet reached Nyen. De la Gardie ordered Wrangel and Cruus to clear Nöteborg County (*uyezd*) and Ladoga Town from invaders as they were passing through.

De la Gardie was confident that this army was sufficiently strong to push back any offensive from inner Muscovy. In late 1613 Prince Dmitriy Trubetskoy had already set out with an army in the direction of Novgorod, demanding that De la Gardie abandon all Swedish conquests in Muscovy. At first, only minor Muscovite contingents moved against the Swedish territory. Some assembled at Staraya Russa in the south, which

---

4 Generalstaben, *Sveriges krig* 1, pp.441–3.
5 Having shown military ineptitude at Gdov, Duke Julius Henry of Saxe-Lauenburg went on to display social awkwardness at court. At a banquet in honour of the Queen Dowager in late 1613, he began to make jokes at the expense of the proven soldier Nils Stiernskiöld, who in a joyous mood participated in the dance despite his leg remaining stiff from the many wounds he had suffered. Finally, the Duke attempted to trip Stiernskiöld so that he would stumble and fall. Enraged by the Duke's uncharitable behaviour, Gustavus Adolphus immediately charged in, slapping the Duke's face so hard that it drew blood. The inevitable outcome was a duel, of which few details are known except that Axel Oxenstierna managed to reconcile the King and the Duke, who became friends again.
6 Generalstaben, *Sveriges krig* 1, p.454.

was defended by Franz Dücker with a company of foot. A few Muscovite contingents, at least some of which were commanded by Prince Yefim Myshetskiy (who after falling into Swedish captivity with the surrender of Nöteborg had managed to escape), advanced towards Bronnitsa. However, Myshetskiy and his men were repulsed by Cobron with a composite force of cavalry and infantry from several units. By 20 November, Muscovites from the direction of Tikhvin had initiated a siege of Ladoga Town. Yet more Muscovite units, under Prince Trubetskoy's personal command, assembled at Torzhok. His intention was obvious: an offensive along the main highway towards Novgorod. However, the offensive soon lost momentum because of heavy snowfall. Even so, concerns over Prince Trubetskoy's offensive was a factor in the decision to abandon the siege of Gdov and recall Horn and his men to Novgorod. For added security, De la Gardie sent calls to Finland for reinforcements.

However, what really worried De la Gardie was the supply situation. Major parts of the Novgorod Lands remained devastated by the years of warfare. If sufficient supplies could not be made available, then De la Gardie, wise from previous experiences, feared that the enlisted soldiers again would mutiny, and plunder Novgorod itself.[7]

By this time, Gustavus Adolphus had given up hope that Charles Philip would become Tsar of Muscovy. On 10 November, he informed the Queen Dowager that he no longer had any hope for Charles Philip's election to the Tsardom, but his brother must nonetheless remain in Viborg so that the Novgorodians would not renounce the treaty with Sweden.[8] A month later, Gustavus Adolphus formally abandoned the previous policy vis-à-vis Muscovy. Henceforth, he wanted to negotiate directly with the Estates in Moscow, or even better, with Tsar Michael Romanov. He was prepared to abandon his father's territorial demands in the Arctic, but he insisted that Sweden's security necessitated the continued control of as a minimum Ivangorod, Jama, Kaporie, Nöteborg, and Kexholm – which constituted a defensive ring around Estonia and Finland – but also Gdov and Ladoga Town.[9] Having discussed the matter further with the Queen Dowager, Duke John, and the Council, in January 1614 the King reached the conclusion that the Swedish demands for Gdov and Ladoga Town could be abandoned, too. Only the defensive ring around Estonia and Finland was non-negotiable, since these fortresses and territories would protect the homeland. Yet, the King also wanted to gain friendly relations with Muscovy, including agreements on trade and hopefully an alliance against the Commonwealth. He was willing to accept the offer of mediation from

---

7   De la Gardie to Gustavus Adolphus, 24 October 1613; cited in Generalstaben, *Sveriges krig* 1, p.455.
8   Gustavus Adolphus to the Queen Dowager, 10 November 1613 (Riksregistraturet, RR); cited in Generalstaben, *Sveriges krig* 1, p.444.
9   Gustavus Adolphus to Charles Philip, De la Gardie, and others, 23 December 1613 (RR); cited in Generalstaben, *Sveriges krig* 1, p.445.

the Union of the Crowns of Scotland and England and took the initiative in inviting the Dutch Republic as a second mediator.[10]

Prince Trubetskoy Invades the Novgorod Lands

In Livonia, a new truce was concluded between Sweden and the Commonwealth in Weltz on 10 January 1614. Although the terms of the truce specified that, unless renewed, it would expire already on 1 May, it was a continuation of previous truces in Livonia. The parties ultimately renewed the truce, which lasted until 29 September 1616.

The truce in Livonia gave De la Gardie the necessary time to deal with the threat from the east. As noted, he did not worry much over Prince Trubetskoy's activities there, and he was right: by late January or early February 1614, Wrangel and Cruus had pushed the Muscovite units out of Nöteborg Country and the surroundings of Ladoga Town, which had been under threat by a Muscovite corps from Tikhvin since November. Cruus had also detached two companies to counter a Muscovite raid into Kexholm County.[11] Later in February, the two commanders continued to Novgorod, which Wrangel reached on 5 March, soon followed by Cruus and the rearguard.

Before then, De la Gardie had sent Horn with an army based on De la Ville's French regiment with orders to make a new attempt on Gdov and also try to capture the fortified Pskov-Pechory Monastery. De la Gardie based his decision on three arguments: (1) an operation against Pechory would threaten Pskov and with some luck prevent the Pskov Army from joining forces with Prince Trubetskoy's corps at Staraya Russa, (2) De la Ville's regiment was already in such a mutinous mood that its further presence in Novgorod was a security risk, and (3) the King had, in an instruction admittedly dated by subsequent events, ordered him to send De la Ville against Pechory.

Horn led the army to Ivangorod, where he arrived in early January. While he made a brief halt there, somebody in Ivangorod sent a letter warning Gdov that Horn was on the way. Gdov prepared its defences. Horn nonetheless attempted to take Gdov, while De la Ville and Corobel attempted a surprise attack on the Pskov-Pechory Monastery. Neither operation went well. Hampered by deep snow and a lack of artillery, the Swedes failed to take either objective. De la Ville lost many men, possibly 200, in their three attempts to storm the monastery; among the dead was his younger brother Jacques, and Corobel was wounded. French morale, already low, deteriorated rapidly. De la Ville's mutinous French regiment self-destructed after the failure at Pechory, and some of the Frenchmen moved into Commonwealth territory towards Dorpat. De la Ville rode

---

10 Generalstaben, *Sveriges krig* 1, pp.446–7.
11 Generalstaben, *Sveriges krig* 1, pp.456–7.

to Borgå in Finland with a lieutenant and 14 cavalrymen, from which he boarded a ship to Stockholm, leaving his escort waiting.[12] Horn rode to Viborg to await the expected arrival of Gustavus Adolphus.

As soon as De la Gardie heard from Wrangel and Cruus that they had cleared Kexholm and Nöteborg Counties and relieved Ladoga Town, he set in motion an operation against the Muscovites at Staraya Russa. As far as the Swedes knew, 2,000 Muscovites stood there. Another 1,200 cossacks, recently stiffened with 400 Moscow streltsy, held Tikhvin (and were those who recently had laid siege to Ladoga Town and sent a raiding party into Nöteborg County). Isay Sunbulov commanded about 1,000 men who had moved to (probably) Kresttsy within a day or two's ride from Novgorod but so far seemed unwilling to approach closer. Yet, Prince Trubetskoy remained at Torzhok with his main army, which only consisted of 3,000 men. At this point, the Swedes had learnt, the men available to Tsar Michael in Moscow were even fewer in number, no more than an estimated 800 hereditary servicemen, 1,500 streltsy, and 1,500 cossacks – and these also had to keep an eye on Zarutskiy, who at this time still held Astrakhan' and the south-east. De la Gardie had little to fear from them. In late February, he accordingly ordered Monickhouen to lead an offensive against the Muscovites at Staraya Russa. De la Gardie assigned Monickhouen a corps consisting of the reconstituted remnants of his regiment, combined with the late Taube's regiment and which hence consisted of nine companies, altogether 1,350 men. As cavalry, Monickhouen received the approximately 200 men of Duke Julius Henry's banner whom he had left behind. He could of course also rely on Franz Dücker, who with a company of foot garrisoned Staraya Russa itself.[13]

Arriving at Staraya Russa, the Swedes found that the Muscovites, under Andrey Palitsyn, had built a strong redoubt, surrounded by a moat. The Muscovites had, in the northern manner, poured water on the walls so that the ensuing ice cover made scaling them all but impossible. Monickhouen immediately laid siege to the redoubt. However, this was easier said than done under winter conditions. Monickhouen launched incendiaries at the redoubt, but the Muscovites had prepared soaked animal hides with which they put out any fires. The Swedes then attempted an assault, but the walls were impregnable, and the mines which they placed at the wall exploded prematurely, killing 50 men of the assault force including one of the captains, Nils Banér. He was a son of a senior noble and two years previously had assisted in saving Gustavus Adolphus's life during a Danish surprise attack.

The redoubt lacked a well, so Monickhouen realised that it would be possible to blockade it into submission. However, there was no settlement nearby, so the Swedes had to camp as best as they could in the snow. They endured for six days, but because of the strong cold, Monickhouen felt

---

12 Generalstaben, *Sveriges krig* 1, p.459.
13 Generalstaben, *Sveriges krig* 1, p.460.

obliged to abandon the siege. Ultimately, it did not matter. Palitsyn and most of the Muscovites at Staraya Russa were recalled to Prince Trubetskoy's main army several months later, and the town remained in Swedish hands.

It took until late March before Prince Trubetskoy finally set out from Torzhok, and joined forces with Sunbulov, who as noted then probably remained at Kresttsy. The information available to De la Gardie suggested that Prince Trubetskoy had no more than 5,000 men, and that he planned to draw to himself the two contingents at Tikhvin and Staraya Russa to enable a full-scale attack on Novgorod. If the city did not fall, Prince Trubetskoy would blockade it.

In response, De la Gardie sent Cobron with some 1,500 horse and foot to offer battle. The Swedish force also included artillery, probably commanded by Erik Jönsson Cremer. Prince Trubetskoy did not oblige; instead, he remained in his fortified camp, apparently expecting his men to fight better in defence of a fortified position than on an open field. Cobron did what he could to lure out the Muscovites, but Prince Trubetskoy did not accept battle.

Yet, the Muscovite camp was too strong to assault without siege artillery. Although few details are known, Sunbulov had apparently spent the time at Kresttsy building strong fortifications, so De la Gardie sent a message to the King, requesting siege artillery in the form of a few 24-pounders. None were available. Because of the inferior road conditions and lack of food supplies, Cobron returned to Bronnitsa. Weather conditions were not expected to allow major operations before the second half of April.

In mid April, Prince Trubetskoy had received the reinforcements that he expected, which meant that he, in the Swedish estimate, now commanded some 8,000 men including fresh reinforcements under Prince Daniil Mezetskiy. At Bronnitsa, Cobron had received reinforcements, too, and now led about 2,000 men.[14]

Prince Trubetskoy finally moved out. His vanguard division consisting of 1,000 men reached Bronnitsa on 20 April. Much of the terrain was then flooded because of the melting snow, so Cobron's cavalry could do little to prevent the Muscovite advance. By 8 May, the Prince had concentrated an estimated 3,000 men at Bronnitsa. De la Gardie sent Monickhouen's reconstituted regiment in support of Cobron's corps, and also called in additional units from the outlying regions.

Trubetskoy's men fortified themselves at Bronnitsa but otherwise remained comparatively passive, since the severe flooding made the roads impassable. There was thus ample time for De la Gardie to assemble his units. He also enlisted Commonwealth mercenaries. A Polish colonel named Konstantin went into De la Gardie's service in late May or early June with his banner of 200 horse. In early July, Colonel Sidor again rode to Novgorod, this time with 500 horse. He had previously been in Swedish service in Kexholm County, under Hans Munck who commanded Swedish

---

14 Generalstaben, *Sveriges krig* 1, p.461.

forces there, but now he entered into a new contract with De la Gardie in Novgorod.

Nothing much happened before July. At this point, De la Garde had concentrated about 3,000 horse (15 banners of Swedish and enlisted cavalrymen and about 900 Polish cavalry) and 4,230 foot for the defence of Novgorod. Prince Trubetskoy had deployed an estimated 5,000 men at Bronnitsa, and had another 3,000 elsewhere in the region. De la Gardie's biggest concern was his lack of food supplies; since no cattle were available, the Swedish army had to slaughter and eat many of their horses. With the customary poor discipline among the enlisted soldiers, infantrymen on numerous occasions stole cavalry horses to feed themselves, occasionally with fighting between the units as the inevitable outcome. As usual, the lack of food intensified the outbreaks of disease that always accompanied an army.[15]

And, as usual, the enlisted soldiers complained that their wages had not been paid. In early July, both Cobron and Monickhouen formally reported to De la Gardie that for this reason, they could no longer be held responsible for the behaviour of their men. Between 30 and 50 men from their regiments defected to the Muscovites, and more would probably have followed, had they known how to communicate in Russian and trusted the Muscovites more. Expecting another major mutiny of the type that had destroyed his armies at Klushino and Ivangorod, De la Gardie deliberately remained behind in Novgorod, foreseeing that his presence without money only would trigger further mutinies.

Cobron, by then promoted to major general, commanded a fairly strong army consisting of five banners of Finnish cavalry, Cobron's own three understrength banners of cavalry, the 900 Polish cavalrymen, Cobron's Regiment, Monickhouen's Regiment, and parts of De la Ville's and Jacob Velamsson's (formerly Rechenberger's) regiments. Other Swedish units nearby, at Novgorod, Porkhov, Saris, and Tyosovo, included about seven banners of cavalry, the Commanding General's Regiment, Cruus's Regiment, and other fragments of De la Ville's and Velamsson's regiments.[16] Prince Trubetskoy was probably outnumbered. But, would the enlisted units actually fight for Cobron and De la Gardie?

The stand-off at Bronnitsa developed into a siege. The flooded terrain did not allow for cavalry operations, and Trubetskoy's men did not move out. By this time, he had developed his camp into a fortified position consisting of a main camp and two forward redoubts east of the River Msta, and at some distance, two additional redoubts built for the vanguard division west of the River Msta in the direction of Lake Il'men'. Cobron commanded the main force, deployed facing the Muscovite redoubts west of the Msta, while Monickhouen deployed his regiment facing the Muscovite main camp. The two defensive lines were so close that the soldiers regularly exchanged

---

15   Generalstaben, *Sveriges krig* 1, pp.463–4.
16   Saris was a settlement located 10 km west-north-west of Ingris (Russian: Izhora).

THE SIEGE OF GDOV

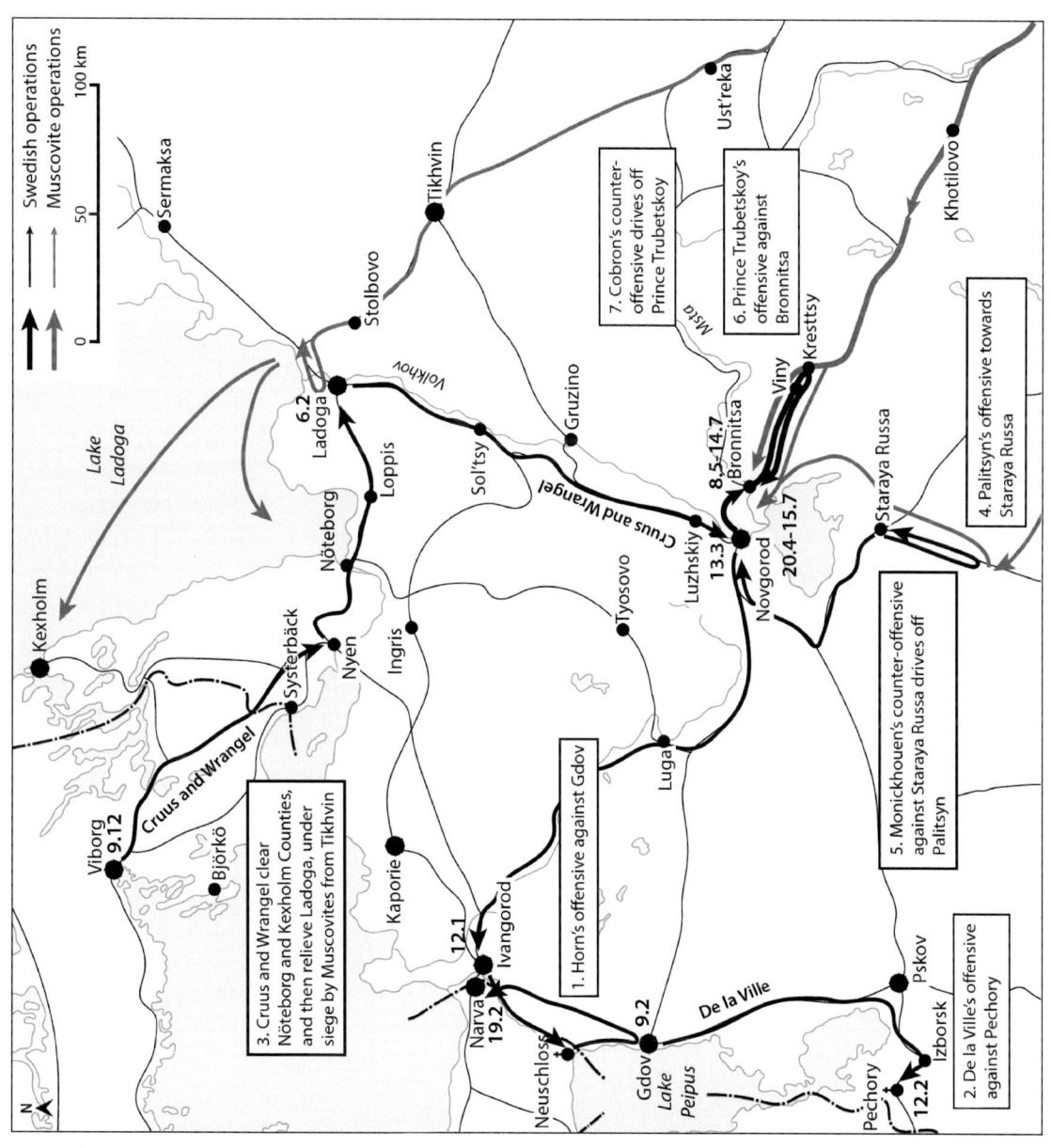

Map 10. Swedish and Muscovite Operations in 1614.

musket fire. Monickhouen was a skilled field engineer, so the Swedes also built a temporary bridge on commandeered boats so that the two commands could reinforce one another as needed. On the night of 27 June, Cobron stormed one of the Muscovite redoubts west of the Msta. Muscovite losses were reportedly 300 men. Trubetskoy was not passive; he received a few hundred men in reinforcements from Ust'reka and dispatched cossacks to both Tyosovo and Porkhov in attempts to cut Swedish supply routes. Yet, the Swedes dealt with these detached units without major difficulties. Moreover, Trubetskoy this time faced a full display of west European siege warfare techniques, and Monickhouen's skillful use of mortars forced the Muscovites to retreat from some of their positions, apparently those east of the Msta. Moreover, the Muscovite army, too, suffered numerous desertions. On the night of 14 July, Trubetskoy ordered his men to retreat. However, the Swedes discovered the withdrawal and attacked, winning a major victory and inflicting severe casualties on the retreating Muscovites. On the following day, the remaining Muscovite redoubt west of the Msta surrendered. The Swedes reportedly massacred its garrison of 400 men. With the victory at Bronnitsa, Muscovite resistance evaporated; Prince Trubetskoy attempted to reassemble his surviving men at Torzhok, but they soon dispersed, their temporary unity under Tsar Michael dissolved by the defeat at Bronnitsa and pre-existing animosities between hereditary servicemen, cossacks, and other groups.[17]

The Fall of Gdov

Meanwhile, Gustavus Adolphus had travelled overland to Finland. At peace with Denmark, the King felt confident to leave the able Field Marshal Jesper Mattsson Cruus and Duke John of Östergötland in charge of Swedish homeland defences. Gustavus Adolphus arrived in Tavastehus on 19 March 1614. He had hoped that negotiations swiftly would resolve the conflict with Tsar Michael's government in Moscow, so that instead he could focus on renewing the war with King Sigismund and the Commonwealth. He had even issued orders to prepare the navy for a landing operation in Livonia. However, it soon became clear that the political situation in Muscovy did not allow for a quick peace treaty under terms favourable to Sweden. Hence, Gustavus Adolphus accepted the renewal of the truce in Livonia with the Commonwealth, and decided instead to focus on the situation along the Muscovite borderlands.[18]

---

17 Generalstaben, *Sveriges krig* 1, pp.464–7.
18 Incidentally, in Finland the King was visited by Colonel Hans Georg von Arnim, a Lutheran Brandenburger who soon would make a name for himself. Arnim presented a plan to capture Kola Castle and Arkhangel'sk for Sweden with a regiment enlisted in Germany. Although Gustavus Adolphus had already given up his father's Arctic designs, he found Arnim's proposal sufficiently interesting

THE SIEGE OF GDOV

The requested reinforcements from Sweden arrived in several groups during the summer, until the Swedish army on the eastern front in late July 1614 consisted of more than 10,200 men.[19] The King was eager to advance against either Gdov or Pskov. The geographical location of Gdov settled the matter, since logistics and communications lines from Pskov by necessity must pass Gdov, which therefore became the priority objective. On 27 July, Gustavus Adolphus gave Horn the task of assembling the army at Narva and then lay siege to Gdov, which was defended by the aforementioned Fyodor Aminov whom we last met in Swedish captivity in 1609.

Logistical and other problems nonetheless delayed the ensuing campaign, so Horn marched out towards Gdovin early August. Cobron's and Monickhouen's Regiments joined the siege soon after 15 August. Gustavus Adolphus personally arrived at Gdov on 25 August with the Drabant Company. Ultimately, more than 4,800 men (1,399 horse and 3,441 foot) participated in the siege of Gdov.[20] It was a major undertaking.

Gustavus Adolphus assumed personal command of the siege, although he was certainly well aware that he had never led a siege operation and relied on the advice of more experienced specialists such as Monickhouen. Logistics were handled by riverine *lodja* transports from Narva along the River Narova and Lake Peipus under the command of naval captain Zakarias Simonsson. Gdov repulsed two Swedish assaults, but on 10 September Aminov surrendered the town before the third. However, Monickhouen fell during the siege. His death cost Gustavus Adolphus an experienced military engineer. Another casualty was Fromhold von der Burg, the commander of the Drabant Company.

Because of the obvious difficulties in taking a fortified town such as Gdov, and the late season, Gustavus Adolphus chose not immediately to carry the offensive onwards against the far more strongly fortified Pskov.

While the operation against Gdov proceeded, a Muscovite corps moved to the mouth of the River Volkhov where they built a redoubt and *lodja* base in an attempt to cut the communications line between Nöteborg and Ladoga Town. This caused problems, and also prevented the Swedes, under Richard Isaacsson Rosencrantz, from shipping five large-calibre cannons and six heavy mortars from Novgorod to Finland. The Swedes estimated the Muscovite corps as some 2,000 in strength, primarily consisting of

---

to revive the plan and gave him a patent for this purpose. Arnim then returned to Germany, but for one reason or another, failed to carry out the design. Generalstaben, *Sveriges krig* 1, pp.471–2.

19 Generalstaben, *Sveriges krig* 1, pp.594–5.

20 Cavalry: Six Swedish banners including the King's Life Banner (altogether 999 horse), Evert Horn's cornet (100), Per Hansson's banner (100), and Samuel Cobron's two banners (200). Infantry: Drabant Company (205 men), Svante Banér's Regiment (1,320), Monickhouen's Regiment (1,166), Samuel Cobron's Regiment (400), Johan Andersson's company (150), Jürgen von Heiden's company (200), and possibly one or two unidentified Finnish companies. Generalstaben, *Sveriges krig* 1, pp.594–5.

SWEDEN'S WAR IN MUSCOVY 1609-1617

cossacks and peasant levies, but with about 30 *lodja*-type river vessels. In response, De la Gardie ordered cavalry against the Muscovites, and simultaneously had a squadron of some 10 *lodja* vessels and one pinnace sent from Nöteborg under Bertil Wessel, commander of the Swedish Ladoga Squadron. In August, the Swedes stormed the Muscovite redoubt, while Wessel's men captured 33 of the Muscovite *lodja* vessels.[21]

A pair of sixteenth-century Muscovite 40-pounder cannons, since 1623 at Gripsholm Castle in Sweden. One was probably captured by Evert Horn at Ivangorod in 1612 and the other probably by De la Gardie's father Pontus at Narva in 1581. There is other speculation that instead they were among the guns shipped from Novgorod in 1614. Originally, they were known in Sweden as *Rysseulvarna* ('Russian wolves') but were later renamed *Galten* and *Suggan* ('Boar' and 'Sow'). (Photo: Janders)

In late autumn, Gustavus Adolphus returned to Sweden with De la Gardie. Evert Horn assumed overall command on the eastern front. In early 1615 he assisted Aminov, who by then had managed to smuggle his family out of Pskov, to go into Swedish service. At this point, the latter's son, Isay (or Isaac) Fyodorovich Aminov, assumed the post of governor of Gdov. Aminov himself was appointed governor of Ivangorod.[22]

Gustavus Adolphus instructed Horn to defend existing conquests and to continue the attempts, already initiated in autumn, to persuade Novgorod to secede from Muscovy. Swedish policy had switched from the introduction of a Swedish tsar to persuading Novgorod to join Sweden. Novgorod was, as we have seen, an old independent principality which Sweden now controlled *jure belli*, by the right of conquest. However, the Novgorodians were reluctant to secede, saying that they remained bound to the oath to Charles Philip. However, some declared their willingness to die rather than leave Muscovy; this response may have derived from feelings of religious solidarity, but equally likely it may have resulted from despair. Whilst Horn made as good use of Novgorod's limited resources as he could, it was still not enough. During the autumn and winter of 1614/1615,

---

21 Generalstaben, *Sveriges krig* 1, pp.479–80; Generalstaben, *Sveriges krig 1611–1632*, Suppl. Vol. 1 (Stockholm: Generalstaben, 1937), p.125.
22 Rabinovich, 'Gdov v smutnoye vremya', p.26.

Novgorod suffered from famine and diseases, which caused the death of some 8,000 people from 1614 to the end of April 1615.[23] However, after the defeat at Bronnitsa Tsar Michael had no men to resume operations against the Swedes in Novgorod or elsewhere. The war had become a stalemate.

---

23   Generalstaben, *Sveriges krig* 1, p.510.

22

Gustavus Adolphus at Pskov

The main threat to the Swedish army in Novgorod was not Tsar Michael's army, which after the defeat at Bronnitsa remained weak and dispersed. A bigger threat was the presence of thousands of Commonwealth mercenaries, mutineers, and assorted freebooters who had moved into Muscovy in search of plunder or the capture of some fortress that might return them in good standing with King Sigismund. All were cavalry, and the mercenary threat could easily be handled by hiring them. However, the Swedish commanders at most times lacked the cash to pay even their already present enlisted units. Another, related problem was the lack of hay for the army's horses and food supplies for both soldiers and the general population.

Gustavus Adolphus wanted to take Pskov before he entered into negotiations with Tsar Michael's court. If he conquered and annexed Pskov together with Swedish-held Novgorod, then it would be difficult for Moscow to insist on a peace treaty that obligated Sweden to return the occupied lands. Beyond the importance of Pskov as a mercantile centre, the city dominated the main highways from the interior of Muscovy to the Baltic ports of Riga, Pernau, and to some extent even Reval. If Sweden could gain control over Pskov, this would secure Novgorod from both overland and shipborne (across Lake Peipus) Commonwealth offensives. As a further bonus, the city could also be used in preparation for future offensives into Commonwealth-held Livonia. All things considered, an annexation of Pskov would put Sweden in a very favourable position.

However, Pskov was strongly fortified, with a castle, an impressive city wall, and water-filled moats. Horn had already made preparations to blockade the city, not least from relief by barge across the Lake Peipus. While the blockade had never been complete, perhaps more success could be had this time?

During the winter of 1614/1615, the Swedes again attempted to cut the supply lines leading to Pskov. However, problems caused by shortages in horses, supplies, and cash to pay soldiers hampered the effort, as did the strong cold and snowfall. Ultimately, the blockade failed.

The Swedish army in the eastern borderlands in 1615 consisted of about 3,000 horse and 10,500 foot, altogether 13,500 men. The figures take into account the shortage of horses. It took time to replace cavalry horses, so many cavalrymen would have to fight on foot.[1]

The fact that Tsar Michael's limited resources and fighting men were stretched over too many fronts did not preclude his commanders from going on the offensive when they could. In early June, Prince Nikita Volkonskiy led some 2,000 men in an offensive from Tikhvin towards Ladoga Town. However, Cobron drove them off, with a combined army consisting of Cobron's Regiment, Adam Richard de La Chapelle's Dragoon Company, and Commonwealth mercenaries in Swedish service. Cobron pursued the fleeing Muscovites to Tikhvin, where he defeated the town's garrison as well. The news of the Swedish successes apparently spread so far and wide that even Tsar Michael's army under Boris Luk'yanov at distant Vologda retreated further inland.[2]

This meant that Horn could prepare the operation against Pskov without worrying much about what the opposing forces might do. Since boat transports across the Lake Peipus were necessary to maintain an army laying siege to Pskov, the Swedes brought in *lodja*-type vessels to protect them. By early summer if not before, naval battles took place between them and Pskov's own *lodja* fleet. Pskov's fleet was victorious, and among other successes, re-established communications with Dorpat in Livonia, from which food supplies could be brought into the city.

Because of the time needed to raise a substantial army and fleet in Sweden, it took until 28 June before Gustavus Adolphus could set out from Stockholm with the Swedish main fleet and the army bound for Pskov. He and the fleet arrived in Narva on 8 July, having stopped briefly at Reval on the way.

Following the disembarkation of the Swedish units at Narva, Gustavus Adolphus commanded a sizeable army of about approximately 2,000 horse and some 4,800 foot. The infantry was divided into five regiments: His Royal Majesty's Life Regiment, consisting of enlisted units already in theatre; His Royal Majesty's Own Regiment, raised in Sweden; Hans von Rechenberger's Regiment, raised in Finland; the Commanding General's Regiment, of enlisted units; and Samuel Cobron's Regiment, also of enlisted units. However, the three enlisted regiments immediately mutinied, refusing to serve without receiving their pay. As usual, the Swedish Crown lacked the necessary cash, so this caused further delays before the men could be satisfied. Gustavus Adolphus also faced immediate difficulties in supplying his army with gunpowder, and in particular, food supplies. The logistical effort, although functioning better than only a few years ago, remained deficient to maintain the army's needs.

Notwithstanding these difficulties, Gustavus Adolphus stood at Pskov with the Swedish vanguard on 29 July. Two days later, the Swedish main army arrived. The mutinous regiments remained behind until mid August,

---

1   Generalstaben, *Sveriges krig* 1, pp.496–7.
2   Generalstaben, *Sveriges krig* 1, p.511.

awaiting their pay – which only could be raised by taking loans. Meanwhile, additional Swedish units and a few other units already in the theatre arrived, which brought up the total further, to some 9,300 men (Table 13).[3] At the same time, another 4,600 men garrisoned Viborg, Narva, Novgorod, Nöteborg, and other strongholds.[4] It was a formidable army that laid siege to Pskov.

Table 13. Gustavus Adolphus's army at Pskov, 1615[5]

Cavalry		
The King's Life Banner, under Herman Wrangel	1	187
Nils Assersson Mannersköld's Banner	1	181
Commanding General's Life Cornet, under Lorentz Wagner	1	200
Evert Horn's Life Cornet, under Otto Grothusen	1	248
Per Hansson's Banner	1	227
Lindved Claesson Hästesko's Banner	1	186
Henrik Månsson Spåre's Banner	1	308
Anders Paul's Banner	1	240
Composite Banner, under Henrik Fleming (?)	1	91
Estonian Retinue of Nobles	1	160
Claes Wachtmeister's Livonian Banner	1	130
Samuel Cobron's Banner	1	150
Polish Banner	1	120
In total	13	2,428
Dragoons		
Adam Richard de La Chapelle's Dragoon Company	1	142
In total	1	142

---

3 For information on the raising of the army, see Generalstaben, *Sveriges krig* 1, pp.496–7, 516, 524, 528. See also Barkman, *Kungl. Svea livgardes historia* 3:1, pp.232–42.

4 Julius Mankell, *Uppgifter rörande svenska krigsmagtens styrka, sammansättning och fördelning sedan slutet af femtonhundratalet, jemte öfversigt af svenska krigshistoriens vigtigaste händelser under samma tid*, Vol. 2 (Stockholm: C. M. Thimgren, 1865), pp.19–21; Generalstaben, *Sveriges krig* 1, pp.596–7.

5 Generalstaben, *Sveriges krig* 1, p.596.

Infantry		
His Royal Majesty's Life Regiment (enlisted, already in theatre)	8	1,658
His Royal Majesty's Own Regiment (raised in Sweden)	5	905
Svante Banér's Regiment	2	177
Jesper Andersson Cruus's Regiment	4	774
Hans von Rechenberger's Regiment	5	1,107
Commanding General's Regiment	8	1,077
Samuel Cobron's Regiment	7	1,049
In total	39	6,747
Grand total	53	9,317

Pskov was defended by an estimated 700 or 800 cossacks and streltsy, as well as the townsman militia which Swedish reports estimated as 1,500.[6] Other accounts described a garrison of 4,000 men, a figure which seems too high:[7] the entire city's population then was only 14,000, after years of wars, famine, and diseases.[8] The townsman militia had to take a major responsibility for defending the large city. The days when Pskov supported pretenders were long since gone; the suffering induced by famine and diseases and the persistent threat posed by the Swedish presence had turned the city into a staunch supporter of Tsar Michael. Since 28 April 1615 the defence was led by Vasiliy Morozov from Moscow and his deputies Fyodor Buturlin and Prince Afanasiy Gagarin. There was friction within the command, because Buturlin and Prince Gagarin constantly argued about who outranked the other. But among the defenders was also the fiery Bishop Silvester from Kexholm, since then promoted to Archbishop of Pskov, who hated foreign heathens no less now than in the past, and constantly preached defiance against the Swedes.

Tsar Michael and his advisors had not only sent Morozov as a governor, they also sent Fyodor Sheremetyev with an army in an attempt to relieve Pskov. Sheremetyev set out from Moscow, but his army never reached the area of operations in the north-west.

Tsar Michael had hitherto refused negotiations for peace. However, an English mediator, John Merrick, chief agent of the London-based Muscovy Company, managed to get negotiations underway. The negotiations took place with De la Gardie in Novgorod, who acted on behalf of Gustavus

---

6 Generalstaben, *Sveriges krig* 1, p.522.
7 Smirnov, *Den svenske tsaren*, p.225.
8 Johan Rudbeck, 3 November 1615; in Jonas Hallenberg, *Svea rikes historia under konung Gustaf Adolf den stores regering* 4 (Stockholm: Johan A. Carlbohm, 1794), pp.1005–1013, on p.1007.

Adolphus and with his approval. Meanwhile, Gustavus Adolphus retained the military pressure on Pskov, with Horn in charge of the campaign. Gustavus Adolphus argued, correctly, that peace negotiations were far more likely to produce a beneficial result for Sweden if they took place while the Swedish army made military gains.

For reasons of logistics and geography, the Swedes had to concentrate their forces against the northwestern side of the city, despite it also being the most strongly fortified. On 30 July, Gustavus had his army march out in full force against this sector of the city's defences. The action was presumably intended as a demonstration, to show the defenders the overwhelming strength of the Swedish army. However, a number of cossacks then sallied out and engaged Evert Horn who led his life cornet in a cavalry charge against the Muscovite cavalry. Then disaster struck the Swedes: Horn suddenly fell to a gun shot. Apparently by coincidence, he had worn conspicuous armour on the occasion, and contemporaries believed that this enabled the Muscovites to target him with well-aimed shots. This deprived Gustavus Adolphus of one of his most accomplished commanders.

The Muscovites continued to sally out, which resulted in daily skirmishes. It was obvious that Pskov had no intention of surrendering. While Gustavus Adolphus at first moved into the well-protected Snyatnaya Mountain Monastery on an island in the River Velikaya north-west of Pskov, he ordered the construction of five separate fortified camps for his army. The first to be completed, across the river from southern Pskov, was a full bastion, which housed an artillery battery as well as Johan Rytter (Reuter)'s company. Then followed, in this order, the King's large, primary camp directly facing the heavily fortified northwestern side of the city, Rechenberger's strongly fortified camp just across the River Velikaya, Cobron's camp facing eastern Pskov, Asmus von Glasenap's camp in the south, and finally Lieutenant Colonel Paul Gottberg's camp south-east of Pskov. The men in Cobron's, Glasenap's, and Gottberg's camps were there to protect the army against any relief force that might arrive along the Pskov Road from Muscovy. The north was already in Swedish hands. Gustavus Adolphus had two bridges built across the River Velikaya, but he had apparently neither the manpower nor the resources to erect defensive lines of countervallation (facing the fortress) and circumvallation (facing the country) to protect his men from sallies and the arrival of any relief force while they laid siege to the town. Based on surviving maps from the siege, no such defensive lines were built.[9]

On 14 August the senior quartermaster, Robert Moore, fell during the construction of the fortified camps. This deprived the King of his remaining senior siege professional. He still had a skilled civilian fortification officer, Andreas Serrander, but nonetheless called for Lieutenant Colonel Andreas

---

9   Generalstaben, *Sveriges krig* 1, p.525.

Goossen van der Maan, a Dutchman, from Svante Banér's Regiment as a replacement for Moore.[10]

Despite these setbacks, by 20 August Pskov was cut off from its supply lines. Preparations were made for an assault to be staged from the King's and Rechenberger's camps. However, the Swedish siege artillery was delayed, arriving at Pskov only on 3 September. Batteries had already been prepared immediately in front of the city walls in the northwestern sector: three batteries for 10 cannons and one battery for two cannons. An additional battery for flank fire was built on the opposite side of the River Velikaya, next to one of the numerous monasteries around Pskov. The siege artillery is believed to have included both 48-pounder and 24-pounder siege cannons, together with several mortars. Apparently both the national chief of artillery (Swedish: *rikstygmästare*) since 1612, Johan Månsson Ulfsparre, and the artillery officer Erik Jönsson Cremer were present to direct operations.[11] Yet, more preparations had to be carried out, and the Swedish artillery set to work only on 17 September. Unfortunately for the Swedes, the heavy artillery cannonballs were in short supply, and it took until 23 September before the artillery could open up a breach in the city wall. However, by then the Swedes were out of artillery ammunition so could do little to prevent the defenders from carrying out makeshift repairs. Then a debilitating disease broke out in the Swedish camp. Henceforth, not only logistical problems but also rampant disease severely affected the Swedish performance. Moreover, the siege of Pskov put a temporary end to the peace negotiations, since neither Muscovites nor the English mediator felt comfortable negotiating while the siege took place. Realising that the siege operation did not proceed well, Gustavus Adolphus began to make preparations for going into winter quarters. On 30 September, he decided in favour of a drawdown.

First, however, the Swedish King would make one serious attempt to storm Pskov. On 8 October he again commenced an intensive bombardment of the northwestern sector of the city. The Swedish artillery managed to open up part of the repaired breach in the city wall. On the following day, 9 October, Gustavus Adolphus attempted to storm Pskov. He picked what should be the best and most experienced units in the army: the Drabant Company and His Royal Majesty's Life Regiment, under Jost Clodt von Jürgensburg. Yet, the operation failed.

Even so, Swedish losses were small. Perhaps a second attack would be more successful? In the evening of 10 October, the Swedes switched to launching gun barrel incendiaries. Some 20 houses burned down, but the results were otherwise poor. The bombardment intensified on 11

---

10   In Swedish sources, the Dutch officer is generally known as Anders Gosen von der Maa (fl. 1607–1616). He must have been an experienced military engineer because in the Kalmar War, in which he served as captain, his expertise was called for during the defence of Kalmar Castle.
11   Hedberg, *Kungl. Artilleriet: Yngre vasatiden*, p.195.

October, and one of Pskov's towers collapsed. However, one of the Swedish incendiaries then accidentally set fire to part of the gunpowder depot, which exploded, killing several artillerymen and badly wounding another 50 or 60.

The worst part of this setback was perhaps the loss of gunpowder. Gustavus Adolphus cancelled the planned assault, and ordered the artillery to be embarked upon riverine transports. The army then commenced a general retreat. The units destined for Novgorod set out on 13 October and Gustavus Adolphus left Pskov with the main army on 17 October, bound for Narva, where he arrived 10 days later.

Tsar Michael and his advisors may not immediately have realised that it was Swedish weakness that had resulted in their abandoning the siege of Pskov. The English mediator, Merrick, claimed that he personally had persuaded the Swedish King – against the recommendation of the Dutch mediators who had recently arrived and obviously supported the Swedish cause – to raise the siege as a concession to Muscovy in the ongoing peace negotiations. Merrick possibly, at least for a while, even believed this. When the truth soon enough came out, Gustavus Adolphus in a devious mood sent Merrick a congratulatory letter, thanking him for suggesting the concession. Merrick then had to play along, claiming that he indeed had persuaded Gustavus Adolphus to pull out – or he would jeopardise his reputation as a mediator.

The failed siege of Pskov again showed Gustavus Adolphus how weak and obsolete the Swedish army was. Work to reform his military establishment began as soon as the army was back in Sweden. Even so, it would take many years – and harsh experiences in the subsequent Thirty Years' War – before the Swedish army developed an adequate capability to conduct siege warfare.

The Pskov Army and militia successfully defended their city until the end of the war.

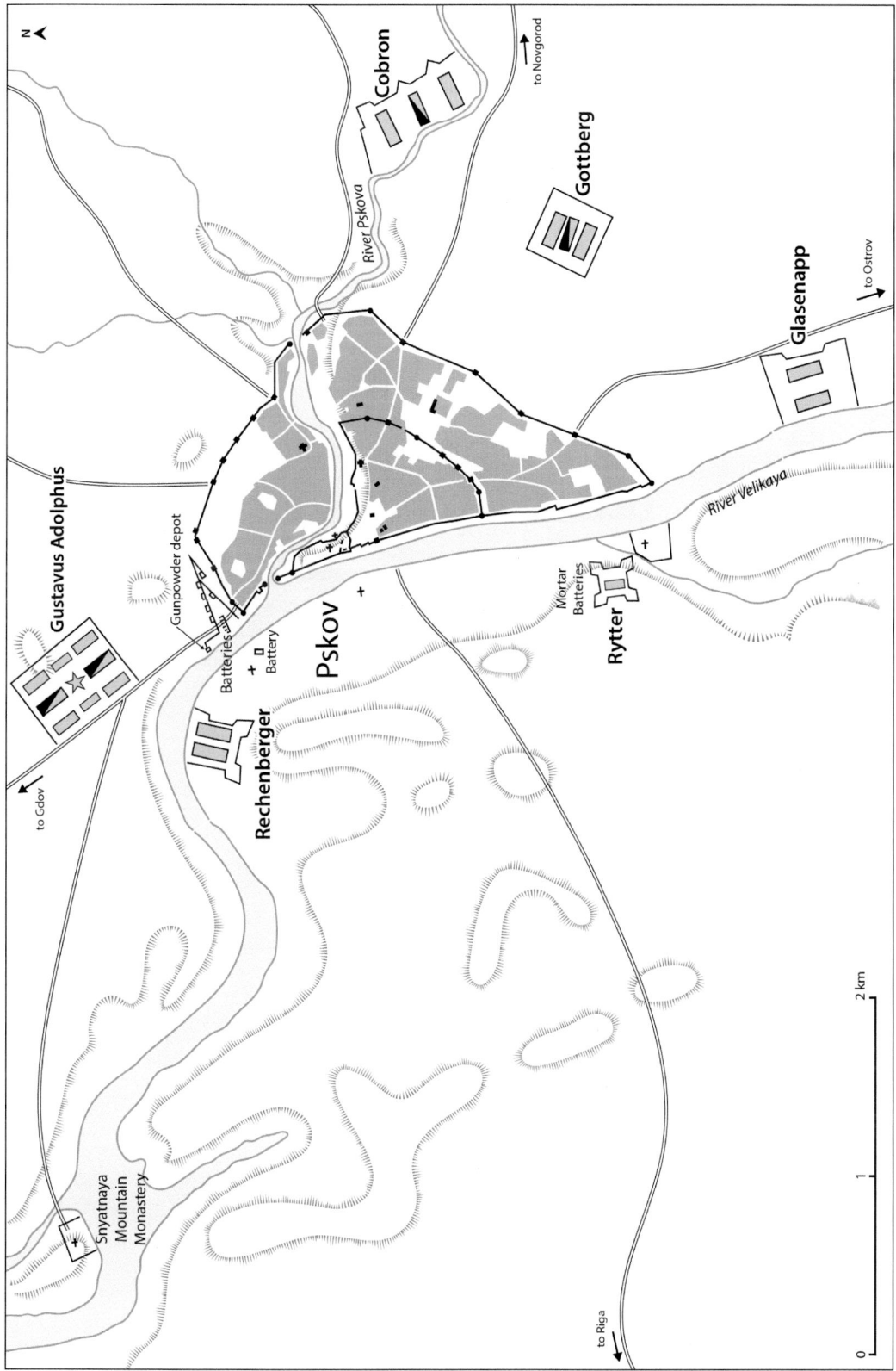

Map 11. The Siege of Pskov, 1615.

23

The Finnish-Muscovite Borderlands

We have seen that Sweden carried out several attempts to take and gain control over the Kola Peninsula. None achieved any lasting results. In 1614, the governors of Uleåborg and Kajaneborg in Finland and the Solovki monastery negotiated a local border truce.

However, it never really became quiet in Kexholm County. The territory was too vast for either Swedes or Muscovites to fully control. While Anders Boije was governor of Kexholm, the Swedish commander of Kexholm County, Hans Munck, in 1612–1613 operated far east of Lake Ladoga in the region between Lakes Belozero and Onega, where he established a presence and managed to raise taxes. Swedes and Muscovites fought naval battles on the lakes and rivers using vessels of the *lodja-type*. In spring 1613 the Swedish navy established a Ladoga Squadron, consisting of *lodja-type* vessels and the occasional pinnace, under navy captain Alexander Foratt, who had previously fought Danish warships in the Kalmar War. By the end of the year, Army Captain Matts Sigfridsson assumed command of the squadron. At the same time, Anders Boije's nephew Hans Boije was appointed commandant of Nöteborg.

Muscovite raiding in the Lake Ladoga region continued throughout the war. Since the Karelian cavalry could hardly cover the entire region, we have seen that Munck hired Colonel Sidor and possibly other Commonwealth mercenaries as auxiliaries. But there were naval activities as well. Skirmishes between Swedish and Muscovite *lodja* vessels took place repeatedly. On 19 May 1614, an engagement took place, in which 11 Swedish *lodja* defeated a Muscovite squadron, capturing three *lodja* in the process. Soon after, Munck had to confront a large-scale Muscovite landing in Swedish-held territory. The invasion force, which crossed Lake Ladoga by *lodja*, consisted of an estimated 750 Muscovites (of whom 400 were streltsy, 200 cossacks, 100 peasant levies from northern Kexholm County, and 50 forcibly conscripted men). Munck confronted them already as they landed, and managed to push them back to their boats. The Muscovites lost 30 dead, 15 men taken captive, and two standards. Then the Muscovites observed that they

THE FINNISH-MUSCOVITE BORDERLANDS

outnumbered the Swedes, who were fewer than they thought, and made another attempt. The decisive battle was fought on 27 July 1614 at Ristilahti in Uukuniemi, a promontory in Lake Pyhäjärvi next to Lake Ladoga. Munck awaited the Muscovites on an open field some distance from the landing site. At this point, the Muscovites preferred to dig in on the shore. Munck then led a charge against them and was wounded in the action, but his second in command Hans Stålhandske managed to rout them. No other details of the battle are known.

In the following month, a confrontation took place at the mouth of the River Volkhov, where Muscovites had built the aforementioned redoubt to house a *lodja* squadron intended to cut the communications line between Nöteborg and Ladoga Town. However, we have seen that a combined Swedish force took the redoubt, and 33 *lodja* vessels fell into Swedish hands.[1] This completed the Swedish victory in the Lake Ladoga region. Henceforth, the Swedish Ladoga Squadron held naval supremacy on the great lake.

As a result, in the winter of 1614/1615 Olonets District (*pogost*), east of Lake Ladoga, agreed to pay tax to the Swedish authorities.

In 1615, command of the Ladoga Squadron was transferred to navy captain Hans Andersson. In addition to the *lodja* vessels, Andersson had two pinnaces at his disposal. He had to repulse a Muscovite shipborne raid in May 1615, but this seems not to have been overly difficult. The Muscovites at Olonets were never sufficiently many to pose a real threat. Moreover, Gustavus Adolphus sent additional riverine vessels to Lake Ladoga. Soon after, Munck again had to carry out an expedition to Olonets to re-establish a presence there. Yet, in the summer of 1615 additional Muscovite raids took place into Swedish-held territories.

We have seen that in Eastern warfare, raiding and looting were frequently used as a weapon of terror, to reduce the enemy population's will to fight so as to ensure its subjugation. This military objective also characterised much of the raiding that went on in the Finnish-Muscovite borderlands. However, here the population was smaller and more scattered than further south, so in this context, subjugation in reality meant acceptance of taxation (in previous centuries, the paying of tribute). Raiding and looting also formed a means to feed and thus retain one's fighting men, since in the sparsely populated north, there often was not enough food to feed full-time soldiers. As a result, most fighting was conducted by what in reality was no more than large raiding parties.

In more densely populated areas, northern armies including Swedish ones employed raiding and looting as part of a defensive strategy, as the chief means to make sure that the devastated territories could not be used as base areas for a subsequent enemy attack on one's own territories. This objective was best accomplished by devastating towns and villages – and the associated agricultural industry that produced food supplies – on the

---

1   Widekindi, *Thet Swenska i Ryßland*, pp.606–12; Generalstaben, *Sveriges krig 1611–1632*, Suppl. Vol. 1 (Stockholm: Generalstaben, 1937), p.125.

enemy side of the border, thus denying the enemy the resources and supplies that were vital to launch an invasion. In addition, large-scale raiding and looting constituted the logical outcome of a deliberate strategy to win the war by applying pressure on the enemy in the ongoing or expected peace negotiations. When neither party was strong enough decisively to defeat the other, the best option was to maintain a defensive strategy, but one which actively prevented the other side from launching a full-scale invasion in the first place.[2]

The Armistice of Diderino

The peace negotiations that got underway in late 1615 continued in Diderino, near Novgorod. Sweden by then had a strong representation in the region, with Gustavus Adolphus (in the early stages), Axel Oxenstierna, and Jacob De la Gardie all taking part in the deliberations of the various proposals (but as was customary, the King did not hold a formal post in the delegation). Tsar Michael was represented by a delegation under Prince Daniil Mezetskiy, who to ensure divine assistance brought with him a copy of the holy icon Our Lady of Tikhvin Mother of God, previously so effective in resisting Swedish hostility. John Merrick mediated on behalf of Scotland and England. The Dutch delegation included notables such as Reinhold van Brederode, Dirck Baas, and Albrecht Joachimi. The rivalry between the Dutch delegation and Merrick was obvious during the negotiations. Gustavus Adolphus correctly regarded the Dutch as being on his side, while Tsar Michael and his advisors, equally correctly, trusted Merrick to guarantee that no unnecessary concessions were made.

The first formal meeting for peace negotiations in Diderino took place on 3 January 1616. In reality, this was the culmination of a long process that already had been ongoing for more than a year.

On paper, Sweden held all the cards. Despite the failure to conquer Pskov, Swedish armies occupied vast areas of territory. Moreover, Tsar Michael lacked the men and resources to go on another offensive against the Swedes, at least for as long as he was also at war with the Commonwealth. Yet, as De la Gardie pointed out, the territories conquered by Sweden were devastated, indeed ruined, and by this time completely unable to supply the Swedish army, any new military operations, or for that matter, the surviving civilian population. Furthermore, the Swedish Crown as usual lacked ready cash

---

2   For the inhabitants of the border region, this strategy spelled disaster and caused all sorts of human suffering. However, from a military point of view the strategy was rational and, we should remember, not unlike the deliberate destruction of the enemy's strategic resources that took place in later centuries (including the extensive campaigns of strategic bombing by air forces in modern times which also are aimed primarily at production facilities, that is, industrial and civilian targets).

THE FINNISH-MUSCOVITE BORDERLANDS

to pay the enlisted units, so De la Gardie could not rule out another major mutiny. In short, it was vital that Sweden negotiated a lasting peace before the conquests were lost to the tide of starvation and epidemics.

Spying took place as well. The Novgorodian noble Yakov Boborykin had earlier taken the oath to Charles Philip, yet because of a number of poor decisions then found himself sentenced to death. Merrick advised Gustavus Adolphus to pardon Boborykin, which he did. Afterwards, the unsuspecting De la Gardie brought Boborykin to Diderino as part of the Swedish delegation. However, Boborykin had other plans. He recruited as a spy one of the Swedish interpreters, the hard-drinking Arn Brook, and when not inebriated the interpreter secretly copied Swedish letters, which Boborykin then handed over at night to his Muscovite counterpart. A key document for the Swedish position was the late Tsar Vasiliy's order to cede Kexholm County to Sweden. Prince Mezetskiy ordered Boborykin to locate and steal the signed original, so that the Muscovite side could claim that no such transfer of territory ever had been authorised.

However, the Swedes had a spy too. This was a Muscovite under-secretary (Russian: *pod'yachiy*) called Mikhalko Klement'yev, who revealed Boborykin's game to the Swedes before the theft could take place. Boborykin, warned by another Novgorodian in De la Gardie's service – the cossack officer Ugrim Ivanovich Lupandin – managed to escape, yet his mother, three brothers, and three sisters were deported to Sweden in retaliation for Boborykin's treason, and the Crown confiscated the family's belongings.[3]

Armistice negotiations in Diderino, December 1615–January 1616. The two delegations with their respective honour guards arrive from opposite directions, with the tents of the mediators in the centre. (Anthonis Goeteeris)

Regardless of the cloak-and-dagger activities, the negotiations on 22 February resulted in the Armistice of Diderino, which allowed a three-month truce in the hope that additional negotiations would result in a peace treaty acceptable to all parties. However, it was soon found that neither side was satisfied with what had been achieved so far, and both prepared for continued war. Yet Gustavus Adolphus was acutely aware of the difficult logistical situation, so he proposed a defensive strategy for 1616. He reduced the army on the eastern front by sending home numerous Swedish and Finnish units, and by paying off eight enlisted foreign companies. The King ordered the construction of three new redoubts, one at Sermaksa at the mouth of the River Svir' in Lake Ladoga and one on each side of

---

3   Smirnov, *Den svenske tsaren*, pp.232–3.

the River Velikaya at its outlet into Lake Peipus. The first would protect Ladoga Town from Muscovite expeditions from Tikhvin and also house the Swedish Ladoga Squadron.[4] The two others would cut off Pskov from its supply route across Lake Peipus, house the *lodja* squadron from Narva, and would serve as a Swedish base area for a renewed operation against the important city. The King also advised the conquest of Pechory, Izborsk, and Ostrov near Pskov, not least to prevent King Sigismund from taking them first.[5]

When negotiations finally collapsed, the question arose as to how to continue the war. In addition to the defensive measures already mentioned, De la Gardie argued for an attack on Tikhvin. However, Gustavus Adolphus considered such a campaign too ambitious with present resources. Instead, he decided upon another action against Pskov. For this campaign, the King promoted Carl Gyllenhielm, his half-brother and De la Gardie's old friend, to field marshal. Gyllenhielm had now returned home after spending 13 years in chains in Polish captivity. He received orders to conquer Pskov, build the aforementioned base at the mouth of River Velikaya in Lake Peipus, make sure the base was manned, and then if time allowed also conquer Pechory, Izborsk, and Ostrov.

Gyllenhielm received an army consisting of, at most 1,268 horse, 120 dragoons, and 2,148 foot for the campaign against Pskov – barely a third of the military force the Swedish Crown had employed for this purpose in 1615. The men were taken from a number of regiments, with the majority being Finns from Rechenberger's Regiment and enlisted soldiers from the Commanding General's Regiment. The horse primarily consisted of Finnish cavalry and La Chapelle's dragoons.[6]

The campaign began cautiously, because rumour had it that a Commonwealth army was already advancing against Pskov. While this rumour turned out to be false, the Swedish hesitation together with the lack of men precluded any overly ambitious plans. Gyllenhielm marched out of Narva on 28 July, bound for Pskov by way of Gdov. He reached Pskov on 9 August. As expected, it was difficult to find food supplies for the army. Moreover, on 17 September a Muscovite surprise attack on the Swedish *lodja* squadron with food supplies from Narva, commanded by Rechenberger, severely disrupted the Swedish logistical effort. The Muscovites captured all the supply vessels and Rechenberger had to continue to Pskov on foot.

Lacking food supplies, Gyllenhielm had little choice, and he abandoned the siege of Pskov on 23 September. He retreated to Narva, only leaving a small detachment of 280 Finnish infantry and 40 cavalrymen under

---

4   For practical reasons, the construction of a redoubt at Sermaksa was first postponed and then cancelled. However, a palisade was built in 1616 to protect the Ladoga Squadron. This turned out to be sufficient to safeguard the river mouth for the duration of the war.
5   Generalstaben, *Sveriges krig* 1, pp.549–50.
6   Generalstaben, *Sveriges krig* 1, pp.553–4.

Björn Borge and Matts Olsson in the newly built fortified camp near Pskov. Ominously, the garrison could be given food supplies for only two months.[7]

Having reached Narva, Gyllenhielm immediately made preparations to resupply Borge's and Olsson's garrison. Additional *lodja* vessels became available on 24 October. Unfortunately for the Swedes, this was the time when Lake Peipus began to freeze, which made a riverine mission impossible.

Besides, on 11 October the Pskov Army laid siege to the camp. Despite daily sallies and skirmishes, the garrison was cut off until 13 November. Then, after a two-day break, the Muscovites resumed the siege on 15 November. When the news reached Narva, Gyllenhielm immediately sent a Swedish relief expedition under Rechenberger. However, out of food for at least 10 days, the surviving Swedes at Pskov on 11 December surrendered under terms of free departure. Rechenberger's relief expedition encountered the retreating Swedish survivors three days later, upon which all returned to Narva.

---

7   Generalstaben, *Sveriges krig* 1, pp.555–6.

24

The Treaty of Stolbovo and Truce of Deulino

Regardless of the Swedish setback at Pskov, by the end of 1616 the two sides had agreed on terms for peace. The war ended on 17 February 1617 with the Treaty of Stolbovo, in which Muscovy ceded Kexholm County and most of Ingria including Nöteborg, Ivangorod, Jama, and Kaporie to Sweden, while the Swedish Crown renounced its claims to the Muscovite throne and recognised Michael Romanov as Tsar of Muscovy. Sweden returned Novgorod, Staraya Russa, Porkhov, Gdov, Somero Region, and Ladoga Town, while Muscovy again renounced all claims on Estonia and Livonia. Muscovy also agreed to pay a monetary restitution of 20,000 roubles. Both parties agreed on the establishment of a free trade regime, with Swedish trade representations to be established in Moscow, Novgorod, and Pskov, and Muscovite ones in Stockholm, Reval, and Viborg.

Modern historians have made much of the contribution to the Treaty by John Merrick. His mediation benefited Sweden in that it excluded Muscovy from the Baltic Sea, which was a means to prevent the Muscovites from establishing trading stations of their own. However, Merrick is also generally believed to have had a hand in ensuring that Sweden never came close to achieving the original war objective of Gustavus Adolphus's father, which was to gain control over Arkhangel'sk on the White Sea and the important northern trade route between western Europe and Muscovy through this port. Merrick had personal interests in the Anglo-Muscovite trade through Arkhangel'sk, so he preferred not to see any Swedish influence there. Yet, we have seen that already in December 1613 Gustavus Adolphus was prepared to drop this objective because of the outcome of the Kalmar War. He was equally prepared to drop Novgorod, since he was aware that his army lacked the strength to control the territory. In fact, the Swedish gains in the treaty corresponded exactly to those non-negotiable territorial demands that Gustavus Adolphus decided upon in January 1614. With or without Merrick, Gustavus Adolphus gained exactly what he set out to achieve. Conspicuous evidence of this is the fact that Tsar Michael and his advisors ordered the treaty terms to be kept secret from the

Muscovite population.[1] Their revelation might have caused further unrest and uprisings. Nonetheless, the treaty ultimately served both Sweden and Muscovy well. After the war, Sweden became the first country to maintain a permanent diplomatic representative in Moscow. The two countries grew into allies, a relationship that supported both during the coming Thirty Years' War.

At some point shortly before the Swedish garrison finally pulled out of Novgorod, the city's tax records fell into Swedish hands. The aforementioned interpreter and intelligence officer Erik Andersson was presumably the one who expropriated key census documents from Novgorod for later Swedish use. Such a task would certainly have been delegated to a man who was familiar with the region and could understand the documents, and sure enough, Andersson was later accused by the city authorities of having stolen key documents. From the occupation of Novgorod to the final peace treaty, Andersson spent much of the war in the city where he also was responsible for the army's logistics – another task traditionally carried out by army intelligence officers. The expropriated census documents came in handy for the Swedish surveyors when the new Swedish–Muscovite border was delimited after the war, and as could be expected, Andersson accompanied the surveyors on their travels to determine the new border.[2] Andersson had certainly acted upon orders. An annotation in the Swedish National Archives offers an excerpt of a 1617 letter from Gustavus Adolphus to De la Gardie, in which the former notes:

> Moreover, considering that our border commissioners are to mark out the new border, it is probably the case that we lack particulars of how far the lands around the fortifications ceded to us by the Muscovites extended. It has been said that the best particulars of this were to be found at the Novgorod Chancellery, and we can only assume that you have now arranged to search for them there.[3]

After the campaigns in Muscovy, Gustavus Adolphus turned his attention to the Polish-Lithuanian Commonwealth. King Sigismund still laid claim to the Swedish throne. Before the late King Charles had secured Finland, there had been a measure of support for Sigismund there, which Charles had purged without mercy, just as he purged Sigismund's supporters everywhere. Hence, a number of Swedish Catholics had relocated to the Commonwealth.

---

1 Smirnov, *Den svenske tsaren*, p.245.
2 Erik Andersson was ennobled in 1626 for his years of valuable service. Assuming the family name Trana, he then held several high posts, until he fell at the siege of Minden in Germany in 1634.
3 Swedish National Archives (Riksarkivet, RA), RR, SE/RA/1112.1/B/128 (1617). Translation based on Elisabeth Löfstrand and Laila Nordquist, *Accounts of an Occupied City: Catalogue of the Novgorod Occupation Archives 1611–1617*, Vol. 1 (Stockholm: Riksarkivet 24, 2005), p.35.

King Sigismund had excellent Catholic credentials, including marriages into the Habsburg family; he also made the Commonwealth a centre for Jesuits. This was the time of the Counter-Reformation, the period of Catholic resurgence which took place in response to the Protestant Reformation. Many Swedes suspected, at times correctly, that the Jesuits in the Commonwealth constantly plotted against Lutheran Sweden, and already in 1612, Gustavus Adolphus had expressed his concern over the threat that Sigismund would return on the wings of a Catholic invasion army. In a letter, Gustavus Adolphus noted that a Commonwealth army, if it set out from Livonia or Pskov, could reach Viborg in Finland in only a few days. And from Viborg, it would be easy for Sigismund to regain control over Finland, either by promises or threats.[4] In 1614–1615, when Gustavus Adolphus was personally engaged in Muscovy, King Sigismund began to lay plans for a new offensive against Sweden, planned to take place as soon as the truce lapsed in September 1616. Sigismund's designs against Sweden continued in 1616, when a Commonwealth parliament promised to support the King's dynastic ambitions, in this case to confirm his son as Tsar of Muscovy.

While the late King Charles and his supporters, especially within the Church, had instilled a strong belief in the Swedish population that Sigismund's claim to the throne was merely a Popish plot to reintroduce Catholicism in Sweden, Gustavus Adolphus's distrust of Sigismund, Catholics, and Jesuits was not the result of mere paranoia. King Sigismund and his supporters regularly sent agents with letters to incite strife in Sweden. We have seen that in 1612 Hetman Chodkiewicz, followed in 1613 by King Sigismund, sent letters to Jacob De la Gardie in Novgorod, inviting him to join Sigismund's faction. De la Gardie immediately forwarded the letters to Gustavus Adolphus and Chancellor Oxenstierna, so as not to be suspected of treason. By 1615 at least one more such letter, to the Bishop of Strängnäs, a town in the Swedish heartland, ended up in the hands of Oxenstierna. In 1616 a letter from Sigismund was even directed to Gustavus Adolphus's cousin John, Duke of Östergötland, who upon receipt handed it over to the King, unread. The letter to Duke John was carried by a young man named Henricus Petri Hammerus, the son of a Swedish mayor; it turned out that Sigismund's men had recruited Hammerus, then a university student down on his luck. In early 1617 he carried two letters to Sweden, one to Duke John, which was concealed in the shaft of a hunting knife, and the other, an enciphered letter destined for an already present agent in Sweden, hidden in a sheep's leg bone. Hammerus subsequently buried the sheep's leg bone under a particular spruce tree in the cemetery of the log church in Långasjömåla, Härlunda parish, where the recipient was supposed to retrieve it (in twentieth-century intelligence tradecraft, this procedure would be referred to as a dead-letter drop). Hammerus was arrested and

---

4 Mirkka Lappalainen, *Det nordiska lejonet: Gustav II Adolf och Finland 1611–1632* (np: Fischer & Co, 2016), p.61.

THE TREATY OF STOLBOVO AND TRUCE OF DEULINO

convicted to death for treason, but not before he revealed that he had been authorised to tell Sigismund's Swedish supporters that a Commonwealth army would attack Sweden in the spring of 1617. There would be naval landings in Stockholm and Kalmar, he said, together with a simultaneous invasion of Estonia and Finland from the east.[5]

The plans sounded credible. News from Danzig mentioned preparations for war. The then Emperor Matthias had permitted King Sigismund to have one of his Swedish Catholics, Gustav Sparre (1582–1629), enlist soldiers within the Empire for an invasion of Sweden, and the Polish king had sent an envoy to Lübeck, demanding that the old Hanseatic city supply an invasion fleet. Spain, too, promised to support the coming war with 6,000 men and a fleet of ships and indeed requested permission from Denmark to move the fleet through Danish waters. In response, Sweden prepared its defences. However, the troops enlisted in the Empire never arrived, since the Emperor suddenly needed them in Silesia and Bohemia (where the Thirty Years' War soon would break out). Oxenstierna had his own agents in the Commonwealth, so he presumably knew that the invasion threat, although real enough, was unlikely to materialise; however, he could hardly ignore the persistent pattern of Commonwealth plots against the Swedish king. Nor could Gustavus Adolphus, who was the direct target of the plots. The next winter, the Swedish leaders again suspected that a Commonwealth army would cross the ice of the Gulf of Finland to invade the province of Nyland in Finland. In response, military forces were deployed to the small town of Helsingfors (modern-day Helsinki).[6] The fear of a Commonwealth invasion army would continue to haunt Swedish foreign policy until 1632, when both Sigismund and Gustavus Adolphus ultimately died.

Unable to find the means to invade Sweden, King Sigismund in March 1617 instead sent a Commonwealth army under his son Władysław and Hetman Chodkiewicz into Muscovy. Having secured Muscovy, the King thought, it would be easy also to conquer Sweden. However, a Muscovite army under Princes Dmitriy Pozharskiy, Dmitriy Cherkasskiy, and Boris Lykov-Obolenskiy ultimately repulsed the Commonwealth army near Mozhaysk, west of Moscow. Nonetheless, the Commonwealth–Muscovite war continued, not least because in 1618 a large Ukrainian cossack army of reportedly some 20,000 men under Hetman Pyotr Kononovich Sagaydachnyy (also known as Pyotr Konashevich; c. 1582–1622) launched a second invasion, this time from the south by way of Kiev, in support

---

5 Hunting knife letter and dead-letter drop: Oskar Garstein, *Rome and the Counter-Reformation in Scandinavia 2: Until the Establishment of the S. Congregatio de Propaganda Fide in 1622* (Oslo: Universitetsforlaget, 1980), pp.392–9. General background: Axel Norberg, *Polen i svensk politik 1617–26* (Stockholm: Stockholm University, dissertation, 1974), p.34; Stefan Östergren, *Sigismund: En biografi över den svensk-polske monarken* (np: Fredestad, 2005), p.175; Lappalainen, *Det nordiska lejonet*, pp.160–63; citing archival sources.

6 Norberg, *Polen*, pp.40–41; Östergren, *Sigismund*, pp.173, 181; Lappalainen, *Det nordiska lejonet*, pp.160–63, 186.

Hetman Pyotr Sagaydachnyy, 1622.

of the Commonwealth cause. King Sigismund had promised the Ukrainian cossacks a one-time payment for the effort but what really attracted them was the opportunity to plunder. They accordingly operated in the same manner as Lisowski's marauders (who, by then under Stanisław Czapliński, continued their reign of terror under the protection of Chodkiewicz). Some reports suggest that the carnage inflicted by Sagaydachnyy's and Czapliński's marauders on rural Muscovy were worse than anything previously seen in the Time of Troubles.[7] This time, Chodkiewicz applied a scorched-earth strategy on Muscovy in order to force Tsar Michael to negotiate.

Neither invasion army managed to conquer Moscow, but it was equally obvious that Tsar Michael lacked the resources to reciprocate with an invasion of the Commonwealth. On 1 December 1618, Commonwealth and Muscovite representatives met in a small town near Moscow to sign the Truce of Deulino, which granted the Commonwealth new territories, including the city of Smolensk and the Chernigov region of Severia. Among Tsar Michael's reasons for surrendering so much territory was his desire finally to have his father, Patriarch Filaret, returned from his years in Commonwealth captivity, something that King Sigismund would not accept unless he first received compensation in lands. In 1619, King Sigismund released Patriarch Filaret and returned him to Moscow. The Truce of Deulino, not the ascension of Michael Romanov, can be said to mark the end of Muscovy's Time of Troubles. The 14½-year truce of Deulino marked the failure of King Sigismund's attempt to put himself or his son Władysław on the throne of Muscovy, yet the agreement also marked the greatest geographical expansion ever of the Polish-Lithuanian Commonwealth. This state of affairs lasted until the Swedes under Gustavus Adolphus returned to conquer the Commonwealth-held Livonia.[8]

---

7   On 20 April 2022, Ukrainian Metropolitan Epifaniy canonised Hetman Sagaydachnyy as the patron saint of the modern Ukrainian army.
8   On this invasion, see Fredholm von Essen, *Lion from the North* 1, pp.27–38.

THE TREATY OF STOLBOVO AND TRUCE OF DEULINO

Map 12. Border changes after the Treaty of Stolbovo and the Truce of Deulino.

25

The Legacy and Implications of the War

The Treaty of Stolbovo was Gustavus Adolphus's first great political success. In a speech to the Estates at the Stockholm parliament immediately after the conclusion of the Treaty in 1617, he summarised its results, with pride but also accuracy:

> For what could be more glorious than to have driven back this our mighty neighbour, with whom we have for ages lived side by side on uncertain terms and with precarious safety, so that he has been forced to yield up those robber-nests from which he was wont to harm us, and is now, by the grace of God, separated from us by lakes, morasses and rivers over which he will not easily be able to do us harm. In the past his near neighbourhood was hurtful to us, since he was so close at hand, and for the greater part of the length of the frontier on that side of the sea. Moreover, he had the advantage of convenient rivers with their numerous river-craft – rivers which rise deep within his best and most populous lands; and by their means it was very easy for him to concentrate his forces, and bring them downstream to fall upon us. …
> Finland is now separated from Muscovy by the great Lake Ladoga, which is as broad as the sea between Sweden and Åland, or between Estonia and Nyland – and over that no Pole so far has ventured. And I trust in God that in future it will be no easy matter for the Muscovite to leap such a stream. And if he should get over it, which God forbid, next after God's power the fortresses of Kexholm and Nöteborg – strong both by art and nature – should hold him up for a while, and bar his way into Finland. Estonia is protected by Narva and Ivangorod, as well as by the rapid river Narova, which rises in the beautiful Lake Peipus, which is no easy stream to overpass. Nor are Narva and Ivangorod easy to capture; and unless they be captured no soldier will be very anxious to venture to the other side

THE LEGACY AND IMPLICATIONS OF THE WAR

of the Narova. ...

Ingria is protected on three sides by the Baltic, by Lake Ladoga, and by Lake Peipus; and where it abuts on Muscovy is defended by vast swampy marshes, which divide Swedish territory from that of Muscovy. Lake Ladoga also covers the flank of a good deal of Kexholm County, and of Karelia, and the latter runs up to the Arctic fells, where no army can pass. Thus, it seems as though God had intended, in this hour of victory, to give us the protection of Nature itself against our false foe the Muscovite ... for he cannot now launch a single *lodja* on the Baltic without our permission. Nöteborg lies athwart the Nyen; Ivangorod and Narva stand on either bank of the Narova, and past these he cannot come.[1]

For Sweden, the Treaty of Stolbovo has been described as the most successful peace ever negotiated with Muscovy or its successor Russia. It secured Finland from Muscovite attacks and excluded the Tsar from the Baltic Sea. For Muscovy, the treaty signified the ascension of the House of Romanov. For both countries, the war led to significant military reforms which, in time, would make both the Swedish and Muscovite military establishments forces to be reckoned with. For Gustavus Adolphus, the war in Muscovy proved a significant step on his path to success in the subsequent Thirty Years' War.

Gustavus Adolphus realised that a reform of the Swedish military establishment was a key task to ensure his and his dynasty's right to the Swedish Crown in the face of opposition from the Polish King Sigismund. The ongoing wars that he inherited at first allowed little time for reform. Time finally became available only with the end of the war with Muscovy in 1617. De la Gardie's cavalry had already held its own against Commonwealth hussars at the battles at Tver' in 1609, yet this had not erased the memory of Kircholm. And the infantry had not yet fully adapted to the requirements of modern warfare, or the Dutch model. Moreover, soldiers enlisted abroad were seldom dependable and might switch sides at any moment, were they not regularly paid – and the Swedish Crown had limited monetary revenues.

Gustavus Adolphus needed to modernise the army's organisation and tactics, but he also needed to modernise its arms and equipment, which demanded substantial imports which Sweden hardly could afford.

Gustavus Adolphus, 1618. 'The Lion from the North', as he would become known in the Thirty Years' War and to posterity. (Gold medal, Economy Museum – Royal Coin Cabinet/SHM, Stockholm)

---

1 Speech to the Estates at the opening of the Stockholm parliament, 26 August 1617, Carl Hallendorff (ed.), *Tal och skrifter av Konung Gustav II Adolf* (Stockholm: P. A. Norstedt, 1915). Pp.46–55, on pp.46–53.

The answer then became to establish a domestic arms industry, ensure the import of necessary raw materials, and preferably simultaneously, raise a modern army. There was also the need to reform the economy so as to enable the establishment of an arms industry in the first place. Gustavus Adolphus and Oxenstierna accordingly sought to apply a three-pronged model to Sweden: the Crown would provide security throughout the realm through a modern army; this secure environment would enable modernisation, which they interpreted as the introduction of a functioning administration and modern industry, including an arms industry; and the private and Crown-supported economic initiatives inherent in modernisation would enable the economic reform necessary to pay for the costs of building security. The three concepts – security, modernisation, and economic reform – were interlinked. Gustavus Adolphus understood that to succeed, he could not have one without the others.

This was a serious problem, which might have killed the modernisation process before it got underway. Gustavus Adolphus did not have the economic resources to begin the process. The Kalmar War had shown that Sweden could not even support its own army on Swedish territory. During the wars of 1609 to 1617, we have seen that the total Swedish military establishment rarely reached an actual strength exceeding 15,000 men, and expeditionary forces were usually no larger than from 3,500 to 7,000 men. Yet, the simultaneous wars against Denmark, the Commonwealth, and Muscovy had needed significantly higher numbers. Around 1615, Axel Oxenstierna prepared a proposal on the number of soldiers that were needed in times of peace. It concluded that Sweden needed 22,200 foot, 4,000 horse, and 544 artillerymen. The navy needed 4,560 sailors, 776 artillerymen, and 3,160 shipboard troops for its warships. In total, Oxenstierna's proposal suggested a total military establishment of 35,240. To this he added the existing garrisons, some 3,700 men, producing a grand total of 38,940. In similarity to many other of Oxenstierna's troop strength proposals, then and later, this was an ideal that ultimately could not be reached, For instance, in 1620 the real number of soldiers was listed as 19,356 foot and 2,177 horse.[2] Two years later, in 1622, the total number of sailors was still just above 2,000.[3] As for the army, it only reached the proposed numbers around 1623. Yet, the proposal shows that Sweden's military needs were significantly larger than what the country's economy could sustain.

To fund the army, the Crown needed to move the army abroad to live off another monarch's territory, receive financial subsidies from other rulers, or both. Abroad, Gustavus Adolphus could raise money by the then prevailing system of requesting contributions. A contribution (German: *Kontribution*) was an impost in money or kind, levied under the threat of

---

2   Hamilton, *Afhandling*, pp.56, 57.
3   Lars Ericson, *Krig och krigsmakt under svensk stormaktstid* (Lund: Historiska Media, 2004), p.112.

THE LEGACY AND IMPLICATIONS OF THE WAR

force. The concept seems to have derived from, and absorbed elements of, the old custom of demanding money to ransom property which under then prevailing law of war could be looted or burned (*Brandschatzung*).[4]

Yet, while this might sustain the army for a while, it would not sustain the much-needed military, industrial, and economic reform. For this, Sweden needed to gain control over the Baltic trade routes to raise sufficient revenue to finance the modernisation process. King Charles had hoped to gain control over the Muscovy trade through control of the Arctic route over Arkhangel'sk as well as the Gulf of Finland route over Narva. The Kalmar War had shown that Sweden could not realise the former, and the Arctic route remained under Danish sovereignty. And while the Narva trade was important, other powers could trade with Muscovy through the Commonwealth's Baltic Sea ports. It was accordingly imperative to gain control over the latter, in particular Riga but also the Prussian ports including Danzig.

A successful campaign in Livonia and Prussia would raise revenue, while the war would sustain the operational expenses of the army and simultaneously, with a little luck, deal with King Sigismund. There really was no other solution. Foreign subsidies were unavailable, and the Swedish Crown was already at war with the Commonwealth. Gustavus Adolphus accordingly chose to move his army overseas, into enemy territory.

It turned out to be the correct decision. Over time, Gustavus Adolphus succeeded in developing Sweden's natural resources, establishing new manufacturing, ending the commercial isolationism of most of his predecessors, and creating an economy that could sustain his security and foreign policy objectives.[5]

Jacob De la Gardie had shown his worth during the years when he was in overall command on the eastern front. He had learnt to understand the region, and on policy issues he had not always agreed with distant Stockholm.

---

4 F. Redlich, 'Contributions in the Thirty Years' War', *Economic History Review*, New Series 12:2 (1959), pp.247–254.

5 On this, see Fredholm von Essen, *Lion from the North* 1. Gustavus Adolphus's policy initiatives also enabled continued rapid population growth. Twentieth-century historians failed to see the growth in population during Sweden's time as a great power because of preconceived notions of a century in which the agricultural population, burdened by conscription, war-related taxation, epidemics, and famines, struggled for survival. In reality, Sweden's new-found political and military power enabled fresh and lucrative opportunities in the export of iron, copper, and essentials for shipbuilding such as tar, pitch, hemp, flax, and especially timber to Dutch and English ports. This in turn opened up employment opportunities outside the agricultural sector which stimulated the economy, increased social mobility, reduced barriers to marriage and the forming of new households, and effectively reduced the age of marriage for women, which in turn stimulated fertility and population growth. By the second half of the century, Sweden imported huge volumes of grain from overseas to feed the growing share of the population engaged in non-agricultural production. Palm, *Sweden's 17th Century*, p.32.

Losing his proconsular powers after the war must have felt like a demotion. Possibly as a small token of consolation, and surely in recognition of his expertise, Gustavus Adolphus in 1621 appointed De la Gardie Governor-General of Livonia, and seven years later Grand Marshal of the Realm. But before this, in an unrelated move, De la Gardie in 1618 married Ebba Brahe, the former sweetheart of a youthful Gustavus Adolphus, who by then had come to terms with the fact that a King's marriage was not a matter of personal choice but an affair of state. While we do not know Ebba's views on the match with De la Gardie, the marriage was harmonious and the couple ultimately had 14 children.

For King Sigismund, the annexation of vast territories in the east was a great success. However, the ambition to bring Muscovy into the Commonwealth and possibly also spread the Catholic faith to the east had failed as miserably as his previous attempt to bring Sweden into a union with the Commonwealth. Worse, his successes in battle against Swedes and Muscovites instilled in the latter an understanding of the need for military modernisation and further increased the tendency to centralisation that already was underway in the governments of both countries and henceforth grew yet stronger. Meanwhile, the same successes instilled overconfidence and complacency in Warsaw and engendered a belief among Polish nobles that the Commonwealth needed neither modernisation nor centralisation. King Sigismund's policies towards Sweden and Muscovy constitute a classic case of overextension and unnecessary escalation that ultimately caused far more harm than good. In the long term, this would doom the prospects of the Polish branch of the House of Vasa and prove disastrous to the Commonwealth, which grew increasingly sidelined as a European power and ultimately was partitioned out of existence.[6]

For Muscovy, the Swedish intervention had formed but one part of the nightmarish Time of Troubles. Despite the Swedish occupation of Novgorod and the fighting around Pskov, Sweden had mostly come across as an ally. A greater problem had been the opportunistic meddling in Muscovite affairs by King Sigismund – and in extension the Commonwealth. Muscovy would not soon forget the threat posed by what it correctly perceived as Commonwealth dreams of expansion.[7] That the meddling, in reality, to

---

6   For the end of the Polish branch of the House of Vasa and the beginning of the end for the Commonwealth, see Fredholm von Essen, *Charles X's Wars* (Warwick: Helion, 3 vols, 2021–2023).

7   The memory of King Sigismund's invasion remains alive in modern-day Russia. The introduction by Russia's President Vladimir Putin of a 'National Unity Day' on 4 November 2005 was no more than a reinstatement of the 'Day of Moscow's and Russia's Deliverance from the Poles in 1612', commemorated in Russia prior to the 1917 Russian Revolution, in remembrance of the day when Prince Pozharskiy and his men on 22 October (O.S.) drove the Commonwealth garrison out of Moscow's Kitaygorod through the divine intervention of the holy icon Our Lady of Kazan'. With the icon's traditional feast day being 25 October (O.S.)/4 November (N.S), this date was chosen as a national holiday.

THE LEGACY AND IMPLICATIONS OF THE WAR

a far higher extent was the result of King Sigismund's personal dynastic ambitions than any objectives of the Commonwealth nobility, which not always gave their unreserved support to King Sigismund's plans, was perhaps less apparent to the Romanov tsars than the fact that a largely Polish army had occupied Moscow for more than two years. Yet another lesson learned for Muscovy was the potential risk of what increasingly had come to be seen as the cossack problem. During the Time of Troubles, cossack bands from the Ukraine, Don, and Caucasus again and again intervened militarily and politically in Moscow politics. Throwing their support behind pretenders to the throne, or abandoning them, enabled some cossack leaders to set themselves up as kingmakers. Others, such as the false Peter, claimed the

The ambiguous legacy of the Swedish intervention in Muscovy is evident from the modern-day monument to the military glory and achievements of Novgorod. This bronze panel shows the liberation of Moscow in 1610. Novgorod's commander, Mikhail Skopin-Shuyskiy, rides into Moscow by the side of his Swedish friend and ally, Jacob De la Gardie ...

... while this suggestive bronze panel illustrates the fall of Novgorod in 1611 to Jacob De la Gardie's Swedish invaders. For the glory of the Orthodox faith, the *protopop* Amos and a handful of streltsy remain defiant until the end, even in the face of the overwhelming might of the Swedish military machine. The modern-day artistic rendition is correct in so far that it was the Church which was most hostile to any non-Orthodox candidate to the throne. (Sculptures by Salavat Aleksandrovich Shcherbakov, 2010)

throne for themselves. Although cossack bands ultimately had endorsed the enthroning of young Michael Romanov, they had proven a military and political force of considerable power. Meanwhile, cossacks had plundered the country far and wide, essentially making a shambles of any attempts of central power. The ease with which destitute peasants 'went cossack' when faced with starvation had only made the problem more acute.

Moreover, the cossack problem was a threat to both Muscovy and the Commonwealth. Ultimately, the emergence and growing numbers of cossacks in both states was the result of widespread peasant flight to the sparsely populated southern frontier in order to escape the rapidly expanding tax burden imposed upon the taxpaying groups of society. The flight of peasants to cossack communities simultaneously deprived the state of revenue, caused a labour shortage in the agricultural sector, and in Muscovy impoverished the servicemen who could no longer find the labour necessary to tend to their lands while they went on active military duty. The phenomenon became a vicious circle, in which peasant flight meant that the tax burden on those who remained increased further, which persuaded yet more men to abandon their fields, which ultimately made the situation unsustainable for both peasants and low-ranking servicemen – and deprived the central government of tax revenues, food supplies, and manpower for the army. The problem had been known for some time, but no government had yet found any solution. The Time of Troubles intensified and aggravated the situation further, and added the ironic twist that henceforth, cossack bands had grown sufficiently strong and numerous to challenge central government on their own terms. The lesson learned in both Moscow and Warsaw was that something had to be done with the cossacks. They would have to be brought under central control, or at least their ambitions must be deflected to foreign targets.

The Swedish conquest and annexation of Kexholm County immediately led to significant migration eastwards towards Muscovite Olonets. Later, after the peace treaty between Sweden and Muscovy, Gustavus Adolphus on 25 February 1618 signed a general amnesty for former inhabitants of Kexholm County. He wanted the Muscovite population to return, so he promised any returnee an exemption from taxation for the first five years and pledged to accept their Orthodox faith. Officially, the Tsar agreed with the Swedish king. However, because of the labour shortage in Muscovy, Muscovite officials made repeated attempts to persuade the migrants to remain where they had settled. Since their key argument was that Orthodox believers could only thrive under Orthodox rule, few returned to Kexholm.

The religious argument was persuasive, because the Orthodox Church was one of the big winners of the Time of Troubles. Following his return from Commonwealth captivity, Patriarch Filaret presided over the development of a powerful and pervasive clerical bureaucracy, which rivalled that of his son, the Tsar. Henceforth Church power, landholdings, and wealth increased greatly. By mid century, the then Patriarch owned some 35,000 serfs. Moreover, the Church used the destruction caused by evil foreign invaders and interventionists during the Time of Troubles as a powerful argument for the preaching of hatred towards the non-Orthodox. All foreign influences were held as evil. As a result, the Church for the best part of a century managed to fuse religiosity with nationalism in a manner not previously seen (and which ultimately faded away following Tsar Peter the Great's reforms), turning the faithful towards increasing xenophobia.[8] We have already seen that the Church had formulated an ideology according to which Mongols, Tatars, and other easterners were evil, had contributed nothing to Orthodox Muscovy, and had to be resisted at all costs. This ideology was now applied to all foreigners. In the view of the Church, the faithful must be continuously encouraged to regard all non-Orthodox as heathens worthy of nothing but hostile contempt. Half a century later, following decades of religious propaganda, foreigners in Muscovy, including foreign embassies, almost daily were faced with obscene gestures and verbal abuse inspired by the Church as the appropriate treatment of heathens.[9] In the plain words of the Swedish intelligence officer Erik Palmquist active in Muscovy at the time: 'They despise all foreigners.'[10]

The Church did not, of course, win over all souls. Some chose to settle in less-regulated territories. Neither Kexholm County nor Ingria, or Nöteborg County as Ingria also became known, were included as part of geographical Sweden or Finland. Although Swedish administrators and garrisons were brought in, some administrative procedures remained different from elsewhere in the kingdom. The population of Kexholm and Nöteborg did not have representation in parliament, but they enjoyed several privileges. The need to persuade the population to remain in place, and the hope that some of those who had migrated would return, ensured that neither of the two counties became subject to the burdens faced elsewhere. They were exempt from conscription. They were also exempt from the new taxes introduced to pay for the ransom of Elfsborg Castle, which was the economically most onerous burden that resulted from the Kalmar War. These exemptions, in particular that of exemption from conscription, meant that the two counties soon became the favoured destination of deserters from other parts of the kingdom – and from Muscovy. Yet worse, the urgent need to get abandoned farmsteads back into production meant that officers of the Crown received authorisation to sign amnesties for past crimes, in particular but not necessarily those committed during the war, for any man who agreed to take over an abandoned farm. As could be expected, a fair number of brigands and rogues took advantage of this deal, and then used the amnesty as a license to carry out fresh robberies and murders. This led to all sorts of complicated legal proceedings, and many hardened criminals

---

8   Dunning, *Russia's First Civil War*, pp.472–4.
9   Ulla Birgegård (ed.), *J. G. Sparwenfeld's Diary of a Journey to Russia 1684–87* (Stockholm: Kungl. Vitterhets Historie och Antikvitets Akademien, Slavica suecana Series A, Vol. 1, 2002), pp.83, 265 n.170.
10 Erik Palmquist, *Några observationer angående Ryssland, sammanfattade av Erik Palmquist år 1674* (Moscow: Lomonosov, 2012), p.98.

escaped justice. In particular the population of Kexholm County, always something of a frontier territory, henceforth grew increasingly lawless and possibly yet more wilful than in the past. Many found smuggling and occasional private raiding a profitable sideline to subsistence farming.[11]

---

11   Kexholm remained under Swedish sovereignty for more than a century, until the Treaty of Nystad in 1721, which formally ended the Great Northern War between Sweden and Muscovy's successor Russia, and terminated the 'Swedish Century' begun with the 1617 Treaty of Stolbovo. The 'Swedish Century' was the time when Sweden rose from the position of a small, northern kingdom into a regional great power which dominated northern Europe and whose influence reached far and wide, throughout the Holy Roman Habsburg Empire but also to eastern powers such as the Commonwealth, Muscovy, Transylvania, the Khanate of the Crimea, and Ottoman Turkey. Many modern-day historians call seventeenth-century Sweden an empire, and for sure, the Swedish Crown also established (admittedly short-lived) colonies in North America and West Africa. In Sweden, the century is usually referred to as the Great Power Period (Swedish: *Stormaktstiden*). The 1721 Treaty of Nystad obligated Sweden to cede to Russia all its gains in 1617 as well as Estonia and Livonia.

Colour Plate Commentaries

1. Swedish Cuirassier, Finnish Retinue of Nobles, 1610

The retinue of nobles provided most of the few cuirassiers that Sweden had. They also contributed men to the heavily armoured Finnish cavalry that served under De la Gardie in Muscovy. This Finnish cuirassier wears full armour, that is, a visored helmet, gorget for the neck, and three-quarter armour that covers the entire upper body and both arms as well as the front half of the upper legs. Many suits of armour came with both a visored helmet and a burgonet. The visored helmet was intended for battle, while the lighter and more comfortable burgonet was worn in camp, on the march, and whenever the need for observation was deemed more important than the need for protection. On the Continent, cuirassiers by this time customarily wore armour that reached down to and included the knees, but contemporary Swedish depictions (almost exclusively found on grave memorials) typically do not show this additional level of protection. Although the Continental style was in the process of reaching Sweden, it clearly had not yet become common there. In a similar manner, this cuirassier wears a breastplate of the peascod belly or goose belly type, which already was falling out of fashion on the Continent. Even in Sweden, professional soldiers mostly wore blackened armour if they expected to use firearms. Yet this noble cuirassier, armed with wheellock pistols and rapier, apparently remains committed to the old school of shining armour, which was kept alive within the nobility.

2. Swedish Harquebusier, Hans Ekholt's Finnish Cavalry Banner, 1617

Harquebusiers constituted the primary type of cavalry in the Swedish army. This harquebusier carries a 16-bore (16.8 mm) wheellock arquebus as his primary armament. The cavalry arquebus is hung from a swivel attached to a bandolier across the left shoulder. It can be fired without unhooking from the bandolier. On the left side of the gunlock, a fairly large leather flap was screwed in place which could be folded over the gunlock so as to protect it. On his right side, the harquebusier carries a special leather strap from his belt with a powder-horn, priming flask, ammunition pouch, and wheellock spanner. As additional armament, a harquebusier might also carry one or two wheellock pistols on his horse, and certainly a sidearm of some kind. This cavalryman carries a modern rapier as sidearm. Other may instead have carried a cavalry cutlass. Although little is known about this weapon, the cavalry cutlass was presumably a cheap cutting sword shorter than a rapier.

This Finnish harquebusier is well-protected. He wears a breastplate and a helmet which might be a morion or a cabasset, which in Scandinavia often is called a pear helmet, because of its pear-shaped, some say almond-shaped top, with a small point.

Units raised in Finland often wore garments of blue or grey woollen cloth, since such cloth was easy to obtain. Hans Ekholt's Finnish harquebusier banner was issued grey cloth at least in 1617. This Finnish harquebusier equally well represents previous Finnish cavalry banners during the war in Muscovy.

3. Swedish Guardsman, Drabant Guard, 1617

The Drabant Guard was not only a fighting unit but also attended upon the King when foreign emissaries visited him. On such occasions, it was imperative that the King's entourage displayed a suitably dignified public façade that was fully consistent with the elevated standing in European affairs that the Swedish Crown claimed. For this reason, the guardsmen were frequently issued new cloth for uniforms. The new cloth was not necessarily of the same colour as the previous issue, so while the Drabant Guard always presented a uniform appearance, there was no permanent uniform as such. For the 1617 coronation of Gustavus Adolphus, the Drabant Guard received yellow garments, with blue trimmings, and feathered hats. The colour of the stockings is unknown, so in this reconstruction we conjectured them as white.

The Drabant-style halberd with concave cutting edge was introduced from Germany in the 1570s and known under this name from 1582 onwards. As a sidearm, this guardsman carries a swept hilt rapier.

4. Swedish Pikeman, Olof Bryngelsson's Karelian Company of Foot, 1615

As noted, units raised in Finland often wore garments of blue or grey woollen cloth. The men of Bryngelsson's Karelian Company were no exception, and were issued grey woollen cloth for garments in 1615. The Crown regularly distributed cloth for garments to common soldiers, which meant that the men of a given unit commonly presented a uniform appearance, with garments of the same style and colour. This pikeman equally well represents other Finnish infantry units during the war in Muscovy.

COLOUR PLATE COMMENTARIES

Pikemen were expected to wear a full set of armour consisting of both breastplate and backplate, gorget, and tassets to protect the upper thighs. Most were issued blackened armour. A pikeman would also wear a helmet. The cabasset seems to have been the most common type, but this pikeman wears a burgonet, an older style which, no doubt, remained in use in remote areas such as Karelia. Pikemen were issued rapiers or cutlasses as sidearms, in this case a rapier. Some might even be issued axes instead of other sidearms.

5. Swedish Arquebusier, the Commanding General's Regiment of Foot, 1614

The Commanding General's Regiment, that is, Jacob De la Gardie's personal regiment, was active in one form or another during the entire war in Muscovy. The men of the regiment were enlisted throughout the Swedish realm as well as on the Continent. In 1614, the men of this regiment were issued grey cloth for garments. The regiment included both pike and shot.

This arquebusier carries a 16-bore (16.8 mm) snaplock arquebus. Unlike musketeers armed with the new but in Sweden still quite rare Dutch 10-bore (19.7 mm) matchlock musket, he needs no fork rest. This soldier wears a helmet of the morion type but is otherwise unarmoured. He carries a rapier as sidearm, with a kind of hilt with S-shaped quillons that was growing increasingly common in the Swedish army, and from the next decade indeed can be called the Swedish style.

6. Swedish Ensign, the Commanding General's Regiment of Foot, 1611

The ensign carried the company colour in battle (but not on the march; this was the task of the company standard-bearer). This ensign carries a colour generally attributed to the period 1611–1615. However, the year 1611 seems the most likely option since the cypher G A stands for Gustavus Adolphus. Following his ascension to kingship, Gustavus Adolphus instead adopted the royal cypher GARS. (*Gustavus Adolphus Rex Sueciae*; Gustavus Adolphus, King of Sweden).When Jacob De la Gardie in 1609 set out on his march into Moscow, and when he in 1611 advanced against Novgorod, he formally did so in the name of Gustavus Adolphus, Grand Duke of Finland. A colour of this type seems very appropriate for either, or both, of these occasions. The colour is 330 cm in breadth and was at least 393 cm in length. The hand grip was short and covered with green wax, with the grip itself covered in cloth.

The ensign is dressed as any officer. He wears no armour, but carries a rapier for self-defence.

7. Polish Hussar, Aleksander Zborowski's White Hussar Banner, 1610

Because of the Polish hussars' origin in the medieval knighthood of western Poland, some hussars by this time still carried as their weapon of choice a knightly longsword akin to the command sword used elsewhere in the region, for use when their lance had shattered. Most, however, would bring a backsword (palash) or an armour-piercing sword instead. As an additional sidearm, this hussar carries a sabre. As protection, he wears half-armour and a *szyszak* helmet.

Many hussars favoured a dress that included a fur cloak, yet most hussars of Aleksander Zborowski's White Hussar Banner instead wore a long rich cloak of woven cloth. The details of the cloak presented here are taken from the painting of the battle of Klushino by Szymon Boguszowicz, the court painter of Field Hetman of the Crown Stanisław Żółkiewski who commissioned the work to commemorate his victory, so we can assume that they are reasonably accurate in its depiction of the dress of a hussar of this unit.

Unlike many easterners, Polish hussars rode in the European manner, with spurs instead of the Mongol-style short whip which was more common among other horsemen in the region.

8. Polish or Lithuanian Cossack-style Cavalryman, Jan Piotr Sapieha's Banner, 1610

Cossack-style cavalrymen were primarily armed with composite bows, carried in a bowcase on the left side and with a quiver of arrows on the right. As a sidearm, this cavalryman carries a sabre. A Lithuanian cavalryman would usually also carry a bear spear (*rogatina*). He is well-protected, being in effect a *pancerni* cavalryman. He wears chainmail armour and a *misiurka* helmet, beneath the round metal plate of which he wears the characteristic flat padding, which makes the helmet look taller. The *misiurka* helmet came with a long chainmail coif or neck guard, which was fastened under the chin when preparing for battle. This cavalryman must feel quite safe, or perhaps it is very warm, because he wears the coif unfastened. Under the armour, he wears the customary dress: a *żupan* undergarment, caftan, and soft leather boots. A cossack-style cavalryman would carry a short whip for guiding his horse instead of wearing spurs.

9. Polish Reiter Cavalryman, Jacques Margeret's Banner, 1610

In the Commonwealth, a cavalryman of the Continental style was known as a *Reiter*, the German term for 'horseman'. Reiter units generally rode heavier horses than those used by native Commonwealth cavalry, especially if heavily armoured in the style of a cuirassier. This fully armoured Reiter wears a helmet, a gorget for the neck, three-quarter armour that covers the entire upper body and both arms as well as the front half of the legs, and high riding boots. Moreover, he wears knee-length cuisses, the additional protection that reaches down to and covers his knees. This Reiter has clearly been in Polish service for some time. This is evident from his ornate cuirass, which is of the style favoured by Polish hussars, and the lobster-tailed pot helmet of the *szyszak* type, which was more comfortable than the burgonet but provided the same level of protection. Germans returning from Polish service were among those who since the late sixteenth century propagated the helmet type in Germany as well, and then under the name *zischägge*. There was otherwise little difference in organisation, equipment, dress, and training between those cavalry units which enlisted for Commonwealth service and those which served in the Swedish army. This Reiter is armed with two wheellock pistols, carried on the horse, and a rapier in the customary manner.

10. Polish *Lisowczyk* Cossack-style Cavalryman, 1610

For years, the Polish soldier of fortune Aleksander Józef Lisowski led a mercenary force that served, among others, the false Dmitriy. Because Lisowski and his men received no formal wages, they were allowed to loot and plunder as they pleased. Lisowski accordingly made a name for himself as a successful marauder. After Lisowski's death in 1616, his men adopted the name *Lisowczycy* or *Lisowczyki* ('Lisowski's men') as a means to profit further from his legend. This cossack-style cavalryman can be taken as typical of those Commonwealth soldiers of fortune who ravaged large areas of Muscovy during the Time of Troubles. His war hammer identifies him as a noble. Of course, the possibility remains that he simply stole the war hammer from somebody he killed. The rest of his dress is of the customary type used by Polish nobles: a *żupan* undergarment, caftan, folded up on one side and fastened to the waist for increased mobility, soft leather boots, and high, fur-lined cap. Armed with a sabre and a long-shafted war hammer, he in addition carries a composite bow in a bowcase on the left side. To this he would add a quiver on the right side. A cossack-style cavalryman would carry a short whip for guiding his horse instead of wearing spurs.

11. Polish Haiduk Infantry Arquebusier, 1610

The national autorament included a few infantry companies, mostly of a type inspired by the Hungarian haiduk system. Haiduk infantry were primarily musketeers. This haiduk infantryman brings the full haiduk armament, that is, an arquebus, sabre, and axe. He has wound a burning slow-match around his left arm, and carries the gunpowder flask and ammunition pouch at his belt. He wears a traditional *magierka* felt cap with several small pipes stuck into the brim. His dress is the customary one: a *żupan* undergarment, a short-sleeved *delia* overcoat with passementerie loops and buttons, folded up on one side and fastened to the waist, tight trousers, and *trzewiki* short boots. When on the march, he would protect his arquebus by carrying it in canvas bag over the left shoulder. Although very significant in sixteenth-century Commonwealth armies, by this time the haiduk companies were already growing obsolete in comparison to Continental companies of foot.

12. Muscovite Voivode, 1609

A voivode was in the Muscovite cavalry army the title used for the commander or deputy commander of a division. Selected from high-ranking princes and boyars, voivodes could afford elaborate mail or scale armour of traditional Turco-Mongol type, with metal plates, joined by straps, to protect the chest, back, arms, and legs. A suit of armour of this type was known as *zertsalo* ('mirror'). This style of armour, in part often covered in silk brocade or velvet, was regularly used in battle by voivodes and well-to-do cavalry. At other times, voivodes wore the traditional garments of the wealthy aristocracy, which like most garments worn by Muscovites at the time were of Inner Asian origin, including the caftan, a long narrow gown, and high, soft boots. Noblemen's clothes were lavish and of high quality, often including silks and expensive furs.

In addition to his sabre, a voivode would typically carry a mace as a symbol of command. He would also bring a pair of pistols in saddle holsters on his horse.

13. Muscovite Cavalryman, 1609

The Muscovite army consisted almost exclusively of cavalry, organised along Mongol lines. This cavalryman carries a composite bow as his primary weapon, which like the accompanying bowcase and quiver, both suspended from the belt, is of Mongol type. A complete set of cavalryman's armaments, including a bow in its bowcase and a quiver full of arrows, was known as a *saadak*. Those who could afford it often carried a bowcase and quiver covered in fabric decorated with embroidery or in appliqué. In addition to the bow, this cavalryman is armed with an axe and a dagger. Most would also carry a sabre. Some would add a pair of pistols (wheellocks or snaplocks) and a musket to their armament.

Like most Muscovite cavalrymen, he wears a short-sleeved, high-collared, densely padded hemp coat (*tegilyay*, from the corresponding Mongol term). Sometimes the *tegilyay* included iron bands or even armour plate fastened inside. In addition, he wears a *shishak* helmet, which also was of Inner Asian origin and which in Poland was known as *szyszak*. He protects his arms with vambraces.

The man's arms, armour, and equipment suggest that he is a provincial hereditary serviceman or a serving man from the retinue of a noble. He rides in the Mongol style, with a saddle and short stirrups, and like all Muscovites at the time, uses a Mongol-style short whip (*nagayka*) instead of spurs.

14. Muscovite Strelets Infantry Musketeer, 1609

The streltsy (sing. strelets, 'shooter') formed the solid backbone of the Muscovite army. The Moscow-ranked streltsy were the most important, but streltsy were also raised in provincial towns as well as on behalf of major monasteries. This strelets carries a matchlock musket as his primary weapon. He carries an ammunition pouch and gunpowder horn at his belt. In addition to the musket, this strelets carries the customary *berdysh* poleaxe which he used as a musket rest as well as for hand-to-hand combat, in particular against cavalry. In addition to these weapons, he carries a sabre as sidearm. He wears the customary Muscovite dress of caftan, high pointed fur or felt hat (*kolpak*), and high, soft boots. The lower edge of the hat could be turned inside-out to display the fur or lining inside. Caftans were often longer, in particular in winter. Streltsy were issued cloth for garments, so the soldiers of a unit would present a uniform appearance. This reconstruction of an early seventeenth-century strelets is based on the depiction of such a soldier in the two maps of Moscow known as the *Tabula Russiae ex autographo, quod delineandum curavit Foedor filius Tzaris Boris desumta*, by Hessel Gerritszoon, and the *Moscovia urbs metropolis totius Russiae Albae*, by Georg Braun and Frans Hogenberg, both based on drawings from the early 1600s.

15. Muscovite Don Cossack Cavalryman, 1609

There were several types of cossacks, ranging from the town cossacks who were voluntary recruits who served as infantry in exchange for wages to the free cossacks who lived in distinct communities along primarily the Don and Volga rivers and often technically were not subjects of the Tsar but were paid money, weapons, cloth, and grain in return for their support in protecting the border against incursions by Crimean and occasionally Ottoman invaders. They were not all horsemen; many were expert boatmen since the communication lines usually followed the major rivers. Cossacks were also hired for service elsewhere and played a prominent role in the expansion into Siberia. This cossack cavalryman, armed with a composite bow, dagger, and sabre, is typical of those who fought for the various pretenders during the Time of Troubles.

16. Muscovite Service Tatar Cavalry Officer, 1613

There were several Tatar enclaves in Muscovy, including, most importantly, those in Kasimov and Temnikov, which raised cavalry units under their own chiefs. However, many Tatars also served within the Muscovite army as servicemen or 'service Tatars' (*sluzhilyye tatary*). Most Tatar soldiers were expert horsemen and often operated in conjunction with cossack cavalry, since their style of fighting was very similar. The main difference between Tatar cavalry units and other Muscovite cavalry was that the former less frequently carried firearms and accordingly were limited to the light cavalry role. Yet, light cavalry was vital for patrolling the southern border, which frequently was under threat from the Crimean Tatars.

This Tatar cavalry officer carries a composite bow in its bowcase and a quiver, as well as a sabre and the mace customarily carried by officers. There is little to distinguish him from a cossack. He may have worn chainmail or splint-mail armour under his caftan, and he has hung his *misyurka* helmet from the belt.

This service officer wears the customary Tatar dress of caftan, high pointed fur hat, and high, soft boots. In contrast, the military elite of the Tatar enclaves within the Muscovite state wore lavish arms and armour, often of the same type as used by the Muscovite boyars and the wealthiest hereditary servicemen.

Flags

1. Sweden: Nyland Cavalry Cornet

Based on the description in the epic poem *Carolomachia*, written by Laurentius Bojerus, the Nyland cavalry from Finland (later to be known as Nyland and Tavastehus regiment) flew a cornet with a helmet crowned with two flags (presumably blue with a cross of yellow or white – that is, heraldic gold or silver).
Colour illustration by Lesley Prince

2. Sweden: Finland Infantry Colour

The Finland infantry was raised in western Finland. According to Bojerus, the Finland infantry (later to be known as the Åbo and Björneborg regiment) flew a colour with a standing bear wielding a sword. Based on later flags, including the national banner flown at the 1617 coronation of Gustavus Adolphus, the field may have been bicolour, in that case blue and yellow.
Colour illustration by Lesley Prince

COLOUR PLATE COMMENTARIES

3. Muscovy: Prince Dmitriy Pozharskiy's Personal Banner

The red silk banner of Prince Dmitriy Pozharskiy depicts on one side Jesus Christ, and on the other, in a scene from the Bible, the Archangel Michael with Joshua kneeling before him removing his boot. The banner was retained by the Pozharskiy family until 1827 when it entered into the Kremlin Armoury in Moscow.
Colour illustration by Fyodor Grigor'yevich Solntsev, 1846–1853

4. The Polish-Lithuanian Commonwealth: King Sigismund's Grand Royal Banner

King Sigismund's Grand Royal Banner (*chorągiew wielki królewska*), carried by Sebastian Sobieski, Grand Standard-bearer of the Crown (*chorąży wielki koronny; vexillifer regni*, a court rank) at the King's wedding procession, as depicted on the anonymous Stockholm Roll, c. 1605. King Sigismund's coat of arms combines the eagle of Poland and the chase of Lithuania with the three crowns and the lion of Sweden, and, in escutcheon, the wheatsheaf of the House of Vasa. The coat of arms is surmounted by a royal crown and framed by the chain of the Order of the Golden Fleece. The original was surrendered to Swedish King Charles X in 1655, following the war popularly known as the Swedish Deluge, and is currently in the Army Museum, Stockholm (AM.084018).

The reconstruction is based on the original and a detail from the Stockholm Roll, which depicts the 1605 wedding procession in Cracow of King Sigismund and his second bride, Constance of Austria. The Stockholm Roll, too, formed part of the trophies surrendered to Swedish King Charles X in 1655. In 1974 Sweden's Prime Minister, Olof Palme, returned the Stockholm Roll to Poland as a goodwill gift to persuade the Polish government to release a former Polish airman, Arkadiusz Korobczyński, who in 1949 defected to Sweden, acquired Swedish citizenship, but then was arrested in Poland on charges of desertion and subversion. The Polish government transferred the Stockholm Roll to the Royal Castle, Warsaw, and released Korobczyński in 1975. (The Stockholm Roll, attributed to Balthasar Gebhardt, 1605)
Reconstruction artwork by Olek Remesz

5. The Polish-Lithuanian Commonwealth: Hussar Officers and Hussar Banner, 1605

Top: Splendidly armed and attired officers in hussar armour and leopard furs, each carrying a mace or war hammer as a symbol of rank and each with a wing of feathers inserted into a wooden frame affixed to his saddle. To add further splendour, at least two have had their horses dyed in white and red, an Eastern practice that remained alive and popular in Poland well into the seventeenth century and perhaps beyond.

Bottom: A formation of fully armed and equipped hussars, each rank attired in uniform furs or cloaks and with identical lance pennants. It remains unknown whether the different ranks, so splendidly uniformed, belonged to the same banner or had been detached as an honour guard from several different banners. Either way, their appearance was spectacular. (Details from the Stockholm Roll, attributed to Balthasar Gebhardt, 1605)

6. The Polish-Lithuanian Commonwealth: Colour of Gostomski's Haiduk Company and King Sigismund's Trabant Guard, 1605

Top: Gostomski's Haiduk Company consisted of 100 men, here formed up in 10 ranks of 10. The under-officers, armed with polearms, have formed up in the front rank. A mounted officer in chainmail supervises the procession.

Bottom: King Sigismund's Trabant Guard, at the time consisting of 66 men, here accompanying clergymen and other notables. The guardsmen are armed with halberds and uniformed in German dress. (Details from the Stockholm Roll, attributed to Balthasar Gebhardt, 1605)

Further Reading

Although a number of books that include brief descriptions of Sweden's war in Muscovy have been published in Polish and Russian, most focus on the conflict between the Commonwealth and Muscovy, with the Swedish participation in the events either downplayed or, in the writings of some nationalist historians, ignored altogether. A first Swedish history of the events, Johannes Widekindi's *Thet Swenska i Ryßland*, was published in 1671. The best modern military history of the Swedish involvement in the war remains the first part of the multi-volume *Sveriges krig 1611–1632* by the Swedish General Staff, published in 1936–1939. This work contains many valuable archive documents relating to the Swedish army under Gustavus Adolphus and is reliable in its use of official records including orders of battle, casualty lists, and logistical inventories. However, its conclusions on tactics and strategy cannot always be taken for granted due to bias in favour of Gustavus Adolphus and extrapolation from developments which took place much later. Moreover, the volume's coverage of the wars before Gustavus Adolphus's accession to kingship does not quite match the standards of the later volumes. Perhaps this can be explained by the fact that this volume was the first which the General Staff historians produced, and that they were primarily interested in events that took place under the direct leadership of their hero, Gustavus Adolphus.

The other key reference work to the military history of Gustavus Adolphus is the multi-volume *Kungl. Svea livgardes historia*, by Bertil C:son Barkman and others, which describes the history of the Swedish Royal Life Guard. Although this work covers a far longer period of time than the General Staff work and, since it focuses on the Life Guard, does not cover every incident of the war, it updates and often provides a better reading of the sources than the General Staff work (in which Barkman indeed was involved). Publication started in 1937 and was not concluded until 1983.

Among Swedish regimental histories, the first two volumes of the multi-volume *Kungl. Artilleriet*, by Jonas Hedberg and others, which describes the history of the Royal Artillery, give a detailed overview of in particular artillery equipment, organisation, and operations during the war. Publication began in 1975 and apparently reached its conclusion in 2011.

For a political history of Sweden's war in Muscovy, the most comprehensive work remains the works by the Swedish historian Helge Almquist (*Sverge och Ryssland 1595–1611*), published as a Ph.D. dissertation in 1907, and the subsequent paper 'Tsarvalet år 1613', published in 1908). A modern study is Alexej Smirnov's *Den svenske tsaren* (first published in Swedish in 2017). Although writing as a journalist, Smirnov's work seems to be the first modern Russian reinterpretation of the election of Gustavus Adolphus as Tsar and the events which ultimately brought Michael Romanov to the throne.

In comparison, more recent *general* works in Swedish on the wars under Gustavus Adolphus are most often derivative and contain little new analysis, although particular aspects have been the subject of often excellent articles and monographs. The beautifully illustrated *Gustav II Adolf och hans folk*, by Göte Göransson, should be mentioned, since it includes a wealth of information on events and dress at the time, including those relating to military matters. Published in 1994, it was the result of years of research into primary sources.

For a modern treatise and re-assessment of the Time of Troubles, currently the most comprehensive work is Chester Dunning's *Russia's First Civil War* (2001). Dunning's treatise, which primarily was written as a refutation of Soviet Marxist interpretations of the Time of Troubles, is wide-ranging, yet suffers from two weaknesses which reduce the power of its arguments. First, and most relevant in the present context, Dunning disregards, and seems to be unfamiliar with, the entire corpus of documentation on the Swedish involvement in the Time of Troubles. The developments in Muscovy cannot easily be understood without also examining the three foreign powers that regularly intervened in Muscovite events. We have seen that Sweden and the Commonwealth played a significant role in respectively northwestern and western Muscovy, and the Khanate of the Crimea played an equally momentous role in southern Muscovy. Second, Dunning's interpretations might be influenced by his very positive assessment of the first False Dmitriy which contrasts with his correspondingly negative views on Tsar Vasiliy.[1] One could also argue with Dunning's continuous and somewhat anachronistic references to 'patriotic forces' for those Muscovites who fought on one side or the other in the

---

1   Dunning goes out of his way to rehabilitate Dmitriy as one of Russia's greatest rulers ever, not least because the young man was 'an exceptional person', 'charismatic and popular', and 'his subjects loved him'. Having gained Moscow, Dmitriy was 'a popular ruler who was not facing an impending social revolution or any kind of rebellion'. Until the very end, the talented Dmitriy 'was utterly fearless and extremely confident of the devotion of his subjects'. Dunning, *Russia's First Civil War*, pp.203, 225, 231, 258. Dunning paints a correspondingly negative picture of the aged and nearsighted Tsar Vasiliy, whom he describes as 'wily', 'treacherous', 'panicky', 'unloved by many of his subjects', and 'widely regarded as an evil, false tsar'. In conclusion, Dunning argues that 'many Muscovites would gladly have killed [Tsar Vasiliy] as a traitor'. Dunning, pp.239, 258, 259, 270, 382, 388. Possibly so, but it was not the Muscovites who killed Vasiliy but Commonwealth captivity and the reason was that King Sigismund preferred his own candidate on the throne.

FURTHER READING

war. We have seen that their motives ranged from greed for power to utter desperation, and from fanatic religiosity to self-defence against plundering marauders. While some, no doubt, preferred to see a countryman on the throne, proximate reasons for taking up arms were quite different from what much later was relabelled as patriotism.

Primary sources to the Time of Troubles are numerous. The early events are described in two important contemporary books by the Swedish diplomat Peder Pedersson (Petrus Petreius). The first, *Een wiss och sanfärdigh Berättelse* (1608), was written in support of Swedish policy but also contains interesting highlights from Pedersson's own observations. The book was reprinted in facsimile in Margareta Attius Sohlman's *Stora oredans Ryssland* (1997). Pedersson's second book, *Regni Muschowitici sciographia* (1614–1615), is less political and more descriptive.

Another eyewitness was the Dutch merchant Isaac Massa (1586–1643), who lived in Muscovy from 1601 until 1609 and described the early years of the Time of Troubles in several manuscripts, primarily *Een cort verhael van begin en oorspronck desser tegenwoordighe oorlogen en troeblen in Moscouia totten jare 1610*. Composed in 1610, it is better known from the combined Dutch and French edition *Histoire des guerres de la Moscovie (1601–1610)*, published in 1866. An English translation was published under the title *A Short History of the Muscovite Wars* (1982). Unfortunately, Massa's work only mentions De la Gardie's expedition in passing on the last few pages. In the 1620s, Massa went into Swedish service and ultimately was ennobled in Sweden.

Konrad Bussow (1552 or 1553–1617) was a German officer in Swedish employ who in 1601 offered his services to and ultimately went into the employ of Tsar Boris. The Tsar employed him, together with the voivode of Ivangorod, as a tool to plot against Narva at a time when the then Duke Charles's rule over Sweden and Estonia was comparatively weak. Among other tasks, Bussow spread rumours that the Commonwealth would move against Narva, and that Tsar Boris was the only ruler who had the power to save the town. The plot was intended to lead up to a coup in Narva in May 1603, but was discovered and foiled, so Bussow fled to Muscovy.[2] He then served Tsar Boris, the first False Dmitriy, and even joined Bolotnikov's army but seems not to have participated in any decisive battle. Later, Bussow likewise joined Sapieha and False Dmitry in Tushino. Bussow produced several manuscripts, primarily *The Disturbed State of the Russian Realm* (*Verwirrter Zustand des russischen Reichs: Moskowitische Chronik*, written in 1614–1617), although their primary focus is on the first False Dmitriy. The events in northwestern Muscovy and De la Gardie's expedition are barely mentioned. Similarly to many of those who wrote histories of the events

---

2   Aleksandr Vladimirovich Tolstikov, 'Narva 1603: K biografii Konrada Bussova', V. D. Nazarov and P. Yu. Uvarov (eds), *Tri daty tragicheskogo pyatidesyatiletiya Yevropy (1598–1618–1648): Rossiya i Zapad v gody Smuty, religioznykh konfliktov i Tridtsatiletney voyny* (Moscow: IVI RAN, 2018), pp.321–9.

during the Time of Troubles, Bussow's intention was to promote himself and justify his personal actions, for which reason his work, although highly entertaining and journalistic in style, is tendentious and often unreliable.

The French soldier Jacques Margeret (c. 1570–1619) described the events in *Estat de l'empire de Russie et Grande Duche de Moscovie*, published in 1607. An English translation was published as *The Russian Empire and Grand Duchy of Muscovy* (1983). Having served numerous Muscovite and Commonwealth notables, Margeret in 1621 went into Swedish service.

One soldier who fought in De la Gardie's army was the Englishman Henry Brereton, who published a brief relation that include details about Horn's campaign in February–June 1610 and the battle of Klushino. Known as *News of the Present Miseries of Russia* (1614), it was reprinted in 1916 with the anonymous *Narrative of an Englishman serving against Poland*, written by a soldier from John Craul's company of foot. Both Brereton and the anonymous soldier seem to have belonged to those who changed sides and went into Commonwealth service during the battle of Klushino, and their narratives may have been written in an attempt to redeem their soldierly honour.

Matthias Schaum, a German priest in the Swedish army, in 1614 published a little book named *Tragoedia Demetrio-Moscowitica*. Although Schaum primarily depended on Petreius's first publication, he also included a brief but unique narrative of the Swedish army from the battle of Klushino to the conquest of Novgorod. Schaum participated in these campaigns, during which he provided spiritual services.

Pierre De la Ville in 1611 provided information about the Time of Troubles and his conquest and subsequent surrender of Ladoga in 1610–1611. His narrative was included in a longer work, *La Chronique de Nestor* (1834).

Many Commonwealth officers wrote about their experiences during the war. Jan Piotr Sapieha employed a secretary who in the years 1608–1611 wrote a diary describing the turbulent activities and constant negotiations with both the Muscovites and King Sigismund at Smolensk. The diary ultimately ended up in Sweden and is preserved in the Swedish National Archives (Skokloster Collection). It was later published by Aleksander Hirschberg in his work *Polska a Moskwa w pierwszej połowie wieku XVII* (1901).

The Crown Field Hetman Stanisław Żółkiewski left us memoirs, known as *Początek i progres wojny moskiewskiej* (probably written in 1612). Although he did not personally witness everything that he described, he was a key participant in the campaigns against Sweden and Muscovy and produced a very readable work.

Numerous other Commonwealth nobles involved in the events wrote memoirs, too. One was Hussar Captain Mikołaj Ścibor Marchocki, who served Dmitriy. About 15 years later, he described his war in *Historya wojny moskiewskiej* (written after 1625, published in 1841). Another was Samuel Maskiewicz, who served King Sigismund. He published his experiences in memoirs probably written between 1625 and 1631, that is, again at least

FURTHER READING

15 years after the events he described. The memoirs were published as *Pamiętniki Samuela Maskiewicza początek swój biorą od roku 1594 w lata po sobie idące* (1838).

Primary sources are necessary for the historian, but they must be read with care. Some are tendentious. Later studies are often helpful to gain an overview of the time and place. A number of these are included in the bibliography. However, since most works on the war in Muscovy are published in other languages than English, the following bibliography is limited to the works most frequently referenced in notes and most useful for continued research. Other works are only mentioned in the notes.

Bibliography

Printed Contemporary Sources and Compilations

Becke, Berthold von der, *Soldaten-Spiegel: Historische Anweisung welcher Gestalt ein Guarison oder Vestung nicht allein mit aller jhrer Notturfft vnnd Zugehörung wohl zu versorgen hohen vnd nidern Aemptern recht anzuordnen* (Frankfurt am Main: Johann Spieß und Johann Jacob Porschen, 1605)

Berry, Lloyd E., and Robert O. Crummey (eds), *Rude & Barbarous Kingdom: Russia in the Accounts of Sixteenth-Century English Voyagers* (Madison: University of Wisconsin Press, 1968)

Birgegård, Ulla (ed.), *J. G. Sparwenfeld's Diary of a Journey to Russia 1684–87* (Stockholm: Kungl. Vitterhets Historie och Antikvitets Akademien, Slavica suecana Series A, Vol. 1, 2002)

Brereton, Henry, *Newes of the Present Miseries of Rushia, Occasioned by the Warre in that Countrey, Commenced betweene Sigimond now King of Poland, Charles late King of Swethland, Demetrius, the last of the name, Emperour of Rushia, Together with the Memorable occcurrences of our owne Nationall Forces, English, and Scottes, vnder the Pay of the now King of Swethland* (London: John Bache, 1614)

Buganov, Viktor Ivanovich (ed.), *Razryadnaya kniga 1475–1598 gg.* (Moscow: Nauka, 1966)

Bussow, Conrad, *The Disturbed State of the Russian Realm* (Montreal: McGill-Queen's University Press, 1994). Translated and edited by George Edward Orchard.

Cotossichin [Kotoshikhin], Grigori Carpofsson, *Beskrifning om muschofsche rijkets staat* (Stockholm: Ljus, 1908)

Danckaert, Jan, *Beschryvinge van Moscovien ofte Ruslant* (Amsterdam: Broer Ianszoon, 1615)

De la Ville, Pierre, *Discours sommaire; De ce qui est arrivé en Moscovie depuis le règne de Ivan Wassiliwich, empereur, jusques à Wassili Ivanovitz Sousky*, par Pierre de Laville, sieur de Dombasle (1611). Paris, Louis (ed.), *La Chronique de Nestor, traduite en français, d'après l'édition imperiale de Pétersbourg (Manuscrit de Kœnigsberg) accompagnée de notes et d'un recueil de pièces inédites touchant les anciennes relations de la Russie avec la France*, Vol. 1. (Paris: Heideloff et Campé, 1834: pp.404–28)

Gheyn, Jacob de, *Die Reitschule oder Übungen der Kavallerie* (Amsterdam: C. J. Visscher, 1599–1600)

Gheyn, Jacob de, *Wapenhandelinghe van Roers, Musquetten ende Spiessen* (Amsterdam: Robert de Baudous, 1608, first published 1607)

Gheyn, Jacob de, *The Exercise of Arms for Calivers, Muskets, and Pikes* (The Hague: n.p., 1607)

Goeteeris, Anthonis [Anton Goeteer], *Journael van de legatie ghedaen in de Jaren 1615, ende 1616* (The Hague: Hendrik Hondius, 1639, first published in 1619)

Hallenberg, Jonas, *Svea rikes historia under konung Gustaf Adolf den stores regering* 4 (Stockholm: Johan A. Carlbohm, 1794)

Hjärne, Harald. 'Utdrag ur ryska krönikor, hufvudsakligen angående Jakob De la Gardies fälttåg 1', *Historiskt bibliotek* 6 (1879): pp.605–18.

Hjärne, Harald, 'Utdrag ur ryska krönikor, hufvudsakligen angående Jakob De la Gardies fälttåg 2', *Historiskt bibliotek* 7 (1879): pp.208–42

Howe, Sonia Elizabeth (ed.), *The False Dmitri. A Russian Romance and Tragedy, Described by British Eye-witnesses, 1604–1612* (New York: Frederick A. Stokes, 1916). Includes the narratives of Henry Brereton and the anonymous soldier from Craul's company.

John of Nassau. 'Grefve Johans av Nassau relation angående kriget i Livland 1601–1602', *Historiska Handlingar* 20 (Stockholm: P. A. Norstedt, 1905: pp.396–438)

Löfstrand, Elisabeth; and Laila Nordquist, *Accounts of an Occupied City: Catalogue of the Novgorod Occupation Archives 1611–1617*, 2 vols (Stockholm: Riksarkivet 24 and 31, 2005 and 2009)

Mankell, Julius, *Uppgifter rörande svenska krigsmagtens styrka, sammansättning och fördelning sedan slutet af femtonhundratalet, jemte öfversigt af svenska krigshistoriens vigtigaste händelser under samma tid*, 2 vols (Stockholm: C. M. Thimgren, 1865)

Marchocki, Mikołaj Ścibor z Marchocic, *Historya wojny moskiewskiej* (Posen: Orędownik, 1841)

Margeret, Jacques, *Estat de l'empire de Russie et Grande Duche de Moscovie; avec Ce qui s'y est passé de plus memorable et Tragique, pendant le regne de quatre Empereurs: à scavoir depuis l'an 1590. jusques en l'an 1606. en Septembre* (Paris: Jacques Langlois, 1669; first published in 1607 by Mathieu Guillemot)

Margeret, Jacques, *The Russian Empire and Grand Duchy of Muscovy: A 17th-Century French Account* (Pittsburgh: University of Pittsburgh Press, 1983). Translation of the above by Chester S. L. Dunning.

Maskiewicz, Samuel, *Pamiętniki Samuela Maskiewicza początek swój biorą od roku 1594 w lata po sobie idące* (Wilno: Teofil Glücksberg, 1838)

Massa, Isaac, *Een cort verhael van begin en oorspronck desser tegenwoordighe oorlogen en troeblen in Moscouia totten jare 1610*. Published in Dutch and French as *Histoire des guerres de la Moscovie (1601–1610)* (Brussels: J. Olivier, 2 vols, 1866)

Massa, Isaac, *A Short History of the Muscovite Wars* (Toronto: University of Toronto Press, 1982). Translation of the above by George Edward Orchard.

Oxenstierna, Axel, *Rikskansleren Axel Oxenstiernas skrifter och brefvexling*, multiple volumes and database. (Stockholm: P. A. Norstedt/Swedish National Archives (Riksarkivet, RA), 1888–2018)

Palmquist, Erik, *Några observationer angående Ryssland, sammanfattade av Erik Palmquist år 1674* (Moscow: Lomonosov, 2012)

Petreius, Petrus, *Regni Muschowitici sciographia: Thet är: Een wiss och egenteligh Beskriffning om Rydzland* (Stockholm: Ignatius Meurer, 1614–1615)

Petreius, Petrus [Peder Pedersson; Peer Peersson], *Een wiss och sanfärdigh Berättelse om några Förandringar som j thesse framledne åhr vthi Storfurstendömet Muskow skedde äre* (Stockholm: Andreas Gutterwitz, 1608)

Sapieha, Jan Piotr, *Dziennik Jana Piotra Sapiehy*, Aleksander Hirschberg (ed.), *Polska a Moskwa w pierwszej połowie wieku XVII: Zbiór materyałów do historyi stosunków polsko-rossyjskich za Zygmunta III* (Lviv: Ossoliński, 1901: 167–332)

Schaumius, Matthias, *Tragoedia Demetrio-Moscowitica: Warhafftige Histori der Wunderseltzamen und Gedenckwürdigen Geschicht, wie es mit dem Demetrio… eigentlich einen anfang und ende gewonnen …* (Rostock: Joachim Fuess, 1614)

Sohlman, Margareta Attius (ed.), *Stora oredans Ryssland: Petrus Petrejus ögonvittnesskildring från 1608* (Stockholm: Carlssons, 1997). Translation of the above.

Sverges Traktater med främmande magter 5: 1 (Stockholm: P. A. Norstedt, 1903)

Ufano, Diego, *Tratado de la artilleria y uso della* (Brussels: Juan Momarte, 1613)

Ufano, Diego, *Artillerie, ou vraye instruction de l'arttillerie et de ses appartenances* (Rouen: Jean Berthelin, 1628; first French edition published in 1614 by Johann Theodor de Bry)

Wallhausen, Johann Jacobi von, *Kriegskunst zu Fuß* (Leeuwarden: Claude Fontaine, 1630, first published 1615)

Wallhausen, Johann Jacobi von, *Kriegskunst zu Pferdt* (Frankfurt am Main: Johann Theodor de Bry, 1616)

Waaranen, Johan E. (ed.), *Samling af urkunder rörande Finlands historia 3 (1609–1611)* (Helsinki: Finska Litteratur-Sällskapet, 1866)

Widekindi, Johannes, *Then fordom Stormächtigste, Högborne Furstes och Herres Herr Gustaff Adolphs den Andres och Stores Sweriges, Götes och Wändes etc. konungs Historia, och Lefwernes Beskrifning, Then Första Deel* (Stockholm: Niclas Wankijf, 1691). A history of Gustavus Adolphus based on archive documents, some of which are now lost.

Widekindi, Johannes, *Thet Swenska i Ryßland Tijo åhrs Krijgz-Historie: Hwilket under twänne Sweriges Stormächtige Konungars, Konung Carls IX. Och K. Gustaf Adolphs den Andres och Stoores Baneer, Storfursten*

Ivan Vasilivitz Suischi och Ryßland til hielp, först emoot the Rebeller och Lithower, sedan the Påler, på sidstonne emoot sielfwe Muskowiterne, ifrån åhr 1607. in til 1617. Aff Feldtherren Gref. Iacob De La Gardie uthfördt, och medh en reputerligh Fredh bijlagdt är, i lijka många Böcker fördellt och sammanfattat (Stockholm: Niclas Wankijff, 1671). A history of Sweden's war in Muscovy based on archive documents, some of which are now lost.

Widekindi, Johannes, *Historia belli sveco-moscovitici Decennalis, quod junctis armis cum Magno Moscorum Duce Johan Basilio Svischio, Primum adversus Rebelles & Lithuanos, mox Polonos, tandem data causa contra ipsos Moscovitas auspiciis Regum Sveciae Caroli IX et Gustavi Adolphi, Ducta Jacobi De la Gardie, Varia fortuna ab Anno seculi hujus Septimo, in decimum septimum gestum, & ardua pace compositum est, Totidem Libris distincta*. Stockholm: Niclas Wankijff, 1672. Reworked Latin edition of the above, with deletions and additions including from works of other historians.

Żółkiewski, Stanisław, *Początek i progres wojny moskiewskiej* (Paris: Rouge, Dunon et Fresné, 1866; probably written in 1612 but only published much later)

Later Studies

Alm, Josef, *Blanka vapen och skyddsvapen från och med 1500-talet till våra dagar* (Stockholm: Rediviva, 1975, first published 1932)

Alm, Josef, *Eldhandvapen 1: Från deras tidigaste förekomst till slaglåsets allmänna införande* (Stockholm: Rediviva, 1976, first published 1934)

Alm, Josef, *Arméns eldhandvapen förr och nu* (Stockholm: Kungl. Armémuseum, 1953)

Alm, Josef, 'Flottans handvapen', *Sjöhistorisk Årsbok 1953-54* (Stockholm: Föreningen Sveriges Sjöfartsmuseum i Stockholm, 1954: 67-147)

Almquist, Helge, *Sverge och Ryssland 1595-1611: Tvisten om Estland, Förbundet mot Polen, de ryska gränslandens eröfring och den stora dynastiska planen* (Uppsala: Uppsala University, Ph.D. dissertation, 1907)

Almquist, Helge, 'Tsarvalet år 1613: Karl Filip och Mikael Romanov', *Historiska studier tillägnade Prof. Harald Hjärne på hans sextioårsdag den 2 maj 1908* (Uppsala: Almqvist & Wiksell, 1908: pp.197-224)

Artéus, Gunnar, *Till militärstatens förhistoria: Krig, professionalisering och social förändring under Vasasönernas regering* (Stockholm: Probus, 1986)

Barkman, G. Bertil C:son, *Gustaf II Adolfs regementsorganisation vid det inhemska infanteriet: En studie över organisationens tillkomst och huvuddragen av dess utveckling mot bakgrunden av kontinental organisation.* (Stockholm: Meddelanden från Generalstabens krigshistoriska avdelning, 1931)

Barkman, G. Bertil C:son, *Kungl. Svea livgardes historia 2: 1560-1611* (Stockholm : Stiftelsen för Svea livgardes historia, 1939)

Barkman, G. Bertil C:son and Sven Lundkvist, *Kungl. Svea livgardes historia 3:1: 1611–1632* (Stockholm: Stiftelsen för Svea livgardes historia, 1963)

Bellander, Erik, *Dräkt och uniform: Den svenska arméns beklädnad från 1500-talets början fram till våra dagar* (Stockholm: Kungl. Armémuseum/P. A. Norstedt, 1973)

Björklund, Jaakko; and Sebastian Schiavone, S 2021, 'Networks of Recruitment: Fiscal-military Operations to Contract Foreign Soldiers for Sweden, 1605–1610', *Northern Studies* 52 (2021): pp.53–97

Bohun, Tomasz, 'Polish-Lithuanian Mercenaries in the Service of Jacob de la Gardie', *Vestnik SPbGU Istoriya* 63: 3 (2018): pp.718–728

Borisov, Nikolay Sergeyevich, *Ivan III: Otets russkogo samoderzhaviya* (Moscow: Akademicheskiy proyekt, 2nd edn 2017)

Broomé, Bertil, *Nils Stiernsköld* (Stockholm: Stockholm University, Ph.D. dissertation, 1950)

Chernov, A. V., *Vooruzhennyye sily Russkogo gosudarstva v XV–XVII vv.: S obrazovaniya tsentralizovannogo gosudarstva do reform pri Petre I* (Moscow: Voyennoye Izdatel'stvo Ministerstva Oborony Soyuza SSR, 1954)

Delbrück, Hans, *History of the Art of War 4: The Dawn of Modern Warfare* (Lincoln: University of Nebraska Press, Bison Books, 1990)

Dunning, Chester Sidney Larson, *Russia's First Civil War: The Time of Troubles and the Founding of the Romanov Dynasty* (University Park, Pennsylvania: Pennsylvania State University Press, 2001)

Dunning, Chester S. L., 'The Richest Place in the World: An Early 17th-Century English Description and Military Assessment of Solovetskii Monastery', Chester S. L. Dunning, Russell E. Martin, and Daniel Rowland (eds), *Rude & Barbarous Kingdom Revisited: Essays in Russian History and Culture in Honor of Robert O. Crummey* (Bloomington, Indiana: Slavica, 2008: pp.309–25)

Dunning, Chester, 'James I, the Russia Company, and the Plan to Establish a Protectorate over North Russia', *Albion* 21: 2 (1989): pp.206–26

Dunning, Chester, 'A "Singular Affection" for Russia: Why King James Offered to Intervene in the Time of Troubles', *Russian History* 34: 1–4 (2007): pp.277–302

Dunning, Chester S. L., 'Captain Jacques Margeret: A Remarkable Huguenot Soldier in Russia's Time of Troubles', *Vestnik VGU Istoriya, Regionovedenie, Mezhdunarodnyye otnosheniya* 24: 2 (2019): pp.76–102

Eerikäinen, Lauri Juhani, and Bengt M. Holmqvist, 'En kondottiärs villkor på Karl IX:s tid', *Meddelande* 35, Stockholm: Armémuseum, 1974–75: pp.45–57

Ericson, Lars, *Krig och krigsmakt under svensk stormaktstid* (Lund: Historiska Media, 2004. First published in 1987).

Fagerlund, Rainer, 'De finska fänikorna under äldre Vasatid: Forskningsläge och problem'. *Turun historiallinen arkisto* 38 (Turku, 1982): pp.94–116.

Filjushkin [Filyushkin], Alexander, *Ivan the Terrible: A Military History* (London: Frontline Books, 2008)

BIBLIOGRAPHY

Fredholm von Essen, Michael, *Muscovy's Soldiers: The Emergence of the Russian Army 1462–1689* (Warwick: Helion, 2018)

Fredholm von Essen, Michael, *Lion from the North* 1–2 (Warwick: Helion, 2 vols, 2020)

Fredholm von Essen, Michael, *Charles X's Wars* 1–3 (Warwick: Helion, 3 vols, 2021–2023)

Fredholm von Essen, Michael, *The Kalmar War 1611–1613: Gustavus Adolphus's First War* (Warwick: Helion, 2023)

Gawron, Przemysław, 'The Battle of Klushino', Grzegorz Jasiński and Wojciech Włodarkiewicz (eds), *Polish Battles and Campaigns in 13th–19th Centuries* (Poznań: Wojskowe Centrum Edukacji Obywatelskiej im. płk. dypl. Mariana Porwita/Stowarzyszenie Historyków Wojskowości, 2016)

Generalstaben, *Sveriges krig 1611–1632*, Vol. 1: *Danska och ryska krigen* (Stockholm: Generalstaben, 1936)

Generalstaben, *Sveriges krig 1611–1632*, Suppl. Vol. 1: *Sveriges sjökrig 1611–1632* (Stockholm: Generalstaben, 1937)

Glete, Jan, *Navies and Nations: Warships, Navies and State Building in Europe and America, 1500–1860*, 2 vols, Stockholm: Almqvist & Wiksell International, Acta Universitatis stockholmiensis (Stockholm Studies in History) 48:1, 1993.

Glete, Jan, 'Vasatidens galärflottor', Hans Norman (ed.), *Skärgårdsflottan: Uppbyggnad, militär användning och förankring i det svenska samhället 1700–1824* (Lund: Historiska Media, 2000: pp.37–49)

Göransson, Göte, *Gustav II Adolf och hans folk* (np: Bra Böcker, 1994)

Grill, Erik, *Jacob De la Gardie: Affärsmannen och politikern, 1608–1636* (Gothenburg: Gothenburg University, PhD Dissertation/Wettergren & Kerber, 1949)

Gullberg, Tom, and Mikko Huhtamies, *På vakt i öster 3: 1600-talet* (np: Schildts, 2004)

Halperin, Charles J., *Russia and the Golden Horde: The Mongol Impact on Medieval Russian History* (Bloomington: Indiana University Press, 1987)

Hamilton, Henning, *Afhandling om krigsmaktens och krigskonstens tillstånd i Sverige, under Konung Gustaf II Adolfs regering* (Stockholm: Kongl. Vitterhets Historie och Antiquitets Academiens handlingar 17, 1846)

Hedberg, Jonas (ed.), *Kungl. Artilleriet: Medeltid och äldre vasatid* (Stockholm: Militärhistoriska Förlaget, 1975)

Hedberg, Jonas (ed.), *Kungl. Artilleriet: Yngre vasatiden* (Stockholm: Militärhistoriska Förlaget, 1985)

Heleniak, Mark, *The Policy of King Sigismund III of Poland-Lithuania towards Muscovy during the War of 1609–1619* (Bundoora, Victoria: La Trobe University, PhD dissertation, 2017)

Hellie, Richard, *Enserfment and Military Change in Muscovy* (Chicago: University of Chicago Press, 1971)

Höglund, Lars-Eric, *Från Karl Knutsson till Kristina: Svenska fälttecken och beklädnad från senmedeltid till trettioåriga kriget* (Karlstad: Acedia Press, 2012)

Ilyushin, B. A., 'Rossiyskiye sluzhilyye tatary v voynakh protiv polyakov i shvedov v 1613–1618 gg.', *Golden Horde Review* 6: 4 (2018), pp.766–782

Jakobsson, Theodor, *Lantmilitär beväpning och beklädnad under äldre Vasatiden och Gustav II Adolfs tid*. Published both separately and as Suppl. Vol. 2 in Generalstaben, *Sveriges krig 1611–1632* (Stockholm: Generalstaben, 1938)

Kargalov, Vadim Viktorovich, *Moskovskiye voyevody XVI–XVII vv.* (Moscow: Russkoye slovo, 2002)

Keep, John L. H., *Soldiers of the Tsar: Army and Society in Russia, 1462–1874* (Oxford: Clarendon Press, 1985)

Kotljarchuk, Andrej, *In the Shadows of Poland and Russia: The Grand Duchy of Lithuania and Sweden in the European Crisis of the mid-17th Century* (Södertörn University College, dissertation, 2006)

Kovalenko, Gennadij, and Elisabeth Löfstrand (eds), *Novgorodiana Stockholmiensia* (Stockholm: Stockholm University, Stockholm Slavic Papers 19, 2012)

Kurbatov, Oleg Aleksandrovich, *Tikhvinskoye osadnoye sideniye 1613* (Moscow: Zeughaus, 2006)

Lappalainen, Mirkka, *Det nordiska lejonet: Gustav II Adolf och Finland 1611–1632* (np: Fischer & Co, 2016)

Malov, Alexander, 'Standards of Russian Cossacks in 1613–1619', Karin Tetteris (ed), *In Hoc Signo Vinces: The Vexillological Seminar, Stockholm 2011 & 2013* (Stockholm: Armémuseum, 2016: pp.79–88)

Munthe, Ludvig W:son, *Kongl. Fortifikationens historia 1: Svenska fortifikationsväsendet från nyare tidens början till inrättandet af en särskild fortifikationsstat år 1641* (Stockholm: P. A. Norstedt, 1902)

Nossov, Konstantin, *Russian Fortresses 1480–1682* (Oxford: Osprey Fortress Series 39, 2006)

Östergren, Stefan, *Sigismund:En biografi över den svensk-polske monarken* (np: Fredestad, 2005)

Ostrowski, Donald, *Muscovy and the Mongols: Cross-Cultural Influences on the Steppe Frontier, 1304–1589* (Cambridge: Cambridge University Press, 1998)

Palm, Lennart Andersson, *Sweden's 17th Century: A Period of Expansion or Stagnation?* (Gothenburg: Gothenburg University, 2016)

Petander, C.-B. J., 'Anteckningar om österbottniskt fotfolk före år 1625', *Österbotten 1964: Svensk-Österbottniska Samfundets årsbok* (Vasa: Svensk-Österbottniska Samfundet, 1964: pp.7–108)

Petri, Gustaf, *Kungl. Första livgrenadjärregementets historia 1: Östgötafänikorna till och med år 1618* (Stockholm: P. A. Norstedt, 1926)

Rabinovich, Yakov Nikolayevich, 'Gdov v smutnoye vremya, 1610–1621 gg.', *Voyenno-istoricheskiye issledovaniya v Povolzh'ye* 8 (2008): pp.17–32

Rabinovich, Yakov Nikolayevich, *Gdov v smutnoye vremya (1604–1621 gg.)* (Novgorod: A. N. Odinokov, 2011)

Rabinovich, Yakov Nikolayevich, (*Staraya Russa v smutnoye vremya: Istoricheckiy ocherk* (Novgorod: B. i., 2011)

Rabinovich, Yakov Nikolayevich, *Porkhov v smutnoye vremya* (Saratov: Nauka, 2013)

Rabinovich, Yakov Nikolayevich, 'Ivangorod, Yam i Kopor'ye v smutnoye vremya (leto 1610–vesna 1612 gg.)', *Vestnik TGU* 10 (126), 2013: pp.61–73

Seitz, Heribert, *Svärdet och värjan som armévapen* (Stockholm: Kungl. Armémuseum, 1955)

Selin, Adrian A., 'Communications in the Novgorod Region during the Crisis Period of the Time of Troubles', *Vestnik SPbGU Istoriya* 63: 3 (2018): pp.748–762

Sikora, Radosław, *Kłuszyn 1610: Rozważania o bitwie* (Warsaw: Instytut Wydawniczy Erica-Fundacja Hussar, 2010)

Sikora, Radosław, *Battle of Kłuszyn (Klushino) 1610* (Lębork: online publication, 2010. Summary of the above in English.)

Sikora, Radosław, 'Klushinskaya bitva 4 iyulya 1610 goda', *Kray Smolenskiy* 6, 2011: pp.10–15. Summary of the above in Russian.

Skrynnikov, Ruslan Grigor'yevich, 'The Civil War in Russia at the Beginning of the Seventeenth Century (1603–1607): Its Character and Motive Forces', Lindsey Hughes (ed.), *New Perspectives on Muscovite History* (New York: St Martin's Press, 1993: pp.61–79)

Skrynnikov, Ruslan Grigor'yevich, *The Time of Troubles: Russia in Crisis, 1604–1618* (Gulf Breeze, Florida: Academic International Press, 1988). Translated by Hugh Graham.

Smirnov, Alexej, *Den svenske tsaren* (Stockholm: Karneval, 2017)

Stevens, Carol Belkin, *Russia's Wars of Emergence 1460–1730* (London: Routledge, 2013)

Stevens, Carol Belkin, *Soldiers on the Steppe: Army Reform and Social Change in Early Modern Russia* (DeKalb: Northern Illinois University Press, 1995)

Svensson, S. Artur (ed.), *Svenska flottans historia* 1 (Malmö: Allhem, 1942)

Szcześniak, Robert, *Kłuszyn 1610* (Warsaw: Bellona, Historyczne Bitwy 117, 2004)

Viskovatov, Aleksandr Vasil'yevich, *Istoricheskoye opisaniye odezhdy i vooruzheniya rossiyskikh'voysk'*, vol. 1 (St Petersburg: Voyennaya tipografiya, 1841)

Biographical Databases

Murdoch, Steve, and Alexia Grosjean, *The Scotland, Scandinavia and Northern European Biographical Database* (SSNE). Website <https://www.st-andrews.ac.uk/history/ssne/>

Riksarkivet (Swedish National Archives), *Svenskt biografiskt lexikon* (SBL). Website <https://sok.riksarkivet.se/SBL/>

Other titles in the From Retinue to Regiment series:

No 1 *Richard III and the Battle of Bosworth*
      Mike Ingram

No 2 *Tanaka 1587: Japan's Greatest Unknown Samurai Battle* Stephen Turnbull

No 3 *The Army of the Swabian League 1525*
      Doug Miller

No 4 *The Italian Wars Volume 1: The Expedition of Charles VIII into Italy and the Battle of Fornovo* Massimo Predonzani & Alberici Vincenzo, translated by Irene Maccolini

No 5 *The Commotion Time: Tudor Rebellion in the West, 1549* E.T. Fox

No 6 *The Italian Wars Volume 2: Agnadello 1509, Ravenna 1512, Marignano 1515* Massimo Predonzani & Alberici Vincenzo, translated by Rachele Tiso

No 7 *The Tudor Arte of Warre Volume 1: The Conduct of War from Henry VII to Mary I, 1485-1558* Jonathan Davies

No 8 *The Ethiopian-Adal War 1529-1543: The Conquest of Abyssinia* Jeffrey M. Shaw

No 9 *The Ōnin War: A Turning Point in Samurai History* Stephen Turnbull

No 10 *One Faith, One Law, One King: French Armies of the Wars of Religion 1562-1598* T J O'Brien de Clare

No 11 *The Italian Wars Volume 3: Francis I and the Battle of Pavia 1525* Massimo Predonzani & Alberici Vincenzo

No 12 *On the Borderlands of Great Empires: Transylvanian Armies 1541-1613* Florin Nicolae Ardelean

No 14 *The Art of Shooting Great Ordnance: A History of the Development, Manufacture and Use of Artillery, 1494-1628* Jonathan Davies

No 15 *The Italian Wars Volume 4: The Battle of Ceresole 1544 - The Crushing Defeat of the Imperial Army* Massimo Predonzani & Simon Miller

No 16 *The Men of Warre: The Clothes, Weapons and Accoutrements of the Scots at War 1460-1600* Jenn Scott

No 17 *The German Peasants' War 1524-26* Douglas Miller

No 18 *The Tudor Arte of Warre Volume 2: The conduct of war in the reign of Elizabeth I, 1558-1603: Diplomacy, Strategy, Campaigns and Battles* Jonathan Davies

No 19 *The Kalmar War 1611-1613: Gustavus Adolphus's First War* Michael Fredholm von Essen

No 20 *Hōjō: Samurai Warlords 1487-1590* Stephen Turnbull

No 21 *The Battle of Castillon 1453: The Death Knell for English France* Peter Hoskins

No 22 *The Tudor Arte of Warre Volume 3: The Conduct of War in the Reign of Elizabeth I 1558-1603: The Elizabethan Army* Jonathan Davies